THE PHILOSOPHY OF HENRY GEORGE

BY

GEORGE RAYMOND GEIGER, Ph.D.

ASSOCIATE PROFESSOR OF PHILOSOPHY
UNIVERSITY OF NORTH DAKOTA

INTRODUCTION BY

JOHN DEWEY

NEW YORK
THE MACMILLAN COMPANY
1933

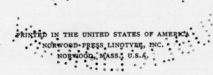

PRINTED IN THE UNITED STATES OF AMERICA
NORWOOD PRESS LINOTYPE, INC.
NORWOOD, MASS., U.S.A.

TO

MY FATHER

PREFACE

I SHOULD like to express here my great indebtedness to Professor John Dewey for his patient and kindly help with most of this work. During the several years of its preparation he has been a constant and attentive critic, although in no way can he be held responsible for the possible errors of emphasis or interpretation that may appear in this discussion. To my former teachers at Columbia University, Professors John J. Coss and Herbert W. Schneider, must go my very sincere gratitude for their painstaking and considerate efforts in reading and correcting a good part of the manuscript. Their criticism has been immensely valuable and has been of specific service in pointing out mistakes of expression and content. I am also indebted to Professor R. G. Tugwell for his helpful suggestions in economic theory.

To the Robert Schalkenbach Foundation I am deeply grateful for the financial assistance which has largely made this volume possible. The Hon. Charles O'Connor Hennessy, its president, and the late Arthur C. Pleydell, one of the members of the foundation, have been particularly helpful, and I sincerely appreciate their advice and encouragement. Mr. Joseph Dana Miller, editor of *Land and Freedom,* and Mr. Harold Benedict are both entitled to my thanks and appreciation for their kindness and their patience in reading and correcting the entire manuscript, and for their inestimable help in the reading of proof. Finally, I should like to take this opportunity to thank my father, Mr. Oscar H. Geiger, for his never-failing inspiration and stimulating advice, and for having aroused my interest in Henry George.

His specific criticisms and his tireless aid with the manuscript and proof have made this book almost his own.

The division of the volume into two parts is perhaps self-explanatory. Part I deals largely with material of exposition and historical reference, while Part II suggests certain more theoretical implications. In this place I may also mention that the splendid bibliography published by the New York Public Library would seem to make gratuitous any general listing in this work of books dealing with Henry George. I refer to "Henry George and the Single Tax. A list of References to Material in the New York Public Library" (Parts I through VII), compiled by the Economics Division of the library, and published in the July, August and September, 1926, issues of the *Bulletin of the New York Public Library* (Vol. 30, Nos. 7, 8, 9). This bibliography was later published in separate pamphlet form. The Manuscript Division of the library has also given me courteous access to its large collection of George's papers.

I should like to thank the editors of the *Journal of Philosophy* for their kind permission to reprint part of Chapter IX, which has already appeared as "The Place of Values in Economics" in the June 19, 1930, issue of the *Journal*.

GEORGE RAYMOND GEIGER.

New York City, January, 1933.

FOREWORD

The life history of Henry George is typically American even though it has few parallels in this country. There are many instances of rise from poverty and obscurity to wealth or fame or both in the realms of business and politics, and there have been many self-made thinkers in various fields. But Henry George stands almost alone in our history as an example of a man who, without a scholastic background, succeeded by sheer force of observation and thinking that were dictated by human sympathy, and who left an indelible impress on not only his own generation and country but on the world and the future. He is an outstanding example of something of which we hear a good deal, but mainly in the way of unjustified boasting, since the quality in question is more marked in talk than evident in conduct: Practical Idealism. He is an example of what may be accomplished by unswerving devotion and self-sacrifice to a dominating idea. He was, we might say, a man of a single idea, but the statement would be misleading unless we also said that he broadened this one idea until it included a vast range of social phenomena and became a comprehensive social philosophy.

Henry George is typically American not only in his career but in the practical bent of his mind, in his desire to *do* something about the phenomena he studied and not to be content with a theoretic study. Of course he was not unique in this respect. The same desire has been shared by many British economists. John Stuart Mill's theoretical writings were ultimately inspired by interest in social reform. But there is something distinctive in the ardent crusade which

George carried on. His ideas were always of the nature of a challenge to action and a call to action. The "science" of political economy was to him a body of principles to provide the basis of policies to be executed, measures to be carried out, not just ideas to be intellectually entertained, plus a faint hope that they might sometime affect action. His ideas were intrinsically "plans of action."

Unfortunately, in some respects, the American public was practical-minded in a much narrower sense and shorter range than was Henry George himself. It is perfectly true that the culmination and indeed the meaning of his social philosophy is to be found in his proposals regarding taxation. It is also true that many persons accept and are justified in accepting his taxation scheme without having knowledge of or interest in the background of principles and aims with which this scheme was organically associated in the mind of Henry George himself. But nevertheless the connection between the theoretical part and the practical part was vital in the thought of George himself. Something vital in acquaintance with his thought is lost when the connection is broken. One may understand the plan of tax reform by itself but one comes far short in that case of understanding the idea which inspired Henry George.

In spite, therefore, of the immense circulation of George's writings, especially of *Progress and Poverty* (which I suppose has had a wider distribution than almost all other books on political economy put together), the full sweep of George's ideas is not at all adequately grasped by the American public, not even by that part which has experienced what we call a higher education. Henry George is one of a small number of definitely original social philosophers that the world has produced. Hence this lack of knowledge of the wider and deeper aspects of his thinking marks a great intellectual loss. In saying this, I am not speaking of acceptance of his

ideas but of acquaintance with them, the kind of acquaintance that is expected as a matter of course of cultivated persons with other great social thinkers, irrespective of adoption or nonadoption of their policies.

I should hesitate to write in this way, lest I might be
thought to depreciate the practical importance of his plan
of social action were it not for two things. One of these
things is the fact which I have already stated. His theoretical
conceptions and his program of social action are so closely
united that knowledge of the first will inevitably lead on to
a better understanding of the second. The other reason is
more immediately applicable. Actual social conditions (like
those for example of the present) are bound to raise the
problem of reform and revision of methods of taxation and
public finance. The practical side of George's program is
bound in any case to come forward for increased attention.
It is impossible to conceive any scheme of permanent tax
reform which does not include at least *some* part of George's
appropriation by society for social purposes of rental value
of land. For instance, we are just beginning to understand
how large a part unregulated speculation has played in
bringing about the present crisis. And I cannot imagine any
informed student of social economy denying that land speculation is basic in the general wild orgy, or that this speculation
would have been averted by social appropriation, through
taxation, of rent. To a large extent, then, some knowledge
of the directly practical side of George's thought is bound, in
the long run, to result from the movement of social forces.
A corresponding knowledge of George's theory of the importance of land—in the broad sense in which he uses the
word—in social development, of the causes of moral progress
and deterioration, cannot be secured, however, without an
understanding of his underlying philosophy.

The importance of a knowledge of this underlying philoso-

phy is urged in spite of the fact that the present writer does
not believe in the conceptions of nature and natural rights
which at first sight seem to be fundamental in the social
philosophy of Henry George. For, as I see the matter, these
conceptions are symbols, expressed in the temporary vocabulary of a certain stage of human history of a truth which can
be stated in other language without any serious injury to the
general philosophy implied. It has repeatedly been pointed
out that the real issue in the "natural rights" conception is
the relation of moral aims and criteria to legal and political
phenomena. Personally, I have little difficulty in translating
a considerable part of what George says on nature over into
an assertion that economic phenomena, as well as legal and
political, cannot be understood nor regulated apart from consideration of consequences upon human values, upon human
good: that is, apart from moral considerations. The question
whether a "science" of industry and finance, of wealth, or of
law and the State, can exist in abstraction from ethical aims
and principles is a much more fundamental one than is the
adequacy of certain historical concepts of "nature" which
George adopted as a means of expressing the supremacy of
ethical concepts, and on this fundamental question I think
George was in the right.

This statement brings me to the connection which exists
between the foregoing remarks and the work of Dr. Geiger
to which the remarks are introductory. In connection with
every topic he discusses, Dr. Geiger makes it clear that a
vital connection between ends, human values, and economic
means is at the basis of George's distinctive treatment. This
fact alone gives a distinctive and timely color to this book.
Moreover, the significance of Dr. Geiger's treatment does
not stop at this point. There is no phase of the work and
the influence of Henry George which is not considered. The
account of his life and development forms a personal thread

which binds all the parts together. Dr. Geiger has given us
a book which meets the contemporary demand for an adequate interpretation of the thought and activity of Henry
George regarded as a vital whole and not as an aggregate of
isolated parts. It will enable the reader to obtain a clear and
comprehensive view of one of the world's great social philosophers, certainly the greatest which this country has produced.

JOHN DEWEY

CONTENTS

PART I

CONTENTS

PART II

IX—ECONOMICS AND ETHICS 479

Contrast between descriptive and normative approaches to economics (479). Historical shift in economics away from earlier ethical and logical emphasis (480). Difficulty of judging the nature of contemporary economics (481). The questioning of the anti-ethical emphasis that characterizes at least part of contemporary economic theory (484). Danger of separation of facts from values (488). This introduces a discussion of natural rights (491). The doctrine must be interpreted ethically, not "metaphysically" (493). Example of that newer interpretation in contemporary jurisprudence (494). The new "hypothetical" approach to natural rights and natural law in legal philosophy (500). The presumptive "as if" interpretation of natural rights (502). This "presumptive" approach to rights not that of George (508). Yet his interpretation was completely ethical (510). Important need for a synthesis of fact and value in economics (513).

X—GEORGE'S ETHICAL SOLUTION 516

George's "ethical" interest in the social problem; the individual determined by his social environment (516). Necessity of "economic" interpretation of ethics (517). George's statement of the economic effects of his solution (518). His economic approach to a "philosophy of history"; his law of human progress (523). George's ambitious correlation of the rise and fall of civilization with the private ownership of land (530). Discussion of the "eugenic" approach to social reform (536). Criticism of such an approach (539). Formulation of George's Utopia (543). Limitations and functions of Utopias; they demand an instrumentalist approach (545). A definition of ethics

PART I

CHAPTER I

THE PROBLEM

PHILOSOPHY needs no definition. It may be taken to mean whatever is called up in the mind by the word itself. Yet there may be a need to examine the type of material that should be admitted to the "ivory tower." Philosophers themselves have never been averse to extending their dominion over all branches of human speculation; they have been the synthesizers of thought, and their work that of intellectual unification. Too often, however, that synthesis has not been a completely catholic one, but has instead been confined to a select group of disciplines, to mathematics, logic, metaphysics, and a mythological psychology. It is true that much more recently biology, and now physics, that charmer of contemporary philosophy, have gained recognition, but sciences as dismal as economics or as worldly as sociology have not yet found a complete welcome in that philosophic melting-pot. Perhaps social and economic problems, unlike those of metaphysics and epistemology, have been too workaday and crass for the refinement that characterizes much of the technique of philosophy.

Such problems have been too earthy even for moral theorists, and so ethical systems have sailed gaily on their way to some goal of good without any overnice concern with the very conditions that have given birth to social and moral problems. The riddles that have attracted the ethical theorist have been so often only the product of metaphysical workshops, while those infinitely more direct and immediate

1

ethical problems that are the consequences of a basically maladjusted social order here and now have been carefully put
aside. Of course, if we translate such problems into the language of a more abstract vocabulary and call them the "problem of evil," then moral philosophy has concerned itself
with such affairs—but how? Chiefly by attempting to explain away, to deny, even to justify, this "evil" by desig-
nating it as some form of good in disguise, by making it the
shadows in the great cosmic landscape, or the discords which
go to consummate the eternal harmony of things. That is
hardly an efficient procedure for handling any problem of
evil. Something more operative than stoic resignation, or
metaphysical explanation, or any other philosophic ano-
dyne, is required if the direct, recurring, practical problems
of poverty, vice, crime, misery—which make up what we
mean by social evil—are to be solved. Philosophy traditionally has discussed evil; perhaps there should be an attempt
to do something about it.

Is it not possible that philosophy's synthesizing function,
at least so far as moral philosophy is concerned, has failed
to include the very material that would be instrumental in
making intelligible the background of moral difficulties? Certainly there has been no lack of concern over the traditional
ethical questions throughout the history of philosophy, but
just as certainly has there been a lack of anything approaching a clear-cut realization of the social ills that underlie
moral problems, and of the social conditions that underlie
moral theories. There is no intention here, however, of suggesting that philosophy must in any unseemly fashion attempt to cope hand-to-hand with social problems; that perhaps would be demanding too much of a discipline whose
traditions point in another direction. And neither is there
any intention here to transform philosophy into economics or
sociology. In fact, it is clearly recognized that these problems

of economic and social maladjustment must first be phrased in moral terms if they are to be handled by professional philosophy. But that is the all-important step, for such a rephrasing will necessarily suggest that, in a complementary fashion, moral problems must be translated into the vocabulary of the social sciences. The two must function, as shall be noted later, in the rôles of ends and means, the ends relating to the characteristic moral goals and goods, and the means to those methods, largely social and economic in nature, through which moral ends may be approached. And the statement that ethical theory and social theory must cooperate if moral philosophy is to become operative and significant, is nothing else than the statement that ends and means can never function as discontinuous entities, but must always act as a unit. There can be no divorce, as has been customary in moral theory, between ends which are intrinsic (moral) and those which are merely instrumental (social and economic).

But what has this brief mention of social instrumentalism [1] to do with the work of Henry George? Just this. If a new conception of moral philosophy is beginning to alter the very province and function of ethical theory, and if philosophy is to be not only permitted but indeed obligated to busy itself with political and social and economic matters, then no serious and carefully elaborated contribution to social ethics can be disregarded. If the riddles of poverty,

[1] It is well realized, of course, that these expressions are perhaps trite repetitions of what may be very familiar material, but still it is felt that the pragmatic approach to ethics is of such significance that repetition may not be too much out of place; these pages do not constitute an exposition but are merely sketchy outlines of an exposition. The classic statement of the thoughts that are inadequately expressed here is undoubtedly Professor Dewey's *Reconstruction in Philosophy*, particularly Chapters V and VII, and more specifically those challenging passages of pages 123–126. For this relation between ethics and economics, see also his recent essay in *Living Philosophies* (New York, Simon and Schuster, 1931), pp. 29–31.

and the human wretchedness and despair born of poverty, are to be answered (and has philosophy a nobler task?) then no earnest proposal can be slighted. In the war against misery there is a need for every weapon. Perhaps the concepts of Henry George will suggest a new technique to be employed in economic pathology, new, that is, in respect to its use (or lack of use) by those who should be directing the consideration of social problems. Perhaps his work may offer a sane and realistic approach to the traditional moral problems and suggest a fusion of ethics and economics. Whether or not his proposals are of value in such a reorganization and restatement is a matter of polemics, but a knowledge of his work must be an essential part—essential, it is insisted, for those interested in the problems of social philosophy as well as for those more directly concerned with economics—of the equipment of any one who approaches this type of material with sincerity and acuteness. As Professor Dewey writes: "No man, no graduate of a higher educational institution, has a right to regard himself as an educated man in social thought unless he has some first-hand acquaintance with the theoretical contribution of this great American thinker." [2]

[2] "An Appreciation of Henry George," the Introduction to *Significant Paragraphs from Progress and Poverty,* edited by Professor Harry Gunnison Brown (New York, Doubleday, Doran, 1928), p. 2. Professor Dewey continues:

"The fact that Henry George has an ardent group of disciples who have a practical program for reform of taxation has tended to obscure from the recognition of students of social theory that his is one of the great names among the world's social philosophers. It would require less than the fingers of the two hands to enumerate those who from Plato down rank with him. Were he a native of some European country, it is safe to assert that he would long ago have taken the place upon the roll of the world's thinkers which belongs to him, irrespective, moreover, of adherence to his practical plan. But for some reason we Americans are slow to perceive and celebrate intellectual claims in comparison with the merits of inventors, political leaders and great industrialists. In the case of the author of 'Progress and Poverty' the failure has doubtless been accentuated in academic circles by the fact that Henry George thought, wrote, and worked outside of them. And in the world at large, in spite of the fact that no works on political economy have had the circulation and reading obtained by his writings, discussion of the practical merits of his plan of reform of taxation has actually

The "theoretical contribution" of George which Professor Dewey suggests, it may be anticipated here, was first of all an insistent attempt to clarify the relation between ethics and economics. Was it possible, George asked, to construct or realize a sane and rational system of ethics in an economically unbalanced society such as that in which man finds himself? Were not moral theories doomed to sterility because of their persistent refusal to recognize that moral problems were real, not philosophical, that instead of being "absolute" they were symptomatic of a social environment? George's demand for economic and social reform was a demand for a new approach to the foundations of ethical concepts, and it was his moral purpose that gave life and richness to the fiscal details of his economics. For him, the superstructure of moral philosophy required a groundwork of political economy. That is to say, George assumed that there was no distinct dualism between the realms of morals and of economics, that there was no insulation which prevented the one from coming into contact with the other. Such a cleavage has been one of the characteristic distinctions made by traditional philosophy; the moral order has been not only divorced from the problems of economics—that is, the problems involved in man's efforts to satisfy his material wants— it has been made superior to such affairs, and has often been given authority over what was regarded as the less exalted and abstract business of a cruder and more "impure" realm.[3]

tended to blur his outstanding position as a thinker. This has been the case because the enormous inertia of social habit and the force of tremendous vested interests have depreciated his intellectual claims in order to strengthen opposition to his practical measures. . . ."

This is a serious indictment of the usual academic neglect of George's work, and suggests that such neglect may indeed be dependent upon something entirely extrinsic to his work.

[3] Yet even Plato, despite his fierce insistence upon an ideal realm of eternal essences, opens the discussion of his perfect city with those most material demands for "food," "a dwelling," and "clothing." (*Republic*, II, 369.)

Such a separation of a moral order from a discipline that treats of the satisfying of human wants must be, of course, subject to all the dialectical difficulties that arise from any discontinuity between ends and means. An end detached from the means by which it may be approached must necessarily remain meaningless, and the attempt to make a discrete end sovereign over an equally discrete means can be nothing else than futile. Ends and means cannot function independently; if they are to operate at all they must do so as functions of each other. To be of service a system of final moral ends cannot be set out in some great aloof void beyond or above "economic" life; it cannot hope to function, as did the Aristotelian Unmoved Mover, merely by the force of a subtle and compelling magnetism. It is clear that such a suggestion in no way invalidates the utility of ends in any system of ethics, but it does hold that the end is valuable only as it remains in contact with the means. The ideals of the Good, Duty, or Right, inasmuch as they are postulated as the *ends* of ethical life, cannot hope to command the *means* of life, which are fundamentally economic in character, without having some earthy and "impure" commerce with them. In plainer words, before men can live well or nobly, they must just live. Before ideals can be realized, there are wants that must be satisfied.

Between "ideals" and "wants," moreover, there still must be no sharp distinction. The two may be qualitatively different, but only to the degree in which wants among themselves qualitatively differ. Wants are not, as were the pleasures and pains of early Utilitarianism, completely homogeneous, and neither do they vary only quantitatively; they are "higher" and "lower," "intellectual" and "material." Therefore it is easy to see how those yearnings and desires that are created by man's unsatisfied "higher" life will readily come to be dignified and perhaps hypostasized as lofty ideals and final ends, while his more material wants will be relegated to the status of animal necessities. There can be no quarrel with such an æsthetic division,[4] provided, however, that this distinction does not develop into a cleavage that will prevent the one order of wants from having any intercourse with the other, or into an aristocratic moral domination that will attempt to subjugate and chasten the common herd of "lower" wants without any real understanding of their function, or their potential capacity for "upward" redirection.

This last suggestion as to the possibility of a readjustment of wants (wants in this particular discussion are understood to be those that have been socially developed and modified rather than the cruder and less articulated biologic wants) brings us again to George's attempted fusion of economics and ethics, and, more particularly, to the problem that always haunted him—the riddle of poverty. George's reaction to poverty was not simply the sentimental revolt against misery and injustice that motivates every social reformer. It was rather the realization of what might be termed the pathological function of want and the fear of want. Poverty for him was much more than the squalid, unæsthetic sight that greets the social worker; it was, in addition, a conditioning element of much of our social life, the background against which were formed so many of man's habits. It was poverty that elevated man's material wants to their dominant position, and it was poverty that laughed at the higher wants, at those social ideals of man, for they were ludicrously remote from the problems of earning one's daily bread. It was in this directive power of poverty and the dread of poverty that George found what he felt to be the dis-

---

[4] This suggested "æsthetic" emphasis may recall Croce's division of the Practical into the Economic and the Ethic, the former concerning immediate, utilitarian ends, and the latter universal and transcendental ones. Yet notwithstanding his interest in political economy, he does not appear to have realized sufficiently the effect of the more common matters of "economic" upon such ethical and transcendental ideals.

tortion in man's outlook upon the social order. Poverty—
or, if it is preferred, the precarious conditions of economic
life—played a major part in the normal fixation of wants, and
it was thus a conditioning factor, not merely economically
but ethically.

Economic precariousness accounted for the emphasis upon
material wants that ethical systems have always deplored.
The exaggerated stressing of those capacities for ruthless
self-advancement, which has seemed so remote from the pure
standards of moral conduct, must be traced in part to the fact
that the social order, as it is at present constituted, places a
premium upon the power to satisfy certain wants, and penalizes whatever attention is paid to other wants. It can hardly
be taken for granted, for example, that all the artificial energies that go into business are merely the result of man's
natural interest in making a living. The insecurity of economic life, the fact that there are countless thousands who
are living on the bare margin of subsistence—and this marginal existence is not confined only to the lowest classes in
the economic order—must suggest possible causes for such
a direction of energies to the service of the material wants.
And that a change in the condition of economic precariousness, were that possible, might effect some shifting of this
habitual emphasis is an implication that cannot very well
be disregarded.

Thus, George offered the assumption that social wants
and social ideals do not occupy separate universes of discourse, that economics and ethics are not divided one from
the other by an unbridgeable chasm. A dualism that excluded the problem of poverty from moral philosophy was
an anomaly, for poverty has been an ever-present condition
of man's life, of that strange life which has created all ethical theory. *George was certain that it was the determining
influence of poverty that had warped man's realization of*

*what constituted the real "goods" of life, and he was just as
certain that only the removal of poverty could clear the channel through which human energies might finally reach those
vague ideals which had not yet been obscured by the economic struggle.* There was then, for him, a direct and obvious relation between economic conditions and the moral
life of man, a relationship that was certain, immediate, and
clearly understandable.[5]

[5] George's approach is illustrated by many eloquent passages in his
work. For example:
"It is not without reason that the wise crow in the Ramayana, the crow
Bushanda, 'who has lived in every part of the universe, and knows all events
from the beginnings of time,' declares that, though contempt of worldly
advantages is necessary to supreme felicity, yet the keenest pain possible
is inflicted by extreme poverty. The poverty to which in advancing civilization great masses of men are condemned, is not the freedom from distraction
and temptation which sages have sought and philosophers have praised;
it is a degrading and embruting slavery, that cramps the higher nature, and
dulls the finer feelings, and drives men by its pain to acts which the brutes
would refuse. It is into this helpless, hopeless poverty, that crushes manhood and destroys womanhood, that robs even childhood of its innocence and
joy, that the working classes are being driven by a force which acts upon
them like a resistless and unpitying machine. . . .
"Carlyle somewhere says that poverty is the hell of which the modern
Englishman is most afraid. And he is right. Poverty is the open-mouthed,
relentless hell which yawns beneath civilized society. And it is hell
enough. . . . For poverty is not merely deprivation; it means shame, degradation; the searing of the most sensitive parts of our moral and mental
nature as with hot irons; the denial of the strongest impulses and the
sweetest affections; the wrenching of the most vital nerves. . . . And thus
the sting of want and the fear of want make men admire above all things
the possession of riches, and to become wealthy is to become respected, and
admired, and influential. Get money—honestly, if you can, but at any rate
get money! This is the lesson that society is daily and hourly dinning in
the ears of its members. . . . And so in society, as at present constituted, men
are greedy for wealth because the conditions of distribution are so unjust
that instead of each being sure of enough, many are certain to be condemned to want. It is the 'devil catch the hindmost' of present social adjustments that causes the race and scramble for wealth, in which all considerations of justice, mercy, religion, and sentiment are trampled under
foot; in which men forget their own souls, and struggle to the very verge of
the grave for what they cannot take beyond." *Progress and Poverty,* pp. 354,
455–463. (The edition is Vol. I of the ten-volume set of George's complete
works, the Fels Fund Library Edition, published by Doubleday, Page & Co.,
Garden City, N. Y., 1906–1911. This edition will be used throughout, and,
unless otherwise noted, the quotations from George's works will be from it.)
"The fact is, that the qualities that raise man above the animal are
superimposed on those which he shares with the animal, and that it is only

Throughout this brief discussion it may have been noticed that the fact that our economic system is in so sadly a muddled state that any permanent and worth-while adjustment of moral values under present conditions is almost impossible has confidently been taken for granted. And there will be no attempt made in this essay to justify that assumption. Social maladjustment is so apparent that any elaborate attempt either to prove or disprove its existence would seem almost ludicrous. This does not refer to the phenomenon of recurring depressions. The social maladjustment that is being taken for granted as obvious here is a chronic rather than an acute condition. It is, for example, even more glaringly apparent during the sway of prosperity myths. In other words, it is being accepted as patent that poverty (if the correct relative rather than absolute criteria are em-

as he is relieved from the wants of his animal nature that his intellectual and moral nature can grow. Compel a man to drudgery for the necessities of animal existence, and he will lose the incentive to industry—the progenitor of skill—and will do only what he is forced to do. Make his condition such that it cannot be much worse, while there is little hope that anything he can do will make it much better, and he will cease to look beyond the day. Deny him leisure—and leisure does not mean the want of employment, but the absence of the need which forces to uncongenial employment—and you cannot, even by running the child through a common school and supplying the man with a newspaper, make him intelligent. . . . Poverty is the Slough of Despond which Bunyan saw in his dream, and into which good books may be tossed forever without result. To make people industrious, prudent, skillful, and intelligent, they must be relieved from want. If you would have the slave show the virtues of the freeman, you must first make him free. . . .

"No sooner are his (man's) wants satisfied than new wants arise. Food he wants first, as does the beast; shelter next, as does the beast; and these given, his reproductive instincts assert their sway, as do those of the beast. But here man and beast part company. The beast never goes further; the man has but set his feet on the first step of an infinite progression . . . away from and above the beast. The demand for quantity once satisfied, he seeks quality." (*Ibid.*, pp. 307–308; 135.) And it was upon that "infinite progression," upon those restless attempts of man to satisfy the wants of "quality," that George founded his Utopia.

In another connection George states: "I speak of this for the purpose of showing how nearly the field of material desires and satisfactions, within which the sphere of political economy lies, comes to including all human desires and satisfactions." *The Science of Political Economy*, p. 84. (This work comprises Vols. VI and VII, consecutively paged, of the edition mentioned above.)

ployed) is nowhere permanently and significantly on the decrease; that crime, both in quantity and quality—i. e., in degree of viciousness—is decidedly on the uptrend; that the stupendous triumphs in medicine are persistently and relentlessly opposed by the negative forces originating in the lack of social hygiene (technological being opposed by economic forces); that monopoly and "big business," the whole "merger" technique of modern industry is slowly concentrating wealth and power, and ever widening the gap between the two extremes in the distribution of the product of economic enterprise. The solutions of the problems arising in the field of economic production have not been met by like advances in solving the infinitely more urgent and menacing problems presented to us by an archaic and vicious system of economic distribution—again that sad contrast between "technical" and "social" progress.

Is there any need of figures and reports to demonstrate that poverty and crime and vice exist, and all the despair and degradation that flow from want? Do we require statistics to realize that we are no nearer a solution of fundamental moral and social problems than we ever were? Can it be anything but obvious that "scientific" and "technical" advances have nowhere been paralleled by progress in advancing human welfare? "Where is the moral progress that corresponds to our economic accomplishments? . . . How undeveloped are our politics, how crude and primitive our education, how passive and inert our morals . . ." [6] It is surely a serious indictment that the problem of social misery is still unsolved, and it is an indictment not only of economics but one that must be answered by philosophy as well, for it can be only a short-sighted view that sees in the phenomenon of poverty [7] simply the need for a more efficient adjustment

[6] Professor Dewey in *Reconstruction in Philosophy*, pp. 125–126.

[7] "Poverty" in this discussion is intended to bear a heavy burden. It should connote the misery and wretchedness and injustice that fester in a

of economic operations. Moral philosophy as well as economic philosophy must share the burden, for an instrumentalist ethics cannot hope to function, as did perhaps rational or absolutistic ethics, in a "passive" and "inert" dimension.

The problem, therefore, that George faced was the problem of changing the economic background against which man's life was lived, so that man himself might be changed. It was an attempt to approach morals by way of economics. It was a conviction that there could be no dualistic severance of ethical ideals and ends from material means. George's purpose, his goal, was the same as that of every social reformer, the introduction of an order of society in which some of man's ethical visions might be realized. His method of reaching such a goal was a unique and essentially an original contribution to the history of reform programs, but in this preliminary approach to George, it is his fusion of moral ends and economic means that is being emphasized. His work contained, on the one hand, a scathing, passionate indictment of existing conditions, and a vision of a new order of things; and, on the other, a penetrating and profound economic treatise that analyzed the causes of those conditions and pointed the way to a solution which would realize that vision. Indictments and visions, however, are so often mere pious protestations and vague dreams; and economic treatises, in their scientific pretensions, are sometimes unwittingly and many times almost deliberately shortsighted. But in George ethical visions and schemes of economics functioned together. He recognized that moral hopes and Utopian prophecies must be related to things fundamentally tangible. There was no divorce between "higher" and "lower" as applied to ideals and wants, but rather a

society that is economically unbalanced. It is the very symbol of social evil. Furthermore, it is being assumed here that poverty is something to be remedied and not merely accepted, and so those attitudes of complacent acceptance or of bored resignation or of æsthetic distaste will be disregarded.

synthesis of the two. They were not separate realms, but different levels or different points of view of one process, just as is the case with all ends and means. His ultimate concerns were dominantly ethical; his immediate attention was with economics; but between "ultimate" and "immediate" there was no chasm.

There must be the insistence, then, that the problem of poverty with which George was contending is essentially, despite its economic phrasing, an ethical and philosophical problem. In fact, this entire approach to George's work may be characterized either as an economic interpretation of ethics ("economic," in this discussion, applying to questions of means, of programs, of "environmental" changes, and "ethics" to that group of ends and ideals and goals that stand out before every social reformer as his guide and vision) or as an ethical approach to economics. George must be appreciated not as just the "single taxer," as is so often the case, not as an economist concerned primarily with the technical details of a practical scheme of taxation, but as a moral and social philosopher who has attempted to secure an inseparable union of economics and ethics. His particular program of means was, of course, vital, but back of his fiscal proposals and back of his detailed and elaborate analysis of economics, lay a zealous endeavor to contribute to a solution of the age-old moral problems. It is unnecessary to mention that this insistence upon the ultimate moral destination and purpose of an economic program must not in any sense be interpreted as a disparagement or belittling of such a program. That would be not only a stupid slighting of what is really George's distinct contribution to economic theory, but also a contradiction of what has just been stressed as the important functional relationship between ends and means. It would be of a piece with the traditional, abortive failure on the part of so many moral theorists to become sufficiently concerned with the specific methods through which alone goals can be reached. It is always a question of means with which one deals directly and immediately. Ends are present, to be sure, but only as the last step in a progression of means, and not as something which lies across the hill or at the end of a rainbow. Ends can never function without means, whereas means, to some extent, can generate their own ends. Thus, once more, the major problem of George—that of poverty and its effects—was a problem of economics *and* morals, and its solution demanded the fusion of means (economic) with ends (moral).

As a corollary of that more fundamental problem, or rather as the background against which it appeared in relief, was the paradox that alliterated through George's work, the paradox of "progress and poverty," of "wealth and want." Poverty itself was indeed a problem, but it was doubly a puzzle when it appeared in connection with a set of social conditions in which wealth and private property were constantly on the increase. Why did advance in material civilization mean a direct and corresponding advance in those vicious by-products of crime, want, misery? Was there a necessary connection between them, or was that connection pathological rather than normal? Was there a wedge being inserted into the very structure of society, which, as wealth increased, pried apart the two ends of the system of economic distribution?

It was this paradox that provided the stimulus that launched George upon his career of social reform, and it was with such a question that he opened his work. The introductory chapter to *Progress and Poverty* asked the challenging quesion: Why, in spite of the fact that "the utilization of steam and electricity, the introduction of improved processes and labor-saving machinery, the greater subdivision and grander scale of production, the wonderful facilitation of exchanges, have multiplied enormously the effectiveness of labor," has there been no corresponding advance in the technique of economic adjustment? Production of wealth had increased, but the distribution of wealth had increased only the disparity between those who had and those who had not. The methods of dividing the product of economic enterprise could show no progress parallel to that achieved in the methods of its creation. This was an amazing problem for George, and one that demanded solution. It seemed to him that the very forces of knowledge as they were applied to industry had produced only downright misery on the one hand and swollen luxury on the other. Certainly such an effect was a perversion and not a legitimate concomitant of economic science.

Had one in the eighteenth century been endowed with the gift of prescience and had he been permitted to look forward into the age of the Industrial Revolution, what would have been the logical inference from the sight of labor-saving machinery, of increased wealth, of vast production—what would have been the logical inference, that is, had his foresight been limited to industrial rather than to social conditions and had his economic philosophy been still naive and free from cynical realism? Would he not have visioned, George asks, "these new forces elevating society from its very foundations, lifting the very poorest above the possibility of want, exempting the very lowest from anxiety for the material needs of life?" Would he not have seen "these slaves of the lamp of knowledge taking on themselves the traditional curse, these muscles of iron and sinews of steel making the poorest laborer's life a holiday, in which every high quality and noble impulse could have scope to grow?" [8]

[8] *Progress and Poverty*, p. 4.

But had he looked more carefully into that supposedly wondrous future he would have seen something far different.

And do not we, in the twentieth century, hearing of the untold energies that science is just beginning to tap, learning of attempts to disintegrate the atom and release its power, or to employ directly the heat of the earth and of the sun, or the power of wind and water; seeing the development of synthetic foods and fuels, of mechanical men; and realizing that there is approaching an industrial age which will need but little or no human labor, a literal machine age—looking forward into that infinitely more important industrial revolution of the twenty-first century—do not we sometimes romantically, hopefully, even scientifically, predict a period in which labor problems will be solved and poverty and deprivation will have vanished? Do we not sometimes, forgetting economics realism in the face of the romance of technology (or of "technocracy"), forgetting problems of distribution in the glare of the solutions in the field of production, also look forward to a day in which the "slaves of the lamp of knowledge" will take on themselves "the traditional curse"?

The prophet of the eighteenth century, had his prescience been omniscient, would have seen that now "some get an infinitely better and easier living, but others find it hard to get a living at all. The 'tramp' comes with the locomotive, and almshouses and prisons are as surely the marks of 'material progress' as are costly dwellings, rich warehouses, and magnificent churches. Upon streets lighted with gas and patrolled by uniformed policemen, beggars wait for the passer-by, and in the shadow of college, and library, and museum, are gathering the more hideous Huns and fiercer Vandals of whom Macaulay prophesied." [9] And is it not a fairly certain inference that the next industrial revolution

[9] *Progress and Poverty*, p. 7.

will bring a picture painted, not by Haldane, but by Bertrand Russell?

"This association of poverty with progress is the great enigma of our times. It is the central fact from which spring industrial, social, and political difficulties that perplex the world, and with which statesmanship and philanthropy and education grapple in vain. From it come the clouds that overhang the future of the most progressive and self-reliant nations. It is the riddle which the Sphinx of Fate puts to our civilization, and which not to answer is to be destroyed." [10]

These, then, were the problems that Henry George attempted to solve. First, the riddle involved in that economic dichotomy, the separation of the product of industry into two unequal shares—one, enriching the few; the other, impoverishing the many—a separation which, for him, was fundamental; it underlay the entire structure of economic enterprise. It was a principle of division that was demonstrated by every increase in the productivity of economic forces, and its cause was the wedge that was driving into the social order and widening the gap between wealth and want. This was the paradox of progress and poverty.

As a direct product of that economic maladjustment was the ethical distortion that followed. Given a social order in which some had too much and others not enough, given an economic arrangement that placed a premium upon the predatory elements in the human organism and penalized, at the same time, those attempts to satisfy qualitatively different wants, there could be no sane and permanent adjustment in the realm of morals. Given this background of a fundamental economic cleavage, the necessary effect upon ethical concepts was either to remove them from affairs here below and place them as inhabitants of some

[10] *Ibid.*, p. 10.

other intellectual world of ends and goals or to transform them into an elaborate system of apologetics. It might be added that even the traditional dualism in moral theory could possibly be linked up with that more existential dualism in the economic realm. Perhaps the characteristic severance of means from ends in ethics may be correlated with a refusal on the part of the moral theorist to concern himself with the possible causes of problem situations in social ethics. May we not, in fact, say of moral philosophy what William James said of God: That in this world of sweat and dirt, God cannot be a gentleman. He cannot refuse to get His hands soiled.

Further discussion of this ethical emphasis must be postponed until the second part of the work; first there must be presented an exposition of George's solution of that economic maladjustment. But there may be kept in mind the basic ethical problem that George sought to handle. His economic solution was not an *ad hoc* one; it passed beyond the horizons of economics to the land of ethics. Man must live before he can live well or nobly, and wants must be satisfied before ideals can be reached. Moral problems cannot be divorced from the economic and social situations which give rise to those problems; moral ends cannot be divorced from the economic and social means through which alone they can be approached. Therefore, George directed his immediate attention to economics, to means, but there was always before him that vision of ultimate moral ends.

CHAPTER II

BIOGRAPHY

THE conceptions of philosophers have not always been accorded biographical interpretation. Thought, unlike the more overt action, has often been treated as something a little removed from the exactitudes of circumstance, as something that has sprung full-armed from the philosopher's head, and that can stand in its own right quite without need for explanatory support. Perhaps, in a sense, this is correct, and it may be that pure thought can be more suggestively and impartially appreciated when it is considered as if it were really a pure and incorruptible essence. Whatever may be the advantages, however, of an approach to philosophy without regard for biographical detail, such a policy cannot be followed in discussing a figure like Henry George, whose thought was determined by the same factors that moulded the very character of the man. His concepts were a living integral part of his being, and they could not possibly be completely understood were they divorced from the peculiar surroundings in which they originated and functioned. The singular uniqueness of George's life and training, strange and bizarre as compared with the biographies of other thinkers, must be grasped by any one interested in his ideas. It is certainly quite unusual and perhaps not just the thing for a philosopher to have been a sailor and a printer, a journalist, tramp, and political candidate powerful enough to have worried Tammany Hall. The story of his life, so removed from the commonplace of both the academic and the every-day worlds, is interesting in itself;

19

it becomes significant when it is correlated with the development of his thought.

There has been only one comprehensive biography of Henry George, and that is the truly great piece of work done by his son.[1] Nearly all of the other biographical material about George has appeared in journalistic or essay form, either in newspapers—particularly in his obituaries and in the stories published during his two candidacies for the New York City mayoralty—or in periodicals and pamphlets.[2] The completeness of the *Life* would afford little excuse for the introduction of any new material were it not for the fact that a number of hitherto unpublished letters have come to light since the date of the book's appearance; and while they do not at all change the picture that the son has given us, they may bring to the foreground some of the less appreciated aspects of George's character. The large collection of letters and diaries that Henry George, Jr., had access to has been examined again, and several selections from them which are not found in the biography have been included here.[3]

Henry George was born in Philadelphia on the 2d of September, 1839, in a small two-story brick building [4] on Tenth Street, south of Pine, just a short walk from the historic State House of Revolutionary fame. In the Philadelphia of 1839 there were still traditions harking back to the days when the city was the shipping center of the new world, when its devout skippers filled the seven seas with commerce and

---

[1] *The Life of Henry George*, by Henry George, Jr., 1900. (George's *Works*, Vols. IX, X.) The biographical details of George's life will be taken largely from this work of his son; other material will be specified separately.

[2] The greater part of this material may be found in the 28-volume collection of Henry George Scrap Books in the Economics Division of the New York Public Library. Of especial interest in this connection are Vols. 1, 3, 4, 6, 7, 10, 11, 13–16, 21, 27, and 28.

[3] The passages from the letters and journals have not all been placed in this chapter; some selections have been used where they may have been found helpful in a fuller appreciation of George's thoughts.

[4] This building has been purchased by the Henry George Foundation of America, and is to be preserved as a memorial.

religion. These traditions of piety and salt water were deeply rooted in the George family. The grandfather, Captain Richard George, a native of Yorkshire, England, had become one of the leading shipmasters of Philadelphia, and up to the days of the embargo and the second war with Great Britain his clippers were a familiar sight in the harbor. His son, Richard Samuel Henry George, born in New Brunswick, New Jersey, was more devoted to the religious side of the family tradition, and, although himself a good sailor, he gave up the idea of going to sea and also a position in the Philadelphia Custom House in order to publish Episcopal Sunday school books. He was for a time the publisher for the General Episcopal Sunday School Union, the Bible and Prayer Book Society, and the Tract Society. Later he returned to the Custom House, but remained a vestryman of St. Paul's Episcopal Church and continued to regard "high church" tendencies with horror. He married twice; his second wife, who was Catherine Pratt Vallance of Philadelphia, was Henry George's mother. She was of Scottish and English descent, and her father, John Vallance, who came from Glasgow to Philadelphia, made a reputation for himself as an engraver; his name may be seen on some of the commissions signed by George Washington. Henry George was one of ten children, the second child and the oldest son.

Young George might well have been headed along the path which perhaps would have led to the position of Episcopal bishop had the financial means of the family been at all adequate; certainly there was no lack of pious sincerity or of clerical respect. But as it was, the $800 income of the father was little enough to feed and clothe the dozen members of the household, and consequently George's schooling never went beyond the elementary stage. At six years of age he was sent to a Mrs. Graham's private school and stayed there until he was nine; then he entered the Mount Vernon Grammar

School, and a year later the Episcopal Academy. The academy, under the direction first of Bishop Alonzo Potter and later of the Reverend Doctor Hare, had achieved a leading position among the schools of Pennsylvania and had turned out a goodly number of Episcopal bishops and college presidents. George's father, although no longer in the religious publishing business, was yet able to obtain for his son the reduced tuition available for clergymen's sons. The boy, however, looked upon this as an unmerited concession, and perhaps that accounted for his inability to get along with his fellow students. He left after a short time and prepared for high school under a private tutor, but his high school studies lasted only five months, and then, when he was not yet fourteen years old, an age at which John Stuart Mill, having mastered Greek, Latin, French, mathematics and logic, was helping his father write political economy, George left school, never to return, and went to work as an errand boy and clerk.

Compared with the training of nearly all the leading figures in English and Continental thought of the day, men who when they were no older than George at the time his formal education ended had completed their preparatory studies or were already enrolled in universities, George's schooling seems almost nonexistent. Its technical incompleteness may be appreciated by the fact that he never became familiar with mathematics, languages or science except in a popular form. Whether a formal education would have broadened George's "one-idea" philosophy to a degree that would have made it unimportant, or whether it would have buttressed his concepts with additional knowledge, must remain an idle although interesting question. It is perhaps easier to believe that the unique and varied experiences of his career, bringing him into contact not so much with the world of academic thought as with the world of perplexing situations and immediate problems, played a more compelling rôle in the formulation and direction of his thinking than could have been achieved by any scholastic training.[5]

It must not be thought, however, that George was at all unaware of the deficiencies in his education, or that he in any way neglected the limited opportunities for instructing himself.[6] His search for knowledge was an eager and private one, and while he was not able to fill in the gaps left in his learning in such a manner as that, for example, employed by Herbert Spencer, yet he did seize upon every means of adding to his fund of information. Before he left school he had already formed the habit of wide if not systematic reading, and upon the foundations that he laid in these early years he later built a rich storehouse of knowledge. The acquaintance with books that is manifested throughout his writings shows a surprisingly catholic range of interest, one that could have come only from an omnivorous and unselective program of early reading.

The literature that the boy found at home was quite natu-

[5] Elbert Hubbard says: "Henry George was right in the class with Spencer, Huxley and Tyndall, none of whom, happily, was a college man, and therefore all were free from the handicap of dead learning and ossified opinion, and saw things as if they were new. Ignorance is a very necessary equipment in doing a great and sublime work that is to eclipse anything heretofore performed. The mind of Henry George was a flower of slow growth. At thirty-seven he was just reaching mental manhood." *Little Journeys to the Homes of Great Reformers* (East Aurora, N. Y., The Roycroft Press, 1907), Vol. XX, p. 67.
(It may be remarked that both Huxley and Tyndall did hold university degrees. The former received his medical degree at London and taught for a while at the School of Mines in Edinburgh. Tyndall studied in Germany and won his doctor's degree in physics at the University of Marburg.)

[6] An interesting side-light on George's educational views appears in this letter to his son Dick, December 17, 1880: "I have come to the conclusion that if you can find a place to learn to set type it will be best for you not to go back to school after Christmas. I don't like your leaving school until you have got further along, but you are getting so old now that it is important that you should learn to make a living for yourself, for that is, by far, the most important part of education. . . . Education never ceases. There is always something to learn and something to try for. . . . But try in the beginning to acquire correct habits, and above all things acquire the habit of working hard when you do work. Whatever you do, learn to do it with your might." Economic conditions being what they were, "making a living" was "the most important part of education."

rally of a religious character, and his grounding in Scripture and in the exegetical works of the Episcopal Church was almost as thorough as if he were being prepared for the ministry. In the books of his father's library [7] he found also strange tales of missionaries in foreign lands and rousing stories of the sea—again that mingling of the pulpit and the forecastle, the fruitful mixture of idea and action that was to characterize George's entire career. The boy had access to the old Quaker Apprentices' Library and to the library of the Franklin Institute, and while there is no record of the precise nature of his reading at this time, we do know that, in addition to the books of fiction and travel, and works like Franklin's *Autobiography*, that he read, he also concentrated upon the study of history and was particularly influenced by Buckle, with his emphasis upon the power of law in historical development and upon the correlation of physical conditions and mental development.

Young George also attended the popular scientific lectures of the Franklin Institute, an organization that had been founded in 1824 for the "promotion and encouragement of manufactures and the mechanic and useful arts." In his diary, which he began early in 1855 and which was kept up intermittently throughout his life, there is mention of his going to the lectures [8] almost every evening and of his youth-

[7] The pietistic tradition in the George family would not permit certain books to be read in the house, and consequently the boy had to do much of his reading in his attic bedroom. Even such a romance as *Scottish Chiefs* came under the ban. The same censorship applied to the theatre, and George's mother, although an ardent reader of Shakespeare, never allowed herself to see a Shakespearian play.

[8] Regarding "lectures" and also the pietistic tradition in the George family, Henry George tells this story of a distinguished fellow American: "I was educated in a very strict faith. My people and the people whom I knew in my childhood, the people who went to our church and other churches of the same kind, had a notion that the theatre was a very bad place, and they would not go to one on any account. There was a celebrated fellow citizen of mine of the name of Barnum. Barnum went to Philadelphia, and he recognized that prejudice, and he saw that, although there were a number of theatres running for the ungodly, a theatre he could get the godly

ful interest in "climatology," "organic chemistry," "electricity," and "the panorama of Europe."

But now the lure of the sea put aside any further thought of lectures or reading; the boy was in his sixteenth year, and the only thing that really mattered was to ship before the mast and sail the South Pacific. An old East Indiaman, the *Hindoo,* was to leave New York harbor early in April of 1855 bound for Melbourne and Calcutta. It was captained by a friend of the family, and Henry persuaded his father—not with too much difficulty, for there was a George tradition to be carried on—to let him sign up as foremast boy. So, after Sunday school on the 1st of April, with a copy of the Bible [9] and *James's Anxious Enquirer* under his arm, the boy left for New York, and ten days later he was off for Australia and India, names whose very sound called up strange images of distant lands and wondrous seas. There is a journal record of the trip to Melbourne, written in a small regular hand with not too much care for the rules of spelling or punctuation, but it is largely in the form of a ship's log with notes of winds

to go to would pay extremely well. But he did not start a theatre. . . . He started a lecture room, and we had in that lecture room theatrical representations, and it was crowded every night in the week and there were two matinées." (Quoted in the *Life,* p. 11, n. 1.)

[9] In addition to the Scriptures the boy took with him much religious advice, and the letters that the young sailor received from home were filled with a pious spirit that was calculated to dispel any of the ungodly thoughts that might lurk in the hold of an East Indiaman. He was told that "the same God who is about you and sees all that you do," is about them, "and He hears and answers prayer, though you may be many thousands of miles away," and that "there are many trials and temptations in a sailor's life; but there are also many things in it calculated to favor serious feelings. See how David speaks of it in Psalms 107: 23–31. I have often felt as if on many accounts sailors ought to be the most religious of men." And his mother wrote him of this kind of news: "The best news just now is the religious news —a great work going on in New York and Philadelphia and all the principal cities of the Union; prayer-meetings all over the land; all denominations uniting together in solemn, earnest prayer; Jayne's Hall (you know its size) is crowded to excess, even those large galleries literally packed with men of the highest respectability—merchants, bankers, brokers, all classes. Those who have never entered a church and have hitherto scoffed at religion meet at this prayer-meeting every day to hear the word of God read and solemn prayer offered for their conversion."

and weather and the daily incidents of life on board, enlivened, however, by some passages of vivid description.

The *Hindoo* arrived at Hobson's Bay, Melbourne, on the 25th of August and left a month later for Calcutta. George visited the Australian city only once and, according to Captain Miller,[10] was not impressed, for instead of gold and riches in this new island continent, times seemed to be "very hard ashore, thousands with nothing to do and nothing to eat."[11] India proved to be a like disillusionment, and in the 80-mile trip up the Hooghly branch of the Ganges river from the sea to Calcutta, and in the visits to Barrapore and other places of interest, he found much to shatter his boyish dreams of the land of the Arabian Nights. After a short stay in India, the *Hindoo* set sail for home and arrived at New York on June 14, 1856.

After fourteen months of a sailor's life it was not easy for young George to settle down once more in the pious Philadelphia family. He "found it full of restrictions, for with all the heavy toil and hard discipline of sea life, there was during the preceding year and a quarter complete freedom of thought and of actions, too, in the hours off duty. And now to come back to conditions where the most innocent of card-playing was regarded as an evil and riding in a public conveyance on Sunday as a desecration of the Lord's Day, made the energetic, masterful boy . . . see new charms in the sea life."[12] Some time later he did sign as ordinary seaman for a short trip from Philadelphia to Boston on a topsail schooner laden with coal, but the life of the sailor was not to be his. The advice given him by Captain Miller of the *Hindoo*,[13] and the opposition of his parents, who perhaps were alarmed at the

---

[10] *Life*, p. 32.   [11] *Ibid.*, p. 31.   [12] *Ibid.*, p. 41.

[13] The captain wrote to George: "I hope you will find some agreeable and profitable employment before long. Take my advice and never go to sea. You know the troubles of a sailor's life before the mast. It never gets any better. A second mate leads proverbially a dog's life. The mate's and captain's are very little better." (Quoted in *Life*, p. 41.)

change that one trip had made in him, turned his thoughts landward; from now on he was to learn to set type. He worked for several Philadelphia printing establishments and newspapers, but his general restlessness and his growing reaction to the strict discipline at home, together with the small wages and insecure position of a typesetter, made some decisive change inevitable. That change was to come shortly, and it was to transform him from a printer's boy in Philadelphia to the "Prophet of San Francisco."

It was at this time that George and some of his young friends formed the "Lawrence Literary Society" for the purpose of discussing "poetry, economics and Mormonism." The club was patterned undoubtedly upon the "Junto" of Franklin's *Autobiography,* although it was hardly of the same character as that Junto which later was to grow into the American Philosophical Society. The Lawrence Society was by no means confined to literary endeavor, however, as a letter from one of the members, Charles Walton, to George some years later will show:

I have often thought of the time gone by when the "Lawrence" in Jerusalem Church was in its palmy days. . . . Can you or I forget the gay, refreshing and kindred spirits that formed that association and gave it a character so unenviable and noticeable as eventually to cause it to be ordered out peremptorily; its sympathy with ghost stories, boxing gloves, fencing foils and deviltry; its exercises tending to promote muscular rather than literary ability; and its test of merit and standard of membership—to drink Red Eye, sing good songs and smoke lots of cigars? [14]

[14] Some letters from his best friend, Joseph Jeffreys, written to George later when he was in California, also indicate that, as the biography states (p. 50), "the fact of knowing anything whatever about liquor or of card playing was significant of the breakdown of the old home influences." Here is a paragraph from a letter of May 6, 1858: "I would have given anything to have you there this evening, my dear fellow, for we are going to kick Hell up again to-night. We have got plenty of the very best imported brandy and port wine, for we have a first rate fellow in our room who is in a wholesale drug house on Market Street and he brings all the liquors home with him, so that they don't cost us anything, and his employers are very willing that

There are still in existence two of George's essays which he prepared for the society, one a quite devastating attack upon "Mormon Polygamy," and the other on the "Poetry of Life," a flowery piece of boyish rhetoric ending with the "Psalm of Life." The youthful introspection of these adolescent years also caused George to conduct a "phrenological examination of head by self," and it is with surprising accuracy that the chart, which may still be seen among his papers, delineates some of the characteristics that the youth discovered in himself. Among the general remarks which follow the detailed degrees of Amativeness, Philoprogenitiveness and the rest, are found these paragraphs:

Will be more likely to make a general than a critical scholar. May have bold and original ideas upon a variety of subjects, yet will not without effort or excitement have a train of connected thoughts upon any; . . . generally takes sides on every contested question. . . . Desires money more as a means than as an end, more for its uses than to lay up; and pays too little attention to small sums. . . . Is inclined to enter largely into business and to push his projects with so much energy and zeal as to appear rash and nearly destitute of caution . . .

The opportunity now presented itself to George to leave Philadelphia and to break away from the home ties which were becoming a little too binding upon one who, according

he should have them at his room for the purpose, as they suppose, of trying experiments, though they little imagine what kind of experiments they are used for. You would have had a splendid time if you had been there." And here is some youthful advice given with the awful seriousness of the teens (May 19): "But Harry, I am truly sorry to hear from yourself that you have been dissipating so much of your time, so much of your money, in pleasures which are not only evanescent but entail sickness upon the frame, injure the fairest and most promising prospects, blight the loftiest ideals of lofty minds, and paralyze the intellectual powers of God's noblest creatures. You have enjoyed yourself—that is right. You have endeavored to repay yourself for restraint and confinement by indulgences which fire the brain and madden the soul, and in the wild excitement you have perhaps forgotten your aims, your hopes, your ambition, and here you have been wrong. Look around you, Harry, and learn from the bitter experience of those who have gone before you, that fame if wanted must be strived for and that perfect success is only to be acquired by slow and steady progress."

to his own phrenological investigations, was "extremely fond of traveling and has an insatiable desire to roam about and see the world and afterward to settle down." Some neighbors had gone out to the Oregon Territory, where their nephew, George Curry, was acting governor, and they had invited Henry George to emigrate to the new West. The magic of the coast, where the gold rush was not yet a memory but a living drama of riches and power, needed no hard times in Philadelphia, nor low printers' wages, nor youthful wanderlust, to add to its magnetic charm, and so George made the traditional nineteenth century American decision of going West. His sailing experience solved the transportation question, which was still a problem in those pre-Civil War days when the Conestoga wagon and not the train was the commonplace. He secured a position as steward or storekeeper on the United States Lighthouse steamer *Shubrick*, [15] which sailed from the Philadelphia Navy Yard for San Francisco on December 22, 1857. The long trip down the Atlantic coast, through the Strait of Magellan, and up the Pacific to the Golden Gate was finally completed in May of the following year, and George found himself in that strange new city of the West, the city of adventure and strength and youth, where a nation was staking out its last frontier. Except for a few occasional visits he was not again to return to Philadelphia and his home.

No satisfactory news arrived from Oregon, and there followed for George a period of feverish and restless drifting. He did not remain long in San Francisco, especially since in June of '58 there came the siren call of gold from Canada. A strike had been made on the Fraser River in the British possessions

[15] The *Shubrick* was the first steam tender in the government lighthouse service, and, in addition to its regular duties, "she was intended to give protection to government property along the seashore of Oregon and Washington from the depredations of Indian tribes and was armed with six brass guns and a novel contrivance for squirting scalding water on the redskins when at close quarters." (*Life*, pp. 56–57; for details of the trip see *ibid*. and pp. 63–67.)

just north of the American line, and George worked his passage up to Victoria on a schooner; but the gold had given out and he soon was back in California. For a time he held a position as printer and lodged in the "What Cheer House," a temperance hotel in San Francisco that boasted a small library of several hundred volumes, including a copy of Adam Smith's *Wealth of Nations.* Here George again began to cultivate his reading, although there is no evidence that in these early days he became acquainted with the work of Smith.[16] His letters home and his diary notes, especially those of April, 1859, which contain what is apparently an outline of English and American history, indicate that for a time at least he followed a definite plan of study; but that was again interrupted by the charmed call of the mines. Once more he set out for the gold fields, this time in northern California, and he made his way as a farm hand, as a weigher in a rice mill, and finally was reduced, to use his own words,[17] to "sleeping in barns and leading the life of a tramp." He never reached the mines; in fact, it was only after the severest of physical hardships that he was able to make his return to San Francisco. Here again his thoughts turned to the sea, but another printing offer kept him ashore and perhaps determined his career.

Some idea of the crudeness of his own writing at the time, and also a glimpse of the circles of the "intelligentsia" of the 1860 Pacific coast, may be had from his letters to his sister Jennie. This is from a letter of April 18, 1859:

I don't read much now except the newspapers and you are getting far ahead of me in that line. It takes pretty much all my spare time to keep posted on the current topics of the day. What

[16] See *Life,* p. 86.

[17] An account of this trip is included in some autobiographical material that George, shortly before his death in 1897, related to Ralph Meeker, a newspaper friend. These "Meeker Notes" may be found scattered throughout the *Life.*

a time we live in, when great events follow one another so quickly
that we have not space for wonder. We are driving at a killing pace
somewhere—Emerson says to heaven and Carlyle says to the other
place, but however much they differ, go we surely do.

I am invited out to-morrow evening to join a reading circle and
if it don't rain will make my début in polite society on this coast.
Would you like to see me make my bow, or hear me break down
when I come to some hard word? But I will do no such thing,
I ain't as bashful as I used to be. I am simply "Henry George,
at your service, no more, no less, if you don't like him, stand to
one side, and let him pass."

You do some pretty heavy reading for a young girl. I wouldn't
be so afraid of novels. A good one is always instructive and your
taste is sufficiently cultivated to allow you to like no other. I never
read them, but then it is solely because I have not time, and am
obliged to take my mental food in as condensed a form as possible.

The advice he received from home shows no let-down in religious interest, and even his own letters manifest some concern with church affairs, although he himself had rejected
formal religion. He wrote home (Jan. 4, 1859):

The only Episcopalian clergyman that I have heard out here was
formerly an actor and is now a tip-top high churchman, keeps all
the saints' days and feasts and fasts of the church, and preaches
that if you get baptized when eight days old you are all right; at
least that was the substance of a sermon I heard, and I didn't
go there to hear another. California is sadly in want of missionaries and I think that it would be a good notion for the Sunday
school to send a few out, provided they were gold-fever proof.

And again (April 18):

I went last evening to hear a sermon preached to young men by
Doctor Cutler of the First Unitarian Church, subject: "Idleness."
It was the best discourse I have heard since I left home. The congregation, though, was rather small. . . . In fact, the theatres here
have a better attendance on Sunday evenings than the churches.

For a time George did turn to religion, and the persuasion
of two of his more ardently pious friends led him to join the

Methodist Church. It was not the effect of any revival—the San Francisco of 1860 was hardly a fruitful field for whole-sale conversion—that made him a church member, but rather the realization of how completely he had broken away from his home influences, a momentary reaction to his own lack of religious faith. His membership was quite casual and certainly did not merit the ecstatic joy of his family, especially since his parents were as yet unaware that it was the Methodist and not the Episcopal Church that he had espoused.

When the Civil War broke out George was setting type for the *Evening Journal,* in which he had bought a small interest. The war did not mean to California what it did to the East, although the slavery question had been burned into the State in the bloody election of 1859. The effects of the war west of the Rocky Mountains, however, were indirect and the significance of the struggle could hardly have been thoroughly appreciated. George, who had been opposed to slavery since boyhood,[18] and who had but recently come from the East, perhaps better realized the meaning of the war than was the case with the average Californian. The letters from home, particularly the news of the enlistment of his boyhood friends, could not help but make the war real to him. His father wrote (June 10, 1860):

You cannot feel it as we do. All around us is warlike, and young men are crowding into the ranks of the forces being raised. Nothing now but the sound of the drum and the march of troops South. . . . But, my dear boy, this is what I think I predicted to you long ago. We are now approaching times and scenes such as never have been seen in these United States; and we old men have come to the conclusion that it is best that it should now be declared whether we are a National Government or not, that our children may know the truth, and what they are to depend upon.

[18] See *Life,* pp. 43–44.

In George's own letters there is some mention of the war,[19] but at this time his thoughts were far more concerned with a growing personal realization of the depressing results of poverty. His writing during these months reveals a decided conviction as to the effects of material wants, a conviction, moreover, that had not been reached vicariously. It was the product of an experience that, already bitter, was soon to become desperate. Here in embryonic stage was the thought that later was to dominate his entire approach to the concepts of economics and ethics; here was an attitude that was to create for him a characteristic and singular interpretation of some of the most fundamental problems of moral theory. He writes: [20]

What a constant reaching this life is, a constant stretching forth, and longing after something . . . and so it will be until we reach the perfect. . . . If civil war should pass over the country leaving nothing but devastation behind it, I think my faith in the ultimate good would remain unchanged. . . . On great events and movements we can philosophize, but when it comes down to ourselves, to our homes, to those we love, then we can only feel— our philosophy goes to the dogs, and we can but look prayerfully to Him who hath more care for us than for all the sparrows . . .

I do not get time to read now; in fact, I have read very little for eighteen months—hardly more than the newspapers. . . . How I long for the Golden Age, for the promised Millennium, when each one will be free to follow his best and noblest impulses, unfettered by the restrictions and necessities which our present state of so-

---

[19] "Am glad Bill Horner and Jim Stanley have gone to the wars. I should like to see them. If I were home, and situated as they are, I would go, too. Not that I like the idea of fighting my countrymen—not that I think it is the best or pleasantest avocation, or that the fun of soldiering is anything to speak of; but in this life or death struggle I should like to have a hand. If they die, they will die in a good cause; and if they live, they will always feel prouder and better when this time is mentioned than if they had remained safely at home while others faced the danger and did the work. I have felt a great deal like enlisting, even here, and probably would have done so, had I not felt that my duty to you all required me to remain." (Letter to sister Jennie, Sept. 15, 1861.)

[20] *Ibid.*

ciety imposes upon him; when the poorest and the meanest will
have a chance to use all his God-given faculties and not be forced
to drudge away the best part of his time in order to supply wants
but little above those of the animal . . .

Is it any wonder that men lust for gold and are willing to give
almost anything for it, when it covers everything—the purest and
holiest desires of their hearts, the exercise of their noblest powers!
What a pity we can't be contented! Is it? Who knows? Sometimes
I feel sick of the fierce struggle of our highly civilized life, and
think I would like to get away from cities and business, with
their jostlings and strainings and cares, altogether, and find some
place on one of the hill-sides which look so dim and blue in the
distance, where I could gather those I love, and live content with
what Nature and our own resources would furnish; but alas,
money, money is wanted even for that. It is our fate—we must
struggle, and so here's for the strife! . . .

And again:

I am not one of those who love work for its own sake, but feeling
what it brings I love it, and am happiest when hard at it. It is no
wonder that wealth is sought by all means, good or bad; for it
expresses almost everything. With it, it seems to me I should be
supremely happy . . . it is but the want of a few dollars that keeps
us separate, that forces one to struggle on so painfully, that crushes
down all the noblest yearnings of the heart and mind . . .[21]

In November, 1861, George lost what little money he had
saved, and yet, two weeks later, with a defiant and characteristic recklessness, he was married. The *Journal*, in which he
had invested his savings, became unable to compete with
papers holding the press association franchises after the
completion of the transcontinental telegraph, and George
was left with but a single coin to his name. In fact he showed
this coin to the young lady when he proposed and gravely
declared that it comprised all his property—and still he was
accepted. His wife was Annie Corsina Fox; she was only

[21] Letter of June 5, 1862.

eighteen at the time of the marriage, while George was twenty-two. Mrs. George had been born in Sydney, Australia, but had come to California and was living in San Francisco; she was of the Roman Catholic faith, of English and Irish descent, and had been educated in a convent at Los Angeles, then a Mexican town. The marriage was an elopement, since the bride's guardians—she was an orphan and lived with her two uncles—were not greatly impressed with the financial condition of the groom. After several days George and his young wife went to Sacramento, where he secured some printing work on the *Union,* a daily morning newspaper.

The next few years were to find poverty and despair hanging grimly over George. His printing work was irregular, he lost his savings again, in some mining stock, and finally, after peddling clothes-wringers for a time, he returned to San Francisco. The first child, Henry George, Jr., was born November 3, 1862, and the second, who was named Richard Fox, on January 27, 1865. The diary notes of these years are mute testimony of the fight that the young father was making against destitution. Most of the items are lists of debts and notices of small sums that he was able to earn at printing. On Christmas Day of 1864 there is this note in the diary:

Struck by something read in library; determined to live more methodically and energetically. Saw landlady and told her I was not able to pay rent . . .

Two days later there was this entry:

Very blue—seem to have got down to bedrock.

Determined to keep a regular journal and to cultivate habits of determination, energy and industry. Feel that I am in a bad situation, and must use my utmost effort to keep afloat and go ahead. Will try to follow the following general rules for one week:

1—In every case to determine rationally what is best to be done.

2—To do everything determined upon immediately or as soon as an opportunity presents.

3—To write down what I shall determine upon doing for succeeding days.

This was followed by his own poem on "The Cross," and a list of debts.

The Meeker Notes reveal his pitiful condition: [22]

I came near starving to death, and at one time I was so close to it that I think I should have done so but for the job of printing a few cards which enabled us to buy a little corn meal. In this darkest time in my life my second child was born.

Mrs. George had already sold her few pieces of jewelry, the delivery of milk had been discontinued because of the expense, and on the day the baby was born there was no money in the house to buy food for the mother. What George did at this crisis of his life he related sixteen years later to a friend: [23]

I walked along the street and made up my mind to get money from the first man whose appearance might indicate that he had it to give. I stopped a man—a stranger—and told him I wanted $5. He asked what I wanted it for. I told him that my wife was confined and that I had nothing to give her to eat. He gave me the money. If he had not, I think I was desperate enough to have killed him.

His diary continues:

Feb. 17, 1865. . . . I am now afloat again, with the world before me. I have commenced this little book as an experiment—to aid me in acquiring habits of regularity, punctuality and purpose. I will enter in it each evening the principal events of the day, with notes, if they occur, errors committed or the reverse, and plans for the morrow and future. I will make a practice of looking at it on rising in the morning.

I am starting out afresh, very much crippled and embarrassed, owing over $200. I have been unsuccessful in everything. I wish

[22] *Life*, p. 148.   [23] *Ibid.*, p. 149.

to profit by my experience and to cultivate those qualities necessary to success in which I have been lacking. I have not saved as much as I ought and am resolved to practice a rigid economy until I have something ahead.

1st. To make every cent I can.

2nd. To spend nothing unnecessarily.

3rd. To put something by each week, if it is only a five-cent piece borrowed for the purpose.

4th. Not to run into debt if it can be avoided.

1st. To endeavor to make an acquaintance and friend of every one with whom I am brought in contact.

2nd. To stay at home less, and be more social.

3rd. To strive to think consecutively and decide quickly.

The journal shows that fortune began to treat him more considerately for a time, and although he did not faithfully live up to his resolutions, he was able to earn money to support his family and pay some of his debts. But a condition such as he had passed through could hardly have failed to impress a man like George, not with a sense of personal bitterness so much as with a wondering dismay at the state of affairs that could cause an honest man to contemplate violence in order to feed his wife and children. And poverty was to be his unwelcome visitor again and again.

George now definitely set out upon a career of writing, and in his diary for March, 1865, there are several notes that show he was consciously endeavoring to develop the literary ability he felt he possessed. He wrote several essays for practice and then composed a fantastic sketch, "A Plea for the Supernatural," which was published by the *Californian,* a literary weekly numbering among its contributors Mark Twain and Bret Harte. News of the assassination of Lincoln swept San Francisco a few weeks later and the boisterous city gave vent to its feelings by destroying four "copperhead" newspapers. George, after helping to hurl type and furniture and machinery out of various newspaper office windows, went home and wrote a fiery article on the murder, "Sic Semper Tyrannis." He placed it in the editor's box of the *Alta California,* the paper on which he was setting type, and it appeared as the leading editorial the next day. Another unsigned article of his on the character of Lincoln was used a few days later as the lead of the editorial page, and George, after his identity was discovered, found himself a reporter. He was first sent as the "war correspondent" of a filbustering expedition that was to invade Mexico in the cause of freedom and help Juarez overthrow Archduke Maximilian, but the overambitious Americans in their water-logged old bark were stopped by a revenue cutter before they could leave San Francisco harbor, and George's services as reporter were no longer needed.[24] He continued to write, however, and devoted himself to free-lance newspaper work, which consisted mainly of descriptive articles built around incidents he had experienced in his early sailing voyages, and also accounts of State politics.[25] His work finally won recognition and he obtained a steady position as reporter on the San Francisco *Times;* he was soon advanced to editorial writer and managing editor.

In December of 1868 George left the *Times* and joined the San Francisco *Herald,* a Democratic paper that had just been founded, and he was sent to New York in order to secure a press association franchise for the new journal. The franchise was refused and George had his first contact with the ugly effects of monopoly when he attempted to run an independent press service from Philadelphia for his California paper. To-

[24] Years later, when George ran for Mayor of New York City, this incident was brought up to show that, in addition to his many other bogyman characteristics, he was also somewhat of a pirate.

[25] He went to Sacramento again for a time and did some official State printing. In a debating society, the Sacramento Lyceum, he was converted from a protectionist to a free trader. For an account of these early tariff beliefs, see his *Protection or Free Trade,* p. 29.

gether with another member of the *Herald's* staff he opened an office on Third Street and sent news to San Francisco over the Western Union wires by means of a special code. The plan was successful for a time, so successful in fact that he "scooped" the Associated Press upon several occasions. The association protested to the telegraph company, the service was discontinued and George's paper lost its Eastern news. George appealed to the officials of the Western Union company and then drew up a news letter attacking the monopolistic features of the Associated Press. His protest was printed only by the New York *Herald*.[26] George returned to California poorer, since there were unpaid salary and expense accounts, but perhaps a bit more sensitive to the power of privilege.[27]

Before George had left San Francisco he had written an article for the *Overland Monthly* on "What the Railroad Will Bring Us." Here he first showed an appreciation of what were really to become his first principles, for previous to this his interest in industrial and economic matters, as indicated in several editorials on the labor question, had lacked analytical examination. It had been an interest largely personal in character and hardly different from what might have been expected of any intelligent American workman of the '60s who was at all conscious of labor problems. In the *Overland*

---

[26] Before the press war had started, George, in a letter to the New York *Tribune,* had delivered an attack upon some railroad and express abuses of the time, particularly the overcharges and reckless handling of the mails on the part of the Central Pacific Railroad and the Wells Fargo Express Company.

[27] A detailed account of the entire affair is found in a letter-press copybook that George kept from January 11 to June 25 of 1869; it is in the New York Public Library and may be of interest to any one concerned with the early development of American journalism. Some years later, while George was editing the Sacramento *Reporter,* the official Democratic organ of the State party, he engaged in another contest with the Associated Press. The press fight resulted from the establishment of the Atlantic and Pacific telegraph system, a rival of the Western Union; this made it possible to set up a competitor of the Associated Press, but the newly formed American Press Association was destined to be short-lived.

article, however, there is expressed a definite conviction, the realization that wealth and want increase together with a disconcerting symmetry. The germ of what was to be perhaps George's most productive thought is found here, although the economic technicalities are necessarily of the crudest sort. A few passages will show the significant direction of George's mind at the time (the article was published in October, 1868):

Amid all our rejoicing and all our gratulation let us see clearly whither we are tending. Increase in population and wealth past a certain point means simply an approximation to the conditions of older countries—the Eastern States and Europe. Would the average Californian prefer to "take his chances" in New York or Massachusetts, or in California as it is and has been? Is England, with her population of twenty millions to an area of not more than one-third that of our State, and a wealth which per inhabitant is six or seven times that of California, a better country than California to live in? Probably, if one were born a duke or factory lord, or in any place among the upper ten thousand, but if one were born among the lower millions—how then?

But however this be, it is certain that the tendency of the new era—of the more dense population and more thorough development of the wealth of the State—will be to a reduction both of the rate of interest and the rate of wages, particularly the latter . . .

The truth is, that the completion of the railroad and the consequent great increase of business and population, will not be a benefit to all of us, but only to a portion. . . . Those who have, it will make wealthier; for those who have not, it will make it more difficult to get . . .

And as California becomes populous and rich, let us not forget that the character of a people counts for more than their numbers; that the distribution of wealth is even a more important matter than its production.

Another bit of writing, much less important in the development of George's ideas, but of considerable consequence in the establishing of his reputation, appeared in the New York *Tribune* of May 1, 1869. It was a demand for the restriction of Chinese immigration, and while the attack seems anomalous when compared with the broadly sympathetic and universal scope of George's later thinking, it is readily explainable in its particular setting; indeed, a Californian of that day (or perhaps of any day) and especially one interested in popular and working class matters, could hardly have been required to preserve a detached and altogether scientific attitude toward the Asiatic problem in this period that preceded the agitation of Dennis Kearney. George, at least, was not quite able to see more than one side of the question. The *Tribune* contribution, however, came into importance some months later through the medium of a letter of commendation written to George by John Stuart Mill. Recognizing Mill's authority in political economy, George had sent him a copy of the article and had received a very gracious letter in reply. The incident caused something of a sensation in the West, where the Chinese question was the all-important one, and from a local newspaper man with but a small circle of friends, George became known throughout the State. In fact, there was some talk of sending him to the Legislature as a Democratic Assemblyman, but he was unable to pay the necessary assessment and the nomination was not forthcoming.[28]

It was in New York that George saw at first hand an example of the bewildering coincidence of progress and poverty that he had been vaguely conscious of in the *Overland* article. Here in that mighty city of the East—where wealth and prestige were written on every brownstone front and the very air seemed charged with power—misery and wretchedness

[28] Some years later George was nominated as Assemblyman from a San Francisco district in a campaign which was directed against the growing power of the Central Pacific Railroad; the campaign was unsuccessful and the Democratic party, including Governor Haight, who had become a close friend of George, was swept out of power.

were already smugly accepted and the slums were beginning to fester. The young man walked the streets and wondered and made a vow. Years later he told of that silent vow:

Because you are not only my friend, but a priest and a religious, I shall say something that I don't like to speak of—that I never before have told any one. Once, in daylight, and in a city street, there came to me a thought, a vision, a call—give it what name you please. But every nerve quivered. And there and then I made a vow. Through evil and through good, whatever I have done and whatever I have left undone, to that I have been true.[29]

And again:

Years ago I came to this city from the West, unknown, knowing nobody, and I saw and recognized for the first time the shocking contrast between monstrous wealth and debasing want. And here I made a vow from which I have never faltered, to seek out, and remedy, if I could, the cause that condemned little children to lead such a life as you know them to lead in the squalid districts.[30]

Another experience, of a similar revelational character but more directly related to economic conditions with which he was familiar, occurred shortly after his return to California. He had been riding one day through a district where the magic boom of land speculation had filled the scrubby countryside with a feverish collection of land offices and claim-jumpers. George relates:

Absorbed in my own thoughts, I had driven the horse into the hills until he panted. Stopping for breath, I asked a passing teamster, for want of something better to say, what land was worth there. He pointed to some cows grazing off so far that they looked like mice, and said: "I don't know exactly, but there is a man over there who will sell some land for a thousand dollars an acre." Like a flash it came upon me that there was the reason of advancing poverty with advancing wealth. With the growth of population,

[29] Quoted from a letter to the Reverend Father Thomas Dawson of Glencree, Ireland, February 1, 1883.
[30] From his acceptance of the New York mayoralty nomination in 1886.

land grows in value, and the men who work it must pay more for the privilege. I turned back, amidst quiet thought, to the perception that then came to me and has been with me ever since.[31]

In the East he had seen the problem; in the West he thought he had found the solution.

George now definitely busied himself with elaborating that solution, and in July of 1871 he published his first comprehensive piece of economic writing, his first attempt to solve the problem of "advancing poverty with advancing wealth." It was a 48-page pamphlet entitled *Our Land and Land Policy, National and State,* which he printed himself; in it he proposed the apparently simple solution for the problem that had forced itself upon him in the speculative rise in the price of Western lands, the solution of absorbing the "unearned increment," that had been recognized by Adam Smith and John Stuart Mill, by means of a tax on the value of land. This proposal, which was to be later known as the "single tax," [32] comprised the fifth section of the pamphlet, the others

[31] "Meeker Notes," *Life,* p. 210.

[32] The words "single tax" appeared in *Progress and Poverty,* p. 425; but it was not until 1887, at the suggestion of Thomas G. Shearman, the economist, that they were used to designate George's proposals (see *Life,* p. 496, n. 1). The phrase has never met with great favor; George himself did not regard it very highly, since its connotation was fiscal and purely methodological. The opposition to the use of "single tax" has largely centered about this failure of the name to indicate the fundamental issues and ethical scope of the land question. The national political party in this country changed its name from the Single Tax Party to the Commonwealth Land Party some years ago, and at the same time the *Single Tax Review,* the leading American periodical of the movement, became *Land and Freedom.* In Great Britain "single tax" has not been adopted generally as a title, and the land reform party has been known there as the Commonwealth Land Party.

The first use of the phrase "single tax" appears to have been in 1743 (that is, the first English use of the term, which is, of course, a literal translation of *l'impôt unique* of the Physiocrats) in a book published in that year by an Englishman, Matthew Decker, on *Serious Considerations on the Several High Duties.* The phrase was also used in 1806 in an English translation of Filangieri's *Science of Legislation* (see *infra,* p. 187), and again in Gourlay's *Statistical Account of Upper Canada,* London, 1822, Introd. p. 9. Robert Fleming Gourlay was a Scotchman who went to Canada in 1817 and proposed a "single tax" on land that was to be based on population. His work was one of those startling anticipations of George's doctrines (see *infra,* Chap. IV). For these early uses of the phrase "single tax," see in the

having dealt with a short historical sketch of the gradual exhausting of the country's public lands, especially in California, and with a statement of the dependence of labor upon land. George himself realized that the work was hasty and incomplete, and that an adequate interpretation of his ideas—perhaps he would have preferred to call them his vision—demanded a more thorough and well-grounded approach. It was eight years before such a work was to be accomplished, for George had now temporarily put aside a more comprehensive consideration of political economy to become editor of his own paper.

He had entered into a partnership with two other men, and with a very small capital they founded the San Francisco *Daily Evening Post*. Its first issue appeared on Monday, December 4, 1871, and the immediate effect was to introduce to California the one-cent piece. The *Post* was the first penny paper west of the Rocky Mountains, and as the one-cent piece was not yet in commercial use on the coast, one thousand dollars' worth of pennies had to be brought from the East. The *Post*, however, did more than merely popularize the penny. It was a vigorous reform sheet, opposed to Grant and pro-Greeley, and according to its own words was to be "the organ of no faction, clique or party." The editorial columns, written by George, emphasized at every opportunity "little Harry George's fad," the taxation of land values, and they contained relentless attacks upon that complacent acceptance of the growing coincidence of wealth and poverty. Characteristic passages such as these appeared during the first month of the paper's existence:

There are in England millions of people who are constantly hovering on the very verge of starvation—white, Christian people,

Single Tax Year Book (New York, 1917) the article by Samuel Milliken on the "Forerunners of Henry George," pp. 306–343; also *The Single Tax Movement in the United States*, by A. N. Young (Princeton University Press, 1916), pp. 109–111.

men, women and children, who are not fed and housed as well as the dogs which are kept at such expense for the amusement of the rich. It will not be otherwise. When some men take to themselves more than their share, others must get less than their share. . . . These are things for working men to think about; for every wrong there is a remedy. (Dec. 7.)

It [disquietude of labor] cannot be put down by cries of "communism," "socialism," "agrarianism," for it is neither the one nor the other of these, but simply an attempt to set aside the principle of competition upon which society is now based and to substitute for it a system based upon the conception of the State as in the main a family, in which the weaker brethren shall not be remorselessly pushed to the wall. It is the exaggerated individualism of our existing social system, the free scope it gives to cruel selfishness and monstrous greed, that calls aloud for its overthrow. The world that is to come out of the social crisis now being inaugurated will not be a phalanstery, nor one in which the rights of property will be disregarded. It will not be introduced by a general scramble on the part of the needy for the wealth of the prosperous; but neither will it be a world of mere remorseless, competitive effort, like a great nest of hissing and wriggling vipers, every one struggling to lift its head above the heads of the others. (Dec. 8.)

If we go back to first principles, none should own the land but those whose toil makes it productive. (Dec. 19.)

A consideration of Mill's opinions on the land question appeared in April of 1873, and a month later, when news of the great Englishman's death came from France, the *Post* paid a warm tribute to his fame and suggested that "his best monument" in America would be a memorial edition of his complete works.

This was the day of personal journalism, when, in the West at least, "personal" meant not so much the dominating influence of a vigorous and whimsically autocratic editor of the Greeley or Godkin type, nor much less the present-day intimate revelations of the columnist, but rather an ability to maintain editorial opinion in the presence of an opposition that usually was armed with something more than strong arguments. George's aggressive tactics, especially in forcing unwelcome prosecutions of political grafters and influential murderers, drew down upon him more than once the threat and even the act of personal violence, and his experiences during these years of newspaper work would have made a stirring chapter in any saga of frontier journalism. George ended his connection with the *Post* late in 1875, when the paper was sold, and then in the Tilden-Hayes presidential campaign of 1876 he was brought into active politics and for the first time deserted the editor's desk for the platform. His success in the campaign was immediate; he "stumped" the State, made the final rallying speech, and soon became known as one of the best political speakers on the coast.[33] But even in a campaign such as this he did not fail to introduce the problem that would not let him rest, and while speaking for Tilden he continued to emphasize such thoughts as—

Food, raiment and lodging are essential not merely to animal existence but to mental development, to moral growth, to the life of the affections. Personal independence, the ability to get a living without trembling in fear of any man, is the basis of all manly

[33] In reference to these speeches he wrote to his mother (Nov. 13, 1876): "I did my best, for my heart was in it, and that is a consolation; and personally what I accomplished was very gratifying. I have shown that I could make myself felt without a newspaper, and shown that I possessed other ability than that of the pen. I have always felt that I possessed the requisites for a first class speaker, and that I could make one if I could get the practice, and I started into this campaign with the deliberate purpose of breaking myself in. It was like jumping overboard to learn to swim. But I succeeded. I think no man in the State made as much reputation as I have made. From not being known as a speaker, I have come at once to the front. I wanted to do this, not as a matter of vanity, or for the mere pleasure of the thing, but to increase my power and usefulness. Already well known as a writer, I knew this kind of reputation would aid me immensely in the future. And so it will—whether I go into politics, into the law, or into the newspaper business again. I do not intend to rest here, but to go ahead step by step. You must not be afraid, though, of politics doing me any harm. I do not propose to mix in lower politics, nor do I propose to chase after nominations. I will wait until they seek me. I propose to read and study; to write some things which will extend my reputation, and perhaps to deliver some lectures with the same view. And if I live I will make myself known, even in Philadelphia. I aim high . . ."

virtues. Ignorance is the companion of poverty; want is the parent
of crime. These are the grand questions . . . yet these are the
questions to which we have been paying least attention.

George's speaking ability, however, was not to be confined
to politics, for in March of 1877 he was asked to deliver an
address on political economy at the University of California.
Indeed, there was some talk of his appointment to the
unfilled chair of political economy at the university. His
interest in economics was known throughout the State, and
for a university that was as yet young and unpretentious,
his lack of scholastic training might possibly have bowed
to a forceful personality and an enviable reputation as a
writer and a talker. But whatever favorable feeling the
California academicians might have had for George soon
vanished when they heard what the editor had to say:

For the study of political economy you need no special knowledge, no extensive library, no costly laboratory. You do not even
need textbooks or teachers, if you will but think for yourselves.
All that you need is care in reducing complex phenomena to their
elements, in distinguishing the essential from the accidental, and
in applying the simple laws of human action with which you are
familiar. Take nobody's opinion for granted; "try all things;
hold fast to that which is good.". . . All this array of professors,
all this paraphernalia of learning cannot educate a man. They
can but help him to educate himself. Here you may obtain the
tools; but they will be useful only to him who can use them. A
monkey with a microscope, a mule packing a library, are fit em-
blems of the men—and, unfortunately, they are plenty—who pass
through the whole educational machinery and come out but learned
fools, crammed with knowledge which they cannot use—all the
more pitiable, all the more contemptible, all the more in the way
of real progress, because they pass, with themselves and others, as
educated men. . . . You are of the favored few, for the fact that
you are here, students in a university of this character, bespeaks
for you the happy accidents that fall only to the lot of the few,
and you cannot yet realize . . . how the hard struggle which is

the lot of so many may cramp and bind and distort . . . but you cannot fail to see enough want and wretchedness, even in our own country to-day, to move you to sadness and pity, to nerve you to high resolve; to arouse in you the sympathy that dares, and the indignation that burns to overthrow a wrong.[34]

George, of course, did touch on detailed questions of political economy, but this "monkey with a microscope," the "mule packing a library," the questioning of "educational machinery" and "learned fools" was too much. Such expressions might have been applauded as obvious had they been the opinion of a dean, but they hardly could have been appreciated as the ideas of an untutored layman. George's address was received with polite and dignified attention on the part of the faculty, and even with some enthusiasm by the students, but there was no more talk of "Professor" Henry George, which perhaps was quite fortunate for both the university and for George's later work.[35] He did, however, retain his circle of friends at Berkeley, including President John Le Conte, his brother, Professor Joseph Le Conte, the noted geologist, and Professor William Swinton.[36]

Several months later George was chosen as the Fourth of July orator of the San Francisco celebration, and in the old California Theatre he was to make what up to then was his greatest effort. The oration was perhaps to those who heard it

[34] Vol. VIII (Our Land and Land Policy) of complete works, pp. 148–150.

[35] Whatever else George may have been, and he did manage to become acquainted with a number of occupations, he scarcely was temperamentally fitted for a professor's position; yet he did tell his wife that the only title he ever cared to have was that of professor. If a professorship were really George's aim, then he undoubtedly made a deliberate sacrifice of his ambitions in this address, for he could not possibly have been unconscious of its effects. He was always willing, however, to sacrifice everything but his convictions.

[36] Professor Swinton was one of George's most intimate friends, and was to exert a great influence on his later work. He was a brother of John Swinton, the New York liberal, had been educated at Amherst and had served as a brilliant Civil War correspondent for the New York Times. His wide scholarship, or else the youthful character of the university, was responsible for his holding the chair of "English language and literature, history, rhetoric, and logic."

a typical Fourth of July spread-eagle affair, and one of the papers reported that the "gas measurer"[37] . . . kindly spoke for several hours on the Goddess of Liberty and other school-reader topics." But George's worship of freedom, his "ode to liberty," was something that his hearers certainly did not grasp; his fervent sincerity they undoubtedly appreciated, but hardly the boundless implications he was suggesting, for the liberty that George was apotheosizing was not merely the product of political democracy and it was much more than the economic equality demanded by labor. It was an almost metaphysical conception, a very *sine qua non* for all enduring and legitimate human activity, and it is only in the context of the tenth book of *Progress and Poverty,* where these lines on liberty are printed with practically no change, that the complete significance of George's thought can be recognized.[38]

Progress and Poverty, according to a note in his diary, was begun by George on September 18, 1877. For a time, however, he was unable to devote all his attention to the book. He interrupted his work first to deliver a lecture which he hoped was to open a speaking campaign that was to be a companion effort for his writing. The lecture, "Why Work Is Scarce, Wages Low and Labor Restless," was first delivered in the Metropolitan Temple of San Francisco in March of 1878, but with the exception of one other address George was unable to follow the plan that he had laid out for himself. That address, which is believed by many to have been

[37] George had secured something of a sinecure from Governor Irwin, whom he had helped to elect, in being appointed State Inspector of Gas-Meters, a position which with little work gave him enough money to live, and, what was more important, permitted him to devote his time to writing; it was thus instrumental in paving the way for the completion of *Progress and Poverty*

[38] This "ode to liberty" has been recognized by critics as one of the most eloquent passages in American literature, and it has appeared in many anthologies, although that is faint praise for philosophic purposes. However, even a Fourth of July oration may rise above mere declamatory significance.

the most polished and fervent talk he ever delivered, was "Moses," and was first presented to the Young Men's Hebrew Association of San Francisco. His interest in politics also took his attention from his work. He had declined a nomination for a State Senatorship in 1877, but the following year he became a Democratic nominee for the position of delegate to the State constitutional convention, only to be defeated in the election. It was at this time also that he helped to found the Free Public Library of San Francisco and became the first secretary of the original Board of Trustees.[39] Still another interruption, his fourth child,[40] was to demand the major part of his interest for a time. Finally, however, after a period of intense concentration, he succeeded in completing *Progress and Poverty* in March of 1879.

George's library during these years consisted of some eight hundred volumes, chiefly standard works on political economy, history and philosophy. In working on his book he also drew upon the bibliographical resources of his university friends, and upon the four libraries of San Francisco and the State library at Sacramento. He was a wide reader and possessed the happy faculty of seizing upon the important ideas of a book, or rather the ideas that seemed useful to him; he was thus able to achieve an astonishing power of rapid reading. He did "chew and digest" some works, especially those on political economy, although, strangely enough, he confessed that they gave him the most difficulty;

[39] The interest in public libraries had remained with George ever since his boyhood days in Philadelphia. In one of his undated note-books there is a discussion of the value of libraries based on Carlyle's "the true university is a collection of books."

[40] This fourth child was Anna Angela, who later became the wife of William C. De Mille, the motion picture producer. George's first-born, Henry George, Jr., his biographer, became a writer on economic and sociological subjects and was later elected to the national House of Representatives from a New York City district. Richard, who was born in the darkest hour of George's life, became a noted sculptor, perhaps his best work being the bust of his father. The third child, Jennie, was later married to William J. Atkinson of New York.

his reading of law, to which he devoted himself for several years, he found of aid chiefly in helping to cure his infrequent insomnia.

George ended his first great task with a feeling of deep and almost holy reverence. He had felt within him the fire of the prophet, the zeal of the crusader, and his finished work had for him all the solace of religion. The burning conviction that had never let George rest since it had first forced itself upon his mind, the seeming apocalypse that here in the private ownership of land lay the root of all the social and moral problems that had perplexed mankind, that the denial of the equal opportunity to the use of the planet was the cancer that had brought on the symptom of that mysterious increase of want with the increase of wealth, had now been given to the world, and for George it was the realization of a profound religious experience. He wrote to his friend Father Dawson in Ireland some years later (February 1, 1883):

. . . When I had finished the last page, in the dead of the night, when I was entirely alone, I flung myself on my knees and wept like a child. The rest was in the Master's hands. That is a feeling that has never left; that is constantly with me. And it has led me up and up. It has made me a better and a purer man. It has been to me a religion, strong and deep though vague—a religion of which I never like to speak, or make any outward manifestation, but yet that I try to follow.

To his father in Philadelphia he sent this accurate prophecy:

It is with a deep feeling of gratitude to Our Father in Heaven that I send you a printed copy of this book. I am grateful that I have been enabled to live to write it, and that you have been enabled to live and see it. It represents a great deal of work and a good deal of sacrifice, but now it is done. It will not be recognized at first—maybe not for some time—but it will ultimately be considered a great book—will be published in both hemispheres, and be translated into different languages. This I know, though neither of us may ever see it here. But the belief I have expressed in this book, the belief that there is yet another life for us, makes that of little moment.

While George undoubtedly believed that his work was an almost inspired revelation of truth, yet he also felt that the demonstration was as logically clear as the most valid of syllogisms; he was confident that his reasoning could be grasped in a sweeping comprehension of first principles, in a lucid deduction that was to be an almost mystic intuition; and this assurance remained with him always.[41] Yet despite George's confidence that his work was a logically impregnable revelation, it was not easy to convince the publishers that the book would pay. The manuscript was first sent to Appleton's in New York, but the author received only a polite card of declination, which stated:

We have read your MS. on political economy. It has the merit of being written with great clearness and force, but is very aggressive. There is very little to encourage the publication of any such work at this time and we feel we must decline it.

Harper's considered the work revolutionary, and Scribner's, after some hesitation, also refused to accept it. Finally, however, William H. Appleton, head of the publishing firm, was interviewed by some of George's friends in the East, among whom was Professor William Swinton, and the result was that he reconsidered his decision and consented to publish *Progress and Poverty,* but with the understanding that the company would not make the plates for the work. George therefore gave the manuscript to an old newspaper partner,

[41] He wrote to a friend from London in 1884: "I do not think the fault is in the book—it arises from its scope, and the necessary connection between the links of a logical chain. When you once grasp this connection and once see the relation of the central ideas, it will be to you like a demonstration and you will never afterward lose it." And again in 1890: "I do not think that there is any point you make that was not threshed over in my mind in writing that book. . . . If I am wrong now the wrong is in the original thinking, not in my subsequent deviation."

and the author himself began to set the type. From these plates there was first published in 1879, the Author's Edition of five hundred copies (San Francisco, William M. Hinton). The Appleton edition appeared in January of the following year.

The book attracted little attention at first. In California the newspaper reviews for the most part ridiculed the fad of their little editor and Democratic orator, and predicted that the work would remain unnoticed. Some encouraging remarks, however, did come from several distinguished figures to whom George had sent complimentary copies. Gladstone wrote from Hawarden (Nov. 11, 1879): "Accept my best thanks for the copy of your interesting work, which reached me to-day, and which I have begun to examine. There is no question which requires a more careful examination than the land question in this and other countries, and I shall set great store on whatever information you may furnish under this head." The Duke of Argyll, with whom George was later to engage in a bitter controversy, courteously acknowledged the receipt of the book, although Herbert Spencer did not. Sir George Grey, the leading Liberal in New Zealand, wrote (Auckland, N. Z., Jan. 27, 1880): "I have already read a large part of the book. I regard it as one of the ablest works on the great questions of the time which has come under my notice. It will be of great use to me. . . . It has cheered me much to find that there is so able a man working in California upon subjects on which I believe the whole future of mankind now mainly hangs."

But George was now in the grip of another period of discouragement. All the time and energy and money that had been put into the writing and printing of *Progress and Poverty* seemed for the moment to have been wasted; George also was without a position, for a change in party success in California had cost him his political sinecure, and his financial condition was again becoming desperate. While waiting for his book to be published he had attempted to put out another newspaper, a weekly called *The State,* but after the eleventh issue it was forced to suspend.[42] The situation in California finally forced George to turn his thoughts East. John Russell Young, managing editor of the New York *Tribune,* and Charles Nordhoff, chief editorial writer of the New York *Herald,* whose friendships George had made during his earlier New York attempt to secure an Associated Press

[42] The few numbers of the paper show a combination of forceful thought and polished diction. This attack upon the complacency of an optimistic view of society's ills appeared April 19, 1879: "Without equal opportunity there can be no freedom; and all our talk and declamation is but babble in the presence of the indubitable fact that . . . there is not equal opportunity. . . . That which is in its very nature and essence unjust never has lasted and it never will last. . . . We are not alarmists. We simply give voice to that which is in the mind and heart of every thoughtful man. To suppose that the few very rich and the many very poor can forever jog along peaceably together is to suppose something that never has happened and that never will happen. It is opposed to the very nature of man—it is forbidden by the eternal laws that rule the universe. But this is not to say that such evils cure themselves. The comfortable doctrine that evils cure themselves is disproved on every page of history. . . . This world is not a fool's paradise in which all will come out right in the end; it is a world in which a people make their own conditions; it is a world in which the eternal laws punish ignorance and recklessness and injustice as remorselessly as the glacier grinds the rock. . . . Are men free when they have to strain and strive and scheme and worry to satisfy the mere animal wants of life? Are men free when, pressed by the fear of want, they are forced to starve their higher natures and to tread under foot in the fierce struggle for wealth, love, honor, justice and mercy? . . . It is the institutions of man not the edicts of God that enslave men; it is the greed and ignorance of mankind not the niggardliness of nature that show themselves in poverty and misery and want-produced vice. Yet while we prate of freedom we strangle freedom; while we thank God for liberty we load liberty with fetters."

George, it also appears, was somewhat of a pioneer in the discussion of the Nordic question: "We of the Anglo-Saxon race do not know how to enjoy ourselves; we do not know how to get the most out of this life that flies so rapidly. . . . Open Plato's 'Dialogues' or Plutarch's 'Morals' and you catch glimpses of society to which ours is as the pow-wow of naked savages or the dance of lunatics. This thirst for wealth, it is the draught of Tantalus." (April 12.) "We are by no means inclined to insist upon the natural superiority of the Caucasian." (May 10.)

Besides *The State* and the *Post* of 1872–1875, George had made one other venture into California journalism. In 1875 he had started the publication of the *Ledger,* a small daily paper with an illustrated Sunday edition, perhaps the first in American journalism. The paper was also novel in that it did not solicit advertising but waited for the advertisers to bring in their business. It is not necessary to add that it did not live very long.

franchise, advised him that there might be some newspaper work in New York, and so in August of 1880, his fare having been paid by Young, George came East unknown and almost penniless. He found himself again in the great city where he once had made a silent vow.[43]

George's arrival in the East seemed to launch *Progress and Poverty* into a truly phenomenal popularity. Here was a voluminous work on political economy and ethics that almost overnight had created a demand that sent its sales later into the millions of copies and made it a rival of the most successful works of fiction. Reviews appeared in all the leading newspapers and magazines, books of commentary and criticism were begun, Appleton's put out a cheap paper edition, Kegan Paul in London arranged for an English publication of the book, and the first of many translations was struck off in 1881.[44] For a short time even the academic

[43] The Garfield-Hancock Presidential campaign first provided an opportunity for George to make himself known. The New York Democratic leaders had heard of the California spellbinder and had persuaded him to speak for General Hancock. They soon regretted their action, however, for they found that the Westerner was one of those rare examples of the real free trade species, and held no brief for revenue tariffs or local schedules. They did not ask him to stump again. Within six years this unknown free trader was to threaten New York's powerful political machines.

[44] This first translation was in German and was the work of C. D. F. von Gütschow; two other German editions, one translated by F. Dobbert, appeared soon after. A French translation was made by J. L. Le Monnier. In 1886, Concordia Löfving and H. Wennerstrom translated the book into Swedish at Upsala; Jakob E. Lange made the Danish translation, and V. Ullman, the Norwegian in 1886. The Spanish translation is the work of Jaime Jepús y Roviralta and was published in Barcelona in 1893. Ludovico Eusebio translated it into Italian in 1888 and published his work at Turin. The Dutch edition, the work of J. W. Straatman, appeared in 1882; Robert Braun is the Hungarian translator, and S. D. Nikolaev the Russian. There is also a Chinese edition of *Progress and Poverty*, which was translated by Professor W. E. Macklin at the time of George's death; Dr. Sun Yat Sen assisted him in the work of translation.

There are more than a dozen editions of the book in English, with nearly as many publishers; the work also appeared in serial form in several newspapers, such as *Truth*, a New York publication, and the Chicago *Express*. It is almost impossible to estimate the exact number of copies of *Progress and Poverty* circulated. The highest figure is seven million, which is obviously too large. The lowest estimate is two million. But there can be no question that the book has had a greater circulation than any other volume on political

world, especially in England, took an active interest in the work; several students of John Stuart Mill, among whom were Dr. Montague R. Leverson and Professor William Ellis, came out in praise of *Progress and Poverty*. Émile de Laveleye, the French economist, William D. Le Seur in Canada, and Professor E. L. Youmans, the American popularizer of Herbert Spencer, were others influenced by George, and also Alfred Russel Wallace, the biologist, who later was to head the English land reformers and who stated that the book was "undoubtedly the most remarkable and important work of the present century." [45]

The popular interest in *Progress and Poverty* perhaps is not difficult to explain. The country was in the grip of violent labor agitation which followed the widespread industrial depression of 1873 to 1877, and which had flamed out in the riots and bloodshed of the great railroad strike of the latter year. An unmistakable labor class consciousness was now at the point of crystallizing. The first bitter strikes and wage wars of the late '60s and early '70s, the murderous activities of the "Molly Maguires," the workers' struggles of the middle '80s, were all overt indications not only of the gradual development of labor organizations but also of the intangible realization of labor's self-awareness.[46] It was a period of industrial upheaval, a day when labor sensed its growing importance, and George's book could not have appeared at a more favorable time for its popular reception. Its prophetic fervor and almost holy sincerity, together with the practical

economy. For complete details on this matter of translations and editions see Part IV of the complete Henry George and Single Tax bibliography of the New York Public Library. All of George's important books, especially *Protection or Free Trade*, also appeared in many editions and translations.

[45] See letter of George to Dr. F. R. Taylor, Sept. 7, 1881, quoted in the *Life*, pp. 353–354.

[46] For a discussion of this period of labor agitation, see Commons and Associates, *History of Labour in the United States* (New York, Macmillan, 1918), Vol. II, Chap. V, and bibliography, *ibid.*, pp. 573–576; or any labor history dealing with the times.

and simple suggestions that it offered, could hardly have failed to impress the working man [47] or the thinker interested in social reform. But while the vivid style and compelling originality of the work, together with the conditions that greeted its publication, were surety for its success, the events of George's meteor-like career carried the knowledge of his ideas still further, especially in Great Britain, where the work became even more popular than in this country.

He first entered the lecture field and traveled all over the United States and Canada speaking on the land question and attracting great crowds by the power of his oratory and the challenge of his book. Of even greater importance, however, was his connection with the Irish land movement. Michael Davitt in 1879, just a month after the completion of *Progress and Poverty,* had roused all Ireland with his attack upon the absentee English landlords, and had rallied the nation under his cry of "The land for the people." The Irish National Land League was formed to supersede the Home Rule League, and even Parnell, despite his conservative leanings, was swept into the agitation and came to the United States with the backing of the *Irish World,* a weekly paper published in New York by Patrick Ford. Later Davitt came to this country, met George, and pledged the Land League to "push *Progress and Poverty* in Great Britain." [48] George seized the extraordinary opportunity presented by this Irish land movement and threw himself into the fight. He lectured for the League in the campaign that had been organized in the United States, and then dashed off a pamphlet, *The Irish Land Question,* which was later changed to *The Land Question,* since George felt that the issues raised were not

[47] To understand George's popularity with labor it must be remembered that, unlike the present time, the 1880 connotation that was suggested by "working man" was one that implied the attributes of "American" and "skilled"; the appeal of *Progress and Poverty* could hardly have had the power that it did without the existence of that type of laborer.

[48] See a letter to Dr. Taylor, quoted in *Life,* p. 341.

confined to Ireland alone. The tract was published in New York, England and Canada and gained a wide circulation. George, in fact, so allied himself with the Irish cause that he was finally sent to Ireland under the auspices of the *Irish World* to lecture and to conduct the Irish correspondence of the paper. He left for Europe in October of 1881.

George's growing reputation, however, had not raised him above the ever-watchful eye of poverty. He had no steady income and was always in debt, borrowing on the strength of some expected lecture or on some future royalties; and it was a bitter experience, as his letters indicate, for him to realize that he could not remove himself from the grasp of want and yet remain faithful to his vision. Here are some extracts from his correspondence with his most intimate friend, Dr. Taylor:

I am afloat at 42 poorer than at 21. I do not complain, but there is some bitterness in it. It is at such times that a man feels the weight of a family. It is like swimming with heavy clothes on. Still, if I keep my health I do not fear. (Dec., 1880.)

One of my creditors has been after me, and I fear some of them may make an attempt to garnishee the proceeds [of the lecture] to-night. (Aug. 11, 1881.)

I have now just $25 in the world, about half a week's living with economy; no, not that. However, this is no new experience to me. (Aug. 12, 1883.)

I want to ask you to do something for me, if you can, and that is to pay my life insurance, some $50 or $60, to Colonel Hawes, and I will send you the money when I get able, which will be in a few months. This sort of work straitens me. (Sept. 28, 1886.)

Immediately after finishing *The Irish Land Question,* and when his reputation was beginning to become international, he yet could write to Dr. Taylor (May 12, 1881):

Inclosed find check for $20. . . . You do not know, and I cannot readily tell you, how much this little accommodation has been to me. It is not so much the want of money as the mental effect it produces—the morbid condition. The man who does not understand that, does not know how it is possible for people to commit suicide. This thing has weighted me very much. Could I have felt free and been relieved of the terrible anxiety, I could have in the same time accomplished many times as much. But yet it has seemed as though a Providence helped me through. When I drew on you for this $20 it seemed my darkest hour. I was weak and weary in mind and body.[49]

The Henry George that Ireland was to see was a short, stocky figure with thinning hair and a full red beard, a sandy red, however, rather than the flaming Barbarossa type. The beard and a flashing pair of deep blue eyes and a nobly shaped head with a great bulging forehead were the striking features of the man. About his appearance George was singularly careless, and he had acquired a habit of almost an academic absent-mindedness. Don Seitz believes that "in the Capitoline Museum at Rome there is a bust of Socrates that bears a most extraordinary resemblance to Henry George." [50] The comparison is hardly a fit one. The Socratic connotation is undoubtedly meant to be a bit flattering, but the Socratic countenance scarcely so. George was not quite a Silenus. On the lecture platform his listeners were to see a restless, moving bundle of energy. He walked up and down, turning to the audience at critical points with arms thrown out in an appealing gesture, or, in a more characteristic pose, with one hand in his pocket, he hung over the speaker's table and by the very power of his sincerity burned his thought into the crowd below. His voice was characteristically persuasive rather than bellowing or rasping; he was an orator who talked directly to his hearers, trying to take each one of them by the coat lapels and convince him individually of the great truths he felt to be surging within him. This subdued style, how-

[49] For George's own explanation of his financial condition, see also *Life*, p. 508.
[50] *Uncommon Americans* (Indianapolis, Bobbs-Merrill, 1925), p. 256.

ever, frequently gave way to great bursts of animated power, particularly when George met with opposition; a friendly and quiet audience might hear only an impressive and carefully planned address, but an antagonistic and heckling one would be greeted with a great booming voice and an inspired emotion driven home with all the favorite devices of the platform. It was the George in this mood who was ranked by the London *Times* as the oratorical peer of Cobden and Bright; it was this George about whom Thomas Beer relates the following newspaper anecdote:

Charles Dana, editor of the New York *Sun*, sent a novice to report Henry George. The boy was made imbecile and covered papers with words of which he now recalls only "lyrelike voice." This went into Dana's cell and came out with the editor's comment on its face: "You sound like Wendell Philips reporting Saint John the Baptist. I asked you to see a Mr. Henry George.". . . The rhapsodist went hurrying for sympathy to the office of *Puck* and showed Dana's cruel remark to Henry Cuyler Bunner. But the humorist was curiously cool after reading the description of Henry George, and limited his sympathy to saying: "Mr. Dana's wrong. I think it sounds like Hall Caine." [51]

This fervent sincerity which perhaps befuddled the cub's pen or typewriter was George's distinctive characteristic as a speaker—and as a man—and it was this unmistakable honesty that Ireland saw and admired.

The Ireland that Henry George saw was a country filled

[51] *The Mauve Decade* (New York, Knopf, 1926), pp. 110–111. Here is another George story that Beer relates: ". . . the parent of the single tax could conceive art only as a vehicle for 'good and noble' purposes. But George was touched by the Fair [the Chicago World's Fair of 1893]. He stood one night with Charles Nolan watching the crowds of the Midway, and dreamed aloud: The people had done all this. It was 'of the people, by the people, for the people.' The lawyer argued: 'No, most of the money was subscribed by rich men. The people had nothing to do with designing these buildings.' The economist pulled his beard and sighed. Anyhow, the people were enjoying it, and his friend Altgeld would govern Illinois. Perhaps the Kingdom of God was a little nearer. He strolled among the crowd and scandalized a waiter at the Auditorium by demanding for late supper cold stewed tomatoes, sugared, while his host drank champagne." (*Ibid.*, pp. 37–8.)

with fifteen thousand military constables and forty thousand picked British troops; five hundred political prisoners, including Parnell and John Dillon, had been jailed under the provisions of the Coercion Act, and, because of its no-rent manifesto, the Land League had been suppressed. George himself came under the strict supervision of the government authorities as soon as he landed, but he at once entered upon an active speaking campaign, starting with a lecture in Dublin that was the occasion for a great popular demonstration; he soon found himself ranked along with Parnell and Davitt, Justin McCarthy and Patrick Egan, as one of the leaders of the Irish cause. He made several trips to England and formed many friendships in the liberal circles of London; Helen Taylor, stepdaughter of John Stuart Mill and one of the leading women in the Irish movement, acted as hostess to George and his wife for several weeks, and later the Georges were guests at the homes of Henry M. Hyndman, the socialist, and Walter Wren. At the Hyndmans' George met Herbert Spencer. The affair was "a 'London crush,' the drawing-rooms thronged and many notables present, among them Tennyson, tall, careless and dreamy—in appearance every inch a poet; and Browning, on this occasion at least, smart and dapper, and, so far from appearing a great poet, looked, as Mrs. George said, 'like a prosperous merchant draper.' " [52] George and Spencer commenced to argue as soon as they were introduced; they differed upon the Irish question, and when Spencer declared that the imprisoned Land Leaguers "have got only what they deserve; they are inciting the people to refuse to pay to their landlords what is rightfully theirs—rent," George abruptly left him.[53] He wrote to Dr. Taylor (March, 1882): "Discount Herbert Spencer. He is most horribly conceited, and I don't believe really great men are. So far as I can judge his reputation here

[52] *Life*, p. 369.   [53] *Ibid.*, p. 370.

is on the wane." The following year he wrote to his doctor-friend: "What you say of Spencer is true. He is going the way of Comte—going insane from vanity." Upon other occasions George met Joseph Chamberlain, John Bright and Walter Besant, and in Ireland he became acquainted with Bishop Nulty, who had risked Rome's displeasure for his views on the land question.

The final split between Parnell and Davitt,[54] the former standing for peasant proprietorship and the latter demanding land nationalization (not under George's single tax method, however, but rather following the purchase plan of Wallace), disrupted organized work for a time, and George realized that there was a growing estrangement between himself and the Irish leaders and that his presence was proving somewhat of an embarrassment even for his friends. He left for Scotland, delivered several lectures at Glasgow, and then traveled to western Ireland in the company of James Leigh Joynes, a master at Eton, who had come to Ireland to see at first hand the condition of the peasants. At the little town of Loughree George and his companion were arrested under the Crimes Act as "suspicious strangers," and although they were soon released, the next day George was rearrested in Athenry, a village some few miles away. He was again set free after some delay and inconvenience, but the incident aroused unfavorable comment in the House of Commons. George later wrote of the affair: [55]

The whole thing struck me as infinitely ridiculous. There was, after all, a good deal of human nature in Artemus Ward's declaration that he was willing to sacrifice all his wife's relatives to save the Union. And in my satisfaction in seeing an Eton master lugged through the town as too suspicious a stranger to be left at large I

[54] George wrote to Francis G. Shaw from London in July of 1882: "The truth about Parnell is that he is really a weak, impossible man who 'flunked' when he had everything to gain by holding firm. . . . Davitt is the strongest man in Ireland."

[55] *Life*, pp. 392–393.

lost all sense of annoyance at my own arrest. In fact, my only regret was that it was not Kegan Paul. . . . I could not feel angry . . . but the Eton master could not see the joke. To come to Ireland only to be mistaken for an emissary of sedition, a would-be assassin of landlords, or maimer of cattle, was something that had not entered into his calculations.

George left for home in October of 1882, but not before he had spoken twice in London, once at a working men's meeting in Memorial Hall presided over by Alfred Russel Wallace,[56] and again to a gathering of Church of England clergy.

He returned to New York with an international reputation that won for him the acclaim of the press and a complimentary dinner at Delmonico's. The dinner was attended by the usual host of notables, including Henry Ward Beecher, and George characteristically forgot the hour and arrived late and with his shoes unpolished. Of more significance than the banquet was a huge mass meeting at Cooper Union at which George was formally welcomed by the labor unions. He was now in great demand as a lecturer and a writer, made several speaking trips, and then started a comprehensive volume on the tariff question, a work that he had planned for many years. He was unable to complete the book for some time, however; the loss of more than a hundred pages of manuscript proved a setback in the early stages of the book, and later George interrupted his work to write a series of articles for *Frank Leslie's Weekly* on "Problems of the Times," which was planned as a counter-attraction to the articles of Professor Sumner of Yale which were appearing in *Harper's Weekly*. In the summer of 1883 George published these essays in book form, naming the work *Social Problems*.[57]

[56] It was at this meeting that George Bernard Shaw, not much past twenty-five, heard George and became, of course, a convert—for a time. See *infra,* pp. 233–234.

[57] *Works,* Vol. II.

Further literary work was then put aside by George's acceptance of an offer to lecture in England under the auspices of the Land Reform Union. Public discussion in Great Britain had been profoundly affected by the land question, and particularly by the work of Henry George; [58] more than forty thousand copies of a sixpenny edition of *Progress and Poverty* had been sold; Professors Fawcett at Cambridge and Toynbee at Oxford had formally attempted to answer George's arguments; newspapers, debates and lectures were concentrating upon the problem of property in land; the "Liberty and Property Defence League," through Lord Bramwell, had delivered a violent attack upon the American economist; and Herbert Spencer, in a letter to the *St. James Gazette,* had made his first demurrer against having his own views on land ownership connected with those of George. With such an interest in what for George was the all-important land problem, he felt that his efforts should be directed to England. He opened his tour in London on January 9, 1884, with a great meeting in St. James's Hall [59] and George was at his best. The *Standard,* leader of the Tory press, described him correctly, albeit sarcastically: "He is perfectly simple and straightforward; a man with a mission; born to set right in a single generation the errors of six thousand years." He found himself next day the center of England's attention; Gladstone could hardly have had more praise or abuse heaped upon him. George wrote to his wife: "I am getting advertised to my heart's content, and I shall have crowds wherever I go. . . . I could be a social lion if I would permit it. But I won't fool with that sort of thing." He talked throughout England and Scotland, and before re-

[58] J. A. Hobson has said that "Henry George may be considered to have exercised a more directly formative and educative influence over English radicalism of the last fifteen years than any other man." (*Fortnightly Review,* Dec. 1, 1897.)

[59] John Ruskin was to have presided at the meeting, but was prevented by illness, and his place was taken by Henry Labouchere, editor of *Truth.*

turning to London lectured at Oxford and Cambridge. At Oxford, where he was the guest of Max Müller, his talk was interrupted by a hostile undergraduate demonstration, and the shouting and jeering of his audience forced him to cut short his address.[60] He talked once again in Dublin,[61] and then left for home in April of 1884.

George's next work appeared soon after his return to New York. It was a reply to an attack that the Duke of Argyll had made while George was lecturing in Scotland. In a bitter article in the *Nineteenth Century* the Duke, whose *Reign of Law* had won considerable recognition in philosophic circles, denounced this "Prophet of San Francisco," declaring that the "world has never seen such a Preacher of Unrighteousness." George's answer, "The Reduction to Iniquity," appeared in the July, 1885, issue of the *Nineteenth Century,* and the two contributions were later circulated in Scotland by the Land Restoration League in a pamphlet, *The Peer and the Prophet;* the same pamphlet was published in this country as *Property in Land.*[62] The crofter uprisings in Skye and the other Western Islands were at that time agitating Scotland, and the controversy with the Scotch Duke, titular chief of the great Campbell clan, made George almost as popular in Scotland as he had been in Ireland. He was again invited to speak in the British Isles and made his third trip to Europe in the fall of the year and, in addition to his tour of Scotland, lectured at Belfast, Liverpool and twice in London.[63] Popular enthusiasm over his campaign almost persuaded him to stand for Parliament, but he decided to

[60] Shortly afterward, when Michael Davitt was invited to lecture at Oxford, the students locked him in his hotel room so that he was unable to appear.

[61] While in England George met Cardinal Manning. Wilfred Meynell, editor of the *Weekly Register,* later described this conversation between the two: " 'I loved the people,' said Henry George, 'and that love brought me to Christ as their best friend and teacher.' 'And I,' said the Cardinal, 'loved Christ, and so learned to love the people for whom He died.' " (*Life,* p. 438.)

[62] *Works,* Vol. III.

[63] During this trip to England George met Lord Bryce.

return to the United States and complete his long-delayed work on the tariff.

The book had been appearing in serial form in a newspaper syndicate late in 1885, but in the summer of 1886 George finished the work and published it himself.[64] *Protection or Free Trade* is perhaps the best example of George's lucid and persuasive reasoning, and in the literature of free trade it remains a classic along with works such as those of Bastiat and Lieber. It is intentionally a deduction from what George accepted as basic, general principles of economics,[65] and its scope included more than an attack upon protectionist fallacies, for George endeavored to show that real free trade, unrestricted laissez-faire, meant not only the abolition of tariffs but of all taxes, and that it demanded the appropriation of land values.

Late in the summer of 1886, with the tariff book now finished and published, George was approached by the New York labor unions with an offer to be their candidate for Mayor in the fall election.[66] George had not intended to

[64] *Protection or Free Trade, Works,* Vol. IV. The book enjoyed a tremendous circulation, chiefly through the efforts of Tom L. Johnson, then Congressman from Cleveland and later the city's great reform mayor. In collaboration with several other Democratic Congressmen he had the entire book placed in the *Congressional Record,* under the "leave to print" privilege, and then the printed matter was franked throughout the country. The Republican members of Congress quite naturally objected to this manner of tariff debate, but the nation-wide commotion that was raised in political and economic circles served only to increase the popular demand for the book. Tom Johnson sent two hundred thousand copies into Ohio; more than one million copies were distributed in the other States; a two-cent paper edition was published later; there were earlier newspaper and cloth editions, and it is estimated that within eight years after its first publication nearly two million copies of *Protection or Free Trade* had been circulated, a figure approached by no other work in the history of political economy with the possible exception of *Progress and Poverty* itself.

[65] George wrote Doctor Taylor (Sept. 14, 1885): "My view of the matter is the reverse of yours. I do not think induction employed in such questions as the tariff is of any use. What the people want is theory; and until they get a correct theory into their heads, all citing of facts is useless." Quite a characteristic utterance.

[66] The wage-earning classes throughout the country, had not become politically organized, and the labor unions were distinctly reticent about

enter politics; he had planned a year of literary and lecture work and had hoped to start a weekly paper in New York. Furthermore, he realized that the disappointing vote for the labor candidates the year before [67] had indicated a lack of organization and unity among the labor factions. He did not consider the proposed nomination for several weeks, but finally the opportunity to bring the land question before the public in an important election convinced him that his candidacy was a necessary method of propaganda. He wrote to his friend Doctor Taylor (Sept. 10): "It is by no means impossible that I shall be elected. But the one thing sure is that if I do go into the fight the campaign will bring the land question into practical politics and do more to popularize its discussion than years of writing would do. That is the only temptation to me." Again, when he was told by a New York official that "you cannot be elected, but your running will raise hell!" he replied: "You have relieved me of embarrassment. I do not want the responsibility and work of the office of the Mayor of New York, but I do want to raise hell!" [68] George required as a condition for his nomination a petition of thirty thousand signatures so that there would be definite assurance of a representative vote at the election; he feared that without such an indication of labor sentiment the support given the unions might be so small as to discredit the movement, as had been the case previously. The petition was secured, despite the fact that such a demand on the part

entering politics as independent parties. By 1880 the Greenback movement had been almost completely deserted by the working men, leaving the bulk of the Greenback strength in the agricultural districts, and the sporadic attempts at political organization in the East had been for the most part unsuccessful. (See, Commons and Associates, *History of Labour in the United States*, Vol. II, p. 251, and pp. 439–442.) The Central Labor Union of New York City (which had resulted from a strike and a political campaign in 1882), had, however, assumed a leading position and was now able to enter politics with a better show of organized strength than it had been able to present before, and it chose Henry George as its most suitable candidate for Mayor.

[67] Commons, II, p. 444.
[68] See *Life*, p. 463.

of a candidate was unprecedented, and at an impressive mass meeting in Cooper Union George became the candidate of the United Labor Party.

His opponents were Abram S. Hewitt, the Democratic candidate, and young Theodore Roosevelt, the Republican nominee. The campaign was bitterly abusive; and all the horrors of the French Revolution were conjured up as an example of what would happen if George and his followers, "the anarchists, socialists, communists, nihilists and theorists," were successful.[69] George made a spirited fight, speaking every day for a month and appearing at as many as twelve or fourteen meetings a day; and as election approached he felt confident of victory. The final results showed that he received 68,110 votes, while Hewitt had won with 90,552; Roosevelt secured 60,435 votes.[70] George realized that the results of the election were in no sense indicative of failure. He had not been elected, but without party support, organization, funds, political experience or newspaper backing, and fighting an admittedly corrupt and powerful political machine, he had polled a vote that would have been representative of either of the major parties. The support given him was an unmistakable crystallization of labor opinion. The New York papers paid tribute to the vote in apprehensive editorials that "viewed with alarm," while in England, where the election was watched with keen interest, the St. James Gazette warned "respect-

[69] For a full account of the election see An Account of the George-Hewitt Campaign in the New York Municipal Election of 1886, by Louis F. Post and Frederic C. Leubuscher, New York, J. W. Lovell Co., 1887; Commons, II, pp. 450–454, and other histories of the American labor movement; and Young's History of the Single Tax Movement in the United States (Princeton University Press, 1916), pp. 95–107.

[70] It has been the general belief among those interested in the political aspects of the campaign that George really was elected but that he was "counted out" by Tammany Hall; as much, in fact, has been admitted by police and district officers. George himself realized the prevalence of fraud (hundreds of ballot boxes were actually cast into the East River), and after the election he continued in his efforts to introduce the Australian ballot system. (For this matter of corruption, see Commons, II, p. 453.)

able Americans to forget the trumpery of party fights and political differentism and face the new danger threatening the commonwealth." The *Pall Mall Budget,* however, held that the 68,000 votes "meant an embodied protest against the kingdom of this world, which after nineteen centuries, alike under democracies and monarchies and empires, is still ruled by Mammon, 'the least erected spirit that fell from heaven.' He [George] stood as the incarnation of a demand that the world should be made a better place to live in than it is to-day; and his candidature was a groan of discontent with the actual, and therefore of aspiration after the ideal." George was not discouraged, and several days after the election he told a large gathering of sympathizers in Cooper Union, "It is not the end of the campaign, but the beginning. We have fought the first skirmish."

He was now in a position to carry out a project that had long interested him, the founding of a weekly newspaper in New York, and finally, after gathering a staff of trained journalists, including William T. Croasdale and Louis F. Post, he put out the first issue of the *Standard* on January 8, 1887. The early issues of the paper were given over to a discussion of the McGlynn case,[71] and the popular interest in the excommunication of the eloquent priest won for the *Standard* a first issue circulation of seventy-five thousand. For a reform journal the paper enjoyed much more than average success, and it was not until the end of August, 1892, that publication was suspended. It was in the office of the *Standard,* on Ann Street, that the Anti-Poverty Society was formed, whose object was "to spread, by such peaceable and lawful means as may be found most desirable and efficient, a knowledge of the truth that God has made ample provision for the need of all men during their residence upon earth, and that involuntary poverty is the result of the human laws that

[71] See *infra,* Chap. VII.

allow individuals to claim as private property that which the Creator has provided for the use of all." The Society held its meetings in the old Academy of Music, and the fervent crowds gathering every Sunday evening, inspired by the pleading of orators like Father McGlynn, who lent the zeal and fire of religion to political and economic reform, were a remarkable example of the emotional strength behind the George movement.

George again entered politics the year after the mayoralty election and ran for the office of New York Secretary of State on the labor ticket, but a schism within the party, which resulted in a break with the socialistic element in the labor movement,[72] brought about the collapse of the organization and George received only 72,000 votes throughout the State. In 1888 he gave his support to Cleveland and free trade,[73] but the continued progress of his ideas in England again turned his attention there. He made a short two weeks' visit to Great Britain, and then, after some further lecture work in this country, returned in the spring of 1889 for an extended English speaking tour.[74] Before sailing for home, George went to Paris, where he attended an international land reform conference and had an opportunity to meet the Continental thinkers who were concerned with the same problems that had confronted him. Michael Flürscheim of Germany was one of the outstanding figures whom he met at the conference.

While still in England George was requested to make a lecture trip to Australia, where the principles of the single tax

[72] For an account of the rise of the socialistic political organization, and of the split with the George faction in 1887, see *infra*, pp. 240 ff.; Commons, II, pp. 269–290 and 456–461; and the various histories of American socialism.

[73] It was in this campaign that William Lloyd Garrison, the younger, came out in active support of George.

[74] During this trip George debated socialism with Henry Hyndman in St. James's Hall in London.

proposals were being incorporated into many of the dominion's acts of law. George still retained memories of his boyhood trip to Melbourne, and he now welcomed an opportunity to revisit a country which, with its secret ballot
system and publicly owned utilities, had now become a
pioneer in progressive legislation. Mrs. George was also
anxious to return to her birthplace, Sydney. The Georges
accordingly came to New York and then left for San Francisco, whence they were to sail for Australia. On the trip
across the continent George spoke in several cities, and in
San Francisco the former editor, gas inspector, Democratic
campaigner and "faddist" was greeted, after his ten-year
absence, in the boisterous manner that the still young city
reserved for the welcome of its native sons. He met his old
newspaper and political associates, and to them he was not
a world figure but just "little Harry George."

He left for Australia on February 8, 1890, and stopped at
Honolulu and at Auckland, New Zealand, where he visited
the veteran Liberal leader Sir George Grey, before arriving
at Sydney. For three and a half months George toured the
island continent in a strenuous campaign of lectures, and
everywhere he was received with an enthusiasm greater than
anything he had experienced before—not even Ireland had
welcomed him with such an outburst of popular acclaim. He
was fêted and banqueted, and the constant round of speeches
and official dinners proved later to have been too great a drain
upon his strength; he spoke every evening and sometimes
twice a day during his entire stay in Australia. His journey
back to the United States completed a trip that had taken
him almost around the world, for from Australia [75] the
Georges sailed up past India, through the Red Sea and the
Suez Canal and across the Mediterranean to Italy. Visits

[75] George sailed for home from Adelaide, South Australia. The province
of South Australia at that time already had a State tax on land values.

around
the
world

were made to Brindisi, Naples, Pompeii and Herculaneum, Rome and Venice; thence they traveled through Switzerland to France, and across the Channel to England, and from there to the United States.

The years of constant activity, the unbroken stretches of speaking and traveling and writing, the bitter denunciation, and the praise that was even more exacting, and with it all the relentless struggle to make a comfortable living, finally demanded their price, and in December of 1890 George was stricken with aphasia. The attack, caused by a slight brain hemorrhage which affected his power of speech, was acute but brief, and within a month he was sufficiently recovered to go to Bermuda for a period of convalescence; and although he returned after some months apparently with renewed strength and energy, and with a determination to complete several volumes that he had already started, yet his physical condition was never afterward vigorous. He was only fifty-one years old, but the rugged body that had carried him through so many feverish years was now tired and old beyond its age.

George first began intensive work on what he thought was to be a primer of political economy, but which broadened under his hand until it assumed the scope of a complete treatise on economics, a treatise that was to relate the science to all human activity. It was a more ambitious undertaking than anything he had hitherto written, more ambitious in intention, indeed, than even the classics of Smith and Ricardo and Mill, for George was to attempt not only to weld all the material that could be grouped under the shadowy classification of political economy into a unified and comprehensive system of thought, but, of more significance, also to form this refashioned science into a foundation for still another synthetic scheme of a universal philosophy.

But, as with *Progress and Poverty* and *Protection or Free Trade*, he again was to interrupt his work in order to turn his attention to controversy, for George was always an opportunist when there was occasion to do battle. As a result, *The Science of Political Economy*, which was the name he chose for what was to be his masterpiece, was never finished; it was cut short by his death. The manuscript, however, was posthumously edited and published by his son, Henry George, Jr., and although the work is not much more than half complete, many of the chapters and book divisions still remaining in outline form, with often only a title sentence to indicate the nature of the material, yet the plan of the volume is evident.[76]

The first of the interruptions that delayed work on the more important treatise was an answer to the encyclical letter of Pope Leo XIII which had been sent out in the spring of 1891. The encyclical was on the "Condition of Labor," and while it did not specify any particular labor movement and hopelessly merged socialism, anarchism and land reform, it took the position of an attack upon all secular attempts to improve the position of the laborer. George's reply was in the form of an open letter to the Pope, some twenty-five thousand words long, and was published in book form[77] in the United States, England and Italy. The work was a polished piece of criticism, suave and subdued, and contained nothing that might have been regarded as bad taste; it was an indication that George's illness had robbed him of none of his intellectual acuteness.[78]

Of a different nature, however, was his next book, which incidentally demonstrated that his polemical vigor was likewise unimpaired. Herbert Spencer in his first work, *Social Statics*, published in 1850, had included a chapter on the

[76] See *Works*, Vols. VI and VII.
[77] *Works*, Vol. III.
[78] For an account of this controversy, see *infra*, Chap. VII.

"Right to the Use of the Earth," which had expressed opinions so like the later proposals of George that the section had been used as propaganda, and Spencer's name had come to be linked with that of the American land reformer. In 1892, Spencer revised this earlier edition of *Social Statics* and published it along with *The Man Versus the State,* a volume in which all mention of the inequity of property in land was omitted. George was aroused to fury by this supposed apostasy of Spencer. This, for him, was intellectual treason, and Spencer a deserter from the ranks, and in *A Perplexed Philosopher* [79] George loosed all the power of taunting ridicule and overt denunciation in an analysis of the great Englishman's change of heart. The book included not only a review of Spencer's opinions on the land question and a bitter declaration that the about-face was the result of pressure brought to bear upon him, but contained also an attack upon what George regarded as the "materialism" of the entire synthetic philosophy. This section of the work made some of George's followers apprehensive, and although most of his sympathizers welcomed a passage at arms with the philosopher of evolution, his friend Doctor Taylor wrote: "In your own particular field I am satisfied you are invincible; but I should not feel so sure of you in metaphysics, philosophy or cosmogony. Remember that life is short, and the powers of the human mind limited, and that you have not yet produced (what you should produce) a monumental work on political economy." *A Perplexed Philosopher* drew no reply from Spencer and the book never became as popular as George's other works. He again devoted his attention to *The Science of Political Economy.*

In this drama of Henry George there had been moments of tragedy and a few of comedy, but the last scene was fittingly

[79] *Works,* Vol. V, and see also *infra,* Chap. VI.

reserved for the climax. It was a scene that once more shifted to a political stage, and the final curtain found George again playing his part as one of those who could never refuse to listen to that vague and compelling call of duty. It was in 1897. In the preceding year George had swung his support, as had all "theorists, visionaries and enemies of sound government," to Bryan, and so had kept unspoiled his record of having always been on the losing side of every important election in which he had been actively interested. Now George was asked to run again as an independent candidate for the New York mayoralty, and this time it was not only his work but his health that advised against entering politics. He had been unwell for several years and his failing vitality seemed hardly capable of withstanding a strenuous New York campaign. But there was that insistent, even Kantian, appeal of duty, an almost plaintive responsibility to serve that fleeting will-o'-the-wisp of "humanity." George was to run as the candidate of the "Party of Thomas Jefferson," and Jefferson was, if any man, his patron saint. The great vote of the liberals of all denominations in the Presidential election of 1896 had seemed to indicate that this was the time for George again to carry his message into a political campaign. It was his duty. In his speech of acceptance, which he delivered while scarcely strong enough to stand, George declared:

I believe . . . that unto the common people, the honest democracy, the democracy that believes that all men are created equal, would bring a power that would revivify not merely this imperial city, not merely the State, not merely the country, but the world. No greater honor can be given to any man than to stand for all that. No greater service can he render to his day and generation than to lay at its feet whatever he has. I would not refuse if I died for it. What counts a few years? What can a man do better or nobler than something for his country, for his nation, for his age?

This conception of an exacting duty is even more strikingly revealed in his conversations and letters. Dr. Montague R. Leverson tells of the following talk: [80]

> Mr. George said to me:
> "Tell me, if I accept, what is the worst that can happen to me?"
> I answered:
> "Since you ask, you have a right to be told. It will most probably prove fatal . . ."
> Mr. George replied:
> "Dr. Kelly says the same thing, only more positively. But I have got to die. How can I die better than serving humanity? Besides, so dying will do more for the cause than anything I am likely to be able to do in the rest of my life."

George wrote his friend Dr. Walter Mendelson in the same spirit (Sept. 30):

> I thank you very much for your friendly counsel. I shall take it, unless as I can see it duty calls. In that case I must obey. After all, how little we can see of the future.

And again, the *Life* records this conversation of George with his wife: [81]

> Annie, remember what you declared Michael Davitt should do at the time of the Phœnix Park murders in 1882—go to Dublin and be with his people, even though it should cost him his life. I told you then that I might some day ask you to remember those words. I ask you now. Will you fail to tell me to go into this campaign? The people want me; they say they have no one else upon whom they can unite. It is more than a question of good government. If I enter the field it will be a question of natural rights, even though as Mayor I might not directly be able to do a great deal for natural rights. New York will become the theatre of the world and my success will plunge our cause into world politics.
>
> Mrs. George answered, "You should do your duty at whatever cost."

The first hectic flush of the campaign, the smell of battle, this righteous war of his, seemed to summon forth the shadow

[80] *Life*, p. 594.   [81] *Ibid.*, p. 597.

of his former strength, and for three weeks he carried on a
last desperate fight, speaking often at half a dozen meetings
in an evening.[82] "And then came the last night, Thursday,
October 28—five days before election." George had spoken
four times that evening, and as the night advanced it was
evident that he was becoming weaker. He returned to his
hotel, the Union Square, after midnight, and before retiring
complained of feeling ill. In the early hours of the morning
his wife arose and found him "standing, one hand on a chair,
as if to support himself. His face was white; his body rigid
like a statue; his shoulders thrown back, his head up, his
eyes wide open and penetrating, as if they saw something;
and one word came—'Yes'—many times repeated, at first
with a quiet emphasis, then with the vigor of his heart's
force. . . . Mr. George was entirely unconscious when Doctor Kelly arrived. A stroke of apoplexy had fallen. The great
heart had worn out the physical body, and a thread in the
brain had snapped." George had died as he had wished to
die—in battle.[83]

The election was almost forgotten in the city's grief, and
as the body lay in state all of Sunday in the Grand Central
Palace the world paid its homage to the power of sincerity.
One hundred thousand mourners filed before his bier, while
another hundred thousand, unable to gain admittance,
prayed in the street outside, and the vast funeral cortège that
followed the body down to City Hall and across the Brooklyn
Bridge proved to be one of the deepest tributes ever paid to

[82] His opponents conducted a very quiet campaign. The Democratic
candidate was Judge Robert Van Wyck; the Republican nominee, General
Benjamin F. Tracy; Seth Low, who twice had been Mayor of Brooklyn (the
election of 1897 was the first of Greater New York) and who had been
president of Columbia University, ran as an independent Republican. In
1902 Low became Mayor of New York.

[83] After George's death, his party in a last brave gesture substituted
Henry George, Jr., for his departed father, but his vote was negligible,
despite the fact that had George lived there are many who believe he would
have been elected. Van Wyck was the winner.

a private citizen. George was buried in Greenwood Cemetery. On his stone were carved these words from *Progress and Poverty:*

The truth that I have tried to make clear will not find easy acceptance. If that could be, it would have been accepted long ago. If that could be, it would never have been obscured. But it will find friends—those who will toil for it; suffer for it; if need be, die for it. This is the power of Truth.

CHAPTER III

GEORGE'S ECONOMIC SOLUTION

An elaboration of George's economic system, an elaboration that, as has been previously suggested, is necessary in order fully to grasp his ambitious correlation of economic data and ultimate ethical consequences, must start with a realization of his dependency upon classical economic theory. George accepted with but little qualification the fundamental groundwork of the classic approach, and the theoretical technique of Smith, Mill, Ricardo, was, for him, the genuine method in political economy. Economics, in other words, was a subject that was thoroughly deductive and demanded for its complete comprehension nothing but an unclouded and unprejudiced rational faculty. Its fundamental assumptions were clearly derived from the laws of nature and needed but to be discovered by philosophic effort.

Political economy, furthermore, was a discipline that was essentially a simple one. It did not require complicated statistics or graphs or the investigations of trained research students.[1] All that it demanded was common sense and popular intuition, or, at most, a philosophic bias. And it was an exact science, for it traced through, by means of infallible causal or logical sequences, the workings of indubitable first principles, "truths of which we are all conscious and upon which in every-day life we constantly base our reasoning and our actions." Among such familiar axioms was the psychol-

[1] See *supra*, p. 47.

ogy of the "economic man": "Men seek to gratify their desires with the least exertion." [2]

Finally, to complete the classic hierarchy, political economy was to be ethical. It is realized, of course, that the classical economists overtly repudiated any "sentimental" concern with ethical judgments; political economy was an exact, natural science which included no explicit moral valuation. Yet it has been pointed out repeatedly by historians of economic theory that, despite this insistence upon the "scientific" character of the subject, the classic writers were in a sense rationalizing their own ethical predilections, or rather those of their backgrounds. Classical economy was implicitly ethical in spite of its insistence upon the natural; its very natural laws, in fact, were largely ethical principles and implied the direction that economic processes "ought" to take, e. g., laissez-faire and economic men. George differed from the classic approach, in this respect, only in his more deliberate emphasis upon the ethical factors. If the classicists stressed the fact that economics is "right" because it is "natural" (although that may be considered a rationalization), George insisted that economics must be natural because it must be right. [3]

Here in George, then, was a restatement of the classical

[2] *Progress and Poverty*, p. 11. However, George felt that Adam Smith was wrong in his corollary of the economic man's "selfishness." That selfishness (the correlate of the universal sympathy upon which Smith founded his moral philosophy—see Buckle's "Examination of the Scotch Intellect During the Eighteenth Century," Chap. VI of Vol. II of the *History of Civilization in England*) was not the basic motive in economic life; such a motive was this "conservation of energy" in desire-satisfaction, and from this and other similar fundamental premises could be rationally deduced the whole structure of the science.

[3] There is another interpretation of the ethical motif in George's work, and that is as a defense of his political and economic proposals. It is pointed out that the major part of George's argument is descriptive and that he defends his solution, in his search for rational sanctions, on any and every current basis of morals. This point will be illustrated further on in the discussion of George's ethical justification of his economic proposals. (*Infra*, pp. 139–140.)

interpretation of political economy. The science was to be one of theory, and was to be a product of introspection, a rational grasp of the rational natural laws that regulated the interaction of economic phenomena. It contained nothing tentative or empirical; much less was economics a descriptive portrayal of the history of a certain group of theories. It could not function without eternal and absolute axioms, and any other interpretation that sought to qualify or temporize was, for George, unworthy of serious consideration.

Such a wholesale acceptance of the classical approach is explicable enough, since whatever economic background George had was entirely a classic one. He first wrote in 1879 (although his earliest economic thoughts had appeared in journalistic form for some ten years previous to that date), and at that time there was little break in the classic tradition.[4] George regarded the work of John Stuart Mill as characteristic of political economy, and thus whatever divergency there was between his own work and that of the great English writers was in application rather than in general outlook. In fact, George's approach, including particularly his ethical emphasis, was the same as that of his American contemporaries and immediate predecessors, such as the Walkers, Wayland and Perry, despite the fact that his acquaintance with their work disclosed to him little similarity with his own. The same theoretical background had made them all followers of the economic tradition, although perhaps George's hand-to-hand contact with economic conditions and their functional significance had made his ethical

---

[4] It is true that in George's last work, *The Science of Political Economy,* he was aware of the new historical approach and of the "break-down" of the classical school. But it was in *Progress and Poverty* that his economic thoughts not only originated but reached their highest development. As he himself wrote in the *Science* (p. 203), he saw no reason for changing his earlier opinions, and so his approach was formed entirely upon the basis of the classic presentation. (For a further discussion of George and classical economy, see *infra,* Chap. IV.)

approach more real and vital than that of the academic tradition.

It is necessary to mention this classic formulation in order to prepare the way for an economic discussion that must be directed along the lines of George's theoretical approach. For example, he must begin his argument with "the meaning of the terms," since, in any deductive presentation, definitions are paramount. They are the formulation of the material that is to be used as the basis for discussion. Definition directs the entire argument, and thus classical political economy invariably prefaced its work by some form of "first principles" which were to organize and test material. That is George's technique in *Progress and Poverty*. He uses as the motto for the entire volume that passage from Aurelius which opens: "Make for thyself a definition or description of the thing which is presented to thee . . ." and his second chapter is on the "meaning of the terms."

Before launching into his argument, however, George finds it necessary first to clear ground by repudiating two of the doctrines that had made political economy the "dismal" science. One was the wages fund theory and the other was the thesis of Malthus.

The specific problem that stimulated George, as has been noted in the opening chapter, was that presented by the persistence of poverty, and particularly the fact that want appeared as a concomitant of wealth. That problem was for him expressed in the simple economic statement that the prevailing tendency in industrial society was to force wages to a minimum—a minimum, it is unnecessary to add, which was not absolute but relative to the worker's share in the product of his labor. Therefore, at the very beginning of his work there was required an investigation of wages, and particularly an attempt to solve the problem of low wages.

The popular doctrine of the late '70s still solved such a problem quite simply: Wages tended to a minimum because there was a fixed fund of capital set aside for the payment of wages, and every increase in the number of laborers necessarily decreased, by an elementary arithmetical process, the individual share of the laborer. As George phrased it, this quite famous "wages-fund" theory, which had received its classic statement by John Stuart Mill, held that

wages are fixed by the ratio between the number of laborers and the amount of capital devoted to the employment of labor, and constantly tend to the lowest amount on which laborers will consent to live and reproduce, because the increase in the number of laborers tends naturally to follow and overtake any increase in capital. The increase of the divisor being thus held in check only by the possibilities of the quotient, the dividend may be increased to infinity without greater result.[5]

This, for George, was the "current doctrine" of the relation between wages and capital, and he realized that it was a doctrine that must be attacked if any dynamic cause of low wages was to be sought. Were it true that wages could not be permanently increased because of the fact that they depended upon a specific sum of capital, it would be well-nigh hopeless to proceed any further with an investigation of low wages.

George's attack upon this wages fund theory affords an interesting example of his approach to the work of his contemporaries. That is, he was acquainted with the very complete attacks upon the theory—attacks which practically removed the early wages fund formulation from economic

---

[5] *Progress and Poverty*, p. 17. The theory of a wages fund was first formulated by Nassau Senior and others, but it was definitely based upon the earlier and more fundamental work of Ricardo. However, while the concepts of Ricardo directly prepared the way not only for the wages fund theory but also for the "iron law" of wages developed later by Lassalle, he himself did not hold that there was a predetermined and inelastic amount of capital set aside for the payment of wages.

theory—by men like Francis A. Walker and William Thornton [6] (although he does not seem to have been familiar with Mill's own repudiation of his earlier position) [7]; and yet, George insists that the wages fund had not been seriously challenged and that it was still completely acceptable to the academic world. The explanation seems to lie in the fact that the approach which George emphasized was not the characteristic argument of these other attacks. He did not confine himself to the more usual challenge of the rigid, inelastic character of a wages fund, but instead criticized the whole concept that wages depended in any essential way upon capital. However, his major position, that of a "productivity" theory of wages, had been given thorough exposition by Walker.[8]

Wages are paid not out of capital but out of the product, was George's main contention. He felt that an attack upon the "fixed," "predetermined" characteristic of a wages fund was something merely incidental; the fundamental doctrine that was to be controverted, a doctrine which gave rise not merely to fund theories but to "iron laws" and other pessimistic approaches to low wages, was that which held that labor is directly dependent upon the capitalist. George argues that the mother of wages is not stored-up wealth, but continuing productivity; both wages and interest are paid out of the joint product of labor and capital, and any seemingly obvious payment of wages out of capital was simply an "advance" to be interpreted temporally and not functionally. By "temporally" is meant here those cases of long-time production in which wages are continually being paid before the product is completed; such advance wages, George holds,

---

[6] See *Progress and Poverty*, p. 18, n.
[7] That amendment on the part of Mill is found most significantly in his essay on "Thornton on Labour and Its Claims," in *Dissertations and Discussions* (New York, Henry Holt, 1875), Vol. V, particularly pp. 47–52.
[8] In his *The Wages Question* (New York, 1876).

are simply forms of guarantee, "retainers," and in no way a functional dependent upon capital. These "advance wages," George believes, are paid out of wealth produced, even if there is only a partial increase in wealth such as in agriculture or in long-time manufacturing. In other words, the worker has "finished" as much of the product as the productive process will permit up to the time of receiving wages. Some value must be created before wages can be paid.

The static concept of a supply of capital upon which depend not only wages but industry itself is hardly tenable, George points out, in the light of a reproducing, moving, transformable industrial order, but of much more importance, he feels, is the realization that were labor to cease, capital would become so much "illth" instead of wealth. That is, the production of wealth is essentially dynamic in character. Labor is not functionally dependent upon past accumulated labor, or capital, as the classic theory taught; a stock of subsistence from which labor is maintained by capital is not at all necessary. All that is required is diversified, contemporaneous production. Subsistence is not furnished by a previously accumulated stock but by an exchange of goods produced in the present. As George formularizes this point: "The demand for consumption determines the direction in which labor will be expended in production." [9] Present labor maintains itself. An accumulation of stock, in connection with the payment of wages, is at most a convenience and in no sense a *sine qua non*.

George's decisive criticism of a wages fund thus occupies a peculiar position. It is in good part a reworking of an argument that had been elaborated by his immediate predecessors—one, moreover, with which he was admittedly familiar—but George felt that his attack upon the concept of a capital origin of wages was really a complete break with the eco-

[9] *Progress and Poverty,* p. 75.

nomic tradition. There is certainly this to be said in reference to George's criticism of a wages fund theory: He was definitely instrumental in popularizing the academic criticism of such a doctrine. Even if belief in such a fund was becoming unacceptable to economists, it still remained either a quite satisfying shibboleth or the most dismal of realities for the layman. But George's forceful and intelligible disposition of the fund doctrine provided not only a summary of the criticism that had been appearing for some years previous to his work; in addition, it helped to dispel from the popular mind some of the dismalness of political economy.

The cause of low wages, then, and ultimately of poverty and all its social consequences, was not to be found in the oppression of labor by capital through a wages fund. And neither was the cause of poverty anything in the nature of Malthusianism. George followed his attack upon the "current doctrine" of a wages fund with a much more bitter onslaught upon Malthus; these two pessimistic doctrines, he felt, accounted for much of the hopelessness of economics and constituted a barrier which firmly held in check any efforts on the part of the science to increase wages or remove human suffering. Were the proponents of a wages fund correct, then efforts to increase wages must be essentially in vain; and were nature insufficient to support the earth's population without the aid of the checks accepted by Malthus, those grim "four horsemen," then misery and social evil were not only inevitable—they thereby received a tacit "scientific" justification.

It is not necessary, however, to say more than a word regarding George's almost savage criticism of Malthus.[10] His arguments, especially the emphasis upon the potency of human intelligence and ingenuity in meeting the spectre of

[10] Book II of *Progress and Poverty*, "Population and Subsistence," is devoted to that attack.

overpopulation (although even that spectre is being rapidly dispelled by contemporary birth-rates), are familiar enough now, although they were by no means welcome or even presentable at the time he wrote. While George may have been mistaken in attributing to economists the wages fund as current and acceptable doctrine, he was by no means mistaken in his recognition of the academic popularity of Malthus (a popularity, in fact, that has not waned appreciably despite the translation of Malthus's "law" into the more innocuous "tendency"). Even the theorists such as Walker who attacked the wages fund theory were sympathetic to Malthus, and Mill's famous passage [11] was still the most complete and unequivocal expression of a well-received doctrine. Here, then, George's break with economic theory was more pronounced.

These attacks of George upon the statements of overpopulation and of a wages fund constituted a process of ground-clearing, as has been noted before, which was necessary before he could attempt to present his solution of the riddle of progress and poverty. Only when these remains of the pessimistic era in political economy have been removed does George feel that he can direct his attention to his own proposals.

It will be recalled that George's constructive argument, following his thoroughly deductive approach, was to open with a definition of terms. The concepts "wages" and "capi-

---

[11] *Principles of Political Economy*, Book I, Chap. XIII, Sec. 2. The fierce optimism with which George met the gloom of Malthusianism is illustrated in his direct attack upon this "niggardliness of nature" statement of Mill: "I assert that in any given state of civilization a greater number of people can collectively be better provided for than a smaller. I assert that the injustice of society, not the niggardliness of nature, is the cause of the want and the misery which the current theory attributes to overpopulation. I assert that the new mouths which an increasing population calls into existence require no more food than the old ones, while the hands they bring with them can in the natural order of things produce more.

tal" are first defined by him, since his opening problem was the attack on the wages fund theory. With the term wages there does not appear to be any serious difficulty, except, as he points out, to remember that the "return to labor" includes any return, no matter what form it may take, for any type of exertion, whatever may be its form. With the concept capital, however, there is introduced a whole series of controversies originating with the very attempt to define what is meant by the word.

In discussing George's treatment of capital, and of the concepts wealth and value into which he is necessarily led, there is always the difficulty of avoiding a possible accusation of atavism. That is to say, these concepts have undergone such wholesale revision at the hands of more recent theorists that an exposition of the nineteenth century presentation may seem out of place to those who are perhaps impatient with the logical formulations of the classical approach. But George's completely classic heritage must be kept in mind, and therefore his definition of capital as "wealth used in the production of more wealth," and his subsequent discussion of wealth and value,[12] must not be placed against a background of later criteria, especially since those canons themselves are by no means above suspicion.

The concepts of capital, wealth, value, have been perhaps more affected by the subjectivistic tendencies that have characterized modern economics than have any of the other

---

I assert that, other things being equal, the greater the population, the greater the comfort which an equitable distribution of wealth would give to each individual. I assert that in a state of equality the natural increase of population would constantly tend to make every individual richer instead of poorer." (*Progress and Poverty*, pp. 141–142.)

[12] George does not attempt any complete discussion of capital or wealth in *Progress and Poverty*. His thorough exposition of wealth and value—upon which, as will be seen, his interpretation of capital depends—is reserved for *The Science of Political Economy*, especially Book II on "The Nature of Wealth."

traditional terms. With the objectivity of economic concepts being increasingly removed because of a fundamentally psychological approach to the science, there is introduced a definition of capital, for example (although there is no intention here of summarizing or reconciling the many conflicting handlings of the term), as the present worth of future income rather than as a given stock of wealth. It is being interpreted as an abstract, mobile fund, in which cost of production is slighted and land included, whereas the more classical view considered capital as an aggregate of concrete goods and so excluded land and emphasized cost. There is no need, however, to elaborate this ideational contrast; it is familiar enough. The only point that is being raised is the warning that George's exposition is to be the classic one, with psychological considerations conspicuously absent.

It has been noticed that George's definition of capital is in terms of wealth, "that bane of political economy," a concept whose difficulties have tempted some theorists to drop the consideration of the term altogether. Such a disposition of wealth, George felt, would be of a piece with discussing mathematics without considering the concept of number. He held that there could be no proper orientation of political economy unless the meaning of wealth were definitely fixed, and he essayed therefore to present an acceptable definition of the term. His efforts to give a logical meaning to wealth demanded, as has been suggested, that value be handled first, and he opens his exposition with an appeal for at least the theoretical retention of Adam Smith's distinction between "value in use" and "value in exchange."

George realized that the successors of Smith had repudiated such a distinction, and he makes it clear, further, that "value in exchange" is recognized by him to be the only type of value handled by economics. But nevertheless he insists upon pointing out what appears to him a serious fallacy in refusing to admit a fundamental, if ideational, distinction between these two types of value.

The criticism of Smith's differentiation between value that was based on usefulness and value founded upon desires that were expressed simply through exchange, was directed to showing that he was attempting to introduce an essentially moral test of value in a discipline in which ethical considerations must be absent. Value in exchange, it was held, was dependent upon some type of use value. Demand followed utility, and Smith's efforts, for example, to show that diamonds had great exchange but little use value, were believed to bring forward the question of standards of usefulness, hence moral evaluation. Anything that was in demand, it was pointed out,[13] had usefulness.

George criticizes this attack upon Smith in a passage that, to the present writer at least, seems a striking parallel to the later attacks upon Mill's notoriously classic fallacy in the use of "desire" as it appeared in his *Utilitarianism*. George argues that Mill makes the fundamental error of stating that whatever satisfies a "use" is thereby "useful." "The use of a thing in political economy means its capacity to satisfy a desire, or serve a purpose," wrote Mill, and therefore diamonds are useful—a statement which follows from the premised definition but which does havoc to the normal connotation of the word "useful." That which "satisfies a desire or serves a purpose" may be the furthest removed from the "useful";[14] if it is desired or serves a purpose it certainly will have value but it will be a different aspect of value from

[13] See, for instance, John Stuart Mill's *Principles of Political Economy,* Book III, Chap. I, Sec. 1.

[14] Of course, some of this word difficulty is removed by more recent economic theory in its substitution of "utility" for "usefulness," and its specific designation that utility means the ability to satisfy any possible use. Yet it is still felt that a happier word than even "utility" might have been employed for such a connotation.

that which depends upon definite use. This distinction of Smith is not a moral one, but rather one that follows customary usage; it is an attempt to employ words as they are commonly employed. That which is "useful" and has value in use is not that which is merely "used," in the sense of satisfying some desire or serving some purpose, however esoteric or mischievous that desire or purpose may be. The "useful" is that which is "normally" and "legitimately" used, that which "ought" to be used—and the distinction is moral only in so far as such moral tinge is precisely what the word "useful" implies.

That which satisfies a desire is "desirable," wrote Mill in his *Utilitarianism,* just as anything which is heard is audible. If "desirable" means that which *is* desired, the statement is sound; but "desirable" means that which *ought* to be desired, and Mill's induction did not prevent him from falling into such an egregious fallacy that it has been used ever since as a horrible example in elementary texts in logic.[15] And the distinction here, it must be insisted, as with "useful," is not basically a moral one—despite the fact that a moral element is introduced. The distinction is nothing more or nothing less than an effort to use words in the sense in which they are ordinarily employed. That is the point George is making. He is endeavoring to handle the word "useful" to designate "that which is worthy of being used," a meaning which is the com-

---

[15] This distinction between the "is" and the "ought" of desire must not be misinterpreted. That is, it must not be understood as the belief in a functional separation between data and norms. It is of course realized that "ought" standards are "givens," just as is the material they judge; any acquaintance, say, with the instrumentalism of Professor Dewey must make that point clear. It is not at all being denied that the "desirable" is as psychologically conditioned as the "desired," nor is there any intention of defending a dualistic severance of values from facts. However, it is not felt that any such instrumentalist position can be used in defending Mill at this point. Certainly there was an important difference in word emphasis that he overlooked—whether deliberately or not is a matter for students of Utilitarianism. And just as certainly was there the lack of any clear realization on the part of Bentham and his followers of an instrumentalist interpretation of their ethical concepts, e. g., happiness.

mon one, in the same way that "desirable" connotes, in fact, denotes, "that which is worthy of being desired." [16]

The failure to accept Smith's distinction, George attempts to point out, paved the way not only for the development of the marginal utility approach to value of Jevons, but ultimately of the Austrian school, where marginal utility is psychologically fixed by intensity of desire, thus doing away with any objective distinction within the realm of value. But even without the thesis of the Austrians, George realized that the "current teachings of political economy" made value no more than the power of goods to command others in exchange. Value is a ratio between all exchangeable things and is measured by demand rate—such demand being determined by the operation of marginal utility. An absolute value, or, to put it in another way, a general increase or decrease in values, is contradictory to the meaning of value. Value is completely relative.

Such a viewpoint, for George, was logically "swimming in vacancy." Values may be relative to one another, but if there is to be any measure of value there must be some fixed unit or standard. An interaction of infinitely relative values without some absolute measuring unit was to him inconceivably absurd. The precise value that belongs to anything is a product of exchange, a proportion, it is true, but what is it that gives "Value" itself? Relativity in values indicates a relation to some source and measure of all values, and that measure and source, for George, was the factor of human exertion.

An exposition of George's theory of value will provide a variation of the classical labor theory. Of course, a labor approach to value has meant many things in the history of

[16] There is a passage in George in which he specifically discusses this difficulty in using "desirability" as the capability of being desired, just as the word "usefulness" was used by Mill to signify the capability of being used. George suggests the word "desiredness" as a possible substitute (*The Science of Political Economy*, pp. 214–216, n.), although he does not offer any substitute for "usefulness."

economic thought. There is, for example, the pure labor-cost theory of Ricardo (although in his later work he slightly modified the "pure" character of his doctrine) and of Marx, with his emphasis upon an abstract social labor-time. Then there is what might be designated as the "ethical" labor theory of Rodbertus, in which it is argued that labor cost "ought" to be the basis of value and would be in a properly organized economic society (compare also the labor approach of Locke). And then the approach of Smith, in which not labor-cost but labor-saving is the determiner of value.[17] (All such objective value theories are, of course, at variance with more recent psychological utility theories.) George's argument is essentially that of Adam Smith.

Smith had written, to select a few characteristic remarks, that:

. . . the value of any commodity, therefore, to the person who possesses it, and who means not to use or consume it himself, but to exchange it for other commodities, is equal to the quantity of labour which it enables him to purchase or command. Labour, therefore, is the real measure of the exchangeable value of all commodities. The real price of everything, what everything really costs to the man who wants to acquire it, is the toil and trouble of acquiring it. . . . It was not by gold or by silver, but by labour, that all the wealth of the world was originally purchased; and its value, to those who possess it, and who want to exchange it for some new productions, is precisely equal to the quantity of labour which it can enable them to purchase or command. . . . Labour, therefore, it appears evidently, is the only universal, as well as the only accurate, measure of value, or the only standard by which we can compare the values of different commodities at all times and at all places.[18]

[17] There is obviously a difference between labor as the *cause* of value and labor as the *measure* of value. The cause of the quality of being valuable does not necessarily measure the quantity of value. In Smith, labor as cause rather than as measure of value becomes more dominant as he presents the intricacies of production, and the uncertain standard of "the higgling of the market."

[18] From the opening pages of Chap. V, Book I, of *The Wealth of Nations*.

In these sentences George felt that the standard of value was perfectly clear. Human exertion was involved in all production of goods, and so value was

equivalent to the saving of exertion or toil which the possession of that thing will save the possessor, or enable him, to use Adam Smith's phrase, "to impose upon other people" through exchange. Thus it is not exchangeability that gives value; but value that gives exchangeability . . .[19]

It must be remembered, however, that George's interpretation of value as a function of labor applies not to expended past labor but to present labor that is needed in production; it is a dynamic labor theory.

It is not the toil and trouble which a thing *has* cost that gives it value. . . . It is the toil and trouble that others are *now* willing, directly or indirectly, to relieve the owner of, in exchange for the thing, by giving him the advantage of the results of exertion, while dispensing him of the toil and trouble that are the necessary accompaniments of exertion. . . . In other words the value of a thing is the amount of laboring or work that its possession will save to the possessor. . . . Value in exchange, or value in the economic sense, is worth in exertion. It is a quality attaching to the ownership of things, of dispensing with the exertion necessary to secure the satisfaction of desire, by inducing others to take it. Things are valuable in proportion to the amount of exertion which they will command in exchange . . .[20]

Thus, George holds that value is dependent upon the command over present labor, a belief, it may be seen, which is tantamount to a cost of reproduction concept, so far at least as the labor element in production is concerned. ("Cost of reproduction" is perhaps a better phrase than the usual "cost

[19] *The Science of Political Economy*, p. 245.
[20] *Ibid.*, pp. 246, 249. Value, for George, was thus *determined* by labor. However, value was *measured* by effective demand. That is, George disagreed with Smith's distrust of the "higgling of the market"; exertion was subjective —George made at least that concession to psychology—and could be objectified for purposes of measurement only by the competition which judged demand.

of production," [21] for George's argument applies not to past labor but to the expenditure of labor that would be required in the present to produce a similar thing.) And therefore George is led to make a fundamental distinction within the general realm of value, a distinction between goods which are amenable to this characteristic of "reproduction," and those which are not. That is, value itself was simply the ability to command present labor, yet this quality of being valuable became attached to goods for entirely different reasons. On the one hand, there was the class of economic goods—one which included the great majority of goods—that commanded present labor, i. e., were valuable, because labor would be required to duplicate them. They were reproducible goods and could be made again by labor were it necessary to replace them. But their very existence embodied labor and so they were able to save present labor; therefore they had value. Thus, there was a type of value which arose from that exertion of past labor which made possible a saving of present labor, and that, for George, was "value from production."

Now, on the other hand, there is another source of command over labor-power, i. e., of value. There is a type of goods whose value in no sense depends upon "production" or "reproduction" possibility. The examples that the text-books give, such as original paintings of old masters, heir-

---

[21] A very interesting interpretation of "cost of production," one which attempts to compromise its character of objectivity with the subjective marginal utility approach to value, is found in the work of Professor Harry Gunnison Brown. His definition of cost of production is: "the amount of *other* goods which the same effort and sacrifice would produce. . . . The cost of production of any good comes finally to be expressible as the amount of some other good or goods which the same labor, land and saving could produce." Marginal factors are introduced, since demand is limited (at least as far as ordinary commodities are concerned) in the case of one good by the marginal sacrifice involved in the production of other goods, and likewise in the case of supply, since goods will be supplied up to a point where the marginal disutility of production is balanced by the marginal utility of goods which are received in exchange. "On the supply side then, as on the demand side of the market, in the case of any goods, the cost of production is an important consideration." (See especially Chap. II, Part II, of his *Economic Science and the Common Welfare;* Columbia, Mo., Lucas Bros., 1925.)

looms, trinkets of historical value, and the like, will illustrate. Such articles are unique; they cannot be reproduced or duplicated, and while they undoubtedly had a cost of production, while labor was expended in their manufacture, their present value is in no way dependent upon what it would cost to make them again. It depends solely upon the fact that there is demand for these goods, and that, by their very nature, they are not reproducible. Their quantity is limited and values may soar to any limits, depending only upon demand; the supply is fixed. Obviously, demand is paramount even when power of reproduction is included as a factor in determining value, but one type of goods depends upon two variables, that of supply (power of reproduction) and that of demand, whereas the other type which cannot be reproduced depends only upon one variable, demand, since the supply remains constant.

To these unique articles, such as old paintings and the rest, which, after all, have no importance as fundamental elements in economic consideration, George adds the concept of land. Land, as far as possibility of reproduction is concerned, has no more value than air. Its value, just as that of those articles which cannot be reproduced (filled-in and reclaimed land is clearly of so limited and negligible a quantity that it can have no appreciable bearing upon the static supply of land), depends solely upon demand. The value of land is not limited by the possibility of producing other land; its value arises from competitive desire for it.

Here, for George, was a type of value entirely distinct from that created by labor-saving, a value that had nothing to do with power of reproduction. The value of unique, non-reproducible goods, of which land was the most important, was dependent not upon the exertion of labor, not upon any actual, tangible product or any addition to the general stock, but upon a peculiarly fortunate type of ownership. Yet it was just as potent in commanding the efforts of labor—which, of course, was what value meant for George. This was "value from obligation."²² It was the result of an "obligation" laid upon present labor. Or, to phrase the distinction in another way: One type of value was indicative of an addition made to the general stock of a nation and hence was socially beneficial; that was "value from production." The other type simply gave evidence of a transference of command over labor-power and was therefore of benefit to none but the possessor of that value; such was "value from obligation." One was, and the other was not, "socially" valuable. These two types of value, George held, must in no way be confused if a sound definition of wealth—the transition to that concept will begin to become apparent—was to be achieved.

What, then, was wealth? Its definition, for George, should be clear from this distinction within the realm of value. Wealth was definitely "value from production" and never included goods which had nothing to recommend them for economic consideration except obligatory value. Wealth always consisted of tangible, produced things; real wealth, as Smith held, was "the annual produce of the land and labour of the society," or, in George's definition, wealth "consists of natural products that have been secured, moved, combined, separated, or in other ways modified by human exertion, so as to fit them for the gratification of human desires. It is, in other words, labor impressed upon matter in such a way as to store

²² To quote George, there was ". . . (1) the value which comes from the exertion of labor in such a way as to save future exertion in obtaining the satisfaction of desire; and (2) the value which comes from the acquisition of power on the part of some men to command or compel exertion on the part of others, or, which is the same thing, from the imposition of obstacles to the satisfaction of desire that render more exertion necessary to the production of the same satisfaction. Value arising in the first mode may be distinguished as 'value from production,' and value arising in the second mode may be distinguished as 'value from obligation'—for the word 'obligation' is the best word I can think of to express everything which may require the rendering of exertion without the return of exertion." (*The Science of Political Economy*, pp. 260–261.)

up, as the heat of the sun is stored up in coal, the power of human labor to minister to human desires." [23] Real wealth always constituted some definite contribution to social wealth. Wealth was the wealth of the community and therefore value from "obligation" was not wealth; *it was no more than a redistribution of goods within the sum total and added nothing to that social wealth.* Value from obligation was as little "productive" as the value of gambling earnings. The value of land, for example, just as the value of slaves, could contribute nothing to national "wealth." In other words, community wealth was not the sum of the wealth of individuals; such a compositive process was as fallacious as the analogous relation between community and individual happiness.

All that is valuable, according to this view, is by no means wealth. Land has value, slaves had value, money is valuable, but they do not make up the "wealth of nations." (Smith's interpretation of wealth, George feels, was essentially the same as his own.) The term wealth, insists George, must be used strictly economically and not figuratively (or psychologically), and it is a figurative use of the word that includes everything valuable as wealth. Value itself is the ability to command the product of labor, but wealth is made up of those products of labor, and the confusion of the species wealth with the genus value was, for George, perhaps the most fertile source of the failure of political economy to define its subject-matter. Wealth depends upon labor expenditure; value, upon labor saving. In other words, George made value dependent upon effort saved, and wealth dependent

[23] *Progress and Poverty*, p. 40. Here again the contrast between the classical and the modern approaches is clear, the contrast always between objectivity and subjectivity. The more recent interpretation of wealth, as Hobson, for example, has always taken great pains to point out, emphasizes not the material connotation of the term, but rather that of subjective. psychological "welfare." Wealth is to be a state of mind, almost, instead of a quantity of matter.

upon effort expended, while Ricardian economics postulated the reverse, wealth resting on saving and value on expending. (The Austrians may be said to have based wealth upon utility secured, value, of course, depending upon marginal utility. In this sense, the Austrians were monistic, abolishing the distinction between labor and utility, whereas the older theory retained a dualism.)

There is no need of entering further into this discussion of value theory, but it is felt that it is perhaps necessary to elaborate George's distinction between wealth-value (particularly capital-value) and land-value. That elaboration is believed essential if for no other reason than to challenge the continual shift away from the classical separation between land and capital, a shift, as has been noted, which is becoming more and more a characteristic element of present-day theory. Moreover, it is a distinction that is a crucial one for George's economic system.

To return, then, to George's definition of capital as "wealth used in the production of more wealth," we find again that, as with the relationship between value and wealth, wealth here is the genus and capital the species. All wealth is not devoted to direct consumption; part of it is stored up and is used to produce new wealth; such wealth is capital. Capital, George held, was not different from wealth; it was a part of wealth, distinguished only by the use to which it was put. All capital is wealth, thus, but all wealth is not capital, and both, moreover, are forms of stored-up labor. Nothing, then, can be capital that is not wealth, and ultimately nothing can be capital that is not the product of labor.[24]

Land is not the product of labor, the argument continues,

[24] "Wealth, in short, is labor, which is raised to a higher or second power, by being stored in concrete forms which give it a certain measure of permanence, and thus permit of its utilization to satisfy desire in other times or other places. Capital is stored labor raised to a still higher or third power by being used to aid labor in the production of fresh wealth or of larger direct satisfactions of desire." (*The Science of Political Economy*, p. 296.)

and therefore must be kept carefully separate from the concept of capital. Such a view, of course, has been severely attacked by more recent economic critics; in fact, its fate has been the same as that of all the corollaries of labor theories of value. Professor Davenport was perhaps the most characteristic critic of this type of distinction.[25] His work is mentioned in this connection, not because his interpretation of economics—one which repudiates the classical attempts to make the science primarily a logical or ethical discipline and which instead stresses a strictly "cost" approach—is felt to be necessarily representative of modern economic theory, but simply because of his decisive treatment of this particular problem.

The definition that Professor Davenport gives of capital, "all durable and objective sources of valuable private income," [26] one which obviously includes land, is, he holds, a functional definition. Capital and land must not be considered in relation to their origin, but in relation to their use. The fact that land has a distinct and unique origin, a "natural" origin, he readily admits,[27] but that, for him, is of no technological, no economic, significance; it is essentially an ethical matter. He even recognizes a distinction between "natural" and "artificial" wealth,[28] and does not deny that the owner of one type of wealth, i. e., the landlord, enjoys a peculiarly advantageous status; but that again, following his strictly "economic" and technical approach, is a matter for social ethics—even of tax reform—and does not concern

[25] See especially *The Economics of Enterprise* (New York, Macmillan, 1919), Chaps. XII and XIII; and *Value and Distribution* (University of Chicago Press, 1908), Chaps. X and XI.

[26] *The Economics of Enterprise,* p. 161. It will be noticed that he at least retains the "objective" characteristic of capital, an attribute which would not be admitted by all the modern definitions of the concept.

[27] *Ibid.,* p. 169.

[28] His definition of wealth is simply "all valuable property" and property itself, he holds, is a legal rather than an economic concept. This is again indicative of his completely descriptive approach to the subject; ethical consideration of any kind is taboo.

economics. The classic distinction between land and capital has been based either on logical or ethical grounds, or even upon an oversimple rationalizing of a given state of society—the historical division of economic classes into landowners, capitalists and workers. It should have been approached, is the contention of Davenport, from the angle of function, an approach which would have tended to remove such a distinction between land and capital. If the standard of function is appealed to, the argument runs, land cannot be distinguished from capital in the productive process. That the source of one is, to put it roughly, labor, while the other has a natural origin, that one should therefore be treated differently from the other in its status as property—these, for Davenport, are not questions for economics but for other disciplines.

In his attempt to disprove the classical assumption—which was the assumption of George—that land and capital are dissimilar, Professor Davenport presents Böhm-Bawerk's catalogue of reasons for distinguishing the two,[29] and this summary, which he feels to be an adequate one, he essays to riddle point by point. The Austrian economist held that land and capital are distinct because: (1) One is movable and the other not; (2) one is the product of labor and the other of nature; (3) one is reproducible and the other not; (4) the owner of land enjoys a special type of privilege not enjoyed by the owner of capital; (5) and (6) there are economic peculiarities connected with land (such as that of diminishing returns) and that, in general, land processes obey different economic laws from those governing the processes of capital. Points (2) and (4) are definitely eliminated in this connection by Davenport's refusal to admit ethics into economics; (1) seems to be, as Davenport suggests, of little consequence;

---

[29] From *The Positive Theory of Capital*, p. 55. (Quoted in *The Economics of Enterprise*, p. 168.)

points (5) and (6) will be discussed further on, since they appear to be more directly connected with marginal utility and the work of Ricardo and Clark than with this specific question of land and capital; so (3) seems to be the only point in Böhm-Bawerk's analysis that need be mentioned here.

The attempts, based upon this argument of reproducibility, to demonstrate that land and capital cannot be *functionally* similar simply emphasize the fact that land is a given, static element which can neither be increased nor decreased to any significant extent by the efforts of man. Labor applied to land results in the production of a factor other than land; it does not affect the amount of land itself. Capital, on the other hand, is definitely a product of labor, and therefore can be reproduced and duplicated; its quantity is in no real sense fixed. This is not the "source" argument all over again, but rather the insistence that two economic elements, one of which is capable of being reproduced upon an increasing demand and whose value therefore is determined by a dynamic ratio between that demand and the contraction or expansion of supply, while the other is not so amenable to demand pressure since its supply is not variable, cannot be treated as similar *functioning* factors in economic processes. "Natural" and "artificial" in this argument refer not to the method by which land and capital have come into existence, but to the fact that one applies to a relatively unchanging element, while the other suggests that which can be made again.

Professor Davenport's arguments questioning this type of distinction center about his challenge of the absolute and unchanging character of land's irreproducibility. He does not proffer the admittedly insignificant fact that land is reclaimed or filled-in as an example of land's reproducibility; instead, he concentrates upon the point that increasing knowledge, particularly in the field of transportation, can prove a substitute for an increased quantity of land. Greater accessibility means more land, he suggests, and the trend of modern industry is constantly to increase accessibility. Moreover, he presents the familiar argument that there is a variation in quantity of land if different kinds of land are considered, that land is not a fixed and given factor so long as there is a distinction based on the amount of land available for different uses. And again, there is the fact that many instruments of capital have a limited supply, and thus, as far as the criterion of irreproducibility is invoked, are of the same nature as land.

This type of objection to the concept that capital can, and land cannot, be reproduced may be technically correct, but it seems unsatisfactory in its attempt to fuse these two economic elements. Every suggestion that Professor Davenport brings forward may be admitted, and still the only region that seems to be affected is that twilight zone between land and capital; the littoral of each realm may be extended by such arguments, but there is a great hinterland behind. Not even the most rabid follower of Henry George or the most classical of economists would deny that, excepting for purposes of logical classification, there is a merging of land and capital at their borders. The well-worn example of the fence or ditch or irrigation trough that has been on a piece of land for generations and has become indistinguishable from the land itself, may be genuinely accepted as offering a difficulty in drawing a hairline between what is land and what is an improvement upon land, or capital, but it is quite another thing to elaborate that type of difficulty into a sweeping condemnation of any distinction between land and capital.

Professor Davenport's suggestions are obviously far less trivial, but they do appear to be in the same category. It may be admitted, for example, that there are certain forms of capital which are difficult, even impossible, to reproduce, great bridges or irrigation dams perhaps, but to use these limited and peculiar expressions of capital as one of the challenges to the concept of the varying reproducibility of land and capital seems to indicate something like a lack of proportion. The existence of an intermediate category affords no justification for the disregard of the two end or limiting categories. (The presence of mulattoes does not vitiate the existential character of whites and negroes.) It may be further admitted that the supply of some types of land, e. g., timber or mining land, is decreasing whereas that of other kinds such as agricultural or building lands may be increasing, and likewise that, because of greater transportation accessibility, land supply itself has been "increased," but to deduce from such evidence that land itself is essentially, or characteristically, or even in any significant aspect a fluctuating and reproducible element, seems quite confusing.

The argument of Davenport is an endeavor to show that in this matter of reproducibility land and capital are not absolutely but only relatively dissimilar, that the distinction between them in this dimension is one of degree and not of kind. Such an argument may be accepted if we make, however, the reservation that the degree of dissimilarity involved is a very large one. It cannot be denied that absolutes have no place outside of logic, that hard and fast rigid distinctions, carefully insulated, have no more existence in economics than in any other science; but that is by no means a refutation of the validity of distinctions. It may be that some land is "made," that land supply is increased by scientific knowledge, that some lands are increasing and others decreasing in area, that some forms of capital cannot be reproduced; and yet the much broader claim that land space is set by natural agencies and that it is not as susceptible to control as is the supply of capital, remains fundamentally unchallenged. If there are to be any distinctions at all in economics (although Professor Davenport's definitions of wealth and capital would seem to indicate that distinctions are of little value), that between reproducible and nonreproducible goods seems a significant one, significant, that is, for functional purposes.[30]

This "functional" approach, while it seems a valid and useful one in the dimension to which Davenport restricts all economic theorizing, is not, however, altogether satisfactory as a foundation upon which to base a crucial difference between land and capital. To essay a fundamental separation, it seems necessary to have recourse precisely to those arguments that are deliberately excluded by Professor Davenport, the ethical arguments (although it must be pointed out that even these "ethical" arguments are in terms of processes,

---

[30] There is, however, a most interesting article by Professor Davenport himself in which this very distinction between land and capital is made. It is "The Theoretical Issues in the Single Tax" in *The American Economic Review* of March, 1917, Vol. VII. He writes: "Viewed in the large, doubtless land is human opportunity rather than human achievement, primary equipment rather than product." (P. 8.) This surely would imply that since land is opportunity rather than achievement, that fact would force it to *function* differently. It is difficult, in fact, to understand how the genetic can be legitimately distinguished from the functional characteristics of land, a distinction that seems always present in his argument.

The passage continues: "The single taxer insists, *and rightly and wisely I again agree,* that most or all of this original bounty should have been held as a joint possession and heritage among men, in equal and common right, to the end that, so far forth, there be always for all men an equality of opportunity. *The fiscal requirements of society, the expenses of the joint community life, should be to the utmost possibility covered by the payments into the common treasury of the funds derived as rent from the social estates."* (Italics mine.) From this expression, and others that will be quoted further on, it will be noted that in his appreciation of the work of George, Professor Davenport was decidedly more sympathetic than most economists; but ideationally he refused to burden economics with the type of ethical problem that George insisted upon. In another connection, he stated: "It may be said with approximate accuracy that the economists have never seriously attacked the theoretical validity of the single tax program. . . . In fact, they have come nearer to ignoring than to condemning." (The *Quarterly Journal of Economics,* Feb., 1910, Vol. XXIV, p. 279, in an article "The Single Tax in the English Budget.") He goes on to state that the economists have been wrong in looking upon the single tax as a fad or hobby offering no practical discussion possibilities, and to praise the theory of the movement, although he criticizes its fiscal methods.

and to that degree functional; that is, while they may be formulated as types of value, yet they imply much more than judgments based upon arbitrary and static value standards). These arguments for retaining the classic distinction between land and capital are chiefly the "origin" approach, viz., that land is not the creation of labor but is a natural element in the production of wealth, and so unlike capital; and secondly, the argument that the ownership of land confers a special privilege which is not present in the ownership of capital, the privilege of taking advantage of the socially created unearned increment of rent. (It must be remembered that Professor Davenport himself admits, and not reluctantly, the force and validity of these arguments,[31] but his point is simply that such matters are for sociology and social ethics, and not for economic science.)

A word may be said in elaboration of this second argument, since it is one that has drawn down upon itself serious criticism, criticism, however, which does not always seem appropriate. The objection of economists to this special privilege approach is simply the denial that there is any unique or peculiar privilege in the landowner's receipt of the socially created value of land.[32] It is one that belongs as well to the owners of all wealth. The argument holds that unearned increment is present in the domain of capital as well as in that of land. All value is social value and every type of significant income involves an unearned share that has been created by the presence of social forces; therefore land possesses no peculiar status in its ability to confer a surplus product. Because of the fact that all the categories of production and income are social, and completely so, in char-

[31] Cf. *The Economics of Enterprise*, p. 169; also the selections from his previously cited article that will be mentioned throughout.

[32] See following pages for a fuller discussion of this whole matter of land's "unearned increment."

acter, the phenomenon of unearned increment cannot be designated as a peculiar property of land ownership.[33]

An answer to this argument must point out that value is social only to the degree in which everything economic and political is social; more specifically that it is only Value, i. e., the abstract category of value, that is completely a social variable—since obviously exchange itself is completely social. But specific values, variation of values within the general concept of Value, must depend upon such prosaic and "technical" factors as demand rate, cost of production, exhaustibility, and, more important for this discussion, possibility of reproduction. These factors themselves are admittedly social, but again, that use of the word is so broad as to be meaningless as a particular determiner of specific economic value. To state that all value depends upon social forces is either a truism or a tautology; it is merely saying, since all social forces are ultimately expressible in economic demand, that where there is society there is demand. But to say that without demand there would be no value is not to say that demand is the sole determiner of value.

Capital value *is* social value—but *only* to the extent that

---

[33] This endeavor to show that there are unearned incomes other than that of rent, and that therefore the socialization of rent should not be considered unless and until other incomes are affected, is particularly mischievous because of its procrastination tendencies. An answer to this type of argument is found in Professor Davenport himself in his criticism of the "commonplace objections to the public retention of all kinds of ground rent," objections such as "the unearned increments in society are many, land increments only one out of a larger class, and that therefore it is unjust and indefensible to prohibit this one, while leaving the others to flourish." He answers that statement this way: "And yet it must be clear that whatever is accomplished towards the elimination of privilege and the equalization of opportunity is so far good. Remedy must begin with something; it is well to do the next thing next, especially if this next thing be the most important and the least difficult thing. Burglary need not be countenanced or highway robbery tolerated, awaiting the time that murder or counterfeiting shall be no more. No crime, or better no criminal, may claim to go free till all other malefactors are jailed—a vested right in one's particular graft or iniquity." (From the *American Economic Review* article previously mentioned; p. 11.)

capital itself is social; that is, capital both as an instrument and as an object possessing value is a social product. Land value, too, is a social value, *but land itself is not a social product;* it is not a product at all. Capital value, therefore, because of the fact that its *supply* is socially determined, involves something more than social demand. That value, in addition, is a variable dependent upon production difficulty and reproduction possibility. The difference between this type of value and that of land must be clear. Land value, unlike capital value, depends not at all upon factors of production or reproduction. It depends solely upon social pressure as it expresses itself in the demand for land.

In other words (and this may be considered as a concluding summary of the present discussion regarding the advisability of separating the concepts of land and capital), the press of population and all the amenities of civilized society express themselves in the demand for land—as they do in the demand for everything else—but whereas the demand for land *must* raise land rent and land value, the value of consumer goods and of capital goods will rise *or* fall, not merely as demand varies, but also in proportion to the elasticity of a reproducible supply in meeting that demand.[34] And that seems to be the crucial difference between land value and capital value. Given an unmonopolized supply of any economic element, in the production of which there is some measure of competition, increased demand and higher social organization may or may not result in increased value. But since there is essentially a monopoly of land and since it is fundamentally irreproducible, increasing demand and social organization *must* raise land values. To apply this, then, to the "social

[34] Is it not significantly true that where social forces manifest themselves in their most spectacular form, as in the large centers of population, the value of labor products, all other things being equal, is comparatively low? Certainly there is no corresponding increase in the value of such products that can relate it in any essential way to the increased value of land under the same social forces.

value" argument: The phenomenon of the social aspect of value cannot be referred indiscriminately to both land and capital, since with one element, land, it is the sole controlling factor, while with the other, capital, it is only one of several operating forces.[35]

It may be remembered that this lengthy discussion, one which perhaps savors too much of that characteristic classical approach which made early nineteenth century economic theory a rather fascinating branch of philosophy, was provoked by George's "meaning of the terms." Now, with such fundamental concepts clarified, George begins to present the mechanics of his argument. That argument, which is to lead

[35] Before leaving this argument it may be in point merely to mention one other most controversial aspect of this distinction between land value and capital value, and that is the question of cost of production. There is no intention here of entering into this dispute except to call attention to it. Since land is not a product, cost of production cannot enter as a factor in determining its value; that seems clear. Does cost of production, however, enter into the determination of capital value? The answers to that question are various, and economists seem to have divided upon whether they emphasize cost of production, or other factors such as marginal utility, for example. (The great work of Marshall, of course, was an attempt to reconcile these two approaches by means of his temporal emphasis; that is, "long-run" production is determined essentially by cost of production, whereas "short-run" production depends upon demand, i. e., marginal utility.) An emphasis upon cost of production would necessarily force a distinction between capital and land, capital being dependent upon such cost, but land being determined in value by the capitalization of its prospective rent. An emphasis only upon psychological factors, such as utility, would tend to discount such a distinction.

The work of Professor Brown (*op. cit.*) represents a thoroughgoing attempt to base capital value upon cost of production and so to distinguish clearly between capital and land. For an interesting recent controversy on this point, see the articles of Professor Brown and Professor Hewett in *The American Economic Review* for September and December, 1929. (See also the March and June, 1930, issues for a continuance of this argument which includes, among others, Professors Fetter and Cannan as contributors.) The conclusion of the controversy between Professors Hewett and Brown would seem to indicate a large measure of agreement, for the former admits that, largely, land is fixed and capital reproducible, that the two elements must be separated, at least for purposes of economic study (although perhaps not functionally), and that cost of production has a direct bearing upon capital value; whereas the latter admits that in the "short-run"—to use Marshall's phrase—alternative reproducibility is no more present in capital than in land, and that therefore in this case capital, like land, tends to equal the discounted value of its future income.

him to what he feels is the solution of the riddle of progress and poverty, will be centered not upon an investigation of the production of wealth, but upon an inquiry concerning the distribution of wealth.[36] It is an inquiry that needs to be examined with some detail, since the argument is not only a critical one for George's system, but handles a topic that has been a vital one for economic theory from Ricardo to John Bates Clark.

George opens his discussion with an exposition of the classic division of the factors of production into land, labor and capital, and of distribution into the respective channels of rent, wages and interest (he does not include profits), and he holds that the chief problem in the distributive process is that involved in the correlation of the laws of distribution. The then current doctrine, he felt, was totally unable to relate these three laws, or to show that they were interdependent and interacting, a phenomenon that must be demonstrated if there were to be any logical approach to the question of the distribution of wealth.[37] Political economy had taught, George states, that wages were determined by the ratio between the amount of capital devoted to the payment of labor and the number of laborers to be paid; that interest was set by the equation between the demands of borrowers and the supply of capital offered by lenders; and that rent was determined by the margin of cultivation. There was no possibility of a synthesis with such a diversified approach to the laws of distribution. Some one factor, some unit, must be sought which would blend all three laws. The

[36] *Progress and Poverty*, Book III, "The Laws of Distribution."
[37] This synthesizing of the laws of distribution was, of course, the problem that motivated the work of Clark, who, like George, felt that these laws were "natural." (George held the laws of production were physical and those of distribution moral, but both natural; cf. Mill, who stated that only the former were natural.) Clark sought to discover a functional distribution which would be harmoniously determined by the ratio of product to productive function.

laws were laws of proportion, and any variation in one must directly affect the others.

The law of rent[38] is George's first concern, for he believed that not only was this law the sole one that had been correctly formulated by classical political economy, but also that it was going to prove to be the unit which would serve to relate the other two laws of distribution. He therefore presents the Ricardian law of rent, which he believes "has the self-evident character of a geometric axiom," and which he accepts without qualification. Academic political economy and the intuitions of common sense coincided, he felt, in approving the work of Ricardo, and the law that "the rent of land is determined by the excess of its produce over that which the same application can secure from the least productive land in use" was so clear that "there is no necessity for discussion." [39]   It was a self-evident principle that had been

[38] George's interpretation of rent was completely the classic one and, being based upon his clear separation of land from capital, was considered as the return solely to land. That is, more recent interpretations, which define rent as "the product of concrete instruments of production," or as "the aggregate of the lump sums earned by capital goods" (Clark's definition), and which include land-rent as simply a form of the larger category of rent, and which hold that the only difference between rent and interest is that the former is an income from a particular instrument of capital whereas the latter is that from the value of capital—all these would have been to George vicious if not entirely unintelligible uses of the term.

[39] Of course, modern economics has found quite some necessity for discussion. Ricardianism, in fact, has been almost completely repudiated by more recent doctrine (see, e. g., Cannan's latest history). Perhaps the most important criticism of Ricardo has been the challenging of any peculiar application of the principle of diminishing returns and surplus values to land. Even if rent were determined by diminishing returns and increasing demand, and even if it did represent a form of marginal surplus, the same phenomenon, it is argued, applies to every other factor of production. All value, all "rent," depends upon some manifestation of the same principle. The precise formulation of a theory of general diminishing returns, or rather of diminishing productivity applicable to all economic factors, was the important work of John Bates Clark. For him, diminishing returns constituted a "general" and not a "special" theory of relativity.

Another major objection to Ricardo is that based on the familiar recent distinction between a "static" and a "dynamic" approach to economics. Ricardian rent is a static concept, is the criticism, and while it may be accepted as such, it must be confined to a logical system of statics. The residual income of rent-producing land over marginal land, for example,

recognized as such, but its corollaries had not been fully grasped. His task, George believed, was to deduce and clarify these corollaries. The first step was to rephrase the Ricardian law, and in this rephrasing will be evident the angle that George was to emphasize. His form of the law was:

> The ownership of a natural agent of production will give the power of appropriating so much of the wealth produced by the exertion of labor and capital upon it as exceeds the return which the same application of labor and capital could secure in the least productive occupation in which they freely engage . . . To say that rent will be the excess in productiveness over the yield at the margin, or lowest point, of cultivation, is the same thing as to say that it will be the excess of produce over what the same amount of labor and capital obtains in the least remunerative occupation. . . . All that part of the general production of wealth which exceeds what the labor and capital employed could have secured for themselves, if applied to the poorest natural agent in use, will go to the land owners in the shape of rent.[40]

Here the completely monopolistic interpretation of rent is fully presented. Rent, in this characterization, has clearly no direct connection with the productivity or utility of land. The value of land depends not upon the part that it plays simply *qua* factor of production, but upon the demand for it; the richest land has no value or rent if there is equally rich land available to all, while inferior land may command high rent provided there is still poorer land in use. Rent "in no wise represents any help or advantage given to production,

depends on the assumption of "no-rent" land, which assumption Ricardo made, but that assumption, as applying to the dynamic functioning of land, is challenged by modern theorists. That Ricardo's law is static does not, however, constitute a criticism of it even at the hands of these theorists. The point that he is criticized for, as for instance in the analysis of Clark, is that he failed to realize that it was static. Clark himself makes the distinction between static and dynamic a decisive one, and then quite freely proceeds to handle the entire concept of diminishing returns as a static concept with no fear of the contradictions or anomalies of dynamics. Even that frank position, however, is no longer tenable for most contemporary theory with its complete insistence upon a dynamic approach.

[40] *Progress and Poverty,* pp. 169–170.

but simply the power of securing a part of the results of production." [41] It is what producers or dwellers must pay to secure the use of land. The capacity of yielding rent gives value to land, and the capacity of yielding rent is determined by marginal land, by a process of relationship, and not by anything intrinsic, such as cost of production. Land rent is the price of monopoly, and land value is thus an "unearned increment." Therefore, George's interpretation of Ricardo's law of rent finds that the ownership of land, unlike the ownership of other significant factors in the production of wealth, means the ability to appropriate part of the product without the expenditure of productive effort, for rent is simply the result of the bidding, on the part of labor and capital, for a fixed land supply. Land value, to refer back to another of George's distinctions, is value from "obligation"; it depends neither upon labor nor upon use, but is rather the privilege of withholding from use. Rent, therefore, is a passive and not an active element in the distributive process; it does not "produce," but merely "gives leave" to produce, and consequently *the return to land must come out of the product of other elements.*

This characterization of rent as a vampire preying upon the other two factors of production, labor and capital, was a not unfamiliar deduction from the Ricardian law, but nowhere did it receive as important an emphasis as in George's system. If the law of rent discloses that the return to land is the sum that labor and capital must pay for permission to produce, then the corollaries of the law of rent must be the laws of wages and of interest. The process is not a reversible one; that is, neither the law of wages nor the law of interest can be taken as fundamental and the law of rent deduced from it, for land is the basic given element, and its margin, unlike that of the other factors, is fixed. Because of its very

[41] *Ibid.,* p. 166.

nature as an increment arising from competition for an irreproducible primary factor, rent has a prior claim. This prior
payment of rent (prior statically if not dynamically) and
therefore the ultimate dependence of wages and capital upon
rent, are summarized thus by George:

. . . The law of rent is necessarily the law of wages and interest
taken together, for it is the assertion, that no matter what be the
production which results from the application of labor and capital, these two factors will receive in wages and interest only such
part of the produce as they could have produced on land free to
them without the payment of rent—that is, the least productive
land or point in use. For, if, of the produce, all over the amount
which labor and capital could secure from land for which no rent
is paid must go to land owners as rent, then all that can be claimed
by labor and capital as wages and interest is the amount which
they could have secured from land yielding no rent. . . . The
wealth produced in every community is divided into two parts by
what may be called the rent line, which is fixed by the margin of
cultivation, or the return which labor and capital could obtain
from such natural opportunities as are free to them without the
payment of rent. From the part of the produce below this line
wages and interest must be paid. All that is above goes to the
owners of land.[42]

George formularizes the point in this way:

Produce = Rent + Wages + Interest,
Therefore, Produce — Rent = Wages + Interest.[43]

The dependence of interest and wages upon rent suggested
to George a direct synthesis, in terms of the phenomenon of
diminishing returns, of all three factors of distribution. Interest and wages, he held, not only were determined by the
amount of the produce to be divided after the extraction of
rent, but also they were specifically set by the variations in
marginal land itself; that is, the law of diminishing returns as
applied to rent must, in the same measure, be applied to capi-

[42] *Progress and Poverty*, pp. 171–172.   [43] *Ibid.*, p. 171.

tal and labor. Diminishing returns and marginal productivity provided the standard which unified the entire process of distribution, but, differing from the thesis of Clark, George's theory did not apply to diminishing returns within each dimension of the productive factors. Instead, it insisted that marginal land, because of the fundamental position of land, supplied the regulatory basis upon which interest and wages, along with rent, depended. Such a concept would logically follow from that of the direct relationship of capital and labor to land, for the determinants of the rent of land would necessarily set, directly or inversely, the rates of interest and wages. George, in addition, however, attempted to work out the independent relationship of interest and wages to marginal land, but it is not necessary in this presentation to trace his arguments in detail.

The correlation of interest, for example, with marginal land demanded a unique theory of interest, which George proceeded to elaborate, basing his justification for interest only incidentally upon "abstinence" or "impatience" or "roundabout production," and concentrating rather upon the contention that interest results from the increase that the reproductive powers of nature give to capital over a period of time.[44] Interest depends upon the reproductive powers of

[44] In *The Science of Political Economy* (Book III, Chaps. V-VIII) George launches into an elaborate metaphysical discussion concerning the function of time and space in the production of wealth. (Metaphysics, however, "which in its proper meaning is the science of the relations recognized by human reason, has become, in the hands of those who have assumed to teach it, a synonym for what cannot be understood, conveying to common thought some vague notion of a realm beyond the bounds of ordinary reason, into which common sense can venture only to shrink helpless and abashed." (P. 339.) Space and time, he insists, are relationships and not existences, and to speak of them as Space and Time, isolated from any relating qualifications, is sophistical. He specifically attacks Kant and Schopenhauer and their subjective interpretation of space and time as categories of the human mind. (George also offers a similar criticism of Schopenhauer's Platonic Ideas. It may be remarked that the work of Schopenhauer was the only technical work in philosophy with which he was completely familiar.) "When we remember that by space and time we do not really mean things having existence but certain relations to each other of things that have existence, the mystery

capital, which depend ultimately upon the reproductive powers of nature, i. e., land, and so George attempts to link interest directly with marginal land. "The relation between wages and interest is determined by the average power of increase which attaches to capital from its use in reproductive modes. As rent rises, interest will fall as wages fall, or will be determined by the margin of cultivation." [45]

The same independent approach to a marginal land theory of wages was attempted, with George endeavoring to show that because of the transformability of labor from one occupation to another, there was a direct dependence of wages in one occupation upon the rate of wages in another, and that therefore "wages in all strata must ultimately depend upon wages in the lowest and widest stratum—the general rate of wages rising or falling as these rise or fall." [46] The "lowest and widest stratum" is that involved in the producing of wealth directly from natural sources, and therefore the "marginal

is solved and the antinomy disappears in the perception of a verbal confusion." (P. 348.) This savors almost of "relativity."

George then turns to the function of these two, space and time, in economics. Since space, as a relationship, plays a part in all manifestations of matter, it is essential in the production of wealth. In fact, all that we mean by the production of wealth is some process of altering the extension of matter. Matter may be transformed by "adapting or changing natural products either in form or in place so as to fit them for the satisfaction of human desire," by "growing, or utilizing the vital forces of nature, as by raising vegetables or animals," or by "exchanging, or utilizing, so as to add to the general sum of wealth, the higher forces which vary with situation, occupation, or character." (*Progress and Poverty*, p. 186.) As shall be noticed further on, the law of diminishing returns itself is nothing but the law of diminishing space. Time, like space, is also essential in production, for it makes possible taking advantage of the reproductive power of nature. As applied to capital it justifies interest.

[45] *Progress and Poverty*, p. 202. This general discussion of interest, of its cause, of spurious interest, and of the law of interest, may be found in Chaps. III-V of Book III. It is a discussion that, to some of George's followers, does not seem as clear as his handling of rent. There are those who feel that his justification of interest might have more logically been worked out along the lines of his general theory of capital. That is, since capital is wealth, and wealth the product of labor, the use of wealth in production, i. e., capital, is entitled to draw "wages" for this form of stored-up labor; thus, interest would be the "wages" of labor as labor is manifested in capital.

[46] *Ibid.*, pp. 211–212.

men" of labor depend upon marginal land; so "wages depend upon the margin of production, or upon the produce which labor can obtain at the highest point of natural productiveness open to it without the payment of rent." [47]

While, however, George's efforts to deduce wages and interest directly from their relation to marginal land is of theoretical significance, yet logically such an independent approach is not necessary. Given George's interpretation of Ricardo's law of rent, one which made rent the recipient of a prior share of the produce which it had no legitimate part in creating, then the corollaries that wages and interest must vary inversely with rent, and that they, like rent, are thus set by the margin of cultivation, must follow.

Thus we come finally to George's important correlation and coördination of the laws of economic distribution:

Rent depends on the margin of cultivation, rising as it falls and falling as it rises.

Wages depend on the margin of cultivation, falling as it falls and rising as it rises.

Interest (its ratio with wages being fixed by the net power of increase which attaches to capital) depends on the margin of cultivation, falling as it falls and rising as it rises.[48]

Or, put in a less formularized statement:

Three things unite in production—labor, capital, and land. Three parties divide the produce—the laborer, the capitalist and the land owner. If, with an increase of production the laborer gets no more and the capitalist no more it is a necessary inference that the land owner reaps the whole gain . . .

The increase of rent explains why wages and interest do not increase. The cause which gives to the land holder is the cause which denies to the laborer and the capitalist. That wages and interest are higher in new than in old countries is not, as the standard economists say, because nature makes a greater return to the application of labor and capital, but because land is cheaper,

[47] *Progress and Poverty*. p. 213.   [48] *Ibid.*, p. 218.

and, therefore, as a smaller proportion of the return is taken by rent, labor and capital can keep for their share a larger proportion of what nature does return. It is not the total produce, but the net produce, after rent has been taken from it, that determines what can be divided as wages and interest. Hence, the rate of wages and interest is everywhere fixed, not so much by the productiveness of labor as by the value of land. Wherever the value of land is relatively low, wages and interest are relatively high; wherever land is relatively high, wages and interest are relatively low.[49]

Such an interpretation of Ricardianism has, of course, aroused bitter criticism on the part of both orthodox and socialist theorists. It may be mentioned, nevertheless, that much of this criticism has slighted the significance—"historical" significance, to say the least—of George's synthesis of the laws of distribution. A similar synthesis, similar, that is, in its concentration upon the phenomenon of diminishing returns, gave the later work of John Bates Clark a permanent place in economic theory (work, which Clark admitted,[50] was influenced by George's concepts), and yet George's treatment has been largely disregarded in academic circles. It must be realized that George himself recognized the criticism that was later applied to Ricardo, that diminishing returns could not be confined to land; he saw that the presence of a marginal factor was indeed the determining element in setting the amount available for all the different shares of production, but in his logical attempts to reduce divergent concepts to the expression of one fundamental principle (just as in his reduction of value and wealth concepts to those of labor) George

---

[49] *Progress and Poverty*, pp. 220–221.

[50] "It was the claim advanced by Mr. Henry George that wages are fixed by the product which a man can create by tilling rentless land, that first led me to seek a method by which the product of labor everywhere may be disentangled from the product of coöperating agents and separately identified; and it was this quest which led to the attainment of the law that is here presented, according to which the wages of all labor tend, under perfectly free competition, to equal the product that is separately attributable to the labor." (*The Distribution of Wealth*, New York, Macmillan, 1899; Preface, p. viii.)

postulated the phenomenon of diminishing returns in land as the constant to which the other factors, the returns to capital and labor, approached. The concept of diminishing returns itself could not act as a common denominator, since land and capital were distinct, but diminishing returns in land could and did set the limit of the various distributive shares.

This was an almost metaphysical conception, for the broadest interpretation of the law of diminishing returns was simply the realization that earth space was finite, and that all earthly matter—all production of wealth—approached a limiting constant (one, to anticipate here, that was privately owned and exploited).

There is in truth no special law of diminishing productiveness applying to agriculture, or to the extractive operations, or to the use of natural agents, which are the various ways which the later writers have of sometimes stating what the earlier writers called the law of diminishing productiveness in agriculture; and that what has been misapprehended as a special law of diminishing returns in agriculture is in reality a general law, applying as well to manufacturing and exchanging as to agriculture, being in fact nothing less general than the spacial law of all material existence and movement—inorganic as well as organic.[51]

Whatever may be the value of this synthesis of George, it is felt that his attempted unification of the too often incoherent processes of the distribution of wealth merits a more important historical position in economic theory than has been accorded it.

At this point there is a significant pause in George's argument,[52] for he finds that he has concluded the "statics" of the inquiry and is now ready to concern himself with its "dynamics." This distinction between a static and a dynamic ap-

---

[51] *The Science of Political Economy,* p. 338.
[52] The opening of Book IV of *Progress and Poverty,* "Effect of Material Progress upon the Distribution of Wealth."

proach is not the separation effected by recent theory, but is simply the analogue of mechanical statics and dynamics. George realizes that thus far he has been concerned with the "forms" of production and distribution, the moulds or channels which shape or direct economic processes, but now he must devote his attention to the active processes themselves. In other words, economic movement now presents itself instead of economic position, e. g., in the case of rent and wages he shifts his approach from an analysis of the determining structure into which these factors of distribution fall to the way in which the actual increase of the one brings about a decrease in the other. George feels that he has already demonstrated that the statics of distribution will give a certain form to the process of rent and wages, i. e., will set them in opposition to one another; but "to say that wages remain low because rent advances is like saying that a steamboat moves because its wheels turn around. The further question is, What causes rent to advance? What is the force or necessity that, as productive power increases, distributes a greater and greater proportion of the produce as rent?" [53] The change is from an investigation of rest to one of motion, but it does not connote, as does the present-day contraposition of statics and dynamics in economics, the change from logic to technology, or from theory to data. George did not feel in any way that he was introducing a superior element or one that was not to be deductive; the dynamic approach was simply another angle, although, because of the very nature of his inquiry, it was the dynamics of rent that presented the most significant justification for his later proposals. (It may be helpful here, in order to remove a bit of the possible incoherency of this exposition, to review, in a word, what the "statics" of the problem has been: Poverty must be sought for in low wages; why, then, are wages low? The

[53] *Progress and Poverty*, p. 225.

wages fund theory and Malthusianism are unsatisfactory. A discussion of a wages fund introduces the necessity for defining terms, specifically that of capital. Capital is wealth used in the production of more wealth. What is wealth? Wealth is value from production, i. e., a labor-saving theory of value. There is a value from production, but also a value from obligation which is not wealth. Land value is value from obligation, and land is not wealth, and therefore not capital. The factors of production, then, are land, labor, capital; of distribution, rent, wages, interest. To understand why wages are low the laws of distribution must be coördinated. The standard of unification is Ricardo's law of rent; rent arises not from the productive functions of land but because land is a limited supply for which there is an increasing demand, i. e., diminishing returns. Rent is paid from the produce but land contributes nothing to the produce; therefore wages and interest must vary inversely with rent. If rent increases, wages—to concentrate upon George's problem—must decrease. But why does rent increase?)

What, then, are the forces that drive rent up? What factors are they that cause an ever-increasing share of the total product to be diverted to the owner of land? Are the forces those that result from the active part of land in the production of wealth? Is the distributive return to the owner of land the payment for his function as a producer? Or, is the cause of increasing rent purely social in character?

The first force that George presents is that of the increase of population. It had been clearly recognized ever since the work of Ricardo, that increased population raised rent because it lowered the margin of cultivation, and it was this fact that was used to buttress Malthusianism since it showed that population was steadily pressing against the limits of subsistence. While George recognized that an increased population lowered the margin of cultivation by necessitat-

ing the use of poorer land, and thereby raised rent, he did not
concentrate upon this point, for he felt that increased population meant increased production; that, despite the utilization of poorer land, with more labor and more intelligent
control of industry, the aggregate and proportionate produce
would not be diminished (his answer to Malthus), and
therefore he had no desire to press this familiar correlation
of population and rent; he felt it had been wrongly interpreted by the advocates of Malthusianism.

Instead, George devotes the major part of his attention,
not to these more strictly material effects of the increase of
population upon rent and land values, but rather to what
Professor Dewey has termed the "imponderable" elements
in that increase of population.[54] In one of the most vivid
and pictorial passages of the entire book,[55] George traces the
genesis of a settlement in a wilderness, and points out that an
expanding community life is clearly the most potent force
in giving value to land. It is not simply that the greater
economies brought about by increasing population have the
effect of adding to the productivity of land (and thus raising
rent, not, however, by changing the margin or compelling recourse to inferior lands, but by widening the gap between
marginal and productive land), but, of infinitely more im-

[54] "I cannot refrain," writes Professor Dewey, "from pointing out one
feature of his [George's] thought which is too often ignored: his emphasis
upon ideal factors in life, upon what are sometimes called the imponderables.
It is a poor version of his ideas which insists only upon the material effect
of increase of population in producing the material or monetary increment
in the value of land. . . . Henry George puts even greater stress upon the
fact that community life increases land values because it opens 'a wider,
fuller and more varied life,' so that the desire to share in the higher values
which the community brings with it is a decisive factor in raising the rental
value of land. And it is because the present system not only depresses the
material status of the mass of the population, but especially because it
renders one-sided and inequitable the people's share in these higher values
that we find in *Progress and Poverty* the analysis of the scientist combined
with the sympathies and aspirations of a great lover of mankind." (Preface
to *Significant Paragraphs from Progress and Poverty*, compiled by Professor
H. G. Brown; N. Y., Doubleday, Doran, 1928.)
[55] *Progress and Poverty*, pp. 233–239.

portance, land pyramids in value because of its adjacency to the center of social activity. It is to the intangible "ideal factors" that one must look for a real appreciation of the phenomenal land values at the heart of population. All such ideal factors are economically expressible in demand for land, and such demand has the inevitable effect of bringing about the staggering hugeness of urban land values—the examples of which have become so common as to have ceased causing wonder. Rent and land value, thus, are the expressions of community coöperation, of "social service." Land removed from the presence of population is valueless, land at the center of population is ridiculously precious. There is no more accurate barometer of this "imponderable" social progress, no more sensitive register of community welfare, than land value. Given an increasing population and an expanding society, George points out, land values arise—and rise. Remove that population, diminish its social advantages, and rent vanishes. *Land value is social value.* It is the *measure* of society's presence, its needs, its qualities and all of its activities and achievements.

The second social phenomenon that he mentions is the effect of the "improvement of the arts" of production. Such improvement in the productive process has the effect of saving labor. "The effect of inventions and improvements in the productive arts is to save labor—that is, to enable the same result to be secured with less labor, or a greater result with the same labor." [56] It is the latter result, i. e., that greater wealth will be produced with the same labor, that follows from "labor-saving" inventions, since in an advanced state of society demand is not static but steadily increases: "Man is not an ox, who, when he has eaten his full, lies down to chew the cud; he is the daughter of the horse leech who constantly asks for more." [57] (That is George's answer to the

[56] *Ibid.*, p. 242.   [57] *Ibid.*, p. 243.

spectre of general "over-production" and of a "labor-saved" industrial order.) Improvement in the technique of production means increased production of wealth.

Now, what is the effect of such an increase upon rent?

The effect of labor-saving improvements will be to extend the demand for land, and wherever the limit of the quality of land in use is reached, to bring into cultivation lands of less natural productiveness, or to extend cultivation on the same lands to a point of lower natural productiveness. And thus, while the primary effect of labor-saving improvements is to increase the power of labor, the secondary effect is to extend cultivation, and, where this lowers the margin of cultivation, to increase rent. . . . Wealth in all its forms being the product of labor applied to land or the products of land, any increase in the power of labor, the demand for wealth being unsatisfied, will be utilized in procuring more wealth, and thus increase the demand for land.[58]

Increased production of wealth has the same effect upon land values and rent as increase in population or in social life; it creates demand for land and therefore raises rent. This contention of George may well be considered by those who hope that further increase in scientific technique applied to industry, new sources of fuel or additional improvement in the machinery of production and transportation, will ultimately solve economic problems. For George, the one effect of any such conceivable improvement was clearly to increase the production of wealth and thereby increase rent. That is the reason for his eternal insistence that the solutions of economic problems can be sought for only in the dimension of the distribution, and not in that of the production of wealth.

This paradoxical function of machinery in increasing production, raising rent and therefore lowering wages, was, for George, the cause of labor's short-sighted attacks upon labor-saving devices. Labor-saving devices in themselves, he argued, mean increased production, but increasing produc-

[58] *Progress and Poverty*, pp. 243, 247.

tion (that is, general production) can never catch up with an expanding, dynamic demand, and so such devices should not injure labor. It is their effect on rent, he feels, that alone makes them of not unmixed good.

And this is the reason why George had no faith in any half-hearted measures in the solution of economic problems. Even free trade—which has always been connected with his taxation proposals and whose literature must include his *Protection or Free Trade* as a classic perhaps unsurpassed in the clarity and persuasiveness of its arguments—even free trade he regarded as essentially incomplete without any change in the distributive process. It also could do nothing more than increase the production of wealth and therefore raise rent.

A third cause for the increase of rent is land speculation, a phenomenon so typical and familiar that it perhaps does not need to be discussed here. As George phrases it:

> That cause is the confident expectation of the future enhancement of land values, which arises in all progressive countries from the steady increase of rent, and which leads to speculation, or the holding of land for a higher price than it would then otherwise bring. . . . The confident expectation of increased prices produces, to a greater or less extent, the effects of a combination among land holders, and tends to the withholding of land from use, in expectation of higher prices, thus forcing the margin of cultivation farther than required by the necessities of production.[59]

George thus concludes the "dynamics" of the problem. He felt that "statically" he had shown how rent absorbs a share of the produce which it had no part in creating. It arose because of the strategic position of land in production; upon Ricardo's law of rent depended the entire distributive process.

[59] *Progress and Poverty*, pp. 253–254. George's explanation of periodic industrial depression, of the business cycle, was in terms of land speculation. (Book V, Chap. I.) The speculative advance in land values (what Paul Blanshard calls the "land racket") cuts down the earnings of labor and capital, curtails consumption, decreases production and communicates the paralysis through all the interlacings of industry and commerce.

And now, he has pointed out that every increase in population, in social organization, in the production of wealth, has but the effect of increasing rent.

Therefore, the inevitable conclusion: "The reason why, in spite of the increase of productive power, wages constantly tend to a minimum which will give but a bare living, is that, with increase in productive power, rent tends to even greater increase, thus producing a constant tendency to the forcing down of wages." [60] This was the dynamic aspect of the mischievous relation of rent to the other factors of distribution. The forces in economic equilibrium had disclosed the functional connection of rent to wages and interest, and now, setting these processes into movement, George feels that such a significant relationship is even more vividly manifested. Rent was unearned both statically and dynamically; on the one hand, because it was a value created not by productivity, labor, or by any tangible contribution to wealth, but solely by the privation of land supply; and on the other, because its growth and increase were due to social forces, and accrued to the individual simply as the result of monopoly land ownership, not as the return for any expression of productive enterprise. Rent was unearned, and therefore its payment was a drain upon earned income. It contributed nothing to the product—nothing except the permission to produce—and yet it had to be paid out of the product; in fact, every increase in the product still further increased its share, since so much more precious was that permission to produce.

This, then, was the cause that George pointed out for the persistence of poverty amid advancing wealth. The benefits that increasing production and increasing social organization bring are intercepted; that is why civilized man finds his fellows crushed into a degradation that becomes more ghastly as it becomes more familiar—and thus less noticed. Because

[60] *Progress and Poverty*, p. 280.

of the monopoly of land, increasing progress and prosperity could bring in their train only further poverty and social evil. And this tragically ludicrous coexistence of progress and poverty (a phenomenon that must proffer a challenge to any mind sensitive to social maladjustment) had, for George, the comparatively simple economic explanation that has been traced in these pages. As he summarizes it:

> The simple theory which I have outlined (if indeed it can be called a theory which is but the recognition of the most obvious relations) explains this conjunction of poverty with wealth, of low wages with high productive power, of degradation amid enlightenment, of virtual slavery in political liberty. . . . It explains why interest and wages are higher in new than in older communities, though the average, as well as the aggregate, production of wealth is less. It explains why improvements which increase the productive power of labor and capital increase the reward of neither. It explains what is commonly called the conflict between labor and capital, while proving the real harmony of interest between them. . . . It explains the vice and misery which show themselves amid dense population, without attributing to the laws of the All-Wise and All-Beneficent defects which belong only to the short-sighted and selfish enactments of men.[61]

That such an explanation was in accordance with all the facts, George was convinced. Inductively, at this point,[62] he sought to correlate the progression of rent with the companion increase of civilizing factors and misery, "but it were as well to cite historical illustrations of the attraction of gravitation. The principle is as universal and as obvious. That rent *must* reduce wages is as clear as that the greater the subtractor the less the remainder. That rent *does* reduce wages, any one, wherever situated, can see by merely looking around him." [63] This relationship, however, was primarily a logical one, as, for that matter, were all the relations of political

---

[61] *Progress and Poverty*, pp. 284–285.
[62] *Ibid.*, Book V, Chap. II.
[63] *Ibid.*, pp. 289–290.

economy. The examples were clearly at hand, but that was only as it should be. In fact, hypothetical cases themselves would suffice.

Take, for instance, as George did, some emerging no-man's land in the English Channel, and establish, or rather postulate, that land there is to remain unappropriated and of free access—productive land, of course. What would happen to wages in Great Britain? What to rent? What to social conditions in general? The answers to such questions, George held, were as logically certain as the most valid of syllogisms. Wages must rise, rent fall, and social conditions improve. On the other hand, make some little village into a great and glorious city, what would be the result if present economic conditions still remained in effect? Would wages be any higher in that expanded town? Rent? "In the new city you may have a luxurious mansion; but among its public buildings will be an almshouse." Wages and social conditions would be in no way benefited, since all the increase in the production of wealth would be overtaken by the rise in economic rent. The "natural laws" of distribution being what they were, the unearned increment of rent must place itself in opposition to the other economic elements; the return to land must infringe upon the returns to labor and capital. And in this prosaic statement of an economic phenomenon lay hidden all the misery that George saw festering in the city slums.

In all our long investigation we have been advancing to this simple truth: That as land is necessary to the exertion of labor in the production of wealth, to command the land which is necessary to labor, is to command all the fruits of labor save enough to enable labor to exist. We have been advancing as through an enemy's country, in which every step must be secured, every position fortified, and every by-path explored; for this simple truth, in its application to social and political problems, is hid from the great masses of men partly by its very simplicity, and in greater part by widespread fallacies and erroneous habits of thought which lead them to look in every direction but the right one for an explanation of the evils which oppress and threaten the civilized world. . . . It is not in the relations of capital and labor; it is not in the pressure of population against subsistence, that an explanation of the unequal development of our civilization is to be found. The great cause of inequality in the distribution of wealth is inequality in the ownership of land. *The ownership of land is the great fundamental fact which ultimately determines the social, the political, and consequently the intellectual and moral conditions of a people.* . . . Material progress cannot rid us of our dependence upon land; it can but add to the power of producing wealth from land; and hence, when land is monopolized, it might go on to infinity without increasing wages or improving the condition of those who have but their labor. It can but add to the value of land and the power which its possession gives. Everywhere, in all times, among all people, the possession of land is the base of aristocracy, the foundation of great fortunes, the source of power. As said the Brahmins, ages ago—"To whomsoever the soil at any time belongs, to him belong the fruits of it. White parasols and elephants mad with pride are the flowers of a grant of land." [64]

What, then, is the solution? George's is simple and complete. "We must make land common property." Thus from a discussion of processes (economics) George now turns to the presentation of solutions (politics).

We have traced the unequal distribution of wealth, which is the curse and menace of modern civilization, to the institution of private property in land. We have seen that so long as this institution exists no increase in productive power can permanently benefit the masses; but, on the contrary, must tend still further to depress their condition . . .

There is but one way to remove an evil—and that is, to remove its cause. Poverty deepens as wealth increases, and wages are forced down while productive power grows, because land, which is the source of all wealth and the field of all labor, is monopolized. To extirpate poverty, to make wages what justice commands they

[64] *Progress and Poverty*, pp. 292–294. (Italics mine.)

should be, the full earnings of the laborer, we must therefore substitute for the individual ownership of land a common ownership. Nothing else will go to the cause of the evil—in nothing else is there the slightest hope . . .

We must make land common property.[65]

It must be stated at this point, clearly and emphatically, that George's "common property" in land did not mean common ownership in land. That is to say, George was in no sense a land nationalist and did not suggest, as is so often mistakenly attributed to him—even by academic economists —that land was to be owned by the State, or that it should be held in joint ownership by the citizens, or that there should be any essential change in our present system of land tenure. All such concepts were distinctly repudiated by him.[66] It is a

---

[65] *Progress and Poverty*, p. 326.

[66] For example, in *Protection or Free Trade,* he states specifically that: "To treat land as a common, where no one could claim the exclusive use of any particular piece, would be practicable only where men lived in movable tents and made no permanent improvements, and would effectually prevent any advance beyond such a state. No one would sow a crop, or build a house, or open a mine, or plant an orchard, or cut a drain, so long as any one else could come in and turn him out of the land in which or on which such improvements must be fixed. Thus it is absolutely necessary to the proper use and improvement of land that society should secure to the user and improver safe possession. This point is constantly raised by those who resent any questioning of our present treatment of land. They seek to befog the issue by persistently treating every proposition to secure equal right to land as though it were a proposition to secure an equal division of land, and attempt to defend private property in land by setting forth the necessity of securing safe possession to the improver . . . We can leave land now being used in the secure possession of those using it, and leave land now unused to be taken possession of by those who wish to make use of it . . ." (Pp. 279–281.) And in other places George is no less explicit in his condemnation of the crudities of agrarian communism. Is not the fear of land nationalization met by a sane thought such as this?— "Everything could go on as now, and yet the common right to land be fully recognized by appropriating rent to the common benefit. There is a lot in the center of San Francisco to which the common rights of the people of that city are yet legally recognized. This lot is not cut up into infinitesimal pieces nor yet is it an unused waste. It is covered with fine buildings, the property of private individuals, that stand there in perfect security. The only difference between this lot and those around it, is that the rent of the one goes into the common school fund, the rent of others into private pockets. What is to prevent the land of a whole country being held by the people of the country in this way?" (*Progress and Poverty*, pp. 397–398.)

grossly inaccurate version of his proposals that attacks them under the labels of "nationalization" or "communism." Instead, George's interpretation of making land "common property" involved a distinctly novel methodological technique, one that has come to be indissolubly associated with his name; he was confident that his method would make land "common property," but, at the same time, retain all the advantages of the private administration of land.

I do not propose either to purchase or to confiscate private property in land. The first would be unjust; the second needless. Let the individuals who now hold it still retain, if they want to, possession of what they are pleased to call *their* land. Let them continue to call it *their* land. Let them buy and sell, and bequeath and devise it. We may safely leave them the shell, if we take the kernel.[67]

That kernel, of course, will be economic rent, the rent of land, the private retention of which, George has tried to point out, is the inequitable factor in the distribution of wealth. Therefore there was only one way to make land "common property." That was to socialize economic rent. *"It is not necessary to confiscate land; it is only necessary to confiscate rent. . . .* What I therefore propose . . . is *to appropriate rent by taxation . . . to abolish all taxation save that upon land values."* [68] Here, then, is the solution that George had been developing in his long examination of the economic process. Land values were to flow into the hands of society instead of into those of private individuals. A product purely social must be retained by society. Economic rent, the rent of land, is a completely social product, the only completely social product; wealth and capital are not. Economic rent, that creature of social forces and the barometer of social progress, must become completely social; it must be collected, by

[67] *Ibid.*, p. 403.   [68] *Ibid.*, pp. 403–404. (Italics are George's.)

society, through the agency of taxation. *This is the "single tax."*

The promised effects of such a solution cannot be discussed in an exposition such as this.[69] It may be pointed out, however, that the effects of George's proposal would be implicitly a part of his complete deductive system. That is, they must be handled as corollaries of George's pattern of distribution; they are implied by his treatment of the distributive process. The effects, in other words, must lie characteristically in his suggested redirection of the flow of wealth, and depend, therefore, almost entirely upon the crucial rôle played by rent. Rent is the focus of the problem, of the solution, and of the effects of that solution. Wages and interest, it may be remembered, have been fixed, for George, by the marginal line of rent, and rent has been paid out of the legitimate return to wages and interest. With rent socialized, however, labor and capital would receive their full return. Rent would no longer retain its privileged position that enabled it to prey upon the other factors of production. Rent had distorted the "natural" process of distribution. Make rent public property, and wages and interest must rise. Make rent public property, and it will defray all the legitimate expenses of social organization, and this will permit all of wages and interest to remain in the possession of labor and capital.

Yet George did not rest the major justification of his solution on any such essentially pragmatic test. The most crucial of all sanctions was for him the ethical sanction, and in no uncertain fashion he placed the acceptance or rejection of his economic philosophy squarely upon its moral justifications. This is undoubtedly his most unequivocal statement of that moral emphasis:

When it is proposed to abolish private property in land the first question that will arise is that of justice. Though often warped

[69] See also *infra*, pp. 518–523.

by habit, superstition, and selfishness into the most distorted forms, the sentiment of justice is yet fundamental to the human mind, and whatever dispute arouses the passions of men, the conflict is sure to rage, not so much as to the question, "Is it wise?" as to the question, "Is it right?"

This tendency of popular discussions to take an ethical form has a cause. It springs from a law of the human mind; it rests upon a vague and instinctive recognition of what is probably the deepest truth we can grasp. That alone is wise which is just; that alone is enduring which is right. In the narrow scale of individual actions and individual life this truth may be often obscured, but in the wider field of national life it everywhere stands out.

I bow to this arbitrament, and accept this test. If our inquiry into the cause which makes low wages and pauperism the accompaniments of material progress has led us to a correct conclusion, it will bear translation from terms of political economy into terms of ethics, and as the source of social evils show a wrong. If it will not do this, it is disproved. If it will do this, it is proved by the final decision. If private property in land be just, then is the remedy I propose a false one; if, on the contrary, private property in land be unjust, then is this remedy the true one.[70]

It therefore becomes necessary to examine George's ethical justification of the socialization of economic rent, for no exposition of his economic system would be complete without a presentation and discussion of his labor theory of property.

If it is to be in ethical terms that George justifies the socialization of rent, to what will he appeal as the fundamental moral basis for his insistence upon the unearned character of the income arising from land? That appeal, it may be guessed, will be to the authority of natural rights. More specifically, it will be with an appeal to the natural right of property that George presents the dichotomy of earned and unearned income.

The argument is a familiar one: Man has a natural right

[70] *Progress and Poverty*, p. 331.

to himself, to the exercise of his powers, and therefore to the product of his labor. He owns himself (or, at least, "should" own himself, for the whole doctrine of natural rights, as will be suggested,[71] may be phrased not so much in metaphysical, categorical terms as in those of an ethical, hypothetical vocabulary), and hence he owns his product. Here is introduced, of course, a complete labor explanation and justification of property,[72] an approach that was accepted by George as whole-heartedly as he embraced the companion labor theory of value. The original and the only source of property, for George, was man's exclusive right to himself and therefore to the products of his labor. "As nature gives only to labor, the exertion of labor in production is the only title to exclusive possession."

At this point, it is perhaps necessary, in order to avoid too hasty criticism, to recognize that labor theories of property are now generally anathema, and that their academic unpopularity is even greater than that accorded to labor theories of value.[73] The "social utility" theory of property, in contrast to such labor theories, need only be mentioned as the most acceptable of current doctrines. While, of course, there can be no overambitious attempt here to tilt at the social utility theory or to justify a labor approach, still it

[71] See *infra*, pp. 491 ff.
[72] This, of course, will recall the familiar position of Locke.
[73] And yet Professor Davenport could write: "I believe that the principle at the heart of the single tax agitation—that the fiscal revenues should be derived from the social estates (the regalia principle in ultimate essence), *from sources to which the justifications of private property do not attach— is right and vastly important.* . . . As *ethical* basis, whatever other basis there may conceivably be for private property, the single taxer *logically finds nothing but the right of the individual to himself and to the results of his activity—the simple recognition of the meaning of personality and of the ethical relations which it prescribes.* That one has produced an item of wealth, or has it by the voluntary transfer of some one that has produced it, affords the sole ethical claim to it. This is doubtless a labor theory of the ethical right of property. Nothing, therefore, which is natural bounty can rightly have been allowed to serve as a source of individual income, to fall into the category of individual ownership." (From the article, "The Theoretical Issues in the Single Tax," mentioned previously, p. 1. Italics mine.)

must be suggested that the attacks upon the various labor theories seem largely to have failed to grasp the significant ethical foundations upon which they depend. That type of foundation is the insistence that the concept of property must have something more than a legal sanction, and that that something more must be ethical or psychological in character. Such ethical justification has been found by many theorists to lie in the output of human labor, in the results of individual strivings. To them, all wealth is clearly the product of the labor of individuals, expressed in whatever form it may be, and hence the ownership of wealth must imply some justification in terms of that expended labor. Labor sets the sought-after ethical or psychological standard, and such a standard seems to be absent from the historical, legalistic exposition that is a part of social utility theories. The labor theorist feels that the social utility approach is likely to fall into the suave equanimity of the evolutionary thesis to which, of course, it is definitely related. A statement that property is a product of historical forces, that it is the last stage of a slow, tedious process, is too often interpreted as *prima facie* evidence of the fact that it is thereby socially useful, or, at least, that to challenge it would be to tamper with the onmoving mechanism of a painful social evolution. That which has arrived does not necessarily bear a warrant that it is of social service, and if it does bear such a warrant, then, it is argued by the labor theorist, a judgment value is introduced, and the social utility theory is transformed from an historical to an ethical approach (which seems to be just what the proponents of that theory are trying to avoid).

In other words, criticism of labor theories of property appears often to have ignored the ethical motivation at the root of such approaches, and to have concentrated upon arguments which are mainly technical in character. For example, there is this major criticism of every labor theory.

All production is completely social, and the individual's output is swallowed up in the social product. Because of the complexity and social organization of economic processes, it is archaic even to speak of "individual" labor or "individual" production, much less of "individual" property. Any particular contribution becomes an inextricable and indeterminable part of the social fabric. Furthermore, the "individual" in making a possible contribution is so dependent upon social coöperation that in no sense can he as an individual be considered as producing anything; he is merely an incidental factor in the productive machine. The individual himself is not an isolated entity but a definite social product. Yet even waiving that more metaphysical difficulty, the economic facts of specialization and division of labor and complicated distribution lead the economist to question the very existence of any possible basis for a labor theory of property. He can find no "individual," no "individual labor," and therefore no labor right to property.

This type of argument seems a graphic illustration of what is felt to be at least two annoying characteristics of modern economics: One (to digress, for a moment, from the underlying ethical emphasis of these pages) is the increasing tendency on the part of the science to complicate both economic phenomena and economic explanations, to magnify details. Take this particular attack upon an individual basis of production. Is it anything more than the apotheosis of numbers? The concept of labor (and the word "concept" is used advisedly despite its philosophic tinge) is one that signifies the expenditure of human exertion in the production of wealth. It is a concept that, if interpreted, as it must be, in a qualitative rather than a quantitative dimension, is clear, valid and serviceable. That is to say, the expenditure of human exertion, no matter how diversified or specialized

or socialized it may become, must be considered as fundamentally and essentially psychological in character. This
exertion of labor that is required for the functioning of economic processes is the exertion or labor of biological entities,
of "individuals"—the term will be retained as intelligible if
not altogether acceptable. Labor is the elemental factor in
production, but it is not some hypostasized labor; it is the
sum total of individual exertions. It is a "distributive" and
not a "collective" term. Granted that the details and complexities of production are enormously involved, and also
that there are major technical difficulties present in determining both the individual's contribution to and his return
from the social product; still, any failure to realize that by
labor is meant the activity of a human being, of a psychological unit, seems a serious one. The difference between intricate and simple production, between large- and small-scale
production is surely a significant difference, but it is hardly
sufficient to eliminate consideration of the factor at the
basis of all production, i. e., labor, human, individual labor.
Labor is certainly as psychological as demand. Both can be
presented in terms of "round numbers," as vast social functions, but each has a common denominator in the exertions
and wants of working, desiring individuals. And this is what is
meant—or, at least, what is believed to be meant—by labor
theories of property. The "socialized labor" or "labor complexity" approach does not seem an effective challenge to
such a contention. It describes labor perhaps but it does not
remove it; it explains but does not explain away. It paints
labor as large and complex, yet that largeness and complexity are simply expressions or forms of that human exertion to which the labor theorist appeals. In short, the argument that discards a labor element as the basis of property
(or of anything else) because the labor involved in economic
production is so inextricable and socially dependent, seems

to be directed along the now customary channel in economics of ignoring universals in the glare of particulars.

The other perplexing attitude of contemporary economics that is illustrated in this attack upon a labor theory of property will return us to the ethical question. That attitude seems to be the strict literalness with which the science approaches any suggestion of ethical judgment.[74] A labor theory of property, for instance, is repudiated by economics because of its "technical" difficulties, when the fact is that the essence of such an approach is not technological at all; it is a sincere attempt at valuation. Property must be justified as well as accepted, and the labor theorist is striving to find a criterion, a sanction. It would, of course, be quite unfair to state that modern economics is not interested in ethical judgments, but it is perhaps not wrong to feel that the descriptive emphasis has become so dominant that values may seem all but mythological. If not mythological, they appear at any rate (except to the more pragmatic of economic theorists) nothing more than the remnants of a metaphysical era. But a labor theory of property must not be taken in too literal or metaphysical a sense, and that seems to be what economists have done. It is a doctrine of "should" and "ought"—just as was the approach of Rodbertus to his labor theory of value—and its interpretation must invoke some degree of instrumentalism. May it not be said, to suggest a possible compromise approach, that the real test or measure of labor value is contribution to social utility? That is, cannot a labor theory of property be modified so as to include the social use of that which is produced, so that merely working, e. g., piling up sand in the desert, does not constitute a property claim? The labor which is the basis of property must be labor that meets the needs of society. This, at least, is a conceivable reconciliation of these two theories, one that avoids the

[74] For this whole matter see *infra*, Chap. IX.

divorce of the genetic from the functional approaches. There is no intention here of elaborating this point any further, especially since it will be handled in a later chapter, but it is necessary to mention one other thought. That will be the recognition that this whole discussion does not by any means imply an instrumentalist interpretation of George's own doctrine of natural rights, especially the natural labor right of property. Undoubtedly there is the temptation, especially for one sympathetic to social instrumentalism, to make such an interpretation, but it is realized that George's phrasing of natural rights is in terms of absolute values. His descriptive emphasis is too strong to be explained as presenting nothing more than a reformulation of ethical concepts in terms of an economic vocabulary, and his absolutistic approach appears too rigorous to be suggestive of any experimentalist technique. But that criticism of absolutism does not necessarily carry over to every labor theory of property.

In fact, it must be recognized that there is the possibility of a twofold interpretation of the whole place of ethics in George's work. One would insist that George's entire scheme of economic reasoning was but a corollary of his system of ethics, or rather that his approach to economics was in terms of an underlying and more fundamental dimension of morals. That interpretation would look upon his appeal to natural rights, specifically the natural right to property founded upon a labor basis, as an attempt to rephrase, in the light of ethics, the more traditional "metaphysical" status of such rights. In other words, George's entire philosophy, it would be held, was an ethical philosophy with economics acting as but the instrument for the achievement of the ethical goals that were always the motivating vision shining before his work. On the other hand, there is an emphasis that regards George's exposition as largely descriptive, and that looks upon his appeal to ethics as an attempt to defend his political solution by rational sanctions. The point mentioned a few pages back, referring to the contrast between processes (economics) and solutions (politics) would be stressed by such an interpretation. It would be argued that George's examination of the economic structure was essentially a descriptive examination of what he felt to be the natural processes of production and distribution, and required none of the apologetics of ethics, but the solution which demanded (politically) a conscious change in our economic organization must be justified in terms of ethical sanctions; hence his appeal to moral criteria. George, in other words, according to this view, was trying to reconcile his political solution with the terms of current philosophy, so that *if* the right to the product of labor exists, the right to property in land does not. Of course, even this latter approach could in no way challenge what has been stated in the opening chapter as the dominant "ethical" orientation in George's work, namely, the conviction that the economic and social background provided the conditioning element in man's moral life; it is simply the belief of such an approach that ethics *qua* ethics did not play a conscious part in George's economic analysis.

It does not seem necessary, in this particular connection, to enter further into that type of conflicting interpretation, especially since George's ethical sanction for the socialization of rent has not yet been given exposition. Granted a premise such as the labor theory of property, that exposition must be evident. With such a premise George can draw a great dualistic classification of property, a classification that clearly separates landed property from property in wealth, i. e., property in the products of labor. The one, property in land, can have no ethical justification, since it has no labor basis. Yet, by that very fact, it may be argued by George that land value, or economic rent, *does* belong to society, since to society is due its creation, just as to the individual there is due the product of his labor. Not only from this negative standpoint is the private ownership of land unjustified, but George feels that it generates a positive injustice in its appropriation of the one source from which labor must operate. Land is not produced by labor but labor must produce from land, and the ownership of land therefore means the control of labor. Landed property thus involves a double injustice.

This right of ownership that springs from labor excludes the possibility of any other right of ownership. If a man be rightfully entitled to the produce of his labor, then no one can be rightfully entitled to the ownership of anything which is not the produce of his labor, or the product of some one else from whom the right has passed to him. If production gives to the producer the right to exclusive possession and enjoyment, there can rightfully be no exclusive possession and enjoyment of anything not the production of labor, and the recognition of private property in land is a wrong . . . When non-producers can claim as rent a portion of the wealth created by producers, the right of the producers to the fruits of their labor is to that extent denied.

There is no escape from this position. To affirm that a man can rightfully claim exclusive ownership in his own labor when embodied in material things is to deny that any one can rightfully claim exclusive ownership in land. . . .

The essential character of the one class of things (capital) is that they embody labor, are brought into being by human exertion, their existence or non-existence, their increase or diminution, depending on man. The essential character of the other class of things (land) is that they do not embody labor, and exist irrespective of human exertion and irrespective of man; they are the field or environment in which man finds himself; the storehouse from which his needs must be supplied, the raw material upon which and the forces with which alone his labor can act.

The moment this distinction is realized, that moment is it seen that the sanction which natural justice gives to one species of property is denied to the other; that the rightfulness which attaches to individual property in the produce of labor implies the wrongfulness of individual property in land; that, whereas the recognition of the one places all men upon equal terms, securing to each the due reward of his labor, the recognition of the other is the denial of the equal rights of men, permitting those who do not labor to take the natural reward of those who do.[75]

The natural rights argument, then, to which George appeals involved more than this right of a man to the product of his labor, and more than the inferred failure of landed property thereby to measure up to a labor criterion. It introduces, in addition, the metaphysical and ethical position that by the very fact of man's presence he acquires certain privileges and demands that are violated by the individual appropriation of land. The ownership of land meant the ownership of men, "for the right to the produce of labor cannot be enjoyed without the right to the free use of the opportunities offered by nature, and to admit the right of property in these is to deny the right of property in the produce of labor." [76] This was a corollary of George's insistence upon the dependency of labor on land. Men are slaves whether their bodies are actually owned, or whether their opportunities to labor are exploited by other individuals. There was, for him, a necessary connection between labor and land, between production and the source of production; hence control of land, of the source of production, implied control of production. Private property in land was of the same ethical character as private property in men.

For as labor cannot produce without the use of land, the denial of the equal right to the use of land is necessarily the denial of the right of labor to its own produce. If one man can command the land upon which others must produce, he can appropriate the

[75] *Progress and Poverty*, pp. 334–336.
[76] *Ibid.*, p. 334.

produce of their labor as the price of his permission to labor. . . .
If chattel slavery be unjust, then is private property in land unjust.[77]

A point that should be suggested here is the insistence that
this selection by George of land and labor as the original and
primary economic elements (a selection, to refer back to a
previous distinction, which places capital in a secondary position) must introduce the more strictly philosophical problem of nature as physical and as human. There is a very
neat logical consistency present in George's selection of
"nature," e. g., "natural laws" and "natural rights," as his
philosophical basis. Nature in its physical aspect was land
(land meaning, of course, all of man's physical environment);
in its human aspect Nature was labor. All economic processes could be reduced to the fundamental operation of one
of these elements upon the other. Whether or not such a
logical classification within "nature" is appealing to modern
economics, it must be recognized as a distinction that reaches
into the very heart of the age-old problem of man's relationship to his physical surroundings, and one, moreover, that
attempts to translate that interrelation from its comfortable
place in metaphysics to the realm of political economy. It
is this concept of the double aspect of nature that, perhaps,
is the thought at the basis of all "physiocracies," and it is
here suggested as one that offers a more ambitious and profound foundation for labor theories of property than has
usually been granted them.

In this labor theory of property, therefore, and in the argument from natural rights, George found his ethical sanction
for the socialization of rent—a sanction which, as has been
pointed out, may be interpreted as a consciously attempted
justification of a political program, or as the statement of a
fundamental ethical-economic process. That ethical justifi-

[77] *Ibid.*, pp. 339; 345.

cation (or description) is one that has been based upon an ambitious evaluation of property forms, an evaluation directed largely by the completely social character of the factor of land value. The attribute of social is one that applies so specifically and characteristically and significantly to the element of earth surface value that the inclusion of land value in the categories of "individual" and "private" seemed to George as the major economic paradox. He therefore emphasized a property distinction, social in origin and ethical in phrasing, that could point to the unique status of land and thus to the justice of rent socialization proposals.

Before concluding this discussion of ethical sanctions it is of course necessary to recognize that perhaps the most bitter attacks upon George's economic proposals have likewise been formulated in ethical terms. George has been designated as "such a Preacher of Unrighteousness as the world has never before seen," and his proposals have met with the most amazingly savage reception in some quarters because of their "profligate conclusions" and "the unutterable meanness of their gigantic villainy." However, to mention a more sober ethical criticism of George's suggestions, one that is representative of a good bit of the unsympathetic approach to his work, there may be introduced the controversial matter of compensation. The words of Professor Davenport may be considered typical:

Confiscation, at any rate, a program which shall impose on any casual present owner of original natural bounty the penalty for a general and institutional blunder, appears to me to be an incredibly unethical position for a school of thinkers whose essential doctrine is one of practical ethics. . . . The general condemnation—my condemnation also—of the single-tax demand for the confiscation of past increment rests substantially on the conviction that an institutional situation—long established and generally recognized rules of the competitive game—should constitute a social obligation to protect the player who proceeds in conformity with the rule and in reliance upon it. If some change needs be made, if a reform is to come, the society that established the institution, rather than the individual who uncritically acquiesced in it, must bear the costs of getting over to the better way.[78]

The answer of George to this argument based on the landowner's good faith is typical of the rigorous, uncompromising nature of his general approach. In this matter of compensation or of socializing only future rent, the major defect, for him, was the "impossibility of bridging over by any compromise the radical difference between wrong and right." Land is social opportunity or it is not. Land should be administered in the interest of society, or it should not.

If the land of any country belongs to the people of that country, what right, in morality and justice, have the individuals called land owners to the rent? If the land belongs to the people, why in the name of morality and justice should the people pay its salable value for their own? . . . Justice in men's mouths is cringingly humble when she first begins a protest against a time-honored wrong, and we of the English-speaking nations still wear the collar of the Saxon thrall, and have been educated to look upon the "vested rights" of land owners with all the superstitious reverence that ancient Egyptians looked upon the crocodile.[79]

Private appropriation of rent, for George, is robbery, not robbery of the past but robbery of the present. Every bit

[78] "Theoretical Issues in the Single Tax," mentioned above; pp. 2, 7. See also pp. 8 ff.

This matter of the difficulty in doing justice to those who have invested in land has made even some of those who have realized the significance of land's socially unearned increment, such as the Mills and Herbert Spencer, advocate not so much compensation as the socialization only of future unearned income. (See also the discussion of "increment taxes," *infra,* Chap. VIII, *passim.*) The same idea is expressed by Davenport: "I believe also that all times have been propitious times, the present a right time no less than any earlier time, for establishing the provision that future increments of earning power from natural resources shall not be permitted to fall into the hands of private owners." (*Ibid.,* p. 1.) Compare also the statements of other present-day economists, particularly Professor Taussig: *Principles of Economics* (New York, Macmillan, 1924 ed.), Vol. II, especially pp. 108 ff., and also pp. 81 and 106.

[79] *Progress and Poverty,* pp. 361–362; 360.

of creative enterprise pays it tribute. It takes its toll from each stage of production. Why should robbery be paid to cease its depredations? "Because I was robbed yesterday, and the day before, and the day before that, is it any reason that I should conclude that the robber has acquired a vested right to rob me?" [80] That legal possession of land has been recognized is no answer, according to George, to the moral accusations that he has brought against landed property, for the claim of compensation, he points out, is on moral grounds. The State perhaps may be morally obligated to compensate—at least that argument can be made—but it is clearly not legally obligated, since the State would not be invalidating any contractual agreement; it would simply be withdrawing its support from the continuance of an expected practice.[81] It is on a moral basis alone that compensation can be pressed, and if property in land has no ethical justification, as George feels he has demonstrated, then compensation for land whose value is to be taken in taxation has no moral justification.

But compensation would be as little expedient as it would be moral. George insists that the payment of the landowner (obviously through the medium of funds raised by taxation or bonds) would be only a continuation, at least for the present and the immediate future, of the policy of benefiting the "owner" of land out of the pockets of the rest of the population.

Just in proportion as the interests of the land holders are conserved, just in that proportion must general interests and general rights be disregarded, and if land holders are to lose nothing of their special privileges, the people at large can gain nothing. To buy up individual property rights would merely be to give the

[80] *Progress and Poverty*, p. 363.

[81] Legal theorists have always made a distinction between property in land and property in labor products; there is always the State as the prime landowner.

land holders in another form a claim of the same kind and amount that their possession of land now gives them; it would be to raise for them by taxation the same proportion of the earnings of labor and capital that they are now enabled to appropriate in rent.[82]

Not only would gain from the abolition of the private appropriation of rent be reserved for the future, but in addition that postponement would be lengthened by the inclusion of the expectation of future increase in land values in the present market price. Compensation, for George, would thus defeat the very purpose of the socialization of rent.

Questions of compensation, however, can obviously arise only after the more primary ethical character of landed property has been determined—and determined negatively.[83] This is illustrated in Professor Davenport's article in which the failure of George's proposals to square with the land-owner's good faith in existing property institutions is cited as its most damaging moral characteristic; such an accusation, however, is made only after there has been at least a partial recognition of the soundness of the ethical attacks upon land as a category of private and individual wealth. In contrast with Davenport's contention that the good faith of the "player of the game" is the chief barrier to what otherwise might be an acceptable ethical basis for the single tax, the more usual moral attack upon George's scheme, as repre-

---

[82] *Progress and Poverty*, p. 358.

[83] As George puts it: "The idea of compensation is raised and has importance only where it serves as a secondary defense of private property in land. If a man believes in private property in land, it is needless to address to him any argument for the necessity of compensation on its abolition. . . . But if he has come to doubt its justice and to favor its abolition, then the raising of the question of compensation, as though it were a new and separate moral question, may serve the purpose of a second embankment or second ditch in military defense. . . . Thus the idea of compensation with which we are concerned is the idea of compensation for the abolition of something in itself conceded to be wrong." (*A Perplexed Philosopher*, pp. 221–222.)

sented, for example, by Professor Seligman,[84] really never calls upon this secondary defense of good faith or implied compensation, since the first-line ethical trenches, it is held, have not yet been stormed. Thus, once the topic of compensation has been introduced an advance clearly has been made, and it would almost appear that a demand for compensation or for respecting the good faith of the owner of land might be welcomed by the follower of George, for it would definitely indicate that the opposition was perhaps ready for a change.

The most helpful attitude, undoubtedly, with which to approach a matter such as compensation is to treat it, not in the uncompromising fashion of George, but with the realization that it constitutes one of those points of adjustment that would be required by any drastic social change, and that a detailed and intelligent discussion of it must follow, not precede, the more fundamental question of the acceptability of private property in land.

This whole matter of compensation has been presented as an example of one of the more usual ethical attacks upon George's doctrines, although it has been seen that it is not a fundamental moral attack. If George's proposals are to be branded as essentially immoral, there must first be understood and met his ethical distinction between earned and unearned income. The claim that all recognized property institutions must be granted the same status, or the introduction of the argument that other wealth and income besides that accruing from land is unearned, are largely legalistic rather than ethical matters. To meet George's demands, the attack must at least be directed in terms of his labor theory of property, in terms, that is, of the recognition of some form of moral standard, and not in those of legal expediency.

[84] See particularly *Essays in Taxation* (New York, Macmillan, 10th ed., 1928), pp. 79 ff.

That type of standard, for George, determined that income arising from land was social and therefore individually unearned, and thus the focus of his ethical judgment is definitely placed within his basic twofold property distinction. This, for many, may be an unacceptable location, but if it is to be answered it must at least be met on its own ground. Ethical objections which introduce other dimensions may be significant in the light of other property distinctions, but they neglect the dualism that George has attempted to establish between the categories of earned and unearned.

The ethical sanctions that lay behind his proposal to socialize rent were George's first consideration. He could perhaps have stressed the tragic inefficiency of permitting the vast increment created upon land by the press and activity of men to be diverted to the possession of a fortunate few, thereby forcing social agencies to support themselves, not by tapping this product of social processes, but by levying toll upon the product of labor. Or he could have dwelled upon the comic but unæsthetic claim of man to "own" the earth. But he reserved his major emphasis for an ethical approach. "That alone is wise which is just; that alone is enduring which is right." Expediency depended upon ethics. It will be necessary, however, to say a word also in reference to the fiscal, "expedient" sanctions that George found as justification for his single tax.

His proposal to socialize rent was in terms of taxation, and therefore there must be raised immediately the perplexing question as to what constitutes the "canons of taxation." Disputes in this field almost rival the classic economic controversies over wealth, value and property, and, of course, there can be no attempt here to do anything more than suggest the place in that type of dispute occupied by George's taxation proposals.

Perhaps the most significant and typical cleavage occurring within taxation theory—typical and significant, at least, from the standpoint of the present discussion—is that which ranges "benefit" or "privilege" theories on the one side, and what may be termed "political" or "functional" theories on the other. According to the one, which possibly may be more appropriately designated as classical, the only legitimate justification for taxation is found in the fact that social organization definitely brings about certain benefits and privileges that accrue to individuals. There is, as it were, a social service that confers aids upon individuals through the existence of the economies made possible by a political structure, and therefore, the argument runs, the fiscal support of government should be drawn from such individual benefits, presumably in proportion to the social service that is rendered. The opposing type of theory is simply the more or less cold-blooded recognition that, as it has been put, we pay taxes because "the State is part of us." Taxation is an integral function of a political organization. It has a "physical" justification as a process and needs no ethical backing such as that proposed by benefit or privilege approaches. The problem of taxation is an *ad hoc* problem and requires none of the apologetics of ethics. Hence, the apportionment of taxation is not to be determined by any benefit technique but by direct and arbitrary (it is admitted) measures, such, for example, as the ability to pay.

It is quite evident that George's taxation proposals must be ranked under the general classification of benefit or privilege theories. Land values are social benefits, the privileges that result from the interaction of social forces, and therefore they should be the sole basis and source of taxation. Ground rent represents the precise degree to which society has coöperated to produce values; it is the measure of social progress. The rent of land is an exact measure of the unearned privileges that accrue to the owner of land through political and economic organization, and therefore it is consummately fitting that such rent be applied to defray the expenses of the political organization. In fact, this is the only ethical basis that George finds for the very existence of taxation. Taxation, just as everything else, must be justified and not merely accepted, and the only justification was that social fiscal requirements be met out of a social product. There was a supreme neatness in the application of economic rent to the category of taxation. Here was a fund that no individual was instrumental in creating, yet it reverted in our present economic order to individuals; taxation was intended for social purposes, yet in our present economic order society depended upon the contributions (rather sacrificial offerings) of individuals out of individual earnings, without attempting significantly or appreciably to tap the fund that society itself produced. Apply social increment to social purposes, and George felt the taxation problem was clearly and simply solved.

This benefit conception of taxation is explicitly formulated by George in his fourth canon of taxation, i. e., "That it [taxation] bear equally—so as to give no citizen an advantage or put any at a disadvantage, as compared with others," [85] to which he adds, "the tax upon land values is . . . the most just and equal of all taxes. It falls only upon those who receive from society a peculiar and valuable benefit, and upon them in proportion to the benefit they receive. It is the taking by the community, for the use of the community, of that value which is the creation of the community. It is the application of the common property to common uses." [86] He here criticizes Adam Smith's earliest "ability to pay" theory, that "the subjects of every State ought to contribute toward the support of the Government as nearly as possible in pro-

[85] *Progress and Poverty,* p. 406.   [86] *Ibid.,* pp. 418–419.

portion to their respective abilities; that is, in proportion
to the revenue which they respectively enjoy under the protection of the State," and endeavors to show that the only
type of revenue or value enjoyed "under the protection of
the State" is that which owes its existence to social organization; that is to say, the only type of revenue or value which
is solely dependent upon government is that which is *not*
created by labor. It is of course true that all property and
all value, all revenue and all labor, are dependent in a vital
sense upon social organization, but, as was mentioned in
another connection, such a dependence is so broadly obvious
that its recognition is rather truistic; it is simply the recognition that without an economic order there would be no economic order, hence none of the economic categories. Labor
values would certainly not be present *qua* values were they
divorced from social organization, but they would still represent the expenditure of human exertion irrespective of their
background. On the other hand, land values, according to
George, alone were enjoyed "under the protection of the
State," since they were completely the product of society;
therefore, the incomes arising from land values alone "ought
to contribute toward the support of the Government as nearly
as possible in proportion to their respective abilities."

That a tax on land values would coincide with the benefits
and privileges that society confers upon individuals, benefits
and privileges that are directly and precisely expressed by
such values, was not by any means, however, the sole practical advantage that George found in his plan to socialize
rent by taxation. There were three other "canons" that he
felt were essential fiscal criteria by which taxation proposals
must be judged. They were:

That it [the tax] bear as lightly as possible upon production—
so as least to check the increase of the general fund from which
taxes must be paid and the community maintained.

That it be easily and cheaply collected, and fall as directly as may be upon the ultimate payers—so as to take from the people as little as possible in addition to what it yields the Government.

That it be certain—so as to give the least opportunity for tyranny or corruption on the part of officials, and the least temptation to law-breaking and evasion on the part of the taxpayers.[87]

The taxation of land values, tried by such canons—along with that of benefit and equality—was held by George to be secure and expedient; it was sanctioned fiscally as well as ethically.

As to George's first canon, it must be clear that there is a vital distinction between a tax upon a social increment such as that of the value of land, and taxes which fall upon production or upon the income or wealth arising from production. The latter type, which, of course, makes up the great bulk of our revenue system, must necessarily hinder productive enterprise. The "power of destruction" that is inherent in taxation may be accounted for by its restrictive and inhibitory tendencies upon production. Taxes which fall upon either the processes or the products of labor must tend to discourage labor, must curtail the production of wealth. They raise an artificial barrier that must be hurdled by the forces involved in the creation of goods. Taxes on production are a drain upon production. A tax on land values, however, not only fails to hinder production, but acts as a definite stimulant. Land value is not a labor-produced value; its creation is an automatic and gratuitous function of society, and therefore its disposition in terms of taxation could have no negative effect upon the processes involved in the production of wealth by labor. If taxation is to bear as lightly as possible upon production and if society is to cease crippling itself by the continued sapping of wealth through taxation, then the social collection of revenue must be shifted, is

[87] *Progress and Poverty*, p. 406.

George's warning, from that levied against the product of labor to that which makes use of the social fund of land values.[88]

A tax must be easily and cheaply collected and it must be direct, i. e., must fall upon the ultimate payers without any shifting of incidence, is George's second canon. That a tax upon land values cannot be shifted is admitted by almost every economist, including George's most bitter critics. The value of land depends upon its relation to marginal land, or, to put it more simply, upon the supply of available land in proportion to the demand; and as a tax upon land in no way can decrease the supply of land, the owner of land cannot add the tax to the price or to the rent of land. Land taxes cannot enter into rent as an item of increase, since rent is determined antecedently to such taxation and by factors in which a tax does not play a part. This unshiftability of a land tax is almost universally recognized as one of its significant advantages, although a similar unanimity, however, has not been accorded to George's contention that a tax on land values may be simply and efficiently administered—[89]

[88] "Taxes levied upon the value of land cannot check production in the slightest degree, until they exceed rent, or the value of land, taken annually, for unlike taxes upon commodities, or exchange, or capital, or any of the tools or processes of production, they do not bear upon production. The value of land does not express the reward of production, as does the value of crops, of cattle, of buildings, or any of the things which are styled personal property and improvements. It expresses the exchange value of monopoly. It is not in any case the creation of the individual who owns the land; it is created by the growth of the community. Hence the community can take it all without in any way lessening the production of wealth. Taxes may be imposed upon the value of land until all rent is taken by the State without reducing the wages of labor or the reward of capital one iota; without increasing the price of a single commodity, or making production in any way more difficult. . . . Tax manufactures, and the effect is to check manufacturing; tax improvements, and the effect is to lessen improvement; tax commerce, and the effect is to prevent exchange; tax capital, and the effect is to drive it away." (*Progress and Poverty*, pp. 410–412.)

[89] It is not within the scope of this exposition to present or attempt to answer the technical, fiscal objections to George's canons of taxation. Such objections may be found in any economic text, although for a suggestion of objections which are a bit removed from the trite and usual approach, there may be mentioned Professor Davenport's otherwise sympathetic article

that is his third canon, certainty. George feels that a tax on rent could be accurately assessed, and that it would thereby remove the ludicrous corruption and perjury, international in proportion, that are so integral a part of import duties, internal revenues, and income and general property taxes.

In concluding this mention of George's "canons of taxation," those fiscal sanctions behind his revenue system, it may be in point to suggest that in a real sense *his single tax is not a tax at all.* A tax definitely connotes some levy, characteristically of an arbitrary and opportunistic nature, that government is forced to make upon the productive powers of industry in order to support itself. Taxation implies a process of self-mutilation; the popular reaction to it as a necessary evil (to use the most polite of expressions) is perhaps largely a correct characterization. The idea of George, however, was clearly to remove from society the onus that taxation of any kind imposes; it was an attempt to make automatic and self-operative the process of defraying social expenditures. Economic rent was to be directed into public instead of private repositories, and was to be employed in meeting public needs instead of swelling private gains. There was essentially no taxation involved here, that is, no taxation in terms of governmental interference. Instead there was to be simply a direct flow of revenue from the social source of land value to that agency which was responsible for the financing of social needs. It is true that such an agency would be, largely, our present form of government, and also that the flow of revenue would be through the existing channels of taxation; the technical functioning of George's proposal would obviously be by means of a taxation system. But it seems definite that there is a clear distinction between a "single tax" in the light

(op. cit.). George himself attempts very briefly to meet some of the more usual objections (see especially Chap. IV of Book VIII of *Progress and Poverty*), particularly the one involving the difficulty of separating land value from the value of improvements.

of George's interpretation, and a "single tax" [90] which might be tested solely as a variety of our present tax species. The former is a tax simply in structure; its essence and function, however, are something quite different from simply an improvised system of taxation, and it must not be judged solely by criteria which are limited to those of a fiscal nature. George's vision was rather, in the words of Professor Davenport, "not a society single-taxed, but a society free from all

[90] One objection to George's fiscal proposals that may be discussed briefly in this connection is that directed against the "singleness" character of his tax. A major difficulty brought forward by economists is that any "single" tax constitutes a poor fiscal policy. No matter what be the nature of the revenue, academic experts point out, inelasticity is a damaging quality of any tax that is imposed to the exclusion of all others. In fact, in many of the standard arguments against the socialization of rent, it is this "singleness" that attracts the greater share of criticism. Even where there is a tacit approval of a tax on land values—which is found in almost every discussion of the subject—there is always made the sharp distinction between such a tax on land values and a "single" tax, and the arguments in favor of the one are never allowed to carry over for the other. This type of separation ignores the point that is being made above, i. e., that George's proposals involve something more than a taxation scheme; they are essentially agencies for social reform and not simply taxation variations. They are of a piece, for example, with Hobson's continued insistence that all forms of "social surplus," of unearned increment, be amenable to social uses through the agency of taxation. Such a suggestion is much more than a contribution to taxation discussion.

The more specific fiscal attacks upon the inelasticity of any single tax point out that a system of taxation must be able to expand and contract to meet the variable demand for revenue, and that therefore any fiscal income must depend upon diversified incidence of taxation. Government should not have to rely upon one source for its income. Some critics suggest that the revenue derived from land values would be insufficient to defray the expenses of society, and certainly would be unable to meet emergency demands such as those of war. Others, however, hold that the collection of the total ground rent would create a large surplus that would provide a tempting field for corrupt practices! But in either case, the general criticism is that a system of taxation must be elastic. It may be mentioned, however, that land values, for example, of the City of New York are more than sufficient to meet its governmental expenditures. The assessed valuation of land in New York City (1932) is approximately nine billion dollars, which on a 5 per cent capitalization indicates that 450 million dollars of the annual rent of land (actual and potential) is retained by the owners of land; while the city collects, at the average tax rate of 2.68 per cent for all boroughs, 240 million dollars of the annual rent of land. This discloses an actual and potential annual land rent in the City of New York of 690 million dollars. The budget of New York City, admittedly extravagant, is 631 million dollars. Proponents of the single tax claim that the abolition of taxes on buildings and improvements, together with the abolition of income, tariff and excise taxes,

taxes of any sort"—(to which he adds, "a goal well within the reach of a wise and provident public policy.") [91] This is not to say, of course, that the single tax of George either is not susceptible to testing by fiscal sanctions or that it is condemned by them; the attempt has been made to relate his proposal to certain clear canons of taxation. The point that is being made here is rather that the proposal to socialize rent definitely transcends the taxation dimension. Indeed, the phrase "rent socialization" would seem a more felicitous one than "single tax," since it perhaps would connote something larger than mere fiscal characteristics.

And this type of socialization, for George, was the only variety required to produce a healthy economic order. The diverting of rent from individual to social termini afforded the necessary compromise between George's fierce demand for "individualism" and his equally zealous insistence upon a socially directed economic system. Such a compromise may recall the point that was mentioned in another connec-

will immediately reflect itself in an increase in land values and therefore in an increase in land rent and that rent will then be equal to the requirements of Federal, State and local governments. And it does not seem necessary to discuss the converse argument that a surplus would prove dangerous. As for the general inelastic character of a single tax on land values and the fact that occasional emergencies would have to be met, it may be admitted—although such admission would hardly be accepted by the more orthodox of George's followers—that a land value tax would permit of the levying of other taxes when serious expansion of revenue was demanded. That is to say, it is felt that the value of a proposal to socialize rent should not be clouded by the possibility that its inelastic character as a tax might not be adjustable to all exigencies. However, the single taxer will point out that in a fundamental sense a sole tax on land values is highly elastic since it varies directly with the progress and demands of any taxpaying and tax-requiring community.

[91] (Op. cit., p. 1.) The same point, i. e., that the single tax is "not a tax at all," was made by Professor Davenport in an address on "The Taxation of Unearned Increment" delivered before the National Conference on State and Local Taxation at Columbus, Ohio, November, 1907. The address was later printed as a pamphlet by the National Tax Association.

(In the former article in The American Economic Review, he concludes his paper with these gracious words: "Not less perhaps for us single taxers of the looser observance than for our fellows of the stricter faith, is it to be desired that we continually exercise ourselves in the amenities of discussion." P. 30.)

tion referring to George's interpretation of "common property in land." It was suggested then that his method offered something radically different from the programs of land nationalization or agrarian communism with which his name has so often been linked. George's taxation proposals sought to retain the nominal individual ownership of land, while at the same time they attempted to direct the economic product of land into social channels. Now, it must be realized that the collection of the annual ground rent of land by the State through taxation agencies would have the literal effect of destroying even individual "ownership," since the purchase price of land would really vanish, and "sale" and "purchase" of land would have little or no significance. But George's contention was that individual "ownership" and individual "administration" of land were vitally dissimilar. Private property in land instead of being essential for, was inconsistent with, the best use of land. The thesis that George essays to defend in opening his discussion of "the application of the remedy" [92] is that the security required for human labor upon land was not that which resulted from absolute ownership of land, but that which was the product of the inviolability of improvements. Security for the *product* of labor, not security for mere land, the product of nothing human, was essential for the unimpeded expenditure of human effort.

There is a delusion resulting from the tendency to confound the accidental with the essential—a delusion which the law writers have done their best to extend, and political economists generally have acquiesced in, rather than endeavored to expose—that private property in land is necessary to the proper use of land, and that again to make land common property would be to destroy civilization and revert to barbarism.[93]

[92] *Progress and Poverty,* Book VIII, particularly Chap. I.
[93] *Ibid.,* p. 395.

That delusion was similar to an old Chinese custom, as reported by Charles Lamb, the custom of burning down dwellings in order to secure the ineffable delicacies of roast pig. But though a sage was necessary to teach Ho-ti and his disciples that arson and cookery were two generically different categories, it requires no sage, argues George, to point out that ownership and use are as clearly separable. Is not the ubiquitous phenomenon of tenant cultivation a definite refutation (a refutation so clear as to be perhaps ignored) of the belief that private property in land is necessary to the proper use of land? [94] "Would not all this land be cultivated and improved just as well if the rent went to the State or municipality, as now, when it goes to private individuals? If no private ownership in land were acknowledged, but all land were held in this way, the occupier or user paying rent to the State, would not land be used and improved as well and securely as now?" [95] Ownership is one thing and use another. Under George's plan individuals could indeed "own" land—although that type of "ownership" would be technical and legalistic, virtual not factual—but the use of land involves another dimension.

What is necessary for the unrestricted use of land is that the improvements upon land, improvements of labor, and not the land itself, be made secure for the individual. [96] A man

[94] Buildings in large cities are erected by investors on long-term leases, twenty-one, forty-two, ninety-nine years, with the knowledge that at the end of that time the building reverts to the landowner. These are investments which involve millions of dollars. Would such investors be any less disposed to build if the land remained "theirs" to use permanently upon the annual payment of rent in taxes?

[95] *Progress and Poverty*, p. 396.

[96] "It is not necessary to say to a man, 'this land is yours,' in order to induce him to cultivate it or improve it. It is only necessary to say to him, 'whatever your labor or capital produces on this land shall be yours.' Give a man security that he may reap, and he will sow; assure him the possession of the house he wants to build, and he will build it. These are the natural rewards of labor. It is for the sake of the reaping that men sow; it is for the sake of possessing houses that men build. The ownership of land has nothing to do with it." (*Progress and Poverty*, p. 396.)

must be guaranteed that the fruits of his labor are secure, and with that guarantee safe, George is sure that no other is needed. It is not the magic of property but the magic of security to labor that is the stimulus for productive effort. Property itself, in George's approach, is nothing but the legal recognition of such security to labor; that is, property can alone rightfully inhere in the products of human exertion. Men would not refuse to produce nor would civilization revert to barbarism were the essence of private property in land extracted through the socialization of rent. As long as man can use land and profit through its use, it matters not where the ownership is located. The paradoxical fact, maintains George, is that private property instead of contributing to the use of land is actually a deterrent, and stands in the way of the proper administration of Nature's bounty to man. Land is held out of use by its owners either for speculative purposes or because of inability to make improvements, or out of mere caprice. Were land taxed to its full yearly rental value, it would be necessarily forced into use, and George feels that the fact of its ownership being "common" instead of "individual" would definitely forward, and not retard, the full and correct employment of land. "If the best use of land be the test, then private property in land is condemned, as it is condemned by every other consideration. It is as wasteful and uncertain a mode of securing the proper use of land as the burning down of houses is of roasting pigs." [97]

George thus attempts to socialize rent and to retain, at the same time, the individualized use of land. This compromise is a significant one. Not merely will it provide the necessity for contrasting his work with socialism itself, but it will point the way for what he felt would be the economic effects of his solution. Those effects will necessarily reside in that

[97] *Progress and Poverty*, p. 400.

"coöperated" mutual realm where society administers that which belongs to society, and the individual, considered as a creature possessing "ethical" natural rights, retains that property which has been justified in terms of a labor sanction.

To conclude, then, George's economic solution, it will be seen that in the private ownership of land, more specifically in the private appropriation of land values, George located the genesis of the persistence of poverty amid advancing wealth and progress. In the social collection of ground rent through taxation, he located the solution of that economic paradox. It was a solution that he hoped would be not merely a saner approach to our very muddled tax system; it was directed rather to straightening the mischievous tangle in the distribution of wealth. That is why George attempted to elaborate, in classical, deductive terms, a completely integrated interpretation of the science of economics. Poverty was not an *ad hoc* problem. It was the symptom of economic disease. That disease was a form of strangulation; the factors in the distribution of wealth, particularly wages, had been effectively throttled by the operations of rent. The "single tax" was not an *ad hoc* solution. It was the attempt to direct the flow of economic processes into more "natural" channels.

CHAPTER IV

BACKGROUND AND ORIGINALITY

An idea that has reached any degree of maturity has, in the course of its historical development, both borrowed freely and given generously, often borrowing without presuming to acknowledge and giving without a demand for recognition. Quite indifferently the stream of thought seems to flow past, drawing upon many nameless rivulets and supplying a host of unknown fountains; it becomes self-conscious and perhaps a bit vain—that is, if a stream can become so without irreparably disturbing its metaphorical balance—only when subjected to critical interpretation. In other words, the evolution of thought is essentially a cumulative process, and the precise contributions of individual originality are of more importance to biography than to history; they are incidental if the viewpoint is that of a social, cultural process. When psychologists as well as historians intimate that strictly original ideas may well be grouped under the class of fables, they undoubtedly have in mind the dominance of this stream of cultural experience. Certainly there can be no attempt to divorce creative effort from its connection with the general movement of thought or from its ideational background— from that accumulated mass of data preserved and transmitted, often unconsciously, by social agencies; but just as certainly, originality, if the word is to have any meaning, cannot be divested of its peculiar function of reacting, and in a formative manner, upon that intellectual background. If it is not creative in any nicely discriminating use of the

162

term, it is at least reconstructive, and in the history of ideas it is this reworking of given concepts, this reconstructive synthesizing, amending, often distorting, of borrowed thoughts that have taken upon themselves the mantle of originality.

Only in such a sense, then, were the ideas of Henry George original. For him as an individual they were, for the most part, new—startlingly new; they were a vision and a revelation. Yet in the stream of thought they had been flowing for ages. For George they were a synthesis of his own creation, a gathering together of all the intimations that had been suggested by laissez-faire economics, but that synthesis, with different backgrounds and all unknown to George, had been anticipated with disconcerting similarity some half dozen times. The lands that George found had been trod before, yet it was with a feeling of companionship and not of chagrin that he came across an occasional footprint which showed him that he was not the first visitor to a virgin soil. The few intimations he had that his work was not completely original did not disappoint him; instead he was grateful that others also had been granted the privilege of seeing a truth.

If this were to be a study in the history of an idea rather than an inquiry into the precise contributions of one man to that idea, its focus would be upon the onward sweep of thought and not upon any question of originality or indebtedness. It would concern itself with tracing the progress of a concept that has long been in the mind of man. It is the idea that this earth of ours is something entirely distinct from the general classification of private property and wealth, that land and natural resources are a common fund to be administered for the common welfare, that this planet on which man finds himself is a heritage to all generations of men, and that considerations both of utility and equity demand that it be not parceled out among the few for the exploitation of the many. It is the idea that man, since if he is to live at all he must live upon the earth, be allowed the use of the earth— an idea that has, at least, this characteristic of profundity, its simplicity. But though the scope of this study is not ambitious enough to include such a survey, it must at least give some brief attention to George's anticipators. This thought of his has been traveling the course of all thought, making its appearance against the strangest of backgrounds and flowing along with the queerest of companions. Some day there will be the complete story of its meanderings, and perhaps it may suggest something in the way of utilizing this particular current in the stream of thought for the irrigating of lands that are intellectually arid.

A discussion of the forerunners of Henry George obviously cannot include the complete group of thinkers who have been in some degree concerned with the land problem. The questions that are proffered by the relation of man to the earth are so ubiquitous that they could hardly have failed to have found their way into the thoughts of all men. They are a part of that general storehouse of ideas to which primitive man as well as Isaiah [1] and the Gracchi have been contributors. A sketch of the specific anticipators of George must rather be confined to those who in the course of their speculations have definitely proposed that the expenses of government be defrayed by a tax upon the socially created value of the land,[2] or those whose fundamental approach to political economy and political theory would logically point to such a deduction.[3] The appearance of these heralds of the ideas of Henry George has been so sporadic and culturally discontinuous that

[1] For an interesting account of the Biblical discussions on the land question, see *My Neighbour's Landmark,* by Frederick Verinder (London, Andrew Melrose, 1911).

[2] Strangely enough, it was those precursors of a single tax scheme whose work most specifically resembled that of George with whom he was least acquainted.

[3] Specific brief accounts of the predecessors of George may be found in Samuel Miliken's *Forerunners of Henry George,* pp. 306–343 of *The Single Tax Year Book* (New York, Single Tax Review Publishing Co., 1917), and

a chronological arrangement of their work is scarcely required, especially since the most striking of them, and the only one from whom George was specifically accused of plagiarizing, wrote only thirty years before the publishing of *Progress and Poverty*.

DOVE

In 1850, the same year that Herbert Spencer, himself a remarkable although later a reluctant anticipator of George, wrote in his *Social Statics* that "equity . . . does not permit property in land." Patrick Edward Dove published in London and Edinburgh a limited and anonymous edition of *The Theory of Human Progression and Natural Probability of a Reign of Justice*. Dove was a Scotch landed gentleman, a scholar and a traveler; his book he dedicated to Victor Cousin. *The Theory of Human Progression*[4] is an attempt to trace the elements that have been present in the development of civilization and to discover whether there is hope for the coming of the scriptural millennium. It is largely an ingenious attempt, and one that shows definite traces of post-Kantianism, to reconcile Christianity and the sciences by means of a division of the sciences so fine that they gradually pass from their own realm to that of theology.[5]

Chapter I of *The Single Tax Movement in the United States*, Arthur Nichols Young (Princeton University Press, 1916). Other reference to particular anticipators will be mentioned later in the text. For a general discussion of the land question in political economy see the classic of Gide and Rist in economic history, *passim;* also (more particularly concerning a single tax): Escarra, *Nationalisation du sol et Socialisme* (Paris, 1904), and Dollfus, *Uber die Idee der einzigen Steuer* (Basel, 1897).

[4] The edition used here was printed in New York by the Humboldt Publishing Co., 1895. In 1854 Dove wrote *The Elements of Political Economy*, in which he disclosed that he was the author of the earlier book. Another work of his, *The Logic of the Christian Faith*, appeared in 1856. This was dedicated to Senator Charles Sumner of Massachusetts, an enthusiastic admirer of *The Theory*, which he had had republished in Boston.

[5] Science, for Dove, is the "knowledge of Being," and the sciences may be divided into Politic, Metaphysic, Mathematic, Dynamic, Physic, and Economic. Philosophy, for him, can be separated into Critic, Dikaistic, and Elpistic. (*Theory*, pp. 382 and 405.)

However, in a section entitled "Application of the Theory of Progression in Man's Political Condition," Dove advanced the identical solution that was later proposed by George, and while he did not reach his conclusions through a comprehensive discussion of political economy, yet the line of reasoning that he followed was precisely similar to that used later by George.

First, there is the thought, a basic one with George, that human poverty is not the result of divine neglect, but rather of man's ignorance and his failure to follow natural law:

A large portion of the population is reduced to pauperism, to that fearful state of dependence in which man finds himself a blot on the universe of God—a wretch thrown up by the waves of time, without a use, and without an end, homeless in the presence of the firmament, and helpless in the face of the creation . . . neither do we believe that pauperism comes from God. It is man's doing and man's doing alone. God has abundantly supplied man with all the requisite means of support; and where he cannot find support, we must look, not to the arrangements of the Almighty, but to the arrangements of men, and to the mode in which they have portioned out the earth. To charge the poverty of man on God is to blaspheme the Creator instead of bowing in reverent thankfulness for the profusion of his goodness. He has given enough, abundance, more than sufficient; and if man has not enough, we must look to the mode in which God's gifts have been distributed. . . .

Every department of nature, and of man's phenomenology, has its laws; and if those laws are infringed, evil is the immediate, invariable, and necessary result. And if man's social condition is evil; if we find at one end of society a few thousands of individuals with enormous wealth, for which they work not, and never have worked, and at the other end of society millions belonging to the same country, and born on the same soil, with barely the necessaries of life and too often in abject destitution—there is no other conclusion possible than that this poverty arises from man's social arrangements, and that poor the mass of the population must remain until those arrangements are rectified by knowledge.[6]

[6] *The Theory*, pp. 252–254.

Then, there is the statement of the cause of involuntary poverty, and the prediction of a class struggle, not between capital and labor, but between the landed and the landless, passages which are almost word for word anticipations of many of the pages of *Progress and Poverty*, and which contain the same lofty vigor and the same theological note of prophetic warning:

The evil is expressed in a few words; and, sooner or later, the nation will appreciate it and rectify it. It is "the alienation of the soil from the State, and the consequent taxation of the industry of the country.". . . Gradually and surely has the separation been taking place between the privileged land owner and the unprivileged laborer. And the time will come at last when there shall be but two parties looking each other in the face, and knowing that the destruction of one is an event of necessary occurrence. That event must come. Nor is it in man to stay it or produce it. It will come as the result of the laws that govern nature and that govern man. . . . The population must be destroyed or the land must be opened to their cultivation, and not accorded to the landlord. Of the two parties, one must give way. One must sink, to rise no more; one must disappear from the earth. Their continued existence is incompatible. Nature cannot support both. . . . It is a mere fallacy to suppose that serfdom has been abolished in England. It has not been abolished, it has only been generalized.[7]

There is the same attack upon the rule of outworn institutions that is found in George:

The great theoretic change that must take place in Britain is the abolition of the belief that one generation of men can be bound by the arrangements of past generations; and, instead of that belief, the substitution of a belief that men in every age must be governed by reason; that, whatever the arrangement or laws of past generations may have been, these arrangements or laws are binding now only in so far as they are now right, quite independently of any sanction they may have received from legislation. The acts of past men are no more binding on present

[7] *Ibid.*, pp. 259–260, and 284.

men in matters of politics than they are in matters of astronomy or theology; and when we find the soil of Britain disposed of, not according to any scheme that pretends to be now right, but according to the arrangements of men long since dead, who enacted the perpetuity of their arrangements, we may rest satisfied that the nation must ere long turn its attention to the revision of those arrangements, and inquire, "What ought to be the present disposition of the soil, supposing no arrangements whatever had been inherited from past generations?" [8]

The general solution of the problem is then put forward with the same difficulties that George later found:

Let it also be observed that the land is not essentially private property, and that naturally one man has as much right to the land as another. . . . The great social problem, then, that cannot fail ere long to appear in the arena of European discussion is, "to discover such a system as shall secure to every man his exact share of the natural advantages which the Creator has provided for the race; while, at the same time, he has full opportunity, without let or hindrance, to exercise his skill, industry, and perseverance for his own advantage.". . . As no individual and no generation is the creator of the substantive, earth, it belongs equally to all the existing inhabitants. . . . But though the permanent earth never can be private property . . . it must be possessed by individuals for the purpose of cultivation, and for the purpose of extracting from it all those natural objects which man requires.[9]

Division of the land, however, Dove shows to be "absurd," "as useless as it is improbable," and "unjust." Then follows the precise suggestion of a single tax:

The actual division of the soil need never be anticipated . . . How can the division of the advantages of the natural earth be effected? By the division of its annual value or rent; that is, by making the rent of the soil the common property of the nation. That is (as the taxation is the common property of the State), by taking the whole of the taxes out of the rent of the soil, and thereby abolishing all other kinds of taxation whatever. And thus all industry would be absolutely emancipated from every burden,

[8] *The Theory*, pp. 300–301.   [9] *Ibid.*, pp. 44, 305, and 308.

and every man would reap such natural reward as his skill, industry, or enterprise rendered legitimately his, according to the natural law of free competition. This we maintain to be the only theory that will satisfy the requirements of the problem of natural property.

Let it be observed that when the land is taxed, no man is taxed; for the land produces, according to the law of the Creator, more than the value of the labor expended on it [10] and on this account men are willing to pay a rent for land. But when the privileged classes had monopolized the land, they called it theirs in the same sense in which labor is supposed to belong to the laborer.[11]

Dove's realization of the fundamental significance of the land problem amounted to a clear and fervent conviction that without its correct solution the way could not be cleared for the "reign of justice" and human progression would be halted. Yet his book was essentially a theological rather than an economic treatise, and while the concern with the land question never appears as something incidental, still it does not have the vital, all-important function that it had for George. It may not have been a collateral issue for Dove and certainly it never seems incongruous, but there is always the impression that, as compared with the purely dialectical processes of dividing the sciences and specifying the precise content of each, this factual matter of land administration must be of secondary importance. It was rather with the work of Kant and of Cousin, and not of the Physiocrats and the Mills, that Dove was concerned.

The book remained practically unnoticed [12] until 1889,

---

[10] Note the Physiocratic influence of the *produit net*. Dove's work shows the indirect influence of the Physiocrats and the earlier English economists; his thorough education must have acquainted him with their doctrines, yet nowhere in the book is there any specific mention of them—indeed, there is no authority quoted later than Moses.

[11] *The Theory*, pp. 311 and 44.

[12] Dove's work was forgotten despite the fact that the book was praised by Carlyle, Blackie, and Sir William Hamilton in England, and by Charles Sumner in this country. See Alexander Harvey's Introduction to the Humboldt edition, p. 11.

when J. W. Sullivan, a journalist who had been dismissed from the staff of George's *Standard,* wrote an article for the *Twentieth Century* on "A Collapse of Henry George's Pretensions," in which he made the accusation that all of *Progress and Poverty* had been plagiarized from Dove's book. George reprinted the article in the *Standard* of October 19, 1889, and answered the charges by stating in the same issue that:

I first heard of it [Dove's book] three years after *Progress and Poverty* had been published, when, in Dublin, in September, 1882, Charles Eason, head of the Irish branch of Smith and Son's newsdealing company, presented me with a copy.

The two books agreed, George continued,

in the recognition of certain fundamental truths, but there are, as I have always contended, self-evident truths, which any one who will look may see, and which, even when covered up by force and obscured by sophistry, have in every age and among every people had their witnesses . . . for they are a part of the natural order as much as the attraction of gravitation, or as that revelation by which two and two make four. . . . So far from even claiming that there was anything new in the idea that all men have equal and inalienable right to land, I have always contended that this was a primary conception of the human mind, and that private property in land has nowhere grown up but as the result of force and fraud. . . . Not my system or anybody else's system, but the old and natural system, the only one conforming to the natural laws and therefore the one intended by the Intelligence which is behind natural law . . .

When I first came to see what is the root of our social difficulties and how this fundamental wrong might be cured in the easiest way by concentrating taxes on land values, I had worked out the whole thing for myself without conscious aid that I can remember, unless it might have been the light I got from Bisset's *Strength of Nations* as to the economic character of the feudal system. When I published *Our Land and Land Policy,* I had not even heard of the Physiocrats and the *impôt unique.* But I knew that if it was really a star I had seen, others must have seen it, too. And so with *Progress and Poverty*. I said in that book that it would come to many to whom it would seem like the echo of their own thoughts. And beyond what I then knew I was certain that there must have been others before me who saw the same essential truths. And as I have heard of such men one after the other, I have felt that they have been but additional evidences that we were indeed on the true track and still more clearly showed that though against us were ignorance and power, yet behind us were hope and faith and the wisdom of the ages—the deepest and clearest conceptions of man.

In *The Science of Political Economy*, George devotes some attention to the work of Dove,[13] and again declares that his own book was entirely uninfluenced by *The Theory of Human Progression*. Dove's conceptions, then, are significant in the historical development of opinion on the land question, and not because of any bearing upon the particular work of George. They are rather an illuminating piece of independent investigation, and constituted one of those individual convictions which, for George, demonstrated that the recognition of revealed truth was something "which any one who will look may see."

[13] Pp. 189–194. In 1884, two years after he had first heard of Dove, George, while speaking in Glasgow, paid a glowing tribute to the work of this Scotch predecessor.

The absurd extent to which avid seekers after traces of plagiarism will carry their suspicious efforts is strikingly illustrated in the case of George by an obituary notice in the Newcastle (England) *Journal* of October 30, 1897. The notice read: "His (George's) chief book, *Progress and Poverty*, is very largely a repetition of what is to be found elsewhere, fallacies included. He draws largely from former writers on economic subjects, and is especially indebted to the all-but-forgotten author of the *Philosophy of Necessity*, Mr. Charles Bray." Bray's book was published in London in 1863 by Longmans, Green. It resembled somewhat the work of Dove, but was largely a psychological and metaphysical discussion of "Mind" and "Matter." It contains several chapters which give a graphic picture of social conditions in England, and Bray's remedy is free trade, the abolishing of taxes and the private ownership of land, and the vague suggestion of a "single tax" upon land. It is quite true that he was one of the many anticipators of George, but George was hardly enough of a research student or an antiquary to have made his acquaintance.

The Physiocrats

More important than this coincidental similarity between the ideas of George and Dove is the association that the single tax has had with the doctrines of the eighteenth century French Physiocrats,[14] although the connection between the two has been quite generally overemphasized. In fact, due to a loose verbal interpretation of the *impôt unique* of the Economistes, and also to the overzealous wish of some of George's commentators, many obvious and fundamental differences between the two thoughts have been disregarded. George himself, while he believed that his conceptions were a logical continuation of the thoughts of the French economists, yet realized, in his earlier work at least, that his knowledge of their ideas was quite limited and he was cautious enough not to attribute too much to their influence. In *Progress and Poverty* he wrote:

But there has been a school of economists who plainly perceived—what is clear to the natural perceptions of men when uninfluenced by habit—that the revenues of the common property, land, ought to be appropriated to the common service. The French Economists of the last century, headed by Quesnay and Turgot, proposed just what I have proposed, that all taxation should be abolished save a tax upon the value of land. As I am acquainted

[14] The Physiocrats, "followers of the natural order," or Économistes, as they later called themselves, and who are credited with being the founders of the science of political economy (they certainly formed the first "school" of economics) and the inspirers of Adam Smith, flourished in France during the third quarter of the eighteenth century, especially from 1760 to 1780. Their ranks included, among others, Dr. Quesnay, physician to Louis XV and Madame de Pompadour, Mirabeau, father of the Revolutionary orator, Mercier de la Rivière, Baudeau, Dupont de Nemours, Le Trosne, and Turgot, the financial minister of Louis XVI. Gournay is sometimes included in their list, but, as Professor Seligman points out, he still was somewhat of a Mercantilist. The opposition to their teachings in France was led by Voltaire and Condillac, also Mably and Galiani. In Italy the Physiocratic influence was centered in men like Sarchiana and Bandini, Filangieri, Verri, and Ortes; and in Centani in Spain. (See Palgrave's *Dictionary of Political Economy*, Vol. I, p. 90, Vol. III, p. 352, and Vol. II, p. 372. In Palgrave there is mention

with the doctrines of Quesnay and his disciples only at second hand through the medium of the English writers, I am unable to say how far his peculiar ideas as to agriculture being the only productive avocation, etc., are erroneous apprehensions, or mere peculiarities of terminology. . . .

Without knowing anything of Quesnay or his doctrines, I have reached the same practical conclusion by a route which cannot be disputed, and have based it on grounds which cannot be questioned by the accepted political economy . . .

The elder Mirabeau, we are told, ranked the proposition of Quesnay to substitute one single tax or rent (the *impôt unique*) for all other taxes, as a discovery equal in utility to the invention of writing or the substitution of the use of money for barter.[15]

George dedicated his *Protection or Free Trade* to

the memory of those illustrious Frenchmen of a century ago, Quesnay, Turgot, Mirabeau, Condorcet, Dupont, and their fellows, who in the night of despotism foresaw the glories of the coming day,

although, as Professor Gide writes,[16] "his tribute loses its point somewhat when we remember that he admits that he had never read them." In *The Science of Political Economy*, George devotes some attention to the Physiocrats[17] and endeavors to draw a fairly close connection between his

of many "single taxes," not necessarily on land values, and also several vague early intimations of George's precise ideas, but these, for the most part, are too fragmentary to be of much service.) There was also Charles Frederick and Mauvillon in Germany, and Asgill, Cantillon, and Spence in England who may be classed under the general school of Physiocracy.

For an account of their work see: Gide and Rist, Chap. I; Weulersse, *Le Mouvement Physiocratique en France* (Paris, Alcan, 1910); Henry Higgs, *The Physiocrats* (New York, Macmillan, 1897); Hector Denis, *Histoire des Systemes Économiques et Socialistes* (Brussels, Rozez, 1897); W. W. Stephen, *Life and Writings of Turgot* (London, Longmans, Green, 1895). The best edition of their writings is that of Eugene Daire (Paris, Librairie de Guillaumin, 1846); see also Turgot's works (Paris, Belin, 1811).

[15] Pp. 421–422, and 431.

[16] Gide and Rist, p. 45, n. 2. George did not read French and there were no English translations of their complete writings available for him—and there is still no complete English translation. He stated that the best English account of their work was contained in Macleod's *Elements of Economics*.

[17] Book II, Chap. IV.

proposals and those of the French economists, an attempt that shows his knowledge of Physiocracy was incomplete.

It is true that the basic assumptions of the Physiocrats resembled those of George, and the language of the two proposals is identical, but the similarity ceases as soon as the question of conclusions and purposes is reached. The concern with the land, for example, was fundamental with both George and the Physiocrats, but the French economists' interest in land, as George correctly understood in *The Science of Political Economy*, was primarily a peculiar and mistaken conviction that agriculture was the one industry in which a surplus of wealth remained over and above the amount of wealth consumed in production, the one industry in which a *produit net* was realized. This net product of agriculture (some of the Economistes also included fishing and mining as enterprises which produced such a surplus) George identified with economic rent,[18] although further on he distinguishes between the two, especially with reference to the fact that rent was not only a product of agricultural effort, but, as Ricardo and Mill later showed, a socially created value.[19]

It was upon this *produit net* that the *impôt unique* of the Physiocrats was to be levied, a tax that would be collected in lieu of all other governmental revenue. At first glance, this seems identical with the single tax of George, and, as a purely fiscal instrument, the two plans are the same, but the "single taxes" differ very widely in the ends they were to achieve as well as in their quantitative determination. The *impôt unique* was not to be a remedy for social evils but rather a

---

[18] *The Science of Political Economy*, pp. 150–151.
[19] *Ibid.*, pp. 151–152.

For a general discussion of the difference between George and the Physiocrats, see Émile Rivaud's *Henry George et La Physiocratie* (Thèse pour le Doctorat—Faculté de Droit; Paris, 1907). Chapter I contains a specific account of the distinctions between the *produit net* and economic rent.

simplification of the burdensome tax system of eighteenth century France. If the only real wealth-producing activity of society were expressed in the *produit net* of agriculture, then obviously all taxes must ultimately come from it, and the Physiocrats merely wanted to abolish the indirect taxes, which ultimately were paid out of the net product. For George, the single tax was a means, and the only one, through which there could be an equitable distribution of wealth. It was, to be sure, a fiscal measure and, like the *impôt unique*, was to simplify governmental finance by doing away with indirect taxes, but it was to be much more than that. It was to be the instrument that would return the value of land to its creators, a restoration that was to prepare the way for the unimpeded flow of wealth into its proper channels. Further, it was to encourage the production of wealth, first by forcing land into use and second by removing the weight of the taxes on creative effort which George, unlike the Physiocrats, recognized to be a burden upon industry and labor, ultimately being paid not out of any net product but rather by the makers and users of wealth. Moreover, the *impôt unique* was to collect approximately one-third of the net product,[20] whereas all the economic rent of land was to be secured by George's single tax.

But aside from these specific differences between the two proposals for a single tax upon land, there remained the great gap between George and the Physiocrats in their conception of the equity of property in land. The Physiocrats were staunch supporters of the *propriétaire foncier*[21]; they believed that a class of respectable landlords was a necessary part of the social order, and their *impôt unique*, they explained quite acutely, would not be a burden upon the landowners, for the land would be bought at seventy per cent of

[20] See Gide and Rist, p. 39.
[21] Rivaud, Chap. II, especially p. 39; Gide and Rist, pp. 7, and 21–26; Young *(op. cit.)*, pp. 17–18.

its value—that is, the tax would not be bought and sold along with the land. As Dupont wrote: "And so the public revenue is not burdensome to any one, costs nothing and is paid by no one." [22] The Physiocratic respect for private property in land was, of course, not shared by George. He felt that the institution of landlordism with its privileged right to the "unearned increment" of land value was the blight that lay at the root of all social injustice. It was the cause of poverty and all the ills born of poverty, and the single tax for him was the method whereby this privileged power of the landlord was to be broken. Thus, there was a complete antithesis between the views of George and the Physiocrats on this fundamental question of private ownership of land, [23] a dif-

[22] Dupont's works, Vol. I, pp. 357–358; quoted in Gide and Rist, p. 40, n. 1.

[23] In the December, 1890, issue of the *Political Science Quarterly*, Professor Gide declared that "the famous system of Henry George, which has caused such commotion, was taught word for word by the Physiocrats," and he went on to quote extensively, especially from Mercier de la Rivière's *L'Ordre Natural et Essentiel des Sociétés Politiques*. Later, he was criticized and defended for his opinion by two writers in the January and April, 1891, issues of the *Quarterly Journal of Economics,* and in a letter which appeared in Notes and Memoranda of the July, 1891, issue of the *Quarterly Journal of Economics,* he attempted to explain his position:

"I am obliged to decide in favor of my critic . . . No; it did not enter into my mind to undertake any assimilation of the doctrines of Henry George to those of the Physiocrats on the question of landed property . . . I recognized fully that the two doctrines are not identical, nor even reconcilable, since the Physiocrats see in the institution of private property the basis of social order while Mr. George sees in it the cause of all the evils which desolate society. What, then, was my meaning? Nothing more than to establish in favor of the French economists a claim of priority upon a particular point . . . that the Physiocrats long before him had the idea of an *impôt unique* on the land; that, for them, as for him, this *impôt unique* (single tax) was founded on a right of the State as coproprietor, and was intended to constitute a sort of common patrimony of the nation; that for them, as for him, this *impôt unique* was to have for its result the suppression of all other taxes, and was thus to give a vigorous impulse to industry and commerce and to simplify prodigiously the budget of the State. It is true that while the Physiocrats used this weapon of the single tax to consolidate property, Henry George wishes to use it to destroy property. But what difference does this make? It is still the same weapon used for different ends. To avoid all misunderstanding I should have said simply this: 'The Physiocrats were "single taxists," but they were not Nationalists.'"

George, of course, also was not a "Nationalist," a fact which so many economists refuse to see. And the difference between the two "single taxes" does seem quite a fundamental one.

ference, moreover, with which George seemed entirely unacquainted.

The closest resemblance, however, between George and the Physiocrats does not occur in the technical proposals which, chiefly because of language similarities, have been used to associate the two thoughts, but rather in the broad, perhaps vague, issues upon which they based their economic thinking —free trade and laissez-faire, and the existence of a natural order to which each appealed. Between the Physiocrats, the first of academic free traders, and George, perhaps the most complete of free traders, there was no division of opinion; George accepted the laissez-faire of the Économistes, but attempted to reinterpret it. The interpretation that George sought to formulate was the idea that free competition had no meaning unless there were first provided equal opportunity, which, for him, meant the abolishing of the privilege and monopoly arising from the private ownership of land. The cynical and high-handed policy of "hands off" that characterized later economic thinking, especially during the early years of the Industrial Revolution in England, and which has so libeled the meaning of laissez-faire, was much too naive, or perhaps too predatory, to have satisfied George;[24] its stupid passivity would have amazed even the Physiocrats themselves.[25]

Coupled with the Physiocratic conception of laissez-faire was the belief in the "natural order," Physiocracy, of course, meaning—as Dupont specifically defined it—"the science of

[24] George wrote in *The Science of Political Economy:* "They [the Physiocrats] were the authors of the motto that in the English use of the phrase 'Laissez-faire,' 'Let Things Alone,' has been so emasculated and perverted, but which on their lips was 'Laissez-faire, laissez-aller,' 'Clear the Way and Let Things Alone.' . . . The English motto which I take to come closest to the spirit of the French phrase is, 'A fair field and no favor.'" (P. 153.)

The authorship of "laissez-faire" has been ascribed to Vincent de Gournay and to Le Gendre (Gide and Rist, p. 11, n. 2), although Professor Seligman, in his economic lectures, suggests the author to have been d'Argenson.

[25] Gide and Rist, p. 11.

the natural order." [26] Just what was meant by this natural order was not quite clear; it seemed elastic enough to fit almost any rational interpretation, although it certainly was not intended to support any Rousseauesque [27] state of nature. Rather it was a system of rational truths that was held to be almost axiomatic—at least to the Physiocrats. Yet such is the nature of "natural orders" that George could interpret the eternal scheme as demanding the social collection of economic rent, for reasons not at all pleasing to the Physiocrats. A conception of a natural order, even more than belief in laissez-faire, is necessarily a general outline, with the details remaining to be filled in.

It is not of the greatest significance, however, to trace with any completeness the similarities and the distinctions between George and the Physiocrats. [28] George, it is true, was acquainted with their work to some degree, more so at least than with the writing of Dove, but that acquaintance was casual and quite indirect, and, what is of most concern in any question of indebtedness, it was formed after George's early thought had already been shaped. George's own words give the best answer concerning his relation to the Physiocrats, and also indicate his viewpoint as to the place of originality

[26] Gide and Rist, p. 5.

[27] It may be well here to recall Rousseau's well-known opinion on the effect of private property in land as found in the opening lines of Part II of his *Discours*: "Le Premier qui, ayant enclos un terrain, s'avisa de dire, ceci est à moi, et trouva des gens assez simples pour le croire, fut le vrai fondateur de la société civile. Que de crimes, de guerres, de meurtres, de misères et d'horreurs n'eût point épargnés au genre humain celui qui, arrachant les pieux ou comblant la fosse, eût crié aux semblables: Gardez-vous d'écouter cet imposteur; vous êtes perdus si vous oubliez que les fruits sont à tous, et que la terre n'est à personne!"

[28] Dr. Rivaud, in concluding his dissertation *(op. cit.)* states: "Thus, whatever may be our admiration for the illustrious American writer, we are obliged to conclude that he was profoundly mistaken when, from the apparent similarity of a fiscal measure, the single tax, and from the identity of one of its corollaries, complete free trade, he deduced the integral correspondence of the two doctrines; and then paid homage, in one of those pages where he expressed his enthusiasm with such an eloquent power, to these great economists whose dream, he believed, was the restoration to all men of their equal rights to the earth." (P. 94; translation, the present writer's.)

in thought. In *The Science of Political Economy,* after a discussion of the effect of the Physiocrats upon the work of Adam Smith,[29] he writes:

It is a mistake to which the critics who are themselves mere compilers are liable, to think that men must draw from one another to see the same truths or to fall into the same errors. Truth is, in fact, a relation of things, which is to be seen independently because it exists independently. Error is perhaps more likely to indicate transmission from mind to mind; yet even that usually gains its strength and permanence from misapprehensions that in themselves have independent plausibility. Such relations of the stars as that appearance in the north which we call the Dipper or Great Bear, or as that in the south which we call the Southern Cross, are seen by all who scan the starry heavens, though the names by which men know them are various. And to think that the sun revolves around the earth is an error into which the testimony of their senses must cause all men independently to fall, until the first testimony of the senses is corrected by reason applied to wider observations.

In what is most important, I have come closer to the views of Quesnay and his followers than did Adam Smith, who knew the men personally. But in my case there was certainly no derivation from them. I well recall the day when, checking my horse on a rise that overlooks San Francisco Bay, the commonplace reply of a passing teamster to a commonplace question, crystallized, as by lightning-flash, my brooding thoughts into coherency, and I there and then recognized the natural order—one of those experiences that make those who have had them feel thereafter that they can vaguely appreciate what mystics and poets have called

---

[29] In this connection, it is interesting to note that even Smith, whose work has been so largely accredited to Physiocratic influences, had already formed his early thought before he left for France or knew anything of the writings of the Economistes. His early work was modified and enlarged, obviously, by the inspiration and teachings of the French philosophers, but the germ of his interpretation of political economy was already present in his mind. For this early, pre-Physiocratic stage of Smith's economic opinion, see particularly an account of some of his lectures at the University of Glasgow in 1763, edited by Cannan in 1896 under the title of Smith's *Lectures on Justice, Police, Revenue and Arms* (Oxford, the Clarendon Press). The lectures are compiled not from Smith's manuscripts but from a collection of students' notes.

the "ecstatic vision." Yet at that time I had never heard of the Physiocrats, or even read a line of Adam Smith.

Afterwards, with the great idea of the natural order in my head, I printed a little book, *Our Land and Land Policy*, in which I urged that all taxes should be laid on the value of land, irrespective of improvements. Casually meeting on a San Francisco street a scholarly lawyer, A. B. Douthitt, we stopped to chat, and he told me that what I had in my little book proposed was what the French "Economists" a hundred years before had proposed.

I forget many things, but the place where I heard this, and the tones and attitude of the man who told me of it, are photographed on my memory. For, when you have seen a truth that those around you do not see, it is one of the deepest of pleasures to hear of others who have seen it. This is true even though these others were dead years before you were born. For the stars that we of to-day see when we look were here to be seen hundreds and thousands of years ago. They shine on. Men come and go, in their generations, like the generations of the ants.[30]

SPENCE, OGILVIE, FILANGIERI

On the 8th of November, 1775, an Englishman, Thomas Spence of Newcastle-on-Tyne, read a paper before the Newcastle Philosophical Society on the "Rights of Man," for which "the Society did the Authour the honour to expel him." The lecture was later printed as a pamphlet entitled "The Meridian Sun of Liberty, or the Whole Rights of Man Displayed and most Accurately Defined." [31] It was the first of a

---

[30] Pp. 162–164. See also the *Standard* article of October 19, 1889.

[31] A 1796 edition of this pamphlet is in the New York Public Library and the quotations used have been taken from it. Spence represents the Physiocratic influence upon early English economic thought; he was particularly concerned, furthermore, with demonstrating that Locke's doctrine of labor in private property does not apply to landed property. The best review of Spence's land taxation proposals is given in J. Morrison Davidson's *Four Precursors of Henry George and the Single Tax* (London, Henderson, 1899). The other precursors are Dove, Ogilvie, and Paine. Spence's "Rights of Man" also appears in *The Pioneers of Land Reform, Spence, Ogilvie, and Paine*, edited with an introduction by M. Beer (New York, Knopf, 1920). For a picture of the conditions in which Spence's thought was formed and a discussion of his later work, see Menger, *The Right to the Whole Produce of Labour* (London. 1899), Foxwell's Introduction, and pp. 147 ff.

long series of pamphlets which were bound together in 1797 as "Pigs' Meat" [32]—The Honey or Essence of Politics—now published in Seventy-two penny numbers, making three Volumes. This is the Only Book that in a Direct Manner teaches the real, honest, pure Rights of Man, and that shews an easy and practicable way to enjoy Them." One of these pamphlets, written in 1796, but published the year later with a Preface and Appendix attacking Tom Paine's *Agrarian Justice,* was the "Rights of Infants, or the Imprescriptible Right of Mothers to such a share of the Elements as is sufficient to enable them to suckle and bring up their Young." [33] This was a companion to the "Meridian Sun," setting forth the same proposals but from the feminine standpoint (somewhat of a Shavian economic presentation); Spence felt that since men were tardy in demanding their rights, their wives must take the initiative from their "lock-jawed spouses."

Spence's conception of the rights of man was grounded upon what for him was the most basic of all rights, that of the use of the earth. This was the foundation of natural rights and, as with George, he believed that it could be secured only by breaking the monopoly of the landlords through a communal collection of the ground rents. In his "Meridian Sun" he wrote:

It is plain that the land or earth, in any country or neighborhood, with everything in or on the same, or pertaining thereto, belongs at all times to the living inhabitants of the said country or neighborhood in an equal manner. . . . The first landowners were usurpers and tyrants; and all who have since possessed their lands have done so by right of inheritance, purchase, etc., from them. . . . Were all the landlords to be of one mind and determined to take their properties into their own hands, all the rest of mankind might go to heaven if they would, for there would be

[32] This peculiar title originated from one of Pitt's statements concerning the "swinish multitude."

[33] This pamphlet, which is also in the New York Public Library, is in dialogue form between "Woman" and "Aristocracy."

no place found for them here. Thus men may not live in any part of this world, not even where they are born, but as strangers and by the permission of the pretenders to the property thereof . . .[34]

And here is the method whereby man can again come into his heritage of the earth and so bring about the "real, honest, pure Rights of Man":

Therefore a day is appointed on which the inhabitants of each parish meet in their respective parishes, to take their long-lost rights into possession, and to form themselves into corporations.[35]

These corporations were to administer the landed estate of the nation as a joint-stock company, in parochial partnership, by dividing the rent:

. . . You may behold the rent which the people have paid into the parish treasuries, employed by each parish in paying the government its share of the sum which the Parliament or National Congress at any time grants. . . . There are no tolls or taxes of any kind paid among them by native or foreigner but the aforesaid rent which every person pays to the parish according to the quantity, quality, and conveniences of the land, housing, etc., which he occupies in it. The government, the poor, roads, etc., etc., as said before, are all maintained by the parishes with rent; on which account all wares, manufactures, allowable trade employments or actions are entirely duty free. . . . For the government . . . having neither excisemen, custom-house men, collectors, army, pensioners, bribery, nor such like ruination vermin to maintain, is soon satisfied and moreover there are not more persons employed in offices either about the government or parishes than are absolutely necessary. . . . All nations have a devouring landed interest to support besides those necessary expenses of the public; and they might be raised very high indeed before their burden would be as heavy as that of their neighbors who pay rent and taxes, too. . . .[36]

The results of such a plan are glowingly depicted by Spence:

[34] "Meridian Sun," pp. 3–4.   [35] P. 8.   [36] Pp. 10–11.

Oh hearken! ye besotted sons of men. By this one bold resolve your chains are eternally broken and your enemies annihilated. By this one resolve, the power, the pride and the arrogance of the landed interest, those universal and never-ceasing scourges and plunderers of your race, are instantaneously and for ever broken and cut off. For being thus deprived and shorn of their revenues, they become like shorn Samson, weak as other men; weak as the poor dejected wretches whom they have so long been grinding and treading under foot. . . . But what makes this prospect yet more glowing is that after this empire of right and reason is thus established, it will stand for ever. Force and corruption attempting its downfall shall equally be baffled and all other nations, struck with wonder and admiration at its happiness and stability, shall follow the example; and thus the whole earth shall at last be happy and live like brothers.[37]

In his "Rights of Infants," which contains the same suggestion for a joint collection and administration of rent, Spence recognized the peculiar economic phenomenon that all social wealth and all social progress are expressed in the value of land, that creative economic energy manifests itself in rent, and that therefore the accrued benefits go to the owner of the land rather than to the community; although in that recognition there might have been present some of the Physiocratic conceptions regarding the unique status of land as a productive agency:

The more I contemplate human affairs the more I am convinced that a landed interest is incompatible with the happiness and independence of the world. For as all the rivers run into the sea and yet the sea is not full, so let there be ever so many sources of wealth, let trade, foreign and domestic, open all their sluices, yet will no other but the landed interest be ultimately the better. In whatever line of business or in whatever situation the public observe men thrive, thither every one presses, and in competition bid over each other's heads for the houses and shops on the lucky spot, thereby raising the rents till the landlord gets the whole part of their labours. . . . Nay, even abolish the tythes and the rents

[37] Pp. 8 and 12.

of the farms will immediately so advance that the whole advantage shall center in the landlords.[38]

George first heard of Spence in 1882 while lecturing in England. H. M. Hyndman, the socialist, had found a copy of Spence's pamphlet in the British Museum and had told George of his earlier suggestion for a tax on land values. George "urged Hyndman to publish the lecture in tract form, believing that it would do much good. Mrs. George suggested that this might prove disadvantageous to Mr. George, for people might say that if the idea of taxing land values had been proposed a hundred years before and had since been ignored by the world, there was little use of George in his *Progress and Poverty* trying to popularize the principle now. Her husband answered that most people hesitate to accept an idea thought to be new; that if the proposal in *Progress and Poverty* could be shown to be really an old one, it might make much more rapid way. And so he urged Hyndman to publish the lecture, which the latter did; while George himself sent a copy to Patrick Ford for publication in the *Irish World*." [39] That was ever George's ingenuous policy, not any demand for the honor of discovery, but only a desire to "propagate the faith"; if the proposal "could be shown to be really an old one, it might make much more rapid way." [40]

William Ogilvie, Professor of Humanities in King's College, Aberdeen, from 1761 to 1819,[41] published anonymously in 1782 "An Essay on the Right of Property in Land with respect to its Foundations in the Law of Nature." [42]   Al-

[38] Preface, p. 3.
[39] *Life*, pp. 368–369.
[40] George discusses Spence in his *Science of Political Economy* (p. 185) and in the *Standard* article mentioned above.
[41] Ogilvie's professorial chair included Latin languages and literature, political and natural history, antiquities, criticism, and rhetoric. In 1793 Columbia College conferred on him the honorary S. T. D.
[42] The essay was later printed in London in 1838 by Dugdale, an edition which according to Davidson (*op. cit.*) was suppressed, although Milliken

though he does not specifically mention the Physiocrats, there is evidence that he was influenced to some extent by their work, especially in the matter of the "net produce." Ogilvie starts from the assumption that was fundamental with Spence, namely, that men have an inherent right to land, and through his rather vague "progressive agrarian law" he hoped to restore much of the unoccupied land to the landless, and to shift taxation gradually from industry to land. He opens his essay with a discussion of the equity of property in land:

All right of property is founded either in occupancy or labour. The earth having been given to mankind in common occupancy, each individual seems to have by nature a right to possess and cultivate an equal share. This right is little different from that which he has to the free use of the open air and running water; though not so indispensably requisite at short intervals for his actual existence it is not less essential to the welfare and right state of his life through all its progressive stages. No individual can derive from this general right of occupancy a title to any more than an equal share of the soil of his country. His actual possession of more cannot of right preclude the claims of any other person who is not already in possession of such equal share.[43]

Then there is the precise suggestion of a tax on land:

A tax imposed on barren lands and so regulated as to encourage the proprietor in his immediate cultivation, or oblige him to resign them to the community for general distribution, could not be esteemed in the smallest degree unjust. His right to these barren

(op. cit.) suggests that the book was well known. Later, D. C. Macdonald, an English single taxer, found copies of the 1782 edition in the British Museum and the Advocates' Library of Edinburgh, and he printed the essay, together with some biographical material, as Birthright in Land (London, Kegan Paul, 1891). Quotations from Ogilvie will be taken from this edition. The essay is also printed in Beer's book (op. cit.) and selections of it in Davidson. George later became acquainted with the work of Macdonald, and he discusses Ogilvie at some length in the Standard article and in The Science of Political Economy, pp. 185–186.

[43] Pp. 7–9. The effect of Locke's "doctrine of labour," to be discussed further on, is clearly evident in much of the work of Ogilvie.

lands is founded solely on occupation; there is no improved value superadded, no right accruing from labour bestowed, and as he occupies besides, more than his equal share of the soil, the whole unimproved tracts of his estate belong strictly and entirely to the public, and no small indulgence is shown in giving him an option to improve or to resign them. A tax on all augmentation of rents, even to the extent of one-half the increase, would be at once the most suitable, the most productive, the most easily collected, and the least liable to evasion of all possible taxes, and might with inconceivable advantage disencumber a great nation from all those injudicious imposts by which its commercial exchanges are retarded and restrained, and its domestic manufactures embarrassed. . . .

If the original value of the soil be the joint property of the community, no scheme of taxation can be so equitable as a land tax, by which alone the expenses of the State ought to be supported, until the whole amount of that original value be exhausted; for the persons who have retained no portion of the public's stock but have suffered their shares to be deposited in the hands of the landholders, may be allowed to complain if before that fund is entirely applied to the public use they are subjected to taxes imposed on any other kind of property or any articles of consumption. How preposterous is the system of that country which maintains a civil and military establishment by taxes of large amount without the assistance of any land-tax at all! [44]

While Ogilvie did not possess the vigor of Spence's polemical zeal, his clear distinction between land and improvements and his argument for the taxation of the former and the exemption of the latter, on the grounds that the collection of taxes out of any fund other than that furnished by the social value of land was a burden and an imposition upon all forms of industrial enterprise, makes him a remarkable anticipator of the precise economic reasoning of George. Ogilvie also enters into quite an elaborate discussion of land and land values, endeavoring to point out that there are three different types of value given to land, that of occupancy as shown

[44] Pp. 58–59, and 16, n.

above being the least justifiable, but that discussion is not so pertinent to the later work of George.

In 1782, Gaetano Filangieri, son of the Italian Prince of Arinelli, published the first two of eight proposed volumes on the *Science of Legislation*.[45] The second volume dealt with economic problems and showed the unmistakable influence of the Physiocratic teachings, and in chapters thirty and thirty-one he suggested as one of the fundamental tenets of political economy the levying of a *unico dazio*, or the *impôt unique* of the Économistes. Filangieri identified his land tax with direct taxation in general and maintained that it was the only feasible and equitable system of governmental revenue.

A direct tax is no other than a tax on land, which is the true and lasting source of public riches and national revenue, and should bear the whole burden of the public contributions. On first appearance the landowner might be supposed to pay the whole, but every class of the community would in reality bear a part of it, in proportion to its fortunes and abilities.[46]

He went on to show quite correctly that such a land tax was to be introduced only gradually, slowly removing taxes on industry and production and proportionately increasing taxes on land values, the only feasible program for the attempted introduction of any single tax scheme. Filangieri was a very close follower of the Physiocrats and so need not be discussed separately in any detail. Benjamin Franklin, who also sympathized with much of the work of the Économistes,[47] be-

45 The work was translated into English by Thomas Ostello and published in London in 1806. The quotations are from this edition.

46 Vol. II, Chap. XXX, p. 197.

47 Franklin wrote to Du Pont de Nemours, July 28, 1768, from London: " . . . There is such a freedom from local and national prejudices and partialities, so much benevolence to mankind in general, so much goodness mixed with the wisdom in the principles of your new philosophy that I am perfectly charmed with it. . . . It is from your philosophy only that the maxims of a . . . more happy conduct are to be drawn, which I therefore sincerely wish may grow and increase till it becomes the governing philosophy of the human species, as it must be of superior beings in better worlds."

came acquainted with Filangieri's work and distributed some of the volumes of the *Science of Legislation* in this country.

EARLY AMERICAN PREDECESSORS

The American forerunners of George may be considered to start with the days of Revolutionary thought, and especially with the work of Paine and Jefferson, whose conceptions in many instances were accurate anticipations of George's proposals.[48] Tom Paine, the much maligned and defended, proved to have been a remarkable herald of George's fundamental thought when in his pamphlet,

(Bigelow's *Franklin*, Vol. IV, p. 195.) Again he wrote to Alexander Small in 1787: " . . . Our legislators are all landholders; and they are not yet persuaded that all taxes are finally paid by the land . . . therefore we have been forced into the modes of indirect taxes, i. e., duties on importation of goods." (*Ibid.*, Vol. IX, p. 414.) See also his letters to the Abbé Morellet in Sparks's *Franklin*, Vol. X, pp. 300 and 345.

[48] American anticipators of land taxation ideas may be profitably carried back into Colonial days, and certainly the name of William Penn, who perhaps received some of his ideas on the land question from his friend Locke, should not be omitted. In his *Fruits of Solitude*, written in 1693, Penn stated that "if all men were so far tenants to the public that the superfluities of gain and expense were applied to the exigencies thereof, it would put an end to taxes, leave not a beggar, and make the greatest bank for national trade in Europe." (From edition of 1718, printed in London, Freemantle and Co., 1901—this is the seventh edition; Part II of *Reflections and Maxims*, No. 222, pp. 152–153.) Milliken (*op. cit.*, pp. 313–314) quotes other reference of Penn to land; this is from "Certain Conditions and Concessions agreed upon by William Penn and Adventurers and Purchasers," July 11, 1681: "That every man shall be bound to plant, or man, so much of his share of land as shall be set out and surveyed, within three years after it is so set out and surveyed, or else it shall be lawful for newcomers to be settled thereupon, paying to them their survey money, and they go higher for their shares." The following first tax law in Philadelphia, January 30, 1683, was reported as "Put to the vote, as many as are of opinion that a Publick Tax upon the land ought to be raised to defray the Publick Charge, say yea——carried in the affirmative, none dissenting." Of course, it is recognized that these opinions of Penn are quite definitely bound up with his duties as colonizer, and that land taxes naturally put themselves forward in a young settlement, chiefly because there is very little else to tax. Still Penn had the thought that men were to be "tenants to the public."

Other early Americans who are mentioned by Milliken as having opinions which might be classed as anticipations of George included Cadwallader Colden, Surveyor-General of New York in 1752, and later Governor (pp. 316–317) and Governor Peter Stuyvesant (p. 315).

Agrarian Justice,[49] he definitely suggested that as land values are created by society they should be collected by society, although his purpose in such a collection was simply to provide a fund for paying out his proposed doles of ten and fifteen pounds.[50] Paine first drew a picture of civilization which in his opinion, as in that of Rousseau, originated when land ceased to be common property and began to be owned by individuals.

On one side, the spectator is dazzled by splendid appearances; on the other he is shocked by extremes of wretchedness; both of which it [civilization] has erected. The most affluent and the most miserable of the human race are to be found in the countries that are called civilized. . . . Poverty, therefore, is a thing created by that which is called civilized life.[51]

After this exposition of progress with poverty, Paine enters into the discussion of property in land:

It is a position not to be controverted that the earth, in its natural uncultivated state, was and ever would have continued

---

[49] The complete title of Paine's pamphlet, which was addressed as a proposal to the Legislature and Executive Directory of the French Republic, in 1797, was "Agrarian Justice opposed to Agrarian Law and Agrarian Monopoly, Being a plan for Meliorating the condition of Men by creating in Every Nation a National Fund, To pay every person when arriving at the age of twenty-one years the Sum of fifteen pounds stg. to enable Him or Her to begin the world, and also Ten pounds per annum during Life to Every person now Living of the age of fifty years, and to all others when they shall arrive at that Age, to enable them to live in old age without wretchedness, and to go decently out of the World." (The quotations used here will be taken from Conway's edition of Paine's writings, New York, Putnam's, 1895; Vol. III.)

[50] It was this suggestion of a dole that drew down upon Paine the opposition of Spence, who in the same year added a Preface and Appendix to his "Rights of Infants." The Appendix was a comparison of the specific proposals of Spence and Paine taken section by section. In the Preface, Spence wrote: "At last Mr. Paine has thought fit to own with the Psalmist and with Mr. Locke that 'God has given the earth to the children of men, given it to mankind in common.' The poor beggarly stipends which he would have us accept in lieu of our lordly and just pretensions to the soil of our birth, are so contemptible and insulting that I shall leave them to the scorn of every person conscious of the dignity of his nature." (P. 3.)

[51] Conway's *Paine*, Vol. III, p. 328.

to be the common property of the human race. . . . It is nevertheless true that it is the value of the improvement only, and not the earth itself, that is individual property. Every proprietor, therefore, of cultivated land owes to the community a ground-rent (for I know of no better term to express the idea) for the land which he holds; and it is from this ground-rent that the fund proposed in this plan is to issue. . . .

Man did not make the earth, and though he had a natural right to occupy it he had no right to locate as his property in perpetuity any part of it; neither did the Creator of the earth open a land-office, from which the first title-deeds should issue.[52]

Paine constantly distinguished between the land as property and the improvements as property and held that the only justification for considering land as property was that of the act of cultivation—which was Locke's position.

Cultivation is at least one of the greatest natural improvements ever made by human invention. It has given to the earth a tenfold value. But the land monopoly that began with it has produced the greatest evil. . . .

There are two kinds of property. Firstly, natural property, or that which comes to us from the Creator of the universe—such as earth, air, water. Secondly, artificial or acquired property—the invention of man.[53]

Despite George's familarity and sympathy with the doctrines of the Revolutionary thinkers, he does not appear to have been acquainted with this specific proposal of Paine,[54]

[52] Conway's *Paine*, pp. 329–330.

[53] *Ibid.*, pp. 331 and 334. One of the most recent works on Paine, *Thomas Paine, Prophet and Martyr of Democracy*, by Mary Agnes Best (New York, Harcourt Brace, 1927), does not neglect to couple his name with that of George. "The plan he [Paine] worked out [in *Agrarian Justice*] contained the germ of Henry George's *Progress and Poverty.*" (P. 360.)

[54] In *The Science of Political Economy,* George does not mention Paine in his brief sketch of the specific anticipators of the single tax; and yet he does include along with the rest Dr. Thomas Chalmers, the Scotch clergyman and divinity professor at the University of Edinburgh, whose *Political Economy,* published in 1832, advocated collecting ground rents for purposes of revenue. Chalmers, however, while he was influenced by the Physiocratic *impôt unique,* was a strict conservative, and advocated such a tax, as did the Physiocrats themselves, because of its benefits to the landed class.

and likewise he does not seem entirely familiar with the land doctrines of Jefferson, who was his recognized idol. However, Jefferson's opinions on the agrarian question were rather vague and fragmentary, and appeared scattered quite haphazardly throughout his letters. Perhaps the most quoted paragraph of his regarding the right to land was from a letter written in Paris to James Madison: [55]

I set out on this ground, which I suppose to be self-evident, that the earth belongs in usufruct to the living; that the dead have neither power nor right over it. . . . This principle that the earth belongs to the living and not to the dead is of very extensive application and consequences in every country . . . and it renders the question of reimbursement a question of generosity and not of right.

And in another letter [56] Jefferson stated that:

Whenever there are in any country uncultivated lands and unemployed poor, it is clear that the laws of property have been so far extended as to violate natural right. The earth is given as a common stock for men to labour and live on. If, for the encouragement of industry, we allow it to be appropriated, we must take care that other employment be provided for those excluded from the appropriation. If we do not, the fundamental right to labour the earth returns to the unemployed.

The suggestion that a land tax supply the means by which the individual States were to contribute their quotas of revenue to the Federal Government was made by Jefferson in 1797,[57] and in another place [58] he held that our people would continue "independent and moral" and "our Government would re-

---

[55] September 6, 1789, in Ford's edition of *Jefferson's Writings* (Federal Edition, New York, Putnam's, 1904), Vol. VI, pp. 3–4; see also pp. 4 ff.
[56] To Madison's father; written at Fontainebleau, October 28, 1785; Ford, Vol. VIII, p. 196.
[57] In a letter to Fitzhugh, Ford, Vol. VIII, pp. 298 ff.
[58] In a letter to J. Lithgow, Ford, Vol. IV, pp. 86–87, n. This contains the characteristic Jeffersonian conception that American culture must remain rural.

main virtuous" only if "there were vacant lands in any part of America."

More striking, however, than these somewhat indistinct and casual suggestions of Paine and Jefferson on the land question, was the almost unknown work of a Wisconsin tailor, Edwin Burgess, who, in a series of letters written to the Racine *Advocate* in 1859–60,[59] proposed the identical scheme of George. In Letter IX of the series, Burgess wrote:

. . . I say put all the taxes on the land, and repeal your stamp duties, your duties on imports, your inquisitorial excise laws, your robbing legacy duties, which tax nothing for the inheritance of land, because the land monopolists made the laws. Put all the taxes on the land, and then the landlord's rent will pay the cost of government, and keep the land at the lowest price forever; then cultivation, production and plenty will prevail, and much of the manufactures which you are now exporting will be needed at home; your home market will be vastly increased, you will be prosperous and permanent customers to each other, your poor laws will be diminished, your credit will not be needed; then poverty, beggary and a land-robbing aristocracy and a tithe-eating Church and State priesthood will soon be among the things that were.
Then free trade, by removing the necessity for standing armies and navies, would open the reign of peace on earth and good will to all mankind; then arts, industry, commerce and morals would be devoted to the promotion of human good, the supplying permanently and bountifully our wants, and elevating our conditions physically, mentally, morally and socially; all nations would become as one family, in which a wrong done to one would be resented by all. The universal brotherhood of man would be realized, and the earth in its fruitfulness, bloom and beauty would become the Eden home of the free, the noble and the good.

Here, from single tax to free trade, from attacks on land monopolists to Utopia, we have another Henry George. Burgess says in another place:

[59] These letters were later printed by W. S. Buffham of Racine as *The Edwin Burgess Letters on Taxation;* there is no date to this edition.

Were all the taxes on the land, and the people's land free, then the hitherto landless could soon build their own homes on their own land, and raise all they needed to consume or exchange, and no longer need the land, house, or capital of others; and then rent, interest, and even usury would cease for want of poverty to sustain them, for the curse of land monopoly being removed, the effect would cease with the cause. Thus would the happiness of mankind be immeasurably increased, and misery be proportionately diminished; then would the earth be redeemed from the giant sin of land robbery, and the Paradise of the present or future be far above that of the past.[60]

George later became acquainted with the work of Burgess and in the *Standard* of August 5, 1891, he quoted a letter [61] of the Wisconsin man which contained a brief statement of his suggestions:

I want to say a few words on the best means of raising revenue or taxes so as to prevent land monopoly. I know not what are your views on the subject, but should like to have you inquire whether raising all the taxes off the land in proportion to its market value would not produce the greatest good to mankind with the least evil, of any means of raising revenue. Taxing personal property has a tendency to limit its use by increasing its price, and the consequent difficulty of obtaining it.

At the same time that Burgess was writing on land monopoly and land taxation, another rural American, Gerrit Smith, an anti-slavery Congressman [62] from Peterboro, New

[60] *The Edwin Burgess Letters on Taxation,* p. 14.

[61] This was an earlier letter of Burgess, written in 1848, to an Eastern newspaper with the nautical title of the Portland (Maine) *Pleasure Boat,* "J. Hacker, Owner, Master and Crew"; the issue in which the letter appeared was "Excursion No. 45, Clearance No. 3."

[62] Smith had been elected as an independent on a platform which included "the right of the soil is as natural and equal as the right to light and air" and "the doctrine of free trade is the necessary outgrowth of the doctrine of human brotherhood; and that to impose restrictions on commerce is to build up unnatural and sinful barriers across that brotherhood." He was a large landholder, his father having been associated with John Jacob Astor, but during his life Smith distributed thousands of acres of his property to landless persons throughout the State. For a discussion of

York, introduced into the House of Representatives, February 21, 1854, a set of resolutions on the Homestead Bill which read:

Whereas all the members of the human family, notwithstanding all contrary enactments and arrangements, have, at all times, and in all circumstances, as equal a right to the soil as to the light and air, because as equal a natural need of the one as of the other;

And whereas this invariably equal right to the soil leaves no room to buy or sell or give it away; Therefore,

1. Resolved, That no bill or proposition should find any favor with Congress which implies the right of Congress to dispose of the public lands, or any part of them, either by sale or gift.

2. Resolved, That the duty of civil government in regard to public lands, and, indeed, to all lands, is but to regulate the occupation of them; and that this regulation should ever proceed upon the principle that the right of all persons to the soil—to the great source of human subsistence—is as equal, as inherent, and as sacred, as the right to life itself.

3. Resolved, That government will have done but little toward securing the equal right to land, until it shall have made essential to the validity of every claim to land both the fact that it is actually possessed, and the fact that it does not exceed in quantity the maximum, which it is the duty of government to prescribe.

4. Resolved, That it is not because land monopoly is the most efficient cause of inordinate and tyrannical riches on the one hand, and of dependent and abject poverty on the other; and that it is not because it is, therefore, the most efficient cause of that inequality of conditions, so well-nigh fatal to the spread of Democracy and Christianity, that government is called upon to abolish it; but it is because the right which this mighty agent of evil violates and tramples under foot, is among those clear, certain, essential, natural rights which it is the province of government to protect at all hazards and irrespective of all consequences.

In his speech on the resolutions, Smith declared:

Smith's life and work see a pamphlet by William Lloyd Garrison, the younger, *Gerrit Smith on Land Monopoly* (Chicago, Public Publishing Co., 1906).

I admit that there are things in which a man can have absolute property, and which without qualification or restriction he can buy, or sell, or bequeath, at his pleasure. But I deny that the soil is among these things. What a man produces from the soil he has an absolute right to. He may abuse the right. It nevertheless remains. But no such right can he have in the soil itself. If he could, he might monopolize it. If very rich, he might purchase a township or county; and in connection with half a dozen other monopolists, he might come to obtain all the lands of a State or a nation. Their occupants might be compelled to leave them and to starve, and the lands might be converted into parks and hunting grounds for the enjoyment of the aristocracy. Moreover, if this could be done in the case of a State or nation, why could it not be done in the case of the whole earth? . . .

It is a very glaring assumption on the part of one generation to control the distribution and enjoyment of natural rights for another generation. . . . A much happier world will this be when land monopoly shall cease; when his needed portion of the soil shall be accorded to every person; when it shall no more be bought and sold; when, like salvation, it shall be "without money and without price"; when, in a word, it shall be free, even as God made it free. . . . So long, then, as the masses are robbed by land monopoly, the world will be cursed with riches and poverty.[63]

Smith, it is true, did not conceive of any single tax plan to break this land monopoly, but confined his attention chiefly to the public domain. His attack upon the abuses and social evils resulting from the private ownership of land, however, certainly connects his thought with that of George.

SPINOZA AND LOCKE

It is a very, very far cry from these frontier minds to the genius of a Spinoza, but merely for the purpose of illustrating the strangeness of the backgrounds against which this conception of land taxation has displayed itself, there is this sentence from the *Tractatus Theologico-Politicus:*

[63] Garrison's pamphlet, pp. 15, 18, 20–21.

The fields, and the whole soil, and, if it can be managed, the houses, should be public property, that is, the property of him who holds the right of the commonwealth; and let him let them at a yearly rent to the citizens, whether townsmen or countrymen, and with this exception let them all be free, or exempt from every kind of tax in time of peace.[64]

This is obviously but a casual and isolated expression, taken from a more elaborate political program, and, of course, there is no intention here of placing upon Spinoza the burden of having been an anticipator of a nineteenth century American economist (although there is scarcely any concept of philosophy that has not been connected in some way with Spinoza's catholic doctrines), yet it does show that the germ of this thought has flourished in many cultures.[65]

Locke, perhaps, is more easily coupled with the political and economic interest in landed property, a concern that manifested itself in his proposed charters for American colonies. His ideas on the question of land ownership, how-

[64] Chap. VI, Sec. 12.

[65] A reading of Milliken's essay *(op. cit.)* will give a fairly complete idea of the scattered fragments of thought that have appeared on this question of a land tax. We find, for example, that an interest in the land problem was shown by Savonarola (see Villari's *Life*, Vol. 1, pp. 275-277) and by Dio Chrysostom (see *The Hunter of Euboea*, Winans's trans. in *Greek and Roman Classics*, Dr. Marion Mills Miller, ed., Vol. VII, p. 302). In mediæval China there are records of the same thought. In *The Économic Principles of Confucius*, by Dr. Chen Huan-Chang (New York, 1911, *Columbia Studies in History, Economics and Public Law*, Vols. 44–45), are these accounts of land taxes: "Yang Yen was a great reformer. He abolished all other direct taxes, and reduced them to the land tax only. . . . This was the first time that the system of 'single whip' was originated. . . . The only basis of direct taxation was the land, not the person. It was simple and uniform. The officials could not practice corruption, nor could the people evade their dues." (Vol. II of the separately published ed., p. 652); and "In 1581 A. D. the system of 'single whip' was universally established. The total amount of land tax and poll tax of each district was fixed, and the poll tax was equally distributed to the land. . . . All the different kinds of contributions, tribute, etc., were simplified into a single item, and they were supplied by the officials with the money of the land tax. Land was the only object of direct taxation and was taxed according to acreage." (Vol. II, p. 656.) A list of other isolated quotations from many diverse, if partial, anticipators of George, may be found in a series of articles by E. H. Crosby, "The Earth-for-All Calendar" in the publication, *The National Single Taxer* (New York, each month of 1900).

ever, appear chiefly in the treatise on *Civil Government* and in *Some Considerations of the Consequences of the Lowering of Interest*.[66] In the latter essay Locke anticipates the doctrine of the Physiocrats, namely, that all taxes come ultimately out of the land, and he disparages the idea that commodities can be made to bear the burden of revenue:

If, therefore, the laying of taxes upon commodities does, as it is evident, affect the land that is out at a rack-rent, it is plain it does equally affect all the other land in England, too, and the gentry will, but the worst say, increase their own charges, that is, by lessening the yearly value of their estates, if they hope to ease their land, by charging commodities. It is in vain, in a country whose great fund is land, to hope to lay the public charge of the government on anything else; there at last it will terminate. The merchant (do what you can) will not bear it, the labourer cannot, and therefore the landholder must; and whether he were best do it, by laying it directly where it will at last settle, or by letting it come to him by the sinkings of his rents, which, when they are once fallen, every one knows are not easily raised again, let him consider.[67]

The problem of property in land is treated most extensively by Locke in Chapter V, "On Property," of his *Civil Government*. He carefully distinguishes, as have all thinkers on the question, between the land itself as property and the fruits of labor upon land as property, declaring that the first is a common heritage to all men, and that the second constitutes the only legitimate basis of property rights—the well-known labor theory of property. Regarding the land as property in common, Locke states:

[66] The edition used here is the ten volume collection of Locke's *Works*, printed in London in 1823. Both *Civil Government* and the interest letter are in Vol. V. The *Civil Government* is the second of two treatises on government, the first being directed against the monarchic proposals of Filmer. The essay on interest first appeared as a letter to a member of Parliament in 1691. In one section, Locke discusses the distinction between interest and rent, showing that one does not depend upon the other, but both upon the law of supply and demand. (Pp. 32–40.)

[67] Vol. V, p. 60.

Whether we consider natural reason, which tells us that men, being once born, have a right to their preservation, and consequently to meat and drink, and such other things as nature affords for their subsistence; or revelation, which gives us an account of those grants God made of the world to Adam, and to Noah, and his sons; it is very clear, that God, as King David says, Psal. cxv, 16, "has given the earth to the children of men"; given it to mankind in common. . . . I shall endeavour to show how men might come to have a property in several parts of that which God gave to mankind in common, and that without any express compact of all the commoners.[68]

The foundation of private property he then shows to be that of human labor:

Though the earth, and all inferior creatures, be common to all men, yet every man has a property in his own person; this nobody has any right to but himself. The labour of his body, and the works of his hands, we may say, are properly his. Whatsoever then he removes out of the state that nature has provided, and left in it, he hath mixed his labour with, and joined to it something that is his own, and thereby makes it his property. . . . For this labour being the unquestionable property of the labourer, no man but he can have a right to what that is once joined to, at least where there is enough, and as good, left in common for others.[69]

The extent of private property in land, however, he holds must be limited:

But the chief matter of property being now not the fruits of the earth, and the beasts that subsist on it, but the earth itself; as that which takes in, and carries with it all the rest; I think it is plain, that property in that, too, is acquired as the former. As much land as a man tills, plants, improves, cultivates, and can use the product of, so much is his property. . . . God, when he gave the world in common to all mankind, commanded man also to labour, and the penury of his condition required it of him. God and his reason commanded him to subdue the earth, i. e., improve it for the benefit of life, and therein lay out something upon it that was his own, his labour. . . . The measure of property nature has

[68] *Works,* Vol. V, Sec. 25, pp. 352–353.   [69] *Ibid.,* Sec. 27, pp. 353–354.

well set by the extent of men's labour and the conveniences of life.[70]

Making land property by means of labor can injure no one, according to Locke, for land in use is always of benefit; in this section he appears to suggest that there is no injustice so long as there is land left which is "as good"—an intimation of Ricardo's "marginal land."

> Nor was this appropriation of any parcel of land, by improving it, any prejudice to any other man, since there was still enough, and as good left; and more than the yet unprovided could use. So that, in effect, there was never the less left for others because of his enclosure for himself; for he that leaves as much as another can make use of, does as good as take nothing at all. Nobody could think himself injured by the drinking of another man, though he took a good draught, who had a whole river of the same water left to quench his own thirst; and the case of land and water, where there is enough of both, is perfectly the same. . . . To which let me add, that he who appropriates land to himself by his labour, does not lessen, but increases the common stock of mankind; for the provisions serving to the support of human life, produced by one acre of enclosed and cultivated land are (to speak much within compass) ten times more than those which are yielded by an acre of land of an equal richness laying waste in common. And therefore he that encloses land, and has a greater plenty of the conveniences of life from ten acres, than he could have from an hundred left to nature, may truly be said to give ninety acres to mankind. . . .[71]

Locke undoubtedly had no intention of definitely attacking the existing land system of England, although his insistence upon land being improved and his belief that "nature has well set" the extent of private estates, show little sympathy with the traditions of the landed gentry.[72] His

[70] *Ibid.*, Secs. 32 and 36, pp. 356, 357.
[71] *Ibid.*, Secs. 33 and 37, pp. 356–357, 359.
[72] In reference to the communistic land agitation in England during the time of Cromwell, led by the mystic Gerrard Winstanley, see the interesting account given in *The Digger Movement in the Days of the Commonwealth*, by Lewis H. Berens (London, Simpkin Marshall, 1906).

thoughts lay rather in tracing the development and equity of property in land. The recognition, however, of man's right to the use of the earth, based upon, what for Locke was a matter of "natural reason," man's right [73] to his person and to his labor, has made him an anticipator of George's most fundamental doctrine.

THE CLASSICAL ECONOMISTS

George's relation to the great economists of England is an interesting example of what might be designated as a variation of the hypothetical method. He turned his attention to the doctrines of traditional political economy only when he had already formed a theory, and it was to verify and to expand his hypothesis that he consulted the writings of the classical economists. With the solution that had thrust itself forward as a revealed expression of truth still fresh before him, he appealed for confirmation to the English writers, and in their work found much that supported his contentions and also many thoughts which he could not accept. Indeed, this recourse to academic political economy was the only path open for George, for at this early stage of his thought, experimentation hardly offered itself as a means of proof, and he felt that he had already considered the available factual material. Moreover, he realized that, whereas his own thoughts on the land question had been formed before he had "heard of the Physiocrats or even read a line of Adam Smith," the development and elaboration of his conceptions demanded a thorough review of the prevailing economic doctrines, and accordingly he devoted himself to a study of British political economy. [74]

[73] It is not necessary here to go into the part played by the whole doctrine of "natural rights" which was so integrally and fundamentally connected with all of Lockian economic and political philosophy.
[74] See preface to the fourth edition of *Progress and Poverty*.

In *Our Land and Land Policy,* which first presented George's views on property in land, it is evident that the economists whom he briefly mentions, Mill and Ricardo and Malthus, were little more to him than names,[75] but *Progress and Poverty* shows a detailed and critical knowledge of the work of all the English economists with the possible exception of James Mill. John Stuart Mill, to whom as an authority George had turned when he first became interested in political economy,[76] is recognized in *Progress and Poverty* as an

[75] The only mention of the British economists in the book, which was written in 1871, is in these passages: "According to the doctrine of rent advanced by Ricardo and Malthus and generally accepted by the best authorities on political economy, the value of land should be determined by the advantages which it possesses over the least advantageous land in use." (*Works,* Vol. VIII, p. 82.) Speaking of the justice of taking land values in taxation, George wrote: "It is this consideration which makes men like John Stuart Mill shrink from the practical application of deductions from their own doctrines, and propose that in resuming their ownership of the land of England, the people of England shall pay its present proprietors not only its actual value, but also the present value of its prospective increase in value." (Pp. 110–111.) On pages 105–106, George also shows that he had heard of Smith's "canons of taxation," and again in speaking of land values he declares, "I mean what I believe is sometimes called in England the unearned value of land." (P. 106.) There is no further mention of classical political economy in the work.

[76] In *The Science of Political Economy* George wrote concerning the drafting of his article (on Chinese immigration): "Wishing to know what political economy had to say about the cause of wages, I went to the Philadelphia Library, looked over John Stuart Mill's *Political Economy,* and accepting his view without question, based my article on it." (Pp. 200–201.) This is the letter that Mill wrote to George acknowledging the latter's article on Chinese immigration (from Avignon, France, October 23, 1869; see *supra,* pp. 40–41): "The subject on which you have asked my opinion involves two of the most difficult and embarrassing questions of political morality—the extent and limits of the right of those who have first taken possession of the unoccupied portion of the earth's surface to exclude the remainder of mankind from inhabiting it, and the means which can be legitimately used by the more improved branches of the human species to protect themselves from being hurtfully encroached upon by those of a lower grade in civilisation. The Chinese immigration into America raises both of these questions. To furnish a general answer to either of them would be a most arduous undertaking.

"Concerning the purely economic view of the subject, I entirely agree with you; and it could be hardly better stated and argued than it is in your article in the New York *Tribune.* That the Chinese immigration, if it attains great dimensions, must be economically injurious to the mass of the present population; that it must diminish their wages, and reduce them to a lower stage of physical comfort and well-being, I have no manner of doubt. Nothing can be more fallacious than the attempts to make out that thus to lower

anticipator of some of the most important thoughts in the book, but George appears to deal a little harshly with what he regards as some of Mill's errors, especially his acceptance of Malthusianism and his beliefs that land constituted a part of national wealth and that wages were paid out of capital. Perhaps George felt that Mill's suggestion that only the future "unearned increment" of land values be collected by the government was a half-hearted acceptance of a great truth, and George's wrath was always great against those who seemed unwilling to grasp the complete significance of an idea.[77] But if Mill appeared a bit too timid for George, certainly the English landlords did not share that opinion,

wages is the way to raise them, or that there is any compensation, in an economical point of view, to those whose labour is displaced, or who are obliged to work for a greatly reduced remuneration. On general principles this state of things, were it sure to continue, would justify the exclusion of the immigrants on the ground that, with their habits in respect to population, only a temporary good is done to the Chinese people by admitting part of their surplus numbers, while a permanent harm is done to a more civilised and improved portion of mankind.

"But there is much also to be said on the other side. Is it justifiable to assume that the character and habits of the Chinese are insusceptible of improvement? The institutions of the United States are the most potent means that have yet existed for spreading the most important elements of civilisation down to the poorest and most ignorant of the labouring masses. If your Chinese child were compulsorily brought under your school system, or under a still more effective one if possible, and kept under it for a sufficient number of years, would not the Chinese population be in time raised to the level of the American?" (Then follow some passages in which Mill points out that Chinese immigration has been so small that there seems little danger of a serious challenge of the American standard of living, and in which he attacks also the practice of contract Chinese labor.) The letter concludes with this statement: "The opportunity given to numerous Chinese of becoming familiar with better and more civilized habits of life is one of the best chances that can be opened up for the improvement of the Chinese in their own country, and one which it does not seem to me that it would be right to withhold from them."

The letter is typical of Mill's never-failing gracious attitude, and it illustrates some of his most pronounced ideas on education. Also, it seems a bit strange to view Mill questioning and George defending, at least in this one case, "the right of those who have first taken possession of the unoccupied portion of the earth's surface to exclude the remainder of mankind from inhabiting it." The present writer does not know of any of the more mature expressions of George on the Chinese problem.

[77] George, however, never placed Mill in the same class with Spencer, whom he regarded as an apostate; Mill, he wrote, "seems to me a very type of intellectual honesty." (*The Science of Political Economy,* p. 137.)

for Mill's constant attacks upon the "unearned increment," together with his work in helping to found the Land Tenure Reform Association, made him always an object of polite suspicion.

Regarding the increase in land values which he termed the "unearned increment," Mill wrote:

Suppose that there is a kind of income which constantly tends to increase, without any exertion or sacrifice on the part of the owners . . . It would be no violation of the principles on which private property is grounded, if the State should appropriate this increase of wealth, or part of it, as it arises. This would not properly be taking anything from anybody; it would merely be applying an accession of wealth, created by circumstances, to the benefit of society, instead of allowing it to become an unearned appendage to the riches of a particular class. Now this is actually the case with rent. The ordinary progress of a society which increases in wealth is at all times tending to augment the incomes of landlords; to give them both a greater amount and a greater proportion of the wealth of the community independently of any trouble or outlay incurred by themselves. They grow richer, as it were, in their sleep, without working, risking, or economizing. What claims have they on the general principle of social justice to this accession of riches? In what would they have been wronged if society had from the beginning reserved the right of taxing the spontaneous increase of rent, to the highest amount required by financial exigencies? [78]

Mill, of course, goes on to say that only the future increase of rent should be collected by the State, and he also questions whether this right of land value taxation has not been waived by the government because it has not been exercised. Since land values have not been collected as revenue, he believes that a tacit justification has been given to the private retention of the unearned increment and any change might prove an injustice to the landed class. But despite Mill's respect for private property and the intense sincerity

[78] *Principles of Political Economy*, Book V, Chap. II, Sec. 5.

with which he eschewed any proposal that might result in an unjust treatment of a single class, he carefully distinguishes property in land from other property, and declares, as did Locke, that the only justification for landed property is that of usage.

It is seen that they [the reasons for private property in land] are only valid in so far as the proprietor of land is its improver. Whenever, in any country, the proprietor, generally speaking, ceases to be the improver, political economy has nothing to say in defense of landed property as there established. In no sound theory of private property was it ever contemplated that the proprietor of land should be merely a sinecurist quartered on it. . . . Landed property in England is thus very far from completely fulfilling the conditions which render its existence economically justifiable. But if insufficiently realized even in England, in Ireland those conditions are not complied with at all. With individual exceptions . . . the owners of Irish estates do nothing for the land but drain it of its produce. . . . When the "sacredness of property" is talked of, it should always be remembered that any such sacredness does not belong in the same degree to landed property. No man made the land. It is the original inheritance of the whole species. Its appropriation is wholly a question of general expediency. When private property in land is not expedient, it is unjust. . . . It is some hardship to be born into the world and to find all nature's gifts previously engrossed and no place left for the new-comer. . . . Landed property is felt even by those most tenacious of its rights to be a different thing from other property. . . . The claim of the landowners to the land is altogether subordinate to the general policy of the State. The principle of property gives men no right to the land but only a right to compensation for whatever portion of their interest in the land it may be the policy of the State to deprive them of. . . . To me it seems almost an axiom that property in land should be interpreted strictly and that the balance in all cases of doubt should incline against the proprietor. The reverse is the case with property in movable goods and in all things the product of labour; over them, the owner's power both of use and of exclusion should be absolute except where positive evil to others would result from it. . . . To be allowed any exclusive right at all over a portion of the common inheritance, while there are others who have no portion, is already a privilege. No quantity of movable goods which a person can acquire by labour prevents others from acquiring the like by the same means; but from the very nature of the case, whoever owns land keeps others out of the enjoyment of it. . . . When land is not intended to be cultivated, no good reason can in general be given for its being private property at all.[79]

Mill's ideas in political economy perhaps may be traced to the days when, as a precocious youngster, he helped his father write the *Elements of Political Economy*. Certainly on this question of a tax upon land values the conceptions of James Mill, with whose work George seemed unfamiliar, were a quite accurate anticipation of the suggestions that are more commonly attributed to his son. In the work of both the Mills there is not only the same specific proposal for the absorbing of increased land values through the process of taxation, but also the same insistence upon the necessity for using the land, and the same distinction made between the landowner as cultivator and the landowner as speculator. There is also the same caution against the suggesting of any possible injustice; James Mill, for example, holding that whereas in a new country before the land has become institutionalized as private property, "there is a peculiar advantage in preserving the rent of land as a fund for supplying the exigencies of the State," [80] in an older country, where landed property has been established, only the increased value of land should be so collected in taxation. The same caution is present also with both the Mills in the matter of compensating the land-

[79] *Principles of Political Economy,* Book II, Chap. II, Sec. 6. See also essays on landed property in *Dissertations and Discussions.*

[80] *Elements of Political Economy* (3rd ed., London, 1826; Sec. 5 on Taxes on Rent, p. 249). He continues by showing that if the whole rent of land were collected in a country in which private property in land had already been accepted, "it would be partial and unequal taxation, laying the burden of the State upon one set of individuals, and exempting the rest. It is a measure, therefore, never to be thought of by any government which would regulate its proceedings by the principles of justice." (Pp. 250–251.)

owner for any losses. (George was very critical of the compensation suggestions of John Stuart Mill.)

Regarding the phenomenon of economic rent and the absorbing of its increase by taxation, James Mill states:

> It is certain that as population increases, and as capital is applied with less and less productive power to the land, a greater and a greater share of the whole of the net produce of the country accrues as rent, while the profits of stock proportionately decrease. This continual increase, arising from the circumstances of the community, and from nothing in which the landholders themselves have any peculiar share, does seem a fund no less peculiarly fitted for appropriation to the purposes of the State, than the whole of the rent in a country where land had never been appropriated. While the original rent of the landholder, that upon which alone all his arrangements . . . must be framed, is secured from any peculiar burden, he can have no reason to complain should a new source of income which costs him nothing be appropriated to the service of the State.[81]

In another passage he mentions the significant distinction between taxes on rent and taxes on production:

> It is sufficiently obvious that the share of the rent of land, which may be taken to defray the expenses of government, does not affect the industry of the country. The cultivation of the land depends upon the capitalists to whom the appropriate motive is furnished when he receives the ordinary profits of stock. To him it is a matter of perfect indifference whether he pays the surplus in the shape of rent to an individual proprietor or in that of revenue to a government collector.[82]

Although George was not acquainted with the work of James Mill, and was far from completely sympathetic to the

---

[81] *Elements of Political Economy,* pp. 252–253. This passage is interesting not only in showing the phraseology of Smith and the Physiocrats, but also in stating, in a degree, the "law of rent" of Ricardo. Mill wrote in 1821. In Chap. II, Sec. 1, he discusses the problem of the "extra doses of capital" that must be used upon inferior land.

[82] *Ibid.,* opening lines of Sec. 5 on "Taxes on Rent."

suggestions of John Stuart Mill, yet he realized the significance that the proposal to collect the future unearned increment of land had for his own conceptions, and in *Progress and
Poverty* he quotes Mill, the son, as a partial indorser of the
idea of land value taxation,[83] although he felt that Mill
"never saw the true harmony of economic laws, nor realized
how from the one great fundamental wrong flow want and
misery, and vice and shame." [84] George believed that Mill
was too entangled in the web of Malthusianism to realize
that want was not due to the "niggardliness of nature" and
"thus to him the nationalization of land seemed comparatively a little thing, that could accomplish nothing toward
the eradication of pauperism and the abolition of want." [85]

Much of the work of Adam Smith on rent and the relation
of rent to wages appeared to George to have this same tendency to fall short of fundamentals.[86] There are, of course, in
Smith many passages in which he all but states the very proposal of George, and there is expressed likewise the definite
belief that rent is an unearned income that arises and increases without any effort on the part of the landowner, and
that therefore it should be used as a source for taxation. In
the opening words of his chapter on the wages of labor, Smith
states:

> The produce of labour constitutes the natural recompense or
> wages of labour. In that original state of things, which precedes
> both the appropriation of land and the accumulation of stock, the
> whole produce of labour belongs to the labourer. He has neither
> landlord nor master to share with. . . . As soon as the land be-
> comes private property, the landlord demands a share of almost

[83] *Progress and Poverty*, pp. 420–421.
[84] *Ibid.*, p. 361.
[85] *Ibid.* But Mill, if any man, was certainly concerned with the "eradication of pauperism and the abolition of want."
[86] George, however, was not entirely familiar with the work of Smith
at the time of writing *Progress and Poverty*, for in August, 1883, he wrote
to a friend that he had just completed his first thorough reading of the
Wealth of Nations.

all the produce which the labourer can either raise or collect from it. His rent makes the first deduction from the produce of the labour which is employed upon land.[87]

In reference to the nature of rent, there is this:

Every improvement in the circumstances of the society tends either directly or indirectly to raise the real rent of land, to increase the real wealth of the landlord, his power of purchasing the labour, or the produce of the labour of other people. . . . The real value of the landlord's share, his real command of the labour of other people, not only rises with the real value of the produce, but the proportion of his share to the whole produce rises with it.[88]

In the section devoted to taxes upon rent, Smith, as did the Mills later, holds that:

Both ground-rents and the ordinary rent of land are a species of revenue which the owner, in many cases, enjoys without any care or attention of his own. Though a part of this revenue should be taken from him in order to defray the expenses of the State, no discouragement will thereby be given to any sort of industry. . . . Ground-rents, and the ordinary rent of land, are therefore, perhaps, the species of revenue which can best bear to have a peculiar tax imposed upon them. Ground-rents seem in this respect a more proper subject of peculiar taxation than even the ordinary rent of land. . . . Ground-rents (economic rent), so far as they exceed the ordinary rent of land, are altogether owing to the good government of the sovereign. . . . Nothing can be more reasonable than that a fund which owes its existence to the good government of the State should be taxed peculiarly, or should contribute something more than the greater part of other funds towards the support of that government.[89]

While the Mills and Smith anticipated George in many of his basic assumptions, it is with David Ricardo that his work

---

[87] *Wealth of Nations* (McCulloch ed. of 1850), Book I, Chap. VIII, p. 29.
[88] *Ibid.*, Book I, Chap. II, p. 115.
[89] *Ibid.*, Book V, Chap. II, Art. 1, pp. 380–381.

is more closely and more functionally connected; the Ricardian "law of rent" [90] may be taken as perhaps the most important foundation stone of George's political economy. Indeed, Professor Young states that "George's doctrine that 'rent or land value does not arise from the productiveness or utility of the land,' that 'it in no wise represents any help or advantage given to production,' looks remarkably like a corollary of the ordinary statements of the famous 'law of rent' "; [91] and that was precisely what George believed— that his work was a necessary and inevitable corollary of the law of rent, and that it carried one step further the reasoning of Ricardo and demonstrated that a correct statement of the law of rent meant the removal of all justification for the private appropriation of rent.[92] Moreover, George felt that he had correlated the law of rent with the laws of wages and of interest, believing, as did Adam Smith, that rent is directly paid out of the produce of labor, that "wages and interest do not depend upon the produce of labor and capital, but

[90] Ricardo formulated but did not "discover" the law of rent. The credit for such discovery is usually assigned to James Anderson in his 1777 tract, "An Inquiry into the Nature of the Corn Laws, with a View to the Corn Bill proposed for Scotland" (see especially McCulloch's ed. of the *Wealth of Nations*, p. 453). There was a group of economic writers in England who definitely anticipated the statement of the Ricardian theory of rent, men like Rooke, Torrens, West, Malthus himself, and several others who, particularly in the years 1814–1815, were interested in this phase of economic speculation. (For these anticipators of Ricardo see Professor Seligman's important essay, "Some Neglected British Economists," which appeared in *The Economic Journal*, Vol. XIII, Nos. 51 and 52, September and December, 1903.) The first statement by Ricardo of the law of rent was in his essay "On the Influence of a Low Price of Corn on the Profits of Stock," of 1817. For his complete formulation of the law see his *Principles of Political Economy and Taxation*, Chap. II, on Rent.

[91] *The Single Tax Movement in the United States*, p. 21.

[92] "Mr. George has performed upon the economical system of Ricardo an operation similar to that which Hume performed on the philosophical system of Berkeley, when, following the method by which Berkeley had eliminated matter, he likewise eliminated mind." Robert Scott Moffat in *Henry George the Orthodox* (London, Remington, 1885, p. 213); a very interesting account of the reaction to *Progress and Poverty* by an economist who clearly saw George's direct relation to the classical school of English economy. (For a discussion of the modern qualifications of Ricardo, particularly those of J. B. Clarke, see *supra*, p. 111, n. 39.)

upon what is left after rent is taken out; or, upon the produce which they could obtain without paying rent—that is, from the poorest land in use. And hence, no matter what be the increase in productive power, if the increase in rent keeps pace with it, neither wages nor interest can increase." [93] Compare this with Ricardo's statement that "in a progressive country . . . the landlord not only obtains a greater produce but a larger share. . . . The interest of the landlord is always opposed to the interest of every other class in the community. His situation is never so prosperous as when food is scarce and dear." [94]

George's statement of the law of rent was that "the rent of land is determined by the excess of its produce over that which the same application can secure from the least productive land in use," which is expanded into:

> The ownership of a natural agent of production will give the power of appropriating so much of the wealth produced by the exertion of labor and capital upon it as exceeds the return which the same application of labor and capital could secure in the least productive occupation in which they freely engage." [95]

"Ever since the time of Ricardo," George states, "the law itself has been clearly apprehended and fully recognized. But not so its corollaries. Plain as they are, the accepted doctrine of wages (i. e., that wages are drawn from the stock of capital) . . . has hitherto prevented their recognition." [96] And therefore George sought to reinterpret the Ricardian law of rent and to add those corollaries which had not been recognized. [97]

While George realized the intimate relation that his work

[93] *Progress and Poverty*, p. 171.
[94] In the essay on the price of corn (McCulloch's ed. of Ricardo's works, 1871; pp. 375, 378).
[95] *Progress and Poverty*, p. 169.
[96] *Ibid.*, p. 170.
[97] See *supra*, pp. 111 ff.

had with the formulations of Ricardo, he was also aware that his knowledge of the English economist's ideas had followed the fashioning of his own proposals, and that there was not, as some writers believe,[98] any conscious dependence of one upon the other. Certainly the suggestions of the English economists, and especially the rent concepts of Ricardo, prepared the way for the discussion and often the acceptance of George's system, but that was solely because his work fitted in with much of the thought of the classical economists, rather than that it was any direct outgrowth from it. Perhaps George was the legitimate developer of Ricardo,[99] but that must be understood in an objective historical sense and not in one of personal dependence. The fact that George did not bring any new ideas into political economy and that nearly all of his conceptions had been anticipated by the classical economists,[100] does not lessen the importance that his discoveries had in the development of his own thought, and it does not explain away the real significance of his

[98] Cannan, for example, holds that "the movement for 'nationalizing' land without compensation to present owners, on which Mr. Henry George and others have wasted immense energy, would probably never have been heard of, if the Ricardian economists had not represented rent as a sort of vampire which continually engrosses a larger and larger share of the produce." (*Theories of Production and Distribution,* London, 1903, p. 393.) While it is true that for Ricardians "the interest of the landlord is always opposed to the interest of every other class in the community," yet Ricardo himself was not hostile to the landed class.

[99] "I hope to show," wrote Moffat, "that Mr. George in his process of reasoning and construction of dogma, is a legitimate follower of the English master of economical method (Ricardo)." (*Henry George the Orthodox,* p. 4.)

[100] As to the work of some of the other classical economists: Cairnes was mentioned by George in *Progress and Poverty* only in connection with his discussion of the interdependence of wages and interest (pp. 20–22). George was apparently unaware of Cairnes's views on the land question, especially as they were expressed in the essay on "Political Economy and Land," written in 1870. Cairnes wrote: "Sustained by some of the greatest names— I will say by every name of the first rank in Political Economy, from Turgot and Adam Smith to Mill—I hold that the land of a country presents conditions which separate it economically from the great mass of the other objects of wealth." (*Essays in Political Economy, Theoretical and Applied,* London, 1873, p. 189.) In reference to George's connection with Malthus, see *supra,* pp. 86–87.

work, which was much more than his rediscovery and re-vitalizing of already promulgated doctrines with the force of sincerity and eloquence.[101]   George's contribution to the history of political economy lay rather in his attempt to fuse all the facts of economic science into a "true harmony of economic laws." He felt that the English economists had failed to do this. Their seeming inability to reach the systematized and complete statement of their own suggestions, or to correlate their isolated intimations, was, for him, an indication

[101] It was the power of this sincerity, and the obvious success George had in popularizing economic doctrine, that impressed J. A. Hobson, who wrote: "But we must recognize at the outset that the substance of George's land theory and policy was nothing new; he is not to be looked upon as a fanatic, who conjured out of his imagination, or his private experience, some brand-new doctrine which he sought to impose upon the popular mind. Those who would thus conceive him are forgetful or ignorant of the tenor of the peculiarly English science of Political Economy, which, from John Locke to J. S. Mill, may be regarded as continually engaged in undermining the ideas of justice and social utility attaching to private property in land. . . . George did not even originate the policy of the 'single tax' on land, most distinctively associated with his name. The small step from the Physiocratic doctrine that all taxation was, in fact, borne by rent to the position that all taxation ought to be so borne, was taken by more than one would-be reformer of this century. The real importance of Henry George is derived from the fact that he was able to drive an abstract notion, that of economic rent, into the minds of a large number of 'practical' men, and so generate therefrom a social movement. It must be understood that the minds into which George dropped his seed were, for the most part, 'virgin soil'; the teachings of economists to whom allusion has been made had never reached the ear of most of them, or had passed unheeded. . . . His nature contained that flavor of obstinacy which borders on fanaticism and which is rightly attached to the missionary. . . . Henry George had all the popular gifts of the American orator and journalist, with something more. Sincerity rang out of every utterance. . . . In my lectures upon Political Economy about the country, I have found in almost every centre a certain little knot of men of lower-middle or upper-working classes, men of grit and character, largely self-educated, keen citizens, mostly nonconformists in religion, to whom Land Nationalization, taxation of unearned increment, or other radical reforms of land tenure, are doctrines resting upon a plain moral sanction . . ." ("Influence of Henry George in England," *Fortnightly Review* of December 1, 1897.) As so many other critical articles on George, especially in England, this fails to realize, even while commending George as not being a fanatic and a conjurer out of his imagination, that he did actually construct the greatest part of his system out of "his private experience." The same small interpretation of George is present in Ernest Barker, who writes that "The American, Henry George, though adding no new ideas, had added new vigour and 'hustle' to an old doctrine." (*Political Thought in England, from Herbert Spencer to the Present Day*, Henry Holt, Home Library ed., p. 215.)

of short-sightedness. George's system was "his own by right of synthesis and emphasis," [102] and it is as a system-maker that George must be understood.[103]

George is thus placed in a peculiar relationship to the classical economists, for he appears not only as an original thinker, who quite independently arrived at some of the fundamental tenets of English political economy, but also as a correlator of what he regarded as disconnected fragments in the work of the economists. His conceptions, while not a product of other systems of economic science, were understood by George himself, and by those of his followers who were conscious of the historical background of the land movement, as a further development of principles that had already been established by the recognized leaders in economics. In using the ideas of his predecessors (when he had discovered them) as a buttress, where they so permitted, for his own hypotheses, and in attempting to develop the implications that he found in the writings of the British economists, George definitely, although perhaps not intentionally, coupled his reasoning with some of the most widely discussed traditions of economic theory. This connection was of great significance in his own work, for his later conceptions, while still unchanged, were broadened and strengthened through

---

[102] Young (op. cit.), p. 25.

[103] One of the most thorough recognitions of this system-fashioning work of George is that by Moffat in the book previously mentioned: "Mr. George, as a system-maker, in which capacity I wish to invite attention to him, is the legitimate continuator and developer of Ricardo, the great system-maker of political economy. . . . As a combination, Mr. George's book is, perhaps, as original a contribution as has ever been offered to science. Yet his method, with a difference that will be duly noted, is Ricardo's, and there is hardly a particular doctrine in his book that has not been previously propounded by some one. . . . Throughout his system of doctrines, there is hardly one which has not its counterpart in some previous system. . . . Has Mr. George diligently collected all these things, or has he rediscovered them for himself? I believe the latter to be in the main the true explanation. . . . The sublimity his transformations impart to the commonest doctrines remind one that the accusation of plagiarism was brought against Handel" (pp. 3–5). That is probably the best statement of this whole matter of the precise degree of George's originality.

his contact with the opinions of the English thinkers. Certainly their ideas, which entered into his own thought after he had been convinced of the truth of his land proposal but before he had worked it out in complete detail, were of more moment to George than were the concepts of his other anticipators; and their general approach to a consideration of the land problem, as well as their specific suggestions, make the classical economists a real factor in the complete statement of George's proffered solution.

The list of George's anticipators has not, of course, been exhausted in this brief survey. There have been other men, many perhaps still unknown, who have seen the peculiar significance of a tax upon the value of the land,[104] and there have

[104] A discussion of the forerunners of George should not be concluded without some mention at least of the German Bodenreformers, whose work came into recognition just a few years before the appearance of *Progress and Poverty.* These land reformers, led by men like August Theodor Stamm in particular, Samter, and Gossen (the latter of the German mathematical school of economy who, along with Walras in Switzerland and France, was of such importance in the independent discovery of the concept of marginal utility), anticipated not only George's specific proposal for a land tax, but also his synthesis of economic laws. Stamm's book, with the significant title of *Die Erlösung der darbenden Menschheit,* appeared in 1871, and, as with *Progress and Poverty,* it held that poverty and all the misery born of poverty could be abolished only by destroying private ownership of land through the means of land value taxation. Such a tax would unravel the tangle of political economy and prepare the way for a natural order. Unlike George, Stamm favored compensating the present owners of land. He later organized the Society for Humanity, which was devoted to propagating his principles of land reform. Adolph Samter's work, *Das Eigentum in seiner socialen Bedeutung,* was published in 1879, the same year as *Progress and Poverty* appeared. Hermann Heinrich Gossen was the most influential figure among these early Bodenreformers because of his general work in economic theory, but he was preceded by Karl Arnd, who wrote a work on Natural Taxation in 1852. Gossen's book, *Entwicklung der Gesetze des menschlichen Verkehrs und der darausfliessenden Regeln für menschliches Handeln,* which appeared two years later, advocated that the State should purchase the land and then, acting as landlord, should lease it to private citizens. In 1860 Friedrich Held petitioned the Prussian legislature to arrange for a tax upon land values only.

For an account of these early Bodenreformers, see Dollfus, *Über die Idee der einzigen Steuer (op. cit.);* Joseph Danziger's account of the single tax movement in Germany, pp. 145–154 in the *Single Tax Year Book (op. cit.),* Young *(op. cit.),* pp. 10–12.

When George's work became known in Germany it was quickly correlated

been others also to whom has come, what George would have liked to think, a vision, an individual revelation of a certain relationship and harmony between the forces that govern the workings of political economy and the forces that control life itself. George knew of only a few of his host of predecessors, but his faith in the universal appeal of this truth that he had seen is found in what are almost the concluding words of *Progress and Poverty:* "And they who fight with Ormuzd, though they may not know each other—somewhere, sometime, will the muster roll be called."

GEORGE'S BACKGROUND

The origin of George's approach to social problems through an attempted solution of the land problem cannot, then, be traced to the work of other writers, although the same thoughts were present among many of his predecessors in economic theory; but that origin can be quite definitely related to the setting in which his thought was formed. His own account of the manner in which he first became aware of the doctrine that was to dominate his life is largely in terms of inspiration and revelation,[105] but inspiration and revelation are not of much assistance in explaining precisely how a theory originated. In the case of George, however, there is little difficulty in tracing back to their sources the factors that really inspired him; indeed, he himself recognized the importance that his background had for the development of his

with the proposals of these early thinkers, and a new group of Bodenreformers came into existence, with leaders such as Michael Flürscheim, Adolph Damaschke, Theodor Hertzka, and Professors Adolph Wagner of Berlin and Imhoff of Freiburg. An instance of the popular relation of the work of George to that of his German predecessors appeared in a quotation from the *Kölnische Zeitung* (Cologne) at the time of George's death (quoted in the *Literary Digest* of Dec. 4, 1897, Vol. XV, No. 32, article on "Henry George Through European Eyes"): "This theory [the single tax] which originated with the English schoolmaster Thomas Spence, was further spun out by Richard Hale, and was further advocated in Germany by Gossen, Samter, and Stamm."

[105] See *supra,* pp. 42–43 and 179–180.

concepts. While, on the one hand, he could write that "Once, in daylight, and in a city street, there came to me a thought, a vision, a call—give it what name you please. But every nerve quivered. And there and then I made a vow," and that, "Like a flash it came upon me that there was the reason of advancing poverty and advancing wealth," yet he also realized that, "I certainly neither picked it up [his theory] second-hand nor got it by inspiration. I came to it by a long, laborious, and most conscientious investigation . . . and if I have been enabled to emancipate myself from ideas which have fettered far abler men, it is, doubtless, due to that fact that my study of social problems was in a country like this [California], where they have been presented with peculiar directness, and perhaps also to the fact that I was led to think a good deal before I had a chance to do much reading." [106] A revealed vision, of course, is very rarely something entirely cut off from all environing conditions, a phenomenon so completely *sui generis* that it is beyond the realm of the explicable; and George's "long, laborious, and most conscientious investigation," together with the fact that his study of social problems was in a country like California, are quite sufficient to indicate the sources from which his ideas had sprung. Inspiration is perhaps nothing but the result of some form of concentrated thought, a result, however, that may be manifested suddenly in a striking mystical experience. And it is not of little consequence that the records show that revelations, even scientific "hunches"—the whole hypothetical technique, if you will—are likely to occur in those precise lines of endeavor in which the individual has been vitally interested; certainly had George's call been one announcing some new law of chemical combination, instead of one con-

[106] From an article in the Sacramento *Record-Union* of March 27, 1880, replying to a review of *Progress and Poverty*. (Quoted by Young, p. 28, and also in the *Life*, p. 325.)

cerned with a land problem, then indeed and only then would it have been a "vision from heaven."

As it was, those years of formative thought, from 1858 to 1879, which found George in pioneer California, where a new order of society was unmistakably in the process of growth, added to the intimate acquaintanceship that he had made with the debasing effects of poverty, are perhaps sufficient to explain why his ideas were directed to a consideration of social questions.[107] In this new West, George found not only the stimulating tonic of a pioneer community, where ideas, when there were any, were impertinently independent of older and mustier traditions, but also, and more significantly, he saw a growing restlessness and growing uneasiness; amid all the buoyant freedom of a new society there were appearing traces of the symptoms that characterized older and more respectable communities, want and misery and charity. And as the West became maturer and more civilized, those essentially pathological symptoms became aggravated. George himself relates how, shortly after he arrived in the West, he became impressed by the lamentable phenomenon that as a country became wealthier and more populous, conditions grew steadily worse:

Let me, since I am in San Francisco, speak of the genesis of my own thought. I came out here at an early age, and knew nothing whatever of political economy. I had never intently thought upon any social problem. One of the first times I recollect talking on such a subject was one day, when I was about eighteen, after I had come to this country, while sitting on the deck of a topsail schooner with a lot of miners on the way to the Frazer River. We got talking about the Chinese, and I ventured to ask what harm they were doing here, if, as these miners said, they were only working the cheap diggings?

[107] Of course, George's thinking cannot be completely understood unless another controlling element is grasped, that vague force of the political philosophy of a Zeitgeist, the doctrine of natural rights made manifest in Jeffersonian democracy.

"No harm now," said an old miner, "but wages will not always be as high as they are to-day in California. As the country grows, as people come in, wages will go down, and some day or other white men will be glad to get those diggings that the Chinamen are now working." And I well remember how it impressed me, the idea that as the country grew in all that we are hoping that it might grow, the conditions of those who had to work for their living must become, not better, but worse. . . . I remember, after coming down from the Frazer River country, sitting one New Year's night in the gallery of the old American Theatre—among the gods —when a new drop curtain fell, and we all sprang to our feet, for on that curtain was painted what was then a dream of the far future, the overland train coming into San Francisco; and after we had shouted ourselves hoarse, I began to think what good is it going to be to men like me—to those who have nothing but their labor? I saw that thought grow and grow. We were all— all of us, rich and poor—hoping for the development of California, proud of her future greatness, looking forward to the time when San Francisco would be one of the great capitals of the world; looking forward to the time when this great empire of the West would count her population by millions. And underneath it all came to me what that miner on the topsail schooner going up the Frazer River had said: "As the country grows, as people come in, wages will go down." [108]

It was this same thought that George elaborated in his first economic writing, an article on "What the Railroad Will Bring Us" for the *Overland Monthly* in 1868.[109] And, of course, it was this paradox of increasing wealth and want that not only gave the title to his chief work, but was really the underlying problem of all his economic thinking. It was expressed perhaps most clearly in the introduction to *Progress and Poverty*:

It is to the newer countries—that is, to the countries where material progress is yet in its earlier stages—that laborers emigrate in search of higher wages, and capital flows in search of higher

[108] From a speech in San Francisco (February 4, 1890, in the Metropolitan Hall) during George's trip around the world. Quoted in *Life*, pp. 80, 100.
[109] See *supra*, pp. 39–40.

interest. It is in the older countries—that is to say, the countries where material progress has reached later stages—that widespread destitution is found in the midst of the greatest abundance. Go into one of the new communities where Anglo-Saxon vigor is just beginning the race of progress; where the machinery of production and exchange is yet rude and inefficient; where the increment of wealth is not yet great enough to enable any class to live in ease and luxury; where the best house is but a cabin of logs or a cloth and paper shanty, and the richest man is forced to daily work—and though you will find an absence of wealth and all its concomitants, you will find no beggars. There is no luxury, but there is no destitution. No one makes an easy living, nor a very good living; but every one *can* make a living, and no one able and willing to work is oppressed by the fear of want.

But just as such a community realizes the conditions which all civilized communities are striving for, and advances in the scale of material progress—just as closer settlement and a more intimate connection with the rest of the world, and greater utilization of labor-saving machinery, make possible greater economies in production and exchange, and wealth in consequence increases, not merely in the aggregate, but in proportion to population—so does poverty take a darker aspect. Some get an infinitely better and easier living, but others find it hard to get a living at all. The "tramp" comes with the locomotive, and almshouses and prisons are as surely the marks of "material progress" as are costly dwellings, rich warehouses, and magnificent churches. Upon streets lighted with gas and patrolled by uniformed policemen, beggars wait for the passer-by, and in the shadow of college, and library, and museum, are gathering the more hideous Huns and fiercer Vandals of whom Macaulay prophesied.[110]

George had seen this vivid contrast himself, not only in the comparison of early San Francisco with the Philadelphia of his boyhood and with the New York that had shocked him with its display of poverty, but also in the changing conditions in California itself. Where once wages had been spectacularly high and working men independently confident and self-assured, there now came the ominous cry of "hard

[110] Pp. 6–7.

times," and the unemployment and stagnation of a period of depression. California was growing older and consequently sadder if not wiser.

But a more suggestive phenomenon in the early development of California, and one that was more specifically responsible for the direction in which George's economic theory developed, was the prodigal disposal of the public domain and the resulting wild flourish of land speculation.[111] This alienation of the lands of California and their concentration in the hands of a comparatively few owners, was not something accidental nor was it peculiarly characteristic of the State of California. It was the direct result of the general State and Federal land policy which was soon to become traditional in its lavish and thoughtless disposal of Western lands. The status of California lands had been complicated by the Spanish and Mexican grants operative before the State entered the Union, but instead of clearing away the confusion that had resulted from conflicting land titles, the early American policy still further unsettled the situation,[112] and paved the way for the unscrupulous activities of land speculators.[113] Coupled with this attitude of neglect was the more positive Federal policy of reckless land grants to private

[111] For a brief historical account of the land policy followed in early California see Young (op. cit.), Chap. II. The authorities he quotes are: Royce's California; J. S. Hittell, The Resources of California (1863) and History of California; H. H. Bancroft's History of California, and T. C. Donaldson's The Public Domain. The statistical reports of various Federal and State land equalization and census boards are also made use of. See also The Great American Land Bubble, by A. M. Sakolski (New York, Harpers, 1932), Chap. XII.

[112] Young, pp. 28–34. The Federal Government waited from 1848 to 1851 before taking any action regarding the status of the Spanish and Mexican grants, and the act of March 3, 1851, was "nominally to 'settle' private land claims in California, but really to unsettle them and the whole country, and keep them unsettled." (Hittel, Resources of California, pp. 455–456, in Young, p. 31.)

[113] Young traces the beginning of the concentration of land ownership in California to government negligence, and quotes Bancroft's opinion that the policy of the United States resulted in "confiscation, and that not in the real interests of the United States, or of American settlers, but of speculating land sharpers." (Bancroft, History of California, p. 577, in Young, p. 34.)

individuals and particularly to the railroads. The lands of the State were admitted to preëmption by the act of March 3, 1863,[114] and later the railways were granted holdings comprising 16,387,000 acres, more than sixteen per cent of the entire area of California. The State policy was no improvement upon the prodigality of the Federal Government, and "in eighteen years the State had disposed of her vast landed possessions, making no attempt to increase their value by improvements, nor leaving any to rise in value along with the development of the country about them. The money realized was . . . dissipated by the extravagance of the early Legislatures, or fraudulently disposed of by political tricksters in collusion with dishonest officials." [115]

Of even more direct influence upon George than the disposal of the lands of the State and the resulting tendency toward land monopoly and concentration [116] was the spectacular soaring of land values. The natural increase in the value of land, due to the growing population that followed the discovery of gold, was enormously accelerated by speculative ventures, and the fabulous prices that land acquired still remain, as does the gold rush, part of early California tradition. "The San Francisco *Directory* for 1852 (p. 9) describes in a striking manner the arrival of the brig *Belfast* from New York, laden with a valuable cargo of goods. 'She hauled up to the Broadway wharf, the only wharf accessible to such a vessel, and there discharged. No sooner was she known to be landing her cargo than goods of all kinds fell twenty-five per cent, and real estate rose fifty per cent. A vacant lot on the corner of Washington and Montgomery

[114] The fraud and land-grabbing that resulted from the policy of preemption are described in R. T. Hill, *The Public Domain and Democracy* (*Columbia University Studies*, 1910, p. 46), in Young, p. 34, n. 22.

[115] Bancroft (*op. cit.*), pp. 640–641, Young, p. 35.

[116] For figures bearing on this tendency for California lands to concentrate in the hands of a few at this period, see tables in Young, pp. 36–37; see also George's *Our Land and Land Policy, Works,* Vol. VIII.

streets at that time bordering on the water, which had been offered for $5,000 and refused, sold readily the very next day for $10,000.' " [117] In the *Annals of San Francisco*,[118] there is this statement:

> But chiefly it was the holders of real estate that made the greatest fortunes. The possession of a small piece of building ground in or about the center of business was a fortune in itself. Those lucky people who held lots from the times before the discovery of gold, or who shortly afterwards managed to secure them, were suddenly enriched, beyond their first most sanguine hopes. The enormous rents paid for the use of ground and temporary buildings in 1849 made all men covetous of real estate. . . . The temptation to perpetrate any trick, crime, or violence, to acquire real estate, seemed to be irresistible. . . . The richest men in San Francisco have made the best portion of their wealth in the possession of real estate.

It was against such a background that George formed his thought. "He witnessed intimately perhaps the most discreditable episodes in all our checkered public land history," [119] and he felt that he had before him the very manifestation of why progress meant poverty. He saw that already the early prosperity of California was giving way to discontent and hardship,[120] and he believed that here was a miniature of civilization itself. For George it was no mere coincidence that as a community thrived and grew so did it open the door to the grim spectre of want. There was a common cause, he declared in *Progress and Poverty*, for this companion advance of prosperity and misery, a common ground from which

---

[117] Young, p. 39.
[118] By Soule, Gihon, and Nisbet (1855), pp. 498–500. In Young, p. 40.
[119] Young, pp. 40–41.
[120] ". . . As the exceptional opportunities for stumbling upon fortunes or for taking up rich lands were seized by those first on the ground, as multitudes of men came in, eager to compete for what they regarded as the opportunities of a century, the inevitable leveling down process commenced, and rates of wages began slowly to recede toward the levels obtaining elsewhere. . . . The evils of poverty and vice, always most conspicuous in cities, manifested themselves in San Francisco." (*Ibid.*, p. 41.)

sprang both the fruits and the weeds of civilized society. This common cause George thought that he had found in the peculiar action of land values. They came into existence only with the presence of man and his productive labor; they rose as population increased and as a crude way of living gave way to a more cultivated social order. They were, he was sure, wholly a social product; yet they were exploited by individual landowners, and their constant increase absorbed whatever increase in wealth might be produced by labor.

It is evident, then, that George's California environment was largely responsible for his approach to the problems of political economy, and if it was indeed a truth that he had discovered, then his frontier experience must be considered as a moulding influence. To his own brilliant originality was added this invaluable privilege of having been present at the very birth of a new social order.[121] And George was not

[121] The influence of his pioneer surroundings in directing George's thought has been recognized by nearly every writer who has considered his work. For example, Professor Perlman writes: "His [George's] dogmatism was largely a result of environment. . . . He . . . began his philosophical experience on what was then the economic frontier, where as yet there was little manufacturing, but mainly mining and agricultural pursuits having a direct dependence upon natural resources. Wages were high, owing to the abundance of these resources offering rich alternative opportunities to the wage-earner. When the first transcontinental railroad was completed in 1869 and a rapid growth of population began, the free land was quickly preëmpted by speculators, the price of land soared up, and wages simultaneously fell. George drew the conclusion that wages had declined because the landowner was now exacting a high rent for the use of land. He also ascribed to high rent similar effects on profits, whose similarity to wages he could see in a community where the independent miners commonly spoke of washing their 'wages' out of the soil." (*History of Labour in the United States*, Commons and Associates, New York, Macmillan, 1918; Vol. II, p. 447.) He continues, ". . . Furthermore, George keenly observed the severe industrial depression which struck California in 1877 and which served to confirm the idea already ripened in his mind that the monopolization of the land by withholding it from use both reduced wages and decreased the opportunities for employment. Thus, the observation of conditions in California led George to explain the exploitation of labour and the lack of employment by a single cause, the monopolization of land."

Professor Gide's first review of *Progress and Poverty*, in the *Journal des Économistes* (Paris) of May 15, 1883, was entitled "De quelques nouvelles doctrines sur la propriété foncière," and he showed that these new doctrines (which, however, he later stated were not new at all—see *supra*, p. 176, n. 23)

the only Westerner to be impressed by the evils of the prevailing land policy; in the early '70s there was widespread agitation in California against "land monopoly," an agitation that had lasted ever since the trouble over the Spanish and Mexican grants.[122] Yet while George may not have been the first to advocate land reform, even in California,[123] his work proved to be the most significant and the most permanent; whereas others had recognized only a condition of local concern, he attempted to widen the importance of the land question, and from its partially revealed effects sought to work out a complete system of social organization.

Conditions in California at the time when George began

were a direct product of such a state of society as existed in California where, under the eyes of all, free land was being exhausted.

Judge James G. Maguire, who was an early friend of George and who later became a prominent single taxer, has stated that George "could not have discovered the great truths of political economy but for the social and industrial phenomena which transpired within his experience" and that had it not been for "the marvellously rapid evolution manifested in California, in which was shown every stage of land monopolization that was developed in Europe and America in many centuries, we would now have no single tax agitation." (In the single tax weekly, *Justice*, Jan. 5, 1895; quoted in Young, pp. 27–28.)

[122] The most influential agitator for land reform was perhaps James McClatchy of the Sacramento *Bee*. George had formed his friendship during his early days in Sacramento, and it was largely through the efforts of McClatchy, who later became editor of the San Francisco *Times*, that George won his early advancement in California journalism. (For an account of this land reform agitation in California, see Young, pp. 49–52.) Regarding the work of McClatchy, J. H. Barry wrote in the San Francisco *Star* of November 6, 1897: "It was James McClatchy who instilled into George those ideas antagonistic to land monopoly which were afterwards so brilliantly woven in *Progress and Poverty*. In fact, George insisted that James McClatchy should be the man to write that work." (Young, p. 50, n. 25.)

[123] George, however, did consider that he was the first. "So far as we know, we were the first upon the American continent or anywhere else to enunciate the principle which will some day be an accepted axiom, that land is the only thing which should be taxed for purposes of revenue. And when we did, it was some time before we could find anyone else who thought the same way." (In the San Francisco *Evening Post*, April 16, 1874.) Certainly his *What the Railroad Will Bring Us* of 1868, and *Our Land and Land Policy*, written in 1871, were the earliest comprehensive treatments of land reform in California. George's editorial policy in the *Evening Post* from 1871 to 1875 was also the first consistent journalistic attack upon land monopoly, and the hostile criticism with which it was greeted showed that, even in California, land reform was far from popular.

his more intensive work, the actual writing of *Progress and Poverty,* had grown increasingly worse, and when the depression of 1877 made its appearance the Western State found that it was in the grip of the same evils that had overtaken the more developed East. Not only had the State's early prosperity disappeared, but at the time of the panic a drought and a serious falling-off in the silver output of the Comstock Lode still further aggravated local discontent, and while California did not experience the violence that streaked blood and fire through the great Eastern railway centers, the policy of intimidation adopted by the Central Pacific Railroad helped to bring on the Dennis Kearney upheaval in which the Chinese as well as the railroad were made the objects of attack. The effect of this depression, following so soon upon the earlier spectacular display of wealth in California, strengthened George in his conviction that he was watching the pathological development of a social system, and helped to make *Progress and Poverty* a direct and timely protest against what was an evident social maladjustment.

George's vision, then, was not conjured out of a feverish imagination. It was not a mystic experience that had no relation to anything empirical, but a significant revelation that had come to him as an inference from the changing conditions that he was able to observe. His originality was not in the form of some divine apocalypse, but was rather a carefully planned attempt to reconstruct out of the facts of his immediate experience and out of the anticipations of the classical economists a system that would correlate all the implications of political economy, that would indeed transform political economy into an instrument for solving ultimately all ethical problems. It is true that George's conceptions did not bring any new ideas into the stream of thought, and it may be that his originality was more synthetic than creative, but it was this fresh approach to old problems, an approach that was as much a product of his background as the poverty that harassed him, that has stamped his work as unique. It was this concept of his, the idea that a broadening and developing of the province of economic problems would have a direct and significant effect upon problems in other fields of intellectual endeavor, that, more than any specific treatment of the land question, has ranked George as an independent thinker. The fervent eloquence with which he expounded his doctrine, the missionary obstinacy which "bordered on fanaticism," the complete absence of any spirit of diffidence, made George a compelling figure. His comprehensive and original grasp of a new significance in the meaning and scope of political economy made him a profound one.

CHAPTER V

GEORGE AND SOCIALISM

AT the close of Chapter III there was made the statement that George's proposal to socialize economic rent was the only form of "socialism" that he felt to be necessary. It was, moreover (with the possible exception of public utilities), the only socialization that was acceptable to him. This limitation of society's control of economic processes to land values must introduce the question as to the general relationship between the proposals of socialism and those of George, and it is felt that a brief discussion of that connection may be in place here. That discussion will be confined largely to pointing out the interesting historical relation between George and the socialists, and to a mention also of the seeming points of contact between their respective programs, points which, although in superficial agreement, are indicative of fundamental theoretical contrasts. Yet these contrasts, it will be suggested, must not be interpreted as insurmountable barriers that will force the two movements to remain forever implacable antagonists.

An unfortunate characteristic of some of the less thoughtful types of right wing criticism is the tendency to link together, for purposes of joint condemnation, all suggestions for social change, no matter how divergent they may be in aim and method. Too often there has been a noticeable lack of discrimination in appraising the different schools of liberal thought with the unhappy result that social movements which are poles apart find themselves confronted by the same critical formulæ. Proposals almost diametrically opposed to one another have again and again been made unwilling allies and have then been attacked along a single front. Marx and Bakunin, for example, made strange and embarrassed bedfellows, yet how many times have they been anathematized as blood-brothers. But, while the type of mind that considers the Soviet leaders to be both socialists and anarchists may well be disregarded, still this perhaps unconscious proclivity to confuse the issues of attempted political and economic reconstruction is more subtle and pervasive than is generally realized. There seems almost to be a set of associated ideas all ready to greet any suggestion of change, and the precise nature of the suggestion does not appear at all relevant.

The reception of George's doctrines has been not a little influenced by this uncritical attitude and the outcome has been to couple him occasionally with the socialists.[1] Of course, the scorn of socialists and the horror of George's followers at any hint of thus being paired together afford an eloquent proof of the infelicity of such a venture, and that scorn and horror on the part of each are perhaps justified. The confusion between George and socialism, it is true, has most frequently showed itself in the popular mind, but it has by no means been confined to popular opinion. In the most

[1] "Socialism," it is well realized, means many things—especially to socialists—but to discriminate too finely between the different schools is hardly of value in this connection. It is felt, however, that socialism as a word still has an obvious connotation that, although somewhat vague perhaps, may be readily grasped.

George himself wrote that "the term 'socialism' is used so loosely that it is hard to attach to it a definite meaning. I myself am classed as a socialist by those who denounce socialism, while those who profess themselves socialists declare me not to be one. For my own part I neither claim nor repudiate the name, and realizing as I do the correlative truth of both principles can no more call myself an individualist or a socialist than one who considers the forces by which the planets are held to their orbits could call himself a centrifugalist or a centripetalist." (*Protection or Free Trade*, pp. 302–303, n.) This, however, was written in 1886, just before George came into bitter political conflict with the socialists.

academic of discussions George has been often designated as a socialist (or, at least, as a land nationalist), although the term has usually been qualified; he has been treated as a "land socialist," an "agrarian socialist," even a "Christian socialist."

The popular confusion of George with socialism has been quite pardonable, for at the time George came into general notice through the newspapers of the '80s his work was directly connected with that of the socialists. His lecture tours in Great Britain coincided with the formation of the newer socialist groups and the reawakened interest in the labor problem, and he was constantly referred to by the English newspapers as the "prominent American socialist." In the United States he achieved his greatest popularity during the New York City mayoralty election of 1886, and in this campaign all the labor unions and socialist organizations rallied to his support. As a result, he was attacked by the more uncritical of the conservative journals as a socialist (also as an anarchist) and he was welcomed, for a time at least, as a socialist by the labor organizers. It is readily understandable, then, that in some quarters there has been difficulty in divorcing George from this early historical connection with socialism; but that difficulty should not carry over into discussions which profess to have more than a casual acquaintance with the fundamental positions of the two movements.

It is of course obvious that both George and the socialists were united in their criticism of the existing order; both saw the absurd evils of an unbalanced economic organization, and both looked forward to something that would indicate a saner treatment of a diseased society. Yet there seems to be nothing quite so productive of disharmony as this "criticism of the existing social order." All reform movements desire "to change conditions," but that goal has appeared to operate so as effectively to preclude mutual agreement between such movements. Too often the one point of contact has been nothing more than this attitude of criticism and aspiration. And this has been certainly true of the socialists and the followers of Henry George. They may have been made co-defendants by indiscriminate attacks, but they hardly have been coöperators. Even though the ultimate ideal of each may be the creation of a more perfect society, their main traveled roads have led in opposite directions with but chance meetings at isolated by-paths.

The historical connection between George and socialism in England was one of the most interesting episodes in the development of British left wing economics, and if that connection has just been mentioned as a plausible ground for the popular confusion of the two movements, it must also be considered as an example of the legitimate traffic in ideas. George's rôle in the formulation of English socialism in the '80s may not be evidence of any basic sympathy between the two, but it was at least a vivid testimony to the persuasive influence of the American reformer upon the radical movements which came under his sway in their very infancy.

Modern "scientific" British socialism can be quite definitely traced to the work and personal influence of Marx in London from 1849 to 1883. He had come to England just after the downfall of the Chartist movement and during the last stages of the shorter-lived Oxford and Christian socialist agitations. The years of labor apathy in England, which lasted from the collapse of Chartism about 1850 to the time of the American Civil War, were the years in which he began work on what was to be his major effort. Even as early as 1846 Marx had written the "Inaugural Address" for the International Working Men's Association (which was really an attempt on the part of the trade-unions to revivify Chartism), although after the failure of the organization within a few years he became suspicious of the English labor leaders. Of course, there had been a growing trade-union movement and Utopian socialist agitation in England all throughout the nineteenth century, but it was Marx and the brilliant circle he soon gathered about him who ushered in present-day socialism.[2]

Yet despite the personal influence of Marx in England and despite the fact that *Das Kapital* was published twelve years earlier than *Progress and Poverty*, strangely enough it was George and not Marx who exerted the initial stimulus upon the thinkers who within a few years were to organize the Fabian Society and the Social Democratic Federation. It was not that English radicals were unacquainted with Marx's work (although *Das Kapital* was not translated into English until 1886, and up to that time had been interpreted, and often wrongly, only by those socialists in England who were familiar with German or French)[3] but rather that their imaginations and interest were profoundly stirred by the vigor of George's writings and the eloquence and sincerity of his personal propaganda. *Progress and Poverty* was first published in 1879. Within three years a cheap paper edition of the book had been circulated all throughout the United Kingdom, and George was arousing Ireland with a series of lectures on the land question. In 1884 he again came to Great Britain and his talks were received with an almost wild

[2] For a discussion of the rise of British socialism see: *History of British Socialism* by M. Beer (London, G. Bell and Sons, 1921) ; *Socialism in England*, Sidney Webb (London, Swan Sonnenschein, 1893); H. M. Hyndman's *Record of an Adventurous Life* (New York, Macmillan, 1911) ; the historical portions of *Fabian Essays in Socialism*, edited by Shaw (1908 edition, Boston, Ball Publishing Co.) ; and general histories of socialism.

[3] See Beer *(op. cit.)*, Vol. II, p. 227. The French translation of Marx was published in 1873, the same year as the second German edition. *The Communist Manifesto* was not of particular influence at this stage of English socialist thought; its effect, in England, had been chiefly upon the Chartists, who may be considered as the English expression of the revolutionary movements of 1848.

enthusiasm.[4] George was turning the attention of liberals to economic questions, and was crystallizing the vague sentiments against social injustice.

George's work, it must be remembered, fitted in admirably with the economic background against which it appeared, that is, the English background of economic theory and land reform that had been prepared by the work of the Land Tenure Reform Association,[5] of John Stuart Mill, and of the whole school of classical English political economy with whose conceptions the proposals of George were definitely linked. The new alignment of liberal economists which arose after the decline in power of the traditional Liberal political policies in the late '70s found a familiar source of inspiration in *Progress and Poverty*. It is true that the majority of George's English converts soon turned from the land question to the growing socialist movement, but the impetus for a consideration of social reform had been supplied by the stocky red-bearded American orator with the religious vision and almost fanatical confidence of some chosen prophet.

This effect of George upon the beginnings of present-day British socialism is fully realized by the socialists themselves, and, although they now consider the single tax agitation as some strange vestigial reminder of a forgotten epoch, there is much in their literature that pays an almost wistful tribute to the fiery American reformer who first set their faces against economic abuses. Perhaps the most illuminating testimony to George's influence in these early days is given by the prince of Fabians himself, George Bernard

---

[4] For an account of George's tours of Great Britain, see *supra*, Chap. II, pp. 61–63, 64–65, 70.

[5] The Land Tenure Reform Association, founded by Mill in 1870, numbered among its members some of the most noted figures in English thought, including John Morley, Thorold Rogers, Alfred Russell Wallace, Cliffe Leslie, and J. E. Cairnes. (For a discussion of George's connection with the concepts of classical English political economy, see *supra*, Chap. IV, especially pp. 200 ff.)

Shaw. In a letter to Hamlin Garland,[6] Shaw wrote that "Henry George has one thing to answer for that has proved more serious than he thought when he was doing it," and that was the conversion of Shaw to social reform. He then relates how one night in the fall of 1882 he was walking along Farringdon Street in London and chanced to wander into Memorial Hall. There he heard an impassioned orator who must have been an American for he spoke of

Liberty, Justice, Truth, Natural Law, and other strange eighteenth century superstitions and . . . explained with great simplicity the view of the Creator, who had gone completely out of fashion in London in the previous decade and had not been heard of there since. . . . Now at that time I was a young man not much past twenty-five, of a very revolutionary and contradictory temperament, full of Darwin and Tyndall, of Shelley and De Quincey, of Michael Angelo and Beethoven, and never having in my life studied social questions from the economic point of view, except that I had once in my boyhood read a pamphlet by John Stuart Mill on the Irish Land Question. The result of my hearing that speech, and buying from one of the stewards at the meeting a copy of *Progress and Poverty* for sixpence . . . was that I plunged into a course of economic study and at a very early age of it became a Socialist. . . . When I was thus swept into the great Socialist revival of 1883, I found that five-sixths of those who were swept in with me had been converted by Henry George. This fact would have been far more widely acknowledged had it not been that it was not possible for us to stop where Henry George stopped. . . . But I am glad to say that I never denied or belittled our debt to Henry George. If we outgrew *Progress and Poverty* in many respects so did he himself too. . . . Nobody has ever got away or ever will get away from the truths that were the centre of his propaganda; his errors anybody can get away from. . . . Only an American could have seen in a single lifetime the growth of the whole tragedy of civilisation from the primitive forest clearing.

[6] December 29, 1904, in answer to an invitation to attend an anniversary dinner in honor of Henry George which was held in New York, January 24, 1905. The letter may be found in the George collection of manuscripts and letters in the New York Public Library.

An Englishman of Liverpool grows up to think that the ugliness of Manchester and the slums of Liverpool have existed since the beginning of the world. . . . His [George's] genius enabled him to understand what he looked at better than most men; but he was undoubtedly helped by what had happened within his own experience in San Francisco as he never could have been helped had he been born in Lancashire. . . . My ambition is to repay my debt to Henry George by coming over some day and trying to do for your young men what Henry George did nearly a quarter of a century ago for me.

And in the latest Shavian economic advice to women,[6a] Shaw writes in the foreword that:

I wonder this book of mine was not written in America by an American fifty years ago. Henry George had a shot at it; indeed it was his oratory (to which I was exposed for forty-five minutes forty-five years ago by pure chance) that called my attention to it. . . . Still, America can claim that in this book I am doing no more than finishing Henry George's job.

That these expressions of George's influence are not just courteous gestures on the part of Shaw is attested by the biographer, Archibald Henderson, who writes that Shaw "found his way out by following an insistent summons—the clarion call of Henry George," and again that:

Shaw was so profoundly inspired by the logic of Henry George's conclusions and suggested remedial measures that, shortly after reading *Progress and Poverty*, he went to a meeting of the Social Democratic Federation and there arose to protest against their drawing a red herring across the track opened by George.[7]

Shaw's protest must have been singularly ineffective, or perhaps he was persuaded later to help drag the herring.

If Shaw, however, is not a credible witness for the his-

[6a] *Intelligent Woman's Guide to Socialism and Capitalism* (Brentano; Constable; 1928).
[7] *George Bernard Shaw, His Life and Works* (a critical biography, authorized) (Cincinnati, Steward and Kidd, 1911), pp. 56; 96.

torical genesis of present-day British socialist enthusiasm, Sidney Webb surely is; he writes:

Little as Mr. Henry George intended it, there can be no doubt that it was the enormous circulation of his *Progress and Poverty* which gave the touch which caused all the seething influences to crystallize into a popular Socialist movement. The optimistic and confident tone of the book, and the irresistible force of its popularisation of Ricardo's Law of Rent sounded the dominant "note" of the English Socialist party of to-day.[8]

And Beer writes that:

. . . Henry George's books and lectures . . . stimulated many of the younger generation of intellectuals and working men, and caused them to turn their attention to economics. Four-fifths of the socialist leaders of Great Britain in the '80s had passed through the school of Henry George.[9]

William Morris believed that "Henry George's book had been received in this country and in America as a new Gospel," [10] and Hobson's opinion in 1897, mentioned in a previous chapter, was that "Henry George may be considered to have exercised a more directly powerful formative and educative influence over English radicalism of the last fifteen years than any other man." [11] In *Fabian Essays in Socialism* Shaw again traces the transition through which "numbers of young men, pupils of Mill, Spencer, Comte, Darwin, roused by Mr. Henry George's *Progress and Poverty,* left aside evolution and free thought, took to insurrectionary economics, studied Karl Marx" [12]—and so became *bona fide* socialists.

[8] *Socialism in England,* p. 21.
[9] *History of British Socialism,* Vol. II, p. 245.
[10] In *Life of William Morris,* by J. W. Mackail, Vol. II, p. 109. (Quoted in Beer, Vol. II, p. 251.)
[11] "The Influence of Henry George in England," in the *Fortnightly Review* of December 1, 1897.
[12] Essay on "Transition to Social Democracy," p. 169.

A representative of a different type of English socialism, the fiery Tom Mann, pays still another tribute to George's influence:

In 1881, I read Henry George's book *Progress and Poverty*. This was a big event for me; it impressed me as by far the most valuable book I had so far read, and, to my agreeable surprise at the time, it seemed to give an effective answer to Malthus. I was greatly interested in the book. It enabled me to see more clearly the vastness of the social problem, to realise that every country was confronted by it, and the capable and comprehensive analyses of the population question supplied me with what I had not then found in any book in this country before. I must again give a reminder that Socialism was known only to a very few persons and that no Socialist organization existed at this time. . . . I am not wishful to pass any criticism upon Henry George; I wish, rather, to express my indebtedness to him. His book was a fine stimulus to me, full of incentive to noble endeavour, imparting much valuable information, throwing light on many questions of real importance, and giving me what I wanted—a glorious hope for the future of humanity, a firm conviction that the social problem could and would be solved.[13]

Hyndman's opinion of George's influence was one of patronizing and good-natured toleration. Perhaps his Cambridge background, which led him at first to view even Marx with some condescension,[14] never allowed him to become really sympathetic with the work of the agitator from the "San Francisco sand-lots," as he constantly referred to George. Although Hyndman was closer personally to George than practically any of the other English socialists (George was his guest for some time while in England) his impatience, as he himself admits in his book,[15] at not being able to convert him to socialism prevented him from seeing in the American's

---

[13] *Tom Mann's Memoirs* (London, Labour Publishing Co., 1923), pp. 27–28.
[14] Marx's proud and austere personality resented this early patronizing, and for his resulting quarrel with Hyndman, see Beer, Vol. II, pp. 228 ff.
[15] *Record of an Adventurous Life*, pp. 266–268.

conceptions anything more than a possible propædeutic influence upon the growth of British socialism. He wrote, in a passage that is important for containing one of the few references of Marx to George's work, that:

About this time Henry George's *Progress and Poverty* began to produce a great effect upon the public mind, partly in consequence of the land question in Ireland, and even in Great Britain, being more to the front than it has been before or since in our day. . . . Marx looked it through and spoke of it with a sort of friendly contempt: "the capitalists' last ditch," he said. This view I scarcely shared. I saw the really extraordinary gaps in the work and its egregious blunderings in economics, but I also recognized, to an extent that Marx either could not or would not admit, the seductive attractiveness for the sympathetic, half-educated mob of its brilliant high-class journalese. I understood, as I thought, that it would induce people to think about economic problems who never could have been brought to read economic books pure and simple; and although I saw quite as clearly then as I do now that the taxation of land values can be no solution whatever of the social question, I felt that agitation against any form of private property was better than the stereotyped apathy which prevailed all around us. . . . Therefore, I argued, George will teach more by inculcating error than other men can impart by complete exposition of the truth. Marx would not hear of this as a sound contention. The promulgation of error could never be of any good to the people, that was his view. . . . Nevertheless, I still hold that George's temporary success with his agitatory fallacies greatly facilitated the promulgation of Marx's own theories in Great Britain, owing to the fact that the public mind had been stirred up to consider the social question, and political economy generally, by George's easily read book. But that George's fluent inconsequences should be uncongenial to Marx's scientific mind is not surprising. George was a boy with a bright farthing dip fooling around within the radius of a man using an electric searchlight.[16]

[16] *Ibid.*, pp. 267–269.
Practically the only written mention of George by Marx occurred in a letter to his friend Sorge from London, June 30, 1881. The letter appears in *Briefe und Auszüge aus Briefen von Joh. Phil. Becker, Jos. Dietzgen, Friedrich Engels, Karl Marx u.a. an F. A. Sorge und Andere* (Stuttgart, 1906), pp. 175–177. My translation of the letter follows:

238 THE PHILOSOPHY OF HENRY GEORGE

These few quotations will be perhaps sufficient to indicate the part that George played in stimulating the young, and the not-so-young English radicals of the early '80s. To paraphrase Sidney Webb's chemical analogy: George found in Great Britain a supersaturated solution of social discontent, and his contact resulted in the forming of a sediment of socialism (a chemical, of course, and not an ethical sediment) while he himself, as the catalytic agent, remained unaffected. The British socialist movement went confidently on its way,

"I had received two other copies of Henry George before getting yours, one from Swinton and another from Willard Brown, so I gave a copy to Engels and one to Lafargue. For the moment I must confine myself to a very brief judgment of the book. The man is in theory completely 'behind the times' (arrière). He understands nothing of the nature of surplus value, and he wanders about, after the example of the English, although still further behind their old-fashioned speculations concerning the more obvious elements of surplus value—the relations of profit, rent, interest, etc. His fundamental principle [is] that everything would be set in order were the ground-rent paid to the State. . . . This view originally belonged to bourgeois political economy; it was next asserted (without mentioning the similar demands made at the end of the eighteenth century) by the earliest radical followers of Ricardo immediately after his death. I myself said concerning this, in my article against Proudhon in 1847 [the next passage is in French]: 'We realize that economists such as Mill (the elder, not the son John Stuart who reiterated something of the same sort in a modified form), Cherbuliez, Hilditch and others, have demanded that rent be handed over to the State to be used for the payment of taxes. That is simply the frank expression of the hate which the industrial capitalist feels for the landed proprietor, who appears to him as useless and superfluous in the system of bourgeois production.' We ourselves, as already mentioned, adopted this appropriation of ground-rent by the State as one of numerous other transitional measures which, as also remarked in the Manifesto, are and must be, if taken by themselves, self-contradictory. . . . With him [George] so much more inexcusable is the fact that he interpreted inversely the reason why in the United States, where land in comparison with the more developed conditions existing in Europe was and 'to a certain degree' still is accessible to the great mass of the people, the capitalist system and the corresponding servility of the working classes have developed more rapidly and shamelessly than in any other country. On the other hand, the book of George, just as the sensation it has made with you, is significant in that it is a first, if mistaken, attempt to become free from orthodox political economy. For the rest, Henry George appears to know nothing of the history of the earlier American 'Anti-renters,' who were more practical than theoretical. He is otherwise a writer of talent (but to have talent is a Yankee characteristic) as is evidenced by his article on California in the Atlantic. He has, however, the repugnant arrogance and presumption which inevitably mark all such panacea-breeders."

Marx's opinion of George was nicely balanced by George's opinion of

and "the young intellectuals and intelligent working men passed from the meetings addressed by the American land reformer, Henry George, to those addressed by H. M. Hyndman and Sidney Webb." [17] The debate between George and Hyndman in St. James's Hall in 1884 may be taken as a convenient date for the final break between George and the English socialists. In the same year the Fabian Society was formed, with Shaw, Webb and Graham Wallas as its moving spirits, and so the vaguest of the socialist elements was organized. The Social Democratic Federation, under the leadership of Hyndman, Champion, and J. L. Joynes was founded a year later, but it was an outgrowth of the earlier Democratic Federation, organized in 1881 by Hyndman and joined by prominent socialists like Belfort Bax and William Morris, who later, however, in 1884, broke away from the Federation and formed the Socialist League. However, both the Federation and the League proved ineffective in influencing the votes of the British working classes, and in 1893, under the direction of Keir Hardie, definite political action was taken by means of the organization of the Independent Labour Party.[18] The Fabian socialists and the Guild socialists, led by G. D. H. Cole, still are upholding what might be

---

Marx. For example, George wrote to Hyndman: "I know, even if it did not stand out here, your profound admiration for Marx, but your book has convinced me of what I thought before, that however great he may have been in other respects, he lacked analytical power and logical habits of thought. Whatever he may have been, he most certainly was not the scientific man you evidently regard him. . . . Whatever may be the value of his historical researches, he certainly seems to me . . . a most superficial thinker, entangled in an inexact and vicious terminology." (June 22, 1884.) George wrote also to an English friend: "I have been reading Hyndman's 'Historical Basis.' It is a pity to see a man of such force following so blindly such a superficial thinker as Karl Marx. Marx's economics, as stated by Hyndman and all his other followers I have read, will not stand any critical examination." (June 26, 1884.) And in another letter to the same man in 1890, George refers to Marx as the "prince of muddleheads."

[17] Beer (op. cit.), p. 242.

[18] For George's influence upon Labor's erstwhile leader, see H. H. Tiltman's recent biography, J. Ramsay MacDonald, Labour's Man of Destiny (New York, Stokes, 1929).

termed the academic tradition, which has always played an
important rôle in the English socialist movement.

George's connection, then, with British socialism was the
stimulating influence of his sincerity rather than the formative power of his doctrine.[19] His relationship with American
socialism was largely of the same character but not of the
same importance, for in the United States there has been
always a more sharply defined line of cleavage between his
teachings and those of the socialists. For one thing, the
impetus and initial enthusiasm of the American socialist
movement were not at all dependent upon the work of

[19] Continental socialism, of course, need not be considered in its relations
to George, for it was a living force thirty years before his work. Also, it must
not be thought that George's influence upon English radical movements was
completely absorbed in or dissipated by the rise of the socialist organizations.
There always has been a very large and influential Georgist group in Great
Britain. Perhaps the most powerful of such Henry George organizations is
the United Committee for the Taxation of Land Values, formed in 1907,
and directed by men such as John Paul, A. W. Madsen, Frederick Verinder
and others. It is a nonparty body which works through a central London
office and a great number of local committees all over the United Kingdom;
its policies are directed largely to furthering land value taxation activities,
political or propaganda, in England (it was of great influence in the Finance
Act of 1931), popularizing George's works, and providing a focus for the
international movement. There is also a political party group of Georgists
in England, the Commonwealth Land Party, founded in 1919, and headed
by J. W. Graham Peace, W. C. Owen, Matthew Warriner, and the late R. L.
Outhwaite, among others. Of course, the Labour and Liberal parties themselves are committed to some measure of land value taxation. (See *infra*,
pp. 411–424.)

    It was against this group that Hyndman waxed very bitter. He con-
cludes his *Further Reminiscences* (London, Macmillan, 1912) with a scathing attack upon them: "A crew of wealthy Radical resurrectionists have
disinterred Henry George's Single Tax nostrum, which I confess I thought
had been buried for good and all thirty years ago. But no, the 'capitalists'
last ditch,' as Marx called it, has not been filled up finally with the remains
of this bootless, burden-shifting panacea for all economic ills. Baron de
Forest, Joseph Fels, Josiah Wedgwood, Hemmerde, Outhwaite and Co. are
hard at the galvanisation of their exhumed mummy, and George the Second
is waiting close by to see whether their charlatanry can imitate vitality to a
sufficient degree to capture the votes of the people and justify his appearance
on the stage as the true mantle-bearer of the well-meaning but ignorant
prophet of the San Francisco sand lots. . . . This single tax nonsense is
injurious because it diverts public attention from the real difficulties of the
land question." (Pp. 523–525.)

George, and in addition there was no land reform tradition such as had existed in England. The origins of modern socialism in the United States can definitely be placed in the period immediately following the Civil War.[20] It is true that, as in England, there had been earlier socialist agitations, but these had been of the Utopian rather than the "scientific" school and were confined chiefly to the Owenite communities and the "Phalanxes" of Fourier, which had been established in a number of places throughout the country. Even the socialism of the German emigrants who had come to the United States after the revolutionary disturbances of 1848 was generally utopian in character, although its leader, Wilhelm Weitling, had been associated with Marx and Engels in Germany.[21] Weitling's idea of an "exchange bank" for labor was almost identical with Owen's "Equitable Bank of Labor Exchange"; his chief work was in the establishing of the General Working Men's League in 1850, a socialist organization that lasted almost until the outbreak of the Civil War. The war, however, claimed most of the members of the Turnvereins and Turnerbunds, who turned from their socialist discussions to help fight slavery,[22] and after the war the socialists found that a new beginning had to be made.

In the late '60s and early '70s the most powerful theoretical influences exerted upon American socialism were the programs of the International Workingmen's Association that

[20] For a discussion of American socialism, see Morris Hillquit's *History of Socialism in the United States* (New York, Funk and Wagnalls, 1910 ed.); Commons and Associates, *History of Labour in the United States,* Vol. II, Part 6; Engels's *The Labor Movement in America* (New York, 1887); Professor Ely's early works such as *The Labor Movement in America* of 1886, and his *Early American Socialism;* Jessie Wallace Hughan's *The Present Status of Socialism in America* (Columbia University Press, 1911); and general histories of socialism. Hillquit stresses the work of the German historians of American socialism such as Sorge and Von Waltershausen.

[21] In the '50s a more Marxian character was given to German-American socialism by the work of Joseph Weydemeyer, a friend of Marx and Engels.

[22] Hillquit *(op. cit.),* pp. 154–155.

had been founded by Marx in London in 1864, and the Lassalle movement that had been inaugurated in Germany the preceding year. These Continental groups, as Hillquit shows,[23] were able to affect socialism in this country through two channels, the outspoken socialists, chiefly of foreign birth, and the American Labor-Union, an organization that had been formed in 1866 for the purpose of uniting all the American trade-unions in a national movement. But, of course, it was a more direct and tangible stimulus than the doctrinaire statements of European socialists that now prepared the way for the rapid spread of all radical labor agitation—the teachings of George included. The panic of 1873–1877 [24] and the bloody strikes of the latter year that had turned many of the great Eastern railway centers into armed camps, had made labor, already self-conscious, sullen and restless. "The strikes failed in every case, but the moral effect was enormous. . . . The spirit of labor solidarity was strengthened and made national," and the "feeling of resentment engendered thereby began to assume a political aspect, and during the next two years the territory covered

[23] Hillquit, p. 163; also Commons, II, 204 ff.
[24] There can, of course, be no attempt made here to trace the industrial background of either American or English socialism. It may be pointed out, however, that it was only after the Civil War that the factory system in the United States began seriously to affect American industry, and so the American "industrial revolution" must be placed distinctly after that of England, with the obvious result of the later self-consciousness of American labor. Moreover, it may be mentioned that in the United States the origins of socialism seem to have been more directly connected with the labor movement itself than was the case in Great Britain. It was, after all, the leaders of a new economic liberalism in England, thinkers who were a very part of the tradition reaching back from John Stuart Mill to Locke, who became the first prominent socialists. The labor agitators, who, of course, had been connected with the labor movement as such all throughout the nineteenth century, were drawn into socialism later, and although they finally assumed control of the most powerful of the ostensibly socialist organizations, there has always remained, it seems, an element of suspicion between the worker-socialist and the gentleman- and scholar-socialist. In this country there was no such classic liberal tradition, and perhaps that is why socialism in the United States appears more intimately connected with the labor movement itself.

by the strike wave became a most promising field for labor
parties of all kinds and descriptions." [25]

Socialism found in this depression and resentment a fertile
background, and it "emerged for the first time from the
narrow circle of the refugees from Europe, extended its
organizations, and made its appeal to the American working
men." [26] It was in 1877 that the Socialist Labor Party was
formed which was to dominate the American socialist movement until the twentieth century. (The present-day Socialist
Party was formed in 1901.) And it was in these same years
that George completed his *Progress and Poverty*. The same
"hard times" [27] that had driven laborers into the ranks of
socialism had made him sensitive to social problems, and still
later it was the continued labor depression that prepared the
way, as it did with socialism, for the favorable reception of
his doctrines. Both George and socialism, therefore, were
affected by the same conditions, and there was no dependence
of one upon the other, as had been partly the case in England;
there was no need for one to look for inspiration to the other
—both had inspiration right at hand.

The one attempted political union between George and the
socialists occurred in 1886, when George became the labor
candidate in the New York City mayoralty election. [28] It
was admittedly only an opportunistic coöperation. George
was the most popular figure in the reform movement, and
both the labor unions and the socialists subordinated their
own programs in order to unite in what they hoped would be

[25] Commons, II, 191. Professor Perlman adds: "The business depression
of 1873 to 1879 was a critical period in the American labor movement. . . .
It became clear that the 'open union' was not an effective means of com-
bating the tactics of capital." (P. 195.)

[26] *Ibid.*, p. 196.

[27] A vivid picture of the deplorable conditions that existed during the
industrial depression of the '70s is given in the book of Allen Pinkerton, the
detective, *Strikes, Communists, Tramps and Detectives* (New York, 1900
ed.; the book first appeared in 1878).

[28] For a brief account of the election, see *supra*, Chap. II, pp. 66–69.

a successful attack upon privilege—the socialists interpreting privilege as capitalism, the labor unions viewing it as the unrestricted power of the employer, and George having in mind only the privilege and monopoly of the private ownership of land. "From the standpoint of labor, therefore, the platform [of George] was not satisfactory, for the single tax was hardly understood by the working men. But so great was the popularity of the man and so bright the chances for success that this was overlooked. Even the socialists, from whom the harshest criticism might have been expected, raised no protest." [29] The socialists had been greatly weakened by the anarchist agitation which had reached its height about 1883,[30] and were in no condition to support their own candidate; "it was only in 1886 that the Socialist Labor Party was roused from its political lethargy." [31]

The socialists never denied that they were hostile to George or that they favored his candidacy for any save opportunistic reasons. The *Volkszeitung,* for example, stated that it supported George "not on account of his single-tax theory, but in spite of it," [32] and this was the general attitude of socialism. And it is also true that neither did George nor his prominent supporters feel any great friendliness for the socialists. George's platform contained none of the fundamental demands of socialism, and socialist leaders received no important places in the United Labor Party. Such coöperation was not intended to last, and obviously it did not last. Dissension began soon after the election when attempts were made to place the party on a permanent basis, and at the convention in Syracuse in 1887 there was an open break between the supporters of George and the members of the

[29] Commons, Vol. II, p. 449.
[30] In that year the membership of the Socialist Labor Party was not more than fifteen hundred. (*Ibid.,* p. 300.)
[31] Hillquit, p. 247.
[32] *Ibid.,* p. 254.

Socialist Labor Party, each faction declaring that the other sought to dominate the movement. While the socialists were willing to compromise, George held that any compromise would be fatal, and the final result was that the socialist delegates to the convention were declared ineligible. This split in the United Labor Party of George caused its downfall; its candidates, including George, polled a negligible vote in the State election of 1887, and in 1889 the party disappeared, George having left it the year before to support Cleveland. Since that time the socialists and the followers of George have gone their separate political ways.[33] The historical relationship, then, between George and socialism was of real importance only in England, and even that connection, perhaps, was a more interesting than significant one.

However, there has been another more ideational factor that has been partly instrumental in that noticed confusion of the programs of the two movements. It is the obvious yet somewhat disconcerting demand for land reform that is part of every socialist platform. Although the land question has not been elevated to a really prominent position among socialists, except in England, where the age-old concern with the land problem and the historical connection with the classical economic school have inextricably bound up all social reform to some extent with ground rent and "unearned increment," [34] yet it has been necessarily present in all pro-

[33] This may be too extreme a statement, for it is true that socialists and single taxers have coöperated on specific political measures in this country, especially in some of the Western States. (See Young's *History of the Single Tax Movement in the United States,* pp. 307 ff.) Such coöperation has been always the result of opportunism, however, and not of principle, but it is a coöperation that must be encouraged by any one at all interested in social and economic problems. In very recent years, especially since the leadership of Norman Thomas, there seems to be more evidence of sympathy on the part of socialists for the work of George.

[34] "The only country, therefore, in which the problem of the nationalization of the land or of land rent has been in the forefront of socialistic discussion is Great Britain—although we may assume that the socialists of

grams of socialism, for both land and capital (which, for socialism, are in the same category) are to be removed from private control and placed under social administration; the socialization of machinery clearly demands the socialization of sites and natural resources. But the evils of land monopoly, of course, have never been considered by socialists to be on a parity with those of other capitalistic monopolies (and too often also has land reform been interpreted by them as merely an agrarian movement, something that concerns farmers and granges rather than industrial society).[35] Still there is ample testimony to show that socialism is peculiarly sensitive to the necessity of abolishing private property in land.

One of the most unequivocal attacks upon land monopoly has been delivered by Bertrand Russell.[36] It is a passage, however, that must not be interpreted simply by itself, for

other countries will proceed largely along parallel lines." *Socialism of To-Day*, edited by Walling, Stokes, Hughan, and Laidler (New York, Henry Holt, 1916), p. 469. Continental socialism, which has remained more or less orthodox, i. e., Marxian, has been very little concerned with the land problem, although the present Social Democratic Constitution of Germany contains some good Georgian provisions.

[35] In the paragraph just quoted from *Socialism of To-Day* there is a startling illustration of just such a short-sighted confusion. "It is obvious that the agricultural problem is very largely the same as the land problem. But this fact has not as a rule been fully recognized by the Socialists—outside of Great Britain." If that is intended for a tribute to the astute recognition of British socialists, it surely falls very short, for—to be paradoxical for emphasis—it is obvious that the agricultural problem has almost nothing to do with the significance of the land problem. And in the very next sentence this "obvious" connection between the agricultural and land problems is amusingly contradicted (the book was written under the auspices of the Intercollegiate Socialist Society), for the interest of English socialists in the land question is traced to "the natural fact that the land problem, aside from its purely agricultural aspects, is more important in that country than elsewhere. Land rent, especially urban land rent, absorbs a very considerable proportion of the total income of Great Britain, doubtless a larger proportion than in any other of the great nations."

[36] Russell is a Guild Socialist with still a philosopher's love for philosophic anarchism. For him "socialism . . . is rather a tendency than a strictly definable body of doctrine" and is fundamentally "the advocacy of communal ownership of land and capital." *Proposed Roads to Freedom* (London, Allen and Unwin, 1918), p. 23. See also his small volume on *Political Ideals* (New York, The Century Co., 1919).

Russell is even harsher against capitalistic monopoly; it is selected merely to show that, as with almost all other socialists, he realizes the fundamental economic position of land:

Private property in land has no justification except historically through power of the sword. . . . The land became the property of those who had conquered it, and the serfs were allowed to give rent instead of service. . . . It is a singular example of human inertia that men should have continued until now to endure the tyranny and extortion which a small minority are able to inflict by their possession of the land. No good to the community, of any sort or kind, results from the private ownership of land. If men were reasonable, they would decree that it should cease tomorrow, with no compensation beyond a moderate life income to the present holders.

The mere abolition of rent would not remove injustice, since it would confer a capricious advantage upon the occupiers of the best sites and the most fertile land. It is necessary that there should be rent, but it should be paid to the State or to some body which performs public services; or, if the total rental were more than is required for such purposes, it might be paid into a common fund and divided equally among the population. Such a method would be just, and would not only help to relieve poverty but would prevent wasteful employment of land and the tyranny of local magnates. *Much that appears as the power of capital is really the power of the landowners*—for example, the power of railway companies and mine-owners. The evil and injustice of the present system are glaring, but men's patience of preventable evils to which they are accustomed is so great that it is impossible to guess when they will put an end to this strange absurdity.[37]

The Fabians have always been interested in the land problem and so it is no surprise to find the Webbs writing that:

The problem [of rent] has, however, to be faced. Either we must submit for ever to hand over at least one-third of our annual product to those who do us the favour to own our country, without

---

[37] *Why Men Fight* (New York, The Century Co., 1917), pp. 133–135. (Italics mine.)

the obligation of rendering any service to the community, and to see this tribute augment with every advance in our industry and numbers, or else we must take steps, as considerately as may be possible, to put an end to this state of things. . . . It is the very emphatic teaching of political economy that the earth may be the Lord's, but the fullness thereof must inevitably be the landlord's.[38]

And then, these statements again from Shaw:

Here was a vast mass of wealth called economic rent, increasing with the population, and consisting of the difference between the product of the national industry as it actually was and as it would have been if every acre of land in the country had been no more fertile or favorably situated than the very worst acre from which a bare living could be extracted; all quite incapable of being assigned to this or that individual or class as the return to his or its separate exertions; all purely social or common wealth, for the private appropriation of which no permanently valid and intellectually honest excuse could be made. Ricardo was quite as explicit and far more thorough on the subject than Mr. Henry George. . . . *What the achievement of Socialism involves economically is the transfer of rent from the class which now appropriates it to the whole people.* Rent being that part of the produce which is individually unearned, this is the only equitable method of disposing of it. There is no means of getting rid of economic rent. So long as the fertility of land varies from acre to acre, and the number of persons passing by a shop window per hour varies from street to street, with the result that two farmers or two shopkeepers of exactly equal intelligence and industry will reap unequal returns from their year's work, so long will it be equitable to take from the richer farmer or shopkeeper the excess over his fellow's gain which he owes to the bounty of nature or the advantage of situation, and divide that excess or rent equally between the two. . . . *The economic object of Socialism is . . . to carry out the principle over the whole community by collecting all rents and throwing them into the national treasury. . . . The socialization of rent would mean the socialization of the sources of*

[38] *Problems of Modern Industry,* by Sidney and Beatrice Webb (New York, Longmans, Green, 1920 ed.), pp. 240 and 238.

production. . . . This transfer, then, is the subject matter of the transition to Socialism. . . .[39]

A more politically minded British socialist, Philip Snowden, admits that:

Even Socialists are not so omniscient as to be beyond the possibility of learning from others. . . . Like the Single Taxers we recognize the evils of the present land system. Like them, we desire to secure for social purposes the economic rent of land. Like them we believe that much of our social misery is due to the private monopoly of land.[40]

Perhaps of more importance, however, than these expressions on the part of English socialists of the significant part played by land in their conceptions of socialism, are the striking recognitions of Marx himself. There is no intention here, of course, to essay any analysis of his opinions on the land question; all that will be done is to suggest certain passages that seem to indicate that his appreciation of the fundamental character of land was more articulate than his followers generally appear either to have realized or to have

[39] *Fabian Essays in Socialism* (the 1889 London Fabian Society edition); from the essay on the "Transition to Social Democracy," pp. 177–180; (italics mine). In the opening pages of the essay on the "Economic Basis of Socialism," Shaw devotes some attention to the original loss of man's claim to the land, and traces in a typically facetious manner the dire consequences of this primal swindling of Adam. Further on, he states: "On Socialism the analysis of the economic action of Individualism bears as a discovery, in the private appropriation of land, of the source of those unjust privileges against which Socialism is aimed. *It is practically a demonstration that public property in land is the basic economic condition of Socialism.*" (P. 22 of the Boston ed., *op. cit.;* italics mine.) One more expression from Sidney Webb may close these quotations from the Fabians: "The growth of knowledge of political economy makes it constantly more apparent that the Radical ideal of 'equality in opportunity' is absolutely impossible of attainment, even in infinite time, so long as individual ownership of land exists." (*Socialism in England,* p. 20.)

[40] In a preface to a Labour Party pamphlet written by Josiah Wedgwood on "Henry George for Socialists." Snowden has always been concerned with the land problem, perhaps more so than any other leading political figure in the party. Recently (1929) he has written a very flattering preface to an abridged edition of George's *Protection or Free Trade.* (See also *infra,* pp. 416, 421–424.)

admitted. Marx concludes the first volume of his work with a chapter on "The Modern Theory of Colonisation" in which he quotes the book of the English economist, E. G. Wakefield, on *England and America*.[41] After treating of the general contrast between colonies and the more developed countries, and after pointing out very clearly that in the colonies it is the existence of free land that frees labor and makes it independent of the exploitative power of capital,[42] Marx writes:

We have seen that the expropriation of the mass of the people from the soil forms the basis of the capitalist mode of production. The essence of a free colony, on the contrary, consists in this—that the bulk of the soil is still public property, and every settler on it therefore can turn part of it into his private property and individual means of production, without hindering the later settlers in the same operation. This is the secret both of the prosperity of the colonies and of their inveterate vice—opposition to the establishment of capital. "Where land is very cheap and all men are free, where one who so pleases can easily obtain a piece of land for himself, not only is labour very dear, as respects the labourer's share of the produce, but the difficulty is to obtain combined labour at any price!"[43] . . . However, we are not concerned here with the condition of the colonies. The only thing that interests us is the secret discovered in the new world by the political economy of the old world, and proclaimed on the house-tops: that *the capitalist mode of production and accumulation, and therefore, capitalist private property, have for their fundamental condition the an-*

[41] The edition that Marx used was a two volume edition printed in London in 1853. A year later a one volume edition appeared anonymously in the United States (New York, Harpers).

[42] This discussion appears in Chap. XXXIII, Vol. I, of *Capital*. (Edited by Engels and revised by Untermann from the 4th German edition; translated by Moore and Aveling; 3rd edition; Chicago, Kerr, 1919 reprint.) Wakefield relates the story of a Mr. Peel who took from England to Swan River, West Australia, means of subsistence and of production to the amount of £50,000, and also 3000 working-class people. Once arrived at his destination, "Mr. Peel was left without a servant to make his bed or fetch him water from the river." The presence of free land freed the worker from the control of the capitalist.

[43] This last sentence is a quotation from Wakefield, Vol. I, p. 247.

nihilation of self-earned private property; in other words, the expropriation of the labourer.[44]

And explicitly what Marx means by the "expropriation of the labourer" is fairly evident in these sentences:

The expropriation of the agricultural producer, of the peasant, from the soil, is the basis of the whole process [i. e., of the development of the capitalist system].[45] To this extent the monopoly of landed property is an historical premise, and remains the basis of the capitalist mode of production, just as it does of all other modes of production, which rest on the exploitation of the masses in one form or another.[46]

Further evidence that Marx was singularly impressed by the part that land monopoly plays in the development and maintenance of capitalistic exploitation is found in his severe criticism of the Gotha program of 1875, drawn up at the Gotha conference which sought to unify the Marxians and the followers of Lassalle. His criticism of the program appeared in a letter to Bracke from London, May 5, 1875,[47] which was reprinted in the *International Socialist Review* of May, 1908.[48] Marx criticizes specifically two statements of the program, one that, "labor is the source of all wealth and of all culture," and the other, "in Society of to-day the means of labor are monopolized by the capitalist class. The consequent dependence of the working class is the cause of every form of misery and servitude." His criticism of these statements is:

Labor is not the source of all wealth. Nature is just as much the source of use-values (and of such, to be sure, is material wealth

---

[44] *Op. cit.,* Vol. I, pp. 841–842, 848. (All italics in these quotations and in the following ones are mine.)
[45] *Ibid.,* p. 787.
[46] *Ibid.,* Vol. III, p. 723. (Vol. III in this edition is the Untermann translation from the first German edition, edited by Engels.)
[47] The letter appears in Marx's posthumous papers, edited by Engels, in 1891.
[48] Vol. VIII, No. 11.

composed) as is labor, which itself is but the expression of natural forces, of human labor power. That phrase is found in all children's A B C books and is right in so far as it supposes that labor makes use of the objects and means belonging to it. . . . In the society of to-day, the means of labor monopolized by the landed proprietors, [the] *monopoly of landed property is even the basis of monopoly of capital,* and by the capitalists. In the passage in question the international statute names neither the one nor the other class of monopolists. It speaks of "Monopoly of the means of labor," i. e., of the sources of life. The addition, "source of life" shows sufficiently that the land and the soil is included in the means of labor. The improvement was brought forward because Lassalle, for grounds now generally known, attacked only the capitalist class, not the landed proprietors. In England the capitalist for the most part is not even the owner of the land and soil upon which his factory stands.[49]

There are a few other general comments of Marx on landed property which may be mentioned here; some of his more specific statements will be reserved for a later discussion of surplus-value.

From the point of view of a higher economic form of society, the private ownership of the globe on the part of some individuals will appear quite as absurd as the private ownership of one man by another. Even a whole society, a nation, or even all societies together, are not the owners of the globe. They are only its possessors, its users, and they have to hand it down to the coming generations in an improved condition like good fathers of families. . . . That it is only the title of a number of persons to the possession of the globe which enables them to appropriate a portion of the surplus labor of society to themselves, and to do so to an increasing extent with the development of production, is concealed by the fact that the capitalized rent, this capitalized tribute, appears as the price of land, that the land may be sold like any other article of commerce.[50]

Private property in land is then the barrier which does not permit any new investment of capital upon hitherto uncultivated

[49] Pp. 643–646 of the magazine article mentioned above.
[50] *Capital,* Vol. III, pp. 901–902; 901.

or unrented land without levying a tax, in other words, without demanding a rent, although the land to be taken under cultivation may belong to a class which does not produce any differential rent, and which, were it not for the intervention of private property in land, might have been cultivated at a small increase in the market price.[51]

Thus they (landowners) pocket the result of social development brought about without their help; they are born to consume the fruits of the earth.[52]

The capitalist performs at least an active function in the development of surplus-value and surplus products. But the landowner has but to capture his ground rent created without his assistance.[53]

It may be recalled also that the first of the ten measures suggested for the achieving of communism in the *Communist Manifesto* was the "abolition of property in land and the application of all rents of land to public purposes," and further, that the class struggle was considered to have originated only after "the dissolution of primitive tribal society" with its "holding land in common ownership." [54]

---

[51] *Ibid.*, pp. 884–885.

[52] *Ibid.*, pp. 726–727.

[53] *Ibid.*, p. 748. (Marx quotes Dove, the anticipator of George, in this connection.)

[54] Pp. 41 and 8 of the Kerr edition, Chicago, 1915.

This quotation from Bebel may also be in point: "One of the chief means of labour's production in manufacture and exchange, is the soil as basis of labour and fundamental condition of all human existence and society. Society reappropriates at the most advanced stage of its development that which belongs to it from the beginning. We find that common property in land existed among all peoples of the earth, as soon as they attained a certain degree of civilization. This common possession was the basis of every primitive society, which would have been impossible without it. Not until the appearance and development of the various forms of supremacy was the common property put an end to and usurped as private possession, an act which gave rise to the most violent struggles, which have continued down to our time. The theft of the land and its conversion into personal property was the origin of bondage, which has passed through all possible phases from slavery to the 'free' workman of our day, till at length, after a development covering thousands of years, the land will be reconverted into common property by the bondsmen themselves. The recognition of the importance of the land for the existence of the race has made it the chief object of contention in all the social struggles of the world." *Woman* (translation of H. B. Adams Walther; London, William Reeves, undated), pp. 200–201.

Now, there is no intention here of placing too much emphasis upon such fragmentary quotations from socialist writers. It is clearly realized that they are occasional rather than key remarks, and also that they may be interpreted—as undoubtedly socialists would insist—simply as expressions of a particular form that capitalism has taken, since for socialists as well as for the more orthodox economists, land and capital are not to be dissociated. Socialists would argue that land, while indeed a necessary element in production and one therefore that demands socialization, is none the less—at least in modern society—a subdivision of the general capitalist system, and cannot be isolated from its relation to capital. They admit, led by Marx, that in the colonies where land is actually "free," capital could have no power to oppress, but they cannot accept the suggestion that society's collection of the economic rent of land would bring about any significant return of "free" land in an already developed capitalistic community. *(Of course, the one contribution that George felt he offered towards the solution of the land problem was precisely the discovery of how indeed to make the land "free" even if it were not actually in a virgin condition such as in the colonies Marx speaks of. For George free land did not mean the vast untrod ranges of newly discovered continents; it meant that the exploitative power of land, which rests in its value or economic rent, be removed from private control. Then, for all questions involving the production and distribution of wealth, land would really be "free," although it might indeed be under a skyscraper.)*

The followers of George, on the other hand, interpret this type of quotation from socialist writers as an almost inspired recognition of the elemental character of land, and they believe that the unpardonable tendency to fuse land and capital has blinded socialism to the real cause of economic exploitation. Shaw's declarations, for example, that the "private appropriation of land" is "the source of those unjust privileges against which socialism is aimed" and that "the socialisation of rent would mean the socialisation of the sources of production" is for them clear evidence that socialism has recognized the evil at the root of all social maladjustment, but has then turned its back.

But the point that must be admitted here is that socialism's interest in the land question is largely incidental and gratuitous, and no attempt will be made to attach any unwarranted importance to this type of contact between the followers of Marx and those of George. It is one of those contacts that, as suggested in the opening of the present chapter, is but a surface similarity, and really indicates a fundamental cleavage in economic doctrine. It must be evident that land can have only a superficial concern for socialism, and for George's adherents this damning of the problem with the faintest of praise and the slightest of attention is even more painful than the positive ignoring of their proposals. Socialism can see in the suggestions of George only a limited and distorted conception of industrial society; for it, he "does not go far enough" and, as Shaw states, socialists are unable "to stop where George stopped."

Thus, the seeming contact between George and socialism in their joint recognition of the importance of the land question must give way to a realization of the fundamental economic contrast that has set them in opposite directions.[55]

[55] For the little material that specifically concerns the contrast between socialism and the contentions of George, the following may be helpful: The fullest and most scholarly interpretation of the question from the Georgist point of view is contained in Max Hirsch's *Democracy Versus Socialism* (London, Macmillan, 1901). The socialist position is perhaps most effectively presented in A. M. Simons's *Single Tax Versus Socialism* (Chicago, 1899), and in the pamphlets of Laurence Gronlund, "The Insufficiency of Henry George's Theory" and "Socialism versus Tax Reform, an Answer to Henry George" (both published in New York in 1887). The work of Gronlund was directly connected with the political dispute between George and the socialists that resulted from the campaign of 1886; that dispute may be followed in the columns of George's *Standard*, especially

It will be necessary to discuss briefly only one or two essential doctrinal distinctions between the two movements, since these differences will be seen to be crucial and unavoidable.

The contrast between George and socialism can be traced ultimately, of course, to their differing statements as to where the source of exploitation in the distribution of wealth is to be located. Does the oppression of the producer of wealth arise from the private control of capital or from the private ownership of land? The socialists' gravest objection to the work of George is clearly based upon what for them is his essentially deficient conception of the origin of monopoly. They will readily grant that the private ownership of land is an evil and that the socialist State will collect the unearned increment of rent, but they insist that such a move is nothing more than an item in socialist administration, and not a measure upon which to found a permanent social reform. The landowner they class as a capitalist, and consequently the ownership of land is only one of the many subdivisions of the more inclusive control of all the instruments of production. They would lump together all the material elements of production, including land, and thus reach a simple dichotomy of capital on the one hand, and labor, which is dependent upon capital, on the other. From this general twofold division of the means of production, there arises a twofold division in the distribution of wealth: There is that which the capitalist pays the laborer as wages and that which he illegitimately keeps for himself, the "surplus-value" created—as is all value—by labor, but withheld from its rightful possessor because of the private control of capital.

during the summer of 1887. George debated publicly with prominent socialists on different occasions, the more important being with Hyndman, Gronlund, and Schevitch; accounts of these may be found in the pamphlet collection in the New York Public Library. In any of the larger texts on socialism may be found brief reviews of the contrast between Marx and George.

This "surplus-value," Marx's *Mehrwerth*,[56] is distributed among the nonproducing capitalist class in the form of interest, profit and rent, which, instead of being the returns to fundamental elements of production, are merely the different channels through which is poured the value stolen from the laborer. For example, as Marx wrote, "all ground rent is surplus-value, the product of surplus labor," and, "private property in land does not create that portion of value, which is transformed into surplus profit, but it merely enables the landowner, who has possession . . . to coax this surplus profit out of the pocket of the industrial capitalist into his own."[57] This competition between the industrial capitalist and the landowner for their respective shares of the surplus value [58] is the reason, therefore, why "such movements as

[56] A schematic discussion such as this cannot enter into an analysis or a history of the interesting doctrine of "surplus-value," although it may be suggested that among socialists themselves the conception has come into disfavor. Bertrand Russell holds, strangely enough, that the chief merit of the doctrine is its "emotional" significance: "This doctrine [of surplus value] is very complicated, and is scarcely tenable as a contribution to pure theory. It is rather to be viewed as a translation into abstract terms of the hatred with which Marx regarded the system that coins wealth out of human lives, and it is in this spirit rather than in that of disinterested analysis, that it has been read by its admirers." (*Proposed Roads to Freedom*, p. 38.)

[57] *Capital*, III, pp. 743; 758. The discussion of rent, which comprises Part VI on the "Transformation of Surplus Profit into Ground-Rent," opens with the statement that "the analysis of landed property in its various historical forms belongs outside the limits of this work. We shall occupy ourselves with it in this place only to the extent that a portion of the surplus value produced by industrial capital falls into the hand of the landowner." (P. 720.) Marx devotes the concluding chapters of Vol. III to a fairly detailed discussion of ground-rent; see especially pp. 900–932.

[58] The follower of George argues that it is ultimately the landowner who is able to exploit both the laborer and the capitalist because his monopoly is the more fundamental. This point seems almost to be admitted by Marx in these lines: "The peculiarity of ground-rent is rather that in proportion as the conditions develop, in which agricultural products develop as commodities (values), and in which they can realize their values, so does also property in land develop the power to appropriate an increasing portion of these values, which were created without its assistance, and so does an increasing portion of the surplus-value assume the form of ground-rent." (*Ibid.*, p. 749.) ". . . Rent, then, forms a portion of the value, or more specifically of the surplus-value, of commodities, and instead of falling into the hands of the capitalists, who extract it from their labourers, it is captured by the landlords, who extract it from the capitalists." (*Ibid.*, p. 897.)

that represented by Henry George," John Spargo states, "fail to vitally interest the working class," for workers can have no interest in how the "surplus value is divided among landlords, money lenders, creditors, speculators, and actual employers." [59] Labor is the creator of all wealth and under a socialistic system would enjoy all wealth, for the private capitalist would disappear, together with the "landlords, money lenders, creditors, speculators," and their various divisions of the unearned surplus-value. Thus socialism includes land as capital, the landowner as one of the mischievous tribe of capitalists, and rent as merely an arbitrary and more or less convenient division of the loot of surplus-value.

George saw no such similarity between land and capital. Land was a "given" factor, the basic element not only of that production of wealth which technically interests economics but of all life itself. (This "land," it must always be noted, and particularly emphasized in any discussion involving socialism, comprises the entire natural environment of man. Natural resources as well as sea or air were economically "land." Land too often has for the socialist no connotation other than that of the prairie or the farm or agriculture. Factory sites, railroad right-of-way franchises, New York City building lots, he is likely to neglect, and paradoxically enough, it is precisely this nonagricultural "land" with which George was particularly concerned.) Land was the Earth—and "the Earth" seemed to George a charmed phrase, one that summoned land out of the dismalness of economics into the more gracious company of the planets. Land was a cosmic as much as an economic element. Man and life were meaningless without land; man was a very part of the earth. As George wrote, land is

"Private land has nothing to do with the actual process of production. Its rôle is confined to carrying a portion of the produced surplus-value from the pockets of the capitalist to its own . . ." (*Ibid.*, p. 955.)

[59] *Socialism* (New York, Macmillan, 1919), p. 268.

. . . the habitation of man, the storehouse upon which he must draw for all his needs, the material to which his labor must be applied for the supply of all his desires; for even the products of the sea cannot be taken, the light of the sun enjoyed, or any of the forces of nature utilized, without the use of land or its products. On the land we are born, from it we live, to it we return again— children of the soil as truly as is the blade of grass or the flower of the field. Take away from man all that belongs to land, and he is but a disembodied spirit.[60]

Land and labor were the economic rendering of the more metaphysical concepts of nature and man. There was nothing that was not produced by their interaction. Wealth, the economic name for the results of man's productive efforts, was basically land, transformed by the magic of labor into the subject of economics.

In such a schematization of the elemental factors of production, it is clear, as has been given exposition before, that capital could be no more than incidental. Capital itself was already a creation of labor working upon land. It was wealth, and while a necessary and legitimate instrument in economic life, was, for George, a product and not a fundamental determiner of man's energies. He states:

Land and labor are original and necessary factors. They cannot be resolved into each other, and they are indispensable to production, being necessary to production in all its modes. But capital is not an original factor. It is a compound or derivative factor, resulting from the union of the two original factors, land and labor, and being resolvable on final analysis into a form of the active factor, labor. It is not indispensable to production, being necessary, as before explained, not in *all* modes of production, but only in *some* modes. Nevertheless, the part that it bears in production is so separable, and the convenience that is served by distinguishing it from the original factors is so great, that it has

<hr/>

[60] *Progress and Poverty,* p. 293.

been properly recognized by the earliest and by all subsequent writers in political economy as a separate factor.[61]

The statement that capital "is not indispensable to production" may seem ridiculous to socialists and to nonsocialists as well. Yet perhaps the very strength of George's argument is that he did limit the necessity of capital to "some modes" of production. It is true certainly that even in the most primitive economy there is always "capital," some elementary form of tool, but that is not what is meant by the discussers of "capitalistic production." They have in mind the modern system of capitalism, which, just as present-day "scientific" socialism, is a product of the Industrial Revolution of the early nineteenth century, and which is distinguished, especially by socialists, not only from the late feudal and manor systems but also from the domestic manufacturing régime of the eighteenth century. In the system of modern capitalism George, of course, recognized capital to be indeed indispensable, but it was his merit (or, if regarded from another point of view, his ludicrous mistake) to base his economy, not upon a particular form of production, as has been the "scientific" method of socialism, but upon what for him were broad and permanent foundations. Thus the

---

[61] *The Science of Political Economy*, p. 406. (See also *supra*, pp. 99–105.)
Therefore, George could argue that capital monopoly depended upon land monopoly, and with the breaking of the latter through his proposals, the former must be undermined. And perhaps it has not been sufficiently recognized by the socialist that there is such a functional connection between these two forms of monopoly. This is not simply the theoretical dependence mentioned here, one that has been elaborated in another connection, but a more *ad hoc* dependence. That is to say, the monopoly of capital cannot stray very far from natural resources. No matter how complete may be the capitalistic control of machinery and all the actual instruments of production, any significant separation of that "capital" from mineral, timber, fuel, railroad "land," would be fatal to monopoly. The very close connection that our "capitalistic" monopolies maintain with land in all its forms is more than suggestive. It seems that, Antæus-like, capital derives its strength from land, and it would appear that the breaking of land monopoly—which must follow once the value of land has been socialized —might operate upon the very foundations of capitalistic monopoly.

machine age could not bewilder him; he neither cursed nor
worshiped capitalism. His postulates made him unable to
view the capitalist system save as a "mode" of production, a
mode which, while certainly not temporary or of any shorter
life than that of modern culture itself, was nevertheless no
more exempt from the dominance of the economic elements
of land and labor than was any other more primitive method
of producing wealth. Capital, once again, was produced
wealth used for the purpose of producing more wealth, and
whether it was a stone axe in the hands of a Neanderthal
worker or a great Pennsylvania steel plant, it was still a
technique for the transforming of land into wealth through
labor.

The attack upon capitalism was for him only the modern
expression of the perennial protest against want and misery.
Socialism perhaps was applicable to nineteenth and
twentieth century conditions, but what of the evils of the
feudal system, or of Roman society, or even of the problems
of any future civilization? There could be no harmony in
any social order which considered the basis of all production,
of all life, as something to be privately exploited. The control of land, therefore, and not that of capital must be regarded as the source of economic injustice, was George's
argument. Land was the primary, all-inclusive element;
capital was essentially secondary, and a functional dependent
upon land.

This statement of the differing "historical" emphases of
George and of socialism—socialism, that is, considering itself
appropriate for a "capitalistic" order, whereas his own proposals, George believed, applied to all possible forms of economic structures—must suggest what is possibly the most
radical point of departure between the two movements.
That divergency is nothing less than the contrasted ap-

proaches of each to the province of social reform; that is to say, the two economic programs have distinctly contradictory conceptions of what might be termed the metaphysical justification of social reconstruction. Modern scientific socialism does not consider itself as some extraneous reform that is to be foisted upon an unwilling social system, but as the very product of that system. It has definitely insulated itself from the ideas of the earlier Utopian and Christian socialists; no longer does it reach back to Plato or to Jesus as the first of the communists. The socialisms of the late eighteenth and early nineteenth centuries in France and England, it considers as well-meaning but ill-advised philanthropies which interpreted the evils of society as "arbitrary deviations from the eternal principles of 'natural law,' justice and reason," and which quite fallaciously believed that their agitation "seemed equally justified in the eighteenth as in the nineteenth century, and in this country as on the old continent." [62]

Scientific, historical socialism recognizes that instead of any such conception it must be considered as a peculiar yet inevitable companion of modern capitalism, and that without the Industrial Revolution and the development of contemporary machine production it would be almost meaningless. It may be wearisome to retail this familiar doctrine of economic determinism, but it is essential in indicating the fundamentally different foundations upon which socialism and Georgism erected their systems. Socialism willingly admits that its very nature makes it an opportunistic movement, a definitely traceable historical event, and not a universally valid dogma. It "claims to be a theory growing out of modern economic conditions, and relying for its realization largely upon the steadily growing concentration and socialization of industry." [63] It is "realistic," "scientific," "historical,"

[62] Hillquit, *History of Socialism in the United States,* pp. 18, 136.

[63] *Ibid.,* p. 253. And again: "The modern socialist movement presupposes the existence of the modern factory system in a high state of development." (P. 136.) Such quotations are felt to be representative of modern

"evolutionary"; it holds that its theory is nothing more—
and nothing less—than an accurate interpretation of social
and economic evolution, Marx, as socialists feel, doing for
economics and sociology what Darwin did for biology.

Marx himself, it may be recalled, never urged socialism
as any universal panacea or as anything that mankind must
be persuaded to adopt; it was rather an inescapable phase of
industrial development, and Marx felt that his work was
largely one of exposition and not of propaganda.[64] And scientific socialism, following his example, has always discounte-
nanced any ideas of perfect states and eternal principles of
social order as illusions; like Marx, it has no patience with
Utopias. The scope of modern socialism is instead frankly
limited to modern conditions; it is inextricably linked up
with nineteenth and twentieth century industrial development. In this very limiting of its program socialism has found
its strength.

The horizons of George's economic philosophy, it must be
evident, enclose a vastly wider sweep of territory than that
embraced by modern socialism. His system was ambitious
and confident, and limited itself only to the realization of
the perfect state. Whereas socialism denies a natural order
and the eternal operation of universally valid natural laws,
at least in economics, George based his entire reasoning on
just such a conception. His fundamental premises were for

socialistic thought. (See following pages, however, for reference to work of
Norman Thomas.) But it does not appear necessary to document extensively
these most general tenets of historical socialism—even though it is fully
realized that socialists very seldom present unified testimony—since they
are the very essence and heart of the "historical" approach.

[64] Professor Simkhovitch states that "it must be borne in mind that
Marx did not advocate socialism because he believed the socialist state
to be good. Socialism, in his opinion, was simply inevitable because of
the economic tendencies inherent in capitalism. Were not such tendencies
at work, socialism would have been an empty Utopian dream, utterly
lacking an economic basis and hence impossible of realization." *Marxism
Versus Socialism* (New York, Henry Holt, 1913), Introduction, p. viii.
Hillquit writes: "The future of human society must be looked for, not in
the ingenious schemes or inventions of any social philosopher, but in the
tendencies of economic development." (*Op. cit.*, pp. 19–20.)

him justified only by this necessary functioning of a natural order, and it was precisely this belief, i. e., that his ideas were an integral part of a universal scheme of things, that made him apply his proposals to all social maladjustment. While socialism was content to confine itself to modern capitalistic conditions, George felt that his concepts were not circumstanced by any peculiar set of sociological phenomena; they were as apposite to the California of the gold rush as to the industrial centers of England, as binding upon mediæval manors or Roman latifundia as upon a city of factories. It was his fervent belief that a recognition of the natural order and a remoulding of human institutions so as to harmonize with it, would bring to pass the perfect state—and nothing else could achieve that goal. Socialism, for George, was unable to conceive of any Utopia simply because it was "more destitute of any central and guiding principle than any philosophy" he knew of; it proceeded "to make a world for itself as disorderly as that which Alice in Wonderland confronted," a procedure that was an obvious result of its fatal facility for "studying details without any leading principle." [65]

George himself did not devote any specific attention to the historical justification of modern socialism, but it is not difficult to understand what his argument would have been. It would be a feeling that the historical interpretation of socialism explains but does not validate its doctrines. While perhaps challenging some of the materialistic conceptions of socialist historians, George could not deny the obvious fact that present-day socialism, both theoretical and practical, is a direct product of present-day capitalistic society, but that, for him, would be nothing more than the statement of a truism. Tracing a theory to its origin, and synchronizing it with a significant era in human development, is interest-

[65] *The Science of Political Economy*, pp. 198–199.

ing, instructive, even "scientific," but hardly of value in appraising the essential worth of a doctrine—that would undoubtedly have been George's contention. His followers realize that some form of socialism seems inevitable,[66] but that historical "justification" appears as only one more evidence of the pathological condition of society; to them it is no argument for the soundness of socialistic proposals. If socialism is a necessary by-product of the modern industrial state, so also, the argument runs, are poverty and misery and disease, and for Georgists the attempt to establish a social reform upon a decaying foundation seems surely more deserving of the ridicule that has so often been heaped upon their own heads for endeavoring to base a lasting reform upon some vague "natural order." They see in socialism perhaps an eventual stage of social organization, but one that, nevertheless, is heir to the absurdities of present-day society, and so they are not at all impressed by economic determinism even though it bear the magic name of evolutionary. Socialism for them is not "rational" even if it is historical.

In other words, socialism's efforts to secure the privileges and immunities accorded to science and to a philosophy of history would be sharply questioned by George. Why support socialism simply because it is bound to come? Why not test socialism by certain canons of economics, standards which George would insist (not merely admit) were the products of a "logical" approach to the science? Socialism,

---

[66] It does appear that some form of socialist organization seems certain to come into existence, even though, as in this country, it may originate from the "wrong" end of the economic structure. A few of the followers of George who accept the inevitability of socialism, believe that their own reform cannot be achieved under present conditions, but must wait until socialism has indeed been ushered in by the process of capitalism. That is, it is felt by some that there must be a transitional stage between present economic conditions and the introduction of George's proposals, a transitional stage which would take care of the present concentration of capital (a concentration, however, which they believe depends ultimately upon the basic monopoly of land).

he would say, is pathological—just as are all the economic phenomena of the present order—whereas the goal of an economic philosophy is that of discovering a sound social order; it is not that of detailing symptoms. Thus, there is here a difference in ideational emphasis that seems perhaps the most fundamental barrier between the teachings of Marx and those of George. A difference between historical and "rational" science, between description and valuation, between, if one wills, realism and idealism, is the essential contrast between these two approaches to economic reconstruction.

At this point it seems necessary to recognize the probability of an objection, to the effect that all this discussion of "scientific" or "historical" socialism has been concerned with a man of straw. It has been a discussion, such an objection might state, that still deals with an old-fashioned Marxianism, long since discarded; an exposition that savors, perhaps, of atavism or resurrection. Contemporary socialism, at least American or English socialism, it might be shown, must be considered as something more direct and more utilitarian than the doctrinaire Continental school; it is not Hegelian but pragmatic.[67] And such an objection may not be out of place. Certainly the recent work of Norman Thomas [68] is a most ambitious attempt to present an acceptable philosophy of a "democratic collectivism," one that shuns Marx, communism, abstract theory, and the doctrine of the dominance of the State over the individual. And just as certainly, therefore, does his work offer perhaps the most serious obstacle that any nonsocialist of right-wing tendencies will have to

[67] For this pragmatic interpretation of contemporary socialism see especially the work of W. E. Walling.
[68] *America's Way Out: A Program for Democracy* (New York, Macmillan, 1931), and *As I See It* (New York, Macmillan, 1932).

face. Persuasive, intelligent, sober, Mr. Thomas's book proffers to the exponents of the "new" capitalism, or to any of the other apologists for our malformed economic system, a crushing indictment that must force all but the most chronically hypocritical or incorrigibly stupid defenders of our weary economic world to a new inventory of anti-red arguments. No longer can the horrendous cries of "Communism," or "Syndicalism," or even "Doctrinaire Marxist Theory" be raised as rallying slogans by the fearful, and no longer can the Russian bogy-man or the "foreign" radical be set up to be knocked down valiantly by the defenders of "American" liberty. Instead, the socialism of Mr. Thomas seems as "American," as "democratic," and as "common sense" as any hard-headed capitalist could demand.

There is no intention here, however, of entering into the internecine strife of the socialists, no intention, that is, of attempting a selection of any socialist doctrine as more typical or more acceptable than any other. The sole reason for mentioning Mr. Thomas, or for indicating that communism and Marxism need not be made synonymous with contemporary socialism, is simply to recognize the recent trend of, at least American, collectivism. That recognition, moreover, is introduced in order to meet the possible objection just raised, i. e., that contrasting the approaches of George and Marx to economic reform is presenting an antithesis that, as far as socialism is concerned, is no longer appropriate. Now, the point that will be made in this connection is that despite Mr. Thomas's criticism of economic determinism, and despite his most gracious appreciation of the work of Henry George,[69] the same philosophic objection

[69] "Of all forms of private ownership landlordism to-day is obviously least socially defensible and land rent represents the clearest drain out of the stream of natural wealth by and for those who do nothing to earn it. Henry George's statement on land and rent remains the most eloquent eco-

that the follower of George applies to the Marxian may be applied also to "democratic collectivism." That is the criticism that has been presented in these last few pages: Socialism is essentially a parochial reform, one applicable perhaps to a system of developed and organized capitalism, but one which commands no recognition as a program of general social reconstruction. It may derive a narrowly pragmatic strength from its concentration upon the problems of a machine age, yet it seems therefore a technology rather than a philosophy. Such a criticism would suggest that a comprehensive economic reform cannot be limited to any single set of conditions; it must expand its horizons so as to include the very sweep of human culture itself. Mr. Thomas definitely restricts his socialist philosophy to the modern machine age. "This machinery of ours is something new

nomic indictment and plea in the English language." (*America's Way Out,* p. 170.) Mr. Thomas goes on to discuss most favorably the application of a tax upon land values (pp. 170–183), although, of course, he rejects "the single tax as a panacea." Even in that more theoretical realm of the distinction between land and capital, Mr. Thomas suggests many statements which almost verge upon the position of George, statements which, as has been mentioned before, seem so perplexing to the single taxer when they come from the socialist. ". . . Land cannot be appreciably increased or decreased and the landlord takes now all the traffic will bear; that is, all that he gets out of his relative marginal advantage. Buildings can be increased or decreased in size and attractiveness; left to themselves they depreciate in value. Land cannot be increased or decreased; it is permanent in extent and solidity. Although a little land has been reclaimed from the sea or desert by the social action of building dykes or irrigation ditches, land in general is not and never was a man-made product. Land, therefore, has no 'cost' in the sense of a supply price of making or reproducing it, but only in the sense of the 'relative value members of the community attach to possessing it.' " (*Ibid.,* p. 174.) "Since land is limited in amount and the use of it is necessary for life, since it is of uneven fertility and uneven convenience, the owners of land can collect rent for its use in varying amounts depending on its marginal desirability. These differing land values, so far as they are of human origin, are created by society. . . . *This envied wealth means no addition at all to the sum of available goods. A Ford makes something. An Astor takes toll by land ownership of what other men make. Profits from land represent a drain on the productive enterprise of men.* Professor John Ise estimates that this drain to private landowners out of the life-giving stream of wealth, a drain due not to improvements on land but to speculation in land and rents, exceeds fifty billion dollars. . . . *From land and natural resources mankind has extended private ownership to great industries and services which are in reality social creations.*" (*Ibid.,* pp. 26–28; italics mine.)

under the sun. And the failure to recognize it as such impairs the value of many brilliant and profound attempts . . . to read our future in the light of our past." [70] The machine may indeed be new, but not so are economic exploitation, social misery, injustice or tyranny.[71] Such a limitation to contemporary conditions may appear to contain the very power of industrial collectivism, but it is a power that sacrifices the perspective and completion and finality that George saw in his own system. In other words, an economic reform based solely upon the phenomenon of capitalism, this type of criticism would argue, can never possess the fundamental solidity and the broad scope that lie in an attempt to solve the larger and more basic land problem.

For that reason, George proposed his own economic philosophy of history, an ambitious effort to achieve an interpretation based upon his own formulation of the social structure.[72] It was a philosophy which did not confine itself to any specific type of culture or to any single economic system. It may have been rash, but certainly it was not provincial. The land has been privately owned and exploited in all significant civilizations, and therefore George's economic determinism was bounded only by the limits of all civilizations. It was not a philosophy of capitalistic history, but one of history itself. That is why George could see in capitalism only one "mode" of production, and why he felt

[70] *America's Way Out,* p. 1.

[71] It is true that perhaps the most telling point that is made in his introductory chapter on the machine age is Mr. Thomas's demonstration that there is no longer any excuse for poverty. He feels that in all past economic systems there may have been some technological reason for economic privation, but any such apology for former misery as still applicable to present conditions can no longer be patiently heard. Still, it is believed that the magic of "technology" has not permitted Mr. Thomas to appreciate sufficiently the nontechnical, "social" causes which have operated to produce past misery just as they now underlie contemporary poverty.

[72] The tenth book of *Progress and Poverty* on "The Law of Human Progress." See *infra,* pp. 523 ff, for a fuller discussion of such a philosophy of history.

that the exploitation against which the socialist rightfully raged was but the contemporary manifestation of a perennial injustice. Whether George's far-flung interpretation was an element of strength or of serious weakness, it is not in point here to discuss. The only occasion for this brief exposition is to suggest an illustration of the divergency between George's economic philosophy and that of socialism. The socialist finds the justification for his proposals in a specialized approach to the history of the capitalist era. George appeals to the general process of civilization itself, and finds in its operations a fundamental maladjustment. One, again, is "realistic," the other "idealistic."

This immediate discussion has been directed to tracing one of the major ideational contrasts between the philosophies of socialism and of land value taxation, the contrast between the differing "historical" justifications that each movement presents. One program looks to the dimension of capital as the locus of unjust economic privilege, and hence is peculiarly concerned with the complexities and problems of contemporary industrialism; that concern of socialism, moreover, is one that undercuts the various internal strifes within its ranks, e. g., the conflict between an economic determinism which sees in the socialist proposals an inevitable result of capitalistic organization itself, and a "planned" collectivism that offers a pragmatic instead of a fatalistic *raison d'être*. The other program looks to the element of land, and therefore sees nothing unique in capitalism except perhaps the aggravated and spectacular misery that it discloses, a misery, however, which it believes to be rooted in a subsoil beneath the capitalist layer; that subsoil, of course, is the private appropriation of land values. But there are other crucial differences that have effected a separation of these two reform movements, and, while this does not pretend to be a complete exposition of such fundamental contrasts, it is felt that it is necessary at least to mention several further typical divergencies.

It has been suggested that the collectivism of Mr. Thomas is a "democratic" one; it still can speak of civil liberty and of the individual, if not of "individualism." In this point, however, Mr. Thomas is making a rather courageous concession, since the traditional political philosophy of socialism recognizes no "individual," much less any expression of individual rights. That "social" emphasis is familiar enough, and it was that emphasis of socialism against which Henry George's "individualism" reacted most vigorously.

George's conception of the relation between society and the individual [73] was one which held them to be indeed correlative and complementary, but which did not therefore consider them as any the less independent. The social organism was, like the human organism, a union of two independent elements, neither of which could be subordinated or disregarded; it was a union of the conscious and unconscious, of the controlled and the automatic. To the Leviathan of Hobbes, [74] George added his Greater Leviathan, the former being the conscious political commonwealth definitely controllable by will and intelligence, the latter being the unconscious free play of individual activity subject only to the laws of human association. In George's words:

Looking on the bodily organism as the analogue of the social organism, and on the proper functions of the State as akin to those that in the human organism are discharged by the conscious intelligence, while the play of individual impulse and interest performs functions akin to those discharged in the bodily organism by the unconscious instincts and involuntary motions, the

[73] A much more suggestive distinction than this usual one between "individual" and "social" is the differentiation between "private" and "public" that Professor Dewey has emphasized. (See especially Chap. I of *The Public and Its Problems*, New York, Henry Holt, 1927.)

[74] See *infra*, p. 526, n. 3.

anarchists seem to us like men who would try to get along without heads and the socialists like men who would try to rule the wonderfully complex and delicate internal relations of their frames by conscious will.[75]

The analogy may perhaps be involved and forced, as most analogies are, but it does indicate a definite approach that allowed George to retain his cherished doctrine of individualism and at the same time to accept the evident domination of a social order.[76] These two realms of human activity—one, the individual, economic, automatically functioning order; the other, the social, political, regulated system of the State—merged at their boundaries, but, for George, they never could be wholly fused; they were as a pair of gear-wheels which remain separate bodies, although their cogs interact as a unit. Socialism was an illegitimate attempt, therefore, to join two distinct spheres of action; the socialist State was a machine and not an organism, "a great machine whose complicated parts shall properly work together under the direction of human intelligence," and it did not see "in

[75] The Condition of Labor, his open letter to Pope Leo XIII, in The Land Question, Works, Vol. III, p. 57.
[76] Despite George's "individualism," his recognition of the growth of socialization in government was clear and largely sympathetic. In Protection or Free Trade he wrote: "In socialism as distinguished from individualism there is an unquestionable truth," that man is "a social being, having desires that harmonize with those of his fellows, and powers than can be brought out only in concerted action. There is thus a domain of individual action and a domain of social action—some things which can best be done when each acts for himself, and some things which can best be done when society acts for all its members. And the natural tendency of advancing civilization is to make social conditions relatively more important, and more and more to enlarge the domain of social action. . . . Society ought not to leave the telegraph and the railway to the management and control of individuals." (Pp. 303–304.) And again: "There is this truth—and it is a very important one—in socialism: That as civilization advances, the functions which pass into the proper sphere of governmental control become more and more numerous, as we see in the case of the railroad, the telegraph, the supplying of gas, water, etc., but this is all the more reason why we should be careful to guard against governmental interference with what can safely be left to individual action." (In the Standard, July 30, 1887.) Norman Thomas sees that "the followers of Henry George themselves usually add to a plea for the single tax a recognition of the importance of public ownership of some public utilities." (America's Way Out, p. 171.)

the social and industrial relations of men an organism which needs only to be suffered to grow." [77] "The ideal of socialism is grand and noble" and "possible of realization," but it is a state of society that "cannot be manufactured—it must grow . . . It can live only by the individual life of its parts." [78] "Individualism" and "socialism" were correlative, necessary and inevitable complements, and George stated that he could see as little sense in making a basic contrast between the two approaches as he could in distinguishing "centrifugalism" from "centripetalism" in planetary discussions.

George's insistence that economic processes functioned automatically through the "unconscious free play of individual activity" introduces clearly enough the classical concepts of "economic men," laissez-faire, free competition. There will, of course, be no general discussion of such familiar topics here, and no unnecessary statement of that anachronism of laissez-faire which is so well recognized by orthodox as well as socialist economics. (Contemporary discussion, in fact, seems no longer to revolve about individualism *versus* collectivism, as about the merit of different types of collectivism.) But a point that must be raised in this connection is one that challenges socialism's severe criticism of the acceptance by George of a doctrine of "free competition." It must be made clear that George's approach to competition was in no way sympathetic with that specious, fictitious competition that has made the very word almost a travesty. George agreed with the socialist that the "present competitive system" must tend to degradation, insecurity and disaster; but it was a pathological system. That is, Sidney Webb's statement that "an almost complete industrial individualism" had been tried and found wanting could not

[77] *The Condition of Labor*, pp. 61–62.
[78] *Progress and Poverty*, p. 319.

have been accepted by George. Instead, the fact was that real competition had never existed, legitimate laissez-faire had never been given a trial. The sham "hands-off," devil-take-the-hindmost policy was as counterfeit as any of the distorted approaches to economics which ignored the fact that the earth was in the control of a privileged few. There could be no free competition with the sources of the production of wealth monopolized and the channels of the distribution of wealth blocked or diverted. A diseased condition of competition had been taken as the norm.

They who, seeing how men are forced by competition to the extreme of human wretchedness, jump to the conclusion that competition should be abolished, are like those who, seeing a house burn down, would prohibit the use of fire.

The air we breathe exerts upon every square inch of our bodies a pressure of fifteen pounds. Were this pressure exerted only on on side, it would pin us to the ground and crush us like jelly. But being exerted on all sides, we move under it with perfect freedom. It not only does not inconvenience us, but it serves such indispensable purposes that, relieved of its pressure, we should die.

So it is with competition. Where there exists a class denied all right to the element necessary to life and labor, competition is one-sided, and as population increases must press the lowest class into virtual slavery, and even starvation.[79]

Therefore, the doctrine of "enlightened self-interest" and the early nineteenth century belief that a common good must inevitably flow from the interaction of competing individuals were, for George, entirely inapplicable to a society grounded upon a basic institution of monopoly. In no fundamental sense, then, can he be classed with those worshipers of a malformed laissez-faire. His views were not those of the Optimists in classical political economy; his interpretation of the province of competition was not at all represented

[79] *Protection or Free Trade*, p. 307.

by the "Harmonies" of Bastiat or the nursery tales of Harriet Martineau.

This attack upon competition was, for George, of the same character as the traditional socialistic attack upon the wages system; it was a concern with a pathological condition that had been mistaken for the normal. ("Traditional" socialistic attack is suggested, since, with the exception of the recent Shavian resurrection of the doctrine of strict equality of income, contemporary collectivists, e. g., Mr. Thomas, are by no means agreed that the wages system *qua* system must be thrown overboard.) It is clear enough that, from the standpoint of strict Marxian socialism, wages are the evident means through which the owner of capital exploits the wage-slave. They are the channel which diverts the labor-created "surplus-value" from the worker to the capitalist. The laborer must sell his labor as a commodity, and the only buyer is the owner of machinery; hence workers must compete against one another for wages which are paid only by the capitalist. Moreover, this traditional attack upon wages was not confined to such an exposition of the mechanics of the system; it was expanded to include the involved social relations between wage-worker and wage-payer,[80] and so criticized also what might be termed the "æsthetic" disadvantages of wages. The laborer is degraded by his wages and becomes a slave. Wage-slavery not only pauperizes the laborer; it demoralizes him as well.[81]

[80] John Spargo writes that what is meant by "the popular shibboleth of Socialism, the cry that the wages system must be abolished," is that the "social relations involved in the wages system must be abolished." (*The Elements of Socialism,* Spargo and Arner; New York, Macmillan, 1912; pp. 234–235.)

[81] Hyndman, for example, was not impressed even by a condition of high wages; that was only a palliative state of affairs and could not remedy the more basic disease of industrial wage-slavery. ". . . The very highly paid wage-earner, even if, in good times, in the United States, he drives to his daily work in a Ford motor-car, is, economically speaking, just as much a wage-slave as the carefully nourished, educated slave of Crassus remained a chattel-slave." (*The Economics of Socialism,* Boston, Small, Maynard,

All such fear of "wage-slavery" was meaningless for George. It was an essentially emotional reaction and of as little economic worth as Carlyle's attack upon "cash" relations; it was nothing more than an *ad hominem* argument. The only difficulty George found with wages was, to put it baldly, that there were not enough of them. In the opening pages of *Progress and Poverty* he reduces to a formula his conception of the source of misery and poverty, and it is the plaintive question: "Why, in spite of increase in productive power, do wages tend to a minimum which will give but a bare living?" "The cause which produces poverty in the midst of advancing wealth is evidently the cause which exhibits itself in the tendency, everywhere recognized, of wages to a minimum." [82] Wages, then, were a problem only because they were *low,* just as competition was only a problem because it was not genuine. The adjective was alone significant; the problem of poverty was nothing more, or nothing less, than the problem, not of wages, but of *low* wages. Any socialistic attack upon the concept of wages itself was an attack upon some subtly hypostasized power for evil.

Thus, the fact that wages are low, that the laborer does not receive the full value of the product he has created, sent George in search of the cause of low wages, whereas, according to the follower of George, the same phenomenon sent the socialist hurtling against the very concept of wages. This was the prime fallacy of socialism—the habit of seeking no further than the obvious. "Wages are paid by the capitalist

1921; p. 203.) He then quotes the remark of Robert Owen that "under capitalism a man must be either a slave-driver or a slave." And G. D. H. Cole eloquently inquires: "What, I want to ask, is the fundamental evil in our modern society which we should set out to abolish? There are two possible answers to the question, and I am sure that very many well-meaning people would make the wrong one. They would answer Poverty, when they ought to answer Slavery. . . . Poverty is the symptom; Slavery the disease." (*Self-Government in Industry,* London, Bell, 1917; pp. 110–111.)

[82] P. 17.

to the laborer; they are therefore the chain of bondage that fetters the worker to the machine. Laborers compete with each other and drive wages down; therefore competition is the cause of poverty. The worker is dependent upon capital; he does not own it and he is poor. The capitalist controls the tools of production; he employs the worker and he is rich. Therefore, the ownership of capital is the source of industrial exploitation." Such propositions, the Georgist argues, are the essence of traditional socialism, and they illustrate the refusal to dip beneath the superficial.

Wage-slavery exists indeed, but not because of the mere existence of wages; it exists because, in the words of Spargo, "there is always an army of unemployed ready to take the jobs that the discontented may vacate, and the choice that confronts the worker is usually a choice between holding his job or falling into poverty or even pauperism . . . Laboring power is a commodity that is bought and sold on the market, and the price of which at any time is determined by the laws of supply and demand." [83] This would be accepted whole-heartedly by any follower of George. With an "army of unemployed" there must be "wage-slavery," but that slavery has nothing to do with wages simply as wages. It is determined solely by that grim and silent army of the unemployed, those "more hideous Huns and fiercer Vandals." The creator of wealth is a slave, held in bondage by "conditions more effectually coercive than statutes could be"; he is a slave, however, not due to the fact that his precious labor-time is bought by a capitalist who pays him an unjust return, but because the value of his labor is "determined by the laws of supply and demand," [84] and the supply of labor is vastly

[83] *Elements of Socialism*, pp. 9-10.
[84] It is realized that "laws of supply and demand," just as is the case with other "laws," have come into some disfavor with socialists. They hope arbitrarily to regulate such affairs; witness the tremendously ambitious Russian Gosplan.

disproportionate to the demand for labor. This is slavery, and a slavery that is enforced by the weight of an unbalanced social order. No one was more bitter against the enslavement of the worker than George, but he could not have comprehended a system of slavery that was considered to have come into existence simply because one man paid wages to another. He saw nothing of the "unæsthetic" features involved in the mere sale of labor; the absurd disproportions of economic society were, instead, based upon the anomaly that the makers of all the world's wealth could find no market for their labor. To disagree with G. D. H. Cole: Is not Slavery the symptom, and Poverty the disease? There is no wage-slavery because of the concept of wages, but there is a definite, not conceptual, slavery that results from competition among an army of unemployed, from an economic system that is fundamentally unsound in its solutions of the problems of economic distribution.

George's solution of wage-slavery was not the destruction of wages but the destruction of that "army of unemployed." That is, the point of oppression, for him, was the point of hire. In other words, if the abolishing of land monopoly would break the fundamental strangulation that cripples the production and distribution of wealth, as George felt it would; if it would thereby throw open unlimited opportunities for labor and so wipe out that army of the unemployed, then the menace of wage-slavery becomes a phantom.[85] A

[85] The important socialist argument that the major economic problem is to give all workers who produce wealth a share in the direction of industry, that without such an active participation workers are not fully developed individuals, but are at the mercy of an economic system in which they have no controlling power (a point which, of course introduces ethical valuation of the status of individuals—something professedly foreign to the traditional socialist), would have been answered undoubtedly by George in terms of his "free" competition. Removal of exploitation at the point of hire would introduce an industrial order in which labor and capital could not be the cutthroat rivals they are under a monopoly-ridden economic system. Adjustment in the way of more direction in the control of industry on the part of the laborer would follow as a matter of course once the worker were

laborer, uncoerced by the pressure of a competing surplus of labor-power, can in no legitimate sense be considered a wage-slave. Neither can he be considered as dependent upon any bogy-man capitalist. The point that George introduced in attacking the wages-fund theory [86] applies here: Divorced from the activity of labor, capital is just so much inert material, and can in no way victimize the worker whose labor is at a premium. Under a condition in which the laborer's bargaining power is not a fiction, as it is at present, but a working reality (and that condition, George confidently expected, would follow the breaking of land monopoly), the exploitation of the worker by the owner of the machine would be shown to be a myth. The socialist statement that in present-day industrial society the means of production are so vast and technical that their concentration in private hands means the dominance of the worker by the capitalist, since the worker, no matter how free he might be, could not manufacture for himself, or in any way duplicate, the ponderous machinery at which he toils, seems to the followers of George as superficial as the acceptance of any half-truth. If labor is dependent upon machinery for its employment, then in a most real and practical sense is machinery as dependent upon labor for its operation. A cessation of all labor for any appreciable length of time would not only make capital useless, it would irreparably damage it.[87] If machinery is at all a Frankenstein's monster, then, with

regarded as a coöperator instead of a competitor, a condition which, according to George's argument, would be realized once wage exploitation had been removed. The administrative control by labor of industrial processes, in other words, was incidental as compared with the equitable sharing of the product of industry; such control was a technical bit of industrial management that would solve itself once the problems of distribution had been met.

[86] See *supra,* pp. 83–86.

[87] The realm of possibility, of course, presents us with the far-off spectacle of an age devoid of all human labor, the era of robots and mechanical dominance, a real machine civilization. But that will require a new political economy, if not a new physics of perpetual motion.

labor's services at a premium, it could injure no one but its owner. Any basic control of wages by capital disappeared, George felt, with the decline of the wages-fund theory, and the fact that the means of production were in private hands was therefore of no significance other than as a problem of industrial administration. Wages were controlled, not by the capitalist, but by supply and demand, by competition.

In concluding this discussion of competition and wages, and the contrast that these concepts introduce between socialism and the work of Henry George, it must be suggested that George's approach was not confined to this "negative" aspect, i. e., the defense of competition and wages from the socialistic attacks, a defense that attempted to limit the socialist's criticism to a realm of "diseased" competition and "deficient" wages. There was a more positive function that was effected by these economic processes, a function directly connected with the problems of the wage system. George argued that (free) competition acted as a regulator of conflicting services and demands, as a determiner of that product of an individual's labor which is considered by socialism—and by orthodox economics—to be indiscoverably swallowed up in the social fund. Competition secured to "every worker a reward commensurate with the value which the community places on his services." In no other way could there be any possible determination of the worth of a man's labor, and no other way was needed. The value of an individual's labor product could have no other meaning except as a value determined by supply and demand, and under a condition of "free" competition that would be its "true" value. A complicated industrial order in which the individual laborer's efforts were merged with the labor of countless others was, for George, no different in any fundamental aspect from a simple unorganized state of production and barter. It still could not escape that ever-present equilibrating process between demand and supply. In fact, the very concept of value itself could be intelligibly measured in no other way.[88]

It will be seen, therefore, that capitalistic complexity could not overcome George with its intricacy, and it could not undermine his cherished ideal of competition. Indeed, given his insistence upon the dominance of the land problem over that of capitalistic exploitation, and given his differing "historical" justification for social reform, the most highly organized of capitalisms could never present him with more than an incidental problem. Thus, all the minor contrasts between his work and that of the socialists may be traced to these crucial differences: Is economic reconstruction a universal need, one that has been apposite at all times and in all cultures, or is it a peculiar problem of a capitalistic society? Is the institution of private capitalism, that rather recent phenomenon, the source of social injustice, or must such injustice be laid to the private control of land (land, it is insisted, being different from capital)? The divergent answers to these questions have made Henry George and the socialists of all complexions philosophic adversaries.

There is no doubt that socialism has become fashionable. A leaning toward socialistic doctrine, whether within or without the boundaries of the academic world, has been transformed from a cause for suspicion to what is almost an indication of sociological discernment. The casual, perhaps dilettante, acceptance of some form of socialism is now a commonplace. In this country, of course, such a partiality has been of a different character from that intense interest which has appeared to divide Europe into two hostile camps. Here, it has been more a concern with the common or garden variety species of socialism that is typified in the extension of governmental control over what once were considered spheres of individual judgment and action.

[88] See *supra*, p. 94, n. 20.

It is true that in the United States the political fortunes of socialism proper have not yet completely recovered their prewar strength, but that is not of any real significance, for whatever may be the varying success of a political organization there must always be a strong popular and nonovert interest in the movement. The socialist appeal to the popular mind is very patent; [89] it acts obviously as a crystallization of prevailing discontent, as a catharsis, so to speak, of the blind reaction against an inequitable social arrangement that coins the labor of one class into the luxury of another. Such an attitude of revolt will naturally discover in the apparent exploiter of labor, the employer, the indisputable cause of all economic oppression. The struggle between labor and capital is a struggle that can be popularly understood.

The academic (if that adjective can be used with any degree of accuracy) inclination toward socialism is one that cannot be so readily analyzed.[90] Perhaps the most evident explanation of it is that the soundest of the socialist concepts,

[89] This appeal has been clearly outlined by Professor Young in his contrast of the popular success of the single tax and of socialism as reform movements. "It sometimes has been asked why the socialist movement has come into greater prominence and enjoyed a greater numerical growth than has the single tax. A chief reason is that the former lends itself better to agitation. The socialist protest is more simple, being directed against the great inequalities in the distribution of wealth. But the single tax is a step more complex, since it undertakes to introduce a theoretical distinction between kinds of wealth, a distinction not readily grasped by the man in the street, to whom socialism makes a stronger appeal. A protest against the mere magnitude and economic power of individual wealth is simpler, and to the average mind appears more logical, than a protest directed against ownership of one form of wealth, land, and that not necessarily in the hands of the economically strong. The average man notices rather the amount of swollen fortunes than the kind of goods in which they happen at the moment to be invested." (*The Single Tax Movement in the United States,* p. 311).

[90] The fact that Marx was a profound and erudite scholar and a typical "academician," coupled with the Hegelian influence in socialism, may be one of the "smaller" (the word is used with all its connotations) reasons why the Marxist proposals have been given such credence and consideration in the academic field. The reverse, of course, would apply to a man like Henry George, the very antithesis of the "scholastic." It may be doubted whether such a suggestion is either fair or valuable, but it might find possibly some good psychological support.

that of the historical inevitability of collectivism, has been accepted as surety for the soundness of the rest of socialist doctrine. The adjectives "historical" and "scientific" and "evolutionary," all used as modifiers of modern socialism, are words that have a fascination for the scholastic mind—a fascination that is a legitimate tribute to the clearly proven methodological power that is connoted by such terms. Certainly the function of history in explaining and interpreting institutions and movements through the knowledge of their genesis and growth is one that cannot very well be over-estimated, and socialism therefore can perhaps make no better appearance than in its historical garb. It may well be that the historical claims of socialism will be verified; at least, there seem to be good grounds for the socialist interpretation, and perhaps it has been this historical plausibility that has made the strongest appeal to socialism's academic adherents.

Yet it must again be noted that to relate the history of a social movement, especially if the more important stages of that history are reserved for the future, is not necessarily to recommend it. Socialists themselves are not unaware of that fact, for were they completely convinced of the historical inevitability of socialism, as was Marx and the more orthodox of his immediate followers, they would not seek to justify or propagandize their doctrines, but would make their efforts those of expectancy rather than of advocacy. If economic determinism were an almost cosmic force moving majesti-cally and uncontrollably forward like the march of Spencerian evolution, then socialist propaganda would be in the nature of aiding the sweep of the tide with an eye-dropper. But socialists cannot remain so complacently fatalistic; actually they now have more faith in the pragmatic justification of socialism than in the historical (witness Mr. Thomas), realiz-ing perhaps that the march of history may not be so uncon-trollable and majestic that it cannot be tampered with.

Socialism seems to be engaged in a "laboratory" technique at present, substituting experimental, perhaps, for historical science, and, pointing to the results of great social ventures, does not appeal so often to the future class struggle. This, however, does not seem as appealing as historical socialism. The results of these "experiments" appear to offer more problems than the experiments themselves, and perhaps economic determinism still remains the safest argument of socialism.

The same spectacle of the companion existence of poverty and wealth sent both Henry George and the advocates of socialism in search of a saner social order, but their searches led them in different directions. However, the emphasizing in this chapter of the evident contrasts between these two searches will be seriously misunderstood if it is interpreted to mean that the followers of George and those of Marx can be nothing but sworn foes. It is true that the debates between the two groups have usually been characterized by an unnecessary display of polemical bitterness and by the calling of names, yet that appears to be a persistent tendency in the mutual relations of social reformers. It would seem, however, that there is enough of misery and oppression to engage all the efforts of social liberals and leave nothing to be dissipated in intramural wrangling. If, because of their differing concepts, the two movements can coöperate only in smaller details, anyway let there be that coöperation. They can remain, at least, amicable antagonists; as George wrote, they can agree to disagree—but disagree peacefully.

CHAPTER VI

GEORGE AND HERBERT SPENCER

THE crusading zeal with which George approached the realm of philosophy is nowhere better illustrated than in his attack upon what he considered the apostasy of Herbert Spencer. Here in Spencer's change of opinion on the land question was a deliberate attempt, George felt, to compromise with a truth that had been recognized and accepted, and, in almost the spirit of a holy war, he brought all his controversial powers and all the keenness of his logic to bear against this great figure in English thought. The attack upon Spencer included not only an analysis of his views on the land question, but extended also to the vast structure of the synthetic philosophy, and to the philosopher's personal character. It may seem somewhat strange, this furious onslaught upon an ideational process, and even a little unwarranted and in bad taste, but it must be remembered that the nineteenth century took its polemics, as it did everything else, a bit more seriously than is the custom at present. And it must also be remembered that this attack of George—it was not a controversy since Spencer never directly answered it—was not something merely contentious. It was based rather on what, for George, was the most vital of human efforts, that of holding fast to truth, after it had been obtained, and repelling every attempt made against it. The great truth was to be found in the solution of the land problem and in the implications that it suggested, and when once that had been grasped, as George felt Spencer had grasped it, and then abandoned for the flimsiest of motives, such renunciation demanded an answer, especially since so great a thinker as Herbert Spencer was concerned; the vehemence of George's attack was but evidence of the strength and sincerity of his faith in the power of truth.

There will be no attempt made here to present any final summary or estimation of the charges that George made against Spencer, and the only new material offered will be some letters and autobiographical opinion which may throw light on the philosopher's attitude toward George's attack. The work of Spencer on the land question is treated in some detail in order to indicate the importance that the problem had for him at one stage of his thought, for, in spite of his later beliefs, Spencer remains as one of the most remarkable and eloquent anticipators of Henry George's conceptions.[1]

Spencer's first book, *Social Statics* ("Or the Conditions Essential to Human Happiness Specified, and the First of Them Developed"), appeared in 1850. It was largely an elaboration of a series of letters that had been written some eight years previous for the *Nonconformist,* in which Spencer's pronounced views on individualism were first presented. *Social Statics* was an attempt to discover the "proper sphere of government," and to trace the development of society, not from any principles of expediency or hedonism, but from the existence of an individual moral sense correlated with the law that "every man has freedom to do all that he wills, provided he infringes not the equal freedom of any other man." [2] In

---

[1] Spencer was one of the few land reform theorists with whose work George was acquainted before he had completely formulated his own thought. In fact, Spencer may be considered as almost an inspirer of George, for *Social Statics,* George stated, "was the only work of the kind I knew of when writing *Progress and Poverty"* (*The Science of Political Economy,* p. 189), and mention of Spencer appears in several places throughout *Progress and Poverty.* In reference to the anticipators of the work of George, see *supra,* Chap. IV.

[2] Part II, Chap. VI, on the "First Principle." The edition used here of *Social Statics* is that printed in New York, D. Appleton & Co., 1883.

Spencer was, of course, aware that this earliest sociological effort of his

the application of this first principle, Spencer deduced the same corollaries of natural rights that have always been joined to the doctrine of individualism, the inference that men had rights to life, to personal liberty, to the use of the earth, and to all those other activities that may be found in any bill of rights. "The Right to the Use of the Earth" constitutes Chapter IX [3] (Part II) of *Social Statics*, and it may be of advantage to quote it at some length, for here indeed is Spencer the fervent land reformer, even if it might have been only the passing fervor of youth:

Given a race of beings having like claims to pursue the objects of their desires—given a world adapted to the gratification of those desires—a world into which such beings are similarly born, and it unavoidably follows that they have equal rights to the use of this world. For if each of them "has freedom to do all that he wills provided he infringes not the equal freedom of any other," then each of them is free to use the earth for the satisfaction of his wants, provided he allows all others the same liberty. And conversely, it is manifest that no one, or part of them, may use the earth in such a way as to prevent the rest from similarly using it; seeing that to do this is to assume greater freedom than the rest, and consequently to break the law.

Equity, therefore, does not permit property in land. For if *one* portion of the earth's surface may justly become the possession of an individual, and may be held by him for his sole use and benefit, as a thing to which he has an exclusive right, then *other* portions

---

was crude and not always exact. In 1864, when the first American edition was printed, he prefaced a note that the book "must not be taken as a literal expression of his present views," that "the general theory which it enunciates has undergone, in his mind, considerable further development and some accompanying modifications," and that in "the closing volumes of this System [of philosophy] . . . he proposes to set forth in them the developed conclusions of which *Social Statics* must be regarded as a rough sketch." In 1877 he made this explanation more specific, prompted, as he stated in the preface to the American edition of that year, by a criticism that had appeared in the *British Quarterly Review* of January, 1875.

[3] Chap. IX includes pages 131 to 144. The vigor of this chapter on the right to the use of the earth made it an effective piece of propaganda for single taxers, and it has appeared in pamphlet form throughout England and the United States.

of the earth's surface may be so held; and eventually the *whole*
of the earth's surface may be so held; and our planet may thus
lapse altogether into private hands. Observe now the dilemma to
which this leads. Supposing the entire habitable globe to be so
enclosed, it follows that if the landowners have a valid right to
its surface, all who are not landowners have no right at all to its
surface. Hence, such can exist on the earth by sufferance only.
They are all trespassers. Save by the permission of the lords of the
soil, they can have no room for the soles of their feet. Nay, should
the others think fit to deny them a resting-place, these landless men
might equitably be expelled from the earth altogether. If, then,
the assumption that land can be held as property, involves that the
whole globe may become the private domain of a part of its inhabitants; and if, by consequence, the rest of its inhabitants can
then exercise their faculties—can then exist even—only by consent
of the landowners; it is manifest, that an exclusive possession of
the soil necessitates an infringement of the law of equal freedom.
For, men who cannot "live and move and have their being" without the leave of others, cannot be equally free with those others.
(Pp. 131–132.)

Spencer goes on to state that the titles of land ownership
can be traced back only to force, fraud and superior cunning,
all of them—in a system of equitable distribution—invalid
claims to property, and he asks:

. . . What becomes of the pretensions of all subsequent
holders of estates so obtained? Does sale or bequest generate a
right where it did not previously exist? Would the original
claimants be nonsuited at the bar of reason, because the thing
stolen from them had changed hands? Certainly not. And if one
act of transfer can give no title, can many? No: though *nothing*
be multiplied forever, it will not produce *one*. . . . (P. 133.)

And then there is the eloquent passage, in the language of
some fiery eighteenth century pamphleteer, in which Time is
held not to be the "great legalizer":

. . . How long does it take for what was originally a *wrong*
to grow into a *right?* At what rate per annum do invalid claims

become valid? If a title gets perfect in a thousand years, how much more than perfect will it be in two thousand years? . . . For the solution of which they will require a new calculus. . . . (Pp. 133–134.)

And this for the doctrine of expediency:

Whether it may be expedient to admit claims of a certain standing is not the point. We have here nothing to do with considerations of conventional privilege or legislative convenience. We have simply to inquire what is the verdict given by pure equity in the matter. And this verdict enjoins a protest against every existing pretension to the individual possession of the soil; and dictates the assertion, that the right of mankind at large to the earth's surface is still valid; all deeds, customs, and laws notwithstanding. (P. 134.)

Spencer recognized the difficulties that arose from these premises, difficulties in the specific means of providing a condition of equity in the disposal of the surface of the earth, and in the separation of the land itself from the improvements which were the result of labor (George felt that his system effectually made an end to such difficulties), but he declared that they were no insurmountable obstacles in the attaining of justice; he ridiculed instead the shallow thinkers who sought to compromise with truth because of petty obstacles:

. . . There are people who hate anything in the shape of exact conclusions. . . . According to such, the right is never in either extreme, but always half way between the extremes. They are continually trying to reconcile *Yes* and *No*. Ifs and buts and excepts are their delight. They have so great a faith in the "judicious mean" that they would scarcely believe an oracle, if it uttered a full-length principle. Were you to inquire of them whether the earth turns on its axis from east to west, or from west to east, you might almost expect the reply—"A little of both," or "Not exactly either." It is doubtful whether they would assent to the axiom that the whole is greater than its part, without making some qualifications. They have a passion for compromises. To meet their taste, Truth must always be spiced with a little Error. They cannot conceive of a pure, definite, entire, and unlimited law. And hence, in discussions like the present, they are constantly petitioning for limitations—always wishing to abate, and modify, and moderate—ever protesting against doctrines being pursued to their ultimate consequences. (Pp. 138–139.)

These sentences were later, and perhaps rightfully, turned with telling effect against their author, especially since Spencer followed this paragraph with:

But it behooves such to recollect, that ethical truth is as exact and peremptory as physical truth; and that in this matter of land tenure, the verdict of morality must be distinctly *yea* or *nay*. Either men *have* a right to make the soil private property or they *have not*. There is no medium. We must choose one of the positions. There can be no half-and-half opinion. In the nature of things the fact must be either one way or the other. *(Ibid.)*

And in another place, he declares, in no indifferent language, that:

. . . The world is God's bequest to mankind. All men are joint heirs to it; you amongst the number. And because you have taken up your residence on a certain spot of it, and have subdued, cultivated, beautified that part—improved it as you say, you are not therefore warranted in appropriating it as entirely private property. At least if you do so, you may at any moment be justly expelled by the lawful owner—Society. (P. 136.)

Spencer concludes his chapter on the right to the use of the Earth with this summary:

Briefly reviewing the argument, we see that the right of each man to the use of the earth, limited only by the like rights of his fellow men, is immediately deducible from the law of equal freedom. We see that the maintenance of this right necessarily forbids private property in land. On examination all existing titles to such property turn out to be invalid; those founded on reclamation inclusive. It appears that not even an equal apportionment of the earth amongst its inhabitants could generate a legitimate proprietorship. We find that if pushed to its ultimate consequences, a claim to exclusive possession of the soil involves a landowning despotism. We further find that such a claim is constantly denied by the enactments of our legislature. And we find lastly, that the theory of the co-heirship of all men to the soil, is consistent with the highest civilization; and that, however difficult it may be to embody that theory in fact, Equity sternly commands it to be done. (Pp. 143-144.)

In the next chapter on the right of property there is an amplification of the one suggestion that Spencer had made for the administration of land, the proposal that the State lease out the land to individual proprietors, who were to act as tenants to society. In Chapter IX he had stated that to secure a condition of equity in landed property the only "change required would simply be a change of landlords":

Separate ownerships would merge into the joint-stock ownership of the public. Instead of being in the possession of individuals, the country would be held by the great corporate body—Society. Instead of leasing his acres from an isolated proprietor, the farmer would lease them from the nation. Instead of paying his rent to the agent of Sir John or his Grace, he would pay it to an agent or deputy agent of the community. Stewards would be public officials instead of private ones; and tenancy the only land tenure. A state of things so ordered would be in perfect harmony with the moral law. Under it all men would be equally landlords; all men would be alike free to become tenants. (P. 141.)

In Chapter X this is further elaborated and is made to coincide with Locke's doctrine that the only justification for landed property is that of labor.[4]

. . . We have seen that, without any infraction of the law of equal freedom, an individual may lease from society a given surface of soil, by agreeing to pay in return a stated amount of the

---

[4] Spencer, however, did not accept Locke's explanation of the origin of private property, and he ranks him as one of those thinkers who "have commonly fallen into the error of referring back to an imaginary state of savage wildness, instead of referring forward to an ideal civilization."

produce he obtains from that soil. We found that, in doing this, he does no more than what every other man is equally free with himself to do—that each has the same power with himself to become the tenant—and that the rent he pays accrues alike to all. Having thus hired a tract of land from his fellow men, for a given period, for understood purposes, and on specified terms—having thus obtained, for a time, the exclusive use of that land by a definite agreement with its owners, it is manifest that an individual may, without any infringement of the rights of others, appropriate to himself that portion of produce which remains after he has paid to mankind the promised rent. He has now, to use Locke's expression, "mixed his labour with" certain products of the earth; . . . and having fulfilled the condition which society imposed in giving that consent—the payment of rent—society, to fulfill its part of the agreement, must acknowledge his title to that surplus which remains after the rent has been paid. (P. 147.)

That this proposal is not to be confounded with strictly socialistic suggestions, Spencer directly refutes what he considers to be the fallacies of "Socialism and Communism"— the first attack of his long warfare against the doctrines of paternalism—and also critically analyzes the "awkward dilemma" which is presented by the "property is robbery" belief of Proudhon.[5]

These were Spencer's earliest thoughts on the land question, thoughts which, while not always exact, were nothing if not unequivocal. To the later matured judgment of the philosopher-laureate they may have appeared rash and hastily formed, but for the young seeker after the "proper sphere of government," they had all the incisive logical vigor that comes of enthusiasm. And it was thirty-three years before Spencer discovered that his youthful conceptions had been —just youthful.

[5] Proudhon, it may be remembered, epitomized the land problem thus: "Quai a fait la terre? Dieu, sans doute! En ce cas, propriétaire, retire-toi!" (*Qu'est-ce la Propriété*, p. 74.)

His change of opinion on the question of the administration of landed property was first expressed early in 1883 [6] at a time when the work of George was beginning to rouse all England. George had just completed his first lecture tour

[6] As late as March of 1882, when Spencer published Part V of the *Principles of Sociology*, on *Political Institutions*, he appeared to hold much the same opinion that he had indicated in *Social Statics* concerning the question of property in land. In Chapter XV, on "Property," after discussing the basically communal character of the lands of primitive tribes, he asks: "Induction and deduction uniting to show, as they do, that at first land is common property, there presents itself the question: How did possession of it become individualized? There can be little doubt as to the general nature of the answer. Force, in one form or other, is the sole cause adequate to make the members of a society yield up their joint claim to the area they inhabit. Such force may be that of an external aggressor or an internal aggressor; but in either case it implies militant activity." (Sec. 539, p. 546; 1899 edition, printed in New York by Appleton; Vol. II of *Principles of Sociology*.)

Again, after showing that private property, especially in land, is the result of a developing society, he continues: "At first sight it seems fairly inferable that the absolute ownership of land by private persons must be the ultimate state which industrialism brings about. But though industrialism has thus far tended to individualize possession of land, while individualizing all other possessions, it may be doubted whether the final stage is at present reached. . . . At a stage still more advanced it may be that private ownership of land will disappear. As that primitive freedom of the individual which existed before war established coercive institutions and personal slavery, comes to be reëstablished as militancy declines; so it seems possible that the primitive ownership of land by the community, which, with the development of coercive institutions, lapsed in large measure or wholly into private ownership, will be revived as industrialism further develops. . . . In legal theory landowners are directly or indirectly tenants of the Crown (which in our day is equivalent to the State, or, in other words, the Community); and the Community from time to time resumes possession after making due compensation. Perhaps the right of the Community to the land, thus tacitly asserted, will in time come to be overtly asserted; and acted upon after making full allowance for the accumulated value artificially given." (Sec. 540, pp. 553–554.)

Spencer concludes the chapter on "Property" with this: "Complete individualization of ownership is an accompaniment of industrial progress. . . . The individualization of ownership . . . eventually affects the ownership of land. Bought and sold by measure and for money, land is assimilated in this respect to the personal property produced by labour; and thus becomes, in the general apprehension, confounded with it. But there is reason to suspect that while private possession of things produced by labour will grow even more definite and sacred than at present, the inhabited area, which cannot be produced by labour, will eventually be distinguished as something which may not be privately possessed, as the individual, primitively owner of himself, partially or wholly loses ownership of himself during the militant régime, but gradually resumes it as the industrial régime develops; so, possibly, the communal proprietorship of land, partially or wholly merged in the ownership of dominant men during evolution of the militant type, will be resumed as the industrial type becomes fully evolved." (Sec. 541, p. 556.)

of Ireland, had spoken before great crowds in London, and had even met Spencer at the home of Hyndman, the socialist. A renewed and popular interest in the land problem had been developed, and now it was that Spencer's earlier work was coupled with the proposals of George. A discussion of *Progress and Poverty* in the *Edinburgh Review* of January, 1883, was the first comprehensive attempt to link together, for purpose of joint condemnation, the suggestions of Spencer and of this new American economist. After analyzing Chapter IX of *Social Statics* in connection with the doctrines expressed in *Progress and Poverty*, the *Edinburgh* reviewer concluded:

Writers like Mr. George and Mr. Herbert Spencer are at war, not only with the first principles of political economy and of law, of social order and domestic life, but with the elements of human nature. . . . To attack the rights of private property in land is to attack property in its most concrete form. If landed property is not secure, no property can be protected by law, and the transmission of wealth, be it large or small, is extinguished. With it expires the perpetuity of family life, and that future which cheers and ennobles the labour of the present with the hopes of the future. These are doctrines of communism, fatal alike to the welfare of society and to the moral character of man.

An article of much the same tenor had appeared previous to this (October 27, 1882, while Spencer was in the United States) in the staunchly Conservative *St. James's Gazette* of London. It was a consideration of "Mr. Spencer's Political Theories" and, on the subject of the land problem, it stated that Spencer's views in *Social Statics* had been again expounded, "not so fully, but with as much confidence as ever" in *Political Institutions*. Upon his return to England, Spencer wrote a letter to the *Gazette* and attempted to explain his position. As George later stated,[7] this provided him an op-

---

[7] *A Perplexed Philosopher; Works,* Vol. V, p. 57.

portunity to take a definite stand on the question of private property in land: "If he wished to defend himself against the charge of attacking property rights and upholding the doctrines of communism, there was an opportunity for him to show, for all of us as well as for himself, that the denial of the justice of private property in land involves no denial of true property rights. Or if he chose to do so, here was a chance for him straightforwardly to recant, to apologize to landowners, and to plead that he was young and foolish when he asserted . . . that 'equity does not permit property in land, and that the right of mankind to the earth's surface is still valid, all deeds, customs, and laws notwithstanding.' "

Instead, Spencer appeared to content himself with that defense upon which he had poured his scorn in *Social Statics*, the defense of those who are "constantly petitioning for limitations—always wishing to abate, and modify, and moderate—ever protesting against doctrines being pursued to their ultimate consequences." After stating that the work of George was one "which I closed after a few minutes on finding how visionary were its ideas," he continued:

. . . The writer of the article in the *St. James's Gazette* does not represent the facts correctly when he says that the view concerning ownership of land in *Social Statics* is again expounded in *Political Institutions*, "not so fully, but with as much confidence as ever." In this last work I have said that, "though industrialism has thus far tended to individualize possession of land while individualizing all other possessions, *it may be doubted* [italics Spencer's] whether the final stage is at present reached." Further on I have said that "at a stage still more advanced *it may be* that private ownership of land will disappear" and that "*it seems possible* that the primitive ownership of land by the community . . . will be revived." And yet again I have said that "*perhaps* the right of the community to the land, thus tacitly asserted, will, in time to come, be overtly asserted." Now it seems to me that the words I have italicized imply no great confidence. Contrariwise,

I think they show quite clearly that the opinion conveyed is a tentative one.

Spencer then made the distinction between the "purely ethical view of the matter" and the "political-economical view" and stated that they apparently did not harmonize. This contrast between "ethics" and "economics" is one that appears in all of his later explanations of the real meaning of *Social Statics,* a distinction that seems to merit George's later satirical differentiation between "transcendental" and "sublunary" ethics. The letter to the *Gazette* concludes with: "All which I wish to point out is that my opinion is by no means a positive one; and, further, that I regard the question as one to be dealt with in the future rather than at present."

Social Statics was still further to plague Spencer before he finally gave it the *coup de grâce* with the "abridged and revised" edition of 1892, and with the publication of *Justice.* The most troublesome episode was launched by an account in the London *Times* of November 5, 1889 (p. 10), of a political debate in which Spencer had been quoted by an enthusiastic bricklayer as an authority for the justification of land nationalization. Spencer's letter of explanation to the *Times,* which appeared two days later, was of the same nature as his letter to the *St. James's Gazette* in 1883. There was the question of "absolute ethics" again: "The work referred to—*Social Statics*—was intended to be a system of political ethics—absolute political ethics, or that which ought to be, as distinguished from relative political ethics, or that which is at present the nearest practicable approach to it." [8] Then, a long

---

[8] In Spencer's *The Man Versus the State* there is again a mention of actions being theoretically and abstractly equitable: "There is the movement for land nationalization which, aiming at a system of land tenure equitable in the abstract, is . . . etc." (In "The Coming Slavery" in *The Man Versus the State,* p. 319; the edition used is that of 1892, in which this work was published together with the revised *Social Statics. The Man Versus the State* first appeared in 1884. It was a collection of four articles that had

quotation from *Political Institutions* followed by this passage: "The use of the words 'possible,' 'possibly,' and 'perhaps,' in the above extracts shows that I have no positive opinion as to what may hereafter take place. The reason for this state of hesitancy is that I cannot see my way toward a reconciliation of the ethical requirements with the politico-economic requirements." Finally, as to the urgency of a solution of the land problem, Spencer states: "All this [in *Social Statics*] was said in the belief that the questions raised were not likely to come to the front in our time or for many generations," and "what the remote future may bring forth there is no saying; but with a humanity anything like what we now know, the implied reorganization would be disastrous." In the letter [9] Spencer also repeated the demand that he had made in *Social Statics* that, if any change in the administration of landed property were inaugurated, the

been written for the *Contemporary Review* and published in February, April, May, June and July of 1884. They were on "The New Toryism," "The Coming Slavery," "The Sins of Legislators," and "The Great Political Superstition.")

This whole matter of abstract ethics, however, is nowhere better answered than by Spencer himself—as was unfortunately so often the case—in one of those forceful passages in *Social Statics*. Speaking of the supremacy of moral requirements, he wrote: "But why all this laboured examination into the propriety, or impropriety, of making exceptions to an ascertained ethical law? The very question is absurd. For what does a man really mean by saying of a thing that it is 'theoretically just' or 'true in principle' or 'abstractly right'? Simply that it accords with what he, in some way or other, perceives to be the established arrangements of Divine rule. When he admits that an act is 'theoretically just' he admits it to be that which, in strict duty, should be done. By 'true in principle' he means in harmony with the conduct decreed for us. The course which he calls 'abstractly right' he believes to be the appointed way to human happiness. There is no escape. The expressions mean this, or they mean nothing." (Introduction, Sec. 6, p. 64.)

[9] In this letter Spencer also declared that "for the last twelve or fifteen years I have refrained from issuing new editions of that work [*Social Statics*] and have interdicted translations." It will not be necessary here to go into detail regarding this statement, yet if it was supposed to mean that publication of the book had ceased, then it was just not true. In the United States, where *Social Statics* enjoyed a much larger circulation than in England, Appleton & Co. continued to publish the first edition of the book, with the prefaces mentioned previously, until 1892. If the sentence is to be taken literally, then the first edition was recognized to be still in circulation. (For further details, see *A Perplexed Philosopher*, pp. 86 ff.)

present landowners be compensated for their property losses.[10]

Such a Pickwickian explanation could hardly have satisfied any one. The *Times,* on the 9th, said editorially—and wisely—that "Were we asked to point a moral for philosophers, we should bid them beware of meddling with the absolute. Forty years ago Mr. Spencer set forth in search of 'absolute political ethics' and constructed his system to his own satisfaction. But it turns out to have been the most relative of things after all. . . . He does not seem, however, to have abandoned his original quest, for he gives us his revised conclusions as to the absolute ethics of land tenure, which appear to us to contain some of the original flaws which

[10] The following paragraph regarding compensation of landowners appeared in *Social Statics,* Chap. IX, Sec. 9, p. 142. The italicized words are those so emphasized by George (in *A Perplexed Philosopher,* pp. 15–16) for the purpose of showing that this incongruous passage, as George calls it, proved that the thought of compensation was not at all clear in the mind of Spencer, and that apparently he had reference to compensation for "improvements" rather than for the land itself. "No doubt great difficulties must attend the resumption, by mankind at large, of their rights to the soil. The question of compensation to existing proprietors *for their improvements* is a complicated one—one that perhaps cannot be settled in a strictly equitable manner. Had we to deal with the parties who originally robbed the human race of its heritage, we might make short work of the matter, *for their improvements we should be under no obligation to regard.* But unfortunately, most of our present landowners are men who have, either mediately or immediately—either by their own acts, or by the acts of their ancestors—given for their estates, *which include many inseparable improvements,* equivalents of honestly earned wealth, believing that they were investing their savings in a legitimate manner. To justly estimate and liquidate the claims of such *for these improvements,* is one of the most intricate problems society will one day have to solve."

This passage, then, can be readily interpreted as a plea for the compensation for improvements, a plea that would have been readily admitted by George, since improvements on land, which are really capital, would be exempted from his "single tax." However, Spencer need not be forced into too strict a rendering of his language. Probably, as was the case with all English land reformers from Locke to Mill, there was always the idea of compensation in Spencer's mind, and if his reasoning led him to deduce that compensation could be justified only by doctrines of "expediency" and that it was not equitable, since, in his own words, an original wrong could never be transmuted into a right, then its abjuring could easily be placed in that vague and nebulous realm of "abstract political ethics."

were to be found in the older version." The editorial then
attempted to point out the flaws that had reappeared in
Political Institutions, particularly Spencer's statement that
property in land had originated in force and fraud, and that
land tenure had never been recognized as absolute by the
State. There were several letters to the *Times* attacking
Spencer's explanation, the most unkind being one from his
friend Huxley. Huxley stated (in the *Times* of Nov. 12, p. 8)
that he was one of those "to whom absolute political ethics
and *a priori* politics were alike stumbling-blocks," and that
he wished to know definitely whether a piece of land bought
"like a cabbage" by an individual A. B. a score of years ago
was really his property despite all "antiquarian contin-
gencies." Did A. B. according to "absolute political ethics"
have "a moral right to the land or not? If he has not, how
does 'absolute political ethics' deduce the State's right to
disturb him?" Huxley was of the opinion that "absolute
political ethics" should be independent of time and space and
that "it should tell us whether A. B., if he continued to hold
his land under the circumstances supposed, is an honest man
or a receiver of stolen goods." He concluded: "In England . . . the theorems of 'absolute political ethics' are in
danger of being employed to make this generation of landowners responsible for the misdeeds of William the Conqueror and his followers." [11]

[11] Huxley, of course, was bitterly opposed to the work of George, for
the dismay with which he viewed his concepts was no different from his
impatience with any attempt to resurrect a doctrine founded upon "natural rights." George, for him, was but another benighted Rousseau, engaged in a mischievous effort to disrupt the "natural inequality of man."
He wrote to his friend Knowles (Dec. 14, 1889): "Did you ever read
Henry George's book *Progress and Poverty?* It is more damneder nonsense than poor Rousseau's blether. And to think of the popularity of
the book!" (Quoted in *Life and Letters* by Leonard H. Huxley; New
York, Appleton, 1906; Vol. II, p. 261.)

Huxley's essentially biologic conception of society, a conception that
led him to justify methods of force and might in social activity, not only
as necessary processes in evolution, but as the legitimate foundation for

It will not be necessary to examine the replies and counter-
replies that this typically London *Times* letter-to-the-editor

ownership and property rights, was one that in no way could be reconciled with any system that sought to approach the problems of political
economy with ideas of justice and equality. (For this defense of force
in social processes, see especially "On the Natural Inequality of Men,"
written in 1890, and later appearing in the collection of essays, *Method
and Results*—New York, Appleton, 1898.) Huxley's specific criticism of
George appeared in the essay "Natural Rights and Political Rights," written
for the *Nineteenth Century* of London, February, 1890. This also is in
Method and Results, Chap. VIII. See also "Capital—the Mother of Labour,"
Nineteenth Century, March, 1890.

Huxley, as did all of George's critics, recognized the popularity and
vigorous sincerity of his work. He wrote in "Natural Rights and Political Rights": "No better evidence of the fact need be adduced than
the avidity with which the writings of political teachers of this school
[that of Rousseau and natural rights] have been and are being read,
especially among the more intelligent of the working classes; and I doubt
if any book published during the last ten years has obtained a larger
circulation among them, not only in this country, but in the United States,
than *Progress and Poverty*. . . . In some respects, the work undoubtedly
deserves the success which it has won. Clearly and vigorously written,
though sometimes weakened by superfluous rhetorical confectionery, *Progress
and Poverty* leaves the reader in no doubt as to Mr. George's meaning, and
thus fulfills the primary condition of honest literature. Nor will any one
question the author's intense conviction that the adoption of his panacea
will cure the ills under which the modern State groans." (*Method and
Results*, pp. 377–378.)

He continues: "Mr. George's political philosophy is, in principle, though
by no means in all its details, identical with Rousseauism. It exhibits,
in perfection, the same *a priori* method, starting from highly questionable
axioms which are assumed to represent the absolute truth, and asking us
to upset the existing arrangements of society on the faith of the deductions
from those axioms. The doctrine of 'natural rights' is the fulcrum upon
which he, like a good many other political philosophers during the last
130 years, rests the lever wherewith the social world is to be lifted away from
its present foundations and deposited upon others. In this respect, he is at
one, not only with Rousseau and his conscious or unconscious followers in
France and in England, but, I regret to say, may claim the countenance of
a far more scientifically minded and practical school of political thinkers—
that of the French *Physiocrats* of the eighteenth century." (*Ibid.*, p. 338.)

Huxley sums up *Progress and Poverty* in these propositions, each of
which he attempts, with indifferent success, to show to be utterly fallacious: "I. All men have equal rights. II. There is no foundation for
any rightful title to ownership except this: That a man has a right to
himself; to the use of his own powers; to the enjoyment of the fruit of
his own exertions; therefore, to whatsoever he makes or produces. III. The
right to that which is produced is 'vested' in the producer by natural law.
It is also a fundamental law of Nature that her enjoyment by man shall
be consequent upon his exertion. IV. Land is a gratuitous offering of
Nature, not a thing produced by labour; all men therefore have equal right
to it. These rights are inalienable, as existing men cannot contract away
the rights of their successors. . . ." (*Ibid.*, pp. 360–361.)

The most bitter of Huxley's criticisms was that directed against those

warfare called out.[12] Spencer's answer to Huxley, however, which appeared on November 15, was a very ingenious and perhaps successful justification of the function of "absolute political ethics." Such a system of ethics was to be a model upon which existing institutions could be re-formed. " . . . We may fairly assume that, in these modern days at least, all legislation aims at a better; and the conception of a better is not possible without a conception of the best. . . . However much a politician may pooh-pooh social ideals, he cannot take steps toward bettering the social state without tacitly entertaining them." This is quite a legitimate and pragmatically acceptable conception of the use of a social ideal, but first it must prove itself of service in an active attempt to realize the "best." It must not be, as ideals and final ends so often are, something discrete and insulated and nicely cut off from the very aim it seeks to achieve. That this vague and essentially transcendental concept of the province of an ideal was in Spencer's mind is all too readily recognized in his own words, for was not this matter of absolute political ethics proffered only "in the belief that the questions raised

"brave 'ords" of natural equality. It was as if George's eloquence was an attempt to overthrow the biologic "natural inequality" of men, that human heritage of the survival of the fittest. "Big-sounding but empty phrases," he wrote, "may be the making of a stump-orator; but what is to be said of them in the mouth of a professed thinker? . . . Who would not be proud to be able to orate in this fashion? Whose heart would not beat high at the tempest of cheers which would follow stirring words like these addressed to needy and ignorant men? How should the impassioned speaker's ear be able to catch a tone as of the howl of hungry wolves among the cheers?" (P. 379.) The "needy and ignorant" men, of course, were needy and ignorant because of the working of evolution in political economy, and nothing could very well be done about it.

George made no attempt directly to answer Huxley, although he wrote to Dr. Taylor (September 16, 1890) : "I suppose you read Huxley's *Nineteenth Century* articles. What do you think of him as a philosopher? I am itching to get at him and will as soon as I can get a little leisure." He could not, however, reply to all of his critics; their number was legion. And Huxley, for George, was not in the same position as Spencer, for he had never espoused any doctrines on the land question which were later to be repudiated. Indeed, Huxley himself was often impatient with Spencer's reasoning.

[12] Frederick Greenwood, the journalist, and Sir Louis Mallet were others who wrote to the *Times* attacking Spencer; Auberon Herbert undertook his defense.

were not like to come to the front in our times or for many generations"? And was there not "no saying as to what the remote future may bring forth"? The same arm's-length interest in the actual effectuation of his ideal system is even more apparent in his last letter to the *Times:* [13] "I cannot allow the late controversy to pass without disclaiming the absurd ideas ascribed to me. The ascription of these ideas has been made possible only by ignoring the distinction pointed out in my first letter between absolute ethics and relative ethics, or the ethics of immediate practice—a distinction inadequately recognized in my early work, long since withdrawn [sic], but insisted on in a later work. Ill-health has kept me silent while seeing myself debited with the ludicrous results which arise when the one is substituted for the other. The suggestion that an ideal must be kept in view, so that our movement may be toward it and not away from it, has been regarded as a proposal forthwith to realize the ideal." [14] If then, "a proposal forthwith to realize the ideal"

---

[13] November 27, 1889, p. 10. In the previous letter (of the 15th) appeared a passage in which Spencer and George would have found themselves in complete agreement. It was: "It appears to me somewhat anomalous that Professor Huxley, who is not simply a biologist but is familiar with science at large, and who must recognize the reign of law on every hand, should tacitly assume that there exists one group of lawless phenomena—social phenomena. For if they are not lawless—if there are any natural laws traceable throughout them—then our aim should be to ascertain these and conform to them."

[14] It is not easy to understand how this letter could have so thoroughly satisfied Huxley as to lead him to write: "From Mr. Herbert Spencer's letter in the *Times* of the 27th of November, 1889, I gather that he altogether repudiates the doctrines which I am about to criticize. I rejoice to hear it; in the first place, because they thus lose the shelter of his high authority; secondly, because, after this repudiation, anything I may say in the course of the following pages against Rousseauism cannot be disagreeable to him; and thirdly, because I desire to express my great regret that, in however good company, I should have lacked the intelligence to perceive that Mr. Spencer had previously repudiated the views attributed to him by the land socialists." (*Method and Results,* p. 197, n.) This surely seems sarcastic, although it may have been in the nature of an attempt to exert a little added pressure upon Spencer. Certainly Huxley would have required a peculiar type of intelligence, or intuition, to have perceived that Spencer "had previously repudiated the views attributed to him."

is something absurd and ludicrous, just what is the genuine significance of a system of absolute political ethics? Does the word "forthwith" make so great a difference, or were Spencer's ideals mere noumena, inhabitants of the world of his Unknowable? Certainly to merit consideration a system of absolute political ethics must be something more than an airy vision, something more immediate than a contemplation of a far-off future. To be of use in any philosophic enterprise that seeks to deal with the stuff of tangible and relevant experience, a final end cannot be placed in some distant realm where it will remain remotely superior to the means through which it can be reached. There must be some contact between the ideal and the real. Perhaps Spencer's "absolute" ethics was just too characteristically and traditionally "philosophic." [15]

The fate of *Social Statics* was as inevitable as it was tragic. It was not murdered; it was mutilated, and for any self-respecting book that is by far the more deplorable calamity. In 1892, Spencer "abridged and revised" the earlier edition and published it together with *The Man Versus the State.* He wrote in the preface to this edition that he had "relinquished some of the conclusions drawn from the first principle laid down," and also that he had been unable to "prevent misinterpretation of my later beliefs." The "relinquished conclusions" were, of course, man's right to the use of the earth, and in this new edition there was no mention of the land problem. There now could be no possible "misinterpretation" of his beliefs. Chapter IX, "The Right to the Use of the Earth," was omitted entirely and the sections in Chapter X, "The Right of Property," which dealt with his suggestion for a communal administration of the soil, were removed, al-

[15] For a final summary of Spencer's distinction between absolute and relative ethics, see the chapter of that name (Chap. XV) in Vol. I of the *Principles of Ethics* (New York, Appleton, 1898). It comprises pages 258 to 280 of Part I, the "Data of Ethics."

though there was still retained the discussion of Locke's justification of property in land. The policy of deletion was likewise ruthlessly applied to all the miscellaneous passages on land that had appeared in the 1850 edition, and many eloquent pages, like those in Chapter XXV on "Poor Laws," yielded to the author's censorship.

The "cleansing" of *Social Statics,* however, was essentially a negative gesture, a necessary rectification of what might well have been enthusiastic, youthful inaccuracies; something more positive was needed, and in *Justice,* which was the first of Spencer's constructive summaries of "the ethics of social life," [16] he definitely excluded from the program of his synthetic philosophy any attempt to discover a solution of the land problem. *Justice,* he wrote in his preface to the revised *Social Statics,* would endeavor to preserve in "permanently accessible form" the fundamental ideas of his earlier work, and to elaborate those deductions which had "survived" from the days of his more reckless thought. The same first principle, for example, that he had deduced from purely moral reasoning in *Social Statics* was one of the "survivals," although now in *Justice* it was reached after a fairly intricate anthropological argument; it is the principle that "every man is free to do that which he wills, provided he infringes not the equal freedom of any other man." This is Spencer's formula of justice.[17] The corollaries following, however, from this first principle are quite different from those that had appeared almost axiomatic to the mind of youth as expressed in *Social Statics.* The deduction of man's "right to the use of the earth" obviously had not survived. Instead there is a chapter (Chap. IX) on "the right to the

[16] The publication of *Justice* preceded by a year the revision of *Social Statics.* It comprises Part IV of Spencer's *Principles of Ethics,* Vol. II.

[17] Spencer's argument traces justice through "animal ethics," subhuman and human justice, and the sentiment and idea of justice. The "formula of Justice" is found in Chap. VI.

use of natural media" in which Spencer, almost as if further to muddle the consideration of the land question, makes the highly questionable distinction between the right to light and air, and the right to the soil itself. Such a distinction would be more apposite for legal tangles concerning real property nuisances and injunctions; it certainly seems out of place in philosophical or economic discussion. Yet, while Spencer admits the natural right to light and to air, he in no place specifically denies man's right to the earth itself; his argument instead is based on the same differentiation between absolute and relative ethics that had occupied him in his earlier correspondence wrangles. A developed system of ethics must admit, Spencer declares, that human beings have a right to land:

> If, while possessing those ethical sentiments which social discipline has now produced, men stood in possession of a territory not yet individually portioned out, they would no more hesitate to assert equality of their claims to the land than they would hesitate to assert equality of their claims to light and air.[18]

Then comes the restraining gesture of relative ethics, or the ethics of "immediate practice" (or, in other words, the only system of ethical conduct in which we can really make our actions count).

> But now that long-standing appropriation, continued culture, as well as sales and purchases, have complicated matters, the *dictum* of absolute ethics, incongruous with the state of things produced, is apt to be denied altogether. . . . The proposition that men have

[18] *Principles of Ethics* (Part IV, *Justice*), Vol. II, p. 85. "Those ethical sentiments which social discipline has now produced" do not appear to recommend the final "absolute ethics" to which sociological evolution, according to Spencer, is approaching. Certainly he is mistaken when he believes that early man acted in a predatory manner in dividing land simply because his "ethical sentiments" had not yet reached nineteenth century development. In fact, as anthropologists demonstrate, the only semicommunal treatment of land was among primitive peoples—and Spencer had himself declared that such was the case. "Social discipline," if anything, has intensified the status of land as private property.

equal claims to the use of that remaining portion of the environment—hardly to be called a medium—on which all stand and by the products of which all live, is antagonized by ideas and arrangements descending to us from the past . . . They now make acceptance of the position difficult.[19]

Relative ethics, according to Spencer, demands the compensation of landowners, and it is precisely in this necessity for compensation that he finds the right to the use of the earth to be "traversed by established arrangements to so great an extent as to be practically suspended."[20] His argument is, in short, a warning that if mankind attempted to win back its "birthright" the cost would be prohibitive, for it would mean the wholesale purchase of all the land from its present owners. It is not necessary here to enter into a discussion of the question of compensation and purchase; it may be sufficient, for the purpose of illustrating Spencer's distinction between man's right to the use of the earth as countenanced by absolute ethics and the loss of that right as a practical result of relative ethics, to quote George's paraphrase of what would have been Spencer's revised opening of a new volume on *Social Statics:*

Given a race of beings having like claims to pursue the objects of their desires—given a world adapted to the gratification of those desires—a world into which such beings are similarly born, and it unavoidably follows that they have the right to use this world as soon as they have paid the full value of it to those of their number who call themselves its owners.[21]

Spencer's reasoning in this chapter appears a strange mixture of doctrines that seemed almost repetitions of the rash ideas of his first book, and notions that bore unmistakably the appearance of conscious restraint. It was as if his mind were deliberately but not always successfully suppressing his

[19] *Principles of Ethics,* Vol. II, p. 85.   [20] *Ibid.,* pp. 92–93.
[21] *A Perplexed Philosopher,* p. 181.

recalcitrant thoughts. For example, he still declared that primitive communal landownership gave way to the conception of individual property in land only as the result of force and violence,[22] but as if to counteract the significance of such a statement he declares:

If, during the many transactions which have brought about existing landownership, there have been much violence and much fraud, these have been small compared with the violence and the fraud which the community would be guilty of did it take possession, without payment for it, of that artificial value which the labour of nearly two thousand years has given to the land.[23]

The same line of argument is followed in Spencer's final summary of the land question in Appendix B of the *Principles of Ethics*.[24] Admitting that private landownership is a heritage from the predatory course of nature "red in tooth and claw," he definitely states that nothing, surely not in the realm of those relative ethics of practice, can be done to reinherit the nineteen-twentieths of the population for whom he had once been concerned in *Social Statics*. Nothing could be done because "we could not, if we tried, trace back the acts of unscrupulous violence committed during these thousands of years; and could we trace them back we could not rectify their evil results. . . . If the genesis of landownership was full of iniquities, they were iniquities committed not by the ancestors of any one class of existing men."[25] The original evildoers were Scandinavian pirates and Norman robber-barons, and while "the wish now expressed by many that

22 In a typically Spencerian manner the rôle of force in changing the ideas of primitive land tenure is traced, in the course of four pages, through the institutions of the Don Cossacks, the Sumatrans, the Suanetians, the Dahomeans, the Danes and the Normans. (Pp. 85–89.) "How was this relation [of landed property] changed? How only could it be changed? Certainly not by unforced consent. It cannot be supposed that all, or some, of the members of the community willingly surrendered their respective claims." (P. 87.)

23 P. 92.   24 Pp. 440–444.   25 P. 440.

landownership should be conformed to the requirements of pure equity, is in itself commendable, and is in some men prompted by conscientious feeling," [26] yet we can do nothing; how possibly can we find the Celts and the Frisians and the Danes and the followers of the great William who first seized upon the land and made it theirs! The rest of the appendix is of a piece with this specious argument, and concerns itself with showing that even through the names and titles of the present landowners the original landlords could not be traced; and with estimating the amount of indebtedness to which the present landlords would have a legitimate claim.[27] It was these mature reflections that had vitiated the deductions of the youth:

When in *Social Statics,* published in 1850, I drew from the law of equal freedom the corollary that the land could not equitably be alienated from the community, and argued that, after compensating its existing holders, it should be reappropriated by the community, I overlooked the foregoing considerations.[28]

Here ended Spencer's thoughts on the land question, and so was explained, at least for his own and perhaps Huxley's satisfaction, his one-time belief that "equity does not permit property in land."

If George's attack upon this recanting of Spencer were merely anger at a modification of opinion, then it could in no sense have been justified. Certainly there still is recognized at least that one "natural right," the right to change one's

---

[26] P. 441.
[27] One of the items with which Spencer credits the landlords is the payment of the poor-law reliefs. Also, his estimate of the value of the land of England "in its primitive, unsubdued state, furnishing nothing but wild animals and wild fruits" was five hundred million pounds— which might be considered a trifle extravagant when it is considered that without the presence of population, all the wild animals and wild fruits to the contrary notwithstanding, land is worth precisely nothing.
[28] Pp. 443-444.

mind, and George never questioned Spencer's specific act of repudiation. It was rather the reasons given for such an about-face that drew down upon Spencer the truly bitter, almost libelous, onslaught of *A Perplexed Philosopher.*[29] Had Spencer ever openly declared that his early thoughts on the land question were essentially wrong, that they were based on a mistaken premise and had been hastily deduced, that they were nothing more than the reasoning of a young philosopher who had not yet approached the more comprehensive conceptions of a synthetic system, then neither George nor any honest critic could have objected to so frank an explanation. Had Spencer still further elaborated his argument, and had he gone on to demonstrate that such doctrines as he had espoused in 1850 were inherently unethical, and that, whether they were proposed by the mind of youth or that of mellowed wisdom, they had no foundation in fact or logic, he could well have been challenged as to the truth and soundness of his statement, but he could not have been accused of shallow compromising. Finally, had he found himself indeed confronted with a logical distinction between absolute and relative ethics, and had he then admitted that his own solution of the land problem, with its policy of purchase and nationalization, was hardly feasible in any system of practical ethics, but that possibly some other plan might have squared with the demands of equity and of expediency, he could not have made the ludicrous, perhaps insincere, attempts to straddle his absolute and relative ethics, and then to invalidate the one through the fortuities of the other.

That Spencer did fail to justify his completely reversed opinion on the land question with sufficiently cogent arguments, and that, in his attempt to defend landed property by an exposition of the history of land tenure and by an account-

[29] Written in 1892; *Works,* Vol. V.

ing statement that showed the soil was too valuable to be subjected to the meddling of absolute ethics, he appeared to rely upon a superficial consideration of the problem,[30] are, however, no indications that his change of heart was the result, directly or indirectly, of any pressure brought to bear upon him. George assumed that it was, and the meagre arguments of Spencer he explained, not as the result of loose thinking or of indifferent interest, but as the scanty shreds that were used to cover a bald and enforced apostasy. Those verses of Browning, "Just for a handful of silver he left us . . ." open *A Perplexed Philosopher,* and almost its concluding words brand Spencer "as a philosopher ridiculous, as a man contemptible—a fawning Vicar of Bray, clothing in pompous phraseology and arrogant assumption logical confusions so absurd as to be comical." George felt that the growing interest in the land problem, which in the early '80s appeared as if it might sweep England, and which for him had all the glad tidings of a gospel of salvation, had intimidated Spencer and had alienated his support:

Believing in Mr. Spencer's good faith, deeming him not a mere prater about justice, but one who ardently desired to carry it into practice, we who sought to promote what he himself had said that equity sternly commanded naturally looked for some word of sympathy and aid from him, the more so as the years had brought him position and influence, the ability to command attention, and the power to affect a large body of admirers who regard him as their intellectual leader. But we looked in vain. When the Justice that in the academic cloister he had so boldly invoked came forth into the streets and market-places, to raise her standard and call her lovers, Mr. Spencer, instead of hastening to greet her, did

[30] It may be that the unintentionally garbled fragments of Spencer's repudiation which have appeared in this chapter are not completely representative of his thought on the land question, although they have attempted to give a fair summary of his changing beliefs. George, however, in his *A Perplexed Philosopher,* has quoted almost every line of Spencer that applied to the land problem, and while the book may be a bitter attack upon the English philosopher, yet it contains in exact quotation the only unabridged review of Spencer's ideas on this one topic.

his best to get out of her way. . . . When, in 1850, Mr. Spencer had said that the rent of land could be collected by an agent or deputy agent of the community, quite as well as by an agent of Sir John or his Grace, he must have known that if ever his proposition attracted the attention of the interests he thus personified he would be denounced in all the established organs of opinion, and in "polite society" regarded as a robber. *Then*, I am inclined to think he would have hailed with joy such indications of the progress of thought. But in 1882, he no sooner found that Sir John and his Grace had been aroused by such a proposition and were likely to hear that he had made it, than he hastened to get the evidence out of their sight, and as far as he could to deny it.[31]

George's own passionate, even intolerant, sincerity had led him to view any suspicious gesture, any hint of infidelity to principle, as the very act of a Judas. By this token Spencer proved himself "alike a traitor to all that he had once held and to all that he now holds—a conscious and deliberate traitor, who assumes the place of the philosopher, the office of the judge, only to darken truth and to deny justice; to sell out the right of the wronged and to prostitute his powers in the defense of the wronger." [32] For George, Spencer had deliberately and ruthlessly sacrificed his own convictions solely because of the opposition that land reform discussion had aroused among the propertied classes of England, and the faintest suggestion of such a renunciation was enough to loose all the bounds of his scorn:

But as hypocrisy is the homage vice pays to virtue, so the very crookedness of this letter [to the *St. James's Gazette*] indicates Mr. Spencer's reluctance flatly to deny the truth to which he had borne witness. He no more wanted to deny it than Simon Peter to deny his Lord. But the times had changed since he wrote *Social Statics*. From an unknown man, printing with difficulty an unsaleable book, he had become a popular philosopher, to whom all gratifications of sense, as of intellect, were open. He had tasted the sweets of London society, and in the United States, from which he

[31] *A Perplexed Philosopher*, pp. 53–54, 56.   [32] *Ibid.*, p. 191.

had just returned, had been hailed as a thinker beside whom Newton and Aristotle were to be mentioned only to point his superiority. And, while the fire in the hall of the High Priest was warm and pleasant, "society" had become suddenly aroused to rage against those who questioned private property in land. So when the *St. James's*, and the *Edinburgh*, both of them chosen organs of Sir John and his Grace, accused Herbert Spencer of being one of these, it was to him like the voices of the accusing damsels to Peter. Fearing, too, that he might be thrust out in the cold, he, too, sought refuge in an alibi.[33]

Such unbridled criticism seems hardly justified and surely out of place in a discussion of ideas.[34] It was not that an attack upon personal character was in bad taste, for to George's fierce and undiscriminating resentment against insincerity, questions of good form and taste were irrelevant, but rather that it was the product of an unsubstantiated conjecture.

---

[33] *A Perplexed Philosopher,* pp. 63–64. Perhaps the most bitter section of this book is the last chapter on "Principal Brown," in which George tells the strange story of a great Yankee "authority on moral philosophy" who in pre-Civil War days in Vicksburg becomes convinced that his former abolitionist sentiments should be confined to the realm of "transcendental ethics"; he is persuaded that they have no place in the "sublunary ethics" of the South. George refrains from making any comparison between Spencer and the Principal, for "since he was under fear of tar and feathers, that would be unjust to Principal Brown."

[34] It must not be thought, however, that this personal element played more than a secondary rôle in *A Perplexed Philosopher*. The book is, for the most part, a dispassionate and detailed examination of Spencer's arguments, and, in addition, contains several chapters of constructive criticism, such as those on the right of property and the right of taxation, and on compensation. And George does attempt to explain his concern with the question of motive; in the Introduction to *A Perplexed Philosopher* (p. xvii) he states: ". . . A change from a clearly reasoned opinion to its opposite carries the implication of fair and full consideration. And if the reasons for such a change be sufficient and there be no suspicion of ulterior motive, the fact that a man now condemns opinion he once held adds to the admiration that previously we may have entertained for him, the additional admiration we must feel for one who has shown that he would rather be right than consistent. What gives additional interest to the matter is that Mr. Spencer makes no change in his premises, but only in his conclusions, and now, in sustaining private property in land, asserts the same principle of equal liberty from which he originally deduced his condemnation. How he has been led to this change becomes, therefore, a most interesting inquiry, not merely from the great importance of the subject itself, but from the light it must throw on the logical processes of so eminent a philosopher."

George's interpretation of Spencer's change of opinion was based merely upon a feeling of outraged confidence, upon an emotional reaction that led him to attribute to Spencer nothing but the crassest of motives. The philosopher had turned aside from a line of reasoning which, for George, had become the way to the ultimate truth, and the loss of this great figure in English thought, through considerations which had appeared the flimsiest, seemed to him almost as the violation of some sacred trust. Of course, the very nature of his charges prevented any attempt at verification, and George never offered specific corroboration of his indictment except to intimate that Spencer had become affiliated with the reactionary Liberty and Property Defense League, a statement which was later shown to have been groundless.

Unless George's almost fanatical devotion to reform be understood, it is not easy to realize how he could have sincerely believed that a man like Spencer had been swayed by that vague and indeterminate power of a society which "had been suddenly aroused against those who questioned private property in land." His overzealousness prevented him from entertaining a sober consideration of Spencer's position, and the interpretation of the philosopher's final view on the land question as anything but a change resulting from the most unworthy of motives would certainly have appeared to George as a gratuitous bit of charity. Such an interpretation, however, seems perhaps more rational than an explanation that is based solely upon the action of social pressure and of wavering courage. It is much easier to believe that Spencer had turned aside quite naturally from the warm sympathy that once had led him to espouse enthusiastically the reform muse, in order to devote himself to work which he regarded as of more strictly a philosophical and scientific character, than that he had been intimidated by "Sir John and his Grace." It is more plausible that the older man had just lost interest in the vexing and confused problems that had attracted the more ardent mind of youth to the application of absolute ethics, than that he had been awed by Tory newspapers and polite society. To a thinker concerned with the expansive stretches of the synthetic philosophy and with the data of psychological, sociological, biological, and ethical evolutionary systems, the land question might not, as it did with George, have held a commanding position. And there is also the possibility that Spencer may have been sincerely convinced that any attempted solution of the land problem would have infringed his cherished doctrine of individualism, and, while that objection could not have applied to George's proposals,[35] it may have made Spencer suspicious of any proposed administrative remedy.

These possible approaches to Spencer's recanting, it is true, may not make his attitude any the more logically commendable, but they should suggest the unreasonableness of branding him as a frightened apostate. They may not explain the insufficiency of his arguments, but that may well be attributed to carelessness or lack of interest; surely every poor piece of reasoning is not the product of intimidation or faithlessness to principle. It is certainly the more charitable as well the more indicative of common sense to interpret

---

[35] Perhaps the most striking illustration of this lack of understanding of George's fundamental ideas appeared in *The Man Versus the State*, in which Spencer groups George, together with the socialist, Hyndman, as an advocate of communistic theories and as a supporter of the doctrine that society should have complete control of all individual property. He states: ". . . Mr. George and his friends, Mr. Hyndman and his supporters, are pushing the theory to its logical issue. They have been instructed by examples, yearly increasing in number, that the individual has no right but what the community may equitably override; and they are now saying: 'It shall go hard, but we will better the instruction, and abolish individual rights altogether.' " (In the chapter on "The Sins of Legislators," p. 371.) To designate George as one who was endeavoring to "abolish individual rights" would be ideationally tragic were it not so ludicrous. As George well declared: "Charity requires the assumption that when Mr. Spencer wrote these passages he had not read anything I had written; and that up to the present time when he has again reprinted them he has not done so." (*A Perplexed Philosopher*, pp. 69–70.)

Spencer's "conversion" as evidence of a natural change in his outlook upon social problems rather than as proof of a deliberate backsliding. His reversal of judgment may have arisen from that state of mind peculiar to advancing age, or from his loss of sympathy for those misfits cast out by sociological evolution, or from any other more strictly personal source— at least, let it become a psychological rather than an ethical matter.

Unfortunately, Spencer's reaction to George's attack, as expressed particularly in a series of letters written to an American friend,[36] was as petulant as *A Perplexed Philosopher* was bitter. His attitude was one of childish, almost plaintive, reprisal, and demonstrated again that old men, especially old philosophers, are not effective absorbers of criticism. Spencer's only constructive explanation of his final position on the land question appeared in his first letter,[37] and it was largely a repetition of the argument in *Justice:*

I have read the introduction to Mr. George's *A Perplexed Philosopher*, and my secretary, Mr. Troughton, having gone through the book, has read to me sundry of the calumnious and vituperative passages. . . . In the first place, irrespective of numerous utterly false insinuations, there are two direct falsehoods which it may be well to name and to flatly contradict. The first of them is contained in the Introduction, page 9, where he says I have placed myself "definitely on the side of those who contend that the treatment of land as private property cannot equitably be interfered with." I have said nothing of the kind. I have continued to maintain that the right of the whole community to the land survives and can never be destroyed, but I have said . . . that the community cannot equitably resume possession of the land without making compensation for all the value given to it by the labour of successive generations. . . . The sole difference

[36] The letters were written, during the years 1893 to 1895, to James A. Skilton, of Brooklyn. They appeared in *The Independent* of New York, under the title of "Spencer's Unpublished Letters," in the issues of May 26, 1904 (Vol. LVI, No. 2895), and of June 30, 1904 (Vol. LVI, No. 2900).

[37] January 6, 1893.

between my position in *Social Statics* and my more recent position is this: In *Social Statics* I have contended that the resumption of the land by the community cannot equitably be made without compensation, but I have there tacitly assumed that such compensation, if made, would leave a balance of benefit to the community. Contrariwise, on more carefully considering the matter in recent years I have reached the conclusion that to make anything like equitable compensation the amount required would be such as to make the transaction a losing one; more interest would have to be paid for the capital required than would be received for the land. And beyond the conclusion that the transaction, pecuniarily considered, would be a mischief rather than a benefit, I reached the conclusion that the system of public administration, full of the vices of officialism, would involve more evil than the present system of private administration. No change has occurred in my view of the principle of the matter, but only in my view of policy.

This hopeless confusion between the land and the improvements upon land, which are capital, and the unfair emphasis upon the matter of compensation which, in fact, played but a minor part in *Social Statics*, are of a piece with Spencer's naive assertion that, while the soil assuredly does belong to the community, the intruders would drive too sharp a bargain to make it profitable for society to reclaim its own property.[38]

[38] The same line of reasoning is presented in Spencer's *Autobiography* (New York, Appleton, 1904). He wrote: "In my first work, *Social Statics*, it was contended that alienation of the land from the people at large is inequitable; and that there should be a restoration of it to the State, or incorporated community, after making due compensation to existing landowners. In later years I concluded that the resumption on such terms would be a losing transaction, and that individual ownership under State-suzerainty ought to continue." (Vol. II, p. 536.) Certainly, if we had to place George's system under one of these two categories, "restoration of it [land] to the State" and "individual ownership [of land] under State-suzerainty," it would be under the latter—another indication that Spencer never understood, or perhaps never conscientiously examined, George's work.

There is always implicit in the protestations of Spencer the thought that what he was attacking was the bureaucracy of land nationalization. If he were referring unconsciously to his own earlier views on the solution of the land problem, then such a criticism might have been justified, but in no way could it have been applied to the suggestions of George, and the fact that

To charge George with the fabrication of a "direct falsehood" because he interpreted this attitude as one which placed Spencer "on the side of those who contend that the treatment of land as private property cannot equitably be interfered with" is perhaps a bit captious, although George might well have amended his statement. He might have explained that Spencer did not contend that the treatment of land as private property could not "equitably" be interfered with, but rather that his intent was one which concerned the "profitable" interference with land as private property!

The second falsehood with which Spencer charged George was one which indeed showed George to have been inaccurate. He had intimated that Spencer had become associated with the Liberty and Property Defense League, and had then suggested from this supposed connection with a reactionary organization of that type, the source of Spencer's prevailing sympathies.[39] Spencer, in this letter of January 6 and also more specifically in another letter of the 10th, gave evidence to show that he had never been affiliated with the League, and that his only connection with any political organization was his membership in the innocuous London Ratepayers' Defense League.[40] George, undoubtedly, had been a bit confused in his choice of Leagues.

Spencer declared that he had closed George's book "after a few minutes on finding how visionary were its ideas" may help to explain the persistent confusion with which he approached a consideration of George's proposals.

[39] See especially *A Perplexed Philosopher*, pp. 65, 72, and 74.

[40] This explanation also appears in his *Autobiography*: "I am a member of but one political body. This body, which I was in part instrumental in establishing, was subsequently joined by sundry men of title, and among them two dukes!" (Vol. II, p. 537.) That body was the London Ratepayers' Defense League.

Spencer concludes his discussion of George in the autobiography with this complaint: "Here, then, are lessons for one who, dealing with theological, political or social subjects, says candidly what he believes. If his career leads him to set forth views exciting class animosities, or individual animosities, he may count upon greater evils than are entailed by the stupidities and misrepresentations of critical journals; and must take into account the possibility, if not the probability, that he will be injured by utterly false interpretations of his motives and by consequent vilification." (*Ibid.*, p. 538.)

Perhaps the most amusing part of Spencer's justification of the sincerity of his motives was his reaction to George's quoting of Browning's "handful of silver" and "ribbon to stick in his coat." With an almost pathetic indignation, and one that demonstrated his sense of humor to have been woefully underdeveloped, he seriously went on to show that he had never received a bribe, nor had he ever been granted a title! Not satisfied with this, Spencer then carefully explained that he had always been antagonistic to the landed and titled classes, and that he had opposed also the clergy, the military group, the professions, and, in his capacity as scientist, even the general populace. His baiting of the government and the political class he demonstrated by page references to his *Principles of Sociology* and *Principles of Ethics* in which he had definitely criticized Lord Salisbury and Gladstone! "There is, in fact," he wrote, "no class which I have shown the slightest desire to please, but have rather in all cases done the reverse." [41] His final refutation of the charge that he had attempted to ingratiate himself into the favor of the propertied interests was indicative of the really sad preciseness with which he received George's attack; he showed that he could not have enjoyed the pleasures of polite society since for a number of years he had been a semi-invalid.

All this was true enough, but to introduce such evidence as formal proof of his sincerity was to betray too punctilious a concern with the question of personal justification, and like-

[41] For these explanations of his position see particularly the letters of January 6 and March 1, 1893. George's reaction to Spencer's interpretation of Browning's lines was his amazement at the "wooden literalness, so comically shown in Mr. Spencer's treatment of the 'religious ideas'" with which "these lines are taken to mean that he has actually received or sought a pension and a title, and I am 'refuted' by being told that Mr. Spencer has within twenty years spoken disrespectfully of two Prime Ministers!" (In *Herbert Spencer Versus Henry George,* a pamphlet-collection of a group of newspaper articles on the controversy, printed by the Sterling Publishing Company of New York, November 26, 1894.)

wise a lack of a sense of proportion. He might well have ignored the challenging of his motives in order to have concentrated more upon the logical explanation of his changed doctrines. It is evident, however, from his direct statements in these letters, as well as from his suggested methods of retaliation, that Spencer regarded *A Perplexed Philosopher* as simply an attack upon his personal character. He wrote, for example, that, "There is only one short word—not used in polite society—which fully describes Mr. George." [42] Two days later, as if fearful of what the word "liar" might lead to, he stated: "On second thought it occurs to me that it will be best not to use strong language in dealing with Mr. George. He is so unscrupulous and venomous that it is undesirable to give him a handle. A simple statement of fact and inferences will be best." In another letter he wrote: "The 'Synthetic Philosophy' can take care of itself, and I don't care a straw if it is attacked by Mr. Henry George or half a dozen Henry Georges with as many papers to back them. . . . Similarly about the land question. I have never dreamed of entering into controversy with Mr. Henry George about that or anything else, and I should be sorry to see any one take up the land question on my behalf. The only thing about which I am concerned is the personal question—the vile calumny which the man propagates." [43] Certainly this personal question was not the only thing about which George was concerned, and, while his overzealous efforts may have led him to an ill-advised attack upon Spencer's good faith, his interest was always centered upon the logical antinomy that permitted Spencer to retain his belief in the premise of natural rights and yet deny one of its recognized deductions. [44]

[42] Letter of January 8, 1893.
[43] March 1, 1893.
[44] While George may have indeed regarded his questioning of Spencer's motives as incidental, yet his own explanation for introducing the personal question seems a bit too charitable to himself: "I have nowhere spoken of Mr. Spencer except as an exponent of ideas. I have nowhere asked his

Spencer never considered George's attack worthy of a direct reply, but he did believe that it was necessary to attempt to invalidate his charges, and for this service he relied upon his American friends. In fact his series of letters to Skilton was intended to outline a method of refutation, a method which seems suspiciously indirect and needlessly dissembled. There were to be articles, for example, incorporating Spencer's views, but written by his friends in this country, and with no mention of his instigation; they were to be in the form of letters and Spencer's opinions were to be presented in the "third person," as he directed. Regarding one of these articles, Spencer suggested: "Of course, such a letter, if you wrote it, would be written quite independently by you as being based upon my published views—a letter such as, in

motives, except when made necessary to explain facts by the fundamental law of the human mind which beneath expression seeks for cause. If I have been unable to restrain the mingled pity and indignation which all men of true impulses must feel on seeing a great truth repudiated and finally denied, and what might have been a lasting reputation wrecked, yet this is not the essence of my book. *A Perplexed Philosopher* is not an attempt to point out the frailties of a man. It is a careful and conscientious examination, not only of all the pressing social issues of our day, but incidentally of a philosophy which assumes to explain the deepest problems that vex the mind and soul of man." (In the pamphlet *Herbert Spencer Versus Henry George*. This pamphlet was a reprint of a series of letters which had appeared in the New York *Tribune*. G. W. Smalley, London correspondent of the *Tribune*, had started this newspaper controversy by a letter violently attacking George's book; this letter was printed in the *Tribune* on September 23, 1894. George answered with a letter which was published on the 30th. The next attack was an article by a group of American Spencerians, among whom were John Fiske, Professor Youmans, Daniel Greenleaf Thompson, Lewis G. Janes, and James A. Skilton, which appeared on November 12th. The letter was largely a review of Spencer's correspondence with Skilton, which was then unpublished, and it brought in evidence to prove that Spencer was indeed an invalid, that he had never been a member of the Liberty and Property Defense League, that he had never sought a title, and it concluded with a bitter condemnation of George's methods. George's answer, five days later, included the above statement. The articles were then collected and printed in pamphlet form, November 26, 1894.)

The opinion that George expressed above he had likewise held before he had written *A Perplexed Philosopher;* in a letter to Dr. Taylor (April 18, 1892) he stated: "But while I will trim down or rather alter in places my harsher references to Spencer . . . I think they must appear somewhere. . . . In turning his back on all he has said before Mr. Spencer has not argued, and no explanation is possible that does not impute motives."

fact, might be written by anybody, even a stranger." [45] Another suggestion of Spencer illustrates one of his most ungenerous attitudes:

It has occurred to me since writing to you that your flank attack might be usefully extended so as to bring into question Mr. Henry George's motives for his agitation. There are plenty of facts showing that he has been pushing it for his own personal advantage. Clearly that last move of his in issuing a pamphlet [46] is with a view to regain his notoriety, to sell his books and to get money. Probably the raising of such questions would form an effective diversion.[47]

The fact that Spencer could have so grossly or perhaps deliberately misconceived George's purposes in conducting his "agitation" is indicative of the sad and futile results that are generated by any questioning of personal motives. Apparently neither George nor Spencer ever realized that the other could have been sincere. George's introduction of an attack upon character unfortunately nullified the very aims which should have been striven for, a sober discussion of Spencer's change of opinion and of the precise points at issue. The only effect of such an attack was to lead Spencer to ignore everything but the onslaught upon his personal reputation. Historians are assuredly correct when they warn against any probing of motives; that should be left for psychologists—if they could fare any better.

It would be tedious and unprofitable to follow any further the vagaries of this dismal dispute. Nothing came of it but bitterness and fruitless misunderstanding. George himself realized that his book had not accomplished anything,[48] and

---

[45] Letter (to Skilton) of January 23, 1895.
[46] Referring to the pamphlet mentioned above.
[47] Letter of December 29, 1894.
[48] George wrote to James E. Mills of California (September 27, 1893): *"A Perplexed Philosopher* does not seem to have attracted the attention that I had hoped for—I do not say that I expected, for I had a good deal of doubt as to what would be its reception. Spencer's reputation is very strong in the organs of public opinion, but I think the book will do some good at least." Before leaving Spencer's letters to Skilton, it may be interesting to

for Spencer the affair was perhaps no more than a vicious episode. No epilogue need be attached to the controversy except to suggest that George's ardent sincerity and militant enthusiasm robbed him of good judgment, while Spencer's cautiousness and the smallness of his personal resentment clouded his view of the fundamental issue in question. Nothing deranges discussion so much as the questioning of good faith.

But George also attacked the doctrines of the synthetic philosophy. Spencer the philosopher as well as Spencer the man drew down his disfavor.

George's criticism of the synthetic philosophy was suggested by his belief that the change from *Social Statics,* which was written before Spencer entered upon his ambitious task, to *Justice,* which was almost the culmination—at least, in point of order and time—of his evolutionary system, might be partially explained by an examination of Spencer's "materialistic doctrines." [49] Materialism, for George, was simply an attempt to account "for the world and all it contains, including the human ego, by the interactions of matter and motion, without reference to any such thing as intelligence, purpose or will, except as derived from them," [50] and Spencer's omnipotent and omnipresent law of evolution he under-

point out that, just as in his *Principles of Sociology,* there is in them no evidence of his concern with a system of "absolute ethics" such as occupied him in his first book, that is, a concern with an attempt to apply such a system. He wrote, for instance: ". . . But to anything larger, such as you adumbrate—a general conception of the relations of men to the soil based on general sociological principles—I have got nothing to say. If, as it would seem, you think that I have got a scheme for future society in my head, you are altogether mistaken." (Jan. 12, 1895.)

[49] George was undoubtedly persuaded to attempt only a brief review of Spencer's technical philosophy because of the warning of several of his more cautious friends, especially Dr. Taylor, who felt that he was leaving his chosen field for a subject which he was hardly equipped to discuss. (See *supra,* p. 74.) His treatment of the synthetic philosophy, therefore, was confined to some twenty-four pages, Chapter III of Part III of *A Perplexed Philosopher.*

[50] *Ibid.,* p. 115.

stood to be just such a suggestion of a fortuitous "interaction of matter and motion." This conception, he felt, was directly opposed to the central idea of *Social Statics*, the idea, in George's words, that "the universe bespeaks to us its origin in an intelligence of which justice must be an attribute; that there is in human affairs a divinely appointed order to which, if it would prosper, society must conform; that there is an eternal rule of right, by which, despite all perturbations of the intellect, social institutions may be safely measured." [51] Whether or not that had been Spencer's conviction in *Social Statics*, certainly it was George's own outlook upon the ordered arrangement of the world, and it was this essentially theological approach to the problems of philosophy that led him to condemn the most fundamental tenets of Spencer's synthesis.

In the earliest work of Spencer, George thought that he had discovered the ideas "of a living God,[52] of a divinely appointed order, and of an eternal distinction between right and wrong, just and unjust"; in the completed Spencerian system there was an Unknowable but no God, and instead of preordained harmonies and eternally valid mandates, there was the insistence upon the relativity and increasing generalization of knowledge, and the demonstration of an ever-changing dynamic universe. Philosophy had become "completely unified knowledge"; it was no longer a mystical or even rational intuition of already established relationships. Spencer had become for George the "Pope of the Agnostics," [53] while in *Social Statics* George believed that he had recognized a kindred spirit. Spencer had developed—or descended, George thought—from the embryonic social reformer to the

[51] *Ibid.*, p. 113.
[52] The difference between Spencer's earlier conceptions of deity and his later more mature considerations would, of course, be quite striking to a thinker with a pronounced teleological outlook such as George.
[53] In a letter to Father Dawson, November 24, 1892.

speculative thinker, from the young enthusiast to the less sensitive system-maker, and such a change appeared to George obviously to coincide with his alteration of opinion on the land question. He had left a task where there would have been "work enough to have engaged the greatest powers for the longest lifetime; but work that would have involved a constant and bitter contest with the strongest forces—forces that have at their disposal not only the material things that make life pleasant, but present honor as well." [54] And he had entered "philosophy," where there were reputation and authority to be won, but none of the hardship and battle and bitterly won accomplishments which George found in his own holy crusade.

George suggested that such a comprehensive shift of interest coincided with Spencer's change of heart on the land question, and he implied that therefore the same unworthy motives could be seen in this transformation of the social reformer to the synthetic philosopher [55]—an implication that demonstrated an impetuous short-sightedness in George's criticism. Spencer's philosophy, of course, did undergo an essential development from the teleological approach to morals, politics and religion that characterized his early work, to the evolutionary approach of his later volumes; there was obviously a process of maturing in his thought, a growing away from the earlier eighteenth century political and ethical concepts. And, while it must be admitted that in attempting to apply this change of emphasis to the land question Spencer found himself in logical difficulties that he never did overcome, yet the causal connection between his philosophic development from "teleology" to "evolutionism"—or "materialism," as George designated it—and his amended opinion as to property in land, must have been the reverse of that suggested by George, which was the bald hint that the pos-

[54] *A Perplexed Philosopher*, p. 114.   [55] *Ibid.*, pp. 114, 135–136.

sible cause of Spencer's "materialism" was to be found in his lack of sympathy with land reform movements.[56]

The arguments which George brought against Spencer's "materialism" were centered in the familiar line of reasoning that has greeted any philosophical system suspected of agnosticism—the objection that such a philosophy fails to account for an original purpose and fundamental will behind the manifestations of "matter in motion." It is essentially the argument from design, the teleological conception that was so integral a part of George's philosophic outlook. George's world was a living proof of some infinite spiritual force, a force which was not merely an eternally persistent reality, but one that indicated a will and a purpose, and that manifested the working of the "highest of spiritual beings— the Great Spirit, or God." God was perhaps unknown, but not the Unknowable, not a noumenon that forever was cut off from the conceptions of man. He was rather the last link in the chain of causation by which man sought to reach back to the ultimate source of causation; the human mind indeed was so constructed that it could not legitimately halt in its retracing of cause and effect until it discovered a first cause, which, for George, was the divine will. George's deism made the world an orderly creation obeying the laws, natural laws, that had been laid down by its designer. To explain life merely as the integration of matter and motion was, to use George's examples, as futile as an attempt to explain the genesis of a locomotive by a demonstration of the materials

[56] George himself, however, realized the extreme thinness of this assumed cause (*ibid.*, p. 136). It might perhaps be suggested by some that George's opposition to the synthetic philosophy was a by-product of his own absorbing interest in the land question rather than a legitimate philosophic objection; but such a suggestion can be dispelled by the fact that as early as 1879, before Spencer had repudiated his opinions on the land question, George had indicated his opposition to his philosophy of "materialism" (*Progress and Poverty*, pp. 478–479, 485). Also, he wrote to a friend (Dec. 21, 1879): ". . . There are two books I should like to write . . . and the other a dissection of this materialistic philosophy which, with its false assumption of science, passes current with so many."

assuming form in a foundry without the assistance of human effort, or to understand a Madonna of Raphael through an exposition of the self-feeding presses by which the printed reproductions are manufactured. The integrating of matter without the guidance of some cosmic superintendent was for George inconceivable.

It was in Spencer's insistence upon the universal jurisdiction of the evolutionary process that George, together with the others of that host of nineteenth century theists, discovered the perils of "materialism." There was no place here for a God. Evolution made no mention of any primal spirit—nothing but a blind persistence of force, seemingly without original intent, and a mysterious development of some vague cycle of homogeneity and heterogeneity. What was to become of religion, of immortality, of the individual human soul, of moral codes?—and nineteenth century, not to mention twentieth century, homiletics found a new delight.

It must be admitted, of course, that George was some decades behind the advanced if not the popular thought of his time in the matter of evolution, but his blind spot was not so large as to obscure a theological interpretation of the admitted significance of an evolutionary hypothesis. George confidently believed that he could distinguish between evolution as a method of development, and evolution as a cause of development—the distinction that has always been made by those desirous of "reconciling" science and religion. George's position is explained in this passage:

But if the Spencerian philosophy is thus indefinite as to what precedes or underlies matter and motion, it certainly shows no lack of definiteness from the appearance of matter and motion onward. With matter and motion begins its knowable, and from thereforward, without pause or break, it builds up the whole universe by the integration of the one, and the dissipation of the other, in the mode described as evolution, without recourse to any other element.

In this elimination of any spiritual element lies, it seems to me, the essential characteristic of the Spencerian philosophy. It is not, as is largely supposed, *the* evolution philosophy, but *an* evolution philosophy; that is to say, its rejection of any spiritual element in its account of the genesis of things does not follow from its acceptance of the principle of evolution; but the peculiarity of its teachings as to evolution arises from its ignoring of the spiritual element, from its assumption that, matter and motion given, their interactions will account for all that we see, feel or know.

In reality the Spencerian idea of evolution differs as widely from that held by such evolutionists as Alfred Russel Wallace,[57] St. George Mivart, or Joseph Le Conte,[58] as it differs from the idea of special and direct creation. It is only when this is recognized that the real point of issue raised by or perhaps around the doctrine of evolution is seen. We all see that the oak is evolved from the acorn, the man from the child. And that it is intended for the evolution of something is the only intelligible account that we can make for ourselves of the universe. Thus in some sense we all believe in evolution, and in some sense the vast majority of men always have. And even the evolution of man from the animal kingdom offers no real difficulty so long as this is understood as only the form or external of his genesis. To me, for instance, who, possibly from my ignorance of such branches, am unable to see the

---

[57] Wallace also was a pronounced land reformer, his views being directly influenced by Spencer's *Social Statics*. He was convinced of the inequity of private property in land, as were so many others, by his reading of the chapter on "The Right to the Use of the Earth," and when George published his *Progress and Poverty*, Wallace regarded it as "the most remarkable and important book of the present century." In 1881 he became the first president of the newly formed Land Nationalisation Society. Wallace, while a believer in the single tax, was essentially a land nationalist and a socialist. (See particularly his *The Nationalisation of Land.*)

[58] Professor Le Conte of the University of California, who had known George during his early days in the West, was one of the leaders in the attempt to harmonize evolution with Christianity. The thesis of his *Evolution*, written in 1887, was to show that this biologic phenomenon was an illustration of divine agency working through natural processes. (See especially Part III on the "Relation of Evolution to Religious Thought.") Regarding Le Conte, George wrote to Dr. Taylor (April 18, 1892): "Professor Le Conte . . . holds that which I would call the external of evolution, with which I do not quarrel, for though I do not see the weight of the evidence with which it is asserted it seems to me most reasonable. What I do quarrel with is the essential materialism of the Spencerian ideas, and this seems to me to inhere in them in spite of all of Spencer's denials." He adds: "John Fiske does not truly represent Spencerianism, but has grafted his own ideas on it."

weight of the evidence of man's descent from other animals, which many specialists in natural science deem conclusive, it yet appears antecedently probable that externally such might have been his descent. For it seems better to accord with the economy manifested through nature, to think that when the soul of man first took incasement in physical body on this earth it should have taken the form nearest to its needs, rather than that inorganic matter should be built up. And while I cannot conceive how, even in illimitable time, the animal could of itself turn into the man, it is easy for me to think that if the spirit of man passed into the body of a brute the animal body would soon assume human shape.[59]

If this indicates that George's conception of biologic evolution was far from clear, it also illustrates the religious attitude with which he approached the possible absorption of the evolutionary principle into some reconstructed theological system. The same attempt to distinguish between evolutionary concepts is made in *The Science of Political Economy*:

As vegetable life is built, so to speak, upon inorganic existence, and the animal may be considered as a self-moving plant, plus perhaps an animal soul; so man is an animal plus a human soul, or reasoning power. And while, for reasons I have touched on, we are driven when we think of ultimate origins to consider the highest element of which we know as the originating element, yet we are irresistibly compelled to think of it as having first laid the foundation before raising the superstructure. This is the profound truth of that idea of evolution which all theories of creation have recognized and must recognize, but which is not to be confounded with the materialistic notion of evolution which has of late years been popularized among superficial thinkers. The wildest imagination never dreamed that first of all man came into being; then the animals; afterwards the plants; then the earth; and finally the elementary forces. In the hierarchy of life, as we know it, the higher is built upon the lower, order on order, and is as summit to base.[60]

[59] *A Perplexed Philosopher*, pp. 118–120.
[60] P. 85.

In *Progress and Poverty* George's attitude toward Spencer was hostile but apparently more appreciative. For example, he wrote: "That civilization is an evolution—that it is, in the language of Herbert Spencer, a progress from an indefinite, incoherent homogeneity to a definite, coherent heterogeneity —there is no doubt; but to say this is not to explain or identify the causes which forward or retard it." [61] His chief doubt was whether "the sweeping generalizations of Spencer, which seek to account for all phenomena under terms of matter and force" could explain the obvious checks to the growth of human civilization.

Nevertheless George's interpretation of evolution cannot possibly be stretched into any sympathetic appreciation of Darwin's work. Perhaps his temper of mind, with its entire absence of any purely scientific interest, prevented his realization of the immense significance involved in the hypothesis that he attacked or disregarded without real comprehension. Any degree of critical evaluation concerning biological problems would never have allowed him to write (to Dr. Taylor, April 29, 1892): "I simply 'don't see' evolution from the animal as the form in which man has come. I don't deny it . . . I attach no importance to the question." While in some passages George did indicate, as has been shown, a vague awareness of some process of organic development, other of his more thoughtless and controversial statements almost cancel that impression. For example, after attacking some of Spencer's admittedly weak arguments on the land question, George declared: "I commend the study of such logical processes to those who on authority of Herbert Spencer's philosophy believe that man is an evolved monkey, who got the idea of God from observing his own shadow." [62] Again, in discussing Spencer's conception of prehistoric man,

[61] P. 476.
[62] *A Perplexed Philosopher*, p. 188.

a conception which, it is true, was drawn from biological rather than anthropological data, George wrote:

How this sorry monster, this big-bellied, short-legged, bad lot of an ancestor of ours managed to avoid the fate of the Kilkenny cats, and keep in existence, we are not definitely informed; but it seems from the Synthetic Philosophy that he did, and went on evoluting.[63]

Here is another attack upon Spencer which, while its prediction concerning Spencer's reputation was partially substantiated, unfortunately also attempted to include Darwin's future status:

I have no respect for Spencer as a philosopher. He was perplexed even in *Social Statics* and he got worse and worse when he went into the philosophy business. Nor have I respect for any of the authorities quoted except for Mill, and he often went wrong. I think from the very first Spencer as a philosopher is ridiculous, and his descriptive sociology is on a level with his dog stories. And I regard his great reputation as a bladder which will collapse in a few years if not pricked (also Darwin to some extent). Of course I would never touch him but for his attitude on the land question, but some one ought to write a comic description of the evolution philosophy—of course, I don't include Darwin and Wallace in that; they confined themselves, so to speak, to their muttons.[64]

---

[63] *A Perplexed Philosopher*, p. 131.

[64] In a letter to Dr. Taylor, April 19, 1892.

Before leaving George's criticism of Spencerian evolution, it may be interesting to note that he had a profound respect for Schopenhauer's conception of the biologic method. He wrote: "Schopenhauer's explanation of the origin of species is in interesting contrast to that of the evolutionary hypothesis, and to my mind comes closer to the truth. According to him the numberless forms and adaptations of animated nature, instead of proceeding from slow modifications, by which various creatures have been adapted to their conditions, are the expression of the desire or collective volition of the animal." (*A Perplexed Philosopher*, p. 125, n.) He then quotes a long passage from the well-known chapter on "Comparative Anatomy" in *On the Will in Nature*, in which Schopenhauer declares that modifications of animal shapes and organs are the result of the particular strivings of the will.

Schopenhauer, incidentally, was the only philosopher—Spencer, of course, excepted—with whose work George was completely acquainted. He was

If, however, George's arguments against Spencer's "agnosticism" and "materialism" and conception of evolution were hardly adequate, there was another and more valid objection to the synthetic philosophy, an objection that was suggested in *Progress and Poverty* and mentioned again in *A Perplexed Philosopher*. George asked whether the doctrines of a philosophy which was grounded solely upon a belief in a universally functioning evolutionary process would not lead to a passive fatalism. Would not a conviction that all existence was an inevitable and necessary development—and a development from an Unknowable—result in a sense of resignation, and a vague faith in some happy future when evolution shall have transformed things as they are now into some ultimate ideal heterogeneity? George sensed the possible quietistic influence of such a creed, and in *Progress and Poverty* he wrote: [65]

The view which now dominates the world of thought is this: That the struggle for existence, just in proportion as it becomes intense, impels men to new efforts and inventions. That this improvement and capacity for improvement is fixed by hereditary transmission, and extended by the tendency of the best adapted individual, or most improved individual, to survive and propagate among individuals, and of the best adapted, or most improved tribe, nation, or race to survive in the struggle between social aggregates. On this theory the differences between man and the animals, and the differences in the relative progress of men, are

introduced to the work of the German pessimist by a friend, August Lewis, who was interested in Continental speculation. While George revolted from the picture of despair which Schopenhauer presented, yet he was fascinated by his brilliance and acuteness. George, undoubtedly considering his own position, was particularly pleased by Schopenhauer's attack upon the professors—although he was not aware of the strictly personal origin or the specifically anti-Hegelian character of those bitter attacks. In *The Science of Political Economy* (p. 209) George quotes, in connection with a discussion of the ponderosities of the Austrian school of political economy, that passage from the *Parerga and Paralipomena*, in which Schopenhauer ridicules the "monstrous piecings together of words," that senseless "logomachy" of Hegel.
[65] Pp. 477–479.

now explained as confidently, and all but as generally, as a little while ago they were explained upon the theory of special creation and divine interposition.

The practical outcome of this theory is in a sort of hopeful fatalism, of which current literature is full. . . . The individual is the result of changes thus impressed upon and perpetuated through a long series of past individuals, and the social organization takes its form from the individuals of which it is composed. Thus while this theory is, as Herbert Spencer says, "radical to a degree beyond anything which current radicalism conceives," inasmuch as it looks for changes in the very nature of man; it is at the same time "conservative to a degree beyond anything conceived by current conservatism," inasmuch as it holds that no change can avail save these slow changes in men's natures. Philosophers may teach that this does not lessen the duty of endeavoring to reform abuses, just as the theologians who taught predestinarianism insisted on the duty of all to struggle for salvation; but, as generally apprehended, the result is fatalism—"do what we may, the mills of the gods grind on regardless either of our aid or our hindrance."

It would be interesting, although perhaps not profitable, to trace what have been the effects of Spencerianism in this connection. George presents a striking example of such an attitude of fatalism in the person of one of the most important of the American popularizers of Spencer's doctrines, Professor Youmans:

Talking one day with the late E. L. Youmans . . . he fell into speaking with much warmth of the political corruption of New York, of the utter carelessness and selfishness of the rich, and of their readiness to submit to it, or to promote it wherever it served their money-getting purposes to do so. He became so indignant as he went on that he raised his voice till he almost shouted. Alluding to a conversation some time before, in which I had affirmed and he had denied the duty of taking part in politics, I said to him, "What do you propose to do about it?" Of a sudden his manner and tone were completely changed, as, remembering his Spencerianism, he threw himself back, and replied, with something like a sigh: "Nothing! You and I can do nothing at all. It's all a matter of evolution. We can only wait for evolution.

Perhaps in four or five thousand years evolution may have carried men beyond this state of things. But we can do nothing." [66]

Whether Spencer in his immediate political thought was so influenced by such a conception of evolution is difficult to estimate, although it would afford an easy, perhaps too easy, explanation of the change in his position on social reform. Not that Spencer became in any sense a convinced Tory or reactionary, but his later outlook upon social problems was quite different, for example, from that of a man like John Stuart Mill, and his transformation from the youthful violent radicalism of 1850 was certainly complete. His distinction between the relative ethics of present experience—(which, it must again be insisted, is the only system of ethics which we, as active agents, can control)—and the absolute ethics of an evolved future social state, seems to be based upon just such a conviction of some happy and inevitable process of development. The same conception might explain his unwillingness to develop the implications involved in the land question, since "the questions raised were not likely to come to the front in our time or for many generations." In the *Principles of Ethics* [67] there is an evident illustration of this hopeful equanimity in evolution's solution of the labor question:

The pleasures men gain by labouring in their vocations and receiving in one form or other returns for their services, usually have the drawback that the labours are in a considerable degree displeasurable. Cases, however, do occur where the energies are so abundant that inaction is irksome; and where the daily work, not too great in duration, is of a kind appropriate to the nature; and whereas, as a consequence, pleasure rather than pain is a concomitant. . . . Bearing in mind the form of nature which social discipline is producing, as shown in the contrast between savage and civilized, the implication is that ultimately men's activities at large will assume this character. Remembering that

[66] *A Perplexed Philosopher*, p. 136, n.
[67] Vol. I, pp. 262–263 (Appleton edition).

in the course of organic evolution, the means to enjoyment themselves eventually become sources of enjoyment; and that there is no form of action which may not through the development of appropriate structures become pleasurable; the inference must be that industrial activities carried on through voluntary coöperation will in time acquire the character of absolute rightness as here conceived.

The British Labour Party, it appears, is too sceptical or impatient; Spencerian evolution, in time, will make labor a pleasure and not a problem.

Whatever may have been Spencer's optimism as to the "absolute rightness" which all institutions were approaching, or his perhaps consequent inertia in endeavoring to realize such a condition, George's attitude was always one of militant activity. His optimism was one that needed the support of all the fervor and power of a crusading army, support for a divine order that had been twisted and deformed by ignorance. For George "absolute rightness" could never be attained by the gratuitous functioning of a persistent evolutionary force unless "relative" rightness could be established right here in the New York and London of 1892. The manifest attacks upon justice and a sound social order needed more positive and more real resistance than faith in an undirected developmental process. George's impatience with any suggestion of a passive acceptance of social disease was shown even to his most intimate friend, Dr. Taylor. He asked him: "Why, when the great struggle is on, and history is being made, will you go into the woods and play the flute? I would rather see you put your lips to the trumpet." [68] At another time he wrote: "Your life and habits are those of a student. Would it not be well to try something more, to 'pitch in' more. There is, it seems to me, an undertone of sadness in life which engulfs a man, at least a thoughtful man, who does not keep

[68] In a letter of June 1, 1892.

moving. Pleasure is in action, and the highest pleasure in action directed to large and generous social objects. I believe you will feel the stronger and happier if . . . you will strike some blow for what you believe to be the right." [69]

It might be possible to find all the power and sincerity and inspiration of George's philosophy right in these words.

This essentially active and practical outlook of George, with its questioning of the "life and habits of the student" and its scoffing at Spencer's desertion of social reform for "speculative philosophy," may well have been the source of much of the bitterness in his criticism of Spencer. Perhaps it was a temperamental difference between the two men, rather than the unworthy motives and blind stupidity with which each charged the other, that accounted for their divergent interests. That type of explanation, at least, is always a safe and innocuous disposition of personal controversy. And maybe it would be best to conclude the dreary record of the attacks and counterattacks of George and Spencer with just such a recourse to differing intellectual interests— to a distinction between the student and the reformer, both, strangely enough, philosophers.

[69] Letter of August 12, 1883.

CHAPTER VII

GEORGE AND RELIGION

THE one great task of religion, for Henry George, was the justifying of the ways of God to man, and at such a task institutionalized religion had tragically failed. It had failed to demonstrate, he felt, that there was indeed a fatherhood of God and a brotherhood of man, for in a world which piously accepted poverty and wretchedness and flagrant injustice, God's ways were not mysterious but mischievous, and "fatherhood" and "brotherhood" were empty tropes. Religion had appeared to him timorous or indifferent when confronted by glaring wrongs; too often, like philosophy, it had fled to the ivory tower to be shielded from contamination, and then from its lofty seat had thundered against all evil, damning it as some elemental attribute, some primordial corruption or privation of divine essence. But to George it was smug blasphemy to declare that always there shall be the poor and the miserable. It was cowardice to flee from the squalor and brutishness of life even if the path of retreat bore the legend of individual salvation. And charity was hush-money.

Yet George was a devoutly religious man, and all his work breathed a spirit of piety. He was certain that his mission was to justify the ways of the Creator, to show that poverty, and injustice, and all the perplexing absurdities that have made even the faithful wonder, must be traced not to God's forgetful equanimity but to the blindness and ignorance of man. Was not man's inhumanity to man the result of the

336

disregarding of natural law—that natural law which was the very word of God? George's religion meant a faith that revolted against the complacent acceptance of wrong, and scorned an arm's length warfare against it. All the fiery zeal of the prophet and the quiet confidence of the initiate were his, for he was sure that whatever vitality and worth lay in religion depended upon religion itself taking a hand in the battle against evil, and not in the issuing of proclamations condemning it. The religious spirit was to him always the crusading spirit, and it was as a crusade that he regarded his own efforts. Indeed, to describe George's work as essentially religious is perhaps to bring it more within the realm to which he felt it really belonged. He led the attack upon land monopoly in almost the spirit of a holy war; his economic postulates were the sacraments of a religion that was to make all men brothers and God a father whose ways could now be understood. Institutionalized religion had not concerned itself with that poverty and injustice, and to that degree had it failed.

George's distrust of institutionalized religion, however, did not carry over to the basic articles of faith upon which religion rested. The existence of God and the immortality of the individual human soul George accepted with a reverent confidence. In fact, except for a short time when as a young man in California he experienced the usual phase of boyish cynicism and rejected all forms of spiritual belief, he never did completely shake off his early pietistic training. But, as has so often been the case in the histories of individual religious experiences, George reinterpreted the religious discipline of his childhood in terms of his later convictions. The devoutness of his youth returned, after a period of eclipse, in a rationalized form which broadened and justified his early religious beliefs but did not fundamentally change them. The faith that had been taught him reappeared against a richer background; it was transformed from a faith to a philosophy. He accepted the essential teachings of the Christian church, which as an institution he criticized, because he felt that were they correctly understood they would be recognized as a necessary corollary of economic freedom. George was not a Christian Socialist, as he sometimes has been described, for he was never a socialist, but certainly he may be considered a Christian, a Christian who followed the "cross of a new crusade."

Religion as an institution, however, was for George of the same nature as accepted political economy, a set of doctrines rigidly formulated and blindly followed, and acting too often as a method for preserving error, stifling opposition and serving a privileged class. It had become, he felt, almost an opiate to be administered to the discontented. The simple religious experience, so typically illustrated in early Christianity, was something which, in an unbalanced social order, became soiled and distorted, and hardened into an inappropriate apology for the very conditions that debased it. George held that the history of Christianity itself afforded a pointed illustration of how the freshness of a religious faith could be transformed into the stuffiness of a wordy and pharisaical dogma; and such a transformation he interpreted not as any change within religion itself, but as the result of pressure superimposed from without by a malformed economic system. The freshness of Christianity, or of any religion, could not live under institutionalism, for that meant inevitably control by the powerful and the wealthy.

This distinction between religious faith and the religious institution, between primitive or even Tolstoian Christianity and the Christianity of fashionable and richly appointed pews, is one that explains George's contrasting reactions to religion. It also explains why his doctrines were received by converts like Father McGlynn and the members of the Anti-

Poverty Society as a new gospel, a vindication of all that was worthy in Christianity, and why they were also interpreted by others as a justification for an attack upon the church as violent as any made by the socialists. George himself, while he never spared the absurdities of religious cant, always followed his attacks with a plea for a new understanding of religion, one that would bring the power of religious experience to the aid of the conflict against social wrong. If he could write that:

This is a most Christian city. There are churches and churches. All sorts of churches, where are preached all sorts of religions, save that which once in Galilee taught the arrant socialistic doctrine that it is easier for a camel to pass through the eye of a needle than for a rich man to enter the kingdom of God; all save that which once in Jerusalem drove the money-changers from the temple.[1]

He also realized that:

. . . there is in true Christianity a power to regenerate the world. But it must be a Christianity that attacks vested wrongs, not that spurious thing that defends them. The religion which allies itself with injustice to preach down the natural aspirations of the masses is worse than atheism.[2]

He knew that there was a "perverted Christianity to soothe the conscience of the rich and to frown down discontent on the part of the poor,"[3] but there was also this interpretation of its teachings:

Here is the essential spirit of Christianity. The essence of its teaching is not, "Provide for your own body and save your own soul," but, "Do what you can to make this a better world for all." It was a protest against the doctrine of "each for himself and devil take the hindermost!" It was the proclamation of a common fatherhood of God and a common brotherhood of men. This was

[1] *The Land Question, Works,* Vol. III, pp. 94–95.
[2] *Ibid.,* p. 96.
[3] *The Science of Political Economy,* p. 174.

why the rich and the powerful, the high priests and the rulers, persecuted Christianity with fire and sword. It was not what in so many of our churches to-day is called religion that pagan Rome sought to tear out—it was what in too many of the churches of to-day is called "socialism and communism," the doctrine of the equality of human rights! [4]

And "the Christianity that ignores this social responsibility has really forgotten the teachings of Christ." [5]

In a sermon on "Thy Kingdom Come," first delivered in Glasgow in 1889, George stated clearly and eloquently his conception of the significance of Christianity. It was an interpretation that may or may not have been good Christian exegesis, but it does indicate the attitude with which he approached the traditional problems and challenges proffered by Christianity. George believed:

. . . that a very kingdom of God might be brought on this earth if men would but seek to do justice—if men would but acknowledge the essential principle of Christianity, that of doing to others as we would have others do to us, and of recognizing that we are all here equally the children of the one Father, equally entitled to share His bounty, equally entitled to live our lives and develop our faculties, and to apply our labor to the raw material that He has provided. Aye! and when a man sees that, then there arises that hope of the coming of the kingdom that carried the Gospel through the streets of Rome, that carried it into pagan lands, that made it, against the most ferocious persecution, the dominant religion of the world. Early Christianity did not mean, in its prayer for the coming of Christ's kingdom, a kingdom in heaven, but a kingdom on earth. If Christ had simply preached of the other world, the high priests and the Pharisees would not have persecuted Him, the Roman soldiery would not have nailed His hands to the cross. Why was Christianity persecuted? Why were its first professors thrown to wild beasts, burned to light a tyrant's gardens,

---

[4] In an address on "Thou Shalt Not Steal," before the Anti-Poverty Society, May 8, 1887. In *Works*, Vol. VIII *(Our Land and Land Policy)* pp. 251–252.

[5] *Ibid.*, p. 251.

hounded, tortured, put to death, by all the cruel devices that a devilish ingenuity could suggest? Not that it was a new religion, referring only to the future; Rome was tolerant of all religions. It was the boast of Rome that all gods were sheltered in her Pantheon; it was the boast of Rome that she made no interference with the religions of peoples she conquered. What was persecuted was a great movement for social reform—the Gospel of Justice —heard by common fishermen with gladness, carried by laborers and slaves into the Imperial City. The Christian revelation was the doctrine of human equality, of the fatherhood of God, of the brotherhood of man. It struck at the very basis of that monstrous tyranny that then oppressed the civilized world; it struck at the fetters of the captive, at the bonds of the slave, at that monstrous injustice which allowed a class to revel on the proceeds of labor, while those who did the labor fared scantily. That is the reason why early Christianity was persecuted. And when they could no longer hold it down, then the privileged classes adopted and perverted the new faith, and it became, in its very triumph, not the pure Christianity of the early days, but a Christianity that, to a very great extent, was the servitor of the privileged classes. And, instead of preaching the essential fatherhood of God, the essential brotherhood of man, its high priests engrafted on the pure truths of the Gospel the blasphemous doctrine that the All-Father is a respecter of persons, and that by His will and on His mandate is founded that monstrous injustice which condemns the great mass of humanity to unrequited hard toil. There has been no failure of Christianity. The failure has been in the sort of Christianity that has been preached.[6]

George was very bitter against "the sort of Christianity that has been preached." There was this inquiry, for example:

What sort of God is it that the Rev. Dr. Huntington worships and to whom the Episcopal collects and liturgy are addressed? Does the rector of Grace Church really think that the "most merciful Father," "Our Father which art in heaven," is really allowing

---

[6] *Works,* Vol. VIII *(Our Land and Land Policy),* pp. 289–291. George's conception of the cause of the Roman persecutions does appear historically accurate, but it is strange to see Christianity upheld as teaching the supremacy of a kingdom on earth and not a kingdom in heaven. For George's views on the person of Jesus, see *Life,* p. 548.

bitter injustice and want to continue among His children in New York City and elsewhere simply because the Episcopal Church does not formally ask Him every Sunday "to suffer not the hire of the laborer to be kept back by fraud"? . . . Is the want and suffering that exist in the centers of our civilization to-day, the bitter struggle among human beings to merely live, and the vice and the crime and the greed that grow out of that struggle, because of God's neglect or because of man's? Is it in accordance with the will of God or is it because of our violation of God's will? . . . Human laws disinherit God's children on their very entrance into the world. . . . If he [Dr. Huntington] ignores this wrong and robbery, and yet prays to God to relieve injustice and want, his prayer is an insult to God and an injury to man.[7]

And again:

"The poor ye have always with you." If ever a scripture has been wrested to the devil's service, this is the scripture. How often have these words been distorted from their obvious meaning to soothe conscience into acquiescence in human misery and degradation—to bolster that blasphemy, the very negation and denial of Christ's teachings, that the All-Wise and Most Merciful, the Infinite Father, has decreed that so many of his creatures must be poor in order that others of his creatures to whom he wills the good things of life should enjoy the pleasure and virtue of doling out alms! "The poor ye have always with you," said Christ; but all his teachings supply the limitation, "until the coming of the Kingdom." In that kingdom of God *on earth*, that kingdom of justice and love for which he taught his followers to strive and pray, there will be no poor. But though the faith and the hope and the striving for this kingdom are of the very essence of Christ's teaching, the staunchest disbelievers and revilers of its possibility are found among those who call themselves Christians.[8]

George's conception of Christianity, then, was of a militant Christianity, one that fought and crusaded not against infidels but against economic injustice. He attacked the religious institution not because of any peculiarly religious

[7] In the *Standard* of January 1, 1890.
[8] *Social Problems, Works,* Vol. II, p. 78.

shortcoming but because, as an institution, it ignored, either deliberately or unwittingly, the social causes that were the basis of nearly all human misery—and sin. If the church persistently disregarded the economic problems that have thrust themselves ruthlessly into individual life and have so often determined man's reaction to the traditional ethical questions, then, for George, in precisely that measure had it defeated the very ends for which it was ostensibly striving.

This clash between George's interpretation of Christianity and the doctrines of ecclesiastical institutionalism is perhaps nowhere better illustrated than in the Papal attempts to discipline one of George's most powerful and fervent disciples, the priest, the Reverend Dr. Edward McGlynn, one who confidently sought to turn the strength of his religion to solving the riddle of social injustice. Here was an episode that was significant not only as an example of the conflicting religious attitudes that could be evoked by the consideration of an economic problem, but also as one of those rare instances when Rome has voluntarily reversed itself. It may be of some value, then, briefly to discuss the excommunication and reinstatement of Father McGlynn, and to indicate the official position of the Papacy toward George's proposals, for there is offered, in this matter of doctrinal theology, a striking commentary upon certain reactions of the religious institution.

The name of Father McGlynn [9] was first associated with

[9] The best accounts of the work and career of Father McGlynn are found in the New York newspapers and magazines during the first half of 1887 and the closing months of 1892, the periods of his excommunication and reinstatement. (In the Henry George Scrap Books in the New York Public Library, especially Vols. 12–16, there are collections of such articles.) A complete chronological account of the "McGlynn case" can be had from the files of George's newspaper, the *Standard,* for the very first issue, of January 8, 1887, opened with a discussion of the priest's suspension, and the entire course of the theological controversy was traced from that point on. The *Standard's* reports of the meetings of the Anti-Poverty Society, of which Father McGlynn was president, are also useful. Of special importance is the

the land question in 1882 while George was in Ireland on his first lecture trip. In that year Michael Davitt had come to the United States to arouse support for the Irish land movement, and it was at his first meeting in New York, in the old Academy of Music, that Dr. McGlynn delivered an address in which he definitely allied himself to the work of George and of the Irish Land League. This was no unknown priest who had joined the ranks of social reform but one of the most influential Catholic clergymen in the country, and an orator who had been classed with Henry Ward Beecher and Wendell Phillips. He had been born in New York City and had been educated for the priesthood at the Urban College of the Propaganda in Rome, where he spent ten years, finally becoming vice-rector of the newly established American College. In 1860, at the age of twenty-three, he received his Doctor of Philosophy and Sacred Theology degree and was ordained a priest in the Church of St. John Lateran at Rome. He returned to New York, held several pastorates in the poorer sections of the city, was made chaplain of the Military Hospital in Central Park during the last years of the Civil War, and, finally, in 1866, became pastor of St. Stephen's Church, which ministered to one of the largest and best-known parishes in the city. His unceasing work of personal charity among the poor, his constant and active interest in political reform in New York City, his lectures throughout this country and Canada on questions of government and

issue of February 5, 1887, in which Dr. McGlynn wrote a review of his own case. Biographical material and written memorabilia concerning Father McGlynn and selections from his speeches and writings may be found in the book of the late Sylvester L. Malone, *Dr. Edward McGlynn* (New York, Dr. McGlynn Monument Association, 1918). Vol. II of the *Life of Henry George* also contains a treatment of the work and personality of Father McGlynn. See also Professor Young's *Single Tax Movement in the United States (op. cit.)*, especially pp. 111–118, and *The Single Tax Year Book*, compiled and edited by Joseph Dana Miller, editor of *Land and Freedom (op. cit.)*, pp. 407–408 and 414–416.

religion, had brought him recognition as an outstanding Catholic cleric. Long before his association with Henry George he had been known and loved as the "priest of the people."

Dr. McGlynn's first public declaration of his support of the policies of George and the Irish Land League was followed by several other speeches at the Davitt meetings, and when George returned from Ireland one of his first acts was to make the acquaintance of this priest and disciple who was later to exert so powerful an influence upon the popular reception of his own doctrines. George had written from Ireland that Father McGlynn was the Peter the Hermit of a new crusade, and that "if Davitt's trip had no other result, it were well worth this. To start such a man [McGlynn] is worth a trip around the world three times over. He is 'an army with banners.' " [10] The meeting of these two men, both devoutly religious and both believing that in the search for the solution of economic problems lay the true end of religion, began a long friendship which, although interrupted for a time, proved to be not only a source of strength in the spread of George's ideas, but also an example of that real fellowship that comes of devotion to an ideal.

The defense of the Irish land movement by Father McGlynn did not, however, remain unnoticed by his ecclesiastical superiors. He was accused of favoring the "Irish Revolution" and several letters of complaint were addressed to Cardinal McCloskey of New York about the "priest McGlynn" by Cardinal Simeoni, Prefect of the Propaganda. Dr. McGlynn was summoned to an interview with Cardinal McCloskey and the result was, in Dr. McGlynn's words, that:

I voluntarily promised to abstain from making Land League speeches, not because I acknowledged the right of any one to

[10] *Life,* pp. 386–387.

forbid me, but because I knew too well the power of my ecclesiastical superiors to impair and almost destroy my usefulness in the ministry of Christ's Church to which I had consecrated my life.[11]

This was not the first time that Father McGlynn had clashed with the Catholic authorities. Once before he had been reprimanded for his advanced doctrine on the question of education; he had insisted that secular instruction was the concern only of the State and not of the church, and that parochial schools could expect no financial support from the government.[12] Nor was this the first time that a clerical defender of the Irish cause, or more particularly of the Irish land movement, had been disciplined by Rome. All throughout the agitation of the late '70s and early '80s great numbers of the Irish clergy had rallied to the support of the "no-renters," and many had been summarily punished. It was this attempted disciplining of the Irish clergy that had led Daniel O'Connell to demand "as much religion from Rome as you please, but no politics!"[13]

[11] In the *Standard* of February 5, 1887. See also *Life*, p. 386.
[12] This idea was expressed by him most forcibly in an interview which appeared in the New York *Sun* of April 30, 1870, on "No Public Moneys for Private Schools." Later, in 1889, in a speech at Cooper Union on "Public Schools and Their Enemies," he stated his position even more strongly.
[13] This slogan was later used by George in the *Standard* articles on the McGlynn case.
Perhaps the most notable of the Irish priests who were silenced by their ecclesiastical superiors was the Bishop of Meath, the Rt. Rev. Dr. Thomas Nulty. In February, 1881, he had addressed a pastoral letter, devoted largely to the matter of land, to the clergy and laity of the diocese of Meath, which was followed, on April 2, by another letter, written at Mullingar, which contained an "essay on the land question." This second letter was also addressed to the clergy and laity of Meath, but, as Dr. Nulty indicated, he drafted it not in his capacity as bishop but rather as a layman writing an economic treatise. The letter was published in pamphlet form by Joseph Dollard of Dublin in 1881. This is a passage from it: "The land of every country is the gift of its Creator to the people of that country; it is the patrimony and inheritance bequeathed to them by their common Father, out of which they can, by continuous labor and toil, provide themselves with everything they require for their maintenance and support, for their material comfort and enjoyment. God was perfectly free in the act by which He created us; but, having created us, He bound himself by that act to provide us with the means necessary for our subsistence. The land is

Father McGlynn engaged in no further agitation for the Irish Land League; he was so bound by his pledge. He did not, however, interpret his promise to Cardinal McCloskey to mean that he was to put aside all interest in political or social questions, and in 1884 he gave his active support to the candidacy of Grover Cleveland. Then in 1886 he was faced with what is perhaps the most difficult problem that can confront the priest, the problem of conflicting allegiances. George had been offered the United Labor Party's nomination in the New York mayoralty election and it was to Dr. McGlynn that he first turned for advice. He was counseled to enter the campaign, and Father McGlynn, with his wide knowledge of political practices, helped in the early organization of George's followers. And now again the priest met the force of ecclesiastical discipline. Archbishop Corrigan wrote warning him to "leave aside" anything that would seem "to coincide with socialism" and to have no further "relations with Henry George." [14] In another letter, several days later, Father McGlynn was forbidden, under pain of suspension, "to take any part in any political meeting whatever without permission of the Sacred Congregation of Propaganda Fide," and

the only means of this kind now known to us. The land, therefore, of every country is the common property of the people of that country, because its real owner, the Creator who made it, has transferred it as a voluntary gift to them. *Terram autem dedit filiis hominum.* Now, as every individual in that country is a creature and child of God, and as all His creatures are equal in His sight, any settlement of the land of a country that would exclude the humblest man in that country from his share in the common inheritance would be not only an injustice and a wrong to that man, but, moreover, would be an impious resistance to the benevolent intentions of his Creator."

George interviewed Bishop Nulty for the *Irish World,* and the interview, which appeared on November 19, 1881, together with a long article on the land question which the bishop contributed to the *Irish World* on November 26, were the direct cause, as George intimated in his letters to Patrick Ford, editor of the paper, of the clergyman's later enforced silence. George wrote to Ford (November 10) that: "My visit to Bishop Nulty was most delightful. Instead of in anything falling below my anticipation he rather exceeds it. Here is a Christian Bishop. . . . I never met a man that seemed to me to so really fill the ideal of a Reverend Father in God. How I wish he were Pope."

[14] *Life,* p. 465.

specifically to absent himself from a meeting at Chickering
Hall at which he was scheduled to speak.[15] But Dr. McGlynn
did speak, and speak "as if he expected that night to be
his last."[16] The next morning he was suspended from his
church.

The suspension was originally for a two-week period. However, after the appearance of an interview in the New York
Tribune of November 26, 1886, in which Father McGlynn upheld the teachings of George and specifically attacked a pastoral letter of Archbishop Corrigan that had condemned
"certain unsound principles and theories" of private property, the suspension was extended to the end of the year, and
the Archbishop laid the matter before the Cardinal Prefect
of the Propaganda at Rome. Dr. McGlynn was then ordered
to Rome but declined, and in his letter to Archbishop Corrigan he wrote that:

As I cannot go to Rome to give an account of my doctrine about
land, I would say that I have made it clear in speeches, in reported interviews and in published articles, and I repeat it here:
I have taught and shall continue to teach in speeches and writings
as long as I live, that land is rightfully the property of the people
in common and that private ownership of land is against natural
justice, no matter by what civil or ecclesiastical laws it may be
sanctioned; and I would bring about instantly, if I could, such
change of laws all the world over as would confiscate private
property in land, without one penny of compensation to the
miscalled owners.[17]

[15] The meeting, which took place on October 2, was under the auspices
of those supporters of George who were not connected with the labor movement. They included many clergymen and professors, and among those
attending the meeting were Professor Daniel De Leon of Columbia, Professor David B. Scott of the College of the City of New York, the Rev.
John W. Kramer, Charles F. Wingate, and Professor Thomas Davidson.
[16] *Life*, p. 465.
Before Father McGlynn's suspension he had sent George to Archbishop
Corrigan for a personal interview, in order to show the Archbishop the type
of man he was supporting. The meeting was friendly and courteous, but
did not affect Dr. McGlynn's suspension.
[17] Letter of Dec. 20, 1886, which appeared in the *Standard*, Feb. 5, 1887.

The first issue of George's *Standard,* of January 8, 1887, was devoted largely to the "McGlynn Case," and although the disciplining of the priest had aroused attention in New York and throughout the country, the *Standard* was almost alone in its attack upon the church authorities. George, in this first issue, stated that he was devoting the attention of his paper to this purely ecclesiastical matter because he felt that it involved "the attitude of the greatest of Christian Churches towards the world-wide social movement of our times, and its decision will be fraught with the most important consequences both to the development of that movement and to the Church itself."

Father McGlynn was removed from his pastorate at St. Stephen's in the middle of January, but he continued to support the work of George and never for a moment did he consider that there was anything in his conduct that was at all contrary to his priestly vows. He was confident that there was a distinct separation between the realms of religious authority and of political action; the conviction that "in becoming a priest I did not evade the duties or surrender the rights of a man and a citizen," [18] clearly expressed the attitude with which he approached the apparent conflict between his allegiance to the church and his economic reasoning. In fact, for him there was really no conflict between the two; he felt that as a priest his vow of obedience was "simply a promise to obey the church authorities in matters concerning the priest's duties of religion," [19] but that as a man and a citizen and a fervent seeker after social justice, his opinions and actions were free so long as they were not "clearly contrary to the teachings of the Christian religion." After his suspension from his pastorate and even after his later excommunication, Father McGlynn never doubted that he was still a Catholic priest or that his conduct was any-

[18] Letter in the *Standard (op. cit.).*   [19] *Ibid.*

thing but that of a good Christian. Perhaps his most eloquent exposition and defense of the Catholic Church is found in the very address in which he lifted the "cross of a new crusade." [20] Here was a remarkable attempt, in an oration that must certainly be given very high rank,[21] to fuse the tenets of political economy with the ardor of religious enthusiasm. It was an endeavor that ambitiously undertook to uphold the teachings of Catholicism and to bring the power of the church to the service of social reform, at the same time insisting that the Catholic hierarchy had no authority over civil or political opinion. Father McGlynn's efforts to dissociate his church's jurisdiction from temporal affairs and yet to remain faithful to its principles are strikingly illustrated in several passages of his speech:

And while I do not admit that it is the province of the Christian church to minutely control—because of its custody of great general religious truths, and because she is the depository of priceless graces to men—the political interests of nations, or to define to them the complicated, the knotty and what would almost seem the insoluble questions of policies, of politics and of political economy; yet, at the same time, I cheerfully give permission to whomsoever will to denounce me as a traitor to that which I myself hold most precious, if on any platform I shall ever say a word against the truth that I have once taught, and that I shall teach, so help me God, as long as I shall live. . . . I repeat, and I shall never tire of repeating, that I find justification for loving every social cause, every economic cause, every political cause, whose object is the diminution—rather let us say the abolition—of poverty, for the diffusion of knowledge, for the refinement and

[20] "The Cross of a New Crusade" was delivered by Father McGlynn in the Academy of Music in New York, March 29, 1887, before a great audience consisting almost entirely of Catholics and especially of his former parishioners of St. Stephen's Church.

[21] The New York *Sun*, a paper that was by no means friendly to the George-McGlynn agitation, declared that "The Rev. Dr. McGlynn's address is entitled to rank with those great orations which at critical times and from the mouths of men of genius have swayed the course of public opinion and changed the onward movement of nations." (March 31, 1887.)

the civilization of these images of God all around us—a cause
in which I must sympathize, and for which, as far as I can, I must
speak and labor; and I never for a moment fancied on that, to
me, most sacred day, when, full of reverence, I bowed before a
Christian altar, to receive the consecration of Christ's priesthood,
that I was to rise from the prostrate attitude any the less a man,
any the less the citizen.[22]

This religious attitude with which he viewed the new gospel
of George is evident in these words:

This new crusade, then, while, to use a modern phrase, there is
nothing sectarian about it, is necessarily a religious movement.
And permit me to say, and I am not at all singular in the saying
of it, if it were not a religious movement you might at the very
outset count me out of it; for I think that any cause, any movement, any object that enlists the thought of men and the affections
of the hearts of men must have a religious inspiration, a religious
justification and a religious consummation. . . . The cross of the
new crusade is not raised in hostility to the cross of Christ. The
very thought of a crusade and of the honored badge of a crusade—
the holy ensign of the cross—is entirely borrowed from Him.[23]

The direct result of Dr. McGlynn's address was the founding of the Anti-Poverty Society. Such an organization had
been previously suggested by Thomas L. McCready of the
Standard's staff, but it was the religious note in the "Cross
of the New Crusade" that inspired the forming of a society
which sought "to spread, by such peaceable and lawful means
as may be found most desirable and efficient, a knowledge
of the truth that God has made ample provision for the need
of all men during their residence upon earth, and that involuntary poverty is the result of the human laws that allow
individuals to claim as private property that which the Creator has provided for the use of all." The first meeting took
place in Chickering Hall on May 1, with Father McGlynn,

[22] Malone *(op. cit.)*, pp. 18, 26–27.   [23] *Ibid.*, pp. 21, 19.

who had been elected president of the organization, delivering the opening address.[24] Owing to the great crowd that was attracted to this first meeting, the following gatherings of the society were held in the Academy of Music, and every Sunday evening a pious yet militant band of converts listened to the words of Father McGlynn, George and other leaders of the movement.

An organization such as this, which was supported by hundreds of Dr. McGlynn's former parishioners who had remained loyal to him, served to widen still further the gap between the deposed priest and his superiors, and early in May he was notified that if he did not report in Rome within forty days he would be excommunicated. "Dr. McGlynn contented himself with his former reply that grave reasons would prevent his making the journey then," [25] and as it became evident that he would be excommunicated, labor opinion in New York became deeply concerned. A parade of Catholic working men, estimated by the newspapers as numbering from thirty to seventy-five thousand marchers, protested against the impending excommunication at a great demonstration on the 18th of June. Yet the *Standard* still remained almost alone in its denunciation of the Catholic authorities.[26]

[24] George wrote (in the *Standard* of May 7): "Never before in New York had a great audience sprung to its feet and in a tumult of enthusiasm cheered the Lord's Prayer; but it was the Lord's Prayer with a meaning that the churches have ignored. The simple words, 'Thy kingdom come, Thy will be done *on earth* as it is in heaven,' as they fell from the lips of a Christian priest who proclaims the common fatherhood of God and the common brotherhood of man; who points to the widespread poverty and suffering not as in accordance with God's will, but as in defiance of God's order, and who appeals to the love of God and the hope of heaven, not to make men submissive of social injustice which brings want and misery, but to urge them to the duty of sweeping away this injustice—have in them the power with which Christianity conquered the world.

[25] *Life*, p. 493. The "grave" reasons were the advice of Dr. McGlynn's physician, who cautioned him against making the trip.

[26] George waxed very bitter and very eloquent in his *Standard* editorials. He wrote, for example, on June 25: "There stands hard by the palace of the holy inquisition in Rome a statue which has been placed there since Rome became the capital of a united Italy. On it is this inscription: 'GALILEO GALILEI was imprisoned in the neighboring palace for having seen that

Father McGlynn was excommunicated on the 3d of July, 1887. But this heaviest of ecclesiastical punishments made no change in his attitude. He was convinced that "once a priest, always a priest," and he was sure that he had been unjustly disciplined, since never, in any word or act, had he attacked the Catholic Church or departed from his duties as a Catholic priest. Archbishop Corrigan interpreted Dr. McGlynn's excommunication to mean that any sympathy for the deposed priest was in itself an act of disobedience to the church authorities, and he went so far as to refuse burial in the Catholic Calvary Cemetery to several Catholics who, although devout in their religion, had attended Father McGlynn's talks at the Anti-Poverty Society.[27] In addition, he disciplined the Reverend Dr. Richard Lalor Burtsell, one of the most prominent of Catholic scholars and a close friend of Dr. McGlynn, by transferring him from his church in New York City to a small parish upstate.

In the summer of 1887, Father McGlynn took an active part in the State convention of the United Labor Party, and after George's nomination for the position of Secretary of State he stumped the State in an active speaking campaign. The election, however, resulted in the break-up of the party, for not only was the socialist element alienated from the George forces, but also a large Catholic group; Patrick Ford, editor of the *Irish World,* had definitely withdrawn his support and George and McGlynn thereby lost many followers.

the earth revolves around the sun.' In after years when the true-hearted American priest shall have rested from his labors, and what is now being done is history, there will arise by the spot where he shall be excommunicated such a statue and such an inscription. And days will come when happy little children, such as now die like flies in tenement houses, shall be held up by their mothers to lay garlands upon it." And after the excommunication had been definitely announced, George declared in no uncertain language that: "The real cause of this excommunication . . . is that the priest against whom the heaviest bolt of Rome has been hurled has dared to preach the gospel of his Master; has dared to apply to the social institutions of the present day the essential teachings of Christianity." (July 16.)

[27] *Life,* p. 495.

Dr. McGlynn continued his work in the Anti-Poverty Society, but in the following year occurred the break between him and George which caused the latter to withdraw from the organization. The rupture arose over the question of supporting President Cleveland in the election of 1888. The President had definitely identified himself with tariff reform, and since free trade was so paramount an issue in the single tax proposals, George and the great majority of his followers felt that they should support Cleveland and the Democratic Party. To this Father McGlynn was vigorously opposed. Although he was a free trader and an admirer of the President, he refused to ally himself in any way with Tammany Hall and the Democratic Party, chiefly because the New York City Democratic organization had actively defended the church authorities in their disciplinary efforts, and, relying upon its important influence among Catholic voters, had attempted to make political capital out of the excommunication. Father McGlynn insisted that an independent labor party, formed upon the platform of the 1887 State convention, be supported in the national election. The final result of the dispute was that George, together with the members of the executive committee of the organization, withdrew, and Dr. McGlynn kept on with his Sunday evening meetings and retained the name of the Anti-Poverty Society.[28]

The most important episode, however, of the entire controversy between Father McGlynn and the church was yet to occur. It was the full reinstatement of the priest at the instance, not of Dr. McGlynn himself, but of the Papal authorities. The first hint that the Holy See had reconsidered its act of excommunication came in 1889, when Archbishop Satolli, Papal Ablegate to the Church in the United States, who had been sent to this country for the inauguration ceremonies of

[28] For an account of the dispute, see the *Standard* of February 18, 25; March 17, 24, 1889.

the Catholic University in Washington, telegraphed Father McGlynn granting him an interview. Dr. McGlynn, however, was on a lecture trip and was unable to meet the Ablegate before his departure from New York for Rome. But three years later, Archbishop Satolli again visited America and made it known that he had been instructed to inquire into the whole matter. He first interviewed Dr. Burtsell, who presented him with an exposition of the single tax proposals that had been endorsed by Father McGlynn. Father McGlynn himself then drew up a doctrinal statement [29] and submitted it to Monsignor Satolli, who, after examining it, forwarded the statement to the Catholic University at Washington, where it was reviewed by a committee of four church authorities.[30] The statement was declared "to contain nothing contrary to

[29] The statement may be found most conveniently in the *Single Tax Year Book*, pp. 414–416, and in Malone, pp. 47–51. It opens with this assertion: "All men are endowed by the law of nature with the right to life and to the pursuit of happiness, and therefore with the right to exert their energies upon those natural bounties without which labor or life is impossible. God has granted those natural bounties, that is to say, the earth, to mankind in general, so that no part of it has been assigned to any one in particular, and so that the limits of private possession have been left to be fixed by man's own industry and the laws of individual peoples." After upholding the right of private property, Dr. McGlynn states that: "The assertion of this dominion by civil government is especially necessary, because, with the very beginning of civil government and with the growth of civilization, there comes to the natural bounties, or the land, a peculiar and increasing value distinct from and irrespective of the products of private industry existing therein. This value is not produced by the industry of the private possessor or proprietor, but is produced by the existence of the community and grows with the growth and civilization of the community. It is therefore called the unearned increment. . . . The justice and the duty of appropriating this fund to public uses is apparent, in that it takes nothing from the private property of individuals, except what they will pay willingly as an equivalent for a value produced by the community, and which they are permitted to enjoy. . . . To permit any portion of this public property to go into private pockets, without a perfect equivalent being paid into the public treasury, would be an injustice to the community. Therefore, the whole rental fund should be appropriated to common or public uses." Father McGlynn's concluding passages are devoted to outlining the effects of the single tax. It is altogether a concise and unequivocal statement of economic doctrine.

[30] The four professors were: Rev. Dr. Thomas Bouquillon, then Dean of the Theological Faculty; Rev. Dr. Thomas O'Gorman, afterward appointed Bishop of Sioux Falls; Rev. Dr. Thomas J. Shahan, the late head of the Catholic University, and Rev. Dr. Charles Grannan.

Catholic teachings." Thereupon Dr. McGlynn professed his complete acceptance of the doctrines of the Catholic Church and withdrew whatever words of disrespect he might have offered to the Holy See during his period of excommunication. However, he did not go into retreat, as was the custom for those of the clergy who were about to be reinstated, for that, he explained to Monsignor Satolli, would have been interpreted as a punishment for his economic opinions. Furthermore, he insisted that he be permitted to expound his single tax convictions at the Anti-Poverty Society meetings or wherever an opportunity presented itself, and it was with such an understanding that on December 23, 1892, the Papal Ablegate announced from Washington that "Dr. McGlynn was declared free from ecclesiastical censures and restored to the exercise of his priestly functions, after having satisfied the Pope's legate on all the points in his case." [31] On Christmas Day Father McGlynn celebrated mass for the first time in five years. And in the evening he addressed the Anti-Poverty meeting.

Three weeks later Archbishop Satolli drew up a lengthy statement [32] reviewing the case, in which he declared that "Dr. McGlynn had presented a brief statement of his opinions on moral-economic matters and it was judged not contrary to the doctrine constantly taught by the Church, and as recently confirmed by the Holy Father in the Encyclical, *Rerum Novarum.*" In June of 1893 Father McGlynn visited Rome and was graciously received by the Pope, who gave him his apostolic blessing. Dr. McGlynn later became pastor of St. Mary's Church in Newburgh, N. Y., and remained there until his death in 1900. His friendship with George was renewed shortly after his reinstatement, and at George's funeral he delivered one of his most impressive orations. He never relaxed in the advocacy of his economic doctrines and

[31] Malone, p. 6.   [32] *Ibid.,* p. 6.

he remains, with the possible exception of George himself, the most popular and influential figure in the early single tax agitation.

There are several significant aspects of this incident of church discipline that may justify this apparent digression into the details of the McGlynn case. One is suggested in the words of Monsignor Satolli, who found that there was nothing in Father McGlynn's "opinions on moral-economic matters" that was contrary to "the doctrine constantly taught by the church." It would of course be patently absurd to intimate that such an isolated statement, even were it a sentence from a Papal encyclical, might be interpreted as some atavistic reminiscence of early Christian communism. Certainly there are no stronger defenders of all forms of private property than the institutions of present-day religion. Yet there must be a dim recognition, even if it does not lead to any overt action by Christianity, of what George liked to think of as the "social justice" mission of Jesus. And especially in Catholicism must there be some recollection, not perhaps of that first vague aspiration of primitive Christianity, but rather of the unambiguous patristic teachings concerning property, and particularly, in this connection, landed property. It is not necessary, or rather it is not possible, here to discuss the land views of the church fathers, especially since their communistic approach to property is fairly familiar.[33] Moreover, their utterances have perhaps no sig-

[33] A few scattered comments of the patristic writers regarding landed property may be presented here; these are merely casually and accidentally discovered quotations, no attempt having been made, obviously, to have investigated the question.
" . . . This earth, whence their gain came, is given to all men to be held in common, and therefore produces for all men common nourishment. . . . He argues, therefore, wrongly, who argues that he is innocent if he appropriates specially to himself the good things which God gave us for common use. . . . Therefore, when we give the poor what they require, we give them their own, not ours; and we can more rightly say that we pay them a debt, than that we act generously towards them . . . It is reason-

nificance for modern Catholic political economy. Much of the work of the Latin fathers in economics, if not in theology and philosophy, has been recognized, and by the church itself, as anachronistic, and what may have been scattered glimpses of profound social truths have gone the way of the mediæval doctrine of interest. Yet, a nineteenth century Papal Ablegate found in George's single tax nothing contrary to "the doctrine constantly taught by the church." And while it must again be insisted that such a declaration cannot be made the basis for any gratuitous excursion into the teachings of the Catholic Church on the question of private property in land, especially since property in land was specifically defended in the encyclical on the "condition of labor," which shall be considered shortly, nevertheless it has definitely stamped the opinions of Father McGlynn and George as Catholic "free doctrine"—"Catholics are free to hold the doctrine [of the single tax] or not to hold it as they see fit." [34]

The effect of the McGlynn controversy upon George was to widen still further the gap that he had recognized between the religious spirit and the religious institution. On the one hand his own conception of the religious power in

able for us to enjoy in common that which is given to us from the common property." Gregory the Great, in his *Pastoral Care*. (The English translation is that of Henry Sweet from King Alfred's West-Saxon version of Gregory's work; Early English Text Society, London, Trübner, 1871, Vol. XLV to L, pp. 334–336.)

"God has ordered all things to be produced so that there should be food in common to all and that the earth should be a common possession for all. Nature, therefore, has produced a common right for all, but greed has made it a right for a few." St. Ambrose, *On the Duties of the Clergy*, Chap. XXVIII, Sec. 132 (*Nicene and Post-Nicene Fathers;* Shaff and Wace ed., New York, Scribner, 1896, Vol. X, p. 23).

There are several other quotations which the writer has been unable to locate specifically, but which may be mentioned here. One is from Tertullian, "The land is no man's property; none shall possess it as property." Another from Cyprian, "No man shall be received into our communion who sayeth that the land may be sold. God's footstool is not property." There are also several interesting statements from the *Divine Institutes* of Lactantius, which, however, are too long to be quoted —neither have they been verified specifically.

[34] See Malone *(op. cit.),* p. 6.

his "moral-economic" system was strengthened and, in a sense, justified; in the person of Father McGlynn and in the devout gatherings of the Anti-Poverty Society were crystallized all that vague force of fervent protest against social wrong which George felt to be the very basis of religion. And on the other hand his distrust of religious institutionalism, although offset to a degree by the final disposition of the controversy,[35] was confirmed and embittered. He wrote, for example, in 1891: [36] "How sad it is to see a church in all its branches offering men stones instead of bread, and thistles instead of figs. From Protestant preachers to Pope, avowed teachers of Christianity are with few exceptions preaching almsgiving or socialism and ignoring the simple remedy of justice." On the same day he wrote a similar letter to his Irish friend, Father Dawson:

But it is very sad to see the general tendency on the part of all clergymen—and it is quite as marked, perhaps even more so, among the Protestant sects even to the Unitarian—to avoid the simple principle of justice. As Tolstoi has put it, they are willing to do anything for the poor except to get off their backs. This is leading them into the advocacy of socialism, and to all sorts of dangerous

[35] In a letter to Dr. McGlynn, George expressed his intense satisfaction with the act of reinstatement by Pope Leo XIII: "My appreciation of the present Pope, greatly increased by the Encyclical, has been steadily growing, and since the errand of the Ablegate has developed, has reached the highest point. It would previously have seemed incredible that such radical, comprehensive and far-reaching action would have been the work of his surroundings and age. Nothing that I can recall has so surprised and gratified me. For the powers linked against it have seemed too great to be broken down save in long years. It seems indeed as if a greater power had on all sides overruled evil for good." (Quoted by Father McGlynn at a meeting of the Anti-Poverty Society, January 15, 1893; cited by Malone, p. 52.) Even before Dr. McGlynn's reinstatement George appreciated the possible contrast between Catholic doctrine and the Catholic hierarchy. He wrote to Father Dawson (Dec. 9, 1888): "You understand my feelings towards the Catholic Church, but there are many—even of Catholics—who do not understand the distinction Catholic theology makes between the Church and Church officialism. . . . Some time after the fight is over, we shall have a Pope condemning private property in land. We shall not be here; but I have faith we shall be somewhere."
[36] To a friend, James E. Mills (May 18).

things, even to the acceptance and even advocacy of principles which will lead ultimately to atheism.

The spectacle of a priest being disciplined by his superiors because, although a godly and zealous cleric, he had sought to make his religion a force in the search for economic justice was, for George, a travesty upon religion. And therefore the apparent change of attitude on the part of the Catholic hierarchy, as reflected in the reinstatement of Father McGlynn, was of the utmost significance for him, especially since his own work, he felt, had been at least partially responsible for that about-face. This work was his reply to the much-discussed encyclical of Pope Leo XIII on *The Condition of Labor (Rerum Novarum),* and it was a work that may be considered as probably the most important tangible product of the McGlynn case.

On the 15th of May, 1891, there was addressed to "our Venerable Brethren, all Patriarchs, Primates, Archbishops, and Bishops of the Catholic World," a Papal letter [37] which was prompted by the fact that "the spirit of revolutionary change, which has so long been predominant in the nations of the world" had "passed beyond politics and made its influence felt in the cognate field of practical economy." [38] The letter recognized that:

The elements of a conflict are unmistakable: the growth of industry, and the surprising discoveries of science; the changed relations of masters and workmen; the enormous fortunes of individuals, and the poverty of the masses; the increased self-reliance and the closer mutual combinations of the working popula-

[37] For the text of this encyclical see George's *Works,* Vol. III, Part II. The following quotations will be from that volume. In connection with this encyclical *Rerum Novarum,* the recent encyclicals of Pope Pius XI, *Quadragesimo Anno* (May 15, 1931, the fortieth anniversary of *The Condition of Labor); Nova Impendet* (October 2, 1931), and *Charitas Christi* (May 3, 1932), may be mentioned as presenting other important economic essays.

[38] *Works,* Vol. III, p. 109.

tion; and, finally, a general moral deterioration. The momentous seriousness of the present state of things just now fills every mind with painful apprehension; wise men discuss it; practical men propose schemes; popular meetings, legislatures, and sovereign princes, all are occupied with it—and there is nothing which has a deeper hold on public attention. . . . There can be no question whatever, that some remedy must be found, and quickly found, for the misery and wretchedness which press so heavily at this moment on the large majority of the very poor.[39]

Here, then, was a recognition of social problems, and, apparently, a promise of some carefully reasoned attempt to solve the riddle that had sent George and other reformers on their separate paths of investigation. But no such attempt was forthcoming, for, after a cursory examination of the more serious economic and political proposals for changing the conditions of "misery and wretchedness" among "the very poor," they were all condemned as "socialistic," and the remedy offered was, instead, that:

. . . Masters and rich men must remember their duty; the poor whose interests are at stake, must make every lawful and proper effort; and since Religion alone, as We said at the beginning, can destroy the evil at its root, all men must be persuaded that the primary thing needful is to return to real Christianity, in the absence of which all the plans and devices of the wisest will be of little avail. . . . For the happy results we all long for must be chiefly brought about by the plenteous outpouring of Charity. . . .[40]

It will not be necessary to examine the Papal arguments against socialism except to indicate that almost all of the non-theological reasoning against collectivism, that is, those attacks which were strictly economic in character, were con-

---

[39] *Ibid.*, pp. 109–110.

[40] *Ibid.*, p. 150–151. It is true that the Pope also suggested the benefits of benevolent and Christian working men's associations, and of some form of governmental regulation of working conditions; but inasmuch as he condemned the entire theory of socialism, such proposals were necessarily superficial and palliative, not to be ranked with the religious approach.

fined, with little exception, to the suggestions of the land reformers. There is scarcely a mention of capital or interest in the encyclical, and, excluding those passages which concern the more strictly political proposals of socialism, there is no mention of any of the fundamental reasoning of the Continental school. The doctrines attacked are labeled "socialistic," but they are essentially those of George. For example, in referring to the right of private property, the Pope gives, as illustration, only property in land:

> Thus, if he [the workman] lives sparingly, saves money, and invests his savings, for greater security, in land, the land in such a case is only his wages in another form; and consequently, a working man's little estate thus purchased should be as completely at his own disposal as the wages he receives for his labor.[41]

Other types of private property were introduced only parenthetically; land nationalization seemed the only type of "socialism" with which the Pope was concerned.[42] Indeed, the fallacy of confusing the proposals of George and his followers with those of *bona fide* socialism was exhibited so strikingly in the encyclical, and there was so flagrant a disregard of any attempt to discriminate between conceptions which were diametrically opposed, that the Papal letter was

[41] *Works*, Vol. III, p. 111.

[42] For example, in attempting to explain away the traditional demands for a community of property—the Pope does not mention that such demands were characteristic Christian tradition—the letter confines itself entirely to landed property, and furthermore is not beyond employing a bit of unusual reasoning: "And to say that God has given the earth to the use and enjoyment of the universal human race is not to deny that there can be private property. For God has granted the earth to mankind in general; not in the sense that all without distinction can deal with it as they please, but rather that no part of it has been assigned to any one in particular, and that the limits of private possession have been left to be fixed by man's own industry and the laws of individual peoples. Moreover, the earth, though divided among private owners, ceases not thereby to minister to the needs of all; for there is no one does not live on what the land brings forth. Those who do not possess the soil, contribute their labor; so that it may be truly said that all human subsistence is derived either from labor on one's own land or from some laborious industry which is paid for either in the produce of the land itself or in that which is exchanged for what the land brings forth." (Pp. 113–114.)

interpreted by many who were interested in the work of George, and especially in its expression as a theological question in the McGlynn case, as a direct attack upon that work. George himself felt that his proposals were singled out as a special target; [43] Cardinal Manning in London expressed himself the same way, [44] and Archbishop Corrigan in New York "hailed the Papal letter as the highest sanction of his own opposition to the single tax doctrine as preached by Dr. McGlynn and Henry George." [45]

Whether or not the encyclical was directed particularly against the proposals of the single taxers, George took this opportunity to present his doctrine again in a suave and polished piece of polemical writing. Especially did he wish to distinguish his conceptions from those of the socialists and to emphasize the religious and ethical implications involved in his system. [46] The book, for his answer to the encyclical developed into a small volume of some twenty-five thousand words, was published in New York, London and Rome in the form of an open letter to Pope Leo XIII, with the date of September 11, 1891. It was called *The Condition of Labor*, the same title as that of the Pope's letter. A handsomely printed and bound copy was presented to the Pope, but George never received any acknowledgment of his work from the Holy See.

The religious character of George's reply was clearly indicated in the opening words of his letter:

[43] He wrote that: "For my part, I regard the encyclical letter as aimed at us, and at us alone, almost. And I feel very much encouraged by the honor." (*Life*, pp. 565–566.) Also in his letter to the Pope, he stated: "Your Encyclical will be seen by those who carefully analyze it to be directed not against socialism, which in moderate form you favor, but against what we in the United States call the single tax." (*Works*, Vol. III, p. 102.)

[44] *Life*, p. 565.

[45] *Ibid*.

[46] George wrote to his son shortly after the work was finished: "What I have really aimed at is to make a clear, brief explanation of our principles; to show their religious character, and to draw a line between us and the socialists. I have written really for such men as Cardinal Manning, General Booth and religious-minded men of all creeds. . . . I think I have done a good piece of work and that it will be useful and will attract attention."

Our postulates are all stated or implied in your Encyclical. They are primary perceptions of human reason, the fundamental teachings of the Christian faith. We hold: That—This world is the creation of God. The men brought into it for the brief period of their earthly lives are the equal creatures of His bounty, the equal subjects of His provident care. By his constitution man is beset by physical wants, on the satisfaction of which depend not only the maintenance of his physical life but also the development of his intellectual and spiritual life. God has made the satisfaction of these wants dependent on man's own exertions, giving him the power and laying on him the injunction to labor—a power that of itself raises him far above the brute, since we may reverently say that it enables him to become as it were a helper in the creative work. God has not put on man the task of making bricks without straw. With the need for labor and the power to labor He has also given to man the material for labor. This material is land—man physically being a land animal, who can live only on and from land, and can use other elements, such as air, sunshine and water, only by the use of land. Being the equal creatures of the Creator, equally entitled under His providence to live their lives and satisfy their needs, men are equally entitled to the use of land, and any adjustment that denies this equal use of land is morally wrong.[47]

That religious note was continued throughout; indeed, Professor Ritchie characterized the controversy as a "dispute between those two scholastic theologians, Mr. Henry George and Pope Leo XIII." [48] George, however, was writing a letter of criticism to the Pope, and since the encyclical dealt with theology rather than with political economy, there may be some excuse for his rôle of "scholastic theologian." But it is precisely this religious approach to his economic concepts that is of interest in this connection, and it will not be necessary here to examine the arguments of George against the more strictly economic sections of the Papal letter; they were largely a restatement of opinions that had been expressed many times before. George made his usual distinction be-

[47] The Condition of Labor, (Works, Vol. III, The Land Question), pp. 3–4.
[48] Natural Rights (London, Allen and Unwin, 3d ed., 1916), p. 270.

tween the different forms of private property, that is, between property in land and property in the products of labor, and he treated with little ceremony the Pope's proposed criterion of the validity of private property, namely, that it is in "the power of disposal that ownership consists, whether the property be land or movable goods." George quite neatly demonstrated that such a standard of private property completely justified slavery. He also was particularly concerned with the contrast between his proposals and those of socialism, and the very suggestions of the Pope, such as State regulation of employment, of working conditions and wages, which, although they appeared alongside of a violent denunciation of socialism, George showed to be essentially socialistic.

But it is to the religious aspect of George's reply that we must turn again if his attitude in this controversy is to be completely understood; his belief that "the social question is at bottom a religious question" is the explanation of his attempt to join theology and political economy. That such a suggested relation is one that lays itself open to criticism is, of course, obvious.[49] Certainly theology is not political economy, and when the discipline of one is transposed to the other there is, if nothing else, a clash of techniques. But George's conception of the oneness of the social and the religious ideal was something more than merely a trespass upon the preserves of an alien field of thought. It was clearly a method of approach to those ethical considerations which were always his guide; it was an attitude of mind that lent religious fervency to social programs. This view of the coincidence of the social and religious questions is eloquently expressed by George in one of his *Standard* articles (July 28, 1888):

[49] Professor Young, in discussing the activity of the Anti-Poverty Society, holds that it brought about "that confusion of the realms of religion and political economy which is to the detriment of each." (*The Single Tax Movement in the United States*, p. 115.)

The men who have worked, the men who will work, the men who can be counted on everywhere and every time till death closes their eyes, are those to whom this reform appeals from the moral, the religious side; those who see in it not a mere improvement in taxation, but a conforming of our most important social advantage to the law of justice, to the will of God; a restoration to the disinherited of the bounteous provisions which the Intelligence that laid the foundations of the world and brought men upon it, has provided for men. And so, while we point out the fiscal advantages of the single tax, while we show how it will reduce their burdens and increase their incomes, let us never lay aside the appeal to higher principles—never seek to gain recruits by presenting to others in the light of a trading expedition that shall bring back much gain to those who participate in it, what to us is really a crusade. The unenlightened selfishness which brings want amid all the elements of plenty, which forces us to stint where we might enjoy, which converts into barren wastes what ought to be gardens, and makes life a drudgery where it might be a development, cannot be cast out by enlightened selfishness. . . . And it is to the quick and sure moral sense, rather than to the slower and duller intellectual perceptions that we can most successfully appeal.[50]

Yet the line of thought that thrusts itself forward most insistently, and undoubtedly to many most distastefully, in George's letter is not this type of approach to the questions

[50] This religious appeal of George's work is noted by C. B. Fillebrown, the economist: "Some chapters of *Progress and Poverty* were written in a spirit of almost apocalytic fervor, and it was this that gave it its wide currency. It was a beautiful vision to the outclassed and disinherited. . . . Here was a man who had seen a vision and pointed a way to deliverance. So the people read his works and joined in the new crusade against unjust power and privilege. And in their leader there was no pretense. He believed implicitly in himself and in his gospel. . . . All these facts must be understood in order to appreciate *Progress and Poverty*. It is, in a sense, a theological work as well as an economic textbook. It is, on the one hand, an attempt to reconcile the concept of a beneficent deity with the poverty and misery of mankind, and, on the other hand, to analyze the cause of this same poverty and misery by a coldly intellectual process and to find the remedy therefor. . . . His doctrine had come to him as a vision and he preached it with the absolute self-confidence of one of the Hebrew prophets foretelling the new Jerusalem. It was this that gave him his immense popularity with the masses. He held out to them the promise of deliverance from poverty." (*The Principles of Natural Taxation*, Chicago, McClurg, 1917, pp. 40–41).

of ethics and political economy and religion, but is rather the concern with a divine system of teleology in economics. It is a concern that must seem to economists as strange and singular, as a species of scholastic reasoning that has no place outside of a technical theological discussion. George's interest in the manifest purpose of God's will in economic affairs appears as perhaps the most insistent element in the letter, not because of any particularly lengthy treatment but because it is taken by him as almost a self-evident postulate. As an illustration of the point that is being suggested here is this passage from the work:

Nor do we hesitate to say that this way of securing the equal right to the bounty of the Creator and the exclusive right to the products of labor is the way intended by God for raising public revenues. For we are not atheists, who deny God; nor semi-atheists, who deny that he has any concern in politics and legislation. . . . Now, He that made the world and placed man in it, He that preordained civilization as the means whereby man might rise to the higher powers and become more and more conscious of the works of his Creator, must have foreseen this increasing need for State revenues and have made provision for it. That is to say: The increasing need for public revenues with social advance, being a natural, God-ordained need, there must be a right way of raising them—some way that we can truly say is the way intended by God.[51]

And again:

That God has intended the State to obtain the revenues it needs by the taxation of land values is shown by the same order and degree of evidence that shows that God has intended the milk of the mother for the nourishment of the babe.[52]

It is evident, then, that the coincidence between the social and religious ideals, which is probably the most suggestive implication in George's conception of Christianity, was regarded by him (at least in this answer to the Pope) as valid

[51] *The Condition of Labor*, pp. 9–10.   [52] *Ibid.*, p. 15.

only to the degree that it rested upon a supreme intelligence that had disclosed to man, through the operation of natural law, its purposeful consideration of social affairs. In fact, his own economic proposals seemed to George essentially removed from the realm of human control to that of divine prescience. "This we propose," he wrote concerning his fiscal suggestion, "not as a cunning device of human ingenuity, but as a conforming of human regulation to the will of God." [53]

The real strength of George's letter did not, of course, lie in any such presentation of divine purpose; nor did its persuasiveness attach itself to his economic arguments, for, although cogent and convincing, they were not peculiar to this particular work. Its appeal, rather, was in the direct challenge to the power of institutionalized religion, as exemplified in its most majestic figure, to put aside, not its neglect of social evils (for George realized that the encyclical was indeed a sincere effort to investigate the "condition of labor"), but its attempt to solve them by pious exhortations and tepid Christian socialism. It was an appeal that, coming as it did during the period of the McGlynn excommunication, could not have been easily disregarded; but it was more than a bit of opportunism. It was a gallant attempt, on the part of George, not only to turn the Pope's economic reasoning from palliatives to fundamentals, but also to enlist the active and whole-hearted support of religion, as expressed in the Catholic Church, in the cause of social reform. Such an overt interest, George held, was the manifest duty of religion. In fact, he endeavored to shift the attack which had been directed in the encyclical against his own proposals to the neglectful attitude of religion itself; he was not apologizing —he was accusing.

Herein is the reason why the working masses all over the world are turning away from organized religion. And why should they

[53] *The Condition of Labor*, p. 9.

not? What is the office of religion if not to point out the principles that ought to govern the conduct of men toward each other; to furnish a clear, decisive rule of right which shall guide men in all the relations of life? . . . What is the use of a religion that stands palsied and faltering in the face of the most momentous problems? What is the use of a religion that whatever it may promise for the next world can do nothing to prevent injustice in this? . . . Is it any wonder that the masses of men are losing faith? [54]

To ignore social injustice was to defend it, and "Shall we to whom this world is God's world—we who hold that man is called to this life only as a prelude to a higher life—shall we defend it?" [55]

This devoutness, this sincere insistence upon the responsibility that faced religion, and, above all, what may be termed the "God-justifying" tenor of the letter, could hardly have failed to impress the church authorities, sensitive as they must have been to the reactions that had been aroused by the McGlynn case. The conviction of George that his mission was indeed to justify the (economic) ways of God to man, and to demonstrate that social evil and injustice were the results of man's transgressions of God's natural laws, stamped his work with a fervent theistic character that, in the minds of the Holy See, must have distinguished his proposals from those of other social reformers. For example, toward the conclusion of his reply there was this passage concerning God, a passage that would have been almost inconceivable in the work of any other writer on the condition of labor:

What is the prayer of Christendom—the universal prayer? . . . It is, "Give us this day our daily bread."

Yet where this prayer goes up, daily and hourly, men lack bread. Is it not the business of religion to say why? If it cannot do so, shall not scoffers mock its ministers as Elias mocked the prophets of Baal, saying, "Cry with a louder voice, for he is a god; and perhaps he is talking, or is in an inn, or on a journey, or perhaps he

[54] *Ibid.*, pp. 98–100.   [55] *Ibid.*, p. 35.

is asleep, and must be awakened!" What answer can those ministers give? Either there is no God, or He is asleep, or else He does give men their daily bread, and it is in some way intercepted.

Here is the answer, the only true answer: If men lack bread it is not that God has not done His part in providing it. If men willing to labor are cursed with poverty, it is not that the storehouse that God owes men has failed; that the daily supply He has promised for the daily wants of His children is not here in abundance. It is, that impiously violating the benevolent intentions of their Creator, men have made land private property, and thus given into the exclusive ownership of the few the provisions that a bountiful Father has made for all.

Any other answer than that, no matter how it may be shrouded in the mere forms of religion, is practically an atheistical answer.[56]

And finally, at the very close of his answer to the Pope, George addressed this strikingly direct and impassioned appeal to the religious ruler of half the Christian world:

Servant of the Servants of God! I call you by the strongest and sweetest of your titles. In your hands more than in those of any living man lies the power to say the word and make the sign that shall end an unnatural divorce, and marry again to religion all that is pure and high in social aspiration.[57]

There is, of course, no evidence to show that George's letter had any bearing upon Father McGlynn's unsolicited reinstatement. It is probable that this unusual action on the part of the Holy See was instead determined largely on the grounds of general church policy, for Dr. McGlynn's punishment had created a decided schism in the ranks of New York and even of American Catholicism. The excommunicated priest had been supported not only by the great majority of his former parishioners at St. Stephen's, which was one of the most influential churches in the city, but also by a large body of Catholic working men and by those Catholics who, although not directly concerned with the labor movement,

[56] *The Condition of Labor,* pp. 100–101.   [57] *Ibid.,* p. 104.

had become indignant at any interference of the church in local political and economic matters. The fact that as early as 1889, two years before the encyclical was written, Archbishop Satolli had intimated that the Papacy was willing to reconsider the McGlynn case was proof that the direct results of the controversy had been sufficient to arouse some degree of apprehension among the church authorities. But that George's letter played a part in the final act of reinstatement in 1892 there can be little doubt.[58] And so, religion in this case, although it had not entered the ranks and battled for social reform, had nevertheless finally refrained from attacking such efforts at reform—and that was something.

One last point may be mentioned in connection with this discussion of the McGlynn case, and that is the ideational contrast between George's views on the fusion of economics and religion and those of Father McGlynn. It may be said, very roughly, that, while both approached the social question with the same religious zeal, George argued for a marriage of economics to institutionalized religion, and Dr. McGlynn hoped for their divorce. As has been noted, McGlynn constantly distinguished between the priest and the citizen, and

[58] George himself felt that his reply had had more than a little influence. This may be seen in an article of his in the New York *Sun,* during January of 1893, in which he said "that the encyclical on *The Condition of Labour* seemed to me to condemn the 'single tax' theory is true. But it made it clear that the Pope did not rightly understand that theory. It was for this reason that in the open letter to which your correspondent refers I asked permission to lay before the Pope the grounds for our belief and to show that 'our postulates are all stated or implied in your encyclical' and that 'they are the primary perceptions of human reason, the fundamental teachings of the Christian faith'; declaring that, so far from avoiding, 'we earnestly seek the judgment of religion, the tribunal of which your Holiness, as the head of the largest body of Christians, is the most august representative.' The answer has come. In the reinstatement of Dr. McGlynn on a correct presentation of 'single tax' doctrines, the highest authority of the Catholic Church has declared in the most emphatic manner that there is nothing in them inconsistent with the Catholic faith. From henceforth the encyclical on the *Condition of Labour* . . . is evidently to be understood not as disapproving the 'single tax,' but as disapproving the grotesque misrepresentations of it that were evidently at first presented to the Pope." (Quoted in the *Life,* pp. 565–566, n.)

between the church as the depository of religious truths and economic science as the hoped-for source of social justice. That quest for social justice, it is true, was a veritable crusade, and it was "necessarily a religious movement," but it was religious only so far as it proved to be the revealer of that inspiration and fervent sincerity which were demanded by such a quest. There was always the fear in his mind of the dominance of ecclesiasticism over civil affairs, of the Church over the State, and so, while the religious psychological experience must be directed toward a solution of social problems, the religious institution must concentrate upon religious and not economic truths. George, on the other hand, felt that the religious institution itself must turn from such perhaps musty work to the vital task of formulating social programs and directing social reform—the very essence, he believed, of primitive Christianity. Such a difference in emphasis between the two men was possibly an inevitable result of their completely different backgrounds, a contrast which sent George from the arena of social reform to religion, looking upon it always as an instrument of such reform, and which forced McGlynn to hold fast to a distinction between his priestly and his civil duties.

George's definite conviction that there was a divine purpose operating in economic as well as in other affairs may perhaps have been expressed a little baldly in his letter to the Pope. But it must be remembered that this attempted refutation of the Papal encyclical was necessarily a strange combination of moods and arguments, and the almost anthropomorphic suggestions indicated in the passages quoted a few pages back are by no means a fair illustration of George's more articulated theistic conceptions. George's argument for the existence of God was expressed by him most clearly in his last work, *The Science of Political Economy*, and particularly in the chapter on the laws of nature—laws which he identified with the will of God. The argument here is largely that of a primal will rather than the argument from design which he had previously made use of in opposing the hypotheses of Spencer. Reasoning from the two premises of a universal causal connection between phenomena, and of the particular causal power of a conscious will in human activity, George was led to infer that the cosmic processes were dependent upon a spiritual purpose that, at least in its method of operation, was similar to human will. The effect of his interest in Schopenhauer is quite evident here. In the following passage, for example, George's insistence upon the continuous functioning of a cosmic will parallels, except for a certain emphasis which becomes readily apparent, the contentions of Schopenhauer, even to the use of his phraseology and of his slightly exaggerated biological analogies:

> The bird flies because it wants to fly. In this will or spirit of the bird we find an ultimate cause or sufficient reason to satisfy us so far as such action is concerned. But probably no man ever lived, and certainly no child, who, seeing the easy sweep of birds through the open highways of air, has not felt the wish to do likewise. Why does not the man also fly when he wants to fly? We answer, that while the bird's bodily structure permits of the gratification of a will to fly, the man's bodily structure does not. But what is the reason of this difference? Here we come to a sphere where we can no longer find the cause or result in the individual will. Seeking still for will, as the only final explanation of cause, we are compelled to assume a higher and more comprehensive will or spirit, which has given to the bird one bodily structure, to the man another. . . . To find a sufficient cause . . . we are compelled to assume a higher will and more comprehensive purpose than that of man; a will conscious from the very first of what will yet be needed, as well as of what already is needed.[59]

And again:

> What we apprehend as the beginning cause in any series, whether we call it primary cause or final cause, is always to us

[59] *The Science of Political Economy,* pp. 52–53.

the cause or sufficient reason of the particular result. And this point in causation at which we rest satisfied is that which implies the element of spirit, the exertion of will. For it is of the nature of human reason never to rest content until it can come to something that may be conceived of as acting in itself, and not merely as a consequence of something else as antecedent, and thus be taken as the cause of the result or consequence from which the backward search began. . . . I know, by consciousness, that in me the exertion of will proceeds from some motive or desire. And reasoning from what I know to explain what I wish to discover, I explain similar acts in others by similar desires.[60]

A primal will, then, was the first or final link [61] in the chain of causation, and that will George postulated as God. "We are compelled when we seek for the beginning cause and still escape negation to posit a primary or all-causative idea or spirit, an all-producer or creator, for which our short word is God." [62] He recognized that such an argument was not fashionable,[63] but to him it was securely valid; it was, in fact, the inevitable product of "rationalism," that rationalism

[60] *The Science of Political Economy*, p. 49.

[61] George's discussion of "causes," showing the identity of the first and final causes, has somewhat of an Aristotelian flavor: "In a series of causes, what we apprehend as the beginning cause is sometimes called 'primary cause,' and sometimes 'ultimate cause'; while 'final cause,' which has the meaning of purpose or intent, lies deeper still. This use of seemingly opposite names for the same thing may at first puzzle others as at first it puzzled me. But it is explained when we remember that what is first and what last in a chain or series depends upon which end we start from. Thus, when we proceed from cause towards effect, the beginning cause comes first, and is styled the 'primary cause.' But when we start from effect to seek cause, as is usually the case, for we can know cause as cause only when it lies in our own consciousness, the cause nearest the result comes first, and we call it the 'proximate cause'; and what we apprehend as the beginning cause is found last, and we call it the 'ultimate' or 'efficient' cause, or, at least where an intelligent will is assumed, as the all-originator, the 'final cause'. . ." (*Ibid.*, pp. 46–47.)

[62] *Ibid.*, p. 79.

[63] "The 'doctrine of final causes,' now largely out of fashion, is understood to mean the doctrine which, as the last or final explanation of the existence and order of the world, seeks to discover the purpose or intent of the Creator. The argument from the assumption of what are now called final causes for the existence of an intelligent Creator is called the 'teleological argument,' and is by those who have the vogue in modern philosophy regarded with suspicion, if not with contempt." (*Ibid.*, p. 50.)

which had for its purpose the demonstration that "the only way in which we can hope to discover what to us is yet unknown is by reasoning to it from what to us is known." There was, for George, an intelligent order operating in the world, and man, being acquainted with certain finite manifestations of that order, could legitimately essay to discover the complete system. His conception of a primal purpose did not make it some blind, enslaving will to live which substituted, as was the case he felt with Schopenhauer, "for God an icy devil." For George it was not "will" so much as the "will of God." But this will of a Christian God was entirely divorced from Christian revelation and Scripture, and was disclosed to man only by the light of reason. So, to natural law and natural rights was added deism, and the eighteenth century synthesis in George was almost complete.

The evidence for the immortality of the soul, however, was not presented by George in quite the rational form in which he argued for the existence of God. And perhaps that very absence of cool reasonableness contributed to the strength of its almost mystic appeal. It is true, of course, that George's passionate conviction of human immortality was a vital part of his more general ethical conceptions, and therefore it was necessarily a rational conviction, but its exposition was poetic rather than logical. Certainly individual human immortality was required by his ethical system as a fulfillment and completion of earthly striving, but the expression of that desire for an essentially logical closed order took the form, as has so often been true in other discussions of immortality, of a lyrical intimation. The clearest example of this in George's work is at the very close of *Progress and Poverty*, the "problem of individual life." "My task is done," he wrote. "Yet the thought still mounts. The problems we have been considering lead into a problem higher and deeper still. Behind the problems of social life lies the problem of individual life."[64] The thought mounted to those heights where the niceties of discursive proof seem almost empty and trivial, where, from Plato down, the precise arguments for immortality become pale beside the vision of an inarticulate longing they endeavor to express. Those Platonic words of Plutarch with which George closed his book strike the dominant note of this last chapter on the problem of individual life, the problem of immortality:

"Men's souls, encompassed here with bodies and passions, have no communication with God, except what they can reach to in conception only, by means of philosophy, as by a kind of an obscure dream. But when they are loosed from the body, and removed into the unseen, invisible, impassable, and pure region, this God is then their leader and king; they there, as it were, hanging on him wholly, and beholding without weariness and passionately affecting that beauty which cannot be expressed or uttered by men."[65]

Life must continue, if life is to have any meaning; thus George postulated immortality.

. . . If human life does not continue beyond what we see of it here, then we are confronted, with regard to the race, with the same difficulty as with the individual! For it is as certain that the race must die as it is that the individual must die. We know that there have been geologic conditions under which human life was impossible on this earth. We know that they must return again. Even now, as the earth circles on her appointed orbit, the northern ice cap slowly thickens, and the time gradually approaches when its glaciers will flow again, and austral seas, sweeping northward, bury the seats of present civilization under oceans wastes, as it may be they now bury what was once as high a civilization as our own. And beyond these periods, science discerns a dead earth, an exhausted sun—a time when, clashing together, the solar system shall resolve itself into a gaseous form, again to begin immeasurable mutations.[66]

[64] *Progress and Poverty*, p. 553.   [65] *Ibid.*, pp. 562–563.
[66] Compare this with the striking picture Lord Balfour has painted in his *The Foundations of Belief* (New York, Longmans, Green, 1897), p. 31.

What then is the meaning of life—of life absolutely and inevitably bounded by death? To me it seems intelligible only as the avenue and vestibule to another life. And its facts seem explainable only upon a theory which cannot be expressed but in myth and symbol, and which, everywhere and at all times, the myths and symbols in which men have tried to portray their deepest perceptions do in some form express.

The scriptures of the men who have been and gone—the Bibles, the Zend Avestas, the Vedas, the Dhammapadas, and the Korans; the esoteric doctrines of old philosophies, the inner meaning of grotesque religions, the dogmatic constitutions of Ecumenical Councils, the preachings of Foxes, and Wesleys, and Savonarolas, the traditions of red Indians, and beliefs of black savages, have a heart and core in which they agree—a something which seems like the variously distorted apprehensions of a primary truth. And out of the chain of thought we have been following there seems vaguely to rise a glimpse of what they vaguely saw—a shadowy gleam of ultimate relations, the endeavor to express which inevitably falls into type and allegory. A garden in which are set the trees of good and evil. A vineyard in which there is the Master's work to do. A passage—from life behind to life beyond. A trial and a struggle, of which we cannot see the end.[67]

The yearning for a further life is natural and deep. It grows with intellectual growth, and perhaps none really feel it more than those who have begun to see how great is the universe and how infinite are the vistas which every advance in knowledge opens before us—vistas which would require nothing short of eternity to explore.[68]

Immortality, whether expressed as a vague, imaginative yearning, or as still another evidence of the rational order and design of God, was equally convincing to George.[69] While part

[67] *Progress and Poverty*, pp. 560–561.

[68] *Ibid.*, p. 555.

[69] In that more intimate and homely commerce with the problem of immortality which, through the presence of death, carries to every man vague glimpses of faith and philosophy, George, of course, was even more certain of the deathlessness of the human soul. Here, belief was vital and personal, something other than metaphorical and more than the peroration to a social philosophy. For some of his more direct and humble opinions on immortality, prompted by the deaths of those with whom he had been intimate, see the *Life*, pages 545–547.

In a letter from George to Charles Nordhoff, editorial writer on the

of his own personal belief, it was at the same time consolidated into his system of thought as an epilogue. Just as with his other earlier religious conceptions that had been renounced during his turbulent years as a youth, the assurance in immortality returned to strengthen him. "Out of this inquiry has come to me something I did not think to find, and a faith that was dead revives." [70] This restoration of religious faith was perhaps the most interesting personal product of his attempted fusion of political economy and religion; it gave George once more confidence in a spiritual order. His sense of religious reverence which had never wholly left him was now justified.[71]

In this general discussion of George and religion the really significant element, however, is not any such question of the

New York *Herald,* written at a time when some of his opinions were still in a process of formation (December 21, 1879), George expressed the importance he felt to lie in the question of immortality: "Do you know what impressed me so much with you and made me want to talk with you, was that you actually believed in the immortality of the soul. It made you to me almost a curiosity, and I thought of it over and over again. It was like meeting a man whose opinion was worth something who told you he saw something which you would very much like to see; but which you could not make out for yourself and which every one around you whose opinion was worth anything said did not exist at all."

[70] *Progress and Poverty,* p. 555.

[71] In one of George's note-books there is a clear expression of this fundamentally reverent attitude. He wrote that "there are those who think and have the idea that they should war against religion because it has been used for the enslavement of men. I do not think so. The true spirit is that rudely expressed in the ringing song"—and then he quotes the stanza from the "Battle-Hymn of the Republic" which opens: "In the beauty of the lilies, Christ was born across the sea." (In Notes on Conditions in Ireland and England, dated January 9, 1883, to May 9, 1884.)

In the biography there is a specific account of how his economic views were linked to George's revival of religious experience: "He attached himself to no sect, yet his nature was strongly reverent. He wished to have his children say night and morning prayers, and often at twilight or before they went to bed he would lie on his lounge in the library and have them and their mother mingle their voices in the old hymns that he had heard as a child in Philadelphia, and again 'Praise God from whom all blessings flow' seemed to swell and echo through old St. Paul's. Out of the inquiry, why want goes with plenty, religion had come to have a new meaning. In the conviction that he had discovered that it was not by God's will, but because of violation of God's ordinance that men suffered involuntary poverty in the heart of civilization, 'a faith that was dead revived' . . ." (*Life,* p. 252.)

revival of personal faith. It is rather a concern with the challenge that he made to the religious institution. It was a concern that sought to justify a divine plan by demonstrating that natural law—or the will of God—if correctly understood and obeyed, would result in a society nearer the ideal of a city of God. George attempted to shift the cause of social misery from the blunderings of a Creator to those institutions of man which, founded upon a heritage of might and ignorance, had tortured and depraved the race—and such a shift from sacred to remediable sources of social ills he felt would be of value, even to religion itself.

George did not, as is so often the fashion with social reformers, launch into a sweeping denunciation of religion; nor did he demand that religion and economics be kept in carefully insulated compartments. Instead, his demand was that religion, being the alleged interpreter of the divine plan and the defender of its wisdom, be called upon to explain the persistence of the misery and suffering born of poverty. Religion, he felt, must address itself to that problem, not because it was at all expert in economic matters, but because the sin and evil that did constitute its particular province could not be dissociated from that economic paradox of poverty and wealth. This was a diseased and malformed social order, and if religion, ignoring any fundamental consideration of its structure, treated pathological symptoms as the normal attributes of a sane and healthy God-directed society, then perhaps herein was "the reason why the working masses all over the world are turning away from organized religion." His own system of thought, George believed, did direct its attention to this enigma. It did attempt to locate the source of social misery in a humanistic and not in a transcendental realm.

The following passages may fittingly close this chapter, for they exhibit vividly George's conviction—his most fervent religious conviction—that it was man and not God who was responsible for the world's wretchedness. And that conviction, stripped of its religious trappings and translated from theology to the social sciences, remains a direct challenge to all forms of intellectual smugness.

Though it may take the language of prayer, it is blasphemy that attributes to the inscrutable decrees of Providence the suffering and brutishness that come of poverty; that turns with folded hands to the All-Father and lays on Him the responsibility for the want and crime of our great cities. We degrade the Everlasting. We slander the Just One. A merciful man would have better ordered the world; a just man would crush with his foot such an ulcerous anthill! It is not the Almighty but we who are responsible for the vice and misery that fester amid our civilization. The Creator showers upon us His gifts—more than enough for all. But like swine scrambling for food, we tread them in the mire—tread them in the mire while we tear and rend each other! [72]

It is the fool that saith in his heart there is no God. But what shall we call the man who tells us that with this sort of a world God bids us be content? [73]

[72] *Progress and Poverty*, pp. 546–547.
[73] *Social Problems, Works*, Vol. II, p. 69.

CHAPTER VIII

GEORGE'S INFLUENCE

THERE may be some value in concluding this whole discussion of the varying contacts that Henry George and his work have had with other movements and other thinkers by pointing out very briefly the influence of his doctrines. That influence will be found not merely in the specific legislative acts of various countries that have sought for tax reform in the direction suggested by George, but also, and perhaps of more importance, the effects of his work may be seen in that more intangible realm of opinion as it is expressed in the writings and words of the exponents of ideas. This tracing of George's influence will be confined within very narrow limits, chiefly because of the difficulties of determining accurately just how significant has been the part that his work has played and of disentangling his proposals from parallel and independent movements of land value taxation. In addition, there is clearly recognized the danger of overestimating (perhaps, too, of underestimating) the imponderable effect of George upon later thinkers. For example, it is quite true, as single taxers will point out, that his work has been recommended, at least in part, by almost every important figure in subsequent liberal social thought, but to what degree that appreciation has been casual, or how much it has been sincere and significant, is not an easy question to answer. And the question is made more difficult because of the fact that many former professed followers of George in political and economic circles have since wandered very far from his concepts.

381

It may be best to discuss first George's influence upon the definite land value taxation proposals that have been introduced throughout the world. This point will, at the same time, bring forward perhaps the most serious difficulty in estimating the effects of George's work, i. e., the difficulty of dissociating his "single tax" doctrines from similar but independent schemes of land value taxation. That problem is stated most forcibly in the comprehensive volume of Miss Yetta Scheftel.[1] Her consistent attempt to handle land value taxation as merely a fiscal scheme and not as a social reform program,[2] and therefore her intense efforts, especially in the opening chapter of the book, to effect a complete divorce between a "single tax" and a simple tax on land values, necessarily make George's work of negligible significance in her history of land value taxation. In fact, there is no indication at all throughout the treatise that there has been any real influence of *Progress and Poverty* upon the more than fifty years of land value taxation experiments that have followed its appearance.

Now, it will be admitted at the very outset of this discussion that the systems of land value taxation of various countries seem to have arisen spontaneously rather than as a result of doctrine or theory, that they have appeared to be adaptations which have followed local conditions instead of examples of a deliberate social program. And it is recognized also that, in at least two instances, land value taxes were discussed and introduced some years before George's work appeared. Furthermore, there will be no attempt to suggest here that there has been disclosed any new data that would indicate a direct influence of George's teachings upon the proposals

---

[1] *The Taxation of Land Value* (Boston, Houghton Mifflin, 1916).
[2] The conclusion of her most negative chapter on "The Tax as a Social Reform" states that "not as a panacea, then, for all social evils and economic maladjustment, although its influence may be beneficial with regard to these, but as a tax must the expediency of the tax on land value be determined." (P. 421.)

which are to be presented. Despite rather careful investigation, it must be admitted that, with a few exceptions, one cannot find definite, "scientific" evidence connecting George in any overt way with much of the land value tax legislation.

To argue, however, that these admissions justify a neglect of George's influence upon such legislation seems to suggest a serious lack of a sense of proportion. The absence of tangible proof of the inspiration of *Progress and Poverty* may be unfortunate from the scholar's point of view (although it may be pointed out that the very nature and drafting of fiscal acts would permit little inclusion of doctrinal origins, and also that the pioneers who were responsible for much of the work were not always articulate or concerned with indicating sources), but, as with most negations, it must not be taken too seriously or the investigator may fall into a variation of the "scholar's error." More specifically, the nonexistence—at least, the nondiscovery—of testimonials to George's influence by early legislators can in no way preclude consideration of the imponderable force of his work, especially since the few notices that we do have of acquaintance with *Progress and Poverty* on the part of the land value taxationists show that the book was a living inspiration. For example, to believe seriously that, in the English-speaking colonies, where in the decade following the publication of George's book there was a remarkable interest in land value taxation, no effect was registered of the tremendous circulation of *Progress and Poverty* or of George's own widely attended lectures in the British Isles and the British dominions, would indicate a serious prejudice against Henry George or else a curious interpretation of what is meant by the word influence.

But should the researcher be unduly insistent, or should he become quite scornful of any suggestion that George played a rôle in the development of land value taxation,[3] then this point might well be made: Henry George must be considered as part of a great liberal tradition, a tradition that extends far in the past and includes in its ranks many great names. That tradition is more important than the work of any one man. Whether consciously or not, George borrowed from and contributed to that stream of thought; he has become an integral part of it.[4] Therefore, unless one is overconcerned with the difficult questions of originality and influence, it perhaps does not matter too much just what place the individual, Henry George, did occupy in that history of land value taxation. That is to say, the collection of land values for social purposes, no matter how opportunistic or locally conditioned it appears, cannot be divorced from social and economic theory, cannot be entirely cut off from the whole great concept of "unearned increment." The researcher may be quite justified in considering the fiscal measures he is handling *as if* they were autonomous and self-generating; he is indeed correct also in stating that he is unable very often to locate the doctrinal background of such legislative acts. Yet a conclusion to the effect that theory plays no part in the formulation of a land value tax would seem to disclose much too narrow an "opportunistic" approach. The belief, e. g., that land value taxes in Canada and Australasia were in no essential way connected with the whole English economic tradition of the "unearned increment" seems a little farfetched. Granted that the investigator may find no tangible manifestation of such a tradition in the early legislatures of New South Wales or of Alberta, and granted even that most of the settlers had never read a line of Locke or Smith or Mill, still it would be indeed a rash scholar who could

---

[3] Miss Scheftel exhibits such scorn in several places; see especially *op. cit.*, pp. 266–267.
[4] For this whole point consult *supra,* Chap. IV.

glibly set aside the formative influence of a large section of English social philosophy.

This is not to develop into a labored account of function-of-theory truisms. The only point that is being suggested is that George must be considered as one of the determining forces in that tradition which has centered its attention upon land values, and that as part of such a movement he can be slighted only with great danger in a discussion dealing with any phase of that topic. The progress of land value taxation, whether or not it can always be directly connected with his inspiration, must nevertheless be included within an exposition of Henry George's work; any other procedure would amount to both a betrayal of his tremendous efforts and also to a handling of land value taxation that was without vision or horizons. Such, at least, would be an answer to the land value tax researcher who should prove a vigorous skeptic in this matter of the significance of George's influence.

Of course that answer would hardly satisfy any one vitally interested in the work of George. It would seem far too apologetic; it would lean over backward in its deference to "scholarship." But this danger of being accused of either minimizing or of exaggerating historical influence is one that cannot very well be dissociated from the discussion of any controversial theme. It attaches itself inevitably to attempts that seek to trace developments, and therefore perhaps the best policy is to proceed with an historical exposition, trusting that its course will avoid the snares both of belittling and of overstatement.

AUSTRALASIA

This brief account of the progress of land value taxation [5] may more or less arbitrarily open with a consideration of the

[5] A word may be mentioned here as to the procedure of this chapter. Since it is to be a brief exposition of material that is readily available, and

development of such revenues in the English-speaking nations, more specifically, for the present purpose, in Australasia, Canada, Great Britain and the United States itself. The land value tax in Australasia [6] will be handled first, not only because some of the very earliest of the taxes originated in that great laboratory of social experiments, but also because its development there has been perhaps more consistent and of greater extent than in any other country.

The first significant attempt to levy a tax upon the economic value of land in Australasia was in 1878,[7] a year before the appearance of *Progress and Poverty*. In 1877 the Liberal government of Sir George Grey had come into power in New Zealand and it had pledged itself to attack the large landed estates that were becoming so conspicuous and menacing a

since it presents no new data, extensive documentation is not believed necessary. The information has been taken largely from the works mentioned throughout, so it will be only for rather significant or possibly controversial material that specific notes will be used. It is felt that a short, running account will meet the present purpose better than an ambitious attempt to repeat work that has been already very satisfactorily done.

[6] Perhaps the best bibliography on the history of land value taxation will be found in Scheftel (*op. cit.*), pp. 461–483. For bibliography on Australasian taxes see *ibid.*, pp. 478–480.

For material on Australasian taxes consult: *Ibid.*, Chaps. II and III; Miller, *Single Tax Year Book* (New York, 1917), pp. 122–141; E. J. Craigie, "The Taxation of Land Values in South Australia," a series of articles beginning in *The Single Tax Review* of January-February, 1915; W. P. Reeves, *Land Taxes and Rates and the Valuation of Land in New Zealand* (London, Allen and Unwin, 1923; 2 vols.); pamphlets printed by the Fourth International Conference to Promote Land Value Taxation and Free Trade, Edinburgh, 1929: by A. G. Huie, "Progress of the Henry George Movement in New South Wales"; by P. J. O'Regan, "The Progress of the Henry George Movement in New Zealand," and by E. J. Craigie, "Land Value Taxation in Australia for Federal, State and Local Purposes." See also articles by W. P. Reeves on "Land Taxes in Australasia," in *The Economic Journal*, December, 1911, Vol. XXI, pp. 513–526, and by Professor Seligman on the new tax movements in Australasia in *The Political Science Quarterly*, March, 1913, Vol. XXVIII, pp. 71–94. The files of the various single tax periodicals, e. g., *Land and Freedom*—formerly *The Single Tax Review*—(New York); *Land and Liberty* (London); *The Public* (Chicago—no longer in existence), will give historical accounts from the single tax interpretation. For more specific works see especially the lists of Australasian government publications mentioned in Scheftel.

[7] In 1875 a progressive land tax was proposed in Victoria but was withdrawn. Two years later in the same province there was passed a land tax, but it was not levied on the unimproved value. (Cf. Scheftel, p. 24.)

factor in the development of the province. Grey's interest in the land problem may be traced both to a theoretical background and, perhaps of more importance, to the peculiar agrarian situation in New Zealand and in the rest of Australasia. He had behind him the great British Liberal political tradition and he himself was a devoted student of John Stuart Mill, but it was the fact of the serious alienation of the land and its concentration in the hands of a few owners,[8] and also of the spectacular and directly perceptible increase in land values, that provided the immediate demand for a land value tax. The colonists, moreover, were spared the hoary tradition of vested landed property that had sent its roots so deeply into British politics, and so the rapid appreciation of economic rent disclosed to them more readily its social origin and implications.[9]

This earliest levy upon land value, the Land Tax Act of 1878, was a very modest start. It provided for a tax of a half-penny in the pound on the unimproved value of land, i. e., the land minus the value of the improvements.[10] Moreover, it allowed an exemption of £500. Yet the opposition that it aroused among the landowning class was so strong that the Grey government fell immediately and the act was revoked by the following ministry. In fact, the tax was removed before it was even collected, and it was nearly twelve

[8] For figures relating to this concentration of land in Australasia, see Scheftel, pp. 20 ff.

[9] *Ibid.*, 19–20.

[10] "Capital value," or selling value, implies the value of land plus the improvements. For purposes of land value taxation, the taxable value of land is this "capital value" minus the value of the improvements, thus giving the "unimproved capital value." (For the difficulties involved in this point, see Scheftel, pp. 70 ff.) In England the phrase "capital value" is sometimes loosely used, even when denoting unimproved value, in order to distinguish such value from the traditional English use of the annual "rental" value (i. e., land value being determined by the annual rent of land—the ordinary, not economic, rent). Capital value in this connection, as it is defined, e. g., in the English Finance Act of 1931, is held to be determined largely by selling price (but, of course, for the purpose of the Snowden land value tax it is a selling value which assumes the absence of all improvements).

years before a Liberal Cabinet introduced the tax again. Henry George knew of this early work of Grey and when *Progress and Poverty* appeared he sent Grey a copy which drew from the Liberal leader a most flattering response.[11] There is no evidence to show that the New Zealander knew anything of George's earlier work, *Our Land and Land Policy,* which was published in 1871.[12]

In 1890, under the leadership of John Ballance, who had been treasurer in the Grey government, and who was responsible for much of the land value tax agitation in 1877 and 1878, the Liberal party again came into power and forced through another land tax measure, the Land and Income Assessment Act of 1891. This act raised the tax to 1d. in the pound but retained the £500 exemption, and also limited the exemption of improvements to £3,000. On the other hand, the principle of land value taxation was strengthened by an additional graduated tax on land valued at £5,000 or more. This graduated scale, which has since been revised many times, was aimed directly at the large estates, an attack upon landed property that is not found throughout the rest of Australasia with the possible exception of Tasmania.[13] In 1893 the £3,000 limit of improvement-exemption was removed, and the act was further amended in 1900, 1903, 1907 and 1912, but with no significant changes.

[11] See *supra,* p. 53.

[12] However, there is this to be said concerning George's possible influence upon the Australasian measures: Not only *Our Land and Land Policy,* but also the vigorous editorial and political campaigns that George carried on throughout the early '70s, were directed to attacking large land holdings, an attack that was the subject of much popular discussion in California. It was this particular phase of land monopoly that was the object of the early legislation in New Zealand (and also in British Columbia). Now, it must be remembered that communication between California and Australia was by no means difficult; the two were much closer, of course, than Australia and England. In fact, San Francisco was really more accessible to Australia than it was to many American cities at this time. George knew something of the work in Australia (see *infra,* p. 406, n. 60), and it is by no means outside the realm of possibility that the dominion knew of his California agitation and was influenced by it.

[13] Scheftel, p. 41. For details of this graduated scale see *ibid.,* p. 38.

Two important additions to New Zealand's policy were made in 1896. In that year a Government Valuation of Land Act was passed which provided for the separate valuation of land and improvements and which also established a series of periodic revaluations.[14] It is obvious that when the principle of land value taxation is accepted the necessity for approximately accurate land valuation presents itself, and one of the great difficulties that the proponents of such taxation must meet is the ludicrously incorrect report of land values that is so often found where there has been no attempt to separate improvements from land for purposes of valuation. The other significant addition to New Zealand's efforts was the Rating on Unimproved Values Act.[15]

The rating on land values in Australasia does not start with this New Zealand act of 1896. In fact, with the exception of the short-lived Grey budget, local taxation of land values preceded provincial ones; they may be traced back to 1878 in Queensland. Rating is different from State and Federal revenue not merely because of its local nature; its very purpose is distinct. It is clear that the national and provincial land value taxes are almost insignificant as far as revenue is concerned. Their purpose is largely social and is directed toward reducing if not disintegrating the large landed estates. On the other hand, the local rates are levied to gain revenue,[16] and consequently are of a much higher percentage, rising, e. g., in the city of Wellington, New Zealand, to 7¼d. in the pound, and to as much as a shilling in the pound—at least as a possible maximum—in Queensland.[17]

[14] For the technique and difficulties of land valuation consult Scheftel, pp. 61–78. See also "Government Valuation of Land in New Zealand," by C. H. Nightingale; pamphlet printed for the Fourth International Conference to Promote Land Value Taxation and Free Trade, Edinburgh, 1929.

[15] In Australasia, as in Great Britain, the term "rating" is applied to local taxation, "tax" being usually reserved to describe Parliamentary imposts.

[16] Scheftel, pp. 78–79.

[17] See pamphlets by O'Regan and Craigie mentioned before.

For the same reason, i. e., to gain revenue, exemptions and graduations are ordinarily absent in rating as contrasted with the government tax. Finally, rating on land values is the nearest approach to a "single tax," since in the various Australasian districts and municipalities that have adopted it there are practically no other sources of revenue.[18]

A number of amendments were added to the original act of 1896 and the whole was incorporated as part of the general Rating Act of 1925. The rating on land values depends upon rating polls, and thus far in New Zealand about 40 per cent of local governing bodies[19] (132 out of 290 taxing districts, which include 77 out of 119 boroughs, and 55 out of 124 counties; town boards and road districts also make up taxing districts) have adopted land value rating, the large cities of Wellington and Christchurch being included.

Turning to Australia itself we find that there is a three-fold tax on land values, the Federal, the State, and local rating. The Federal Land Tax was passed in November, 1910, and all six provinces (Queensland, New South Wales, South Australia, Western Australia, Victoria, and Tasmania) have State land taxes, the earliest being that in South Australia in 1884. With the exception of Tasmania all of the provinces have local rating on unimproved land values. As was mentioned before, the Federal tax is a low one and has been aimed directly, as it was phrased, at "bursting up big estates." It contains also specific penalties for absentee owners. The State taxes generally incorporate the graduated feature, which also strikes at large land holdings, laying a high tax upon the greater concentrations of land and imposing only a minimal rate upon small holdings.

Queensland was the first province to rate locally upon land values but the last to have a provincial tax. As early

[18] Scheftel, pp. 48–55. See also *infra,* following pages.
[19] O'Regan, *op. cit.*

as 1878 rating was in vogue and in 1879 the Division Boards Act definitely legalized the exemption of certain improvements from rating. More improvements were exempted in 1887, and the Valuation and Rating Act of 1890 excluded all improvements and personal property from local taxation. In 1902 there was passed a general consolidation act, that of the Local Authorities of Queensland, which, while imposing certain limits on the local authorities, made it obligatory for all rating to be based on the unimproved value of the land [20] This 1902 act set the maximum rate at 3d. in the pound, and also provided for revaluation every three years. However, 1921 and 1924 saw important additions, the Amending Act of the former year raising the maximum rate to 1s. in the pound, and the Greater Brisbane Act of the latter year increasing rating power in that municipality.

It was not until 1915 that Queensland inaugurated a State land tax.[21] Like other provincial imposts it was graduated, a tax of 1d. in the pound if the land were valued at less than £500 and rising gradually to a rate of 6d. on £75,000 or more of land values. In addition, the following year found another specific tax placed on undeveloped land, 1d. in the pound in 1916, an additional half-penny the next year, and 2d. from 1918 on.[22]

South Australia began the taxation of land values with the State Taxation Act of 1884, which went into effect the following year. As in the rest of Australasia the early colonial reports were struck by the phenomenal increase in land values, and Treasurer Rounsevell of the Colton Ministry in-

[20] Scheftel, p. 49.

[21] Miss Scheftel's book appeared in 1916 and therefore was still able to point out that this State had not yet adopted the principle of provincial land value taxation. (See p. 34.)

[22] "It is interesting to note that since 1st January, 1917, freehold title to land in Queensland is unobtainable, excepting for land acquired before that date. Under the Crown Lands Act, 1910–1918, land can only be obtained from the Crown on lease. A pastoral lease may not exceed thirty years, the term for agricultural farms is twenty years, other leases are in perpetuity." E. J. Craigie, in "Land Value Taxation in Australia" (*op. cit.*, p. 4).

troduced in 1884 his bill, aimed against the appropriation of such values by the owners of large estates. A tax of a half-penny in the pound upon the unimproved value of land was first levied; certain exemptions were made of park, church, university lands and the like. There was also a provision for periodic assessments. In 1895 an additional half-penny was placed upon values above £5,000, and absentee owners were penalized another 20 per cent. Several changes were made in 1903, increasing the general rate to ¾d. in the pound and amending also the absentee rates, but since 1906 the rates reverted to the ones operating prior to 1903.

Rating in South Australia began in 1893, although the act of that year was generally unsatisfactory.[23] The act was amended in 1900, 1910, and 1914, and in December, 1926, rating on land values was introduced for district councils; the former rating had been for municipalities. While rating is optional in South Australia, sixteen municipalities, including the city of Adelaide, and six district councils rate entirely on unimproved land values.

Following the election of 1894 in New South Wales the Reid government came into power pledged to an attack upon the protective tariff and to the support of land value taxation. The ministry, however, met with stubborn opposition from the upper house—the Legislative Council—in its efforts to tax land values, and it was only after another general election that the Land and Income Tax Assessment Act of 1895 became law. It has been maintained that Henry George's important lecture trip of 1890 in Australasia [24] was of particular influence in this legislation of New South Wales.[25] The act provided for the usual levy of 1d. in the pound, after a deduction of £240 of land values had been made. In 1902 the act was amended so as to clarify the relation between the

[23] *Single Tax Year Book, op. cit.,* p. 130.
[24] See *Supra,* p. 71.
[25] *Single Tax Year Book,* p. 136.

owner and the lessee of land. The revenue derived from the act amounted to as high as £345,497 [26] for the financial year of 1906–1907, but in that year the Local Government Act was passed, introducing local rating, and the State revenues began falling steadily, reaching £2800 in 1926–1927.[27]

Rating in New South Wales [28] contains both the obligatory feature of Queensland's rating and also the optional privilege of the New Zealand act; general shire and municipal rates must be only on the unimproved value of land, whereas special shire or municipal rates, or additional municipal rates, may be either on unimproved or improved value. In 1916 a very significant step in local rating was taken when the city of Sydney voted to exempt all personal property and improvements and to place all rating upon unimproved land value. Sydney, which has a population of more than 900,-000, is thus the largest city in the world to derive all its revenue from a "single tax" on land values. In addition, the new bridge across Sydney harbor, the North Shore Bridge, has been paid for to the extent of one-third out of a rate on the increased land values which have accompanied its building.

It will not be necessary to present in detail the history of land value taxation throughout the rest of Australia. Western Australia began State land taxation in 1907 and local rating in 1902. There was also passed a special City of Perth Endowment Lands Act in 1920. Tasmania, which has no local rating, inaugurated its graduated provincial tax in 1905. Victoria had State levies in 1910 but did not have optional local rating until 1914.

A word, however, must be mentioned concerning the land

[26] *Ibid.*, p. 137.
[27] Craigie pamphlet, p. 1. In fact, for all intents and purposes the State land tax in New South Wales stands suspended. (Scheftel, p. 55.)
[28] The introduction of rating under the Carruthers government is also held to be the direct result of the agitation of George's followers in the province. (See the Huie pamphlet, *op. cit.*, p. 2.)

policy in the new Federal capital district of Yass-Canberra, which, while it does not involve the taxation of land values, certainly is evidence of a most advanced handling of land ownership. In 1911 New South Wales donated some 900 square miles of territory for a Federal district, and two years later work was begun on the new Australian capital. The war interrupted the building and it was not until 1920 that construction of a provisional capital really began. The provisional Parliament House was begun in 1924 and opened three years later. Canberra is governed by three commissioners,[29] the commission form of government having been established by the Seat of Government Administration Act of July 23, 1924.

The land policy of the capital territory is completely in terms of leases; there is no outright private ownership of land, all land being rented from the Government. Lots are leased at public sale, the terms being twenty-five years for agricultural land and ninety-nine years for urban land. The rent is set at five per cent of the capital unimproved value (i. e., the approximate economic rent of land), and after a term of twenty years, thereafter every ten years, the rentals are revalued. Moreover, the lessee must begin to build within two years after receiving the lease, and must complete his improvement within three years. Here, then, seems to be an approach to what Henry George had in mind: land being "owned" by the State but used and improved by private individuals, with the economic rent going into the public treasury to supply public needs.[30]

[29] Material on Yass-Canberra may be found in any of the official Australian government publications. See also the Craigie pamphlet, and articles by Percy R. Meggy in Land and Freedom, especially in the issue of May-June, 1931, and Enclaves of Economic Rent for 1930 (Fiske Warren, Harvard, Mass., 1931), pp. 258–263.

[30] In connection with land value taxation in Australasia it may be in place to point out that in South Africa since 1916 there has likewise been a similar policy. Assessments there all distinguish, for one thing, between land and improvement value, and in the province of the Transvaal all municipalities and

What have been the results of land value taxation in Australasia, and to what degree may the policy be attributed to the influence of Henry George? Miss Scheftel, whose book, as has been pointed out, is generally most negative in its appraisal of George's work and most tepid and detached in its appreciation of the principle (rather concept) of land value taxation, is yet quite gracious in recognizing George's influence in Australasia, and quite confident that such taxation, at least fiscally, has proven successful. There can be no attempt made here to present in a detailed fashion any of the fiscal results of the tax. That may be very readily found in Miss Scheftel's work. All that will be mentioned by way of conclusion are some of the results which she permits to be drawn from her scientific analysis.

It may be well to quote the concluding paragraphs of the chapters on land value taxation in Australasia:

Summary: In so far as the efficacy of the land tax can be gauged at all, the results of the levy have been more or less beneficial economically and socially. Housing conditions continue to improve in the colonies in spite of the increase in population. Had the rates of taxes been considerably higher the effects on land speculation, perhaps too on rents, would have been more notable. To what extent the exemption of business premises from heavy taxes has in turn stimulated business can only be inferred.

In conclusion, two significant facts are to be noted. First, in no case has there been a repeal of the tax except to extend its operation; in other words, after its adoption, however great the opposition may previously have been, the levy of the tax ceased to be a party measure. Indeed, the opponents of the tax seem to have become reconciled to its existence; at best they have attempted merely to disprove the beneficent results predicted by

district councils are required to levy a rate on land values of at least 1d. in the pound, although improvements are also taxed. Pretoria and Johannesburg rate only on land values. Kroonstad in the Orange Free State, where land value rating is optional, taxes land values, and Durban in Natal, and East London in the Cape province both rate much higher on land values than upon improvements.

the sanguine supporters of the land tax. Secondly, the adoption of the tax by one State after another, by the local bodies, and recently by the Federal Government of Australia, argues in its favor and for its expediency in that country.[31]

Miss Scheftel is more sure of the "fiscal" benefits [32] of the tax than of the "social" ones. The disintegration of large estates, the lowering of rent, the shifting of the burden of taxation upon the recipients of the "unearned increment," in general, the predictions of the more radical land value taxationists as to a redirection of the social order itself, are not found by her to be corollaries of the tax, and so "the experience with the tax for over two decades (1916) has both allayed the anxiety of its adversaries and dissipated the extravagant hopes of its most ardent adherents." [33] Of course Miss Scheftel does not, and cannot, take such conclusions very seriously. With the exception of a few municipalities there has been but a pointing in the direction of a "single tax"; consequently the hopes of a Henry George cannot yet be tested in Australasia. For example, in connection with the disintegration of large estates, it is pointed out that, except in New Zealand, the low rates, evasions, and inaccurate valuation systems have nullified any significant effect that the land tax may have had upon the large landed holdings.[34] And in the paragraphs quoted above it is suggested quite clearly why there have been only negligible effects upon rent or land speculation. Yet the fact that there have been any social advantages at all would seem to indicate that instead of Miss Scheftel's rather negative conclusion, there might be an interpretation which would see in the admitted partial benefits of a small tax upon land values a forecasting of greater changes when the "social" in addition to the "fiscal" purposes of such a measure were brought into prominence.

As a background of the land value taxation movement in

[31] Scheftel, pp. 119–120.   [32] Pp. 95–96.   [33] P. 106.   [34] Pp. 96 ff.

Australasia, Miss Scheftel admits the significance of George's writings, of his trip to the islands in 1890, and of the unremittent activity of his followers, especially immediately after his visit.[35] On the other hand, she is also certain that such taxation has had a spontaneous growth in Australasia, being in operation, for example, even before the appearance of *Progress and Poverty*, and she argues, in addition, that there is almost no analogy between George's "single tax" and Australasia's land value taxation.[36] The first point is unquestionably correct and all that the follower of George can do is to suggest, as was mentioned a few pages back, that George must be considered as part of a great theoretic tradition, a tradition that lies at the root of all movements to capture for society any part of the unearned increment of land values. Her second argument does not seem as plausible. For instance, she writes: "The numerous exemptions, low rates, progressive scales, surely do not reflect the striving of the single taxers to make the land tax the sole tax. In fact, since the enactment of the taxes, no attempts have been made, as was predicted, to tighten the screw or to approach anything like the confiscation or the nationalization of the land."[37] Ignoring for the moment the perhaps unwise use of the term "confiscation" or even "nationalization" as applied to the proposals of George, it cannot be legitimately argued that because land value taxation is not the single tax that therefore the two have almost nothing in common. Single taxers were unable to remove exemptions or to raise rates, but that surely is not evidence that no close analogy exists between a low, qualified tax on land value and a high, unqualified one. There are very few followers of George who would not agree that any attempt to introduce his suggestions must originate in some such gradual manner. This is not to say, of course, that Australasia has taken but the first step toward the ulti-

[35] Pp. 31–32.   [36] Pp. 33–34.   [37] P. 33.

mate realization of the single tax. Such a statement would be rash indeed. But it would perhaps be no more unjustified than the contention that land value taxation is completely parochial, that, in other words, it is a step in no direction.

CANADA

There is a very close analogy between land value taxation in Australasia and in the western provinces of Canada.[38] Both regions, at the time of the inauguration of the tax, were in an undeveloped pioneer condition, sparsely populated and with great tracts of undeveloped land. 'In both there was the same striking phenomenon of rapidly increasing land values as population grew, of feverish land speculation, of unimproved land held out of use for further appreciation of value, of absentee landowners. Moreover, there was the same pioneer psychology, the same disregard for the property traditions of the older country and the same determination to settle local problems without too much reliance upon the

[38] For material on Canadian land value taxation see: Scheftel, Chap. VI (bibliography, pp. 481–483); Professor R. M. Haig's report on "The Exemption of Improvements from Taxation in Canada and the United States," prepared in 1915 for the Committee on Taxation of the City of New York; (see also the same author's article on "The New Unearned Increment Tax in Alberta," *The American Economic Review*, September, 1914, Vol. IV, No. 3, pp. 716–718); *Single Tax Year Book*, pp. 81–95; *The Taxation of Land Values in Western Canada*, Archibald Stalker, McGill University (master's thesis), Montreal, 1914; Professor S. Vineberg's *Provincial and Local Taxation in Canada*, Columbia Studies in History, Economics, and Public Law, Vol. LII, No. 1, 1912; "Home Rule in Taxation in Western Canada," California League for Home Rule in Taxation, San Francisco, 1915 (pamphlet); report on "The Financial Condition of Victoria" by Dr. Adam Shortt, Victoria, 1922 (pamphlet, attacks land value taxation); "The Progress of Henry George Thought in Canada," by A. C. Thompson and A. W. Roebuck, paper prepared for the Fourth International Conference to Promote Land Value Taxation and Free Trade, Edinburgh, 1929; F. J. Dixon, "The Progress of Land Value Taxation in Canada," Winnipeg (pamphlet); see also special articles in *The Single Tax Review*, Vancouver special number, May–June, 1911; Edmonton and Grain Growers special number, September–October, 1911; also articles by Schuyler Arnold starting in January–February, 1915, number. Government reports will be found mentioned in Sheftel.

English heritage.[39] As early as 1873 in British Columbia and Manitoba, six years before *Progress and Poverty* was published, there was imposed a "wild land" tax which sought to discourage holding land out of use on the part of absentee owners, at least outside of the limits of incorporated cities, towns and villages. Manitoba also put a special tax on land speculators. A year later British Columbia took another important step when the city of Nanaimo, the coaling station on Vancouver Island, exempted improvements from taxation. In 1876 the province passed an Assessment Act which amended the wild land tax provision but which still discriminated against unoccupied land.

The year 1891 marked perhaps the beginning of the most significant phase of land value taxation in western Canada, the operation of local option in separating land from improvements as far as valuation and exemption were concerned. In that year British Columbia empowered its municipalities, both city and district, to rate improvements at a lower value than the land and made it possible, furthermore, to exempt improvements altogether from taxation.[40] The following year exemption of at least one-half of improvement value was made mandatory upon the municipalities. By 1895 such an exemption was operating in Vancouver. In 1906 the assessment upon improvements was reduced to 25 per cent, and in 1910 improvements were entirely exempted from taxation in that city. Vancouver also levied various types of license fees and similar local taxes, but by 1911 more

---

[39] For example, in the '50s Upper Canada broke away from the English system of basing assessments upon the rental value of land (which, of course, discriminated in favor of unused land) and turned to land value itself, determining that the economic rent, which was set at 6 per cent of the full capitalized value, be the measure of land value. Ontario followed suit in 1869, and at present the city of Quebec alone rates on the annual rental. This breaking from the English system, moreover, was in the east, where there was less of the pioneer spirit. (See Scheftel, p. 252.)

[40] *Ibid.*, p. 261.

than 75 per cent of its revenue was derived from a tax on land values. However, during the war, Vancouver, along with other cities of the Dominion, was forced to resort to heavy taxation, with the result that improvements were again taxed up to the provincial limit, 50 per cent of their valuation. Much has been made of this "failure" of land value taxation in Vancouver, the opponents of such taxation pointing out that it breaks down when confronted by serious emergencies, the supporters arguing that the low rate on land values could not prevent the inevitable speculation that followed the city's building boom. In any case, the abnormal war situation, following the prewar "depression" in western Canada, would make any attempt at impartial judgment very difficult indeed. Victoria, along with Vancouver, also returned to 50 per cent exemption. It had inaugurated local option the same year as Vancouver and by 1911 had exempted all improvements from taxation. Up to the outbreak of the war, twenty-six of the city and district municipalities of British Columbia had totally exempted improvements from taxation; in eleven, improvements were taxed from one-tenth to one-third of their value, land, of course, being assessed at full value, whether used or not; the remaining twenty-five municipalities did not exceed the provincial minimum of 50 per cent exemption. Since the war the figures have changed to: Total exemption of improvements in twelve cities and towns (the district municipalities are not included in these figures), New Westminster, North Vancouver, Nanaimo, Port Moody, Prince Rupert, and Revelstoke being among them; four assess at 25 per cent or under, and twelve at the necessary 50 per cent.[41]

In 1894 the territorial government of the Northwest Territories, out of which Saskatchewan and Alberta were formed in 1905, empowered its municipalities to exempt improve-

[41] Thompson and Roebuck pamphlet *(op. cit.)*, pp. 5–6.

ments from taxation, although adding certain qualifications,[42] and when Saskatchewan and Alberta became provinces this system of local option was continued. In Saskatchewan the Village Act of the 1908–1909 session made it possible for all villages to exempt improvements from taxation and to derive all revenue from land values, and in 1912–1913 the Rural Municipalities Act extended that provision to those divisions. This privilege was soon taken advantage of, and by 1914 all the rural municipalities of the province depended solely upon the revenue (with the exception of certain license fees) from land values.[43] In the cities, towns and villages of Saskatchewan improvements cannot be taxed at more than 60 per cent of their value, and since 1911 cities and towns can make a gradual exemption of all improvements. The exemption reached by Regina, the capital, amounted to 75 per cent of improvement value.[44] In 1914 a special surtax was levied by the province upon absentee land owners.

It was in Alberta, however, that perhaps the furthest extension of "municipal single tax" was reached. Edmonton, the capital, obtained its charter in 1904, a year before Alberta became a province, and the charter provided for a general tax upon land values. Business and income taxes were also levied, but later these were dropped, and "municipal single tax," i. e., a tax on land values to meet the requirements of local expenditures, became the revenue system of Edmonton. Alberta, as did Saskatchewan, provided for local option from its very admission as a province, and the Town Act of 1911–1912 required that all improvements be exempt from taxation in towns and villages; cities with separate charters were not included, but of the six cities, Edmonton, Medicine

[42] Scheftel, p. 263.
[43] Ibid., p. 270.
[44] See ibid., pp. 264–265, for the figures of exemptions in other cities and towns.

Hat, and Red Deer exempted all improvements, while in Calgary 75 per cent, Lethbridge two-thirds, and Wetaskiwin 20 per cent of improvements were exempt from taxation.[45] As in British Columbia, the war forced taxation upon improvements again, and the cities now have the following scale of exemptions: Red Deer has a 50 per cent exemption, Edmonton and Medicine Hat 40 per cent, Lethbridge one-third, and Calgary a 30 per cent exemption.[46] In addition, Alberta passed a special unearned increment tax in 1913 which went even further than municipal single tax and showed that the principle of land value taxation was clearly accepted. A tax of 5 per cent was placed upon all increases in land values, and a year later a 1 per cent tax was levied on undeveloped land in the province.

Manitoba did not emphasize land value taxation to as great an extent as the other three western provinces. The "wild land" tax of 1873 has already been mentioned, and some time later the province exempted farm improvements from taxation, first to the extent of $1,000, then $1,500, and finally all farm improvements.[47] The Municipal Assessment Act provided for the valuation of all land in rural municipalities upon the basis of unimproved land value, and permitted a local exemption of one-half of improvement value from taxation.[48] Winnipeg operates under a separate charter and exempted one-third of improvements from taxation. The other three cities in Manitoba also undervalued improvements but illegally.[49] Here again, however, the war forced certain added taxes on improvements, yet Winnipeg still finances its water supply, some $15,000,000, out of a special tax on land values.

[45] Scheftel, p. 265.
[46] Thompson and Roebuck pamphlet, p. 5.
[47] This legislation is held to be due to the influence of George upon a young Manitoba journalist, W. W. Buchanan, who had the ear of the Greenway government. (*Single Tax Year Book*, p. 85.)
[48] Scheftel, p. 265.
[49] *Ibid.*

In this connection, one of the most interesting land policy instances in Manitoba has arisen in connection with the recent development of Fort Churchill as an ocean port. This development was begun in August, 1927, and in March, 1929, the control of the land passed from the Dominion to the province of Manitoba, but with the provision that, as in Canberra, Australia, the land was to be leased, not sold, and so kept under public control.[50]

Summarizing these efforts at land value taxation in western Canada [51] offers more difficulties than a similar summary of the Australasian system, the chief perplexity arising because of the reintroduction of some measure of improvement taxation in the war finance period. In 1916 Miss Scheftel could point out that, while perhaps not as successful as the experiments in Australia and New Zealand, the taxation of land values in western Canada was definitely a financial benefit. "As a fiscal measure, the tax has responded adequately to the needs of the communities, since it is not only a productive source of revenue, but also since it is least burdensome to industry and capital. The fact that the adoption of the tax in the western provinces has spread and that, even in the recent dire fiscal stress,[52] no attempt to rescind the measure has anywhere been made, is further testimony of its expediency." [53] The same conclusion, although with many more qualifications, was reached by Professor Haig.[54] The tax was not condemned as a local measure, but neither was it made the basis

[50] Thompson and Roebuck, p. 4.

[51] Such taxation has had little success in the older eastern provinces, although there has been a pronounced popular demand for the exemption of improvements. (Scheftel, pp. 300–301.) It may be mentioned that in Toronto the Ontario Legislature permitted the city to exempt houses from taxation on a sliding scale, buildings valued at $2,000 or less being allowed a 50 per cent exemption. (Thompson and Roebuck, p. 6.)

[52] Miss Scheftel finds that the severe prewar depression, especially in the western provinces, did not seriously or peculiarly handicap the municipalities taxing land values any more than those which taxed improvements.

[53] Ibid., p. 299.

[54] Op. cit.

for any wider extension of the principle of land value taxation.

However, since 1916, the opponents of land value taxation can show retrenchments which, although inspired by war exigencies, have not yet been significantly amended. The question, therefore, that must at least be raised in presenting an account, however brief, of the Canadian experiment is one which would inquire into the seriousness of this partial change of policy. That question obviously cannot be answered here. It will be answered differently, of course, by both the supporters and the attackers of land value taxation, and it may be remarked that perhaps the major difficulty that has been noticed in such answers is one of either a deliberate or an unconscious shifting of the issue. Where successful, land value taxation is hailed many times by the single taxer as an example of the ultimate efficiency of his program; where unsuccessful, it is pointed to as but an incomplete and parochial system that was destined to fail. And the same confusion seems present so often with the critics of any Henry George plan; land value taxation when effective is but a peculiar and isolated local phenomenon, applicable perhaps in the particular situation but arguing nothing for the feasibility of any further extension of the principle. When it seems to suggest a failure it is a warning that any further advance in this direction must be avoided. These perplexing interpretations have helped to complicate the Canadian situation, yet even confining the question to land value taxation—or to "municipal" single tax—there is the additional difficulty, even impossibility, of estimating the financial reports of these western cities dissociated from the tangled fiscal conditions of the past decade and a half. Any such analysis or judgment would be clearly outside the limits and the equipment of the present exposition.

If, however, the fiscal advantages of land value taxation

in western Canada were accepted by Miss Scheftel, at least in 1916, the "social" effects, as was also the case in Australasia, she believes to have been negligible, and in this she is supported by both Professor Haig and Professor Seligman. For example, it is pointed out that land value taxation did not have the effect of lowering rent [55]—which perhaps was to be expected, since its rate was not high enough to have prevented land "booms." Nor did such a tax appear to have had any serious effect upon land speculation or upon the holding of land out of use.[56] And the admitted spectacular increase in building, and also the rise in wages, in western Canada are held to be only partially, if at all, the result of the exemption of improvements from taxation.[57] However, one can quarrel with these conclusions only at the risk of falling into the dilemma just mentioned, i. e., of blowing hot and cold—success and failure—with the same breath.

Finally, the influence of Henry George upon these Canadian efforts in tax reform is held to be practically nonexistent. Indeed, Miss Scheftel here becomes quite scornful at any suggestion of such a connection.[58] It is admitted that George made a number of visits to Canada between 1885 and 1890, and also that, at least in eastern Canada, single tax associations had been organized as early as the '80s, but there is the insistence, much more emphatic than in the case of Australasia, that land value taxation in these western provinces was entirely locally conditioned and completely divorced from any setting of theory.[59] Moreover, as in

[55] Scheftel, pp. 295 ff.
[56] *Ibid.*, pp. 296 ff.
[57] *Ibid.*, pp. 292 ff., and 298 ff.
[58] *Ibid.*, pp. 266–270.
[59] Miss Scheftel gives the results of a questionnaire sent to various local authorities inquiring as to the cause of the inauguration of land value taxation (pp. 267–269). The reasons given indeed seem "provincial" enough, with no mention of theory, of George, or of classical political economy. Yet despite this stressing of local fiscal needs, there is nothing in these answers that would preclude an extension of the principle; that is, the reasons given

Australasia, the beginnings of land value taxation anticipated the work of George himself,[60] and so Miss Scheftel can find little reason for associating the work of Henry George with the experiments in western Canada. To attack such a conclusion with justifiable reasons is not easy, even in the most sympathetic exposition of George's work. The investigations of single taxers themselves into the origins of the Canadian movement can find little direct influence, except that a few of the pioneers in the Canadian enterprise were early followers of George.[61] Therefore all that can be appealed to is the admittedly "unscientific" contention that the tremendous popularity of George's writings and the recognized persuasion of his personal propaganda could not have failed to affect a neighboring country, one which he had visited many times. And likewise, the influence of the English theory of "unearned increment" upon western Canadian legislation can merely be presented as an obvious probability; it cannot, unfortunately, be definitely verified—at least by the present writer.

GREAT BRITAIN

If this discussion of the Australasian and Canadian land value taxation movements has appeared to slight the influence of George's work, such a perhaps apologetic attitude

for the adoption of the tax could all be accepted, notwithstanding their partial character, by at least the more "opportunistic" of single taxers.

[60] George himself knew something of the work of his Canadian and Australasian anticipators. "In the *Post* (of San Francisco) of April 16, 1874, George quoted the platform of the 'Land Tenure Reform League of Victoria,' as set forth in a tract by Robert Savage. The seventh plank said: 'The allocation of the rents of the soil to the nation is the only possible means by which a just distribution of the created wealth can be effected.' In commenting on this, George claimed originality for his own idea." (Young, *The Single Tax Movement in the United States*, p. 53, n. 39.) Whether by Victoria was meant Australia or British Columbia is not clear, although it was probably the former.

[61] See especially the series of articles in *The Single Tax Review* mentioned at the opening of this section.

must vanish from a consideration of this phase of social reform in Great Britain itself. This is not to say that George was in any unique way responsible for the English movement. But it is to say that the whole tradition of English classical economy, into which George so neatly fitted,[62] cannot be explained away—as may be possible in Canada and Australasia —as the directing background of the taxation of land values. Neither local conditions nor provincial fiscal needs, but a social reform backed by the greatest names in English political economy, directed the efforts of the land value taxationists.[63] And George's work was accepted as almost the inevitable corollary and the logical development of the whole English land reform movement from Locke to Mill and Wallace. His personal success[64] was relatively—and perhaps absolutely—greater in the British Isles than in the United States, and the same was true of the circulation of his books. Especially in his formative connection with the very beginnings of English socialism[65] did George become indissolubly a part of the reform tradition in that country.[66] Therefore, in any consideration of the theory of English land value taxation—and, it must be remembered, the significance of the English movement is largely one of social principle rather than of fiscal exigency—the influence of Henry George can in no way be neglected. From the earliest unsuccessful local rating attempts, through the famous Lloyd George budget, and down to the late spring and early summer of 1931, when (if one is permitted the use of his imagination) for more than two months the shade of Henry George

[62] See *supra*, p. 196 ff.
[63] Even Miss Scheftel admits this; see especially pp. 207–208.
[64] See *supra*, pp. 55–65.
[65] See *supra*, p. 230 ff.
[66] Hobson's statement, mentioned several times before, may again be kept in mind: "Henry George may be considered to have exercised a more directly formative and educative influence over English radicalism of the last fifteen years (1882–1897) than any other man."

stalked the House of Commons, the effect of *Progress and Poverty,* an effect not merely imponderable but recognized and accepted, has been a moving, pregnant force.

It is perhaps not necessary to trace chronologically the history of English land value taxation. For one thing, with the exception of the Finance Act of 1909–1910, the history of such tangible tax efforts has not been a very full one, at least up to 1931. And again, the most spectacular manifestation of land value taxation is also the most recent, the Finance Act of 1931. However, to suggest some type of legislative background it may be helpful to say a word about the earliest attempts and to mention briefly the provisions of the Lloyd George budget.

Despite the fact that land reform had been an integral part of English liberal thought all throughout the nineteenth century, and that it had been incorporated also among the principles of the Liberal Party itself [67]—Cobden and Campbell-Bannerman being particularly sensitive to this phase of social reform—there was no definite land value legislation until 1910.[68] The chief difficulty, of course, was, and still is, the absence of a system of local option in English taxation, a system such as obtains, at least partially, in practically every other country, including particularly the English dominions themselves.[69] Consequently every attempt at the local exemption of improvement or rating on land values has had to pass through Parliament, where the House of Lords

---

[67] For example, in 1889 at the annual meeting of the National Liberal Federation in Manchester, and again in the famous Newcastle program of the 1891 meeting, the necessity of a tax on land values was made clear.

[68] For a concise account of these early movements in England, see Scheftel, pp. 190–207; for bibliography, pp. 473–478. See also *The Single Tax Review* for January–February, 1913, and the *Single Tax Year Book,* pp. 96–105.

[69] It is interesting to note that the result of all the agitation for local rating and local exemption of improvements finally resulted not in any provision for a local tax but in a national tax. This was true both in 1910 and 1931, and so English local rating on land values is still to be achieved.

proved always an insuperable obstacle. As early as 1884 (the very year, it will be noticed, when George's early influence in Great Britain was at its highest point) the Parliamentary Housing Committee suggested the expediency of taxing land values.[70] From 1891 on Parliamentary committees continued the investigation of the question of local option and local rating on land values, but the reports were largely unfavorable. However, there were minority reports in many cases which did sympathize with land value taxation. For example, while the 1892 report of the Select Committee on Town Holdings did not favor taxation of vacant land or the separation of improvements from the land for valuation purposes, the minority Draft Report Committee advised the taxing of land at a higher rate than that on buildings. The same was the case in the report of the Royal Commission in 1901. Land value taxation was rejected but a separate minority report made recommendations similar to the Draft Report, adding that site value rating by localities be made optional.[71] In 1889 and 1893 the London County Council advised rating on site values and even began a preliminary valuation of all the land in London. The same was true in Glasgow in 1891 and 1895.[72] From 1901 to 1908 there were rather frequent suggestions in Parliament for the separate assessment of land and improvements, and for rating on land values, but all met defeat at the hands of the upper house. This was especially pronounced in the unfavorable reception of the

[70] Of course there had been "land taxes" all throughout English history, as in every other country too, but these taxes were based on "annual rental value" and not on "unimproved value" or even "capital value." Schedule A of the English income tax, for example, is levied on the gross rental of real property. Moreover, the land valuations in England, which were the basis of these land taxes, were centuries old and completely inaccurate. So, it was not until the '80s and '90s that "land value" taxation became a significant fiscal (if not theoretical) issue.

[71] Scheftel, pp. 197–199.

[72] Ibid. As many as 518 local councils, including many of the largest cities of England and Scotland, followed suit and petitioned Parliament for local rating on land values.

rating bills of 1906 to 1908. Such opposition of the House of Lords was one of the reasons that brought it into the tremendous popular disfavor which almost resulted in its dissolution in the following years.

Then came Part I of the Finance Act of 1909–1910, the result of the famous (or, for the Tory, infamous) Lloyd George budget.[73] The unprecedented character of these duties on land value, the wide-reaching political controversy with the House of Lords following its bitter and unrelenting opposition, the general "socialistic" character of this Liberal Parliament with its program of old-age pensions, labor insurance against unemployment and accident, labor exchanges, Irish home rule, and the like, made these political years some of the most interesting that England had seen. To concentrate, however, on the land value duties in the final Finance Act: First of all it must be remembered that these new duties were introduced for social and not for fiscal reasons.[74] For one thing, the taxes were unprecedented in that they turned to "capital value" instead of "annual rental value." This was not a logical outgrowth of local conditions, as had been the case in the English colonies, but a definite and deliberate break with the English system. There was, in fact, a studied attempt in drafting the duties to make clear their discriminatory, "theoretical" nature.[75] Moreover, as was true also, for

[73] There is naturally a great wealth of material, particularly in the economic periodicals, on the provisions of this Finance Act. The following references, as has been the general policy, are intended merely as samples: Scheftel, Chap. V, bibliography, pp. 473–478; Professor Seligman's article on the new English duties in the *Political Science Quarterly*, Vol. XXVII, September, 1912, pp. 454–469; Professor Davenport's "The Single Tax in the English Budget," in the *Quarterly Journal of Economics*, Vol. XXIV, February, 1910, pp. 279 ff. A most interesting summary and criticism of these land value duties may be found in a pamphlet written by Sir Edgar Harper, who, as Chief Valuer to the Board of Inland Revenues, was responsible for a good share of the valuation and collection procedure; the pamphlet, "The Lloyd George Finance (1909–1910) Act: Its Errors, and How to Correct Them," was prepared for the Fourth International Conference to Promote Land Value Taxation and Free Trade, Edinburgh, 1929.

[74] Scheftel, pp. 207–208.   [75] *Ibid.*

example, in most of the provincial land value taxes in Australasia, there was no attempt to justify the duties upon the ground that they would yield an appreciable amount of revenue; they were instead frankly an attempt to translate into the realm of concrete legislation some measure of that theory of social reform which had characterized so much of nineteenth century Liberal politics and Liberal political economy. These duties, in other words, were part of the general reform program of the Liberal group that had come into power in 1906, and therefore this immediate background of Liberalism must be kept in mind, as well as the history of the tangible efforts at local rating and the underlying tradition of English classical economy, in order to understand the final success of the 1909 budget.

Lloyd George introduced his budget on April 29, 1909, but it was exactly a year later before the Finance Act became law. The intervening twelve months witnessed one of the most vituperative, "class" debates in English Parliamentary history, a controversy that precipitated two general elections and resulted finally in the drastic curtailment of the power of the House of Lords. It was not until after January, 1910, that the definite success of the land value duties section of the budget was assured, although even then the exemptions and amendment that were forced into this Part I mutilated and practically nullified, as Lloyd George later admitted, the purpose of the taxes. There were four classes of so-called land value duties,[76] although in reality two of them were in no essential way levied upon

[76] Part I of the Finance Act of 1910, which contains the provisions for these land value duties, is a most complicated document, and this sketch of the taxes is a mere oversimplified skeleton. The complexities of this section of the act, especially in the matter of land valuation (there were, for example, no less than five different types of land valuation to be determined— the gross value, full site value, total value, assessable site value, and agricultural value), later proved to be one of the most potent reasons for the collapse of the land value duties. See the Harper pamphlet *(op. cit.)* for a brief and clear account of these difficulties.

the value of land. First, there was the "increment value" duty, which was a 20 per cent levy on the rise in land value, i. e., 20 per cent of the difference between the assessable site value as first determined (on April 30, 1909) and as it was determined at the time of the death of the owner, or the date of sale, at which time the tax was to be paid. The tax was also to be paid when land was leased for more than fourteen years, and was to be paid every fifteen years in the case of land in the possession of corporate or incorporate bodies that did not change hands. Then there was a "reversion" duty which operated in the case of leasehold property, a 10 per cent duty being imposed upon the difference between the total value at the expiration of a lease and the total value at the grant thereof. This was paid upon the occasion of the expiration of the lease. Both of these, it will be seen, are indirect levies.

The other two land value duties were direct annual levies. There was a tax of a half-penny in the pound laid on "undeveloped land," land which "has not been developed by the erection of dwelling houses or of buildings for the purposes of any business, trade, or industry other than agriculture . . . or is not otherwise used *bona fide* for any business, trade or industry other than agriculture. . . ." And, finally, a duty of one shilling in the pound was placed upon "mineral rights," i. e., the rental value of all rights to work minerals and of all mineral wayleaves. This duty met the fiercest criticism. It may be pointed out that this mineral rights duty and also the reversion duty were in no real sense taxes upon land value. The mineral duty was simply a charge upon the quantity of coal, or other mineral, brought to the surface; it was a tax upon production. And since the reversion duty, unlike the increment value levy, was placed upon the total value instead of upon assessable site value, the increase was almost invariably due in large part to the erection of a building, so that this tax, at least partially, was one upon improvements.[77]

Perhaps the most significant measure in this part of the Finance Act was not these land value duties but the provision for a complete valuation of all the land in the United Kingdom. This was a tremendous undertaking, comparable alone to the Domesday Book of William the Conqueror. Land was to be valued as of April 30, 1909, and every five years thereafter. A separate Valuation Department, under the jurisdiction of the Commissioner of Inland Revenue and in collaboration with the assessors of the income tax, had to be established to value the approximately eleven million hereditaments. However, although an accurate valuation of land was urgently needed and was indeed the very first step in any approach to land value taxation, the provisions of the 1910 act placed almost insurmountable obstacles in the way of the valuers.[78] In addition to the five different types of value that had to be determined, which of course necessitated the valuation of improvements as well as of the land itself, there was the whole cumbrous matter of appeal and adverse court decisions to hinder the work of the valuation department. These added complications greatly increased the cost and the time of the valuation. Also, there was the fact that the valuation results were not open to public inspection, a striking contrast to all valuation for rating purposes. Yet by 1920 nearly all of the valuations had been made, although many of them were subject to objections and appeal and so had not yet become binding.[79]

The difficulties involved in valuation were not by any means the only obstacle in the way of these land value duties. Each section of Part I, especially that relating to mineral rights, was tremendously, and often needlessly, complicated, and from the very formulation of the taxes there was great

[77] Harper, *op. cit.*, p. 2. [78] *Ibid.*; also Scheftel, pp. 233 ff.
[79] Harper, p. 2.

dissatisfaction, not merely among the Conservative group but, of much more significance, even among the most eloquent adherents of land value taxation.[80] The attack on the duties from the standpoint of the landowners was clear enough. It was quite naturally an attack of principle. The small charge on land was in no way distressing, but the precedent of a discriminatory tax upon the capital value of land instead of upon its annual rental value, and the unheralded duty on undeveloped land (a tax, so the opponents argued, on nonincome-bearing land and so contrary to all the canons of taxation!) were felt to augur evil when the Liberals—or, if they could see that far, the Labourites—became more powerful. On the other hand, the attacks of the supporters of land value taxation were directed at the unnecessary complications, the small rates, and, above all, the exemptions that had been included in the act.[81] First of all, agricultural land, or rather land whose value did not exceed the average value of agricultural land, was exempt from the duties. The same was true of small holdings.[82] Land used for games or recreations, and land held by the Government or by and for the King were likewise exempt; other exemptions were also included. Such exemptions, especially those of agricultural land and of small holdings, were held to be direct violations of the principle of land value taxation, introduced solely for the sake of gaining support for the general measure. Yet despite this intense dissatisfaction on both sides the land value duties remained in operation for ten years. The Finance Act of 1920, section 57, repealed all the duties except that on mineral rights, and so the necessity to complete land valuation ceased. However, as was stated above, most of the

[80] Harper; Scheftel, p. 243; *Single Tax Year Book,* pp. 106, 121.
[81] For a contrast of these duties with the German taxes on land value, especially in the matter of exemptions, see Scheftel, pp. 212 ff.
[82] The provisions respecting small holdings may be found most conveniently in Scheftel, p. 216.

valuations had been already completed and were recorded in the offices of the Inland Revenue Department.

It will not be necessary here to bridge the gap between the Finance Act of 1910 and that of 1931. As far as the history of land value taxation in England is concerned, that period was not a very fruitful one. In the budget of May, 1914, it is true, there were proposed by Lloyd George a Revenue Bill aimed at some of the difficulties in the earlier valuation provisions, and, of more importance, a Rating Bill designed to establish some degree of local rating on land values.[83] Both bills were "postponed" and, of course, three months later came the war and the end of the proposals. The year 1920 saw the finish of the Lloyd George act, an end in which he himself, realizing the unworkability and complexity of the duties, concurred, and 1928 witnessed the ambitious Conservative budget of Winston Churchill which turned its back upon the whole theory of land value taxation and free trade,[84] and ultimately precipitated the fall of the Government. Neither will it be necessary here to trace the interest of the Labour Party in land value taxation. From its earliest beginnings and especially because of its heritage of at least the theory of Fabian socialism, there has been a marked concern with the land problem among its adherents. The whole socialist upheaval in the last two decades of the nineteenth century which pre-

[83] Even in 1912 there were three unsuccessful attempts in the House of Commons to introduce local rating on land values.

[84] The land value controversy has embraced two of the most remarkable "apostasies" in English political history. In 1910 Churchill, the great Liberal, was second only to Lloyd George himself in his denunciation of the landed class and in his quoting of arguments from Henry George; in 1928 he was the Tory Chancellor, proposing tariffs and consumption taxes, and exempting land. In this recanting he was soundly berated by Sir John Simon, who virtually led the debate of the Liberals. Then came the Labour budget of 1931, and in the attack upon land value taxation and upon the whole free trade theory Sir John's name led all the rest. Not even Baldwin was more scornful of this "socialistic robbery." The classic onslaught by Lloyd George upon Simon for this alleged treason in the closing days of the budget debate will perhaps remain one of the most bitter and vindictive indictments ever heard in the House of Commons.

pared the background for the organization of a more opportunistic, politically conscious labor group was shot
through with land reform; indeed, with the inspiration of
Henry George himself.[85] As is the case with all (theoretical)
socialists, the laborite must include the collection of the
unearned increment of land values as one of his programs,
although, of course, that is pointed to as simply one plank;
it is a plank, however, that in England, because of the
peculiar appropriateness of the land problem and because of
the tradition of English economics, has captured the imagination of socialists to a much greater extent than on the Continent. And it was this harmony of interest on the question of
the taxation of land values among both Liberals and Labour
that alone made possible the Finance Act of 1931; at least
in this one reform (with the addition also of free trade
maintenance) Lloyd George and Philip Snowden were sworn
allies.

On April 27, 1929, Snowden opened his general election
campaign in Albert Hall, London, with the statement that
"a Chancellor of the Exchequer who taxes land values will
deserve the gratitude of the country. A Labour Chancellor
will do this." Two years later, to the day, he introduced
into the House his famous budget statement.[86] Even in his
first budget, soon after the election, he had anticipated the
taxation of land values, but it was not until 1931 that he kept
his election promise and definitely formulated such a taxation
program. His proposal, as compared with the Lloyd George
land duties, was quite simple. It advised a tax of a penny in

[85] See *supra,* p. 230 ff.

[86] For an account of the provisions and the discussion of this Snowden
budget the English newspapers and periodicals of the months April to July,
1931, will be most helpful. See also both the English and American economic
journals of this period. The official account of the proceedings will, of
course, be found in *Parliamentary Debates,* Official Reports, 5th Series, 1931.
The May–June and July–August, 1931, issues of *Land and Liberty,* London,
contain a succinct and completely accurate summary of the progress of the
budget through the House.

the pound on the unimproved capital value of land,[87] i. e., "the amount which the fee simple might have been expected to realize upon a sale in the open market on the valuation date," assuming, however, that there were no improvements, excepting agricultural, upon the land.[88] This tax was not to go into effect until the financial year 1933–1934, but since for a bill to be certified as a Money Bill (and so not under the jurisdiction of the House of Lords) the revenue included in the bill must be collected within the same financial year, it was necessary to adopt an enabling resolution setting aside that precedent of the English Constitution. Such a resolution was adopted on the 28th of April, the debate took place on the 4th and 6th of May, and on the latter date the resolution was passed by 289 votes to 230. On Report Stage (the next day) the resolution carried 166 to 94.[89] The Finance Bill itself was issued on the 13th of May.

While this Finance Bill differed from that of Lloyd George of 1909 in the greater simplicity of its proposed land value duties, a direct annual tax of a penny in the pound on land value instead of the earlier and more complicated fourfold scheme of taxation, it agreed with the Liberal budget in

[87] In the final draft of the Finance Act, the provision for this tax is found in Part III (which is devoted to the whole matter of the land value tax), Section 10: "Subject to the provisions of this Part of this Act relating to exemptions, there shall, in respect of all land in Great Britain, be charged for the financial year ending the thirty-first day of March, nineteen hundred and thirty-four, and for each subsequent financial year, a tax (to be called 'land value tax' and hereinafter in this Part of this Act referred to as 'the tax') at the rate of one penny for each pound of the land value of every land unit."

[88] Section 11. (In the original Finance Bill the sections of this part were numbered from 7 to 30. In the final draft they are numbered from 10 to 35. Sections 11–16 deal with valuation, objections and appeals; 17–23 with assessment, recovery and recoupment; 24–25 exemptions and relief; 26–34 supplemental; 35 application of preceding sections to Scotland.) Section 11 gives in detail the various improvements that are not to be considered in determining taxable value. Sections 31 and 32 define the meanings of certain controversial terms and expressions.

[89] A suggested reason for the ease in getting such an enabling resolution accepted was the Conservative hope of employing a similar procedure in future tariff proposals.

making certain serious exemptions. Agricultural land, for
example, was exempt from the necessary valuation and
taxation,[90] as were also small holdings whose land value tax
would not exceed ten shillings a year, mineral rights,[91] shoot-
ing and fishing rights, public and railway lands, and also,
of course, charitable institutions, churches, schools, and the
like. These exemptions, with the exception of that of small
holdings, were held by the Chancellor not to infringe upon
the principle of land value taxation. The chief reason for
such exemptions, it was argued, was the difficulty of valuation and the consequent delay in collecting the tax; there
was always the fear that the Speaker of the House might not
accept the budget as a Money Bill, and so the opportunistic
reason for emphasizing the revenue rather than the social
nature of the bill was constantly kept to the front.[92]   As

[90] The provisions for these exemptions will be found in Sections 24–25. (It
will be remembered that the numbering of these sections is that of the final
Finance Act and not that of the original Finance Bill.)

[91] Chancellor Snowden stated during the early debate, on the 4th of
May, that not only difficulties in valuation, but also the hope of future
nationalization, accounted for the exemption of mineral rights.

[92] For this reason, land which is exempt from taxation is not to be valued.
Since the Finance Act was ultimately to be certified as a Money Bill, the
only excuse for valuing land was for revenue purposes. Thus, land not
taxed did not require valuation; such a valuation, although theoretically
demanded and necessary, would have been a social or economic measure
and not simply a financial one. While agricultural land is exempt from
both valuation and taxation, still an attempt is made in the Act (Sections
11 and 19) to distinguish between the actual "land value" and the "cultivation
value" of such land. That is, land which has "purely" or "merely" a value
for agricultural purposes is to be exempt from both valuation and taxation,
while agricultural land which has a value higher than that of ordinary
farming land, e. g., land in the vicinity of cities, is to be valued and taxed
according to the degree in which its "cultivation value" does not approach
its "land" or "building" value. Of course, to determine such an excess some
sort of preliminary valuation must be made, but if the commissioners are
satisfied that there is no surplus of land value over cultivation value, there
is to be no permanent valuation of that land. Such a decision is an arbitrary
one, and this whole complicated distinction has drawn down the severe criticism of the supporters of land value taxation.

Section 19 includes the compromise between the Government and the
objecting Liberal group over the proposed "double taxation" amendment,
and introduces a most intricate plan of subtracting a multiple of the
Schedule A "annual value" income tax determiner from the land value
assessment, with the provision that the amount deducted should not exceed
seven-eighths of the land value tax. ("This means that the minimum charge

with all land value taxation measures, the valuation of the land itself was of prime importance. Therefore the Finance Bill took up the matter of valuation from the point where it was dropped in 1920. Provision was made for the valuation of all land in Great Britain, starting with the original valuation date as of August 1, 1931.[93] (However, the Finance Act changed this valuation date to January 1, 1932.) Valuations every five years thereafter were to be made, August 1, 1936, 1941, and so on. (The Act did not change the dates of these later valuations.)

The Second Reading of the Finance Bill was carried on May 19th after a motion to reject had lost, 270 votes to 230, and on July 3d, after weeks of bitter and exciting Parliament debate, the Third Reading passed the House of Commons by the unexpectedly large majority of 274 to 222. The Speaker of the House certified the measure as a Money Bill and so it passed into law without any possible interference on the part of the House of Lords. At this writing the future of such a highly important step in the progress of land value taxation in England lies in the hands of the new National Government and its fate seems quite certain. The Conservative party, at least, pledged itself during the debates to wipe the act off the statutes should they be returned to power, and Neville Chamberlain has already (1933) promised the neces-

of land value tax on any land, however much improvement it carries, will be equivalent to one-eighth of a penny on the whole amount of the actual land value. There will therefore be a levy on the land value of all land excepting that which is specially exempted under other provisions; and it will be an 'additional tax' despite the protestations of alleged injustice that gave birth to the original Liberal amendment." *Land and Liberty*, July–August, 1931, p. 121.) This Liberal amendment was really a wrecking one and would possibly have proved fatal to the intentions of the bill had it been adopted. It attacked land value taxation as "double taxation" and proposed therefore to set off the amount of income tax collected under Schedule A against the land value tax. The Government vigorously fought this amendment, and the adoption of the compromise Section 19 was felt to have solved a most crucial difficulty, and one which, for a time, seriously threatened the very fate of the bill itself.

[93] Sections 11–16; sections 27–28 give special power to the commissioners; valuation dates are in Section 32, on definitions. The valuation is under the jurisdiction of the Commissioners of Inland Revenue.

sary repeal legislation in the next Finance Bill. Valuation has already been discontinued on the grounds of economy (it had been started before the fall of the Labour Government), and there is little doubt that if the present Government remains in power the next general budget bill will eliminate these Snowden land value taxes. However, the 1931 act is a most significant one despite its present melancholy status, and despite the fact that the numerous exemptions and the low rates [94] are by no means satisfactory to the adherents of land value taxation. For one thing, notwithstanding the exemptions, the principle of a tax on site value remained intact throughout the entire proceeding, and so the British Labour Party became officially identified with the whole policy of land value taxation.[95] The simplicity of the new

[94] Under the caption of "Only a Penny," the July–August, 1931, issue of *Land and Liberty*, p. 113, quotes selections from opposition speeches and the opposition press which show very clearly that the low rate of tax was in no way a comfort to the Conservatives; it was the precedent established, the introduction of the entering wedge, that aroused their resentment. Among the quotations are the following: "Don't be deluded by the mention of a penny in the pound . . . you must remember that a penny in the pound which is now spoken of, and which may reach any figure you like, is on the capital value and not on the income . . . I can say one thing about it— that if we get back to power that tax will never see daylight." This was from a speech of Stanley Baldwin at Southampton, reported in the London *Times*, June 15, 1931. "The proposed tax of a penny in the pound might well be raised to a shilling in the pound in the first budget of a Chancellor of the Exchequer enjoying the support of a clear majority in the House of Commons." *Western Mail*, June 1. "The tax is not taken quite seriously . . . But . . . machinery which the Socialists are setting up with Liberal aid is the most potent weapon that those who are the declared enemies of society as it exists to-day could possibly have. The tax as at present proposed is only a penny in the pound; but it establishes a principle which will enable any Socialist Chancellor to tax property owners out of existence with little more than the stroke of a pen." London *Morning Post*, June 18. "Future Socialist Chancellors need do no more than follow the advice of the Single Taxers, and by steadily increasing the penny tax to 20 shillings, the thing is done . . ." *Truth*, May 27. Many similar quotations of the same nature show that while land value taxationists are not satisfied with the penny rate, neither are the landowners! These opposition complaints demonstrate clearly that England realizes that the Snowden act, as far as this measure is concerned, is one of principle and theory, and not simply a revenue scheme.

[95] At the time of the fourth International Conference to Promote Land Value Taxation and Free Trade, held at Edinburgh in the summer of 1929, more than a hundred members of Parliament, including fifteen Ministers,

tax showed more clearly what had been perhaps obscured by the cumbrous 1910 act, i. e., the direct attack upon land monopoly. Moreover, the adopted program of land valuation can alone prepare the way for the possible future local rating on land values (the Government valuations are certified to the local authorities), a hope which the English land value taxationists always keep before them. Valuation of land irrespective of improvements, and a direct, annual tax levied upon such value, are the very core of land value taxation, and they were present in the Finance Act of 1931.

This whole discussion of land value taxation in Great Britain has emphasized the part played by the theory of such a social venture. It has pointed out that the great English liberal tradition of land reform must be recognized as at least the background of all such fiscal measures. To conclude, then, with what seems to be the clearest expression of such a theory and of such a background, it may be in place to quote some sentences from the speeches of Philip Snowden himself, the financial genius whose temperament is hardly that of the "pure theorist," although that is how his opponents like to picture him. On the 3d of July Snowden concluded the budget debate with these words, words that might have come from the very pages of Henry George, and which, indeed, followed a few seconds after the Chancellor had used the name of the American economist:

The principle underlying this bill is to assert the right of the community to the ownership of the land. I have never made any question about that, nor that that right should be expressed in the

seven of them members of the Cabinet, sent messages of good will and sympathy to the meeting, indicating something of the Liberal and Labour attitude. (See Paper No. 36, published by the conference.) During the budget debate the offices of the United Committee for the Taxation of Land Values, perhaps the strongest Henry George organization in Great Britain, became almost a clearing-house for those Government supporters in the House who sought technical or historical information; the various memoranda issued by the committee, especially in connection with some of the proposed amendments, played an admitted part in the debate.

form of a rent paid by the occupier or rather the owner of the land to the community. As I said just now, this is only the first step in the reform of our land system. The effect of that system has been to place a burden on industry of hundreds of millions a year. It has crowded our people into pestilential slums, and it has driven hundreds of thousands of people from the land into the towns to compete with the town workers, with the result that wages have been depressed and unemployment has been increased. . . .

The party for whom I speak have always put the question of land reform in the forefront of their programme. Although I may not live to see the step that we have taken this afternoon advance still further, at any rate I submit this bill to the House of Commons with the satisfaction that I believe that we have begun a far-reaching reform which some day will liberate the land for the people and abolish once and for all the tyranny under which the people in this country have suffered.[96]

The most fervent follower of Henry George could find nothing to quarrel with in such a sincere and unequivocal statement. And other statements of the Labour Chancellor are no less striking. This is from his opening speech of April 27th:

. . . The scandal of the private appropriation of land values created by the enterprise and industry of the people and by the expenditure of public money has been tolerated far too long. In asserting the right of the community to a share in what has been created by the community, we are taking a step which will be approved not only by the Labour and the Liberal Parties, which have long advocated this reform, but also by a large number of Conservatives, whose sense of justice is outraged by glaring ex-amples of the exploitation of the public by private land monop-olists. The present system stands in the way of social and eco-

---

[96] The precise text from which these remarks are taken is the account of the debate as it appears in the May–June and July–August, 1931, issues of *Land and Liberty*, London. However, reports of the speeches may be obtained in the periodicals and newspapers of these months, and they appear in *Parliamentary Debates (op. cit.)*. The above statement appears in the July–August issue of *Land and Liberty*, p. 106.

nomic progress, inflicts crushing burdens on industry and hinders municipal development. When we have carried this measure, as I am sure we shall, and as we are determined to do, we shall look back upon the budget of this year as a landmark on the road of social and economic progress, and as one further stage towards the emancipation of the people from the tyranny and the injustice of private land monopoly.[97]

During the debate on May 4th Snowden pointed out that "the revenue from the taxation of land values is not by any means the only advantage that we hope to attain. There is, in my opinion, a more important advantage. It will cheapen land; it will throw land open for use." [98] And again:

Land differs from all other commodities in several respects. The land was given by the Creator, not for the use of dukes, but for the equal use of all His people. A restriction in the freedom to use land is a restriction on human liberty and freedom. To restrict the use of land by the arbitrary will of its owner, enhances its price, raises rents, hampers industry, and prevents municipal development and the promotion of social amenities. Every increase in population, every expansion of industry, every scientific development, every improvement in transport, all expenditures of public money, indeed, every child born, adds to the rent of land . . .[99]

These are the thoughts, almost the very language, of Henry George, and whether or not there was the specific debt to the American in their formulation, there can be no doubt that at least the tradition to which his name has become attached was responsible for their expression. But one can be more bold. The name of George himself was frequently heard during the debates—a fact made much of by the American newspapers—and, indeed, each side occasionally chided the other for its failure to comprehend or to state accurately the propositions of *Progress and*

[97] *Ibid.*, May–June issue, p. 82.   [98] *Ibid.*, p. 84.   [99] *Ibid.*, p. 83.

Poverty.[100] Snowden's own personal interest in George is well attested.[101] Therefore it is no "unscientific" assumption to present George's influence upon the English movement of land value taxation. As with any other example of ideational influence, it would of course be palpably impossible to trace a "chapter and verse" dependency, but there is no difficulty in grasping the fact that both the tradition of land reform and also the more specific and concentrated phrasing of that reform as it is stated in the pages of *Progress and Poverty,* have found a degree of expression in the financial legislation of Great Britain.

THE UNITED STATES

There is little doubt that Henry George's own country affords the most disappointment to his followers. While there has been the most strenuous sort of activity, political, educational, propaganda, opportunistic, theoretical, on the part of American single taxers, there has not been, with two or three exceptions, any legislation embodying the significant demands of their program.[102] At least there have been no

[100] In fact, there were times, to any one privileged to hear the debates, when the English House of Commons seemed almost a Henry George convention, or at least a gathering of land value taxation delegates.

[101] That interest is expressed in at least two prefaces written by the Chancellor, both of which have been mentioned earlier in different connections; the most recent (1929) is a foreword to an abridged English edition of George's *Protection or Free Trade,* and the other is a preface to a Labour Party pamphlet written by Josiah Wedgwood, "Henry George for Socialists." Snowden has also given many personal expressions of his admiration for George.

[102] The present section can deal only with the tangible, legislative effects of George's work. There has undoubtedly been a great imponderable influence that cannot very well be measured or discussed.

The chief work on the single tax in the United States is, of course, Professor A. N. Young's *The Single Tax Movement in the United States* (Princeton University Press, 1916); Chaps. VIII, IX, X, and XI contain material handled in this section. See also: *Single Tax Year Book,* pp. 26–66; Scheftel, Chap. X, especially pp. 450–459; "The Progress of Henry George Ideas in the U. S. A.," by John J. Murphy, pamphlet prepared for the Fourth International Conference to Promote Land Value Taxation and Free Trade,

tangible results in the United States proportionate in any way to the outlay of money and energy.

The reason is a little difficult to state—that is, unless one succumbs to an evertempting cynicism. Should one allow himself so to be tempted, then it is very simple to answer why neither single tax, nor socialism, nor a labor party, nor, in fact, any organized opposition liberal or radical group has ever had any real success here. That answer would show that the country has been too young and immature and devoid of tradition; or too hard and selfish and (up to the present) too prosperous and healthy; or too ignorant and contented; that, in other words, it has been too unphilosophic to have fostered the theory or even the practice of social reform. The discontented and disillusioned follower of Henry George can very easily sit down with the discontented and disillusioned liberal or radical of any faith, and commiserate with him (and say, perhaps, with John Chamberlain, "farewell to reform"). But it is not polite to be cynical. Neither is it in order to attempt an exposition of conservative America. It is perhaps sufficient to say that the same reasons that have accounted for the failure—at least up to the present—of all forward-looking ambitious political and social programs must be invoked in tracing George's lack of overt influence in this country.

Should one refuse to be cynical, however, it may be more helpful to point out some more specific reasons for the peculiar and conspicuous absence of tangible success in the development of George's doctrines in the United States. To those inclined to sneer at his work, it is the very coupling of his name and of "single tax" with "land value taxation" that has prevented a progress here comparable with that of land value movements throughout the world. Since, for these critics, land value taxation is completely parochial and

Edinburgh, 1929. Other specific works on different aspects of the movement in this country will be mentioned further on.

of only fiscal, not theoretical, significance, and since in this country, unlike other countries, practically every improvement-exemption or land value tax measure has been, if not espoused, at least attacked under the label of George or of single tax, the reason for failure seems clear. Miss Scheftel, for example, can write that "until recent years, the proposal of the tax on land values, confounded with the Single Tax, remained a dead issue in this country . . . It may well be, however, that the Single Tax bugbear will retard rather than promote the adoption of the tax on land value." [103] And Professor Carver holds, in favoring the inheritance tax over the land value tax:

The inheritance tax, however, has stood on its merit and has not been championed as an engine of social reform. It has had no body of ardent apostles to set up a fiery cross and preach a crusade against a fortunate class. The land tax has been thus handicapped, which may account for its slow progress. In the ardency of reform, arguments are used which ignite certain inflammable spirits but repel all thinking men.[104]

On the other hand, the follower of George can find less damaging reasons for his only slight degree of success. He would show, for instance, that under the American taxation system, with its heavy levies on real estate and especially on general property, land is already taxed to a much greater degree than in perhaps any other nation. There is nothing in the United States similar to the traditional English system which made the taxation of vacant land impossible since taxable value was based upon the annual rent. Land in the United States is assessed upon its selling ("capital") value and although, as even Professor Seligman admits,[105] vacant

[103] Pp. 450–451. (Miss Scheftel, of course, suggests other fiscal reasons for the slighting or inapplicability of such taxation in the United States. See pp. 422–450.)

[104] *Essays in Social Justice,* Cambridge, 1915, p. 304. (Quoted in Young, p. 287.)

[105] *Essays in Taxation,* 1913 ed., pp. 488–489. (Quoted in Young, p. 287.)

lots are generally much under-assessed, still the more spectacular abuses of the older landed property régime in Europe have never been completely present in this country.[106] Due to these heavy taxes on land and to special assessments for local improvements, "it is probably true that a larger percentage of ground-rent is reclaimed by the community through taxation in the states of Massachusetts and New York than in any other territory in the world."[107] At one time in the city of New York 35 per cent of the annual land value was being collected for public purposes.[108] Therefore the already existing heavy taxes on land, even though they bear little resemblance to any theory of unearned increment, offer a serious difficulty to the American advocate for further taxes on land value.

Then, there is the difficulty of the various legislative or constitutional restrictions of the different States which prevent any sweeping national measure of tax reform (the English Finance Act of 1931, for example, would be inconceivable in this country), and also, paradoxically enough, retard the progress of local option.[109] This is one reason, as shall be noted, why in nearly every case movements for local option in taxation have been engineered by single taxers. And again, the emphasis upon the political aspect of land value taxation is another reason given by some single taxers (notably Mr. Fillebrown) for lack of success, although other

[106] Another instance, which will be mentioned a few pages further on, of the advantages of the American system is that from quite early times there has been a separate assessment of land and improvements by the various States.

[107] *Thirty Years of Henry George,* by C. B. Fillebrown (Boston, 1915, 3d ed.), p. 15. Mr. Fillebrown was one of the most successful of the "single tax limited" advocates, and was of particular importance in breaking down the opposition of the more "respectable" citizen.

[108] Murphy, *op. cit.,* p. 3.

[109] "As yet, with the exception of a few isolated instances, reform in local taxation in the United States is still in its infancy. The prospect of the institution of the tax on land value is therefore remote. The momentum of the agitation to introduce the tax will quicken, however, as the fiscal exigencies of the cities assert themselves." (Scheftel, p. 459.)

followers of George maintain that the political medium offers
the greatest possibility for their work. It will therefore be
an appeal to some reason of this type that will be made by
any one sympathetic to the contributions of Henry George,
any one, that is, who is attempting to explain not the theoretical causes for the slow progress of the single tax—which
is a much larger question—but rather the specific conditions which have prevented an acceleration of the land
value taxation movement in the United States.

Since there has been no spectacular or uniquely significant
single step in the progress of American land value taxation,
perhaps the most acceptable procedure for handling that
movement will be a very brief chronological account of the
more important attempts to introduce some measure of a
levy upon the unimproved value of land or to exempt improvements from taxation.[110] It will be noticed that these
efforts include tactics that range all the way from the
establishing of single tax colonies to the support of seemingly
innocuous legislation whose phrasing contains no mention
of "single tax" or of Henry George. It will also be noticed
that, with the exception of the political interest of George and
his early followers in the cause of free trade, the single tax
attempts include no national efforts at tax reform; they are
limited to State and local measures. The reason, of course,
is that Federal financial discussion has taken almost no
account of land taxation, but has confined itself largely to
tariffs and income taxes.

The first recognized attempt to introduce some measure of
land value taxation on the part of single taxers [111] seems to

---

[110] This account will not include the early political campaigns of George
and his immediate followers; these have been mentioned briefly in a preceding chapter on biography. Nor will it include a survey of the various
conferences and educational programs of American single taxers. That may
be found in the *Single Tax Year Book*, and also in Young.

[111] It may be remarked that, differing from the case in other countries,
nearly every movement for land value taxation or for the exemption of

have been as early as 1892 in the town of Hyattsville, Maryland.[112] Due to agitation by the Georgists, personal property had already been exempted from local taxation, and land was (illegally) assessed at a higher rate than improvements; then in 1892 there was secured a charter from the State which permitted the Board of Commissioners to make whatever assessments or exceptions from assessment were thought justified. The board proceeded to exempt improvements wholly from taxation and to levy all the taxes of the town upon land values. In the following year, however, these efforts were declared unconstitutional.

In the neighboring State of Delaware, in 1895, the single taxers made one of the most spectacular campaigns in the history of the movement.[113] An attempt was engineered to capture the State and to use it as a model for their fiscal program. Delaware was selected because of its small size and because one-third of the voters were concentrated in the city of Wilmington; also because of its lack of constitutional restrictions, its proximity to large cities having strong single tax organizations, and its evenly balanced Legislature. The followers of George launched a most colorful and varied crusade, which provoked such excitement that a number of the single taxers found themselves in jail, and the whole question of free speech was added to that of land value taxation. During the campaign a weekly periodical, *Justice,* was published in Wilmington and Philadelphia. However, the outcome of the whole effort was a distinct blow to the hopefulness of George's followers. The election of 1896 found the single taxers with a little more than three per cent of

improvements in the United States has been inaugurated or at least organized by admitted followers of George. The reason seems clear, and may be located in the peculiar conditions (e. g., the existing heavy taxation of land) which have tended to prevent the spontaneous interest in land value taxation that is found elsewhere.

[112] Young, pp. 145–147; *Single Tax Year Book,* pp. 56–59; also New York *Times,* March 16, 1893, p. 1.

[113] Young, pp. 147–152; *Single Tax Year Book,* pp. 35–37.

the total vote cast. However, since this vote was not on a referendum tax measure, but was cast for a direct Single Tax third party, its smallness may be thus partially explained.

The next major effort finds the advocates of land value taxation active in Colorado, where from 1899 to 1902 a serious attempt was made to introduce the Australasian system.[114] A tax commission, under the chairmanship of Senator James W. Bucklin, had been appointed by the State Senate to investigate State and local revenue laws. Bucklin visited Australia and New Zealand and returned with a most favorable report, strongly advocating the installation of some measure of land value taxation in Colorado. The Legislature agreed to submit the proposal to the voters as a suggested amendment to the State Constitution. In the election of 1902 the proposed amendment was defeated.

It was on the Pacific Coast, however, that the most elaborate single tax campaigns were conducted. Starting in 1908 and lasting until 1914 there was a whole series of proposed amendments, especially in the State of Oregon, that sought to exempt improvements and to tax land values.[115] These attempts were financed chiefly by Joseph Fels,[116] and were characterized by their refusal to use the term "single tax," except in the earliest campaign, and by their opportunistic appeal to self-interest and to purely fiscal arguments.[117] The first Oregon amendment, brought forward in 1908,[118]

---

[114] Young, pp. 156–159; Single Tax Year Book, pp. 27–31.

[115] Young, pp. 163–183; Single Tax Year Book, pp. 42–46.

[116] Joseph Fels was a wealthy soap manufacturer who contributed large amounts of money (some $173,000 over a period of five years) for the advocacy of the single tax. His concentration upon Oregon was an effort "to put the single tax into effect somewhere in the United States within five years."

[117] There is a most interesting repudiation of these tactics by W. S. U'Ren, who was the leader of the single taxers in their efforts in Oregon, in the Single Tax Year Book, pp. 44–46.

[118] One of the major reasons for selecting the State of Oregon for these attempts was the fact that it had adopted the initiative and referendum system. The same reason applies to the States of Washington and Missouri, where, at about the same time, other single tax proposals were presented.

proposed an exemption from taxation of all manufacturing and farm improvements; strangely enough, personalty and business other than manufacturing were not included in the exemption provision. In this first campaign the single taxers did not hesitate to state that this was a "step in the direction of the single tax." The measure was defeated by a little less than two to one, although in Multnomah County, in which Portland is located, the amendment failed to carry by only 483 votes. A year later began the active coöperation of the Joseph Fels Fund Commission, and in the election of 1910 another amendment was proposed abolishing the poll tax and granting local option in taxation. However, in this election the single tax group did not allow the use of that phrase, although their opponents made it quite clear that what they were attacking was that "step in the direction of the single tax." The amendment was accepted by 44,171 votes to 42,127. From 1910 to 1912 the single tax battle waged very fiercely in Oregon. In addition to proposed measures for exempting personal property and improvements from taxation in three counties, the single taxers drafted an unusual type of amendment to the State Constitution which accepted the theory of progressive taxation; these were put before the people in the 1912 election following the most vigorous campaign that George's followers had yet made anywhere. Great emphasis was placed upon the success of land value taxation across the border in Canada, and appeals were made to the promised increase in Oregon's prosperity. The result was again a keen disappointment to the single taxers, for all the measures they supported were lost, and the home rule section of the 1910 amendment was repealed. In 1914 there was a similar result; two improvement-exemption amendments were defeated by a vote of more than two to one. Professor Young concludes: "The Oregon single tax agitation has thus far brought no indication of results commensurate with the efforts expended. Analysis of the votes shows that the adoption of any part of the single tax program was no nearer in 1914 than in 1908." [119]

The single tax efforts on the Pacific Coast were not, however, confined to Oregon. In the State of Washington work was begun as early as 1897, and in 1912 one of the few actual adoptions of at least part of the single tax proposal was made by the city of Everett. [120] From 1897 to 1899 single taxers actively supported a proposed constitutional amendment providing for local option in taxation; in the election of the latter year, however, the amendment was defeated. But in the election of November, 1911, Everett, with a population of about 25,000, amended its charter so that improvements were exempt from taxation. The amendment, which had been labeled "Single Tax," provided for a gradual exemption, starting with 25 per cent in 1911–1912 and reaching a total exemption by 1917. In April, 1912, this single tax clause was defeated, but in November of the same year it was again decisively carried by a vote of nearly two to one, despite the fact that the ballots were clearly marked: "Single Tax; For, Against." "The reasons for Everett's adoption of the amendment seem to have been similar to those which have induced cities of the Canadian west to exempt improvements from taxation, the fact that corporations or absentee owners held a considerable area of unimproved land within the city." [121] But this amendment was never put into effect. After 1912 the State Tax Commission ruled it unconstitutional, the single taxers offered no protest, and the assessors were ordered to ignore it. There were two other important single tax campaigns in Washington in 1912 and 1913, in the city of Seattle. In both years proposals were put forward to

[119] Young, p. 182.
[120] Ibid., pp. 184–191; Scheftel, pp. 451–452; Single Tax Year Book, p. 65.
[121] Young, p. 186.

exempt personal property and improvements from municipal taxation, but both were defeated.

In California also there have been a number of significant
attempts to introduce home rule or single tax measures; in
fact, with the exception of the Oregon campaigns, the votes
in the California elections have been regarded as perhaps the
most important practical tribute to the efforts of American
single taxers. In 1912 and 1914 local option amendments
were defeated in California, but in each case home rule was
favored by more than 40 per cent of the voters, and in 1916
an outright single tax amendment to the State Constitution
was submitted and, although defeated, the affirmative
vote was 31 per cent of the total.[122] This campaign, which
was conducted under the leadership of Luke North, was
perhaps the first State election for a straight Henry George
program. Two years later a similar amendment was proposed and defeated; the affirmative vote was 118,688 out of
479,022, the decrease in the single tax vote being attributed,
by many, to the entrance of this country into the war. In
1920 a much more conservative amendment to the State
Constitution was offered to the California voters, but again
lost, although it was favored by 216,714 of the electorate.

These years appear to have been important ones in single
tax activity. In 1912, in addition to the work in Oregon,
Washington and California, there was waged in the State of
Missouri [123] perhaps the most bitter of all single tax battles.
A constitutional amendment had been proposed by initiative
petition which provided for the gradual exemption from
taxation of personal property and improvements, and with
the proviso that land be never exempt from taxation. The
campaign of 1912 was a most active one, and the opposition,
especially that of the "embattled farmers," who felt that

[122] Young, p. 232; *Single Tax Year Book,* pp. 50–51.
[123] Young, pp. 191–197; *Single Tax Year Book,* pp. 38–41.

they were being discriminated against, was so strong that the result was several acts of personal violence against single tax agitators.[124] At the election the amendment was overwhelmingly defeated.[125]

During this period, however, there were other land value tax measures, both legal and illegal, which helped to remove some of the pessimism among single taxers. The record of almost complete political failure was lightened a little. Starting in 1911, the city of Houston, Texas, inaugurated one of the most interesting experiments in the whole history of American land value taxation.[126] Under the direction of J. J. Pastoriza, an ardent single taxer who had been elected Finance and Tax Commissioner of the city, there were first introduced the separate valuation of land and improvements and the Somers system of land assessment. Then, public service franchises were assessed and taxed, and finally Pastoriza took a further extralegal step in reducing the assessment of improvements. The policy of assessment in Houston had already laid the precedent of practically ignoring personal property and generally underassessing buildings; the Tax Commissioner continued this policy and extended it so as to assess all improvements at 25 per cent of their value and land at 70 per cent of its value. In addition, he exempted bank deposits, credits, all household goods, and continued to ignore personal property. This "Houston Plan of Taxation," although extralegal, proved to be very popular and its success and general soundness were attested to by even those who were not advocates of land value taxation.[127]

---

[124] Young, pp. 195–196.

[125] However, in 1914 an "anti-Single Tax" constitutional amendment intended to prevent the use of the initiative and referendum for single tax purposes, was submitted, but beaten three to one (*Single Tax Year Book,* p. 41, and Young, pp. 196–197.)

[126] Young, pp. 197–202; Scheftel, pp. 453–455; *Single Tax Year Book,* pp. 60–61.

[127] Young, pp. 199–202; Scheftel, pp. 454–455.

In March, 1915, however, an unfavorable court decision ended the experiment.

A more legally valid procedure, and one that is hailed by several groups of George's followers as easily the most significant and promising step in the whole American movement, was inaugurated in 1913 by the passage of the Stein Bill in Pennsylvania.[128] This act applies to the second class cities of the State, i. e., Pittsburgh and Scranton, and provides for a gradual reduction of the tax rate upon improvements as compared with that on land. That is, the tax rate on improvements shall not exceed the specified percentages of the tax rate on land. The method of reduction was that for the year 1914–1915 the tax rate upon improvements be assessed at 90 per cent of the tax rate on land, to be followed by further cuts of 10 per cent every third fiscal year, until a 50 per cent reduction was reached. Practically, on the 50 per cent basis, this means that the total of all improvement values shall bear one-third of city expenses, and the total of all land values two-thirds. This "Pittsburgh Plan" has already come into full effect, the opposition has been slight,[129] and its adherents have pictured the striking results of its operation.[130] The success of the tax reduction upon improvements in Pittsburgh and Scranton has started a movement for the ap-

[128] Young, pp. 210–215; Scheftel, pp. 455–456; *Single Tax Year Book,* pp. 62–65.

[129] This exemption measure was, of course, not labeled "single tax" in any way, and was supported by various civic commissions and non-partisan bodies. During the legislative proceedings leading up to the passage of the act, the city of Scranton was not heard from at all, indicating the lack of an organized opposition. The most serious attack upon the act was in 1915, when a repeal of this reduced building taxation was pushed through both houses of the Legislature; it was, however, vetoed by Governor Brumbaugh.

[130] See especially "The Pittsburgh Plan," a pamphlet published by the Allied Boards of Trade of Allegheny County, 1925. This includes, among other statements, a collection of quotations from the more important business and manufacturing enterprises in Pittsburgh. See also "Pittsburgh's Graded Tax in Full Operation," by Percy H. Williams, *National Municipal Review,* December, 1925; and the 1929 *Proceedings of the National Tax Association,* which contains a pro and con discussion.

plication of the law to third-class cities, and even to Philadelphia itself, while in Pittsburgh an effort is under way to lower the percentage further until there will be no tax on improvements.[131]

New York City has witnessed a most interesting struggle for improvement-exemption and the taxation of land values. Starting as early as 1891 with the work of Thomas G. Shearman, one of George's associates and perhaps the leading taxation authority of the whole early movement, and the organization of his New York Tax Reform Association, there was a determined attempt to enact into legislation at least a degree of the single tax proposals.[132] This, of course, was in addition to and even partially independent of George's own work and campaigns in New York City.[133] The first tangible result of the agitation of this association, and chiefly through the work of Lawson Purdy, was in the years 1903–1904, during the administration of Mayor Seth Low, when the State Legislature directed the city to assess separately the value of land,[134] to publish the assessments in printed lists, and so prepared the way for the full valuation of land. In 1911 the Legislature directed other cities of the State to assess separately the value of land. The question of the exemption of improvements from taxation in New York City has been widely discussed since 1908. Under Mayor Gaynor, some years later, two important commissions were appointed to investigate the congestion of population and to ascertain

---

[131] The Pittsburgh legislation is significant as a general trend in policy, since, unlike most American cities, merchandise and similar property, and, more recently, machinery, have been exempted from taxation. Moreover, there are no substitute taxes, so that the real estate tax is the substantial source of municipal revenue in Pittsburgh.

[132] Young, pp. 215–229; Scheftel, pp. 457–458; *Single Tax Year Book,* p. 19; Murphy, *op. cit.*

[133] See *supra,* pp. 66–69, 75–77.

[134] It has been noted before that in the United States the policy of separating the improvements from the land itself had an early origin. It has been estimated that more than twenty billion dollars of land values are separately assessed in this country. (Murphy, p. 4.)

new sources of revenue. The Congestion Committee was appointed in 1910 and made its report a year later, recommending the halving of the tax rate upon buildings, and hinting also at the possibility of a land value increment tax. The New-Sources-of-Revenue Committee was appointed in 1911 and reported in 1913. Its chief suggestion was a 1 per cent increment tax to be based upon the increase (as determined annually) over the 1912 valuation. Unlike the European increment taxes, this was to be collected annually. Legislative bills based upon the recommendations of these commissions were introduced at Albany as early as March, 1911. The Sullivan-Short Bill of that year, proposing halving the tax rate on buildings, the reduction to extend over a period of five years, was not allowed to come to a vote. This bill was reintroduced unsuccessfully several times after its first defeat. The same fate overtook the widely discussed Herrick-Schaap Bill in 1914. This was a proposal suggesting an amendment to the New York City Charter and was based largely upon the Pittsburgh Plan of the preceding year; improved land was to be valued at 90 per cent as compared with a 100 per cent valuation of unimproved land, with a 10 per cent reduction every year, until a 50 per cent valuation was reached. Controversy over the bill lasted for several months and numerous hearings were held, but the opposition was too strong. In 1915 a similar bill was likewise killed in committee.

Further discussion of land value taxation in New York City was stimulated in 1914 when Mayor Mitchel appointed the Committee on Taxation of the City of New York, a body consisting of twenty-five members, including men such as Professor Seligman and Frederic C. Howe. Two important reports were prepared for the committee by Professor Robert Murray Haig of Columbia University, one on "The Exemption of Improvements from Taxation in Canada and the

United States," [135] and the other on "Some Probable Effects of the Exemption of Improvements from Taxation in the City of New York." After a number of public hearings [136] the committee presented its final report in January, 1916. It did not favor the exemption of buildings, nor a "supertax" on land values, but it did propose another 1 per cent land value increment tax, just as had the Gaynor report of 1913. A minority report of seven members favored the exemption of improvements. Despite the interest aroused by these committees and the resulting discussion, there was a decided lull in the New York City movement after this report of 1916, and it was not until four years later that any tangible step was realized. The legislation of 1920, however, may be traceable directly to the great housing shortage and the abnormally high rents of the post-war years; it was only incidentally an outcome of the earlier agitation. In September, 1920, the State Legislature permitted the exemption of new dwelling-houses from taxation for a period of ten years. New York City, along with six other cities in the State, immediately took advantage of that privilege.[137] There is little doubt that the tremendous building boom in the years immediately following 1920 was a direct result of that exemption. In 1927 the New York City authorities also voted to exempt for twenty years dwellings built by limited dividend companies under the State housing law. This emergency im-

---

[135] This report (which contains perhaps the best account of the Canadian movement) has been mentioned before in connection with Canadian land value taxation.

[136] One of the most earnest advocates for the exemption of buildings was Benjamin C. Marsh of the Society to Lower Rents and Reduce Taxes on Homes. Mr. Marsh, however, did not consider himself an outright "single taxer."

[137] The exemption was limited to $1,000 per room, and $5,000 per house or apartment; later, to a maximum of $15,000 per building. At this time also there were passed the emergency rent laws placing certain limits on the power of landlords to raise rents. This exemption of new buildings expired after the ten year exemption period, and such improvements are now assessed for taxation purposes.

provement-exemption measure was one of the very few legislative steps in the whole American movement, but it was, however, the product of local conditions rather than the embodiment of any theory.

There may be mentioned, for the sake of completeness, several other interesting incidents of land value taxation and improvement exemption in the United States. From 1913 to 1915 in Colorado, the seat of the earlier agitation of 1899–1902, the single taxers made active efforts to capture the votes of three cities.[138] Colorado is exceptional in granting extensive home rule power to its cities, and so in Pueblo in 1913, and in Denver and Colorado Springs in 1915, improvement-exemption amendments were proposed. The amendments were defeated in the latter two, but Pueblo accepted a measure providing for a 50 per cent exemption of improvements from municipal taxation in 1914 and a 99 per cent exemption for 1915. After being put into effect in 1914, the amendment was repealed by popular vote in November, 1915.

California inaugurated an experiment in land value taxation in 1909, when the State Legislature provided for the financing of new irrigation districts by means of a special levy on land values alone.[139] Two of the older districts also adopted the plan, Modesto in 1911 and Turlock in 1915, both of them in the San Joaquin Valley. The four new irrigation districts which operate under this system are Oakdale and South San Joaquin, also in the valley, Anderson-Cottonwood in the northern part of the State, and Imperial, near the Mexican border.

One further interesting, although unsuccessful, attempt to introduce special taxation of land value is found in Wisconsin. In 1921 there was proposed in the State Assembly the Grimstad Bill, drafted and supported by Professor John

---

[138] Young, pp. 202–208; *Single Tax Year Book*, pp. 31–34.
[139] Young, p. 208; *Single Tax Year Book*, pp. 52–56.

R. Commons and others.[140] The bill provided for a "surtax" on land values over $10,000; such values were to be subject to a graduated tax starting with a levy of one-half of 1 per cent to 1 per cent, and rising from that minimum rate. (Compare this with the Ralston-Nolan Bill in Congress.) While improvements which were already subject to existing taxes were not affected, land valued at less than $10,000 together with the timber and fertility value of land were to be exempted. Fertility was arbitrarily set at one-half the value of farm land, this being an attempt to equalize the determination of rural and urban land values. At the same time as the drafting of the Grimstad Bill, the Miller Bill in the Assembly and the Johnson Bill in the Senate proposed similar homestead exemptions.[141] Perhaps the most interesting aspect of the discussion over this bill was the supporting argument of Professor Commons before the special Assembly committee.[142] Although he declared himself not to be a single taxer, he stated that the chief aim of the bill was to transfer the burden of taxation from labor products and improvements to land values; in addition, these surtaxes on land value would help to abolish unearned income, to open opportunity for employment, and to attack farm renting. Professor Commons further argued that while there was a natural right to labor products, there could be no such right to social values, and that land values were essentially an illegitimate surplus "allowed to owners over and above the amount of real wealth that they or their predecessors have added to the wealth of the State." On the contrary, the taxation of improvements was unjustified, since the owners of improved land "are adding to the wealth of the State in the

[140] For an account of the drafting and discussion of this bill see especially the following newspaper accounts: The *Capital Times* of Madison for April 20, 1921, and June 14, 1923, and the Milwaukee *Journal* for March 22, 1923.
[141] See the *Journal* article.
[142] An account of Professor Commons's speech may be found in the April 20 issue of the *Capital Times*.

same proportion that they are becoming wealthy themselves." Professor Commons continued with an attack upon speculation and holding land out of use, and concluded with the statement that the crux of the whole problem was whether the increasing burden of taxation was to be laid upon "property whose value results only from an increased demand of the public for something that cannot be increased in supply by labor or by an increase of savings" or upon the improvements of labor. He also argued that the Grimstad Bill was not directed at the farmer, but was devised largely to hit the owners of vacant city lots. However, despite the support of Professor Commons and of other economists and agricultural experts, the Grimstad Bill was defeated in the Assembly in June of 1923 by a vote of 46 to 37. Nothing since has been proposed in Wisconsin in the way of taxing land values peculiarly, except that in 1926 during the gubernatorial campaign Fred R. Zimmerman, who was elected Governor, advocated the repeal of personal property taxes, although nothing was done after the election. In Wisconsin there has been an increasing tendency to reduce the number of classes of taxable personal property, but these exemptions have all been for particular reasons.[143]

Before leaving this discussion of American land value taxa-

[143] There are a number of other minor taxation acts that may be briefly mentioned here in passing: In the State of North Dakota, during the Non-Partisan League activities during the war and in the years immediately afterward, there was a pronounced move in the direction of improvement exemption. In 1917, for example, farm improvements were assessed at only one-sixth of the rate for land, land being assessed at 30 per cent of its value, and farm improvements at 5 per cent. This classification was made possible by a constitutional amendment of 1914. In 1919 farm improvements were totally exempt from taxation, city dwelling buildings were exempted 50 per cent, while land, railroads, utilities, and business buildings were assessed at a 100 per cent valuation. This classification, however, has been somewhat changed since. In Minnesota, starting as early as 1897, the land value of the rich iron mines was taxed, and in 1921 a further tax was placed upon ore value. The Tax Act of 1912 in Rhode Island, in addition to separating land from improvement value, placed a very low rate for its municipalities upon intangible personal property.

tion, it is necessary to say a word concerning the single tax colonies, or, as they are termed, "enclaves of economic rent," in the United States.[144] These social experiments are attempts to establish small societies based upon an approximation to single tax principles. There are at present fifteen such colonies,[145] ten of which are located in this country,[146] the first being founded as early as 1895 and the last in 1932. The tradition of the Owenite communities and of the "phalansteries" of Fourier may be considered to have prepared some type of historical background for such coöperative enterprises in the United States. "All the enclaves are identical in the principle of taking the economic rent and using it for the payment of taxes; in all of them, therefore, improvements are exempt; thus, in essence, the Single Tax prevails; but, on the other hand, in no one of them has there been any attempt to pay either the customs or the excise or the national

[144] The best discussion of these "enclaves" is found in *Enclaves of Economic Rent*, an annual publication starting in 1921 and appearing every year since (Harvard, Mass.). It is a collection largely of legal documents, published by Fiske Warren, with an historical description by Charles White Huntington. See also: *Single Tax Year Book*, pp. 66–80; Young, pp. 250–256. In addition, there have appeared a number of newspaper and periodical accounts of these colonies, especially of Fairhope, Alabama, the earliest and largest of the enclaves; some of these are: J. Bellangee, "Fairhope the Forerunner," *Twentieth Century Magazine*, September, 1911, Vol. IV, No. 24, pp. 483–492; and also an article by the same writer in the May–June, 1913, issue of the *Single Tax Review;* an account by E. M. Elgin in the New York *Evening Post*, "A Single Tax Town," Saturday, Dec. 8, 1900, p. 38; "Fairhope, a Single Tax Colony," by Helen C. Bennett in *Collier's*, Vol. XLIX, No. 26, pp. 24, 44–46 (Sept. 14, 1912). See also *American Communities and Coöperative Colonies* (Chicago, 1908), pp. 505–512; and a short bibliography in Young, pp. 250–251, n. 74.

[145] The five enclaves not in the United States are those of Saint Jordi in the Republic of Andorra in the Pyrenees which was formed in 1916; Liéfra, which began its economic career in 1928 in France near Les Fosses in the department of Aube and not far from Clairvaux; Labuan, begun in 1920, on the Island by that name ten miles from the nearest coast of Borneo; Eden, founded in 1932 in Oranienburg near Berlin, Germany, and Canberra, already mentioned, and which also may be included as an enclave.

[146] There is actually a distinction in the enclaves between those which are and those which are not "colonies." The former attracts settlers to the land, while the latter is based upon an extension of territory for those already living in the settlement. (See Fiske Warren in the *Single Tax Year Book*, p. 66.)

income tax, or to atone to enclavians for the artificial increment in the prices of domestic goods due to the 'protective'
policy." [147] The first of these enclaves was established on the
shores of Mobile Bay sixteen miles from the city of Mobile,
in Baldwin County, Alabama, and was called Fairhope. It
was begun in 1895 (although it was incorporated in 1904
and the town itself was not actually founded until 1907) by
a group of single taxers and socialists who had formed an
Industrial Association the year previous in Des Moines, Iowa.
The group consisted of members from Iowa, Minnesota, Ohio,
Pennsylvania, and British Columbia, five families in all, who
purchased the land and established the Fairhope Single Tax
Corporation, which became the landlord of the settlement.
It now has nearly 4,000 acres of land, the town of Fairhope
itself covering about 1,100 acres; the population of the corporation land is at present about seven hundred, that of the
town itself about six hundred. Originally there were a number of socialistic enterprises connected with Fairhope but
they have now largely disappeared. [148] The corporation holds
the land of the colony as a trustee for the entire membership,
land valuations and rentals are determined annually and the
land is leased by the corporation to its members accordingly
(transfer of leases and the sale of improvements are quite
common), and the rentals thus obtained constitute a fund
from which are paid "all taxes levied by the State, county or
township on the property of the corporation or any of its
members held within its jurisdiction, moneys and credits excepted." [149] Road and poll taxes are also paid thus by the corporation. Fairhope is largely a winter resort town, and it
seems to have prospered, [150] despite the fact of some discontent

[147] *Ibid.*
[148] *Ibid.*, p. 69.
[149] From the Fairhope Constitution, 1911, Art. XIV. (Quoted in Young,
pp. 252–253.)
[150] Young, p. 255, and *Single Tax Year Book,* p. 72.

among the members, and despite also the unfavorable attitude of even Henry George himself.[151]

The nine other American enclaves are much smaller but are governed by the same general principles. Arden, Delaware, near the city of Wilmington, was begun in 1900, and was a direct outgrowth of the single tax campaign waged in that State a few years earlier.[152] In 1922 a suburb, Ardentown, was established as a site for future expansion, and developed into a separate colony. Another enclave was formed in 1909 in the town of Harvard, Massachusetts, some thirty miles west of Boston, and was given the name of Tahanto. It started with but two lots, but by 1921 had expanded to about 650 acres. In 1910 Free Acres was founded; it is in the Watchung Mountains of New Jersey, only thirty miles from New York City. Halidon in Maine was established a year later; it is near the city of Westbrook. The next enclave founded was near Ayer, Massachusetts, and is contiguous to new land added to Tahanto, in Harvard; it is called Shakerton and was begun in 1921. The last three American enclaves were formed in 1926, 1927 and 1932; they are Gilpin's Point, in Caroline County, Maryland, near Preston, and about one hundred miles from the enclave of Arden; Trapelo, in the town of Weston, Massachusetts, near both Shakerton and Tahanto, and the newest known as Wall Hill in Mississippi. While the success or failure of such small enterprises, based largely upon the ideal of local community coöperation, can argue little for the applicability of the general concepts of land value taxation or of the single tax, still it is interesting to note that, unlike the many early socialistic communities in the United States, these enclaves have been

<hr />

[151] See *The Standard*, November 2, 1889, pp. 2–3, for George's views regarding any such general application locally of the single tax, and the *Single Tax Year Book*, p. 67, for his specific reaction to Fairhope itself.
[152] *Supra*, pp. 429–430.

most vigorous and seem to have had a continued increase of vitality.

In concluding this discussion of George's influence in the United States, one may point out that, fortunately or unfortunately, the American land value taxation movement has been indissolubly connected with that of the "single tax" itself, a relationship that is by no means present in the general history of land value taxation. Indeed, the whole progress of tax reform itself in this country has been definitely bound up with the work of George's followers.[153] This is not to say, of course, that the responsibility for the very slight measure of such reform is to be laid at the door of the single taxer, but, as if to compensate for his own lack of ponderable success, the Georgist has thrown his weight against the anomalies of our very muddled tax system. That there has not been more actual progress in land value taxation in the United States is obviously a keen disappointment to the followers of Henry George. They feel that his work has never received a proper recognition, especially in academic circles, and that the theory of land value taxation has not been appreciated here as, for example, it has in England. Whether the future of the single tax movement in the United States is to lie in separate political action, or in an op-

[153] For example, "home rule" or local option in taxation has always been linked with single tax in this country. "A survey of the movement for local option in taxation shows that it originated with single taxers and that nearly every agitation for home rule has been initiated and backed by them." (Young, pp. 233–234.) "Local option in taxation turns out to mean, in most cases, local option in exemption." (A quotation from Professor Bullock in Young, p. 235.) "We have now come to look on 'local option in taxation' and 'single tax' as terms practically synonymous." (*Ibid.*, p. 234; a quotation from a member of the Oregon State Tax Commission in 1910.) In the attack upon the stupidities of the general property tax, the single taxers, as Professor Seligman admits, have done "yeoman service." The same is true with the separate assessment of land and improvements, although such separation anticipated the work of George himself. Even in the nonfiscal agitation for direct legislation, the initiative and referendum, single taxers have taken a commanding part. (See Young, pp. 239–240.)

portunistic amalgamation with the socialists or with a "third party" group, or in the educational and propaganda field; whether there is to be continuance of a localized interest in tax reform or a more ambitious attempt to present the full program of George's proposals—questions such as these must first be answered before one can outline the further possible effect of George's work in this country.

DENMARK

The very rapid progress of Danish land value taxation in the last decade is one of the most significant developments of the entire movement.[154] It is particularly significant for the present survey, since such a development seems to have been directly connected with the work of George's followers in Denmark, who practically took command of the Danish agrarian agitation and turned it almost completely into land value taxation channels. And the work in that country is of still further importance in that it is one of the few examples of a sympathetic approach to land value taxation on the part of farmers. The agricultural worker is almost universally suspicious of the land value tax (too often because he confuses it with a straight land tax), and therefore the fact that Denmark, primarily an agricultural, dairy country, has incorporated the principle of land value taxa-

---

[154] Perhaps the best account of the more recent Danish efforts may be found in the files of *Land and Liberty,* London, especially from January, 1925, to May, 1926. The early movement may be traced in the *Single Tax Year Book,* pp. 164–170. See also a collection of papers prepared for the Fourth International Conference to Promote Land Value Taxation and Free Trade, Edinburgh, 1929 (it is interesting to note that the Third Conference, of July, 1926, met at Copenhagen): "The Work for Land Value Taxation and Free Trade in Denmark, 1926 to 1929," by F. Folke and K. J. Kristensen; "Danish Agrarian and Social Evolution and the Influence of Henry George's Ideas Thereon," by Professor Jakob E. Lange; "Social Democrats and the Henry George Policy: The Political Victory in Denmark," by Sophus Berthelsen; and "Land Valuation in Denmark," by K. J. Kristensen. The various economic periodicals also contain current accounts of the Danish movement.

tion into its legislation is at least partial testimony to its applicability in an agricultural society.

A land value tax was definitely made a part of Denmark's revenue system in 1922, but there had been years of active work on the part of George's followers before that time, work which had prepared the way for such legislation. As early as 1886 *Progress and Poverty* was translated into Norwegian by Veggo Ullmann; in the same year *Social Problems* and in the following year *Protection or Free Trade* were also translated into that language. However, it was not in Norway [155] but in Denmark that a single tax agitation was started. The work of Ullmann himself in Denmark, and also of Johan Hansson, a Swedish liberal, and of Professor Jakob E. Lange, Sophus Berthelsen, and Arvid Jarnefelt, early Danish converts, began the movement for land value taxation. In 1889 a Social Reform Union was founded to teach the principles of George, and in 1902 there was formed a Henry George League.

The first significant result of this pioneer work was the now famous Köge resolution of November 8, 1902. This was formulated at a meeting of the Sealand Husmaend ("housemen," or small holders) Society and urged the adoption of complete free trade and of land value taxation. Similar resolutions were passed at other meetings of the "housemen," and it began to be apparent that the ancient Danish agrarian movement was becoming dominated by the principle of land value taxation.[156] The sympathy toward free trade is, of course, readily understood in an agricultural country such as Denmark. A political step was the next important move. Stimulated by donations from the Fels

---

[155] In Norway and Sweden there has been little success in the direction of land value taxation; there is some single tax activity in these countries (see the *Single Tax Year Book*, pp. 171–175) but nothing definite has as yet resulted.

[156] See Lange, *op. cit.*

Fund in 1909–1910, definite political action was attempted and for a number of years unsuccessful attempts were made in the national legislature to introduce some measure of land value taxation. Finally, at the very end of 1915, the followers of George were successful in pushing through a measure providing for the separation of improvements from land for valuation purposes, and, more important, providing also for the immediate valuation of all the land of Denmark. Provisional valuations were made the following year.[157] In 1920 more acceptable valuation machinery was established, which made a valuation for that year, and also in 1924 and 1927. Valuations are to be made every five years following this last date.[158]

This valuation provision gave the land value taxationists a strong foothold and in the succeeding years they managed to influence the Social Democrats, the Danish Marxist political organization, to turn at least a degree in the direction of Henry George.[159] The final result was that on August 7, 1922, the Danish Government enacted a small national land value tax. Its rate was 1.5 per thousand (1.5 mills) on the capital (selling) unimproved value of land; this rate is equivalent, comparing it, for example, with the English Finance Act of 1931, to about ⅓d. in the pound. In addition, all improvements under approximately $2,700 (10,000 kronen) were exempt from taxation, while other improvements were taxed at the old real estate rate of 1.1 per thousand. On March 31, 1926, this national land value tax was supplemented by an act providing for the local taxation of land values at a higher rate than the tax on improvements. The rates of this local land value tax vary from 6 to 35 per thousand in the rural districts, but the rate is not to rise above 7½ per thousand

---

[157] Trial valuations, however, had already been made in 1911 and 1912.
[158] Kristensen, *op. cit.*
[159] Berthelsen, *op. cit.*

in the city of Copenhagen. Finally, beginning in 1930, there has been a pronounced move in Denmark for a land value increment tax, and also for complete local rating upon land values; nothing, however, has definitely been enacted along this line up to the date of this writing.

It will be seen, therefore, that while the history of actual land value taxation in Denmark covers only a brief period and is limited as yet to two legislative acts, there can be no doubt of the sympathetic reception, in this country of farmers, of the principle elaborated by Henry George. The results of such a fiscal policy have been glowingly portrayed by the adherents of land value taxation,[160] although, considering the very low rate of the tax and the short interval of time involved, such a correlation may seem a little rash.[161] However, it cannot be denied that there seems to be little dissatisfaction with the tax in Denmark, and neither can it be denied that the favorable reaction of this rural community appears to contradict some of the stock attacks upon a land value tax. This fact, together with the direct influence of George's work upon the movement, make the Danish land value legislation a notable contribution to the significance of economic theory.

GERMANY

". . . An increase of the value of land arising without the application of labor or capital to property shall inure to the benefit of the community as a whole." This statement in the German Weimar Constitution [162] is perhaps the first and only expression of the theory of "unearned increment" to be found

---

[160] See, for example, an article by Abel Brink in *Land and Freedom,* New York, January–February, 1932.

[161] As has been the case throughout, there can be no attempt in this brief exposition to analyze or even present any of the results, favorable or unfavorable, that have been attributed to the land value tax.

[162] Section V, Article 155.

in any national organic law. It is, of course, to be understood as one of the programs of Social Democracy, but it
must also be placed against a background of German land
reform that anticipates the work of Henry George himself.
A discussion of the land value taxation movement in Germany has been reserved for the last because that movement
has seemed somewhat independent of the general tradition.[163]
For one thing, the theory of such taxation has received
particular development in Germany, and so, although there
had been contact with the teachings of the English classical
economists, the approach to "unearned increment" and
specifically the elaboration of a "benefit" theory of taxation
appear to have been largely the work of German theorists
themselves. Moreover, the actual local and later the Imperial increment taxes in Germany must be traced not simply
to such a theoretical stimulus but also, and perhaps of more
importance, to certain peculiar conditions in the development of the German municipalities.

The work of the early German "Bodenreformers," men
such as Gossen, Samter and Stamm, has been mentioned in
another connection.[164] These anticipators of George definitely
prepared a theoretical foundation for German land value
taxation. Especially significant was the name of Professor
Adolph Wagner, whose work later in the '70s,[165] directed

[163] For accounts of German land value taxation see: Scheftel, Chap. IV
(Bibliography, pp. 468–473, 483); Single Tax Year Book, pp. 145–159; Single
Tax Review, March–April, 1912 (Special Number for Germany); Professor
Seligman's article on the German increment taxes in the Political Science
Quarterly, Vol. XXVII, December, 1912, pp. 577–604; articles by Anna
Youngman in the Quarterly Journal of Economics, Vol. XXVII, November,
1912, and February, 1913, pp. 151–201 and 329–372; "The Valuation and
Taxation of Land in Germany," by Dr. Alex Paletta, a pamphlet prepared
for the Fourth International Conference to Promote Land Value Taxation
and Free Trade, Edinburgh, 1929. These references, as has been the case
in each instance, are merely suggested samples out of a much larger body
of material.

[164] See supra, pp. 214–215, n. 104.

[165] Die Abschaffung des privaten Grundeigentums (Leipzig, 1870) and
Rede über die soziale Frage (Berlin, 1872) contain the essence of his theory.
See also his more ambitious volumes: Lehr- und Handbuch der Politischen
Oekonomie and Grundlagen der Volkswirtschaft. The work of Alex-

largely to the development of his "socio-political" theory, which argued for the employment of taxation as a means to correct the unequal distribution of wealth, and also for a "social benefit" justification of taxation, was largely responsible for the spread in Germany of the "Umsatzsteuer." [166] As early as 1881 *Progress and Poverty* was translated into German, and the immediate result was the incorporation of George's work into the German tradition and the rise of a new group of Bodenreformers led by Wagner himself, Adolph Damaschke, Michael Flürscheim, and others.[167] There is thus a striking parallel between George's relation to the English classical economists and his contact with the German land reform theorists; in both cases there was an independent development of theory which later, however, developed into an amalgamation, and so made possible the presentation of George's concepts along with a body of existing doctrine.[168]

Yet the immediate stimulus for a land value tax in Germany was not so much this theoretical background, although its directive influence cannot be doubted,[169] as it was the enormous appreciation of land value in German cities and the resulting outburst of land speculation.[170] The need for revenue to meet the great municipal budgets and the realization that urban landowners were not contributing a proportionate share, were the motives that were directly responsible for the increasing interest in land value taxation. Germany's "Umsatzsteuer" has already been mentioned, but

ander Meyer also may be mentioned, especially his "Das Princip der Communalsteuern," in *Preussische Jahrbücher*, Vol. XVIII, Berlin, 1866, pp. 166 ff.

[166] This was a levy collected upon the transfer of real property. It may be traced back to the collection of certain ancient fees. (Scheftel, pp. 125–127.)

[167] *Supra*, pp. 214–215, n. 104.

[168] *Supra*, p. 200 ff.

[169] "For popularizing the principles underlying the increment tax, the propaganda of the 'Bodenreformer' (Single Taxers), since their organization in 1898, has exerted a strong influence . . . The widespread influence of the 'Bodenreformer' may be gathered from the fact that in 1910 the number of societies was 542, and the membership about 750,000 persons." (Scheftel, p. 143.)

[170] *Ibid.*, pp. 128 ff.

a much more important move was the unsuccessful attempt by the city of Bremen in 1874 to substitute capital or selling value for productive value in determining land valuation. An act providing for such a change was passed and, although it was repealed four years later because of valuation difficulties, a precedent had been established. Then, in 1893, came "the epoch-making reform in local taxation," the Prussian "Kommunalabgabengesetz." This was an act providing for a measure of local option in taxation, and it prepared the way for land value taxation, negatively, by forbidding the localities to levy income taxes or certain excise duties, and positively, by permitting the levying of special land taxes.[171]

The next important step did not occur in Germany itself but in the German Chinese colony of Kiao-chau in 1898. Designed to check the inevitable land speculation that followed the marked rise in land value after Germany took possession of the territory the year before, the Kiao-chau land value tax seems to have been purely opportunistic and to have had little connection with any economic theory, much less with the work of Henry George.[172] The tax provisions were threefold: There was to be an annual direct land value tax of 6 per cent. In addition, there was a 33⅓ per cent increment tax levied when the land was sold; this, however, was a tax on the total increment, or net profit, of the sale and not levied on the land value itself, and therefore a 6 per cent exemption was deducted from the gross increment as an allowance for the improved value. Finally, there was the usual land sales tax or Umsatzsteuer. These taxes, however,

---

[171] Scheftel, pp. 124–125.

[172] However, Dr. W. E. Macklin, an American single taxer residing in China and the translator of *Progress and Poverty* into Chinese, states that through his indirect efforts Dr. W. Schrameier, the first Land Commissioner of Kiao-chau and the man largely responsible for the land taxes, became familiar with George's book, and attempted to put it into partial operation. (*Single Tax Year Book,* p. 192.)

were not successful in checking land speculation, and so in 1906, following an act passed in 1903, the annual land value tax was increased wherever the land remained undeveloped. The increase was to 9 per cent for unimproved land, with an additional 3 per cent increase every three years that the land remained unworked, until a rate of 24 per cent was reached. When land was built upon, the tax reverted to the original 6 per cent.

There is little evidence to show that this colonial experiment in taxation had any direct influence upon the local German increment taxes of the following years.[173] It is felt rather that the conditions mentioned above, i. e., the rapid industrial expansion of the German municipalities which brought about increased land values, great land speculation, and also the large city budgets, together with the background of economic theory and of the more tangible "Umsatzsteuer" and the "Kommunalabgabengesetz," provided a sufficient stimulus for the levy,[174] beginning in 1904, of the local taxes on land value increment. In that year the city of Frankfurt-am-Main inaugurated the first attempt at such taxation. This first "Zuwachssteuer" was really a combination of three separate taxes. There was the old transfer tax of 2 per cent on the selling price; then an additional progressive transfer tax which discriminated against unimproved land; and thirdly, the more specific tax on value increment.[175] The increment tax was a graduated tax on the difference between the purchase price and the selling price of land, provided that the increment was not less than 15 per cent and also that the land changed hands within twenty years; additions to the

[173] Scheftel, pp. 134 ff.; 184.

[174] In addition there was the tradition of the long-established German "Erbaurecht," a leasing system resulting from the fact that in Germany much land is owned by the Government itself, i. e., the States and the municipalities; consequently, there has been definite regulation of the use of that land which is leased out to private individuals.

[175] Scheftel, pp. 133–134.

purchase price were made to compensate for permanent improvements and also for any outlay of capital. Thus, while the increment tax was based upon selling price and not upon actual land value, these exemptions for improvements were attempts to place the burden of the tax upon the increment of land value itself.[176] The progressive scale of rates varied from a 2 per cent tax for a 15 to 20 per cent increment to 5 per cent of the increment for a 30 to 35 per cent rise in value, with 1 per cent of tax for every additional 5 per cent of increment after that until the maximum rate of a 25 per cent rate was reached.[177] This "Zuwachssteuer" or "Wertzuwachssteuer" of Frankfurt-am-Main [178] was followed in the next year by similar taxes in Cologne and Gelsenkirchen, and then by increment taxes in Essen, Dortmund, Gross-Lichterfelde, Pankow, and Weissensee in 1906; Breslau, Hessen, and Kiel in 1907; Hamburg (1908), Berlin (1910), and a great number of others, until, by 1911, 652 local German governments, comprising about one-quarter of the population of the Empire, had enacted the principle of land value increment taxation into law.[179]

In 1911 there was passed the "Reichszuwachssteuer," or Imperial Increment Tax. This virtually repealed the local taxes and substituted instead a Federal increment tax; the local governments, however, were to receive 40 per cent of the revenue, the Central Government, 50 per cent, and the State 10 per cent, for administering and levying the tax. It will not be necessary to describe the complicated details and also the difficulties of this imperial tax.[180] Perhaps the most interesting part of the Federal law was the very elaborate and com-

[176] "The system of scientific valuation of land apart from improvements has made little progress in Germany, even though the land and house taxes have long been separately assessed." (Scheftel, p. 132.)
[177] Ibid., p. 144.
[178] Oetzsch and Helbersdorf, small communes in Saxony, are believed to have preceded Frankfurt in levying such taxes. (Scheftel, p. 144, n. 1.)
[179] Ibid., p. 144.
[180] Ibid., pp. 146 ff.

plex system of exemptions and compensations directed to separating the increase in value due to the efforts of labor and capital from the "unearned increment" [181] of land value.[182] The tax, as was the case with the local levies, was graduated, progressing from a 10 per cent tax if the increment did not exceed 10 per cent of the purchase price to as much as a 30 per cent rate for an increment above 290 per cent. However, after two years of experimenting and because of the great difficulties arising from administering the imperial tax,[183] the increment tax was relegated again to the localities, a change that is held to be a victory for the "benefit" theory of taxation.[184] The following year brought the war and the end of any further Federal efforts.

Despite the constitutional reference to "unearned increment" mentioned at the opening of this section, there has been no national attempt to introduce any measure of land value taxation in the German republic.[185] According to the Weimar constitution the taxation of land is left to the German States, but the only State that has availed itself of this privilege in order to tax land values is Anhalt.[186] In fact, only Hessen, Lippe, and Lübeck, in addition to Anhalt, use capital value as the sole basis for land taxation. The other States rely upon a value based upon productivity or a mixed system of capital and product value.[187] And the one tangible effort of the German Government in this whole matter, the

[181] "The imperial law declares that the tax is to fall on the *unearned* increment ('der ohne Zutun des Eigentümers entstanden ist'); *Reichszuwachssteuergesetz vom 14 Februar, 1911*, Sec. 1. In this connection it is interesting to point out that in the British Parliament the proposal to call the increment *unearned* was promptly dismissed." (*Ibid.*, p. 141, n. 4.)

[182] Scheftel, pp. 146 ff.

[183] *Ibid.*, pp. 150 ff.

[184] *Ibid.*, p. 178.

[185] It may be noted that in December, 1919, the city of Vienna enacted a land value tax measure, but it was overshadowed and made of negligible importance by the house rent taxes and the indirect taxes which were introduced at the same time.

[186] See Paletta pamphlet *(op. cit.)*, pp. 6–7.

[187] *Ibid.*, pp. 3–6.

Imperial Valuation Law of August 10, 1925, paradoxically enough, did not provide for the separation of improvement value from land value itself.

Germany's venture into land value taxation thus presents an interesting example of the fusion of economic theory with the fiscal and social requirements of a specific situation. The tradition of the "unearned increment" concept had occupied an important and largely an original place in German political economy, but it was a more immediate municipal problem that translated such theory into the increment tax legislation.[188] Henry George plays an indirect part in this German experiment. Just as with England, his work was not an original stimulus but instead came to be accepted as an integral part of a rather respectable economic tradition; his writings therefore proved to be an added inspiration, as was again the case in England, for the efforts of the German land reformers.

Before leaving this discussion of the various movements in the direction of land value taxation, a word must be said about the agitation in South America.[189] Because of the recognized trend of South America to the culture of France, it is most interesting to see that there was an early Physiocratic influence upon Latin-American thinkers. The most notable expression of that influence is to be found in Argentina in the work of its first President, Bernardino Rivadavia. His agrarian law in 1826, which was in force for two years, established the principle that public land was not to be sold, but was to be leased, with the rent accruing to the Government. In 1882, Dr. Andres Lamas of Montevideo, "the

---

[188] The results of this local taxation are held to be approximately the same as those of the Australasian and Canadian experiments. While the promised social effects, e. g., decreased rent or a significant weakening of land speculation, did not seem to materialize, still the tax as a fiscal instrument has been largely approved. (Scheftel, pp. 179–184.)

[189] See *Single Tax Year Book*, pp. 180–187.

South American Henry George," published *The Agrarian Legislation of Rivadavia,* in which he upheld and elaborated the principle of the social collection of land values. There is little doubt that he knew nothing of the work of George. The work of Dr. Herrera y Reissig in 1913, *El Impuesto Territorial,* was perhaps the most important step in popularizing the concepts of Rivadavia and George, and after 1914 there was a decided single tax agitation in Argentina; one of the most important results of that movement was a partial fusion of socialists and single taxers with the socialists emphasizing land value taxation in their programs. As early as 1906, however, the city of Buenos Aires had separated improvements from land for valuation purposes, and the province of Cordoba, in addition, has actually levied a land value tax. However, if Argentina led the way in land value taxation theory, other South American countries have advanced further in the actual practice of such taxation. In Uruguay, with the exception of the city and department of Montevideo, there is a large land value tax, and in Montevideo itself there is a separate assessment of land and improvements. In Brazil there has been a recent revaluation of the land of Rio de Janeiro, and in the city of Garibaldi improvements are exempt from taxation; Garibaldi is in the State of Rio Grande do Sul.[190] The Brazilian State of São Paulo has also investigated favorably the land value taxation of Uruguay.

There is little further to mention, in this exposition, of actual land value taxation in other countries, although the record of other single tax activities throughout the world will be found in the *Single Tax Year Book.* Little can be said about the Soviet approach to the land problem, since it is too inextricably connected with the general theory of communism.

[190] See also the New York *Herald Tribune* of December 6, 1931, Foreign News Section.

George's Influence upon Later Thinkers

A discussion of ideational influence must necessarily remain either partially in the realm of conjecture or else be limited to the citing of actual expressions of indebtedness. In presenting George's effect upon later figures in political and economic thought,[191] it seems best to choose the latter procedure despite the fact that it may result in nothing but a sketchy catalogue of isolated quotations. The difficulties of attempting any less concrete approach would hardly justify the effort. Those difficulties have already been noted in discussing George's influence upon the various specific measures of land value taxation; it is almost impossible, in most cases, to distinguish the thread of his work from the fabric of economic theory into which it so neatly worked, or to determine the degree of independence and "spontaneous generation" of the different fiscal experiments. To essay, therefore, an exposition not simply of George's effect upon the tangible legislative acts of land value taxation, but upon the much more imponderable "stream of thought" that flowed after him, would seem a little too ambitious for a chapter such as the present one. This is not to say, of course, that no difficulties present themselves in limiting the discussion to the actual mention of George's work by later writers. There is always the danger of attributing too much, or even too little, to such sporadic statements, especially since many of these expressions have been, if not denied, at least somewhat at variance with the more integrated philosophy of their authors. A more technical difficulty is that of verifying such testimonials. There is pamphlet after pamphlet issued by

[191] This present section will not repeat a discussion of George's influence upon the English Fabians, or upon socialism in general, or upon the theorists and legislators responsible for the many acts of land value taxation. It will confine itself to those figures, chiefly American, who have not already been mentioned in other connections.

different single tax organizations which contain lists of quotations illustrating the effect of George's concepts upon more recent thinkers, but only a very small percentage of such statements permit corroboration. Single tax writers would perform a very great service to those interested in the work of Henry George if they would indicate more often the source of their quotations. Therefore, while this section may appear entirely too brief and sketchy and even incoherent, still it is felt that the following treatment of George's influence upon the men who have succeeded him may offer the least serious difficulties.

Perhaps the most spectacular and complete example of a Henry George convert was Tolstoi. The direct influence of George's teachings is found all throughout the work of Tolstoi; [192] there are, however, several specific statements which epitomize his thought. One of the most important of these is to be found in an article which first appeared in the London *Times* of August 1, 1905; it was written the month before by Tolstoi at Yasnaya Poliana. The translation for the *Times* was the work of V. Tchertkoff and I. F. M., and the article itself was later printed many times in American newspapers

[192] The most complete anthology of Tolstoi's expressions of his indebtedness to George and of his general opinion on the land question may be found in a pamphlet, "Tolstoi on Land and Slavery," issued by the Land Values Publication Department, London (no date). This collection includes unequivocal quotations from the following writings of Tolstoi: *Resurrection* (especially in the speeches of Prince Nekhlúdoff); *The Slavery of our Times; Some Social Remedies; The Confessions; What Shall We Do; The One Thing Needful; The Fall and Rise of Hell; The Root of Evil; An Appeal to Russians; How Shall We Escape; The Kingdom of God; What Is Art? The Meaning of the Russian Revolution; The Only Means; Letters on War;* and the Introduction to George's *Social Problems.* In a special letter written for this collection (March 31, 1909, Yasnaya Poliana) Tolstoi states: "Henry George is especially to be appreciated by those who profess Christianity in some sense, for not only are the foundations of his teachings but also his methods truly Christian. . . . In this lies the essence of George's teaching. However those, who need to do so, may endeavor to conceal his teachings, it is so clear and indisputable that it cannot but be recognized by mankind. God help you. On your side are justice, reason, love. On your side is God, and therefore you cannot but be successful."

and journals.[193] "A Great Iniquity" is the title of the essay, and more than four pages out of the thirty-eight are direct quotations from the works of George. Tolstoi's appreciation of the American reformer may be indicated by passages such as these:

Characteristically was this [i. e., neglect] the fate of the activity of the remarkable man who appeared towards the end of the last century—Henry George—who devoted his great mental powers to the elucidation of the injustice and cruelty of landed property and to the indication of the means of correcting this evil by the help of the state of organization now existing amongst all nations. He did this in his books, articles and speeches with such extraordinary power and lucidity that no man without preconceived ideas could, after reading his books, fail to agree with his arguments, and to see that no reforms can improve the condition of the people until this fundamental injustice be destroyed, and that the means he proposes for its abolition are rational, just and expedient . . . (Pp. 15–16.)

The chief weapon against the teaching of Henry George was that which is always used against irrefutable and self-evident truths. This method, which is still being applied in relation to George, was that of hushing up . . . (P. 17.)

People do not argue with the teaching of George, they simply do not know it. And it is impossible to do otherwise with his teaching, for he who becomes acquainted with it cannot but agree . . . (P. 18.)

. . . The method of solving the land problem has been elaborated by Henry George to such a degree of perfection that, *under the existing State organization and compulsory taxation*, it is impossible to invent any other better, more just, practical, and peaceful solution . . . And I think that Henry George is right, that the removal of the sin of landed property is near, that the movement called forth by Henry George was the last birth-throe, and that the birth is on the point of taking place; the liberation of men from the sufferings they have so long borne must now be realized. (Pp. 37–38.)

[193] The text and pages from which these quotations are taken are those of a reprint of the article from *The Public* (Chicago) of August 19, 1905; the reprint is under the auspices of the Joseph Fels International Commission.

It is perhaps not necessary to make any additional quotations from the writings of Tolstoi which deal with the work of George.[194] They all contain the same almost worshipful reverence for Henry George, the same essentially religious interpretation (in this, Tolstoi read the American very correctly), and the same feeling that the single tax offered a compromise, at least as far as present-day social organization was concerned, between the paternalism of political socialism and the ideal of a restrictionless Christian communism. The land problem was the great problem for Tolstoi's Russia, and George, therefore, was for Tolstoi the great economist.

From the Russia of Tolstoi to the China of the republican revolution is a far cry, but this "compromise" appeal of George, the compromise, that is, between outright socialism and the theory of democratic individualism, was one of the directing forces behind the work of Sun Yat Sen. For one thing, he assisted Dr. W. E. Macklin in translating *Progress and Poverty* into Chinese, although his interest in the American economist was of an earlier date, and throughout the program of the first Nationalist Government it was the work of George and not that of the socialists that provided the stimulus for attempted economic reform. This influence of George is recognized very clearly by Wang Ching-wei, formerly the head of the Kuomintang and the direct successor of Dr. Sun Yat Sen himself, in an interview with Paul Blanshard: [195]

We are not Communists . . . I want to assure the American public that the Kuomintang and the Communist Party have come to a parting of the ways . . . Sun Yat Sen, as you know, was greatly influenced by your American radical, Henry George, but

[194] There is a good bit of material concerning this influence of George upon Tolstoi; several references that may be mentioned here are: "Tolstoi Looks at America," by Albert Parry in *Asia*, November, 1930, Vol. XXX, No. 11, pp. 772–777; *The Life of Tolstoi*, by Aylmer Maude (New York, Dodd Mead, 1917), Vol. II, pp. 474, 628; articles by Tolstoi in *Land Values* (London), Vol. XXII, pp. 136 ff., and in the *Review of Reviews*, Vol. XVII, (1898), pp. 73–74.

[195] In the New York *Times*, Sunday, September 11, 1927; p. 5 of feature section.

he was never a Communist. His economic program, which is ours, means three things: Henry George's method of assessing land, definite laws against monopoly under private ownership, and Government ownership of large public utilities. We propose to realize this program without violence and without confiscation.

The one-time popularity of Henry George with the American "liberal" [196] of the late nineteenth and early twentieth centuries may definitely be traced to that same fusion of economic radicalism and Jeffersonian democracy that was so characteristic of his thought. It was George's attempt to found a social program of reconstruction upon the "natural rights" and individualism of early American political theory which appealed to that "liberal crowd" described so accurately by Frederic C. Howe.[197] In the general atmosphere of that great liberal reform era of the Bryan and post-Bryan days, George's work was a most welcome visitor, and almost every member of that liberal "crowd," Hamlin Garland, Lincoln Steffens,[198] Brand Whitlock, Clarence Darrow, Newton D. Baker, Herbert Quick, and a host of others, was at least a partial disciple of George.

Howe, of course, was perhaps the most complete and deliberate single taxer of that liberal group; his numerous works on land value taxation [199] and his persistent advocacy of George's principles made him one of the leaders of the single tax movement. But most of the others were equally enthusi-

[196] Further discussion of George's influence upon later thinkers will be confined to the United States, since his most important foreign followers have already been indicated in other places.
[197] The Confessions of a Reformer (New York, Scribner's, 1925).
[198] His recent Autobiography (New York, Harcourt Brace, 1931) gives perhaps the most vivid and complete picture of this "liberal reform" era. It may be mentioned that Steffens, along with Howe, Mrs. Carrie Chapman Catt, Charles H. Ingersoll, and others, was a member of the Fels Fund Commission. However, in the autobiography Steffens gives little mention to George himself; see Vol. II, p. 475.
[199] See especially: Privilege and Democracy in America (New York, Scribner's, 1910); The High Cost of Living (New York, Scribner's, 1917); The City, the Hope of Democracy (New York, Scribner's, 1905); and The Modern City and Its Problems (New York, Scribner's, 1915).

astic Georgists. Brand Whitlock's appreciation of George may be found in several of his works,[200] and especially in this report of a conversation with Howe during a walk in Brussels shortly after the war: " 'I have gone through every political philosophy,' he [Whitlock] said. 'I can see nothing in Socialism. The philosophy of Henry George of a free state in which the resources of the earth will be opened up to use is the only political philosophy that has ever commanded my adherence. But the world is not interested in such a simple reform. It wants too much government, too much regulating, too much policing. And it may never change.' " [201] This is perhaps the best expression of the appeal that the American liberal found in the writings of George.

It is interesting to remember that the now very public Clarence Darrow was one of these brilliant young liberals, and one of the most sincere admirers of George. In an article in Luke North's *Everyman*,[202] Darrow paid this great compliment:

. . . He [George] wrote a good book, a profound book, the first book on political economy—and I think I am safe in saying the last book on political economy—that people may ever read . . . Henry George did believe in 'natural rights' but his great arguments are based upon the great law which permeates all life— expediency . . . Henry George was one of the real prophets of the world; one of the seers of the world . . . I won't mention them all —Moses, Jesus, Goethe, Henry George . . . [They] were not the wisest men of the age; they were men with an ideal and with a purpose; they were men filled with the divine spark which alone can illumine the world . . . Henry George's work was the work

---

[200] See especially *On the Enforcement of Law in Cities* (Indianapolis, Bobbs Merrill, 1913), and *Forty Years of It* (New York, Appleton, 1925.)
[201] *Confessions of a Reformer*, p. 189.
[202] September–October, 1913, Vol. IX, Nos. 7–8, pp. 20 ff. (This was the report of an address delivered by Darrow before the Chicago Single Tax Club, September 19, 1913.) However, Darrow's recent autobiography gives little sympathetic attention to George; in this it agrees with that of Lincoln Steffens.

of the philosopher, of the dreamer, of the author, of the prophet, and those men never are and never can be politicians. And I think no one knew it better than he . . . Before Henry George learned to write or to speak he had something to say, and he had that something clearly in his own mind so he could make himself understand it before he tried to make any one else understand it . . .

Another of the "crowd" was Newton D. Baker, who received his reform education at the hands of Cleveland's beloved Tom L. Johnson,[203] the city's famous mayor and congressman. As late as 1914, Baker avowed himself a firm single taxer, and hoped that he "might some day see with the vision of his master, Tom L. Johnson."[204] Hamlin Garland and Herbert Quick represented in literature this individualistic, liberal approach, and both were complete exponents of the proposals of George.[205] Bryan himself con-

[203] Men such as Tom L. Johnson and Louis F. Post do not have to be discussed in an exposition such as this. Their work with Henry George, their love and reverence for him, their lifelong efforts to promote the adoption of some measure of the single tax, are perhaps so well known that it would be indeed out of place to treat them as figures "influenced" by George. For an example of the attitude with which they approached George, see particularly Johnson's *My Story* (New York, Huebsch, 1911).

[204] Quoted from a statement by Baker at the fourth Annual Fels Commission and Single Tax Conference, Washington, January, 1914; see *Single Tax Year Book*, p. 25.

A number of Woodrow Wilson's Cabinet members, particularly Franklin K. Lane and William B. Wilson, were at times unambiguous Georgist converts. Woodrow Wilson himself stated: "All the country needs is a new and sincere body of thought in politics, coherently, distinctly, and boldly uttered by men who are sure of their ground. The power of men like Henry George seems to me to mean that; and why should not men who have sane purposes avail themselves of this thirst and enthusiasm for better, higher, more hopeful purposes in politics than either of the present moribund parties can give?" (From *Life and Letters* by Ray Stannard Baker; New York, Doubleday Page, 1927–1931.) Judge Samuel Seabury, now very much in the public eye in New York City, was one of the fervent young men that George gathered about him; he ran for office several times in New York, always receiving the whole-hearted support of single taxers.

[205] See especially Hamlin Garland's article "Memories of Henry George" in *The Libertarian*, Vol. V, 1925, pp. 279–283; here he tells of his conversion to George's principles and of his complete acceptance of them; and the conclusion of Herbert Quick's autobiography, *One Man's Life* (Indianapolis, Bobbs, Merrill, 1925; pp. 400 ff.), in which he points to George as "the

tinually professed his admiration for George, and stated upon one occasion that "it has been said that it marks an epoch in history when God lets loose a thinker in the world. And such a thinker was Henry George . . ." [206]

This "liberal" movement of the early twentieth century contained many other figures appreciative of the work of Henry George. The George dinner just mentioned, at which William Jennings Bryan spoke, included, among others, speakers such as Ernest Thompson Seton, Edwin Markham [207] and William Lloyd Garrison, the younger,[208] and provoked expressions of sympathy from men like Norman Hapgood, Bird S. Coler, George Harvey, Richard Le Gallienne and Albert Shaw. Samuel Gompers,[209] Poultney Bigelow, [210] Charles Francis Adams,[211] Lyman Abbott, Elbert Hubbard, Justice Brandeis, Felix Adler, former Governor L. F. C. Garvin of Rhode Island, John Moody and William Marion Reedy might also be cited as products of that background which welcomed the work of George.[212] Even the Progressive movement of

mind which will make a success" of our civilization, and states that on every vital point he agrees with him. (P. 407.)

[206] *The Public*, February 4, 1905, No. 357, pp. 202–204; from a speech by Bryan, "Equal Opportunity and Moral Truth," at a *Progress and Poverty* anniversary dinner, Hotel Astor, New York City, January 24, 1905.

[207] Markham, along with Garland and Quick, and also Bliss Carman, Luke North and the late Edmund Vance Cooke, represent the "democratic" acceptance of George by the liberal "crowd's" literary figures.

[208] Garrison, like Tom Johnson and Louis F. Post, was so intimate a follower of George that he perhaps should not be included so casually along with other less earnest single taxers.

[209] See his appreciation of George in *Seventy Years of Life and Labor* (New York, Dutton, 1925).

[210] See his *Seventy Summers* (New York, Longmans Green, 1925).

[211] See especially an article in the *Outlook*, Vol. LXVI, No. 16, December 15, 1900, pp. 911 ff.

[212] The only names that are being used here are, of course, those which in some degree have been verified as at least partial sympathizers of George. There are many lists of names which are not included because they cannot be substantiated; see especially a pamphlet put out by the Joseph Fels Fund (no date), "Tentative List of Prominent Americans Who Endorse the Single Tax and Those Who Favor the Taxation of Land Values Rather than of Improvements," which contains some four hundred names, most of them in *Who's Who*; and also "Opinions of Public Men on the Life and Work of

a later date still could point to him as an inspiration.[213]

It is much more difficult to speak of the interest of the contemporary liberal in the work of Henry George. There is no need to point out that, whether for good or for evil, the more recent radical leans to socialism of some complexion and away from the "democracy" and "individualism" that characterized the former American liberal. In fact, the name "liberal" itself is fast becoming a connotation for something old-fashioned. Hence, there has been a corresponding neglect or half-hearted patronizing of George's economic philosophy among the present leaders of social and economic reform, and even where his work has been thoroughly appreciated it is usually given a subordinate position in a larger and more socialistic program; that has been true, for example, with such men as Norman Thomas, John Haynes Holmes, and others. The approach of the *New Republic* and the *Nation* represents the prevailing tendency that refuses to consider men like George as anything but benighted democrats who believed in a mediæval doctrine of natural rights and individual liberty. However, there is a handful of liberal-radicals who, if not single taxers, at least recognize the validity and significance of George's economic program. The former *Freeman,* with men like Francis Neilson, Albert Jay Nock, and the group of brilliant essayists that gathered about them, and then the *New Freeman,* with writers such as Paul Blanshard (although he is a complete socialist), represent this more sympathetic approach to the philosophy of land

Henry George," a pamphlet published by the Dr. Mary D. Hussey Fund, New York (no date).

[213] Amos Pinchot, in particular, was sympathetic to the taxation of land values, and this was the opinion of Theodore Roosevelt: ". . . the burden of taxation should be so shifted as to put the weight of land taxation upon the unearned rise in value of the land itself rather than upon the improvements, the buildings; the effort being to prevent the undue rise of rent." (From an article, "The Progressive Party," in *The Century,* October, 1913, Vol. LXXXVI (n. s., Vol. LXIV), pp. 834–835.) In this article Roosevelt also favored municipal self-government in taxation.

value taxation. Of course it is not being suggested that, outside of the ranks of single taxers themselves, there is any strong affection for George among contemporary radicals. The fact seems to be, instead, that perhaps the most momentous question that the single taxer will have to answer within the very near future is whether he should continue to make his appeal to the traditional "liberal," who has up to now supplied the bulk of his strength in this country, or whether he should throw in his lot, at least for opportunistic reasons, with the gathering strength of a more organized "opposition" group.

In the academic world of political economy the work of George has been received with little favor. Too often there has been a rather pronouced neglect of the implications of his thought, but even when they have been appreciated it has been seldom with sympathy. This attitude, however, holds only for George's "single tax" proposals; the concept of taxing land values has itself met with little opposition, and George's well-formulated attacks upon the anomalies of our present tax system have been gratefully received even by such a severe critic as Professor Seligman. Complete single taxers among academic economists are very few; Professor Harry Gunnison Brown of the University of Missouri is perhaps the most important figure of such a group.[214] But advocates of some degree of land value taxation include many of the most important figures in American economics. The statements of the late Professor Davenport have been mentioned before.[215] Professor Irving Fisher writes:

[214] Others who may be mentioned are: Professor Glenn E. Hoover of Mills College, Dean William H. Dinkins of Selma University, and Professor Joseph M. Klamon of Washington University. Outside of the field of economics itself, Professor Frederick W. Roman, formerly of New York University, may be mentioned. There are, of course, a number of other complete single taxers among academic economists, but it is perhaps not in order to list them, especially since verification is not always available.

[215] *Supra*, pp. 105, n. 30; 107, n. 33; 156–157.

I cannot agree that land value should be the sole source of public revenue. Nevertheless, premising that so important a change should not be made abruptly, I favor the gradual reduction so far as possible of taxes on the products of labor and taking instead the economic rent of bare land.[216]

Professor T. N. Carver of Harvard: "I favor a special tax on land values in so far as these values are the result of location rather than of fertility . . . Location value seems to me to be a good subject for special taxation." [217]   This statement is from Professor Frank D. Graham of Princeton:

. . . The real unearned income is that which accrues to an individual without his having done anything which contributes to production. Of the several types of such income the most important is that which issues from the site-value of land. The recipient of such an income does nothing to earn it; he merely sits tight while the growth of the community about the land to which he holds title brings him an unmerited gain. This gain is at the expense of all true producers or investors in industrial equipment. The taxation of this gain can do nothing to deprive the community of any service since the donee is rendering none. The land will be there for the use of society whether the return from it is taxed or free. Society creates the value and should secure it by taxation . . . The approach to scientific taxation involves a shifting of the burden from productive industry, where it now lies, to such incomes as these which are in truth unearned. Like many other reforms, this must be accomplished only step by step, but the path along which we ought to move lies clearly within our sight.[218]

---

[216] From the Appendix to *Significant Paragraphs from Progress and Poverty*, edited by Professor Brown (with an introduction by John Dewey) (New York, Doubleday, Doran, 1928), p. 77. This appendix consists of a collection of answers to questions sent out by the American Association for Scientific Taxation. Some sympathetic expressions pointing in the direction of land value taxation are, of course, present in the general writings of these economists, but this appendix is perhaps the most concise and specific statement of their views on this question.

The present writer has heard Professor Fisher state that he was "90 per cent a single taxer." His chief objection to George, he stated, was the "metaphysics" of the single tax system, i. e., its absolutism.

[217] *Ibid.*, p. 78.

[218] *Ibid.*

Professor John R. Commons feels that:

. . . this portion [on improvements] of his [the farmer's] taxes should be greatly reduced and even abolished, on the part amounting to more than 60 per cent of agricultural values; but the bare land value, amounting to 40 per cent, or less, should be taxed at higher rates. By no possible effort or expense can he, as an individual, increase his bare land values. These are increased by the labor, management and thrift of other taxpayers and other industries in the form of highways, railways, schools and profitable markets . . . Bare land values, including the value of mere waterpower, are due solely to scarcity, while the value of fertility, improvements, machinery and personal property are due mainly to thrift, good management and labor . . .[219]

And, finally,[220] this expression from Professor Raymond T. Bye of the University of Pennsylvania:

I believe that we should increase the taxation of land, exclusive of improvements, at the same time that we decrease the taxation of the improvements thereon. Such taxation of land should be increased gradually, not suddenly; and if extended over a long enough period of time, it would not be unwise to raise the tax to the point where it would appropriate to the State the greater part, if not the whole of, the economic rent. I do not believe, however, in the Single Tax doctrine that such a land tax should be completely substituted for all other taxes . . .[221]

This last statement is typical both of the favorable approach to land value taxation on the part of many economists and also of their shunning anything that savors of a "single tax." As Professor Davenport phrases this point: ". . . I do not, however, regard as implicit in the principle of the social retention of land rent [which he favored] the requirement

---

[219] *Ibid.*, pp. 78–79. See also *supra*, pp. 439–441.

[220] Similar expressions of opinion were received by the Association from President-Emeritus Arthur T. Hadley of Yale, Professor Paul H. Douglas of the University of Chicago, Professor Tipton R. Snavely of the University of Virginia, and others. The sympathetic approach to land value taxation of the late Professor Seager may also be mentioned here.

[221] Appendix, *Significant Paragraphs*, p. 79.

that economic rent should constitute the sole source of public income. Never is any good revenue method rightly discredited by any other." [222] However, there need be no discouragement to the follower of George in such repudiation of a "single tax." It is perhaps not this "singleness," or negative aspect, of his proposals that needs to be emphasized (at least, in presenting an exposition to the economist) so much as the more positive declaration that the incidence of taxation should fall heavily upon the economic rent of land. And the insistence upon gradualness in the taxation of land value, which all economists express, is not merely acceptable to, but indeed demanded by, nearly every follower of Henry George. Thus, while academic economists hold no overt brief for the work of George, yet many of them are advocating, despite judicious qualification, his very concepts.

Outside of the field of economics itself there have been several expressions in the academic world of admiration for George. The statements of Professor Dewey have been given before.[223] Perhaps the most recent and most articulate statement of such admiration was formulated by President Nicholas Murray Butler, who opened his 1931 Columbia University Commencement address (June 2) by declaring:

It is a full half century since no inconsiderable part of the world was plunged into vigorous and often excited controversy over the thesis and the arguments of a book by Henry George. He called it *Progress and Poverty*. The very title was abundant in challenge, and the argument of the book was more challenging still. Henry George pressed the question as to why it is that with all the vaunted progress that society has made and is making, there should still be so much poverty and want, and such apparently permanent lines of division between the great mass of those who prosper and the great mass of those who do not. While Henry George lived and met the public face to face upon the platform, his vigorous personality gained him many followers and made many advocates

[222] Appendix, *Significant Paragraphs*, p. 77.
[223] *Supra*, pp. 4–5, n. 2; see also *infra*, p. 562.

of his opinions. The years that have passed have set his economic analysis and economic teaching in due perspective, and enable us now to consider them with a just sense of their permanent importance and with regard to the soundness of their underlying principles.

It may be said at once that so far as Henry George pointed to privilege as an unbecoming, unfair and indeed disastrous accompaniment of progress, his teaching has passed into economic theory everywhere. Sound economists in every land accept and support economic equality and economic opportunity as fundamental . . .[224]

President Butler, of course, goes on to state that few economists accept George's concentration upon the land problem as crucial, and that the tendency now is to look for other types of privilege, but his appreciation of the cardinal point in George's social philosophy, the ethical attack upon the paradox of progress and poverty, is a correct and generous one.[225] Even in the realm of natural science there has been testimony to the influence of George, the most outstanding examples being the unequivocal single tax work of Surgeon-

[224] Quoted from the address as it is printed under the auspices of the office of the Secretary of Columbia University (New York, 1931).

[225] Dr. Butler made the very same point a few days later in an address before the American Club of Paris (June 10, 1931). He began his talk by taking the title of "Progress and Poverty" from Henry George, and he asked why George's great question concerning the mischievous relation of the two had never been satisfactorily answered. "Why is it that with all the progress which the world is making in so many directions—science, letters, fine arts, every form of industry, commerce, transportation—why is it that there still exists so much want, so much of all that which for lack of a better name may be summed up under the single word poverty?

"Henry George asked that question fifty years ago. Today everywhere in this world, East, West, North, South, Europe, America, Asia, Africa, that question is being asked—why is it that, with all that man has accomplished to his great satisfaction and pride in this last generation or two, why is it that the world today is in the grasp of the greatest economic, financial, social and political series of problems which have ever faced it in history? Why is it?"

Dr. Butler evidently implies agreement with Henry George's warning that "Not to answer means to be destroyed." (Quoted from the New York Times of June 11.) These statements of President Butler may also be found in his recent volume of collected essays and speeches, Looking Forward (New York, Scribner, 1932), pp. 35, 279–284.

General William C. Gorgas, of Panama Canal fame, and of Professor Lewis Jerome Johnson of the Harvard Graduate School of Applied Science.[226]

It would be very easy to multiply such a list of sympathetic readers of Henry George. However, it is felt that this brief summary may be sufficient to indicate a sample of the approach to his work. The foregoing section in no way professes to be a complete catalogue, and therefore many important figures in the United States and in other countries have been omitted; some of them are known, but their statements have not been verified, while undoubtedly the expressions of many more have just not come to the attention of the present writer. Apologies also may be in order for the possibly inadvertent inclusion of men who no longer consider themselves as sympathizers of George. All that has been attempted in these pages has been a presentation of George's influence in that more vague realm of opinion, and it will perhaps have served its purpose if it has suggested the rather wide effect that his writings have had upon later thinkers.

A conclusion of this treatment of George's influence, and, indeed, a conclusion of this entire first part, might possibly sound a note of complaint. That complaint would be directed largely at the professional world of economics for its apparent neglect of the thought of Henry George. It would insist, for one thing, that there seems to have been, in that seeming neglect, a slighting of the precious historical spirit

---

[226] These two scientists, complete single taxers, have articles appearing in a Joseph Fels Fund pamphlet (no date), "Two Papers on Public Sanitation and the Single Tax." The pamphlet was sponsored by a group of scientists and sanitation experts, including Jacques Loeb, Dean Victor C. Vaughan of the University of Michigan, Thomas Mott Osborne, and a number of other important figures. See also "Taxation Blunders and Their Remedy," by Professor Johnson, Joseph Fels Fund pamphlet (no date). Even Einstein has evinced interest in George's work. (See letter in *Land and Freedom*, March–April, 1932.)

of economics. That is to say, these last chapters have tried
to indicate that George has played a most significant rôle
in late nineteenth and early twentieth century thought; they
have attempted to trace, at least superficially, a concept that
has spread to such culturally discontinuous areas as China,
Denmark and Australasia, and that has impressed itself upon
the opinions of many thoughtful men. They have tried also
to suggest George's pioneer position in economics, a science
that in this country, at the time of his work, was not very far
removed from the pioneer stage itself. Indeed, George may be
said to have been a privileged observer at the quite humble
birth of a new civilization; the industrial unrest of the late
nineteenth century was made strikingly manifest to him at
that last American frontier, the Pacific Coast, and in that
unrest of a still young social order he felt that he was watching no mere children's disease, but a cumulative pathological
condition arising from a maladjusted distribution of wealth.
It was the very appositeness of his conceptions, indigenous
as they were to the opening West of Civil War and Reconstruction days, that, if nothing else, should press for historical consideration, and it is not at all necessary for the
economist to think of Henry George as the "Prophet of San
Francisco" in order to appreciate his place in American
thought. In other words, it is sincerely felt that the work
of Henry George, and the intimate connections that it has
had with other important social and economic movements,
cannot without risk be slighted by the historian of economic
theory.

Another possible complaint that may be raised here would
concern itself with what seems to be the failure of economics
to grasp the significance of a "one-idea" philosophy. That is,
the apparent exaggeration on the part of George against
which economics has directed its heaviest guns, his complete

concentration upon the land problem to the exclusion of anything else, may really be said to contain the very strength of his proposals. It is a truism to state that almost every important ideational contribution that the history of intellectual enterprise has recorded, from a Platonic doctrine of Ideas to a Watsonian behaviorism, has been originally elaborated in an extreme, often bizarre form. Compromise has no place at the initiation of ideas; it enters later, when history has performed its function of erosion. Therefore, while in George's case it may possibly be argued that his refusal to consider any possible economic specific except that of the socialization of rent was not overly pragmatic, still that refusal to compromise must be regarded as one that has cast the brightest kind of focus upon the crucial part played by land in the economic process. That concentrated emphasis upon the operations of land value and rent is essential if the complete functioning of land is to be given exposition, and a thorough treatment of that problem, as it appears in the work of George, is vital if that functioning is to be made familiar to those who are concerned with social problems. The increasing of that familiarity has been one of the major aims of this entire discussion of Henry George.

However, this part should not end upon that note of complaint. It should more suitably close with what may prove a transition to the second section of the present work. Such a transition will introduce again the ethical emphasis that was presented in the opening chapter. George's work must be considered not simply as an economic treatise; it is as much a contribution to ethical theory. President Butler has said that "so far as Henry George pointed to privilege as an unbecoming, unfair and indeed disastrous accompaniment of progress, his teaching has passed into economic theory everywhere." If this statement were expanded so as to include the hope that the recognition of such a "disastrous accompaniment of progress" might likewise pass into moral theory, it would perhaps be a complete expression of George's mission and of his contribution. Let us attempt, then, an examination of that ethical emphasis, and particularly of that emphasis as it appears against the background of economics.

PART II

CHAPTER IX

ECONOMICS AND ETHICS

THE opening chapter of the present work has suggested that economics and ethics must play the rôles of means and ends; more specifically, that moral systems and goals cannot legitimately divorce themselves from economic conditions and processes. A complementary thesis will be proposed in the present chapter: Just as ethics must realize that its hierarchy of values is conditioned by the social background against which it operates, so, in a like degree, economics must look to the directing power of moral concepts.

Such a statement will, of course, introduce the whole conflict between the historical, or descriptive, and the normative approaches to economics, a conflict that has translated into that discipline the classic division made by philosophy, the separation of the sciences of fact from those of value. That division, it need not be added, must not be taken too seriously. There is obviously no fixed and neat differentiation of scientific enterprises, just as there can be no precise separation between the concepts of fact and of value themselves. In the same measure that these concepts necessarily merge into one another, with no clear-cut boundary line between, so do the respective scientific branches blend, with no real possibility of labeling one completely factual or the other wholly interpretive. The most descriptive of scientists limits, if nothing more, his scope of factual material—thus introducing valuation. And a theorist surrounded only by values with no

facts in sight would be a strange creature indeed. Sciences
such as medicine (and economics itself) represent this merger
better than the disciplines ordinarily used to illustrate the
traditional separation: The natural sciences on the one hand,
and ethics, logic, æsthetics on the other.

While, however, this philosophic cataloguing of the sciences need not be interpreted too rigorously, still there is
clearly a difference of emphasis that is indicated by such an
attempt at classification. The descriptive sciences do concern themselves primarily with facts, data, "givens." The
normative disciplines (science might object to the appropriation of its name) deal essentially in standards, norms,
interpretations, values. And it cannot be denied that the
recognition of this direction of attention to the different approaches that any problem may elicit, the difference, putting
it crudely, between an "is" and an "ought" judgment, is of
definite worth. Of equal worth is the recognition of that
other familiar difference in scientific emphasis, really a
corollary of this first distinction, the contrast between a
factual and a "theoretical" approach.

Now, there will be no overambitious attempt here either
to trace that pronounced change in economics away from the
earlier ethical and theoretical approach to a later descriptive
and quantitative one,[1] or to make any general judgment as
to the nature of contemporary economics. The former is
familiar enough, and the latter would imply that present-day
economics is sufficiently unified so that any single statement
might be applied to it, when, of course, the fact is that contemporary economic "theory" is in a most extraordinarily
troubled and unorganized condition. That shift away from

---

[1] A brief and very clear account of the transition from the classical to
the recent approaches to economics may be found in Professor Paul T. Ho-
man's *Contemporary Economic Thought* (New York, Harpers, 1928), especially the Introduction and the first part of the concluding chapter on
"The Present Impasse." See also *The Development of Economics*, by Professor O. F. Boucke (New York, Macmillan, 1921).

classical political economy was the great theme of late nineteenth and early twentieth century economic theory, and it may be said, arbitrarily although conveniently, that Marshall presented the last great example of "ethical" neo-classicism, just as John Bates Clark was perhaps the final expression of the "logic" of neo-classic theory. Veblen's almost savage attack upon the Benthamite felicific calculus and the whole ethical nature of classical political economy, and his own proposed "institutional" interpretation, are supposed to mark the end of such an ethical approach (although, as it has repeatedly been pointed out, Veblen's onslaughts upon the economic anomalies and practices of present-day society certainly indicate a valuating, normative outlook).

The result of such reactions has been to direct at least one major strain of contemporary economic thought into "descriptive" channels. In many large sections of present-day economics, the word "theory" itself has become increasingly suspect and is being supplanted by more characteristic and suggestive terms, "statistics," "quantitative analysis," and the like. Even more unpopular, of course, are the ethical and logical concepts that once constituted almost the entire fabric of the science. The work of the late Professor Davenport with his emphasis upon a "cost" approach and his substitution of "technology" for logic, and even the important researches of Professor Mitchell [2] illustrate the more general thesis that economics must develop technically and statistically, not logically or ethically.[3] And the very teaching of economics, with its absence of the traditional "principles"

[2] However, Professor Mitchell still maintains that ethics cannot be divorced from economics, and that economic operations must be interpreted in terms of some form of standard; see especially his statements and those about him in The Trend of Economics, edited by Professor R. G. Tugwell (New York, Knopf, 1924).

[3] A Critique of Economics by Professor Boucke (New York, Macmillan, 1922), for example, defends this decisive distinction between economics and ethics.

and the reliance upon the "case" system,[4] seems to suggest that there is certainly a representative group of economists who insist that economics must seek for data, but shun standards; correlate facts, but avoid values; be descriptive, not normative.

However, as was mentioned above, there can be made no inclusive characterization of contemporary economics. In fact, it would almost seem that in the last few years there is something of a renaissance in economic theory, an almost wistful longing again for "principles" and "logic," and, at least among those younger economists influenced by pragmatic instrumentalism, there appears to be even a return to ethics.[5] (The work of Hobson and the "welfare" school of economics, which has kept to the forefront of discussion this ethical note, is being excepted, since academic economics has

[4] One of the best and most recent examples of this approach is the text, *Economic Behavior,* published by the New York University department of economics, Atkins and others (New York, Houghton Mifflin, 1931).

[5] The Tugwell volume *(op. cit.)* is a splendid illustration of such a pragmatic, neo-ethical emphasis. Representing the views of a number of the so-called "younger" economists, it presents selections which, with few exceptions, are quite sympathetic to the ethical point of view. Professor J. M. Clark, for example, holds that "economics cannot stop short of ethics," although he points out, of course, that it must be a pragmatic ethics that is being considered. Professor A. B. Wolfe adds that one can have little patience with "pure" science in a world as economically sick as ours. (This was all before the "depression.") A functional economics, he shows, must be ethical, although such ethical characteristics must be founded upon a correct psychology, and not upon the older hedonism. He also suggests that the small minority interested in economic "theory" is increasing. Professor Tugwell himself notes "the feeling of futility among the younger men," and suggests that any experimental approach to economics is "inescapably ethical." He mentions Patten, Hamilton, Mitchell, Clark, and Fisher as all interested in the ethical approach, although he admits that in their works (and this is certainly true of Professor Mitchell) there seems little interest in ethics itself.

Another interesting exposition of the more recent relation between economics and ethics, interesting because of the diverging views expressed, may be found in the *American Economic Review,* Vol. XII, Supplement, March, 1922, pp. 192–201. Here is a record of a discussion of the relation between economics and ethics which took place at the thirty-fourth annual meeting of the American Economics Association, December, 1921. Among the members entering into the discussion are: Professors F. H. Knight, A. B. Wolfe, H. G. Hayes, Jacob Viner, G. A. Kleene, and W. I. King.

not been overly sympathetic to their enterprises.) So, there is no intention in this connection of labeling contemporary economic theory as nonethical or as non-"theoretical"; no intention of selecting any school or any economist as typical of recent work. The following plea for the recognition of ethical standards in economics will be concerned simply with that emphasis in present-day economics which seems insufficiently sensitive to the place of moral judgment, just as the earlier insistence upon a recognition of economic conditions on the part of ethical theory referred only to the more aloof and splendidly isolated of ethical systems. Yet no man of straw, i. e., an unmoral economics, is being set up to be overthrown, for it can hardly be denied that a major ideal of much of our economics is the description of phenomena in terms of passionless, judgment-proof graphs.

Finally, this discussion will not seek to trace the historical record of such a dispute over the place of values in economics. That dispute may be considered to have begun as early as the work of Ricardo,[6] and it perhaps reached its height during the controversies centering around the German historical school, those great controversies in the *Verein für Sozial Politik.*[7] The present treatment of economics and ethics

---

[6] Professor Boucke considers Ricardo to have signalized the expulsion of ethics from economics, although, as has been pointed out previously, the whole classical school of political economy was implicitly ethical. It is true that the great English economists felt that they were laying down the inexorable natural laws of a "natural" science, but their work may very easily be interpreted as a great logical rationalization of the background of ethical theory, e. g., laissez-faire and, later, utilitarianism.

[7] See especially Haney, *History of Economic Thought* (New York, Macmillan, 1928 ed.), pp. 485–498. The whole "historical" approach may well be considered as the corollary, if not the very statement, of the descriptive, as opposed to the ethical, interpretation of economics. Roscher, Hildebrand, and Knies represented the "older" historical school, and, while they attacked classical absolutism, they cannot be considered to have been anti-ethical. (Cf. Keynes, *Scope and Method of Political Economy*, p. 20.) The "younger" school, composed of men such as Schmoller, Brentano, and a number of others, were more positive in their insistence upon an historical, nonmoral interpretation of the science, and prepared the way for the exaggerated statement of the thesis that political economy must be considered

will attempt merely to propose certain difficulties that may result from any serious exclusion of standards from economics,[8] and to suggest possible examples of the return, after a period of banishment, of ethics to social disciplines that are related to economics. An exposition of the part that values played in Henry George's own economic system may illustrate the significance of such a fusion for any integrated social philosophy.

In opening such an argument as this, it must first be recognized that economics can hardly be blamed for turning away

as devoid of principles or direction, and that it must include nothing more than the expression of an historical development.

[8] The bibliography of this economics-ethics topic is not a very full one. In fact, in Professor Jerome Davis's foreword to J. A. Hobson's *Economics and Ethics* (New York, Heath, 1929) that volume was put forward as a pioneer work in the field. Of course all of Hobson's writings have been dominated by the "welfare" approach, but this present work of his presents perhaps one of the finest expositions of such an emphasis. The central theme of all of Hobson's economic philosophy may be considered to lie in his attempt to bridge the gap of coolness between economic theory and social reform, and to attack, therefore, the "pure" interpretation of the science. He is most severe against the ethical "atomism" of classical theory, and feels that he offers a program for "a world that has lost laissez-faire." His ethics, instead, is one of control, one which, while it criticizes the practice of communism, still holds before it the ethical communistic goal as an ideal; Hobson's attacks upon competition, private gain-seeking, and the whole concept of labor as a commodity, are as decisive as any of the socialists' criticisms.

To continue the bibliography: *Economics and Ethics*, by Sir J. A. R. Marriott (London, Methuen; New York, Dutton, 1923)—this is a conservative plea for the retention of the traditional ethical judgments; *The Nature of the Relationship between Ethics and Economics*, C. E. Ayres (The University of Chicago Press, 1918; No. 8 of the Philosophic Studies); "Moral Valuations and Economic Laws," Professor Warner Fite (*Journal of Philosophy, Psychology and Scientific Method*, XIV, 10.); "Economic Values and Moral Values," Professor R. B. Perry (*Quarterly Journal of Economics*, XXX, 445). See also Dewey and Tufts, *Ethics* (New York, Henry Holt, 1908; revised edition, 1932), Part III, especially Chaps. XXII through XXV; and the appropriate chapters in Professor Urban's recent *Fundamentals of Ethics* (New York, Henry Holt, 1930). Some of the older treatments may be found in articles such as the following from the *International Journal of Ethics*: "The Relation between Economics and Ethics." J. S. Mackenzie, Vol. III, April, 1893, pp. 281–308; "The Restoration of Economics to Ethics," C. S. Devas, Vol. VII, January, 1897, pp. 191–204; and Professor C. A. Elwood's "The Sociological Basis of Ethics," Vol. XX, April, 1910, pp. 314–329. See also J. M. Keynes, *The Scope and Method of Political Economy* (London, Macmillan, 3d ed., 1904), especially Chap. II; and Professor E. C. Hayes, *Sociology and Ethics* (New York, Appleton, 1921). Bonar's classic *Philosophy and Political Economy* is, of course, largely historical.

from the earlier dogmatic, hortatory ethics that once greeted the social sciences.[9] A system of values founded upon a mythological psychology and presented in terms of absolutism can have little appeal for an enterprise that is reaching for the goal of science. And it must also be noted at the outset that it is likewise not in the least strange that economics should look to the quantitative and physical ideal. It is trying to achieve scientific formulation at a time when physics and the mathematical approach are the recognized models of science, and when a new and more technical methodology has enormously increased the data of all the social sciences.

Such recognitions, however, are by no means complete justifications. That is, the reaction from a logico-hedonistic ethics is hardly a warrant for a reaction from an instrumentalist ethics. Economics can find little excuse for looking away from an ethics that is a critical valuation of values already socially current, and less excuse for ignoring the (ethical) fact that the consequences of economic processes, consequences which lie in the dimension of human satisfactions, must be part of the material that the science "describes." Such consequences are the satisfactions of material wants, and any "physical science" attempt on the part of economics to operate in a vacuum shut off from the recognition of such wants would seem to be abortive. As consequences, values enter into the very subject-matter of economics. (Even on the "purely" descriptive side of the science, valuation has been introduced, as, for example, in giving

---

[9] In the Devas article just mentioned there occurs a passage which illustrates what should *not* be the relation of ethics to economics: "Now, economics can be looked on somewhat as an ingenuous youth, who, like other youths, is liable to contract low tastes, such as a desire to disregard contracts, to cancel debts, cut up ancestral parks, confiscate inheritances, appropriate accumulations. And general ethics can be looked on as the parent, who, with this young man's eyes upon him, must keep to a high standard of conduct." (P. 203.) Were the relation of ethics to economics that type of Toryism, then certainly there should be little protest against keeping the two disciplines carefully segregated. (Cf. also the Marriott volume, *op. cit.*)

property a legal status.) This implicit presence of values should certainly suggest, moreover, that as economics approaches the goal of science, it must develop more faith in its own subject-matter instead of imitating the technique of other disciplines that deal with a distinctly different type of material.

There is no intention here, of course, of making a positive criticism of much of the technique of contemporary economics. That criticism would be as foolhardy as it would be foolish. Certainly the collection of data and the emphasis upon inductive processes must be welcomed and must be made the foundation of any enterprise that presumes to construct a rigorous discipline. The difficulties that will be suggested here are largely negative ones, and will be located chiefly in presenting the embarrassing situation in which values are placed by such a shift on the part of the social sciences away from ethics (for this "descriptive" emphasis of economics is but the expression of a general trend). Moral values have long since been expelled from the natural sciences, and now they are being squeezed out of the social sciences. Indeed, it would begin to appear that the exorcism of standards and norms is now a prerequisite for any enterprise that desires to achieve respectability. For example, if one should approach the economist [10] with a plea for the recognition of values, if there is expressed the somewhat pious hope that economic data are to be organized in terms of economic welfare, he is politely referred to some of the other social fields, to sociology, perhaps, or to that vague field of

[10] In the entire following discussion the use of "economist" or "economics" will connote this nonmoral interpretation. It has already been recognized that no such general judgment can be made, but, for the purposes of the present argument, it seems unnecessary to qualify every use of the words "economist" or "economics" with some such phrase as "of the nonmoral school." Such qualification is intended in each case, but it will not be made explicit except occasionally.

social ethics. (The work of the late Professor Davenport presents perhaps the best example of this reference of all "ethical" suggestions to some field other than economics. Economics must be technological and descriptive, he argued, not logical or ethical, and such questions, for example, as tax reform, or the distinction between land and capital, have little or no "technological," economic significance. However, it may be pointed out, even if there is no "technological," "economic" difference between the two, i. e., land and capital, still such a distinction must be considered *somewhere*. It does not seem vital that such a realm of difference may not be technically "economic"—according to Davenport's definition of the science—it exists, it must be handled, and the attempt by such economists to shunt it off to some other field of inquiry illustrates precisely the irresponsibility and lack of coöperation that, it is being suggested here, is introduced by the severing of two enterprises of the nature of economics and ethics. Ethics itself cannot be expected to handle such economic concepts as land and capital, and so such a dualism removes the consideration of a crucial, if "ethical," point from the jurisdiction of any responsible agency; the result is to place it literally in some airy land of nowhere. It is not only that mutual aid is precluded by this separation of economics from ethics, but, in addition, the issue, e. g., the land-capital controversy, which is raised is rendered thereby homeless.) But should one follow this suggestion of the economist, with what is he confronted? It will be found that these other social sciences are likewise engaged in a precipitous rush to the goal of description.[11] Should economics, for example, point to sociology for norms, it will be discovered that sociology is

[11] The same qualification that has been made with reference to economics applies here also. That is, no attempt is being made to suggest any general characteristics of the social sciences, but there must be recognized, nevertheless, a prevailing tendency, as with economics, to shift from judgments and values to description and history.

busily engaged in neglecting standards for case histories. The social sciences seem yearning to be natural sciences. They are no longer content with remaining even historical descriptions; they must "go physical." No longer must the stigmas of "theoretical" or "deductive" or "introspective" or "arm-chair technique" or "closet approach" be placed upon them.[12]

This difficulty, therefore, presents itself: Where are values to find a refuge and how are they to exercise control? Of course, the realm of values may again seek a haven from such snubbing in some remote region of ethics, carefully insulated from the more lowly disciplines. That certainly would be nothing new; ethics has always striven to inhabit such an ethereal kingdom and has suffered nostalgia when removed from the upper air, but characteristically it had sought that speculative world itself, while now it seems to be banished there. The danger, then, that may result from the expulsion of values from economics and the other social sciences is the reintroduction, from another angle, of the traditional cleavage between ethics and the humble sciences that was so characteristic a part of former philosophy. That cleavage must be recognized to be present whether the approach be that of classic theory, which held that ethics was too exalted a creature to be hampered by the crudities of empiricist techniques, or that of the modern economist who refuses to be annoyed by the distractions that a consideration of standards would introduce into facts. The certain effect of both approaches is to make values remote and inoperative, to segregate judgment from description, and to present us with a dilemmatic choice between a social science that is without values or a social ethics that is without facts. Yet we must not forget, to distort a famous line, that "facts without values are blind; values without facts are empty."

---

[12] If this appears to exaggerate certain distinctions and approaches, that exaggeration is realized as such and perhaps may charitably be interpreted as suggesting emphasis.

The danger that is suggested here is not one that need greatly concern the physical sciences. They have traditionally—that is, since the birth of modern science—been exempt from the moral justification that has been demanded of the more hybrid social disciplines. Science has been recognized as disinterested and therefore privileged, and ideally ethics has been permitted to trouble the scientist as little as it has the artist. Such an æsthetic point of view, however, will hardly carry over to the enterprise of economics. Here, such "æsthetic," intrinsic values are by no means implicit in the functions and operations of economic concepts, but are bound up inextricably with the meanings and operations of other disciplines of control, that is, of extra-economic social and moral agencies. Take, for example, the concept of property, or the distinction between earned and unearned income. Contemporary economics is attempting to operate with property as a phenomenon that is simply nothing more or less than the last step in a long and arduous evolutionary development. It is a given, an economic datum that is to be approached quantitatively, with perhaps at most a statistical investigation into its internal efficiency; that is to say, for purposes of economic science, it is to be accepted for what it is. Present-day economics likewise seems to be endeavoring to lump together all phases of income, avoiding distinctions between earned and unearned varieties of wealth. (Professor Davenport's definitions of capital and property are particularly suggestive in this connection.) Income, like property, is to be accepted as a concept resulting from the operations of economics, its significance lying within the range of the science itself.

While such a procedure definitely represents the "scientific" aim of economics, namely, the attempt to handle its material dispassionately without the slant or direction that valuation would introduce, still the benedictions that have been reserved for that approach in the physical sciences can with but little success, it seems, be dispensed in fields such as that of economics. Property and income can scarcely be accepted with the same equanimity that is accorded in the natural sciences to paramoecia or spinal frogs or catalysts. The subject-matter that concerns economics has often had too checkered a career to submit gracefully to the calmness that a quantitative or even an historical survey cheerfully bestows. In other words, the exemption of the data of physical disciplines from ethical standards is a unique privilege, and possible only because of the intrinsic values—perhaps dominantly æsthetic—that are present in the creative operations and technique of science; whereas perhaps because the social enterprises are too tainted with earth and Adam, with man and man's possessions, too humanistic (to use a word somewhat inaccurately), the divorce of facts from values in such endeavors would tend to cripple their social significance and to make complete the isolation of ethics.

This, however, must not be interpreted as a plea for the wholesale fusion of economics and ethics. It is rather the suggestion that, since it has been the insistence of much recent philosophy that ethics concern itself with the more prosaic enterprises in order to proceed upon its path of evaluating with sufficient descriptive material, a converse demand should be made upon economics to the effect that it in turn be not too neglectful of the responsibility of judging. One cannot ask too much of ethics. While it must attempt to grasp the significant findings of other studies, it cannot be expected, for example, to delve into the technical and often dismal details of economics. Nor, on the other hand, can an enterprise such as economics be required to act as a surrogate for moral speculation. But it may be demanded that just as ethics must place no insulation between itself and the social sciences, so likewise these alleged descriptive techniques cannot rightfully disavow all consideration of values. Maybe a plea for a little less division of labor would be in order, for so long as economics and ethics each concentrates rigidly upon its specific approach, the one being descriptive and the other interpretive, the significant marginal spheres which surround each enterprise will never be able to coincide. There can be little intelligent coöperation if each social science is to remain descriptively isolated, each one outdoing the other in its disparagement of directing elements.

It has been mentioned above that the slighting of values in economics and the other social sciences has been, in part, a reactionary shift away from the eighteenth- and early nineteenth-century ethical approach. That ethical approach may perhaps be typified by the concept of natural rights. It is realized full well that even a mention of natural rights is always dangerous. Any discussion of the topic, even the briefest—as this will necessarily be—must labor under a genuine embarrassment, the difficulty of examining a cadaver without being suspected of the mutilation or, on the other hand, of the resurrection of the dead.[13]

[13] It is being assumed that a knowledge of the long historical development that lay back of the eloquent expression of natural rights that appeared in the American and French Declarations is sufficiently familiar. The immediate ideational background was, of course, the work of Rousseau and Locke (the latter being of more influence upon American political theory than was "Jean Jacques, the inventor of natural rights"), and the whole social contract tradition (the completely antithetical interpretations on the part of Locke and Hobbes of the state of nature that preceded the forming of the social contract are one of the most vivid testimonials to the caprice of "nature"), while extending further back and underlying the very concept of rights were the forces evoked by the Puritan revolution, the radical Wycliffites, and the entire Protestant movement itself. "The theory of natural rights is simply the logical outgrowth of the Protestant revolt against the authority of tradition, the logical outgrowth of the Protestant appeal to private judgment, i. e., to the reason and conscience of the individual . . . Puritan England had produced the theory of natural rights; but the conditions were not yet favorable for its abundant growth . . . The theory of natural rights is Protestantism transferred to the region of worldly affairs, and stripped of the traditionalism against which at first it did not 'protest.'" (Ritchie, *Natural Rights;* London, Swan Sonnenschein, 1895, pp. 6, 10, 13.)

The concept of "natural," to be sure, has a much more hoary record

Nevertheless, it seems in point here, as a possible example of a reconciliation of fact and value in political and economic theory, to mention the more recent interpretation of the classic doctrine of rights. There must first be taken for granted, in any approach to such a concept, an awareness of the complete disapproval of the traditional formulation of the doctrine. The arguments that have been employed

behind it than that of abstract "rights." The Middle Ages did have rights, but they were rather the authoritative, specific grants of a feudal era—usually the correlates of duties—than the general, innate, "essential" rights of a later day; such a concept, i. e., rights that were inherent and natural, required the individualistic spirit of a Reformation superimposed upon the doctrines of late feudal legal theory. "Natural," on the other hand, traces back its ancestry to the Sophistic and Cynic separation of "convention" from "nature," to Aristotle's natural this and that, and, of more importance, to the natural law of the Stoics. ("Natural law," it must be remembered, was originally a political and ethical concept, the basis of a natural social order; the scientific emphasis, as we characteristically know it, was dependent upon the growth of scientific data which were to be "legally" organized.) The classic transference of Stoic natural law to Latin culture; the work of Cicero; the ultimate incorporation of the concept into Roman law, whence it became part of the mediæval heritage; all that is familiar. Thomas's "law of nature," as has been repeatedly pointed out, is essentially a combination of Aristotle's Nature plus Cicero's law of nature. Then came the work of Grotius, Pufendorf, and also of Hooker, who greatly influenced Locke, and "natural" came into English thought, where it was soon joined to "rights." And the end of the eighteenth century found the doctrine a most powerful weapon for the attack upon political exploitation. The concept of natural rights really affords one of the neatest examples of a thought that, although the definite product of a long historical lineage, yet was seized upon by its popularizers as an intuited revelation of an eternal metaphysical system.

It would be patently absurd to present in this connection any attempt at elaborate bibliography; the history of the concepts "natural" and "rights" boasts of too pretentious a literature to be cavalierly treated. A few direct and specific references, however, may be suggested here simply as characteristic samples: Ritchie *(op. cit.),* Chaps. I, II, III, IV; Carl Becker, *The Declaration of Independence* (New York, Harcourt, Brace, 1922), Chap. II; Berolzheimer, *The World's Legal Philosophies* (Jastrow trans., New York, Macmillan, 1924), Introduction, Chap. V; Bryce's *Studies in History and Jurisprudence* (Oxford, 1901), Vol. II, Chap. XI; R. W. and A. J. Carlyle, *A History of Mediæval Political Theory in the West* (Edinburgh, Blackwood, 1903; 5 vols.), particularly, Vol. I for the mediæval development of natural law; F. J. Goodnow, *The American Conception of Liberty and Government* (Brown University, 1916), Part I; Roscoe Pound, *Law and Morals* (University of North Carolina, 1924) ; *The Spirit of the Common Law* (Boston, Marshall Jones, 1921) ; *An Introduction to the Philosophy of Law* (Yale University Press, 1922). There is a very suggestive article by the late Professor G. H. Mead, "Natural Rights and the Theory of Political Institutions," in the *Journal of Philosophy, Psychology, and Scientific Method* (March 18, 1915, Vol. XIII, No. 6).

against natural rights are now almost commonplace: For example, that the "individual," upon whose metaphysical status as a discrete and autonomous entity the whole problem of rights depends, is a concept quite questionable when tested by an organismic standard of social processes; that the concept "natural" is a very poor methodological instrument, since it demands a criterion essentially unempirical, intuitive, noetic, "rationalistic," and since, as experience has unmistakably shown, it has been used to justify all manner of doctrine; that these rights were too rigid, too absolute, and likewise too many in number, that they "multiplied essences" and were therefore inapplicable for purposes of expediency and utility; that the whole concept of natural rights, instead of being any ultimate and eternal precious charter of liberties, was rather a clearly traceable historical phenomenon that came into such tremendous import largely because it was used as a weapon by eighteenth-century liberals; all this must be recognized as legitimate and familiar criticism of the natural rights approach to the relation of the individual to society, criticism, moreover, which reaches back to early nineteenth-century English jurists and political theorists, Bentham, Burke, Austin.

However, the thought that will be suggested here is that this "metaphysical" interpretation of the doctrine of natural rights, which perhaps well deserved the strictures that have been directed against it, was essentially a narrow and over-rigorous interpretation. It it quite true that "natural" as a political and economic criterion is unsound as a metaphysical concept, i. e., that there is no warrant for postulating an eighteenth-century apotheosis of Nature as the basis of social orders and economic systems, and unsound also—for want of a better word—as an epistemological concept, namely, that there is no way of knowing when the "natural" state is achieved, that no bell rings at its realization. But when corrections and allowances are made in terminology, it may be recognized that "natural" means normative, and that the seeking after the natural is ethical and not metaphysical; it is a demand for standards and criteria, the symbol—perhaps hypostasized—for values. And it is under the aspect of this nonmetaphysical interpretation that the concept of natural rights, and likewise that of natural law, are being subject to a new evaluation, at least in certain disciplines such as that of jurisprudence.

The philosophy of law, just as that of economics, experienced in the nineteenth century a decided revolt against the absolutism of eighteenth-century legal concepts represented, for instance, by the natural law of Blackstone, and jurisprudence became concerned with an historical approach such as that of Eichorn and Savigny, and later with what Roscoe Pound calls the emphasis of the "mechanical sociologists." The scientific spirit of the late nineteenth century could brook no philosophizing in law, and so the law became a social "language" or a set of evolutionary formulas which could be traced and discussed, but which it would be futile to attempt to direct or to evaluate. However, just as the overemphasis of the metaphysical approach by the eighteenth century resulted in the onslaught upon natural rights and natural law, so there has been in legal philosophy a reaction against the overhistoricism and neglect of values of nineteenth century jurisprudence. The work of the Natural Rights school in France, of Kohler and Stammler in Germany, who, although opposed to the natural rights concept, oppose even more vigorously the mere descriptive and historical approach to legal theorizing, and of jurists such as Dean Pound and Justice Holmes in this country—also some of the writings of Professor Hocking and Professor Cohen—definitely point to a changing interpretation of some of the classic concepts, an interpretation that emphasizes the ethical rather than the traditional metaphysical approach. Dean Pound can write that:

Already there is a revival of natural law, not of the natural law that would have imposed upon us an idealized version of the law of the past as something from which we might never escape, but of a creative natural law that would enable us to make of our received legal materials, as systematized by the legal science of the last century, a living instrument of justice in the society of to-day and to-morrow. Such a natural law will not call upon us to turn treatises on ethics or economics or sociology directly into institutes of law. But it will not be content with a legal science that refuses to look beyond or behind formal legal precepts and so misses more than half of what goes to make up the law.[14]

This is, of course, not an essay in jurisprudence and the only point that is intended in these last paragraphs is that the criterion of "natural" is not one that has been summarily and permanently banished. It remains in ethics if not in metaphysics. It is a symbol of the cry for better things—for better laws, better social orders, better economic systems. A "natural" order, a "natural" right, a "natural" law, are postulated because men seek to find some sure basis for the things that "ought" to be. If they can point to Nature, then their demands seem more solidly grounded. Here in Nature is the way things should be; look to the "natural" standard and then criticize, value, improve. It is true that such a standard may be admittedly a creative fiction; granted that there is no "natural" this or that in the nature of things, and granted that, if there were, no one would ever know when it had been reached; still, "natural" has a significance that was certainly not exhausted, perhaps not really understood, by eighteenth-century metaphysicians. The significance is basically that of a dissatisfaction with existing conditions, a discontent with mere description and the colorless technique

[14] *Law and Morals,* pp. 87–88.

of scientific statement, and is instead a reaching forward to ideals and goals.

This point, however, will be misinterpreted if it is thought to imply a serious criticism of the descriptive, historical, scientific approach. It is simply the suggestion that the appeal to norms is one that is corrective of much of the narrowness that may result from too strict a worship of data and too studied a neglect of values. It is an appeal that refuses to accept conditions with equanimity simply because they are facts. All this seems to be suggested by "natural" and perhaps that is why the concept cannot be for long disregarded. As a specific program, "natural" may be of little service, but as a recognition of the place of values, it serves an essential purpose. The argument that is crudely expressed here is summed up, in connection with its presence in the problems of law, by Professor Hocking:

The law of any place and time is either subject to criticism or it is not. Unless the idea of "improvement" and the idea of the "law" are somehow incongruous, there must be at least a logical distinction between what the law is and what it ought to be. This is so evident to common sense that any opposing view would seem possible only by way of reaction from some atrocious misuse of the idea. It was the fate of the Natural Rights schools to provoke such a reaction, and to send an entire century of legal philosophers burrowing among the facts of law past and present for instruction which they agreed could not be found in ideals set up in total independence of history. Now, at the opening of still another century, we find common sense once more taking courage. The Natural Right-ists were right in at least one respect: the question, What ought the law to be? is a pertinent question, and they were even right in assuming that the human will had something to do about it.[15]

This same nonmetaphysical approach to the concept "natural" may also be applied to that of "rights." It may

[15] *The Present Status of the Philosophy of Law and Right* (Yale University Press, 1926), pp. 4–5.

be granted that the notion of an individual existing prior to any social and political system, with rights bequeathed to him by a rational Creator, rights which were inherent, inalienable, imprescriptible, and self-evident, was a myth. It cannot be denied that the idea of a State formed by a compact between autonomous, independent individuals in order to safeguard the rights of all through a mutual respect for the rights of each, was a product of a pre-sociological and pre-anthropological political background. Any conception of man as a completely individualistic animal, whose present political and social status is essentially artificial, one arrived at by contract, is fantastic. All this and more may be granted, and still there remains that important transition from metaphysics to ethics. It may be true that man *has* no rights— rights, that is, according to an eighteenth century pattern; yet there are rights that he *should* have. He must be treated "as if" he had moral claims upon society in order that he *will* be able to realize such claims; the concept is a presumptive fiction.

What is meant by this is simply that if political and economic science is to function at all, it must recognize that the concept of "social," taken by itself, may become as abstract, as empty, and as fruitless as the concept of "individual." Despite the admitted validity of an organismic approach, the welfare of governments and economics orders is not, after all, an abstract conceptual welfare, but the welfare of individual members, members who must be treated psychologically as well as socially; that is, they must be so treated if the social structure is to be subject to criticism and redirection. "Nothing is more evident, I venture to think, as a result of two or three thousand years of social philosophizing, than that society must live and thrive by way of the native impulses of individual human beings." [16] Has not the paradoxical yet

[16] Hocking, p. 68.

frequent attempt on the part of the historical school to consider governments and social systems *qua* governments and social systems, rather than as instruments that serve "the native impulses of individual human beings," been an almost studied effort to ignore the very values and standards by which alone governments and social orders can be judged? And is not the pronounced tendency to study the social organism as a self-sufficient unit, with scant attention being paid to the individual status of its constituent organs (the result, perhaps, of a false physiological analogy, or of an overemphasized biological approach), indicative of precisely that descriptive attitude which refuses to concern itself with critical evaluation? The purely historical treatment of the State and of existing economic structures may well concentrate upon these products of evolutionary social development, to the exclusion of a consideration of purposes and goals, but that approach is not one that can intrigue a seeker after values.

It must be suggested that the historical approach to politics and economics becomes involved in a serious dilemma when it seeks to prefer factual material to that concerning values. Such an approach results either in no valuation judgment at all, or in the erecting of historical events into a standard of values. The former horn of the dilemma certainly cannot be accepted by any philosophic approach; philosophy, in a real sense, may be designated as the science of values. And the latter alternative means a procedure that is as absolute as the traditional natural rights theory, one which indeed might be termed a variant of that theory, interpreting "natural" in this case simply as the historically existential. It may be granted that political and social organization is what it is because of certain historical forces, but there always lurks in the background the demand for a norm, a standard, an ideal, for testing such an organization.

That standard must be, in some form or other, "the impulses of individual human beings." This is not political atomism, but simply a recognition, to repeat, that the category of "social" may turn into an historical, descriptive concept instead of being used as a critical one, that valuation and interpretation of "social" demand the necessary correlative of "individual." In the words of Dean Pound:

. . . Much that advertises itself as social is in truth individualist; it is individualism to be attained through society rather than through individual self-help . . . Just as in the seventeenth century an undue insistence upon public interests, thought of as the interests of the sovereign, defeated the moral and social life of the individual and required the assertion of individual interests in bills of rights and declarations of rights, there is like danger now that certain social interests will be unduly emphasized and that governmental maternalism will become an end rather than a means and defeat the real purposes of the legal order. Although we think socially, we must still think of individual interests, and of that greatest of all claims which a human being may make, the claim to assert his individuality, to exercise freely the will and the reason which God has given him. We must emphasize the social interest in the moral and social life of the individual. But we must remember that it is the life of a free-willing being.[17]

And again:

Toward the end of the nineteenth century a new movement became manifest in law and in the science of law. Faith in the spontaneous development of legal institutions began to give way to faith in the efficacy of effort to make or to shape the law to known ends . . . In particular, whereas the immediate past had

---

[17] This quotation is directly preceded by the following: "But we must not infer that the contribution of eighteenth-century theory to our legal tradition is to be cast out utterly. For the theory of fundamental principles to which law must conform and of fundamental interests which law must secure at all events has another side . . . Men are saying today that material welfare is the great end to which all institutions must be directed and by which they must be measured. Men are not asking merely to be allowed to achieve welfare; they are asking to have welfare achieved for them through organized society . . ." (*The Spirit of the Common Law,* pp. 108–111; this passage is followed by "Much that advertises itself" . . . etc.)

put the whole emphasis upon the general security, greater weight began to be given to the individual human life . . . In jurisprudence it was manifest first in a better understanding of the relation of legal rights to so-called natural rights. It came to be seen that the ultimate thing was the claim or demand or desires of a human being; that out of all such *de facto* claims or demands or desires some were recognized by moralists and jurists as reasonable and were called natural rights, and some were recognized and delineated by law and as so delimited were given effect by legal rights.[18]

This tentative, empirical quality that is thus being attributed to a concept that was originally absolute and intuitional is the one sure basis for a reinterpretation of the natural rights doctrine such as that which has been a characteristic theme in French jurisprudence since the opening of the century. There can be no attempt made here at all to discuss that approach,[19] but it is clear that the more important of the French theorists who are concerned with this question take, if not a fictional, hypothetical attitude, at least the position that any acceptance of "natural rights" must be founded upon social utility, a utility, moreover, that is changing and developing. Whether it be the functional conception of Duguit,[20] or the plea for "idealism" of Charmont, the "reas-

---

[18] *Law and Morals,* pp. 108–109. In this connection see also Professor Dewey's *The Public and Its Problems* (New York, Henry Holt, 1927), *passim.*

[19] For the best brief account of these movements, see *Modern French Legal Philosophy,* by Fouillée, Charmont, Duguit, and Demogue (Scott and Chamberlain trans.), Vol. VII of the Modern Legal Philosophy Series (the Boston Book Company, 1916), especially editorial preface, and Part I, Chaps. VI, IX, XII; Part II, Chaps. I–VIII, XI. For other material see: Beudant, *Le Droit Individuel et l'État* (this book, which appeared in 1891, may be considered as the beginning of the revival of the natural rights concept); Saleilles, "L'École historique et droit naturel" (*Révue Trimestrielle de Droit Civil,* 1902, I, 80, 98); Planiol, *Traité Elémentaire de Droit Civil* (1900); Gény, *Méthode d'Interprétation et Sources en Droit Privé Positif* (1900). These latter two works, representing an attempt—in the words of Duguit—"to adapt the antiquated codes to modern needs by a looser interpretation," have been severely criticized by him. Compare also the more comprehensive works of Duguit, especially his *Les Transformations générales du droit privé depuis le Code Napoleon* (Paris, Alcan, 1912), and of Fouillée and Charmont, particularly the latter's *La Renaissance du Droit Naturel.*

[20] For an interesting and similar functional approach to rights and particularly to the right of property, see R. H. Tawney's *The Acquisitive Society*

suring placard, 'changing content guaranteed,' " is always present. No one, for example, could be more bitter against the metaphysical notion of a social contract and of inherent, inalienable rights than Duguit,[21] yet his essentially psychological postulate of an "individual" and of an "individual will and mind as the basis of all phenomena" reintroduces a doctrine of rights as a necessary condition for that individual's functioning, such functioning, as he attempts to show, being a necessary part of the social process.[22] Rights, according to this conception, have a much different status from the older natural ones; they are socially useful and hence socially necessary. A quotation from Charmont may, in addition, illustrate the variable concept of natural:

> The idea of natural law, then, is differently conceived from the way it formerly was. It rests upon another foundation, and at the same time it undergoes certain transformations. It reconciles itself with the idea of evolution, with that of utility. It loses its absolute, immutable character, for it possesses only a variable content. It takes account of the interdependence of the individual and the community; it thus tends to bring the individual conscience and external law into accord, instead of setting them in opposition.[23]

(New York, Harcourt Brace, 1921). F. and H. Laski in *Law in the Modern State* (New York, Huebsch, 1919) present a functional "public service" rather than "sovereignty" thesis of the law.

[21] See *Modern French Legal Philosophy (op. cit.)*, Part II, Chap. VIII (taken from Duguit's *L'État: Le Droit Objectif et la Loi Positive*).

[22] *Ibid.*, Part II, Chap. IX. Duguit's work is, in a great measure, influenced by that of Durkheim and Lévy-Bruhl. Cf. the doctrines that equality, instead of being any primal attribute, is the definite product of an advanced civilization.

[23] *Ibid.*, p. 146. (From *La Renaissance du Droit Naturel.*) Professor Morris R. Cohen has written a very suggestive paper, "Jus Naturale Redivivum" (*The Philosophical Review*, Vol. XXV, No. 6, November, 1916, pp. 761–777), which is practically a summary of the points that have been made in favor of this whole reinterpretation of natural law and natural rights. He takes up four arguments directed against the classic concept, the historical, psychological, legal, and metaphysical arguments, and shows that each of them is in no sense irrefutable. He is particularly concerned with the value of "ought" in jurisprudence, the distinction between "substantive codes" and a "science of principle," and he warns against too complete an avowal of historicism. He writes, for example, "The essence of all doctrines of natural law is the appeal from positive law to justice, from the law that

Natural rights and natural law, then, "can only creep into sight" in a greatly amended form. They must become empirical, elastic, workable, pragmatic. If all these qualifications really transform the traditional concept into something entirely different, that difference is essentially one of content; although their connotations have undergone a fundamental adjustment, the phrases and the "form" of natural rights and natural law may well remain—as indeed they have—a part of the literature of political and legal theory.

If the "individual," then, is to be treated as the reasonable test of the efficacy of legal and political and social systems, if his "claims or demands or desires" are to constitute a regulative factor, he must be postulated as possessing such claims or demands or desires independent of social arrangement. This is what is meant by the previous statement that even if metaphysically and historically men are endowed with no such claims—or rights—yet they should be so endowed by the political theorist. Take, for example, in this fictional, hypothetical, "as if" [24] approach to the question of rights, the matter of the equality of all men before the law. There is probably no writer on jurisprudence who would be so rash as to hold that such legal equality is based upon the "fact" of man's "natural" equality, upon the actuality that men "are" thus equal. On the contrary, a concept of equality tends definitely to ignore conditions which exist, but only for the purpose of endeavoring to bring about conditions that are held to be desirable. Legal rights are hypothetically

is to the law which ought to be; and unless we are ready to assert that the concept of a law that ought to be is for some reason an inadmissible one, the roots of natural law remain untouched." (P. 769.) This article appears now as Chap. IV of Book III, in *Reason and Nature* (New York, Harcourt Brace, 1931).

[24] Vaihinger does not consider in detail the concept of natural rights in his important contribution to this "as if" approach. Natural law he holds to be one of the "summational fictions." (*The Philosophy of As If,* 1911, Ogden trans., 1924.)

postulated, conditions are presumed to exist, because of an essentially melioristic outlook; the law may operate with fictions, but it does so in order to direct realities—that is, law interpreted ethically, not descriptively. The same is true of the concept liberty; men perhaps are actually as little "free" before the law as they are "equal," but "if most powers develop best in liberty—as they do—liberty will be a presumptive right." [25] In other words (and the argument here will follow closely that of Professor Hocking), what we mean by such presumptions, by the whole category of rights, are those conditions under which individual powers normally develop. "Rights, we say, are the conditions under which we must presume that human powers will best come to their own. . . . It is objectively 'right' that an individual should develop his powers." [26] If we are to assume that the individual must be the regulative factor, the standard in criticizing social institutions, we must realize that individual rights are nothing more—or nothing less—than the social recognition that such an individual is a functioning,[27] developing entity with definite potentialities. That social recognition, however, is manifested in the form of a presumption, or a fiction, since it treats men in a way that is not supported by (historical, scientific) facts—e. g., men are treated as free and equal— but it is a fiction that seeks, on the one hand, to evaluate, for it recognizes that there should be an effort made to bring about these conditions, and, on the other, to develop, for it treats man as if his powers were further progressed. As it has been put, this presumption has the same value as that

[25] Hocking, *op. cit.,* p. 72.
[26] *Ibid.,* pp. 72–73, 71–72.
[27] Duguit's argument for rights is that they belong to a man because he has functions to perform. Hocking does not accept that position but concentrates upon this "development of powers." It is not easy to see the significance of the difference between these two claims. Correct functioning— functioning, that is, in an Aristotelian sense—depends definitely upon the development of powers, and conversely unless those developed powers are correctly directed, function will not be achieved.

of considering a youth to be several years older than he really is. Rights, in this sense, are a necessary and constructive fiction.[28]

The individualism that is being suggested throughout this present argument is thus an ethical, not a metaphysical, individualism, and it may well be asked of the historical school whether it is prepared to deny that individuals as such have a title to basic moral consideration, just as it may be asked of much current political theory whether its emphasis upon the social has any ethical status at all if such claims to (moral) individuality are denied.[29]

It may be in place here to mention just a word further as to the significance of the statement that the standard of "natural" and of "right" is "admittedly a creative fiction." What is meant by this is that a recognition of a presumptive, hypothetical character in an approach to concepts such as those of natural rights and natural law will not only remove much of the absolutism that was so objectionable a feature of the classic doctrines, but will also prepare the only possible way for a readmittance of such concepts into present-day theory. For example, it may be true that from the standpoints of law and politics men are endowed with no innate, imprescriptible, natural rights. Still, as has been seen, for purposes of social manipulation they must be treated, and,

[28] The argument is summed up by Professor Hocking: "If the different presumptive rights are so many ways of promoting the development of individual human powers; if any law is right because it does this promoting, and only so far as it does it, ceasing to be right when and in so far as it fails of this achievement; then this measure or standard by which we test what is 'right' or 'just' gives us the nature of 'rightness' or 'justice.' It defines what we may please to call the absolute right, which is nothing more than to say, it defines what right is. It is right, absolutely right, that an individual should develop the powers that are in him. He may be said to have a 'natural right' to become what he is capable of becoming. This is his only natural right . . . Wherever moral ambition exists, there rights exist." (*Op. cit.*, pp. 74–75.)

[29] For a very recent and penetrating discussion of this whole problem see Professor W. W. Willoughby's *The Ethical Basis of Political Authority* (New York, Macmillan, 1930).

in fact, have been treated, as if they did possess such rights. This is a transition from metaphysics to ethics, and an important transition. An "as if" approach—that of a necessary fiction or a creative presumption—postulates as a regulative factor, not as a categorical statement, that "the claims or demands or desires of a human being" (to use Pound's phrase) must direct legal and social, political and economic thought. A doctrine of rights, therefore, is not one that can be unconditionally expelled from political and social theory, but it needs definite qualification, and this presumptive handling of the concept seems to introduce the most valuable type of qualification. It recognizes that rights are fundamentally a name for ethical claims flowing from the very nature of the individual, and that the concept of rights introduces a theory which includes man as an ethical factor as opposed to a view which excludes such a factor. It is an approach that concerns itself with values, but since the treatment of rights is hypothetical it does not attempt to read them existentially into the social structure. The eighteenth-century natural rights concept, from a metaphysical standpoint, was "pure" fiction, whereas the ethical, "as if" interpretation is a "creative" fiction, a moral presumption.

A presumptive approach, moreover, recognizes no hard and fast order that is eternal and unchangeable. Presumptions and fictions change; they are empirically determinable and mould themselves to fit the exigencies of utility. The natural rights of an "as if" world, for example, would possess the same characteristics as that "as if" world—they would be relative, variable, and not too enamored by the charms of rational absolutism. They do not constitute an immutable ideal system to which the contingent, positive legal right must conform, but they are concepts that vary according to their usefulness. They are "interests which we think ought to be secured; demands which human beings may make which we think ought to be satisfied," and those interests and demands are neither universal nor eternal. Interests and demands are elastic, and therefore presumptive natural rights are elastic. The absolute character of the older doctrine may really be said to have been its basic defect; it disturbed the late nineteenth century because science and history could discover no such absolute nature, and it is even more annoying to present tendencies which attempt to work with and to use concepts. A rigid system of absolutes is not an easy thing to manipulate, to operate with, and that handicap, rather than any metaphysical one, is the damaging feature of classic natural rights. But the characteristic argument against this rigidity of rights cannot be brought to bear upon an interpretation that recognizes and demands that rights be made amenable to conditions which are in a state of transformation, an interpretation that holds that such concepts must be tested by a standard of social efficiency.

It may be necessary to suggest one or two warnings or qualifications, however, in connection with this type of "as if" argument. One is that the insistence upon the recognition and development of individual powers assumes, obviously, that there actually exist such interests and powers. "Rights" [30] themselves may be presumptive and fictional, since they are essentially a social reaction, but those bases upon which they depend cannot be so regarded. Yet this is nothing more than a corollary of the previous postulate that it is by the category "individual" that the concept of "social" is to be measured. This independent existence of certain "interests" that the law concerns itself with is clearly accepted by Roscoe Pound:

A legal system attains its end by recognizing certain interests, individual, public, social; by defining the limits within which these interests shall be recognized legally and given effect through

[30] "Rights" here signify legal rights; cf. the Pound passage above.

the force of the State, and by endeavoring to secure the interests so recognized within the defined limits. *It does not create these interests.* There is so much truth in the eighteenth-century theory of natural rights. . . . They [individual interests] *arise apart from the law . . . The law does not create them, it only recognizes them* . . . The seventeenth- and eighteenth-century theory, however, confused the interest, which exists independently of law, and the legal rights, the creature of law . . . *Natural rights mean simply interests which we think ought to be secured; demands, which human beings may make which we think ought to be satisfied. It is perfectly true that neither law nor State creates them* . . . it is fatal to all sound thinking to treat them as legal conceptions. . .[31]

A more serious qualification, therefore, is that the terms "fiction" and "as if" must not be taken too literally. That is to say, the argument that has been made in these last pages may perhaps be stated in a stronger fashion if it is put solely in temporal terms, in terms of a future. The individual must be treated so that he *will* have certain rights; he must be handled so that his having of rights may be *furthered*. That is the implication and justification of any hypothetical approach. A fictional theory might be interpreted as a static theory, whereas what is intended here is that the "as if" approach is a dynamic one, and in so far a reality. The fictional view must not be thought of as an abstraction, but as an aim, as a directive principle of action which itself is in no way a fiction. Natural rights—as ethical rather than legal concepts—must be understood as directing realities, and in that sense they could be designated as fictional only by those who would treat all ethical claims as fictional. It is recognized, therefore, that there is a possible ambiguity in employing an "as if" phraseology, for if a thing is morally real it is somewhat misleading to designate the approach to it as a fiction.

[31] *The Spirit of the Common Law,* pp. 91–92. (Italics mine.)

There is no intention here, to conclude, of implying that such a hypothetical interpretation of natural rights was in any way the approach of Henry George. No attempt will be made to minimize his absolutistic attitude. For him, natural rights were sacred, eternal, God-given things, derived from the very nature or essence of humanity, and they were never anything less. He himself held that all his economic doctrines were implicit in the bills of rights of the American and French Declarations, and that his political philosophy was a free rendering of the classical presentation of natural rights.[32] And neither will there be any suggestion that for George the ethical emphasis in economics was essentially a provisional one. His statement of the ethical nature of economics was too rigorous to permit such an approach.[33] But there must be introduced the thought that while George undoubtedly relied in terminology and methodological con-

---

[32] These are some of George's characteristic passages: "There are those who, when it suits their purpose, say that there are no natural rights, but that all rights spring from the grant of the sovereign political power. It were waste of time to argue with such persons. There are some facts so obvious as to be beyond the necessity of argument. And one of these facts, attested by universal consciousness, is that there are rights between man and man which existed before the formation of government, and which continue to exist in spite of the abuse of government; that there is a higher law than the human law—to wit, the law of the Creator, impressed upon and revealed through nature, which is before and above human laws, and upon conformity to which all human laws must depend for their validity. To deny this is to assert that there is no standard whatever by which the rightfulness or wrongfulness of law and institutions can be measured; to assert that there can be no actions in themselves right and none in themselves wrong. . . . These natural rights, this higher law, form the only true and sure basis for social organization." (From the chapter on "The Rights of Man" in Social Problems; Works, Vol. II; p. 92.) "The simple yet all-embracing statement of natural rights in the Declaration bears the stamp of primary truth; it includes all partial truths and coördinates all other truths. This perfect liberty, which, by giving each his rights secures the rights of all, is order, for violence is the infringement of rights; it is justice, for injustice is the denial of rights; it is equality, for one cannot have more than his right without another having less; it is reverence towards God, for irreverence is the denial of His order; it is love towards man, for it accords to others all we ask for ourselves." (From a speech on "Wanted—a Democratic Party," at the Brooklyn Reform Club, March 12, 1883.)

[33] See Supra, pp. 139–140.

cepts upon the older formulation of the doctrine of natural rights, the essence of his position lay in an ethical individualism. The ethical status of individuals, the nature and scope of claims morally made in behalf of individuals, were the great sanctions behind any theory of rights. To deny natural rights was "to assert that there is no standard whatever by which the rightfulness or wrongfulness of laws and institutions can be measured." And that is why it is felt that this preceding discussion of the more recent "as if" interpretation of natural rights, an approach that regards such a doctrine as an insistence upon the necessity of standards of judgment, has not been a gratuitous or arbitrary one.

This distinction between the "ethical" and "metaphysical" elements in George's interpretation of the concept "natural" may be illustrated by his handling of property rights. The phrase, "the natural right to property," connotes characteristically a strictly conservative use of the idea. It is familiar that the bulwark of the reactionary individualism that dominated much of nineteenth century thought was precisely this "natural" sacredness of property. Property in land, in goods, and in men (from Aristotle to the pro-slavery constitutions of pre-Civil War days) have all been justified by the sacrosanct qualifications of "natural." [34] In fact, all of the smugness of conservative laissez-faire, all the deplorable effects of an unenlightened, hands-off Manchester policy, found their sure basis in man's natural and inalienable right to himself and to the fruits of his labor. (It was "unnatural," therefore, to prohibit women and children from working sixteen hours a day in mines since their rights would have been violated!)

[34] The absolutistic approach to "natural" always demands the appeal from intuition to intuition. As Bentham put it, the fairest of those who hold things to be natural is "that sort of man who speaks out and says, I am of the number of the elect; now God himself takes care to inform the elect what is right . . . If, therefore, a man wants to know what is right he has nothing to do but to come to me." (*Principles of Morals and Legislation;* Clarendon Press ed., pp. 17–20, n.)

And perhaps the logical, "metaphysical" conclusions from such a premise of natural right might have been that to which the hard-headed Manchester school was led.[35] The attacks of all "welfare" economists, e. g., Hobson, upon classical economy have been precisely that its "natural laws" and "natural rights" sought (although unsuccessfully) to operate outside of the dimension of ethics, and therefore partially prepared the way for the reactionary distortion that followed. A nonmoral, "physical" functioning of natural law and natural right could not be questioned by the social reformer.

George's interpretation of a "natural right to property," however, was an ethical one. That is to say, while George's approach was undoubtedly phrased in absolutistic terms, still the concept of "natural" was used by him critically; "natural," in a word, was that which *ought* to be law. For example, George sought to make an important (ethical) qualification in the classical statement of such a natural right to property, a qualification founded upon a labor basis. That labor amendment distinguished between property in land and property in the product of labor, or capital, and attempted to demonstrate that there was a moral sanction, e. g., for the socialization of rent.[36] There could be no natural right

[35] Of course, it was not logic but good business that led to such an interpretation. Unfortunately, when the concept of property is based upon an uncompromising natural right, there must be those who read the auguries, and the keeping of the intuition of the natural right to property has been so often in the care of property-owners. As Dean Pound puts it: "The theory of inherent moral qualities, while it would serve for interests of personality . . . would not serve as a basis for the so-called natural right of property . . . None of the jurists of that time (seventeenth and eighteenth centuries) questioned the existing social order. On the contrary, they assumed as beyond question a natural right of property." (*The Spirit of the Common Law*, p. 93.) For a brief statement of the various "rights" to property based upon these differing logical or metaphysical emphases, see Ritchie's chapter (XIII) on the "Right of Property." *(Op. cit.)* It was such examples that made him impatiently conclude his discussion with "the dispute between these two scholastic theologians, Mr. Henry George and Pope Leo XIII," over the right of property in hand. (Pp. 270–271.)

[36] See *supra*, pp. 133 ff.

to property in land, since such a right was dependent only upon the expenditure of labor. Now, whether or not such a distinction is appealing, George's efforts show unmistakably that it was the ethical aspect of property that attracted him, and not any logical or metaphysical one. And it may therefore be said that George's concern with natural rights was largely an ethical concern.[37] When the over-rigorous interpretation of rights led to conclusions which, for him, were directed away from economic welfare, he refused to follow them. This is not to say that such a treatment of rights by George was in every case a conscious one. There can be little doubt that the metaphysical dress in which he clothed the whole concept of rights, and the eighteenth-century vocabulary which he employed, were generally uncriticized by him. Yet it does seem evident that it was the function of natural rights in providing a norm that made the concept a very foundation for his joint structure of economics and ethics. And it is believed that this whole previous presentation of the "normative" value of a doctrine of rights may, without any serious distortion, be considered applicable to George's underlying ethical emphasis.

It was such an emphasis, moreover, that may be held responsible for George's classical, "theoretical" phrasing of economics. The attack on the part of all rationalistic systems of ethics upon the fumbling efforts of experience was

[37] Such a concern is made clear in expressions such as these: "Our so-called recognition of the equal and natural rights of man is to large classes of our people nothing but a mockery, and as social pressure increases, is becoming a more bitter mockery to larger classes, because our institutions fail to secure the rights of men to their labor and the fruits of their labor." (*Social Problems,* p. 96.) "What use are political rights unless they can be used to gain social rights? I care not what the form of government may be; I care not how you treat of the rights of men—so long as the equal, inalienable right of men to gain a free, fair living by their own labor is denied." (From a lecture at the Midland Institute, Birmingham, England, January 23, 1884.) It is clear that George's distinctly ethical conception of natural rights insisted upon the moral phase of politics as well as of economics.

implicit in his approach to political economy; the science must be decisive and rigid. It is of course by no means necessary, or, in fact, advisable, to accept such an absolutistic system of ethics as that which appealed to George; indeed, it must be evident that this whole interpretation of his work is attempting to explain ethical significance through another approach. But it is felt that it is necessary to accept his fervent contention that economics derives its significance from a rapprochement with ethical consequences and ethical standards. In other words, the point here is not as to what interpretation is to be given ethics, rationalistic or instrumental, but it is whether economics is to consider itself as ethically determined or not. The only way, for George, that economics could so consider itself determined was to follow the theoretical presentation of the classical school. That is an argument that may or may not be accepted, but the more general contention that the background of economics must be an ethical one is a thesis that can be disregarded, it seems, only with great danger. One does not have to be completely unorthodox to insist that those "nonmoral" efforts of recent economists have as yet achieved scant success. Contemporary economics finds itself as helpless as classical political economy (and much less confident) in the face of the economic evils with which civilization is confronted. Its vocabulary is more "scientific" than the syllogistic terminology of the early nineteenth century, its graphs are imposing, and its researches intricate, but there still are (should not one add that they are increasing?) poverty, misery, economic unrest. Economics must develop further in a quantitative dimension, it is answered. Perhaps. But should that development sacrifice values and standards to statistics, should it become so engrossed with figures as to blind itself to symptoms and cures, then one must evince a polite skepticism.

The question, finally, that must be raised here is whether economics and the other social sciences should seek the goal of description and quantification with a resolute and calm determination to ignore anything that savors of valuation and judgment. Will they be more successful than jurisprudence and better preserve some of their recently won physical science attributes? Or will ethics begin to creep back? Or should there be the definite and unconcealed attempt to thrust values again into economics? Shall a discipline such as economics, which is concerned with probably the most vital and menacing problems that a social order is called upon to face, be praised for accepting the material that comes to it without attempting to evaluate, to criticize, to amend?

Economics, since it is an enterprise that investigates man's attempts to satisfy his material wants, may indeed be considered, in an age of industrialism and competition such as this, in an "acquisitive society," as the "science of survival." Economics, and no longer biology, seems to be the technique that treats of the struggle for existence. Those fittest who survive and flourish in an acquisitive, competitive society must be studied, not by biology or even psychology, but rather as specimens subject to economic analysis. The point is more than a facetious one. It suggests perhaps that the phenomena which are the materials for the operations of economics are too portentous, too indicative of unsolved moral problems, to be accepted uncritically as the subject-matter of a descriptive or historical science. By uncritically is meant here specifically the failure to distinguish between the normal and the pathological, a failure that is not present in some of the disciplines that economics seems to choose as models. Psychology, for example, does not confuse the healthy and the morbid; economics too often does. And the cause may perhaps be located in the absence of norms and standards.

One more point: There have recently been launched attacks upon the overspecialization of contemporary science and technical knowledge (the *Encyclopedia of the Social Sciences* represents a reaction from such specialization in its field), and the plea has been made for the introduction of an intellectual synthesis, of an age of system-construction. Modern physics is being hailed in many quarters as the locus of such a physical synthesis. This challenge directed against an overspecialized concern with minutiæ, against an ignoring-of-the-forest-for-the-trees technique, seems to be even more applicable to the social sciences than to the natural sciences, more applicable, perhaps, because that hyperspecialized technique does not appear to fit the social enterprises as neatly as it does the physical disciplines; great gaps of body show here and there. However, this indictment of overspecialization should not be confined to the realm of fact itself, but must be expanded so as to embrace in its charge a criticism of the exclusion, upon the grounds of specialization, of value from fact, an exclusion that banishes from the social sciences vision along with values. A warning of the dangers of such a type of specialization seems particularly pertinent in the case of economics.

It is felt here that economics may become richer and more vital if it puts aside, at least partially, certain feverish efforts to resemble physics or biology. It need not fear that a reintroduction of values would open the way for a wholesale return of all the concepts of classical political economy, for, as has been noted, when a doctrine of ethical import such as that of natural rights is resurrected it reappears in a new garb; the new form corresponds to the empirical instead of the rational. There is scarcely opportunity in this connection to mention the significant alteration that such a new form effects in ethical as well as in economic operations. It may be suggested, however, that the recent emphasis, as in Professor Dewey, upon the operational point of view (using the expression made current by contemporary scientific thinking) as applied to ethics, namely, that values as well as concepts be tested in terms of their operations, may benefit from a greater degree of coincidence between two such disciplines as economics and ethics. Such an emphasis might disclose a new approach to their mutual operations which would tend to make the one more susceptible to direction and the other less void of content. Certainly, there need be no fear of such a coincidence unless economics, on the one hand, begins to realize that it has been operating largely with surface material, or ethics, on the other, that it has too often neglected material of any nature.

It is a somewhat depressing paradox that facts and values seem so often at odds in economics. The pendulum appears to swing from the thesis that the science must be a branch of logic and ethics, to the antithesis that it must shun the dim region of norms. Surely, there must be a synthesis that unites both in a common field of thought.

CHAPTER X

GEORGE'S ETHICAL SOLUTION

GEORGE'S concern with poverty did not lie within the realm of pity or of charity, as is the case with many of our practical sociologists; that is, his concern was not an æsthetic one. Neither did his interest in economics have a detached, "scientific" character. And if it be said that this concern of his was "ethical," that word must be understood as implying nothing of the nature of pious exhortation. By an ethical interest in the phenomenon of poverty and in the processes of economic life, there is meant the frank realization that human life, with all its ideals and hopes, all its "values," is conditioned by the social setting in which it finds itself. Morality, if it means anything, is an effort to enlarge and enrich the dimension of human personality, to integrate the individual so that his status as a social organism will become more intelligible, more self-conscious. The ethical concepts are concepts of expansion, attempts to widen the boundaries of individual personality, to socialize that personality—to personalize social forces. These ethical values, then, these judgments that seek to develop and to direct personality, can they be operative without a definite social orientation?

Must it not be clear, that is, that the individual, with whom ethics busies itself, is not something complete in himself? Is not individuality rather a potentiality, a capacity for development, and does it not "develop into shape and form only through interaction with actual conditions"?[1] To continue with Professor Dewey's analogy: Individuality is no fenced garden that is to be cultivated in isolation. "Our garden is the world, at the angle in which it touches our own manner of being." Now, does not one angle of that contact point in the direction of economic phenomena? Is not one of those "actual conditions" which have a developmental function in moulding the form of individuality that economic paradox which aroused Henry George? The economic spectacle of poverty, of poverty surrounding wealth, was of ethical import solely because it distorted that development of society within which personality must develop and moral judgments arise. The consequences of economic operations were moral ones; that is why George made economics a branch of ethics. The consequences of poverty were the distortion of all values; that is why George must solve the problem of poverty before he can explore the vistas of ethics.

Whether or not it shocks our "intrinsic" values, the fact that the background of human activity is essentially and characteristically dominated by the spectre of "making a living" cannot be put aside. That spectre, for some, may be tenuous and subtle, nothing but an evanescent myth, yet for too many others it expands into the terrifying proportions of some Brocken-shadow. A precarious, predatory setting cannot be disregarded in any catholic approach to social ethics. It may be that "pure" philosophy can cavalierly dismiss such mundane considerations and withdraw itself tranquilly into some higher sphere of essences. Such philosophy is singularly fortunate; it is to be envied. Metaphysics and logic and

[1] Professor Dewey in *The New Republic*, "Individualism in Our Day" (April 2, 1930, Vol. LXII, No. 800, p. 187). This series of articles on "Individualism, Old and New" (starting in *The New Republic* of January 22, 1930) is perhaps the clearest and most recent expression of the thought that is intended in these paragraphs. (These articles have since appeared in separate form.)

epistemology perhaps need no "economic interpretation," but they must not attempt to draw ethical or political theory up with them. Any divorce of the social philosophies from their evident, if unwelcome, "sordid" surroundings is productive of just that empty formalism that has been so typical of ethics and politics. Ethics and politics, however, are not formal; they are vital, instrumental. The conditions which they handle are menacingly vital, destructively instrumental, since, in our present order of things, those conditions point to economic insecurity. "The most marked feature of present civilization is insecurity . . . In spite of all that is written about unemployment, its emotional and mental effect does not seem to me to have begun to receive the attention it deserves. It is hopeless to look for mental stability and integration when the economic bases of life are unsettled." [2] Mental stability and integration—that is what is sought by ethical values.

Therefore, to preface a discussion of what George confidently expected would be the ethical end results of his solution of the economic problem, there must first be very briefly presented another excursion into the dimension of economics, one concerned with the economic effects of the socialization of rent.

It has been noted before that the solution of the economic problem must be most significantly located in the realm of the distribution rather than in that of the production of wealth. But, asks George, consider first the effect of his taxation proposal upon the production of wealth. Our present system of taxation penalizes production and offers a premium to idleness. It fines the man who builds, who improves, who

---

[2] Professor Dewey in "The Lost Individual" (No. II of *The New Republic* articles; February 5, 1930, Vol. LXI, No. 792, p. 294). He adds that the pathological accompaniments of such economic insecurity cannot "be got rid of by hortatory moral appeal."

increases wealth; it exempts the man who does not. Would not a shift of the burden of taxation away from productive enterprise (George's first "canon of taxation"), the lifting of the enormous weight of taxation from industry, act as an unparalleled stimulus upon the production of wealth? [3] George's plan calls for the redirection of the incidence of taxation from production to a source that is the result of no industry or labor, one that automatically presents itself as the by-product of social organization. Here in land values was a source for taxation that seemed so neatly provided that, for George, its presence could be nothing else but the manifestation of a "natural law" of taxation. Devote this fund of revenue to defraying the expenses of social organization, and the production of wealth will proceed unhampered.

Consider further, George urges, the new opportunities that would be opened to production. Land would be forced into use—and by land is meant building land as well as agricultural land, factory sites as well as mines, transportation opportunities as well as all natural resources. Land could not be held out of use for speculative purposes or because of inability or unwillingness to improve it. No one could keep land unemployed and still pay its ground rent to the State in taxation; the man who improved his land would be penalized no more than the owner who kept his land idle— just the reverse of the strange operations of our existing system. What could be the only effect upon the production of wealth of this opening up to production the opportunities of

[3] "Instead of saying to the producer, as it does now, 'The more you add to the general wealth the more shall you be taxed,' the State would say to the producer, 'Be as industrious, as thrifty, as enterprising, as you choose, you shall have your full reward! You shall not be fined for making two blades of grass grow where one grew before; you shall not be taxed for adding to the aggregate wealth.' And will not the community gain by thus refusing to kill the goose that lays the golden eggs; by thus refraining from muzzling the ox that treadeth out the corn; by thus leaving to industry, and thrift, and skill, their natural reward, full and unimpaired?" (*Progress and Poverty,* p. 433.) As for that rather amusing contemporary spectre of general overproduction, see *supra,* pp. 123–124.

land that is now not used to its full capacity and the land that is not used at all? Increased production of wealth, as George has pointed out before, creates an increased demand for land. When rent is socialized, that increased demand will be met by further land being forced into use, whereas now that increased demand merely swells the rent accruing to the owner of land.

Now, to make the transition from production, how would this disposition of rent and of land monopoly [4] affect the channels through which wealth was distributed? The pattern of distribution that George has elaborated must be recalled, for the effects of his solution lie characteristically in its redirection of the flow of wealth. In fact, it can be only as corollaries that such economic effects can be presented, since they are implicit in his treatment of the distributive process. That is, the part that rent plays in George's approach to the distribution of wealth is crucial; it is the focus of the problem, of the solution, and of the economic consequences of that solution. Wages and interest, he has held, have been fixed by the marginal line of rent, and rent has been paid out of the legitimate return to wages and interest. With rent socialized, however, wages and interest would receive their full return.

Labor and capital would then receive the whole produce, minus that portion taken by the State in the taxation of land values, which, being applied to public purposes, would be equally distributed in public benefits. That is to say, the wealth produced in every community would be divided into two portions. One part would be distributed in wages and interest between individual producers, according to the part each had taken in the work of production; the other part would go to the community as a whole, to be distributed in public benefits to all its members.[5]

[4] George does not have to convince us that the socialization of rent would break land monopoly. But with the fall of that monopoly, all monopoly, he felt, would be undermined. (See *supra*, p. 260, n. 61.)

[5] *Progress and Poverty*, pp. 438–439.

Rent would no longer retain its privileged position that enabled it to prey upon the other factors of distribution. The importance for George's concepts of his synthesis of the laws of distribution becomes apparent. Rent has distorted the "natural" process of distribution. Make rent public property, and wages and interest must rise. Make rent public property, and the expenses of social organization need not be paid out of the return to labor or capital. That is the logical neatness of George's laws of rent, wages, and interest.

Wages and interest thus will rise, he argues, because the negative force of rent will have been removed. But, from a positive approach, consider, asks George, the effect of increased production of wealth and the redirected distribution of wealth specifically upon labor. Obviously demand for labor, for all types of labor, would grow. Were land values to remain private property, however, that demand for labor could not materially raise wages, since, in terms of George's argument, whatever increase might take place within wages would be met and overtaken by an increase in rent. (The same would happen to interest.) But with land values a public fund, with therefore no encroachment of rent upon the other factors of distribution, that pressing demand for labor would not only necessarily increase wages—real, not merely money, wages—but also remove unemployment. Furthermore, to complement higher wages would be the increased supply—resulting from land being forced into use and increased production—of all consumable goods, from food to houses; and prices, building rent—"the cost of living"—would fall.

It may be objected perhaps that this is becoming too humble and homely even for what is frankly a discussion of economic effects. "Wages," "unemployment," "cost of living"—unfortunately they are far from ideational; they are crude, crass, practical. But upon them depends economic se-

curity, and upon economic security depends the healthy development of the individual, and ultimately the judgments
and values of ethics. George is here proposing a system of
distribution—to attempt what is possibly a more gracious
phrasing—which would seek to alter that most vicious of relationships between increasing economic activity and increasing
economic insecurity. That marriage between progress and
poverty, in the light of his examination of the economic
structure, is cemented by rent being diverted into private possession. Rent rises as economic activity grows, and falls as
economic activity diminishes or ceases; thus rent is not only
the creature of communal activity, but seems to be the life-
blood of the community. Any force or instrumentality that
deprives the community of this life-blood—rent—acts as a
parasite upon the forces engaged in the production of wealth.
This was George's argument, and therefore the effects of a
solution that, at one blow, would transform rent from a
negative to a positive factor could, for him, be nothing short
of the removal of economic insecurity.

But this new equilibrium established, further advances in productive power, and the tendency in this direction would be greatly
accelerated, would result, in still increasing rent, not at the expense of wages and interest, but by new gains in production, which,
as rent would be taken by the community for public uses, would
accrue to the advantage of every member of the community. Thus,
as material progress went on, the condition of the masses would
constantly improve . . . For the increasing power of production,
which comes with increasing population, with every new discovery
in the productive arts, with every labor-saving invention, with
every extension and facilitation of exchanges, could be monopolized by none. That part of the benefit which did not go directly
to increase the reward of labor and capital would go to the State
—that is to say, to the whole community.[6]

[6] *Progress and Poverty*, p. 440.

The working out of that type of equilibrium would necessarily be in terms of wages, employment, cost of living, and if to some these terms are æsthetically "materialistic," let us say, as did George, that the effects of the socialization of rent would make progress and poverty enemies, logical contradictories, instead of the boon companions that they are at present.

It may be objected more vigorously that there is no guarantee that these predicted economic consequences would follow the socialization of rent, that, after all, they might exist only in the dimension of George's logic of distribution. That is an objection that by its very nature, of course, is unanswerable except in terms of George's logic. Rent, that is, has not been socialized, and thus the effects that George and his followers have demonstrated would be the consequences of their approach to the distribution of wealth, must still lie within the realm of controversy. But whether the logic of distribution that he has worked out, the "natural" economic process, rather, that he felt he had "discovered," would be justified by economic experimentation depends clearly upon the introduction of the experiment.

There is, however, another approach that may be made to this whole matter of the ethical consequences of the socialization of rent, an approach that introduces perhaps the most fundamental question proposed by George. It is the problem that he raised regarding "the law of human progress" and his discussion,[7] in many points, has almost the flavor of a German philosophy of history. George opens his ambitious argument [8] by questioning the current theory of human

[7] Book X of *Progress and Poverty*.
[8] George wrote to a friend, Charles Nordhoff, editorial writer of the New York *Herald*, that "the chapters relating to the development of civilization are but a bare skeleton of what I would like to say, and do not begin to

progress. That theory was one of hopeful fatalism, i. e., the evolutionary concept of Herbert Spencer.

This I take to be the current view of civilization: That it is the result of forces . . . which slowly change the character, and improve and elevate the powers of man; that the difference between civilized man and savage is of a long race education, which has become permanently fixed in mental organization; and that this improvement tends to go on increasingly, to a higher and higher civilization. We have reached such a point that progress seems to be natural with us, and we look forward confidently to the greater achievements of the coming race—some even holding that the progress of science will finally give men immortality and enable them to make bodily the tour not only of the planets but of the fixed stars, and at length to manufacture suns and systems for themselves . . . In this view, progress is the result of forces which work slowly, steadily, and remorselessly, for the elevation of man. War, slavery, tyranny, superstition, famine and pestilence, the want and misery which fester in modern civilization, are the impelling causes which drive man on, by eliminating poorer types and extending the higher; and hereditary transmission is the power by which advances are fixed, and past advances made the footing for new advances.[9]

Civilization is a slow upward climb, as is everything else, from the suitably qualified homogeneity to the converse heterogeneity, and the pauses that history presents are simply pauses—explicable perhaps in terms such as those of arrested mobility due to a thickening of the "cake" of custom.[10]

To George, however, the evidence of history pointed not to temporary pauses but to cycles, each with its birth, growth, and final "Untergang."

It is not merely these arrested civilizations that the current theory of development fails to account for. It is not merely that men

present the argument as strongly as I feel it." (December 21, 1879, San Francisco.)

[9] *Progress and Poverty*, pp. 479, 487.

[10] Compare, for example, Bagehot's *Physics and Politics*.

have gone so far on the path of progress and then stopped; it is that men have gone far on the path of progress and then gone back. It is not merely an isolated case that thus confronts the theory—*it is the universal rule.* Every civilization that the world has yet seen has had its period of vigorous growth, of arrest and stagnation; its decline and fall. Of all the civilizations that have arisen and flourished, there remain to-day but those that have been arrested, and our own, which is not yet as old as were the pyramids when Abraham looked upon them—while behind the pyramids were twenty centuries of recorded history. . . . If progress operated to fix an improvement in man's nature and thus to produce further progress, though there might be occasional interruption, yet the general rule would be that progress would be continuous—that advance would lead to advance, and civilization develop into higher civilization. Not merely the general rule, but *the universal rule,* is the reverse of this. The earth is the tomb of the dead empires, no less than of dead men. Instead of progress fitting men for greater progress, every civilization that was in its own time as vigorous and advancing as ours is now, has of itself come to a stop. Over and over again, art has declined, learning sunk, power waned, population become sparse, until the people who had built great temples and mighty cities, turned rivers and pierced mountains, cultivated the earth like a garden and introduced the utmost refinement into the minute affairs of life, remained but in a remnant of squalid barbarians, who had lost even the memory of what their ancestors had done, and regarded the surviving fragments of their grandeur as the work of genii, or of the mighty race before the flood.[11]

This was the universal rule of civilization, not a continued progress upward, but a cyclic arrangement of bloom and decay. But this present civilization, this thing of steel and concrete, of printed books and art and learning, but yet of steel and concrete—surely this will not decay! However, George is a veritable Jeremiah. The signs of ruin are becoming apparent. Political liberty and legal equality, for example, upon which the social ideals of present civilization are supposed to rest, are fast becoming empty names. They

[11] *Progress and Poverty,* pp. 482–483.

are forms, he points out, and forms without life are more
deadly than an absence of forms.[12] The dimensions of law
and politics are, and must be by their very nature, subordinate to that of economics,[13] and, given an unbalanced order,

[12] "But forms are nothing when substance has gone, and the forms of
popular government are those from which the substance of freedom may
most easily go. Extremes meet, and a government of universal suffrage
and theoretical equality may, under conditions which impel the change,
most readily become a despotism. For there despotism advances in the
name and with the might of the people. The single source of power once
secured, everything is secured. There is no unfranchised class to whom
appeal may be made, no privileged orders who in defending their own rights
may defend those of all. No bulwark remains to stay the flood, no eminence
to rise above it. They were belted barons led by a mitered archbishop who
curbed the Plantagenet with Magna Charta; it was the middle classes who
broke the pride of the Stuarts; but a mere aristocracy of wealth will never
struggle while it can hope to bribe a tyrant." (*Progress and Poverty*, pp.
527–528.)

[13] This economic determination of the social order is presented perhaps most interestingly by George in *The Science of Political Economy*
(Book I, especially Chaps. III–IV) in a discussion of what he designates as
the Greater Leviathan. The Leviathan of Hobbes, that artificial political
man, can be supplemented, according to George, by a Greater Leviathan
which is formed by the economic integration of men. "This Greater Leviathan is to the political structure or conscious commonwealth what the
unconscious functions of the body are to the conscious activities. . . .
Now, as the relations of the citizen proceed essentially from the relation
of each citizen to a whole—the body politic, or Leviathan, of which he is
a part—is it not clear, when we consider it, that the relations of the civilized man proceed from his relations to what I have called the body economic, or Greater Leviathan? It is this body economic, or body industrial,
which grows up in the coöperation of men to supply their wants and satisfy their desires, that is the real thing constituting what we call civilization. Of this the qualities by which we try to distinguish what we mean by
civilization are the attributes. It does indeed, I think, best present itself to
our apprehension in the likeness of a larger and greater man, arising out
of and from the coöperation of individual men to satisfy their desires, and
constituting, after the evolution which finds its crown in the appearance
of man himself, a new and seemingly illimitable field of progress. This body
economic, or Greater Leviathan, always precedes and always underlies
the body politic or Leviathan. The body politic or State is really an
outgrowth of the body economic, in fact one of its organs, the need for
which and appearance of which arises from and with its own appearance
and growth. And from this relation of dependence upon the body economic, the body politic can never become exempt." (Pp. 22–23; 27.)

George vigorously attacks the Spencerian concept of the priority of
biological and hereditary factors in determining social evolution, and in
Progress and Poverty (Book X, Chap. II) he makes a striking plea for a
recognition of the dominance of social conditions. In his concluding passage of the argument he states: " . . . In short, I take the explanation of
the differences which distinguish communities to be this: That each society,

nothing in civilization can remain healthy. This is how modern civilization may decline:

. . . A corrupt democratic government must finally corrupt the people, and when a people become corrupt there is no resurrection. The life is gone, only the carcass remains; and it is left but for the plowshares of fate to bury it out of sight.

Now this transformation of popular government into despotism of the vilest and most degrading kind, which must inevitably result from the unequal distribution of wealth, is not a thing of the far future. It has already begun in the United States, and is rapidly going on under our eyes. That our legislative bodies are steadily deteriorating in standard; that men of the highest ability and character are compelled to eschew politics, and the arts of the jobber count for more than the reputation of the statesman; that voting is done more recklessly and the power of money is increasing; that it is harder to arouse the people to the necessity of reforms and more difficult to carry them out; that political differences are ceasing to be differences of principle, and abstract ideas are losing their power; that parties are passing into the control of what in general government would be oligarchies and dictatorships; all are evidences of political decline.[14]

Political decline is portentous because it is a symptom of general decay. It would be gratuitous to supplement the evidence that George saw in 1879 with a catalogue of present-day conditions. It would be almost an act of unfairness to an already overharassed social organization to make a parade of the menacing economic unrest, the political anarchy, the moral apathy or smug hypocrisy of the times. "When a

small or great, necessarily weaves for itself a web of knowledge, beliefs, customs, language, tastes, institutions, and laws. Into this web, woven by each society . . . the individual is received at birth and continues until his death. This is the matrix in which mind unfolds and from which it takes its stamp." (P. 502.) George realizes that hope for a civilization that is to display a continuous and upward progress cannot be found in biology. The changes effected within the individual will not accelerate and draw on with them civilization as long as conditions in society act as a brake upon further individual development. Alteration in society must be focussed upon the forces which conditions the individual. (For a fuller discussion of this matter, see *infra*, pp. 536–542.)

[14] *Progress and Poverty*, pp. 529–530.

people become corrupt there is no resurrection." Is that day
of cynical disillusionment far off—not merely political disenchantment but economic and ethic as well? "There is no
mistaking it—the very foundations of society are being
sapped before our eyes, while we ask, *how* is it possible that
such a civilization as this . . . should ever be destroyed?" [15]
It is hardly profitable, however, to dwell upon the promised decay of western civilization or to comment upon our
"detached" study of the monuments of past cultures. George
is only one of many prophets who have announced thus:
"Whence shall come the new barbarians? Go through the
squalid quarters of great cities, and you may see, even now,
their gathering hordes! How shall learning perish? Men
will cease to read, and books will kindle fires and be turned
into cartridges." [16] It is of more instrumental significance to
trace George's theory of the cause of these ever-recurring
cycles of growth and decay. This will lead back to the economic concern that is at the root of his excursion into a philosophy of history. For him the cause of this decay was not
an organic cause; that is, George did not accept that most
dismal of interpretations, i. e., that civilization and culture
must grow old and perish just as do individuals. The cause
is a less hopeless one than that product of a poor analogy;
it is less hopeless because it is an economic cause, and therefore susceptible to control. To preface that economic presentation, however, there must first be understood what, for
George, was the very law of human progress itself.

What is meant, first, by human progress? That progress,
for George, could lie only in one dimension, the dimension of
mental power which was both the instrument by which man
advanced and the measure of that advance. It is the instrument by which man advances, for it makes possible "the extension of knowledge, the improvement of methods, and the

[15] *Progress and Poverty*, p. 532.   [16] *Ibid.*, p. 535.

betterment of social conditions." It is the measure of that advance, for it is in the degree that the extension of knowledge and the betterment of social conditions make possible the satisfaction of man's insatiable desire "to be, to know, and to do" that progress becomes significant. That is to say, by human progress George means, in the social realm, the extension of human knowledge, and, in the individual realm, the satisfaction of man's "higher" wants—intellectual, æsthetic, moral. Human progress is not material progress.

However, does not this statement appear to contradict an earlier contention, namely, that George's interpretation of the social problem is one that keeps clear of the traditional dualism between the "material" and the "ideal"? But consider further. There are, in addition, what George calls "nonprogressive" activities. The nonprogressive activities may be classified as those of maintenance and conflict; "by maintenance I mean, not only the support of existence, but the keeping up of the social condition and the holding of advances already gained. By conflict I mean not merely warfare and preparation for warfare, but all expenditure of mental power in seeking the gratification of desire at the expense of others, and in resistance to such aggression." [17]

To compare society to a boat. Her progress through the water will not depend upon the exertion of her crew, but upon the exertion devoted to propelling her. This will be lessened by any expenditure of force required for bailing, or any expenditure of force in fighting among themselves, or in pulling in different directions. [18]

Neither bailing (maintenance) nor dissension (conflict) is a "progressive" activity. The progressive activity in this case is the propelling of the boat through the water. Neither the mere support of existence nor the resistance to aggression are "progressive" activities in the case of human progress.

[17] *Ibid.*, p. 504.　　[18] *Ibid.*, pp. 504–505.

The progressive activity here is the satisfaction of the desire for knowledge.

The connection, then, between "higher" and "lower" activities, between progressive and nonprogressive ones, may perhaps become clearer. Progressive activity is definitely dependent upon the variable of nonprogressive activity. Mental power can function in progressive lines only after its nonprogressive tasks, chiefly those of sustaining life, have been accomplished; those tasks act as a limiting factor. In other words, human progress is essentially a surplus. It is the mental power that can be devoted to satisfying the "ideal," "higher" wants of man once his "material," "lower" needs have been taken care of. There is indeed no insulation between the two realms, but a direct functional connection.

But what is the law of human progress? That law George locates in the phenomenon of association, of social gregariousness. Man, the social animal, is presented with only one way of efficiently solving the problem of "nonprogressive" activity; that is, by a continuing and everincreasing utilization of communal forces. As the power of social coöperation rises, the less compelling should become the demands of maintenance, and the greater should become the degree of mental power that can be expended in "progress," whereas when the integration of social powers is at a low level the maintenance of life absorbs more and more of the activity of man.

Now, as in a separated state the whole powers of man are required to maintain existence, and mental power is set free for higher uses only by the association of men in communities, which permits the division of labor and all the economies which come with the coöperation of increased numbers, association is the first essential of progress. Improvement becomes possible as men come together in peaceful association, and the wider and closer the association, the greater the possibilities of improvement.[19]

[19] *Progress and Poverty*, p. 505.

Association is not merely the natural condition of man; it is the hope of progress as well, since it sets free the powers that are required for development.

Yet this is only half of the "law of progress." It will be recalled that George's "nonprogressive" activities are divided into those of maintenance and conflict. The first is included within the operations of association, but what is the negative significance of the second? Here the synthesis of George's economic system and his philosophy of history will begin to manifest itself. Just as association, by setting free from nonprogressive activity human powers that can be turned to the further development of man, acts as an upward force, so there is what George terms an "internal resistance" or "counter force" which arises as that association is achieved and as civilization becomes more organized. That resistance must be comprehended if the cycle of civilization is to be explained. It is the resistance, the conflict that arises because of the growth of inequality among the members of civilized society. That inequality, for George, cannot be explained in terms of biology; it is instead the very creature of existing civilizations.

Now, this process of integration, of the specialization of functions and powers, as it goes on in society, is . . . accompanied by a constant liability to inequality. I do not mean that inequality is the necessary result of social growth, but that it is the constant tendency of social growth if unaccompanied by changes in social adjustments. . . . I mean, so to speak, that the garment of laws, customs, and political institutions, which each society weaves for itself, is constantly tending to become too tight as the society develops. I mean, so to speak, that man, as he advances, threads a labyrinth, in which, if he keeps straight ahead, he will infallibly lose his way, and through which reason and justice can alone keep him continuously in an ascending path.

For, while the integration which accompanies growth tends in itself to set free mental power to work improvement, there is, both with increase of numbers and with increase in complexity of the social organization, a counter tendency set up by the production of a state of inequality, which wastes mental power, and, as it increases, brings improvement to a halt. . . .

I am merely attempting to set forth the general fact that as a social development goes on, inequality tends to establish itself, and not to point out the particular sequence, which must necessarily vary with different conditions. But this main fact makes intelligible all the phenomena of petrifaction and retrogression. The unequal distribution of the power and wealth gained by the integration of men in society tends to check, and finally to counterbalance, the force by which improvements are made and society advances. On the one side, the masses of the community are compelled to expend their mental powers in merely maintaining existence. On the other side, mental power is expended in keeping up and intensifying the system of inequality, in ostentation, luxury, and warfare.[20]

The power of association that releases mental power is overweighed by the inequality which, with the great mass of mankind, again reclaims that mental power for nonprogressive activities. Thus, the "law of progress," that of association, must be supplemented:

As the wasteful expenditure of mental power in conflict becomes greater or less as the moral law which accords to each an equality of rights is ignored or is recognized, equality (or justice) is the second essential of progress.

Thus association in equality is the law of progress. Association frees mental power for expenditure in improvement, and equality, or justice, or freedom—for the terms here signify the same thing, the recognition of the moral law—prevents the dissipation of this power in fruitless struggles.

Here is the law of progress, which will explain all diversities, all advances, all halts, and retrogressions. Men tend to progress just as they come closer together, and by coöperation with each other increase the mental power that may be devoted to improvement, but just as conflict is provoked, or association develops in-

[20] *Progress and Poverty*, pp. 511; 515.

equality of condition and power, this tendency to progression is lessened, checked, and finally reversed.[21]

The focus of George's "economic interpretation of history," therefore, must be directed upon this "inequality" that arises as civilization develops and that brings about ultimately the decay of that civilization by raising "nonprogressive" activity to a crucial position. That inequality is, of course, an inequality in economic status, one which lies at the foundation of all varieties of inequality. It is, in other words, nothing less than the central problem of progress and poverty placed now against a background of civilization's rise and fall. That problem was always the great problem for Henry George. Its ramifications were infinite. Economic insecurity was the center from which radiated all the roads of social unhealthiness. In terms of George's brief but ambitious presentation of a theory of human development, it was now the very cause of man's failure to make permanent the progress that association had won for him.

Still further does George press his economic interpretation, and relentlessly, without any sign of diffidence, does he now correlate specifically the fall of civilization with the private ownership of land! Not indirectly does he make that, for him, triumphant correlation; that is, he does not rely upon a circuitous approach by referring back to his previous argument that the economic cause of poverty can be traced to the private appropriation of rent. Instead he appeals directly to his "law of human progress." That law postulated the growth of communal association as essential to the development of progressive activity, since such association tended to remove the onus of nonprogressive activity from the individual. Association developed a collective power that was

[21] *Ibid.*, p. 505. (Italics mine.)

more than the sum of individual efforts, and distinguishable from them. That collective power, that surplus of power, should make possible, therefore, the increasing sloughing off, on the part of the individual, of the concern with non-progressive enterprises.

Now, what is the correlation between this surplus of power that arises from association and George's economic postulates? The connection must be clear. That phenomenon of association creates a communal value which is in no way dependent upon individual efforts. Such communal value is directly and accurately expressed in the economic concept of rent. Land value is association value. It is a value that swells as association becomes more organized, and collapses as that social organization disappears or loses its efficiency. In a literal sense, then, land value is the economic measure of human progress. For George, it is the attendant of association, and association is the foundation of progress. Rent is not merely one of the channels in the distribution of wealth; it is not a rationalization of an economic state and it is more than the formula of an economic process. It is the tangible manifestation of the intangible power of association, the "material" measure of the imponderable elements of human gregariousness. Rent, finally, for George, is the exchange rate of man's development.

Land, however, has been privately owned in all our civilizations. The first occasional primitive insight that land was common property gave way to the psychological and sociological forces that have made for all manner of private property, and land was added to that category. Thus, the value that has been created by the press of men coming together has been gathered by the fortunate few into whose hands, in the course of history, the earth has passed. A social product has become an individual gain. Here, then, is the source of that inequality which, for George, has been the brake upon all cultures. The reason why the natural progress of civilization reaches a climax, decays, and finally collapses, can be traced to the inequality that results from the passing of community value into the sphere of private property. This transfer of value is the most vicious of economic maladjustments, for George realizes that the inequality it produces is a cumulative one. The greater the integration of social forces, the greater is the value of land, and therefore under the economic systems of all civilizations the greater has been the tribute that must be paid by mankind for the very process that draws it together. That tribute has taken different expressions under the different forms of social organization, but the principle of exploitation has remained the same—the diverting of a social fund from its legitimate social function.

There could be no more tragic circle than this continual self-annihilation of progress. Human development, as George saw it, carried along with itself the very instrument that proved its destruction; civilization suffered from auto-intoxication. That instrument could be the very one which, in a saner economic system, might bring about a still further advance in progress, a development which would be boundless, but now that instrument, the social increment of land value, acted as the creature of Frankenstein.

George was asking, in other words, whether human progress itself could continue under a system of economic instability. Economic insecurity, the deadly inequality within the economic status of man, overthrew his "law of human progress." That progress depended upon "association in equality." It depended upon association taking care of the "nonprogressive" activities of maintenance. But what instead has been the effect of that association which was to release man's powers? It has throttled human progress by having been transformed into an "association in inequality." That inequality (for George the result of private property in land) has raised to a position of dominance the satisfaction of "non-progressive" wants. It has diverted mental power, the instrument of *bona fide* progress, into the path of menial pursuits. It has robbed human progress of all that is progressive.

This, then, is an approach to the socialization of rent by which George soars beyond the categories of economics into the very dimension of the rise and fall of civilization. He has attempted to trace the law of human progress itself, but has found that it cannot be severed from the prosaic requirements imposed by economic concepts. The development of culture, he has become convinced, is a function of rent.

Here, then, is George's most fundamental approach to the relation between economics (means) and ethics (ends). Man's moral and social progress is inevitably conditioned by an economic background. He can develop upward only when economic problems have been solved. And the great economic problem is that of the land.

Such a statement, however, conjures up a difficulty that cannot be easily neglected, and cannot be thoroughly handled. It is the problem found upon the scarred and torn battlefield stretching between the warring lines of "environment" and "heredity." The field, it is true, has been plowed anew in recent years by a whole corps of workers; the old war-cries, to vary the metaphor, have been reworded in terms of sociology and social psychology, of biology and anthropology, of intelligence tests, statistical surveys, and the rest, but the basic approach to the problem presented by the conflicting claims of man's racial and family heritage on the one hand, and of his social and economic surroundings on the other, has remained a familiar one. The difficulty that has faced all social reformers still persists: Are the evils that such reformers have attacked, be they termed poverty, crime, injustice, ignorance, or just social maladjustment and inefficiency, a product of man's inherent inability to live sanely with his fellows? Or are they to be located in a social milieu that is amenable to human direction? In other words, are social evils a branch of the etiology of man's moral ills, or are they the symptoms of an ethnic disease?

There is, for example, the approach of George that, basing itself upon the conviction that poverty directly affects the very springs of human action, seeks to launch an immediate attack upon it largely through economic weapons. His own words, quoted a few pages back, present this concept of the functional control of the individual by society: ". . . Each society, small or great, necessarily weaves for itself a web of knowledge, beliefs, customs, language, tastes, institutions, and laws. Into this web, woven by each society . . . the individual is received at birth and continues until his death. This is the matrix in which mind unfolds and from which it takes its stamp." And, on the other hand, there is the attitude that is convinced that, since social and political evils are the indication of some deeply rooted racial deficiency, the remedy must be pointed to the securing of fundamental biologic changes, of direct changes. It is an attitude that challenges the belief that social disease is a fit matter for an immediate attack, and questions whether such disease is really curable in terms of the economic, educational and political programs that have been proffered.

To be more specific: The suggestions that are brought forward by what might be termed the biologico-heredity school of contemporary social psychology constitute an attempt to realize, by means of practical and tangible techniques, the more abstract contentions of doctrinaire hereditarians. Taking as fundamental the dominance of race and family heritage over environmental conditions, of "nature" over "nurture," such an approach holds that permanent improvement of social conditions can be achieved only through methods that are directed to the selection and propagation of superior biologic strains. To remedy the evils of the social world man himself must first be moulded "nearer to the heart's desire." Man makes conditions, the argument runs, and while it is of course not denied that conditions in turn affect man, this latter relation is largely incidental, a relation that has the function of limitation or elimination perhaps, but certainly not of creation or re-forming. Environment may "set off" characteristic and hereditary behavior; it can act as a trigger, but whatever action may result is entirely dependent upon the potentialities of the organism. Factors that are inherent may be drawn forth, produced, or inhibited by conditions, but they cannot be induced.

The sociological implications of such a biologic approach are apparent. Social change must originate *via* individual change, and individual change is a question of direct eugenic control. Man's character cannot be vitally transformed by the social world; to improve men means to handle them as Gregor Mendel handled garden peas. Not economic or political reform, but measures of "positive" and "negative" eugenics are required to abolish the misery and wretchedness of society.[22] For such an approach, class stratification, that veritable caste system of the existing economic order, is fundamentally a matter of heredity.[23] All attempts, then, to transform per-

[22] It is such an approach that leads Professor F. H. Hankins, for example, to conclude his stimulating book with the conviction that social improvement "is solely a question of encouraging or maintaining the multiplication of the more able, regardless of race, and of discouraging the multiplication of the less able. Measures of positive eugenics are difficult to introduce, but widespread education and free discussion will do much. Information is all that the intelligent need. For the less intelligent there should be devised and universalized some effective means of birth control. This would help restore the disparity between the birth rates at the upper and lower social levels. There might also be a gradual extension of the present policies of segregation and sterilization . . . The wisest statesmanship would begin at once the discovery of the gifted strains and seek to introduce social conditions favorable to their preservation and multiplication." (*The Racial Basis of Civilization;* New York, Knopf, 1926, p. 375.)

[23] "It appears to us that since the first work of Francis Galton the steady accumulation of evidence favors the view that social stratification

manently the status of man as a social being through the medium of social reorganization and readjustment must remain of a piece with those quaint efforts of man to elevate himself by tugging at his boot-straps.

The type of problem that presents itself here, however, is not one of eugenics *qua* eugenics. That is, it cannot be directed to a discussion of the peculiar difficulties of such a science, or to what is perhaps even more important, the question of its good faith.[24] This digression is constantly and intentionally limiting the contrast between the eugenic and economic programs to those of approach, to the opposite attitudes of mind that each represents, to difficulties not so much of technique as of temper; and therefore the only difficulty presented by the biologic thesis that will be noticed here is its seeming failure to recognize explicitly that a breeding program is the definite product and peculiar creation of a social system, that it is thus as much dependent for its application upon an economic and political structure as is any other social proposal.

Such a recognition, it is true, is implicit in a paragraph like that quoted above. ". . . Measures of positive eugenics are difficult to introduce, but widespread education and free discussion will do much. Information is all that the intelligent need. For the less intelligent there should be devised

in a democratic society is explained more fully by the variation of inherent qualities than by any other factor." (*Ibid.*, p. 369.) It is a bit difficult to understand what Professor Hankins means by a "democratic society." He cannot seriously mean that political democracy has any significance in an economically unbalanced social order.

[24] What is meant here by a question of "good faith" is one that wonders about the goal toward which eugenic processes aim. Granting that the end of the science is that of the development of a certain type of human being, the question must arise: What type will be instrumental in increasing the welfare and happiness of the race, and who shall determine the type? This point of good faith is introduced, briefly but very acutely, by Bertrand Russell in his essay *Icarus* in the interesting Dutton series. Such a question is, of course, part of that more general challenge to science, the inquiry into the ends which scientific knowledge is intended to serve, that everpresent question as to normative values.

and universalized some effective means of birth control."
These sentences, it seems, represent an attitude that fails,
or perhaps is unwilling, to grasp the fact that social proposals
(even in the realm of biology) are functions of a social environment. "Widespread education," "free discussion," "information," "there should be devised and universalized some
effective [social] means"—are these not the very things the
environmentalist is trying to manipulate? To assume them
as necessary for the functioning of a eugenic solution of society's ills is, if we are endeavoring at all to reach fundamentals, surely circular logic. The very fact that such vital
and characteristically social agencies are introduced by the
eugenic approach only incidentally seems to give evidence
of a genuine difficulty in this concentration upon the suggestions of biology.

This is not intended to be the truistic recognition that
every human proposal is in some degree a socially determined
variable, for that could hardly be designated as a criticism of
any one proposal, but it is a sincere conviction that the
eugenic approach is short-sighted in its discussion of means.
The legitimate end of the science is, of course, the end that
is motivating every attempt, sociological or biological, to
change this life of ours, to create a nobler and more characteristically human being. But—at the risk of becoming increasingly bromidic—individuals can't be reached, even for
the purpose of introducing direct measures of positive and
negative eugenics, except through social agencies. Granted
that the question of ends in this whole discussion is the improvement of the individual, the means, because of the obvious fact that man functions only in some form of social
organization, must be social; this criticism of the biologic approach, therefore, is again one that is based upon the instrumentalist emphasis upon means. The very means of eugenics
must themselves be the product of prior social means. When

it is stated, for example, that "widespread education and free discussion" will be necessary before the difficulties of introducing eugenic measures are overcome, it is implicitly recognized that such eugenic programs are, in fact, themselves the end of other more fundamental processes. But that recognition is made too casually; it appears to ignore the fact that questions of means and instruments are all-important, and that the means to eugenic ends must be of a social character.

The thought that is trying to become articulate here is simply a plea for the recognition of the priority of social factors in any platform of social betterment. Biology's contribution to the social problem cannot be underestimated, or in any way disparaged, but it is felt that it does not afford a short cut to the direct manipulation of the individual. Eugenics must work through the medium of a social structure, and therefore it appears that the more fundamental problem of directly attacking that social structure—the problem that the environmentalist is trying to handle—must remain the characteristic approach of the social reformer.[25]

It is true that the biologist may still introduce the whole psychological problem of motivation, and point out that the social structure itself can be changed only by the action of motivated individuals. Yet, in this connection it seems only necessary to appeal to the fact that the social environment has been and is being changed, that there do appear individuals who are motivated and inspired, and whose efforts have produced definite transformations in society. Were that not so, then indeed would we be revolving in the most vicious of

[25] The words of Graham Wallas may be significant here: "Social psychology can never lead men to wise practical conclusions unless it keeps in view its relation to that science of human breeding which Sir Francis Galton named Eugenics . . . On the other hand . . . one finds one's self wondering whether . . . eugenic science will progress, or eugenic motives and methods be effective in a society unhygienic, uneducated, and unorganized." (*The Great Society;* New York, Macmillan, 1914, pp. 55-56.)

circles, and an attitude of bland resignation would be all that would be left for us.

And so to conclude this digression: Has it not yet been demonstrated, psychologically and sociologically, that the individual (at least so far as the qualities that make him a functioning social organism are concerned) is a product of his environment? Is it not a logical, if not yet a "scientific," postulate to assume that conditions must in some way be altered before any permanent change can be registered upon the individual? Can biology, *via* eugenics, function—or even be applied—in a social order in which the much simpler and less sophisticated problems of providing enough food and shelter for its members have not yet been solved? These are just leading questions. It is unfortunate that they cannot be made definitive statements. Let us end here with that most wise passage from the *Republic*, one not so spectacular as the more familiar Platonic breeding program, but one perhaps more quietly significant:

The regulations which we are prescribing . . . are not, as might be supposed, a number of great principles, but trifles all, if care be taken, as the saying is, of the one great thing . . . education and nurture: If our citizens are well educated and grow into sensible men, they will easily see their way through all these. . . . The State, if once started well, moves with accumulating force like a wheel. For good nurture and education implant good constitutions, and these good constitutions taking root in a good education improve more and more, and this improvement affects the breed in man as in other animals.[26]

The present chapter is devoted to a discussion of what might be termed the ethical effects of Henry George's economic solution. Any elaborate presentation of the economic effects of such a solution is not being essayed for reasons that already have been suggested. For one thing, the exposition of George's solution, which has been attempted, must con-

[26] Chap. IV, pp. 423–424. (Jowett translation.)

tain within it an implicit exposition of its economic consequences. That is, the socialization of rent, according to
George's outline of the economic process, must remove the
mischievous tangle in the distribution of wealth whereby
rent advances at the expense of wages and interest. Land
value was to be transformed from a social liability into a social asset, and only thus could an advancing civilization lead
to economic stability. Such effects were clearly the logical
conclusions of his premises. The presentation of his economic
indictment was at the same time the promise of his solution.
But perhaps a more important reason for not offering an ambitious exposition of such economic effects is one that also
has been noted before: Prediction in the realm of economics
is always a quite dangerous undertaking; at least, predictions must remain predictions until they are subject to empirical verification. And therefore a cataloguing of economic
consequences must either wait upon such verification or else
imply a much more expert handling of economic detail than
this essay can venture.

It is rather what George felt would be the ethical effects
of his solution that must interest us here. Now, to make such
a transition from economics to ethics, and to follow George's
argument, there must first be granted certain assumptions.
That is to say, let it be assumed, for the sake of that argument,
that the economic consequences of George's solution would be
as he had pictured them. Let the imagination, in other words,
wander over the prospect of an economic order in which
poverty and want and misery—economic insecurity, to be
less rhetorical—had disappeared, a social scheme in which
increasing economic activity tended to distribute instead of
to concentrate wealth. And let that exercise of the imagination expand even to Utopian proportions; let it add a word
to that great magic literature of perfect cities. Such an addition would not be in the economic terms of wages, rent,

cost of living; it would be in the ethical language of beauty, justice, noble men and women, and splendid, wise States. In that it would be little different from those charmed lands of nowhere that philosophers have always sought to discover—to invent. And the Utopia of Henry George, if one glances at it hastily, appears as but one more of those poems of man's hope in man. George's hope, however, is not that of the hortatory moralist, and neither is it that of the scientific eugenicist. It is the hope of the economist, and as such it bears a slightly different tinge from those other hopes.

What is meant by this is simply a recognition of a more realistic note in the Utopian hopes of George. That realism is centered in the location of the social ideals and the ethical values to be found in visions within an economic milieu in which alone they would be able to survive. The origin of the ideals and values that are found in social Utopias is not difficult to ascertain. It is an ideational origin, one springing from the dreams of great dreamers, and one therefore that makes those ideals and goals vital as an inspiration and as a directing program. George also dreamed, but of more moment to him than were the ideals he dreamed was the background against which they might flourish. The Utopian visions of the moralist and of the biologist are essentially transcendental; the one by pleas and the other by breeding seek to rise above the conditioning factors that are found in man's immediate surroundings. George instead sought to found his ideal society upon a redirection of those surroundings and not upon an effort to escape them. His—to risk the accusation of a pun—was an immanent Utopia. That is why his perfect state, placed as it was within the realm of economics, appears to offer a hope with a more realistic promise.

Utopias have resided always in the land of ethics, and ethics has characteristically implied a place of hope and good wishes. The divorce of the realm of ethics from the "lower" sphere of the instrumental is, of course, one against which familiar criticism has been attempted throughout this entire discussion of Henry George. The dualism between a moral order and an economic order (by economic order is intended the dimension of man's material wants), between ends and means, is a fatal one for ethical advance. It is a dualism that forces ethics to seek its solutions aided only by those "higher" ideal wants with which ethical theorists have forever been concerned. It limits the field of moral inquiry and excludes the very conditioning factors that make real and vital the whole meaning of morals. That is why the instrumentalist has always been suspicious of the select associates of much of ethical theory. Its very exclusiveness has robbed it of the richness and the material that must be sought in the problems of man's "lower" wants.

But of greater significance, that type of separation has robbed ethics of a comprehension of what may be implied by values themselves. There can be no legitimate cleavage between the values of ethics and the less exalted values of economics. The search for values, as Hobson points out,[27] must begin not in philosophic abstraction but with a consideration of "the instincts, appetites, and behavior of the animal man." The whole concept of a standard of values and of ethical welfare cannot be cut off from the psycho-physical organism or from the social community in which that organism functions.[28] Ethical values are judgments concerning the consequences of action, of action that occurs at the

---

[27] *Economics and Ethics;* see especially Chap. II.
[28] "In working out the basic theory of Welfare in Human Values, I incline to adhere closely to the conception of man as a psychophysical organism, welfare emerging in an organic harmonious coöperation of interrelated physical and mental activities." (*Ibid.,* p. 21.) Hobson goes on to state that physical health, mental development, and a coördination between the two make up this harmonious relation. Welfare in its relations to the community is discussed by him in Chapter III.

level of "the instincts, appetites, and behavior of the animal
man." The meaning of these judgments is therefore not
something absolute or self-sufficient; it must refer back to
the material which is judged, and that reference is in fact
the sole justification of ethical values. Just as in a previous
connection it has been insisted that, because the material
of economics involves consequences which are judged and so
pass into the field of ethics, economics cannot cut itself off
from ethics, so here that same insistence may be applied to
ethics. The material that it judges is "economic"—using
that term in a broad, figurative sense—and so the significance
of ethics, as that of economics, is no self-contained, autonomous, privileged "value." The values of each are instrumental, inter-operating. It is once more the recognition that
ends (ethic) and means (economic) must function as but different stages of one process.

The suggestion has been made before that ethics has a dual
function in that it attempts both to socialize personality and
to personalize social forces. This double function presents
ethics likewise with a dual responsibility. "Morality implies
responsibility, not merely for one's own soul, but for the continued good health of the social order." [29] The moral concepts are those of integration, and that integration involves,
in addition to the adapting of the individual personality to
the social demands, the refashioning of the social order so
that its workings may not be too unintelligible and contradictory to man's comprehensions. Now, the question is
whether it is possible for ethics to accept any kind of divorce
between itself and a discipline such as economics, whose chief
contribution is the understanding of the most vital opera-

[29] Professor Ayres in *The Nature of the Relationship between Ethics and
Economics,* Philosophic Studies of the University of Chicago, No. 8,
November 1918; p. 55. He continues: " . . . Moral insight is insight into
the whole structure of society; the moral interest is an interest that includes
the fortunes of institutions as well as of individuals."

tions of that social order.[30] If the intelligent integration of the individual with society is the goal of that which is of greatest worth in ethics, then ethical theory cannot be oblivious to the economic distortion in that society. If economics is to aid society in managing its affairs, if it "represents one phase of the general moral problem," then ethics cannot continue to ignore that phase.

"Moral insight is insight into the whole structure of society." That is perhaps an ambitious definition of this integrative function of ethics, but it is surely more significant than one that confines the boundaries of morals within the limits of ideals and visions, to the exclusion of the real and the visual. The insight of ethics has so often been directed into the exhortations of theology or the demonstrations of logic. Perhaps that is why ethical theory has failed to concern itself as much with evil as it has with a problem of evil. Poverty and economic insecurity, for example, have been given scant attention by ethics. Is it because they do not rightfully belong in that field, or is it because the ethical insight has not been into the whole structure of society?

This may be straying a bit from the work of Henry George, but it is felt that these thoughts are not entirely gratuitous, since it is in such terms that his economics becomes ethically significant. It may be recalled that this mention—a repeated mention—of the connection between ethics and economics was suggested by a more realistic, because economic, flavor that might be found in George's ethical visions. Specifically, that measure of realism was his conviction that ideals and Utopian hopes could have little longevity unless the matrix in which they took form was a favorable one. In other words,

---

[30] " . . . The one important effect of increased understanding of economic institutions is an increased capacity on the part of society at large to manage its affairs. In this sense the problem of economics is to contribute its study of industrial society to the solution of the problem of living. It represents one phase of the general moral problem." (*Ibid.*, p. 57.)

ethical Utopias, whether the product of the poet, the moralist, or the biologist and scientist, must remain lands of nowhere so long as they refused to consider conditions of settlement. Those conditions were primarily economic in character. Any social order that strove to realize the goals of ethical dreams must first busy itself with the more prosaic matters of economic adjustment. And that is why the bulk of George's work was not in ethical theory but in an examination of the processes of economics. "Thrift and virtue and wisdom and temperance are not the fruits of poverty." Let us turn back then to an assumption made a few pages back, the assumption that the economic results of George's solution would be as he had pictured them. Let a contrast be made between a civilization in which economic security has been attained and that one with which we are more familiar. Would that economic contrast throw any light upon a possible ethical dissimilarity between those two social orders?

Perhaps the most disconcerting spectacle that confronts the searcher for Utopia is that mad scramble of man to satisfy his material wants. That scramble seems an unæsthetic, brutish thing for the dreamer of perfect cities, and so the dreamer becomes ethically aristocratic. That is to say, he either relegates the satisfaction of these "lower" wants to a great third estate which can never achieve the status of philosopher-king (that is actually a bit of realism), or by exhortation he endeavors to chasten these wants, to will them away, or to transmute them by means of maxims. To employ George's terminology, the seeker after a social order that is to embody some of the aspirations of men is concerned particularly with magnifying "progressive activity." He is distressed at the exaggerated emphasis that society places upon "nonprogressive activities." A familiar conclusion, then, of the moralist is to concentrate upon an elaboration of these "higher" wants of man (progressive activity), reserving for the satisfaction of the "lower" desires (nonprogressive activity) a technique of suppression and inhibition. Thus, there enters again that characteristic dualism. The "higher" order is that which is concentrated upon, and the "lower" is neglected; so Utopias remain Utopias. That spectacle of civilization being dominated by a mad, ugly, stupid scramble, however, is amenable not to the well wishes of the traditional moralistic approach but to an examination of psychological motivation in terms of its social background.

"The mental power which can be devoted to progress is only what is left after what is required for nonprogressive purposes." In this way does George phrase that dominance of "materialism" which is the bane of all ethicists. It is economic insecurity, the fact that the "nonprogressive" activities of maintenance demand the major share of mankind's attention, that makes crucial this concern with the "lower" wants. Man becomes a predatory animal because he is conditioned by a ruthless economic order.

Did you ever see a pail of swill given to a pen of hungry hogs? That is human society as it is . . . "Devil catch the hindmost" is the motto of our so-called civilized society to-day . . . We learn early to grasp from others that we may not want ourselves . . .

The greed of wealth, which makes it a business motto that every man is to be treated as though he were a rascal, and induces despair of getting in places of public trust men who will not abuse them for selfish ends, is but the reflection of the fear of want. Men trample over each other from the frantic dread of being trampled upon, and the admiration with which even the unscrupulous money-getter is regarded springs from habits of thought engendered by the fierce struggle for existence to which the most of us are obliged to give up our best energies . . . He must have eyes only for the mean and vile, who has mixed with men without realizing that selfishness and greed and vice and crime are largely the result of social conditions which bring out the bad qualities of human nature and stunt the good; without realizing that there is even now among men patriotism and virtue enough to secure us the best possible management of public affairs if our social and political adjustments enabled us to utilize those qualities.[31]

Whence springs this lust for gain, to gratify which men tread everything pure and noble under their feet, to which they sacrifice all the higher possibilities of life; which converts civility into a hollow pretense, patriotism into a sham, and religion into hypocrisy; which makes so much of civilized existence an Ishmaelitish warfare, of which the weapons are cunning and fraud? Does it not spring from the existence of want? [32]

These are the ethical consequences of a society in which the problems of economic adjustment are still unsolved. It is not simply the overt manifestations of poverty and crime and vice, but the insidious, pervasive atmosphere of the philistine that furnish the indictment of economic insecurity. Man's habits, those habits of reaction that are judged by ethical values, are formed in a mould of materialism. Economic precariousness sets that mould. The complaints of the ethical theorist, of the theologian, directed against the grasping, selfish character of human society—can they be sympathetically received if such complaints are unaccompanied by any interest in the economic health of that society?

Moral philosophy essays a very ambitious undertaking when it seeks to handle by an *ad hoc* technique this "acquisitiveness" in human nature that spells the doom of so many ethical visions. That taint of greed which corrupts everything it touches is not something that can be exorcised by means of categorical imperatives or by an abacus of hedonism. And, unless one refuses to accept the concept that human nature is a function of conditioning factors, neither is it some primal, indelible mark of Adam. To solve a problem such as this, a problem which is at the root of most of the anomalies that ethics and religion are called upon to face,

[31] George in *Social Problems, Works,* Vol. II, pp. 71; 212–213.
[32] *Progress and Poverty,* p. 455.

philosophy must be supplemented by the social sciences; moral problems must be translated into the vocabulary of social problems. Ethics so often has approached its material as if the evils it endeavors to transcend were absolute or logical in character, and that therefore they must be attacked by means of some weapon of demonstration. Ethical problems have been regarded as independent, self-operating, and their solutions have been held to lie in the same dimensions. But the evils that worry ethics are not parthenogenetic. They spring from a fertile origin, a social, economic origin, and any elaboration of moral philosophy must first achieve a comprehension of that pathological source. This is still the plea for a secure economic foundation underneath the structure of ethics.

To return, then, to the possible ethical contrast between two social orders, one of which has and the other has not arrived at a state of economic security, what would be the effect of that security upon "materialism"? That word, of course, just as the word "poverty," must bear a heavy burden in this discussion. By it is connoted that whole shift away from all the values that ethics and æsthetics have ranged in their pantheons. By it is meant the emphasizing of those "non-progressive" activities of maintenance, the loss of all the power that could be directed to the enrichment and expansion of human life, and to the satisfaction of the "higher" ideal wants that still float before the eyes of men. Materialism here signifies not some petty characteristic of man or of an age; it becomes a symbol of the forces that have made man a rather clever animal instead of the son of the gods of whom the philosopher-poets have sung. It is the very hypostasis of the backward drag in human development. And it is this "materialism" which is itself the product of economic conditions, and which acts, in turn, as the source of most of the paradoxes between the real and the ideal that confront the ethical theorist, that is to be acted upon by the removal of economic insecurity. It has been assumed that George's solution would effect such a removal. Let him then go on to paint his Utopia:

Shortsighted is the philosophy which counts on selfishness as the master motive of human action. It is blind to facts of which the world is full . . . It is not selfishness that enriches the annals of every people with heroes and saints. It is not selfishness that on every page of the world's history bursts out in sudden splendor of noble deeds or sheds the soft radiance of benignant lives . . . there is a force which overcomes and drives out selfishness; a force which is the electricity of the moral universe; a force beside which all others are weak . . . To be pitied is the man who has never seen and never felt it . . . He who has not seen it has walked with shut eyes. He who looks may see, as says Plutarch, that "the soul has a principle of kindness in itself, and is born to love, as well as to perceive, think, or remember."

And this force of forces—that now goes to waste or assumes perverted forms—we may use for the strengthening, and building up, and ennobling of society, if we but will, just as we now use physical forces that once seemed but powers of destruction. All we have to do is but to give it freedom and scope. The wrong that produces inequality; the wrong that in the midst of abundance tortures men with want or harries them with the fear of want; that stunts them physically, degrades them intellectually, and distorts them morally, is what alone prevents harmonious social development. For "all that is from the gods is full of providence. We are made for coöperation—like feet, like hands, like eyelids, like the rows of the upper and lower teeth."

There are people into whose heads it never enters to conceive of any better state of society than that which now exists—who imagine that the idea that there could be a state of society in which greed would be banished, prisons stand empty, individual interest be subordinated to general interests, and no one seek to rob or to oppress his neighbor, is but the dream of impracticable dreamers, for whom these practical level-headed men, who pride themselves on recognizing facts as they are, have a hearty contempt. But such men—though some of them write books, and some of them occupy the chairs of universities, and some of them stand in pulpits—do not think.

If they were accustomed to dine in such eating houses as are to be found in the lower quarters of London and Paris, where the knives and forks are chained to the table, they would deem it the natural, ineradicable disposition of man to carry off the knife and fork with which he has eaten . . . Consider this existing fact of a cultivated and refined society, in which all the coarser passions are held in check, not by force, not by law, but by common opinion and the mutual desire of pleasing. If this is possible for a part of the community, it is possible for a whole community. There are states of society in which every one has to go armed—in which every one has to hold himself in readiness to defend person and property with the strong hand. If we have progressed beyond that, we may progress still further.[33]

Give labor a free field and its full earnings; take for the benefit of the whole community that fund which the growth of the community creates, and want and the fear of want would be gone . . . Men would no more worry about finding employment than they worry about finding air to breathe; they need have no more care about physical necessities than do the lilies of the field. The progress of science, the march of invention, the diffusion of knowledge, would bring their benefits to all . . . There would result, not only the utilization of productive forces now going to waste; not only would our present knowledge, now so imperfectly applied, be fully used; but from the mobility of labor and the mental activity which would be generated, there would result advances in the methods of production that we now cannot imagine.

For, greatest of all the enormous wastes which the present constitution of society involves, is that of mental power. How infinitesimal are the forces that concur to the advance of civilization, as compared to the forces that lie latent! How few are the thinkers,

[33] *Progress and Poverty*, pp. 460–464. In contrast to his picture in *Social Problems* of the pail of swill and the hungry hogs as an example of the society that is, George continues in the same place (p. 71): "Did you ever see a company of well-bred men and women sitting down to a good dinner, without scrambling, or jostling, or gluttony, each knowing that his own appetite will be satisfied, deferring to and helping the others? That is human society as it might be."

the discoverers, the inventors, the organizers, as compared with the great mass of the people! Yet such men are born in plenty; it is the conditions that permit so few to develop . . . Had Cæsar come of a proletarian family; had Napoleon entered the world a few years earlier; had Columbus gone into the Church instead of going to sea; had Shakespeare been apprenticed to a cobbler or chimney-sweep; had Sir Isaac Newton been assigned by fate the education and the toil of an agricultural laborer; had Dr. Adam Smith been born in the coal hews, or Herbert Spencer forced to get his living as a factory operative, what would their talents have availed? But there would have been, it will be said, other Cæsars or Napoleons, Columbuses or Shakespeares, Newtons, Smiths or Spencers. This is true. And it shows how prolific is our human nature. As the common worker is on need transformed into a queen bee, so, when circumstances favor his development, what might otherwise pass for a common man rises into a hero or leader, discoverer or teacher, sage or saint. So widely has the sower scattered his seed, so strong is the germinative force that bids it bud and blossom. But, alas, for the stony ground, and the birds and the tares! For one who attains his full stature, how many are stunted and deformed . . .

To remove want and the fear of want, to give to all classes leisure, and comfort, and independence, the decencies and refinements of life, the opportunities of mental and moral development, would be like turning water into a desert. The sterile waste would clothe itself with verdure, and the barren places where life seemed banned would ere long be dappled with the shade of trees and musical with the song of birds. Talents now hidden, virtues unsuspected, would come forth to make human life richer, fuller, happier, nobler. For in these round men who are stuck into three-cornered holes, and three-cornered men who are jammed into round holes; in these men who are wasting their energies in the scramble to be rich; in these who in factories are turned into machines, or are chained by necessity to bench or plow; in these children who are growing up in squalor, and vice, and ignorance, are powers of the highest order, talents the most splendid. They need but the opportunity to bring them forth.

Consider the possibilities of a state of society that gave that opportunity to all. Let imagination fill out the picture; its colors grow too bright for words to paint. Consider the moral elevation, the intellectual activity, the social life. Consider how by a thousand actions and interactions the members of every community are linked together, and how in the present condition of things even the fortunate few who stand upon the apex of the social pyramid must suffer, though they know it not, from the want, ignorance, and degradation that are underneath . . .[34]

Here, then, is the direction to which George points for a glimpse of the perfect state. Man sets foot upon the steps of an infinite progression and seeks to satisfy those higher wants, to reach for ideal values, only when he can put behind him the concern with "nonprogressive" wants. For him to live well, he must first live; before ideals can be realized there are wants that must be attended. But, with that concern over living put behind him, the potentialities that are dormant in man must develop. Those potentialities have displayed themselves when conditions have permitted. George is confident that they will raise man to a new splendor when they are given a free rein—and economic security must free the rein.[35]

Economic security, for George, is but another name for

[34] *Progress and Poverty,* pp. 459, 466–469.

[35] Bertrand Russell phrases one of the most acute objections that may be made at this point. This objection, i. e., that direction and supervision is required in both "nonprogressive" and "progressive" endeavors, that leisure must be organized, seems to be one of the advantages of a "socialistic" over an "individualistic" approach such as that of George to the problem of human development. "Socialism as a panacea seems to me to be mistaken in this way, since it is too ready to suppose that better economic conditions will of themselves make men happy. It is not only more material goods that men need, but more freedom, more self-direction, more outlet for creativeness, more opportunity for the joy of life, more voluntary coöperation, and less involuntary subservience to purposes not their own. . . . Social reformers, like inventors of Utopias, are apt to forget this very obvious fact of human nature. They aim rather at securing more leisure, and more opportunity for enjoying it, than at making work itself more satisfactory, more consonant with impulse, and a better outlet for creativeness and the desire to employ one's faculties. Work, in the modern world, is, to almost all who depend on earnings, mere work, not an embodiment of the desire for activity." (*Why Men Fight,* New York, Century, 1917, pp. 41, 98.) George did not handle this type of question, but undoubtedly would have considered it one of the adjustments that would follow the attainment of economic security.

liberty and justice, and the Utopia that he is drawing turns into a pæan in praise of them: [36]

The poverty which in the midst of abundance pinches and imbrutes men, and all the manifold evils which flow from it, spring from a denial of justice. In permitting the monopolization of the opportunities which nature freely offers to all, we have ignored the fundamental law of justice—for, so far as we can see, when we view things upon a large scale, justice seems to be the supreme law of the universe. But by sweeping away this injustice and asserting the rights of all men to natural opportunities, we shall conform ourselves to the law—we shall remove the great cause of unnatural inequality in the distribution of wealth and power; we shall abolish poverty; tame the ruthless passions of greed; dry up the springs of vice and misery; light in dark places the lamp of knowledge; give new vigor to invention and a fresh impulse to discovery; substitute political strength for political weakness; and make tyranny and anarchy impossible . . .

Our primary social adjustment is a denial of justice. In allowing one man to own the land on which and from which other men must live, we have made them his bondsmen in a degree which increases as material progress goes on. This is the subtile alchemy that in ways they do not realize is extracting from the masses in every civilized country the fruits of their weary toil; that is instituting a harder and more hopeless slavery in place of that which has been destroyed; that is bringing political despotism out of political freedom, and must soon transmute democratic institutions into anarchy.

Civilization so based cannot continue. The eternal laws of the universe forbid it. Ruins of dead empires testify, and the witness that is in every soul answers, that it cannot be. It is something grander than Benevolence, something more august than Charity—it is Justice herself that demands of us to right this wrong. Justice that will not be denied; that cannot be put off—Justice that with the scales carries the sword. Shall we ward the stroke with liturgies and prayers? Shall we avert the decrees of immutable law by

[36] Chap. V of Book X of *Progress and Poverty*, "The Central Truth." The passage on pages 543–545, George's "ode to liberty," is one of the most eloquent in his book, and has been quoted many times in prose anthologies. It is too long to be given here in full.

raising churches when hungry infants moan and weary mothers weep? . . .

In our time, as in times before, creep on the insidious forces that, producing inequality, destroy Liberty. On the horizon the clouds begin to lower. Liberty calls to us again. We must follow her further, we must trust her fully. Either we must wholly accept her or she will not stay. It is not enough that men should vote; it is not enough that they should be theoretically equal before the law. They must have liberty to avail themselves of the opportunities and means of life; they must stand on equal terms with reference to the bounty of nature. Either this, or Liberty withdraws her light! Either this, or darkness comes on, and the very forces that progress has evolved turn to powers that work destruction. This is the universal law. This is the lesson of the centuries. Unless its foundations be laid in justice, the social structure cannot stand . . .

But if, while there is yet time, we turn to Justice and obey her, if we trust Liberty and follow her, the dangers that now threaten must disappear, the forces that now menace will turn to agencies of elevation. Think of the powers now wasted; of the infinite fields of knowledge yet to be explored; of the possibilities of which the wondrous inventions of this century give us but a hint. With want destroyed; with greed changed to noble passions; with the fraternity that is born of equality taking the place of the jealousy and fear that now array men against each other; with mental power loosed by conditions that give to the humblest comfort and leisure; and who shall measure the heights to which our civilization may soar? Words fail the thought! It is the Golden Age of which poets have sung and high-raised seers have told in metaphor! It is the glorious vision which has always haunted man with gleams of fitful splendor. It is what he saw whose eyes at Patmos were closed in a trance. It is the culmination of Christianity—the City of God on earth, with its walls of jasper and its gates of pearl! It is the reign of the Prince of Peace!" [37]

[37] *Progress and Poverty*, pp. 541–542, 546, 545, 549.

George's almost metaphysical concept of liberty may evoke little sympathy in this day of cynicism, yet even that Nietzschean, H. L. Mencken, can write: "Liberty in itself cannot bring in the millennium. It cannot abolish the inherent weaknesses of man—an animal but lately escaped from the jungle. It cannot take the place of intelligence, courage, honor. But the free man is at least able to be intelligent, courageous and honorable if the makings are in him. Nothing stands in the way of his highest functioning. Free, he may still be dull, timorous, untrustworthy. He may be shift-

It is well realized that all Utopias are suspect. Perfect social orders have appeared as but an exercise of poetic license, and their attainment has been smiled at as the dream of a philosopher. Yet it may be well to consider briefly whether this perennial search for perfection in human society is simply a soaring of the imagination.

There is no particular difficulty involved, of course, in the raising of a sneer at the efforts of the founder of ideal cities. It is just as easy, however, to scoff at that "realism" upon which they who ridicule the Utopian dreamer pride themselves. That is, "realism" in comprehending our social adjustments becomes a ludicrous thing when, instead of including, it is transformed into a substitute for values. Too often, as in literature, realism signifies the portrayal of the ugly; the ugly is the realistic, and beauty must reside only with the romanticist. If that connotation is accepted, then, of course, the realist is he who revels in the sordid record of things as they are. But if a more intelligible interpretation of realism is chosen, then, no matter how callous the realist, he must admit into his "reality" the presence of values. These values (whether they are objective or subjective does not concern us here), these social ideals of beauty, happiness, justice, equality, are as "real" as the most tangible bit of ugli-

---

less and worthless. But it will not be against his will; it will not be in spite of himself. Free, he will be able to make the most of every virtue that is actually in him, and he will live and die under the kind of government that he wants and deserves." (In the New York *World*, January 30, 1927.) And Bertrand Russell can write, with an absence of cynicism, that: "I do not say freedom is the greatest of all goods; the best things come from within —they are such things as creative art, and love, and thought. Such things can be helped or hindered by political conditions, but not actually produced by them; and freedom is, both in itself and in its relations to these other goods, the best thing that political and economic conditions can secure." (*Proposed Roads to Freedom,* London, Allen and Unwin, 1918, p. 111, n.)

George, when told by William Lloyd Garrison (the younger) that he did not believe the single tax to be a panacea, replied: "Neither do I; but I believe that freedom is, and the single tax is but the tap-root of freedom." (Quoted by Louis F. Post in *The Taxation of Land Values,* Indianapolis, Bobbs-Merrill, 1915, p. 54.)

ness with which the realist is concerned. (Of course "ugliness" is itself a value judgment, but, with certain exceptions in the realm of æsthetics, it is not elevated as a standard to be attained. The realist insists that he is simply picturing ugliness and not judging it one way or the other.) And just as real, and far more crucial, are the judgments made in this realm of values. "Things as they are" include as a supplement things as they might be, things that ought to be. When the realist testifies that all attempts to change social conditions or to redirect the forces within human nature must be vain ones, the "reality" that he is invoking is the worship of ugliness. It is obvious that that ugliness must be comprehended by the most poetic of dreamers, but that it must be grasped and clung to, that its presence must blind man to the possibility of transcending it—such a procedure is not realism but stubbornness.

A skeptical approach to the prophecies that have been drawn by the painters of perfect states may not rightly be quarreled with, but surely a challenge can be made against that attitude of bland complacency that is affected by the "realist." It is not merely that he is implying that values are unreal things, the stuff of dreams, but of more "realistic" importance, he is blocking whatever possible road there may be that leads to social improvement. By refusing to admit the possibility of any type of change he is most effectively precluding any change. It may be that all of the hopes that have been expressed in the literature of Utopia cannot be realized; it may even be that few of them can be reached; but the striving toward the goal that they set up must act as the only vital stimulus for any type of progressive step. Values and ideals do not function in any esoteric sense. They point out directions and raise standards of measurement. They pass judgment and provoke criticism. They are instrumental, not decorative. It is in this way that values become operative, that "ideals"—to risk a professional pun—enter into the sphere of "critical realism." And this is why the sneer of the "realist" at the fervent hopes of the makers of splendid ideals seems such a futile thing.

It is perhaps not so much futile as it is dangerous. There is an increasing familiarity, and hence an increasing neglect, that result from the realist's insistence upon handling "things as they are." The continual commerce with the ugly, the refusal to look beyond and above, can have the effect only of blunting the sensitivity. Social maladjustment, economic distortion, all the bitterness of a twisted society, seem less acute and of little menace when they are handled casually as the "real." It is not in place here to add one more warning of the dangers present in this cavalier acceptance of a pathological condition as the normal, but it does seem necessary to suggest that some type of standard must be sought if there is to be a critical appreciation of the social order that conditions man. That standard is to be found implicit in the models that social philosophers have constructed. Much of the structure they have erected may have to be cut away or refitted, but it is in the path down which they point that even the "realist"—unless his realism is nothing more than the morbid concern with the ugly—must look.

There is no contradiction in this directive function of ideal values provided, as has been insisted again and again, that such "ideals" are not elaborated in total independence of the means by which alone they may be realized. If this is all that is meant by "realism" in its approach to social problems, then its conception would be the only acceptable one. But, characteristically, the "realist" has erred, in the same degree as has the "idealist," by insulating the universe of discourse with which he operates. The Utopian has lived in the light of a rosy future, and the realist has refused to look beyond the day. One has divorced ends from means, while the other has denied the authority of ends. It would appear as almost too obvious to advocate that a compromise between these two extremes must be achieved before an intelligible solution to economic and political problems can be realized. That compromise, it need not be added, is the work of social instrumentalism.

There will be no insistence here that the work of Henry George presents a completely acceptable compromise, but it is felt that his approach does point to the most sane method of handling the social problem. Irrespective, that is, of his particular economic program, there is in George's writings that merging of visions and facts, of ethics and economics, of ideals and reals—a union that appears to offer the most fruitful technique for the social philosopher. His fusion of psychology with the social sciences, i. e., his interpretation of human nature as a social variable, as a potentiality completely subject to the direction and conditioning of external forces; his founding of politics upon economics; his "economic interpretation of history"—the bold correlation of the rise and fall of civilization itself with an economic process; in fact, the whole synthesis that George essayed must be recognized as a thorough attempt to analyze, to value, and to reshape.

George contented himself neither with that indictment of the existing social order which roused him to his work nor with filling in the sketchy glimpse of that nobler society which was his inspiration. He added a comprehensive explanation and a carefully elaborated solution. Whether or not that solution and its promised effects find acceptance, there can be little question that his approach is an instrumental one. He sought that fertile marriage of hopes and methods. In his sweeping gesture of locating the problem, tracing the solution, and cataloguing the results, there is found a realistic confidence and a fervent ideality that cannot fail to capture

the imagination and the respect of all who are sensitive to
the problems of our social structure. That is why, perhaps,
an instrumentalist such as Professor Dewey can feel that
"there have been economists of great repute who in their
pretension to be scientific have ignored the most significant
elements in human nature. There have been others who were
emotionally stirred by social ills and who proposed glowing
schemes of betterment, but who passed lightly over facts.
It is the thorough fusion of insight into actual facts and
forces, with recognition of their bearing upon what makes
human life worth living, that constitutes Henry George one
of the world's great social philosophers." [38]

[38] From "An Appreciation of Henry George," preface to *Significant Paragraphs from Progress and Poverty*, edited by Professor Harry Gunnison
Brown (New York, Doubleday, Doran, 1928). In the same place Professor
Dewey writes: "I do not say these things in order to vaunt his [George's]
place as a thinker in contrast with the merits of his proposals for a change
in methods of distributing the burdens of taxation. To my mind the two
things go together. His clear intellectual insight into social conditions, his
passionate feeling for the remediable ills from which humanity suffers, find
their logical conclusion in his plan for liberating labor and capital from the
shackles which now bind them."

CHAPTER XI

EPILOGUE

HENRY GEORGE was not a professional philosopher. Neither was he a professional economist. Perhaps it would have been with the journalists that he might have ranked himself had the question of his precise classification been presented to him. And perhaps it is as a visionary reformer that the world of academic economics and philosophy has regarded him (although that world has characteristically treated George with the devastating and unanswerable criticism of neglect), or as an interloping layman, unfitted by lack of scholastic training for his ambitious work of social reconstruction. But there really can be no quibble as to the exact nominal qualifications for admittance to the ranks of philosophy. Philosophy itself has been singularly disrespectful to all artificial distinctions when it has sought for recruits, and the slave and emperor, the dramatist, the priest and sculptor, as well as German professors and English gentlemen, have been equally welcome. All that is necessary is that spark of cold (or even hot) flame.

Philosophy, for George, was not "that dear delight." Nor was it literally a love of wisdom. If the ever-doubtful aid of etymology were solicited, "philanthropy," stripped of its popular, patronizing connotation, would perhaps better characterize his thought than "philosophy." The love of wisdom was never an end in itself for him; in all cases it was but a path leading to the love of man. Neither did his philosophy

563

concern itself at all with the traditional problems of epistemology, logic or psychology. George's attitude toward the fascinating difficulties that have made up the very fiber of the history of philosophy was casual rather than appreciative, and his acceptance of the metaphysical world of human sensation and reason was as complete as was his refusal to accept the social world of human institutions. The problems that stimulated him were not those of a theory of knowledge, but of a political and economic approach to morals.

It was this ethical interest that directed his economic speculations. Economics provided the methodology for reaching the summits proposed by ethical concepts, just as ethics was the directing agent of philosophy itself. The suggestion has been made repeatedly in this discussion of George's work that an instrumentalist interpretation of social ethics demands a knowledge and an appreciation of any completely articulated analysis of morals in social-economic terms. Philosophy, as represented in ethics, cannot refuse to accept the challenge that our present social system presents it. The problems and the proffered solutions that have sprung from the misery inherent in existing economic arrangements press for recognition from moral theory. It was the merit of George to confront philosophy and religion with this problem of social evil. Here was a question for those question-asking disciplines, one that had been given scant consideration by the great figures who directed their researches, but one which nevertheless menaced the structures that they were striving to raise.

And further, it may well be asked of philosophy whether it can afford to permit the social sciences to act as its surrogate in the handling of society's ills. If there is any problem that must stimulate the searcher for an integrated "world vision," it is this of remediable human misery. If there is any paradox that must startle the ethical theorist in his quest for the realization of moral values, it is this starving of human power that takes place in front of the greatest expression of human power. Is not the solving of that paradox a vital task for social philosophy? If philosophy lays claim to one characteristic, it is that of catholicity. Surely, then, within its synthesis must be located not merely the vague awareness of the problem of social and economic disease, but also a sincere attempt to contribute to the remedy. This was George's interpretation of philosophy, a frank, urgent, perhaps unsophisticated demand that the love of wisdom be devoted to the love of man.

Indeed, in these concluding remarks it may well be that the challenge George offers to economics is not as crucial as that he offers to ethics. It is true, of course, that his criticism of economics [1] was unequivocal and pertinent. (Indeed, because the existing economic structure seems so unbalanced, so productive of wrong emphases, so tragically indifferent to

[1] "Political economy has been called the dismal science, and, as currently taught, *is* hopeless and despairing. But this, as we have seen, is solely because she has been degraded and shackled; her truths dislocated; her harmonies ignored; the word she would utter gagged in her mouth, and her protest against wrong turned into an indorsement of injustice. Freed, as I have tried to free her—in her own proper symmetry, Political Economy is radiant with hope.

"For, properly understood, the laws which govern the production and distribution of wealth show that the want and injustice of the present social state are not necessary; but that, on the contrary, a social state is possible in which poverty would be unknown, and all the better qualities and higher powers of human nature would have opportunity for full development." (*Progress and Poverty*, p. 557.)

George was puzzled by the neglect of the economists. He wrote, in a letter to his friend Dr. Taylor: "How persistent is the manner in which the professors and those who esteem themselves the learned class ignore and slur me; but I am not conscious of any other feeling about it than that of a certain curiosity." (April 28, 1892.) Two years before that, however, at the conference of the American Social Science Association (Saratoga, New York, September, 1890), Professor Seligman thus spoke to George: "It is grossly unfair to ascribe to the professors of political economy a truckling or even an unconscious subservience to the powers that be. All history disproves this. . . . No one is more desirous of attaining social peace, no one has to-day a deeper sympathy with the unhappy lot of the toilers, no one is more anxious to seek out the true harmony of social interests, than the student of political economy. If we thought you had solved the problem, we would enthrone you high on our council seats, we would reverently bend

human values, it would seem that any unorthodox approach would start with the initial advantage of pertinency. And the onus of academic disapproval that has been placed upon all such economic heresies perhaps may not be taken too seriously until that academic world discloses what solutions it has offered for the problem of poverty.) But that criticism of economics, while more spectacular, was possibly less fundamental than George's implicit examination of ethics, and also, it seems, more subject to possible attack. Although these two enterprises—economics and ethics—cannot legitimately be completely separated, still there is a clear distinction between the demands that he presents to each of them. One is a technical and highly controversial demand; the other is simpler and more compelling. It is the plea that George makes for a hand-to-hand attack upon social evil. That attack, it is true, must take place within the enclosure of economics and politics, but the authority and the strategy for the struggle rest upon social ethics. Moral theory must provide the vision, and it must understand the consequences; the technique of economics must be shot through with the motivation of ethics.

To put it more bluntly: There is an urgent, menacing need for human intelligence to become sensitive to the malformations within the social structure. Economics, in some quarters, appears to be turning away from that type of sensitivity to one more appreciative of the statistical analysis of that structure. Sociology, in part at least, seems to be confining itself rigidly to the collection of data and cases, considering, apparently, that judgments are now taboo. But, on the other hand, there is an indication that ethics itself is becoming more aware of this precise type of problem, more aware of a

the knee and acknowledge in you a master, a prophet." (Quoted by C. B. Fillebrown in a pamphlet, *Henry George and the Economists*, Boston, 1914.) Such an expression of a "welfare" interest is a frank, helpful attitude that might well motivate contemporary economics.

particular form of evil than of the category of evil—which is
nothing short of a revolution in ethical theory. Of course,
that sensitivity is one which must rely upon the material
provided by the laborious researches of the social sciences,
but ethics will add that vital, directive factor of values. It
will make judgments, a procedure that some of the social
sciences seem mortally afraid of. And that is why this problem of poverty, of economic insecurity, may perhaps be
most suggestively laid at the door of ethics.

Some day there will be a story-teller who will write of this
life of Henry George. He will not be wistfully sympathetic
nor will he wear a little patronizing smile. He will be one
who can recognize and estimate the fierce strength of an un-
sullied sincerity. He will understand the use of those vague
shadows of background and setting that play so revealing a
part in any portrait. Unlike the son-biographer who labored
under the disadvantage of having completed his work just
three short years after his father's untimely death, he will
be more able to judge of George's historical position. Perhaps the present vogue, unsurpassed in the history of publishing, for biography and autobiography, for memoirs and letters, will find in George a fitting subject— although he might
not lend himself so easily to modern biographical method, to
that technique of disenchantment. Such a story will try to
make clear why George was confident that his work had led
him to Truth, and why he was confident that ultimately it
must be verified. And it will grasp the great power that lies in
George's statement that with an economic program "has come
to me something I did not think to find, and a faith that was
dead revives." It will illuminate that vision which he kept always before him, and which led him on like the "Cross of a
New Crusade." And it will elaborate those words of Henry
George's great book, almost his very concluding words, in

which he throws down his challenge. *Is it a challenge that can be ignored?*

He who will hear, to him the clarions of the battle call. How they call, and call, and call, till the heart swells that hears them! Strong soul and high endeavor, the world needs them now. Beauty still lies imprisoned, and iron wheels go over the good and true and beautiful that might spring from human lives.

INDEX

A

Absolutism, in law, 494; of classic doctrines, 504, 506; accepted by George, 508

Acquisitiveness, 549–51

Alabama, single tax colony in, 442 n., 443–44

Alberta, land value taxation in, 400–402

Andorra, single tax colony in, 442 n.

Anti-Poverty Society, foundation of, 69–70; George's doctrines a new gospel to, 338–39; Father McGlynn in, 351–54, 356, 359; and Henry George, 352 and n., 354, 359

Arden (Del.), single tax colony, 444

Argentina, land value taxation in, 456–57

Argyll, Duke of, denounces George, 65

"As if," 502, 505, 506, 507

Associated Press, George's encounter with, 38–39

Association, in equality the law of progress, 530–33

Australasia, George's lecture trip to, 70–71; land value taxation in, 70–71, 385–98; George's influence in, 388 and n., 392, 395

Australia, its enthusiastic reception of George, 70–71, 392; land value taxation in, 388, 389, 390–94, 396

B

Baker, Newton D., a disciple of George, 462, 464

Bebel, F. A., on common vs. private property in land, 253 n.

Beer, M., on George's influence in Great Britain, 235

Biology, recognized by contemporary philosophy, 1. See also Eugenics

Blackstone, Sir William, revolt against his natural law, 494

Bodenreformer (German single taxers), 450–51

Böhm-Bawerk, E. von, his distinctions between land and capital, 101

Bray, Charles, and Henry George, 171 n.

Brazil, land value taxation in, 457

British Columbia, land value taxation in, 399–400

Brown, Harry Gunnison, single taxer, 467

Bryan, W. J., on Henry George, 464–65

Burgess, Edwin, forerunner of George, 192–93

Butler, Nicholas M., on George's influence, 470–71, 474

Bye, Raymond T., on land value taxation, 469

C

California, effect of environment on George, 215–25, 234; land speculation in, 220–21; single tax defeated in, 433; experiments in land value taxation, 439

Canada, land value taxation in, 398–406; George's influence in, 405–406

Canberra. See Yass-Canberra

Capital, in wages fund theory, 83, 85; definition of, 87–109; a factor

569

403, 405; on influence of George in Canada, 405–406; on land value taxation in U. S. A., 426, 427 n.

Schopenhauer, Arthur, admired by George, 330 n.; his influence on George, 373

Science of Political Economy, The, writing of, 72–73, 74

Sciences, the dismal, 1; of fact and of value, 479–80

Scranton (Pa.), land value taxation in, 435 and n.

Security, the essential, 158, 159; economic, effects of a state of, 551–57

Self-interest, enlightened, 274

Selfishness, not the master motive, 552–55

Shakerton (Mass.), single tax colony, 444

Shaw, G. B., Henry George's influence on, 232–34; on George's influence in England, 235; on socialism and the rent problem, 248.

Shearman, Thomas G., his work for land value taxation, 436

Single tax: earliest proposal by George, 43; defined, 131–32; effects of, 132–33; attacks on, 147–48; fiscal justification of, 149–61; Dove's suggestion of a, 168–69; the Catholic Church and, 347–50, 352–53, 354–71; land value tax and, 397; municipal, in Edmonton, 401, 402; indissolubly connected with land value taxation in U. S. A., 425–26, 445; campaigns and projects in U. S. A., 428–46; agitations in Denmark, 447; as a panacea, 558 n.

Skill, destroyed by drudgery, 10 n.

Skilton, James A., Spencer's letters to, 315–21

Slavery, involved in private ownership of land, 141–43; wage, 275–80

Smith, Adam, his distinction between "value in use" and "value in exchange," 89–93; anticipates George, 207–208

Smith, Gerrit, forerunner of George, 193–95

Snowden, Philip, on socialists and single taxers, 249; leads in enactment of land value tax legislation, 416–19, 421–23; repeal of his taxes threatened by National Government, 419–20; his interest in Henry George, 424

Social Democratic Federation, its formation stimulated by George, 231, 238–39

Social Problems, writing of, 63; in Norwegian, 447

Social Statics (Spencer's), history of, 286–304; abridged revision of, 303–304

Socialism, confusion of George's ideas with, 227–30; British, and George, 230–40; American, and George, 240–45; evils of land monopoly recognized by, 245–53; contrast between George and, 254–61; fundamental barrier between George's teachings and, 261–66; its philosophical base narrower than George's, 266–70; and individualism, 271–74; its attack on the wage system, 275–80; its present status with relation to George's followers, 281–84

Socialization, of rent, ethical justification of, 133–49; fiscal justification of, 149–61

Society, its functional control of the individual, 537; George's ideal, 542

Sociology, and professional philosophy, 1–3

South Africa, land value taxation in, 394 n.

South America, land value taxation in, 456–57

South Australia, land value taxation in, 391–92

Spargo, John, on cause of wage-slavery, 277

2812-8
58T